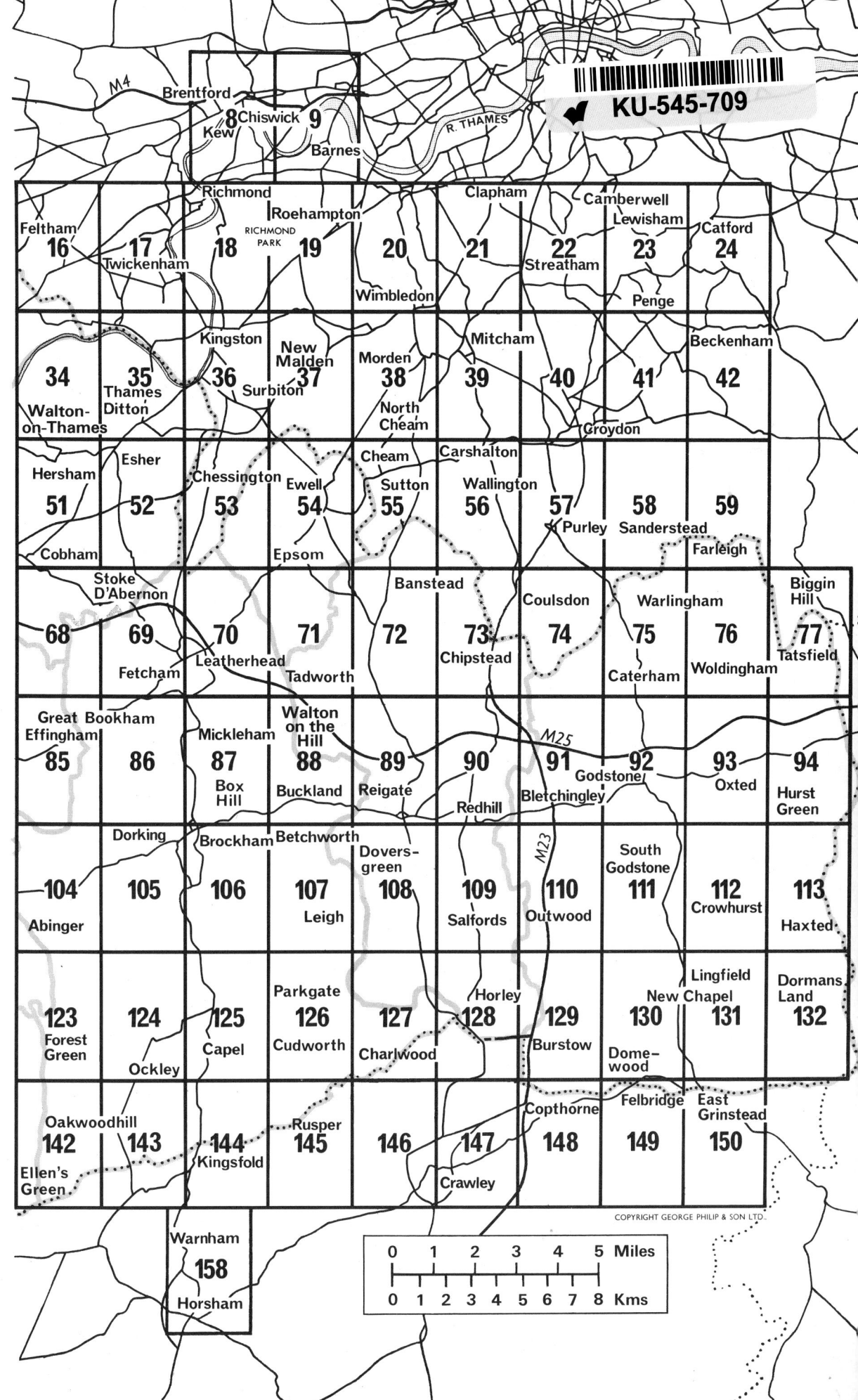

KU-545-709

M4
Brentford
Kew 8 Chiswick 9 Barnes
R. THAMES

Feltham 16 | 17 | Richmond 18 | Roehampton 19 | 20 | Clapham 21 | Camberwell 22 | Lewisham 23 | Catford 24
Twickenham | RICHMOND PARK | Streatham | Penge
Wimbledon

Walton-on-Thames 34 | Thames Ditton 35 | Kingston 36 | New Malden 37 | Morden 38 | Mitcham 39 | 40 | 41 | Beckenham 42
Surbiton | North Cheam | Croydon

Hersham 51 | Esher 52 | Chessington 53 | Ewell 54 | Cheam Sutton 55 | Carshalton Wallington 56 | 57 | Sanderstead 58 | 59
Cobham | Epsom | Purley | Farleigh

Stoke D'Abernon 68 | 69 | 70 | 71 | Banstead 72 | 73 | Coulsdon 74 | Warlingham 75 | 76 | Biggin Hill 77
Fetcham | Leatherhead | Tadworth | Chipstead | Caterham | Woldingham | Tatsfield

Great Bookham Effingham 85 | 86 | Mickleham 87 | Walton on the Hill 88 | 89 | 90 | 91 | 92 | 93 | 94
Box Hill | Buckland | Reigate | Redhill | Godstone Bletchingley | Oxted | Hurst Green
M25

Dorking | Brockham Betchworth | Dovers-green | South Godstone
Abinger 104 | 105 | 106 | 107 | 108 | 109 | 110 | 111 | 112 | 113
Leigh | Salfords | Outwood | Crowhurst | Haxted
M23

123 | 124 | 125 | Parkgate 126 | 127 | 128 | 129 | 130 | Lingfield New Chapel 131 | Dormans Land 132
Forest Green | Ockley | Capel | Cudworth | Charlwood | Horley Burstow | Dome-wood
Horley

Oakwoodhill 142 | 143 | 144 | Rusper 145 | 146 | 147 | Copthorne 148 | Felbridge 149 | East Grinstead 150
Ellen's Green | Kingsfold | Crawley

Warnham 158
Horsham

COPYRIGHT GEORGE PHILIP & SON LTD.

0  1  2  3  4  5  Miles

0 1 2 3 4 5 6 7 8  Kms

# Philips'

# SURREY
# STREET ATLAS

## 12th Edition

**3** INCHES TO **1** MILE

# Surrey Street Atlas

Considerable effort has been made by checking on the ground and by innumerable consultations with various authorities to make the information contained in the maps as up-to-date as possible (although in some congested areas it has not been possible to show certain very small roads and names). However, because of the highly detailed and changing nature of the area it is difficult to be precisely correct in every respect and the publishers would welcome any comments which readers may care to make and which will help towards maintaining accuracy in future editions. Please address correspondence to George Philip & Son Ltd., 12-14 Long Acre, London WC2E 9LP.

We should like to thank the Engineers, Surveyors and Planners of the Authorities throughout the county who have helped so readily and also the many firms and private individuals who have contributed with their local knowledge and expert advice.

First edition 1966
Twelfth edition 1988

British Library Cataloguing in Publication Data
Surrey Street Atlas – 12th edition
    1. Surrey (England) – Road maps
    912'. 422'1 G1818.S8
    ISBN 0 540 05537 9

© 1988 George Philip & Son Ltd

# Contents

# Legend

*The representation on this map of a road, street or footpath is no evidence of the existence of a right of way.*

| | |
|---|---|
| M4 | Motorways |
| A3 | Trunk roads and 'A' roads ⎫ D.O.T. classification and road numbering |
| B376 | 'B' roads ⎭ |
| | Other connecting roads ⎫ These roads may possibly be either private, |
| | Other roads ⎭ narrow, or unfit for road vehicles. |
| 12 | Motorway interchange numbers |
| B | Bridleways |
| | Footpaths |
| | County boundaries |
| | Borough and District boundaries |
| | Railways, stations |
| ⊖ | London Underground stations |
| + | Places of Worship |

Post Offices  Hospitals  Schools  Farms  Public Houses  Town Halls
 (P.O.)        (Hosp.)    (Sch.)   (Fm.)    (P.H.)         (T.H.)

ⓟ  Car Parks

# INDEX OF TOWNS
# AND VILLAGES

**6**

## MAJOR ADMINISTRATIVE BOUNDARIES OF SURREY

County Boundaries
Surrey Boundary prior to April 1965
Borough and District Boundaries

KENT

EAST SUSSEX

LONDON

GREATER

BROMLEY L.B.

LEWISHAM

LAMBETH L.B.

CROYDON L.B.

SUTTON L.B.

MERTON L.B.

HAMMERSMITH L.B.

WANDSWORTH L.B.

KINGSTON UPON THAMES L.B.

RICHMOND UPON THAMES L.B.

EALING L.B.

HOUNSLOW L.B.

HILLINGDON L.B.

EPSOM & EWELL

REIGATE & BANSTEAD

TANDRIDGE

MOLE VALLEY

WEST SUSSEX

prior to April 1974

BUCKS.

SPELTHORNE

ELMBRIDGE

RUNNYMEDE

WOKING

SURREY HEATH

GUILDFORD

WAVERLEY

BERKSHIRE

HAMPSHIRE

0 1 2 3 4 5 Miles
0 1 2 3 4 5 6 7 8 Kms

# Map

A
B
C

1

IVER STA
P.O.
Thorney Farm
BATHURST ST.
WALK
THORNEY LANE
Thorney
THORNEY MILL ROAD
River Colne

Richings Park
JAMES WALK
SYKE CLUAN
SYKE INGS
WELLESLEY AV.
SOMERSET WAY
Sports Grd.
WAY
ST. LEONARDS WK.

PARK
ROAD
North Park
RICHINGS
OLD SLADE LA.
THE POYNINGS
THE RICHINGS

NORTH
LANE
SUTTON LANE
Richings Home Farm
Richings Park
Old Slade Farm

M25 15
M4 4B
M4

2
M4
Sutton Court Farm
Sutton
M4

M. 4
M O T O R W A Y

Bigley Ditch

Colne Brook
Buckinghamshire Boundary
Greater London Boundary

A4
C O L N B R O O K
B Y - P A S S
A4

3
BATH RD.
P.H.
VICARAGE WAY
Chequers P.H.
Nurseries
MOOR LANE
TARMAC WAY
SAXON WAY

WILLOW CL.
HIGH ST.
MILL ST.
BRIDGE ST.
PARK ST.
Nurseries
ACCOMMODATION ROAD
HEATHROW CL.
Longford Bridge

MORELAND DRIFT
BROOK SIDE
COTTESBROOK CL.
ALBANY PK. ALL
LAUREL
AINTREE CL.
MYRTLE
FAWNS
CHESTER CL.
RAYMOND CL.
THE HAWTHORNS
GALLEYMEAD RD.
Surrey Boundary
Longfordmoor
P.H.
Longford

Colnbrook
COLERIDGE
RODNEY
DAVENTRY
Mad Bridge
R. D.
Moor Bri.
STANWELL
Longford
Runway 1

Poyle
DAWLEY RIDE
POPLAR CL.
MEADOW BROOK CL.
ELBOW MEADOW
ROAD

4
Poyle Manor House
MATHISON WAY
BILTON CL.
Duke of Northumberland's River

Manor Farm
COLNDALE RD.
ARKWRIGHT RD.
DAVID RD.
MOTLOW RD.
Wyrandisbury River
A3044
MOOR
Western Perimeter River
Longford
BURROWS HILL CL.

Poyle Farm
PRESCOTT RD.
BLACKTHORNE ROAD
CHRISTINE
Poyle Industrial Area
ROAD

Colne Brook
River Colne
BEDFONT COURT
BURROWS HILL LA.
WESSEX RD.

5
COPPER MILL RD.
Berkshire Boundary
Surrey Boundary
HORTON RD.
Lintell's Bridge
14
A3113
AIRPORT WAY
Nursery
SPOUT LANE NORTH
M5

W R A Y S B U R Y
R E S E R V O I R
M25
LEYLAND'S LA.
HORTON ROAD
TITLOCK CL.
SPOUT LA.
ROAD
A3044

A
B
C

CONTINUED ON PAGES 13 & 14

0    500    1000    1500    1760 Yards (1 mile)

Extended scale suitable for all pages from 7–158

0    500    1000 Metres (1 kilometre)

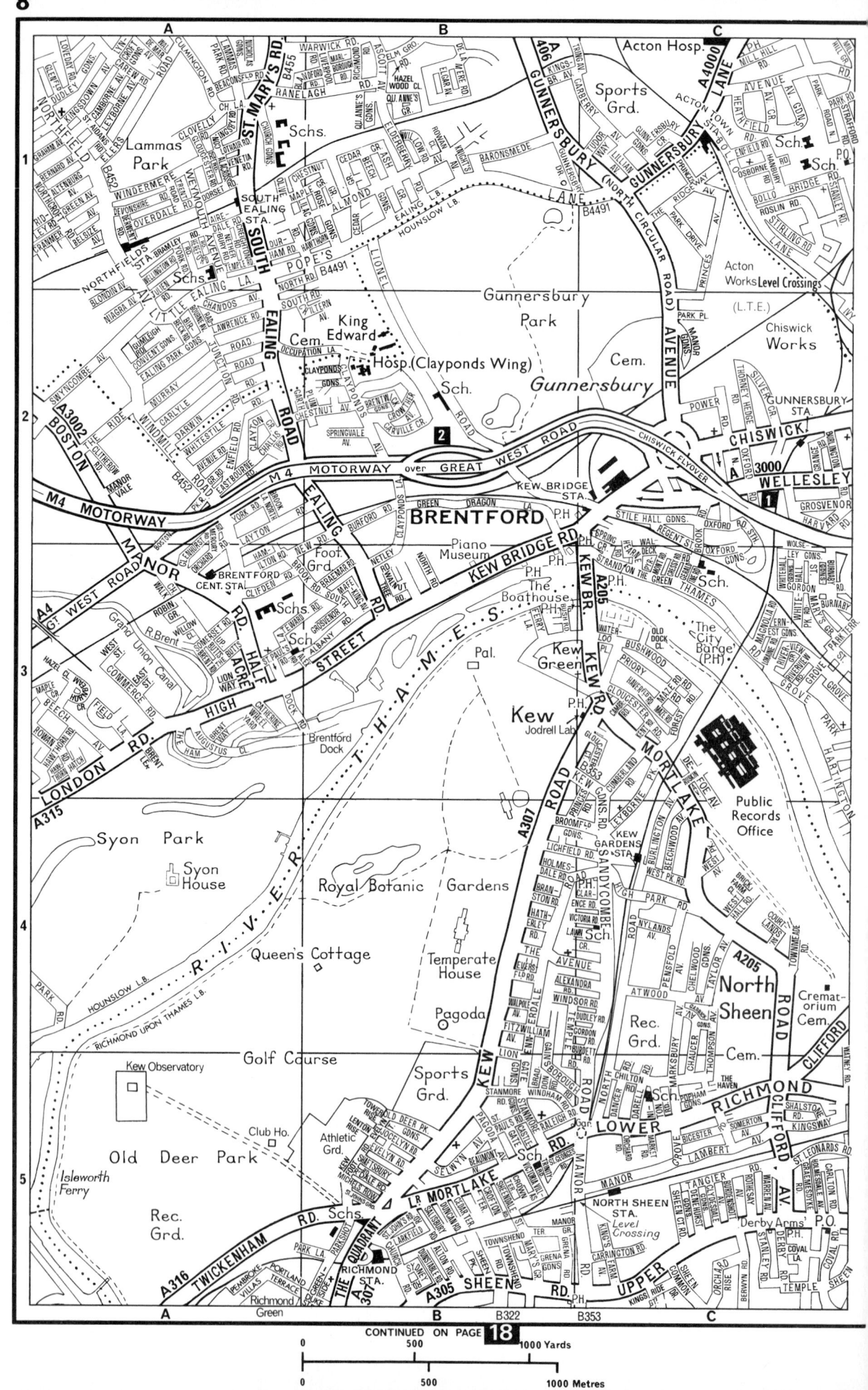

CONTINUED ON PAGE **18**

0      500      1000 Yards

0      500      1000 Metres

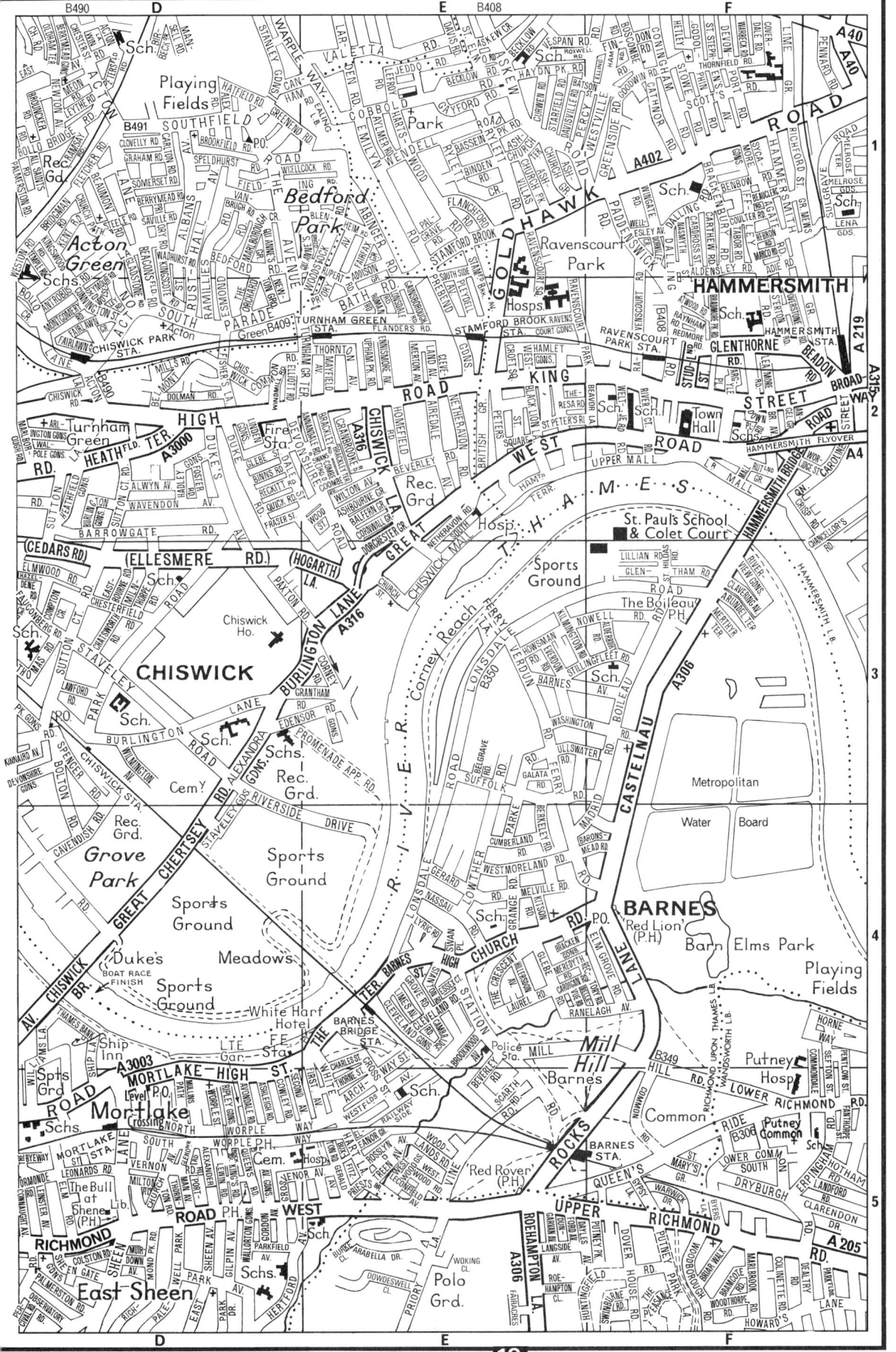

COPYRIGHT GEORGE PHILIP & SON LTD.

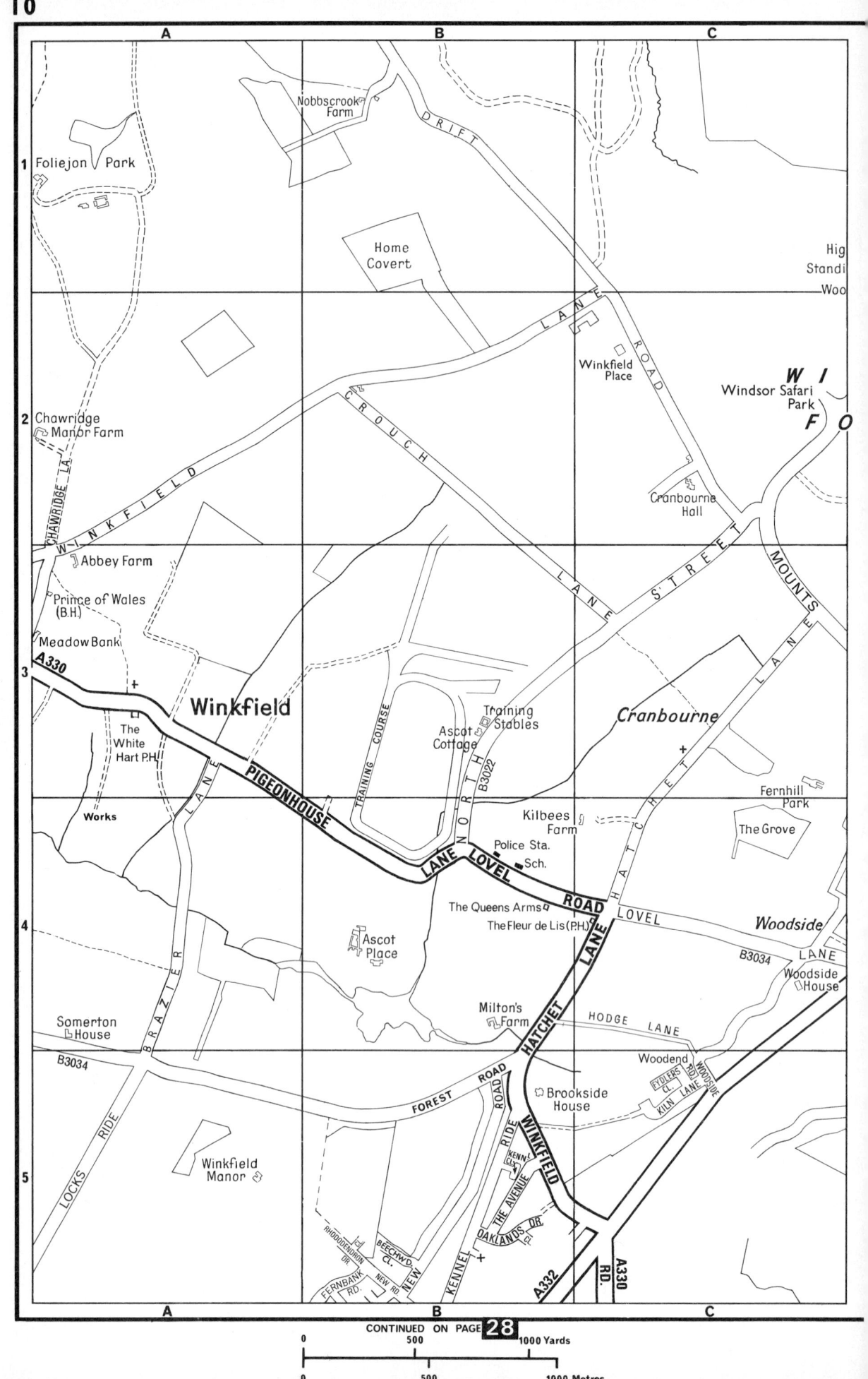

Nobbscrook Farm

Foliejon Park

1

DRIFT

LANE ROAD

Home Covert

Winkfield Place

Hig Standi Woo

CROUCH

Chawridge Manor Farm

2

Windsor Safari Park

W I F O

WINKFIELD

CHAWRIDGE LA.

LANE

STREET

Cranbourne Hall

Abbey Farm

Prince of Wales (B.H.)

Meadow Bank

MOUNTS LANE

A330

3

Winkfield

Training Stables

Cranbourne

+

The White Hart P.H.

Ascot Cottage

HATCHET LANE

Fernhill Park

The Grove

BRAZIER LANE

PIGEONHOUSE

TRAINING COURSE

LANE NORTH

B3022

Works

Kilbees Farm

Police Sta.
Sch.

Woodside

LANE

LOVEL

B3034

Woodside House

ROAD

The Queens Arms

The Fleur de Lis (P.H.)

LOVEL

4

Ascot Place

Milton's Farm

HODGE LANE

Somerton House

HATCHET LANE

Woodend

FYDLERS CL.

WOODSIDE RD.

B3034

KILN LANE

FOREST ROAD

Brookside House

LOCKS RIDE

Winkfield Manor

RIDE ROAD

WINKFIELD

KENNEL FY.

THE AVENUE

OAKLANDS DR.

5

+

A332

A330 RD.

KENNEL RIDE

RHODODENDRON DR.

BEECHW'D. CL.

NEW

FERNBANK RD.

NEW RD.

CONTINUED ON PAGE 28

0    500    1000 Yards

0    500    1000 Metres

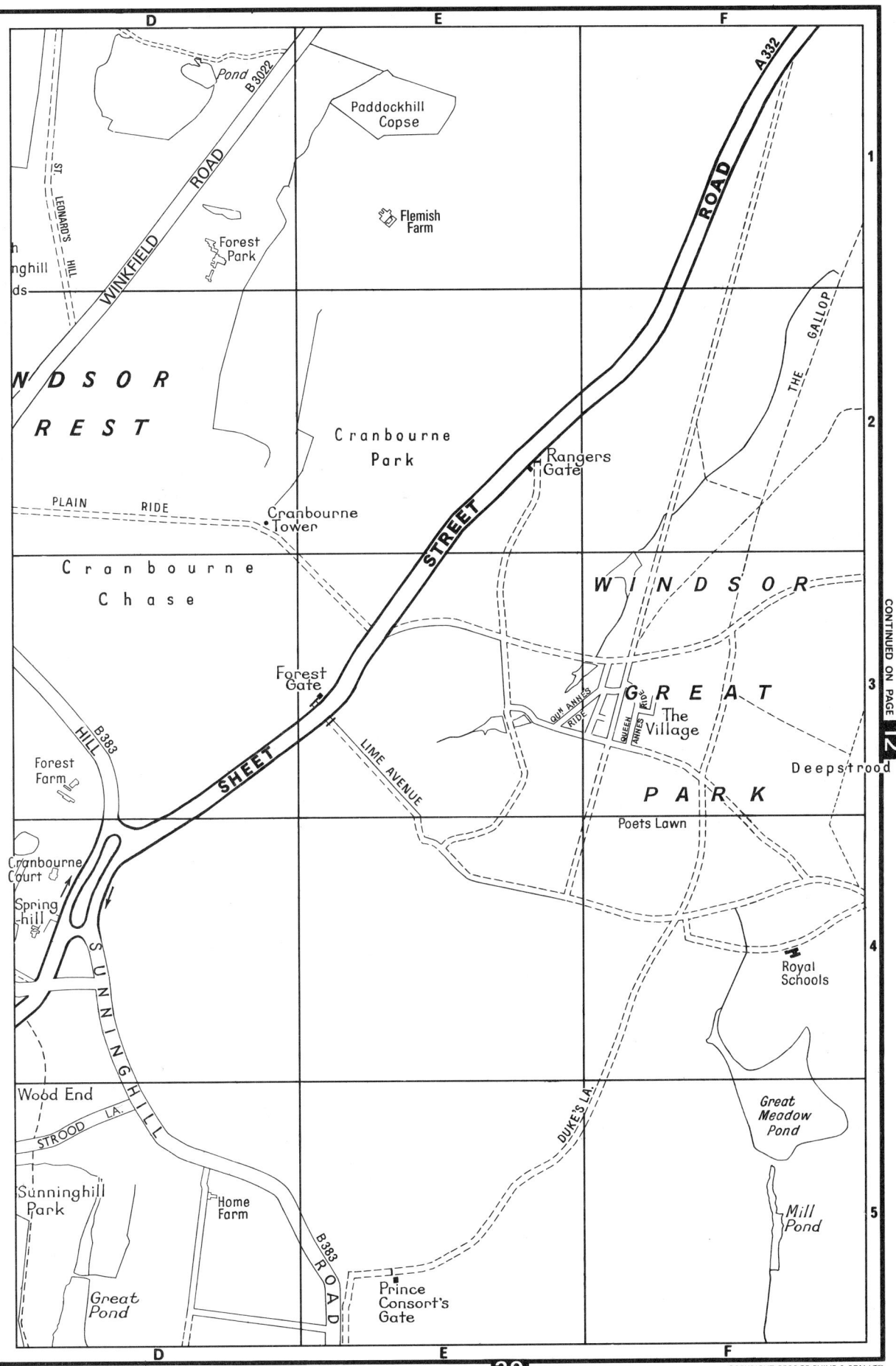

**11**

CONTINUED ON PAGE 12

CONTINUED ON PAGE 29

A308
ALBERT RD.
CLAYHALL LA.
ALBANY
LUKE'S ROAD
STRAIGHT
CHURCH
Pol. Sta.
QUEENS CLO.
WILLIAM
SHAW DR.
ELLIS CL.
ST ANDREW'S CL.
HAM LA.
St. Peter's Ch.
KINGSWOOD CR.
The Manor
Remenham House
PARK AV.
DRIVE

**Old Windsor**

Rec. Grd.
Farm House
School
CORNWELL RD.
Newton Ct.
BURFIELD
KINGSBURY DRIVE
Newton Hotel
Sch.
B3021
NEW CL.
THE AVENUE
MEADOW WY.
MEADOW
FOLLET CL.
Friary Farm
P.O.
ORCHARD RD.
WARD
AYLESWORTH SPUR
MILLS SPUR
MALT CL.
WALPOLE
GROVE CL.
KEPPEL SPUR
THE FRIARY
FRIARY ROAD
St. Peter's Ch.
Manor Farm Estate
FAIRFIELD APPROACH
NURSERY WAY
FAIRFIELD RD.
Old Ferry Drive

Bears' Rails Gate
CRIMP HILL ROAD
King Edward VII Hospital (for Children and Elderly People)
PELLING HILL
WHARF RD.
RIVERSIDE
OUSELEY
COPPICE DR.
GARSON LA.
ROAD
THE EMBANKMENT
WINDSOR ROAD
A308
MEDE MAGNA CHARTA LANE

CRIMP HILL ROAD
THE LONG WALK
WINDSOR
Equestrian Statue of King George III
240 Snow Hill
Runnymede House
Kennedy Memorial (to Freedom) Magna Carta
Boundary
Berkshire
Surrey
St. John's R.C. Sch.
A328
PRIEST HILL

**GREAT**

The Dell
RIDGEMEAD ROAD
BISHOPSGATE ROAD
Brunel University
Cooper's Hill
Commonwealth Air Forces Memorial
OAK LANE
COOPERS HILL LANE

**P**+**ARK**

The Royal Lodge
Bishops Gate House
RHODODENDRON RIDE
HAM LANE
Dell Park
**Englefield Green**
Kingswood Halls of Residence R.H.C. (Univ. of London)
HOLLYCOMBE
CLARENCE DR.
KINGSWOOD CL.
KINGSWOOD RISE
TITE
B388

Cumberland Lodge
Cow Pond
PROSPECT LA.
KINGS LANE
NORTHCROFT
NORTHCROFT GDNS.
NORTHCROFT VILLAS
LAUREL AV.
WILLSON ROAD
SCHRODER CT.
ST. JUDE'S
BEAUFORTS
Sch.
BARLEY MOW RD.
MIDDLE
HARVEST
SPENCER GDNS.
Meth.
WILLOW WALK
PARSONAGE
The Retreat
CHESTNUT
R.C. Ch.

Pol. Sta.
Cumberland Gate
The Savill Garden Restaurant
Towngreen Farm
Car Park & Entrance to Garden.
Parkwood
QUEEN VICTORIA'S AVE.
LARCHWOOD
FIRBANK PL.
ASHWOOD RD.
BEECHTREE CL.
PINE CL.
LINDEN
ELM
HOLLY CL.
CHERRYWOOD AV.
MAGNA CYPRESS WK.
HANOVER
Cemetery
Englehurst AV.
VICTORIA
ALEXANDRA
ST. JUDE'S ROAD
A328
EGHAM HILL
VICTORIA AV.
ALBERT R.
ARMSTRONG
HIGHFIELD CL.
St. Hosp.
BOND LANE

Obelisk
Prince Consorts Statue
Sandylands
Park House
**Egham Wick**
BLAYS LANE
SWALLOWFIELD
RAVENFIELD
CORBY DR.
THORNCROFT
Sch.
SOUTH ROAD
BAKEHAM LANE
SIMONS WALK
ROBERTS WAY
Royal Holloway & Bedford New Coll. (Univ. of London)

Obelisk Pond
Smith's Lawn (Royal Landing Field)
WICK ROAD
A30
St. David's

CONTINUED ON PAGE 11

CONTINUED ON PAGE 30

0    500    1000 Yards
0    500    1000 Metres

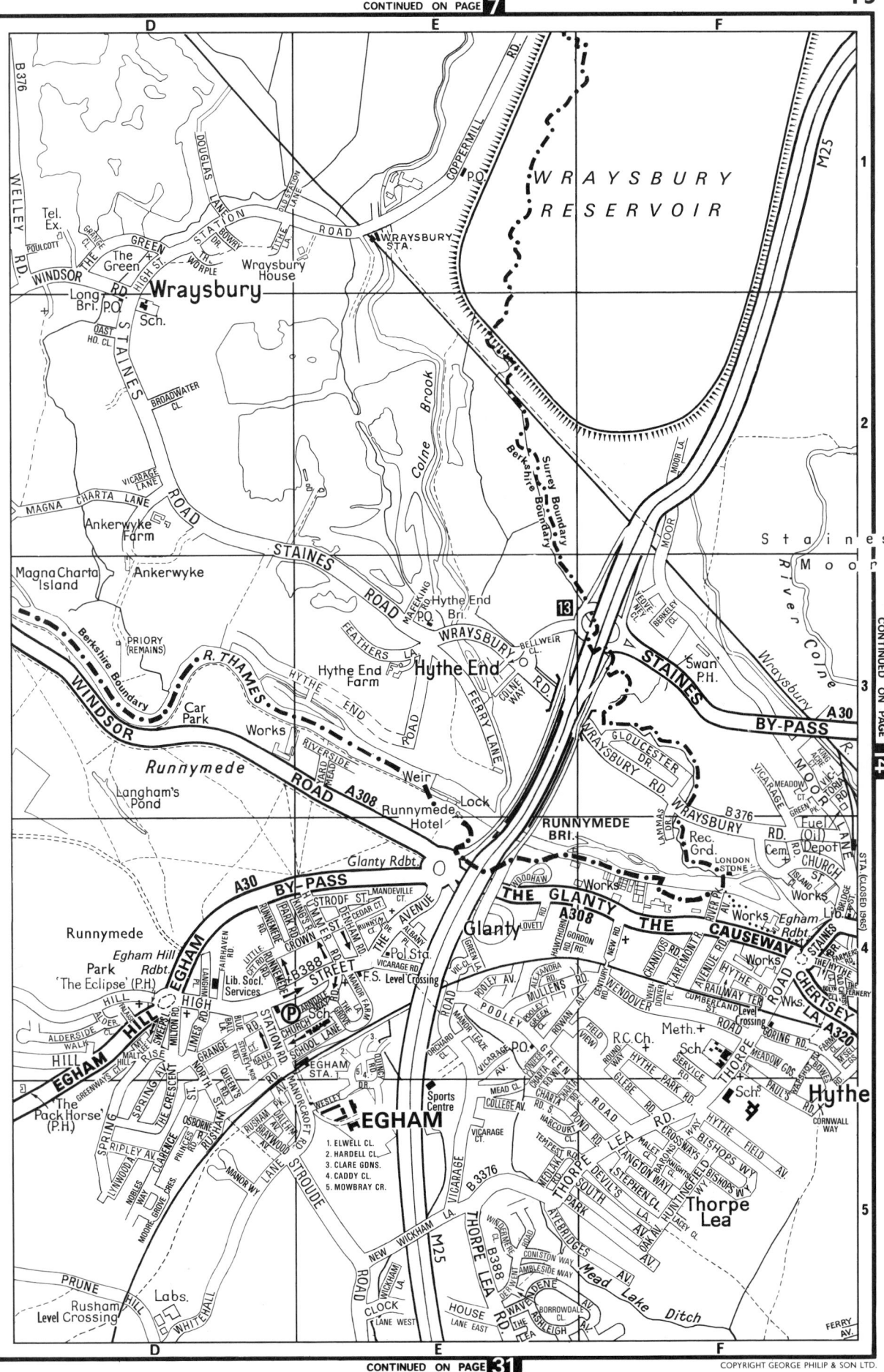

CONTINUED ON PAGE **14**

COPYRIGHT GEORGE PHILIP & SON LTD.

A B C

CONTINUED ON PAGE 13

1

Southern Perimeter Road

Stanwellmoor

Stanwellmoor Farm
Hithermoor Farm
Southern Farm
HORTON RD.
HITHERMOOR
CHELTENHAM VS.
HAWS LA.
Lower Mill
Stanwell Place

A3044
MOOR

PARK ROAD
HIGH ST.
Swan
Sch.
Stanwell
Rec. Gd.
RIVERSIDE RD.
BEDFONT
SHOREHAM
STIRLING RD.
SUNDERLAND RD.

2

KING GEORGE VI. RESERVOIR

STAINES

RESERVOIRS

B378

Cemy.
Sch.
Sch.
HADRIAN WAY
CLARE RD.
CORDELIA GDS.
RAVENSBOURNE AV.
THE HEATHERS
CRANFORD AV.
OSBOURNE AV.
EXPLORER AV.
KINGS-WAY
VIOLA AV.
Ashford Hospital
Cem.

Borehead Ditch

3

A30
STAINES BY-PASS
'The Crooked Billet' (P.H.)
STANWELL NEW RD.
Sch.
Billet Bri. Rdbt.
Shortwood Pond
Hengrove Farm
Cemy.
LONDON ROAD
STANWELL RD.
ASHFORD RD.
KENILWORTH
CUMBERLAND RD.
AVONDALE RD.
DORSET RD.
PORTLAND RD.
SALCOMBE RD.
THETFORD RD.
CRESCENT
STATION
School & Lib.
Education Off.
Wel. Sch.
B378
Ashford Sta.

Pol. Sta.
LONDON STAINES
A308
Shortwood Common

4

A308
HIGH ST.
STAINES
Sch. Lib.
Town Hall
THAMES ST.
KINGSTON ROAD
LEACROFT
Swimming Pool
Knowle Green
PRIORY GREEN
Aqueduct
R. Ash
BROOKSIDE AV.
BOUNDARY
Remand Centre Hosp.
WOODTHORPE RD.
MARLBOROUGH
CHESTERFIELD RD.
STANLEY RD.
CHAUCER RD.
WOLSEY RD.
TENNYSON RD.
NELSON RD.
Links Hotel
FORDBRIDGE
BY-PASS
Ford Bri.

5

A320
CHERTSEY LANE
R. THAMES
Sand Pit
COMMERCIAL RD.
Council Depot
P.O.
ALEHAM
B376
WORPLE ROAD
WORPLE AVENUE
School
Cherry Tree
HURSTDENE RD.
HAZEL GROVE
TEMPLEDENE
PAVILION GDNS.
Sch.
ELIZABETH AVENUE
ARNOLD RD.
BERRYSCROFT RD.
GLOUCESTER
CHARLES AVENUE
CRESCENT ROAD
River Ash
ASHFORD
B377

0 500 1000 Yards

0 500 1000 Metres

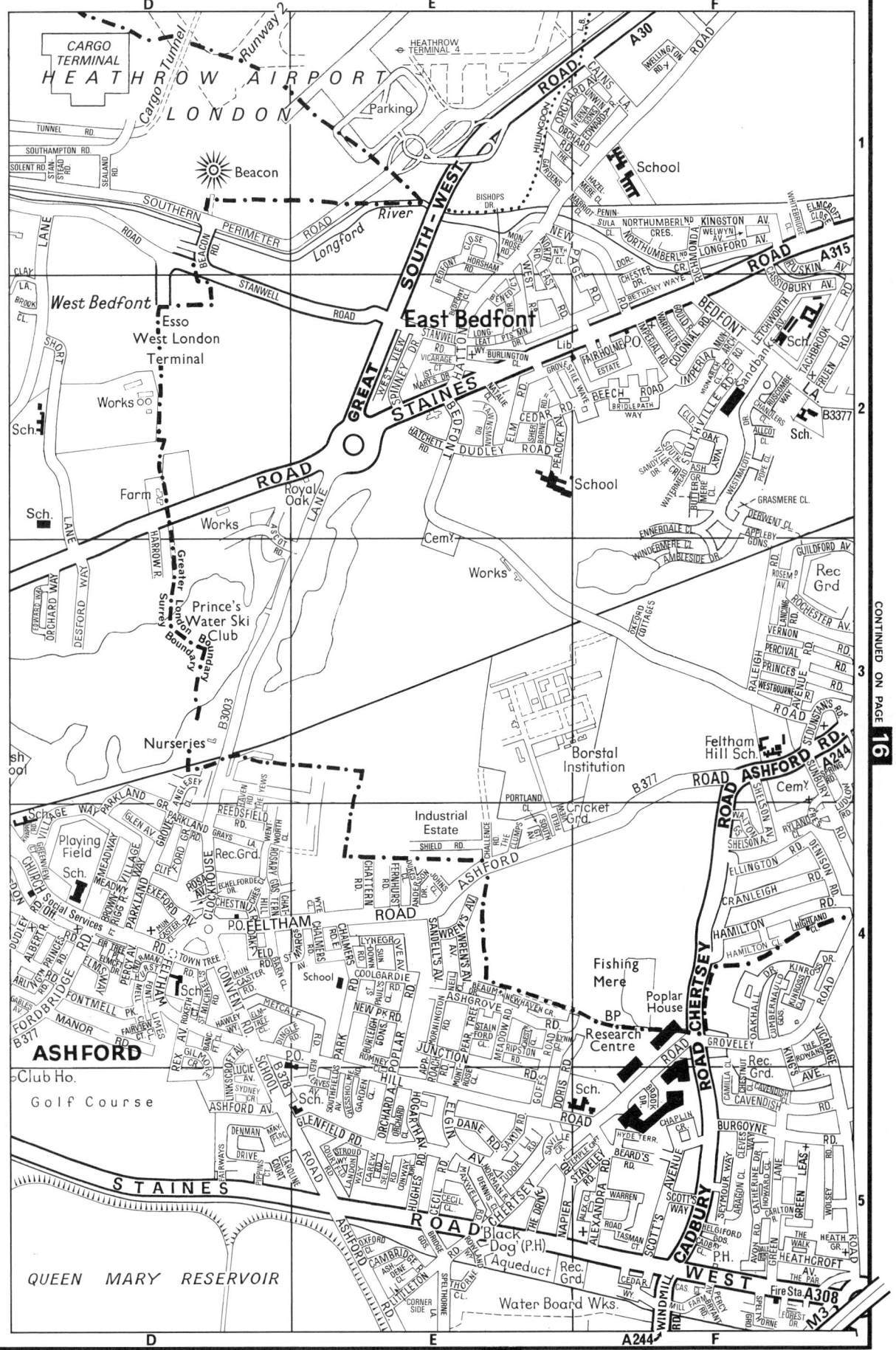

CONTINUED ON PAGE **16**

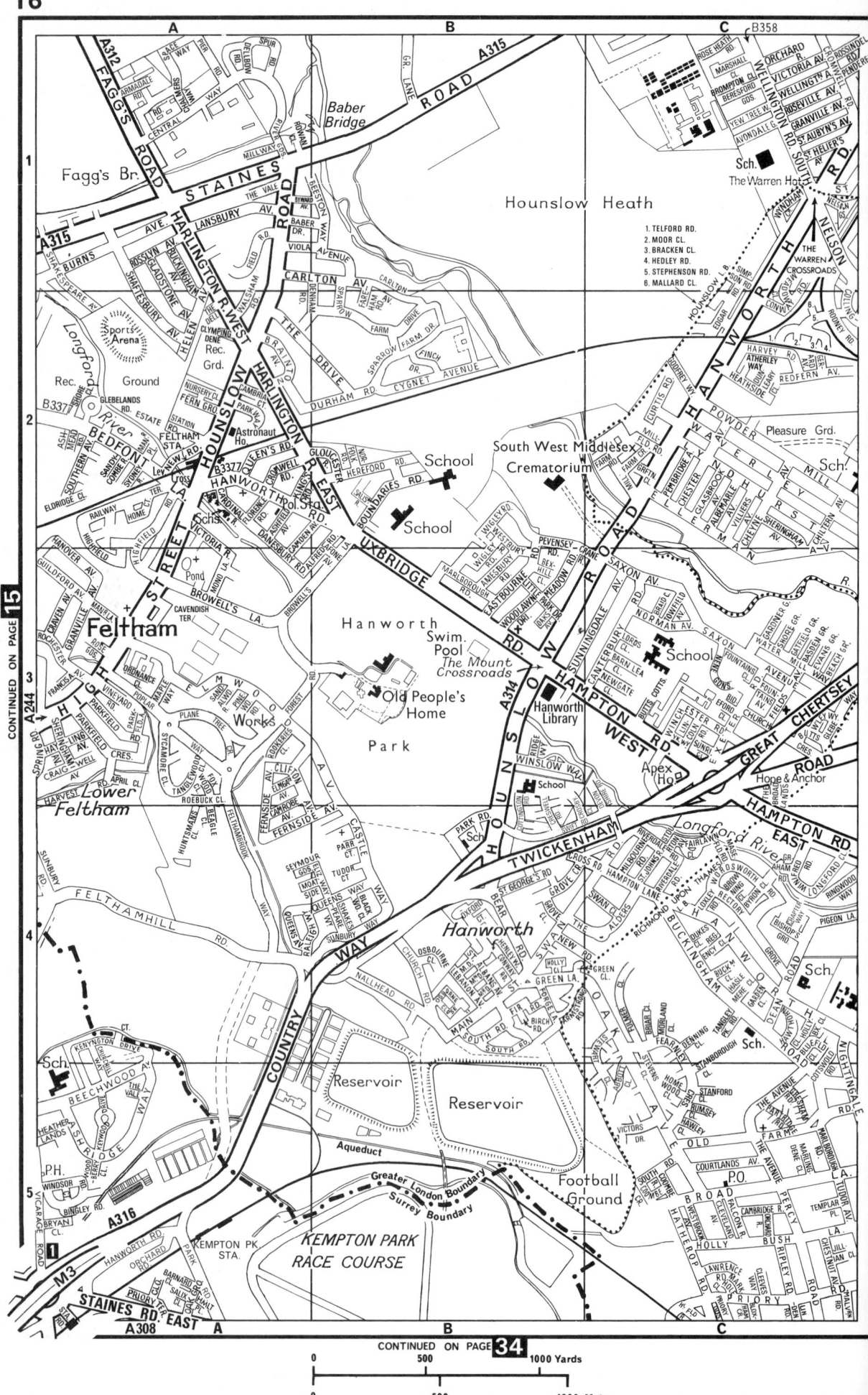

B358

CONTINUED ON PAGE 15

A312
FAGG'S ROAD
A315

Fagg's Br.

STAINES ROAD

Baber Bridge

Hounslow Heath

WELLINGTON RD SOUTH
NELSON RD

Sch
The Warren Hotel

THE WARREN CROSSROADS

1. TELFORD RD.
2. MOOR CL.
3. BRACKEN CL.
4. HEDLEY RD.
5. STEPHENSON RD.
6. MALLARD CL.

HARLINGTON RD WEST

THE DRIVE

HARLINGTON RD EAST

BEDFONT

Sports Arena

Rec. Grd.

Rec. Ground

River

School

South West Middlesex Crematorium

Pleasure Grd.

Sch!

FELTHAM STA.

Astronaut Ho.

HANWORTH Pol. Sta.

School

School

UXBRIDGE RD.

Feltham

Pond

HANWORTH

Swim. Pool
Old People's Home

The Mount Crossroads

HOUNSLOW RD.

HAMPTON WEST

Hanworth Library

School

Apex Ho.

GREAT CHERTSEY ROAD

Hope & Anchor

Lower Feltham

Park

School

Winslow Way

HAMPTON RD EAST

Longford River

Sch.

TWICKENHAM

Hanworth

Sch.

A244
A316

FELTHAM HILL RD

COUNTRY WAY

Sch.

BUCKINGHAM

Sch.

P.H.

Reservoir

Reservoir

Football Ground

P.O.

P.O.

M3
A316

STAINES RD. EAST
A308

KEMPTON PK. STA.

Aqueduct

Greater London Boundary
Surrey Boundary

KEMPTON PARK RACE COURSE

0    500    1000 Yards

0    500    1000 Metres

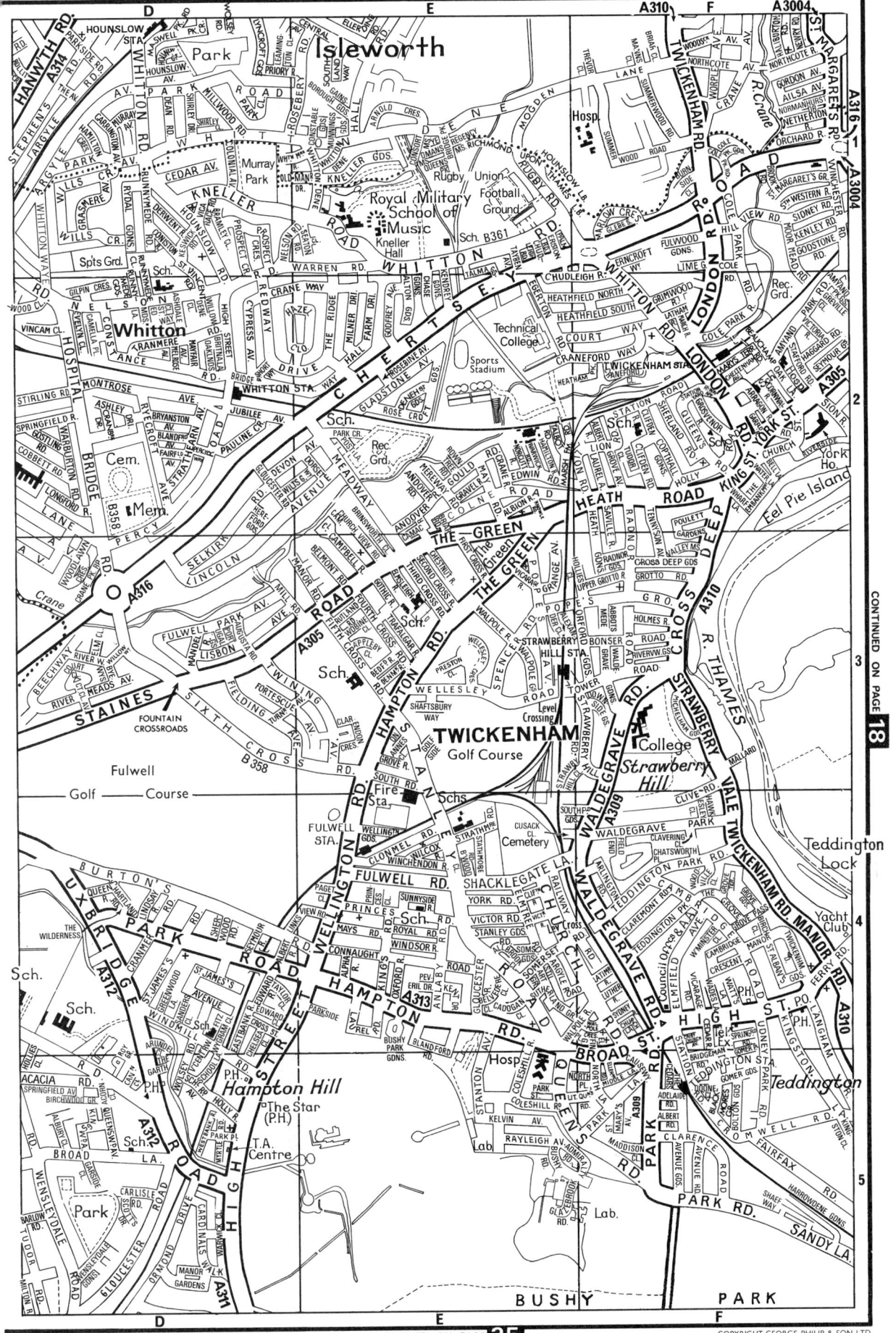

CONTINUED ON PAGE 18

CONTINUED ON PAGE 8

CONTINUED ON PAGE 17

# Richmond

A316  A307  A305

St. PETERS  St. GEORGE'S  RD.  RANELAGH RD.  Richmond Green  SHEEN RD.  WORPLE WAY  Sch.  SHEEN COMMON DR.  CHRIST CHURCH

THE AVENUE  TWICKENHAM BRIDGE  RED LION ST.  PARADISE  PRINCES RD.  East Sheen Common

HOUNSLOW RD.  RICHMOND RD.  RICHMOND HILL  KING'S RD.  QUEENS RISE  Cem.  Sch.

RICHMOND ROAD  CROWN RD.  St. MARGARET'S RD.  Ice Rink  FRIARS  QUEEN'S RD.

Marble Hill Park  Star & Garter Home  PETERSHAM RD.  The Lass of Richmond Hill (P.H.)  Bog Lodge

Spts. Grd.  Richmond Gate  30 m.p.h. motor car road

R. THAMES  Meadows  Band Stand  Sidmouth Wood

Petersham  Petersham Park  Leg of Mutton Pond

Ham House  Pembroke Lodge (refreshments)  Oak Lodge  Car Park  R  Pen

Sudbrook Pk. Club Ho.

Ham  Sudbrook Pk.  Golf Course

THE COMMON  UPPER HAM RD.  PETERSHAM RD.  Ham Common  B352  HAM GATE AVENUE  Isabella Plantation

Hosp.  CHURCH FARM RD.  Common  THE SHIRES  Ham Gate  Pond  Ham Cross  Pond

Angler's Hotel (P.H.)  Fire Sta.  BARNFIELD  The Cardinal (P.H.)  Thatched Ho. Lodge

Aircraft Works  T.V. Studios  RICHMOND RD.  PARKLEYS  Cowper Park  30 m.p.h. motor car road

R. THAMES  Rivermead  Sports Fld.  Boys Sch.  Spts. Fld.

KINGSTON RD.  Girls Sch.  Sch.  Car Park  Kingston Gate

Sch.  P.O.  Yacht Marina  Kingstonian F.C.  St. Agatha's  Sch.  Spts. Fld.

Hosp.  Normansfield Av.  KINGSTON HILL  The Albert Hotel (P.H.)  George & Dragon (P.H.)

A310  B358  SANDY LANE  A307  A305  A308

CONTINUED ON PAGE 36

0    500    1000 Yards
0    500    1000 Metres

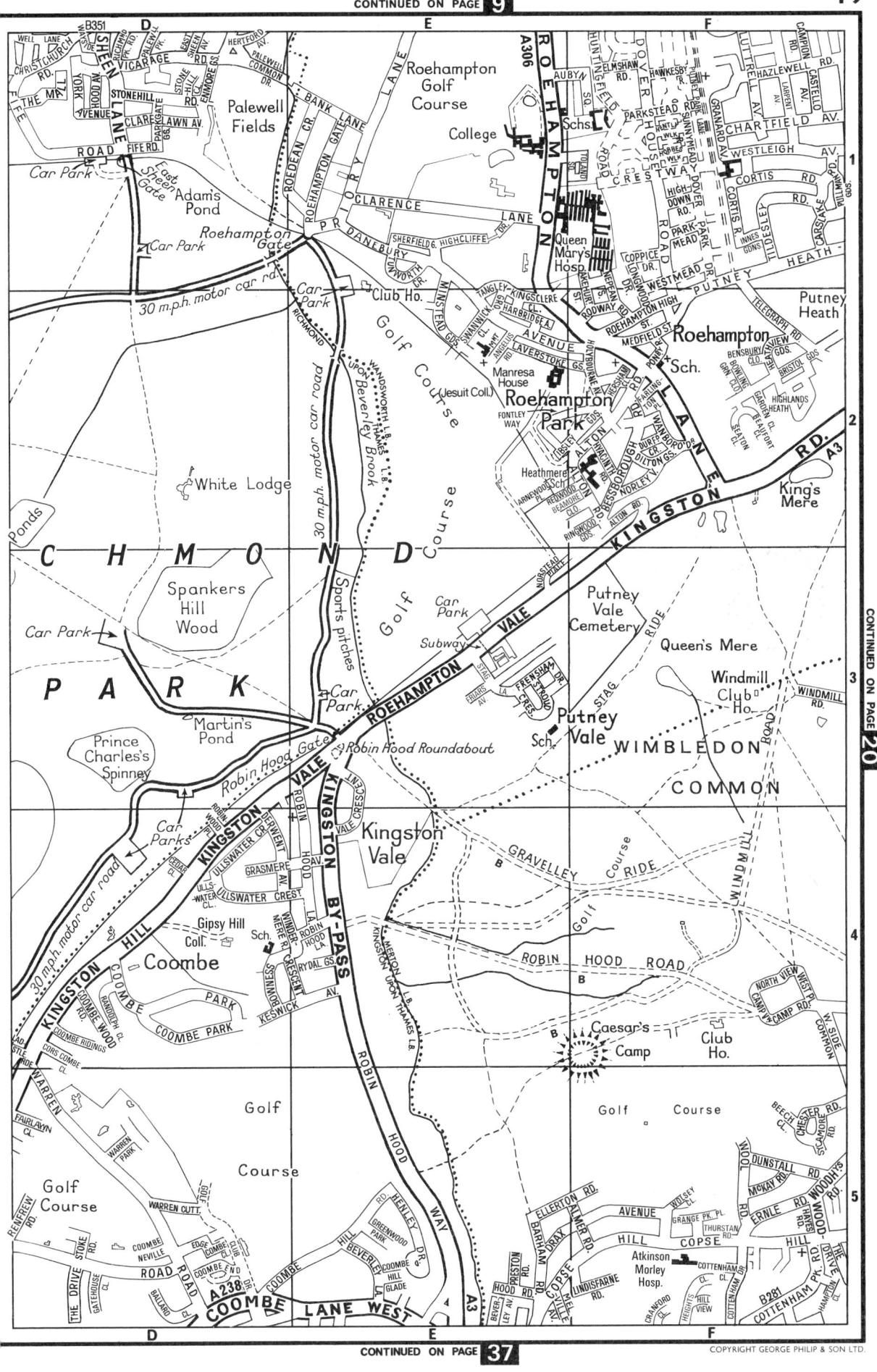

CONTINUED ON PAGE 20

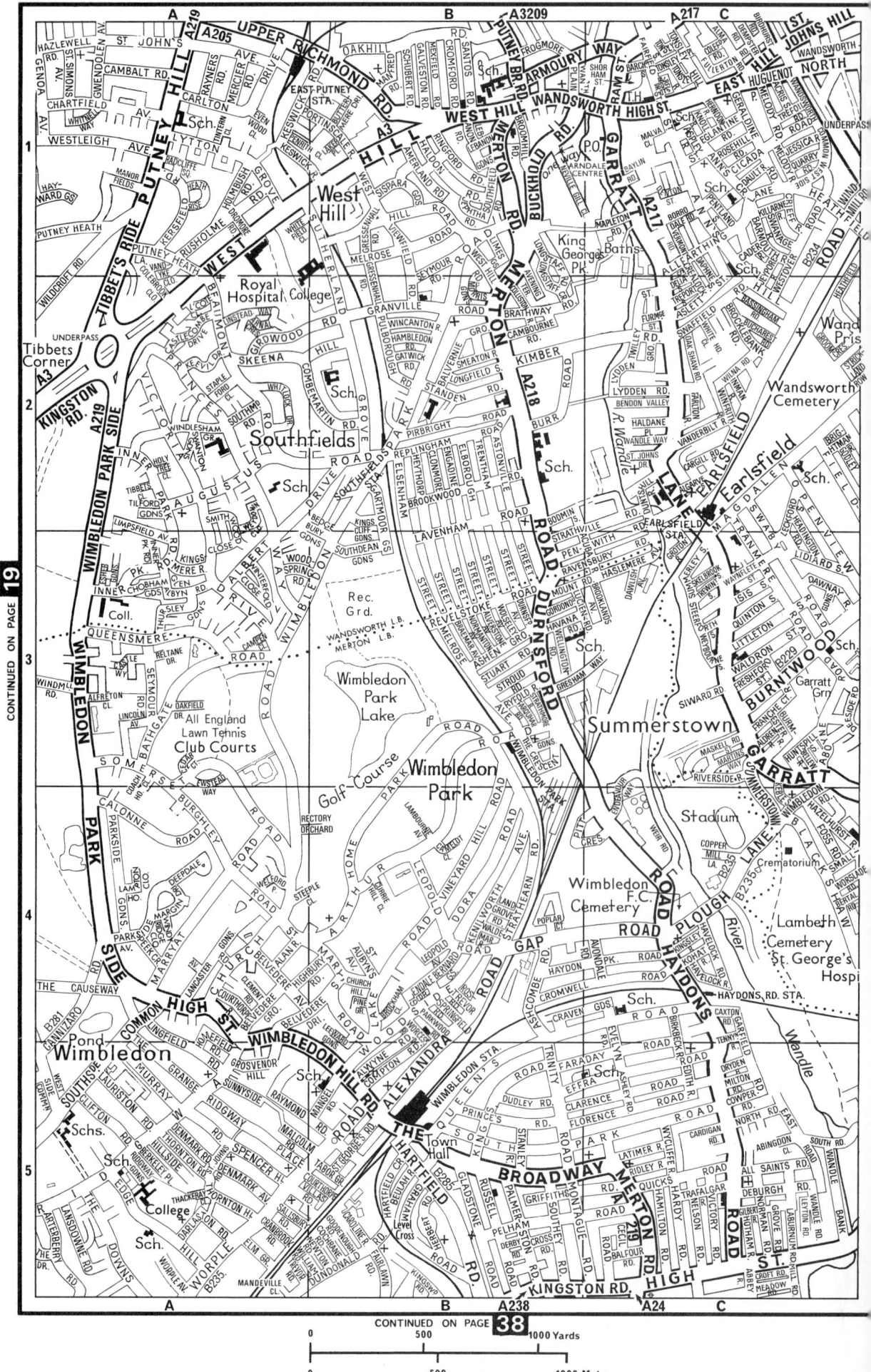

CONTINUED ON PAGE 19

0    500    1000 Yards

0    500    1000 Metres

Clapham

Clapham Common

Spencer Pk.

SIDE

Training Coll.

Wandsworth Common

BROOMWOOD

NIGHTINGALE

Springfield Hospital

Upper Tooting

Streatham Cemetery

BALHAM

CAVENDISH

POYNDERS RD. A 205

Tooting

Tooting Bec

Common

Tooting Bec Hosp.

Athletic Ground

HILL

GARRADS

BEC ROAD

TOOTING BEC

MITCHAM

Streatham Sta.

Streatham Vale

STREATHAM COMMON STA.

CHRISTCHURCH

CONTINUED ON PAGE 22

CONTINUED ON PAGE 21

CONTINUED ON PAGE 40

0   500   1000 Yards

0   500   1000 Metres

DULWICH
Dulwich Park
Sports Ground
Golf Course
Club Ho.

CAMBERWELL
Alleyn's Sch.

Peckham Rye Park
Camberwell Cemetery
Convent

LEWISHAM
Honor Oak Park Sta.
Stillness Schs

STANSTEAD RD. A205
Forest Hill
Forest Hill Sta.

Horniman Gdns. Mus.
LONDON ROAD
Firecup Sta.

Upper Sydenham
Lower Sydenham
Sydenham Sta.

DARTMOUTH RD.
KIRKDALE
SYDENHAM HILL
SYDENHAM ROAD

PECKARMANS WOOD
Sydenham Hill Sta.

WESTWOOD
B.B.C. Television Mast
CRYSTAL PALACE PARK RD.
Crystal Palace Park
Stadium
Crystal Palace Sta.

ANERLEY HILL
HIGH STREET
PENGE
Penge Sta.
Beckett Walk

WESTOW HILL
CHURCH RD.
A212

PARISH LANE
GREEN LANE
A213 A234

CONTINUED ON PAGE 24

CONTINUED ON PAGE 41

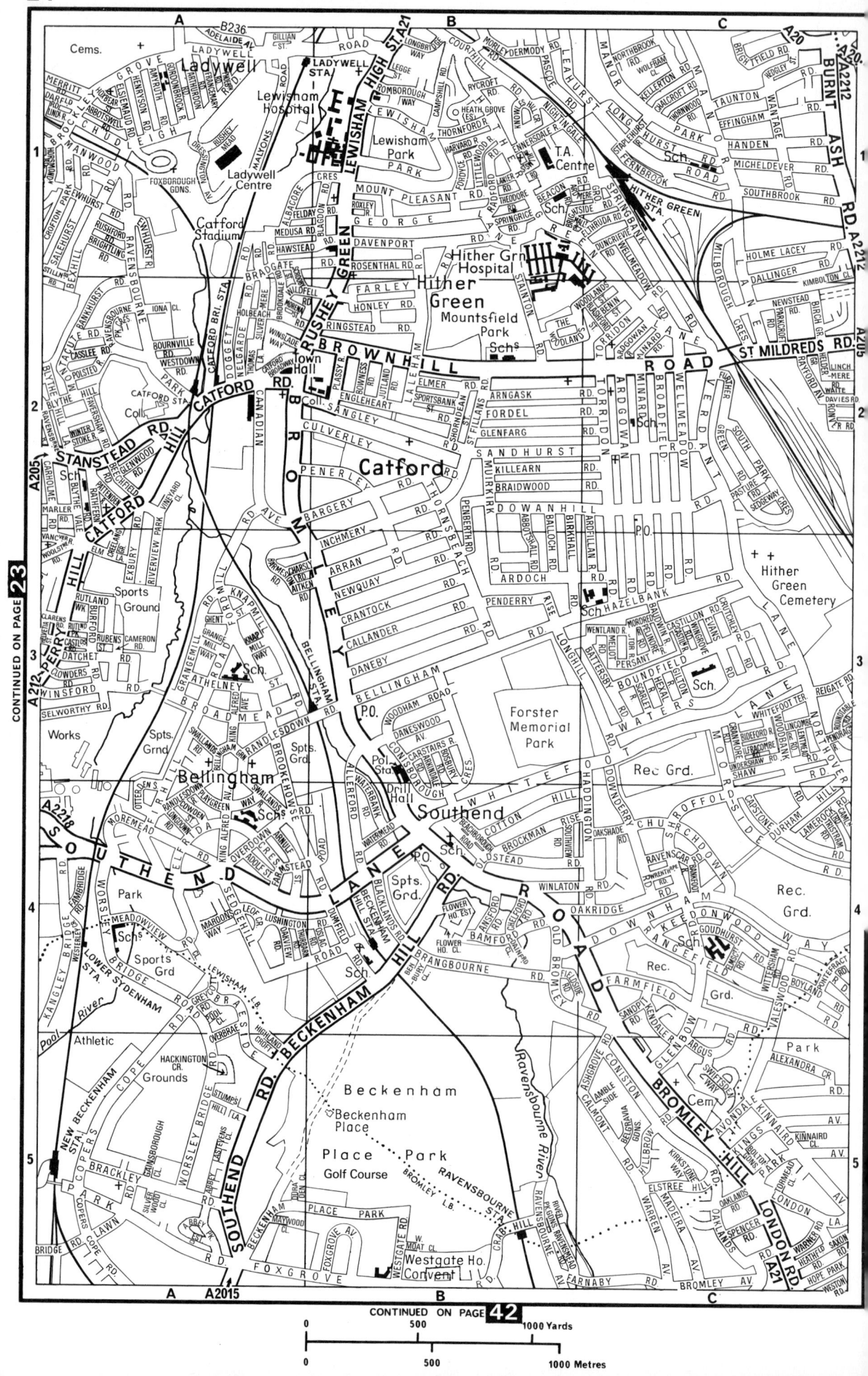

CONTINUED ON PAGE 23

CONTINUED ON PAGE 42

0 500 1000 Yards

0 500 1000 Metres

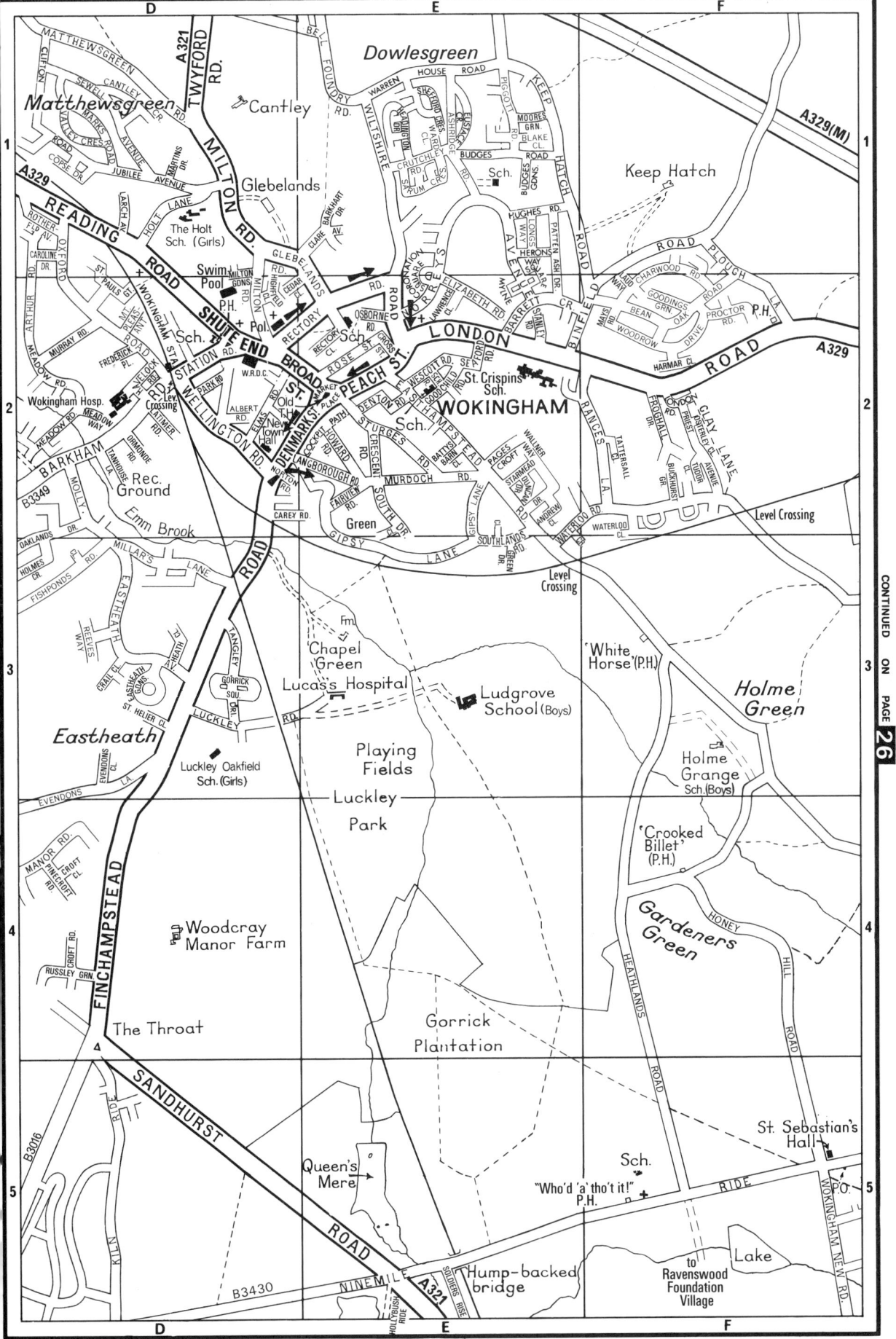

CONTINUED ON PAGE 26

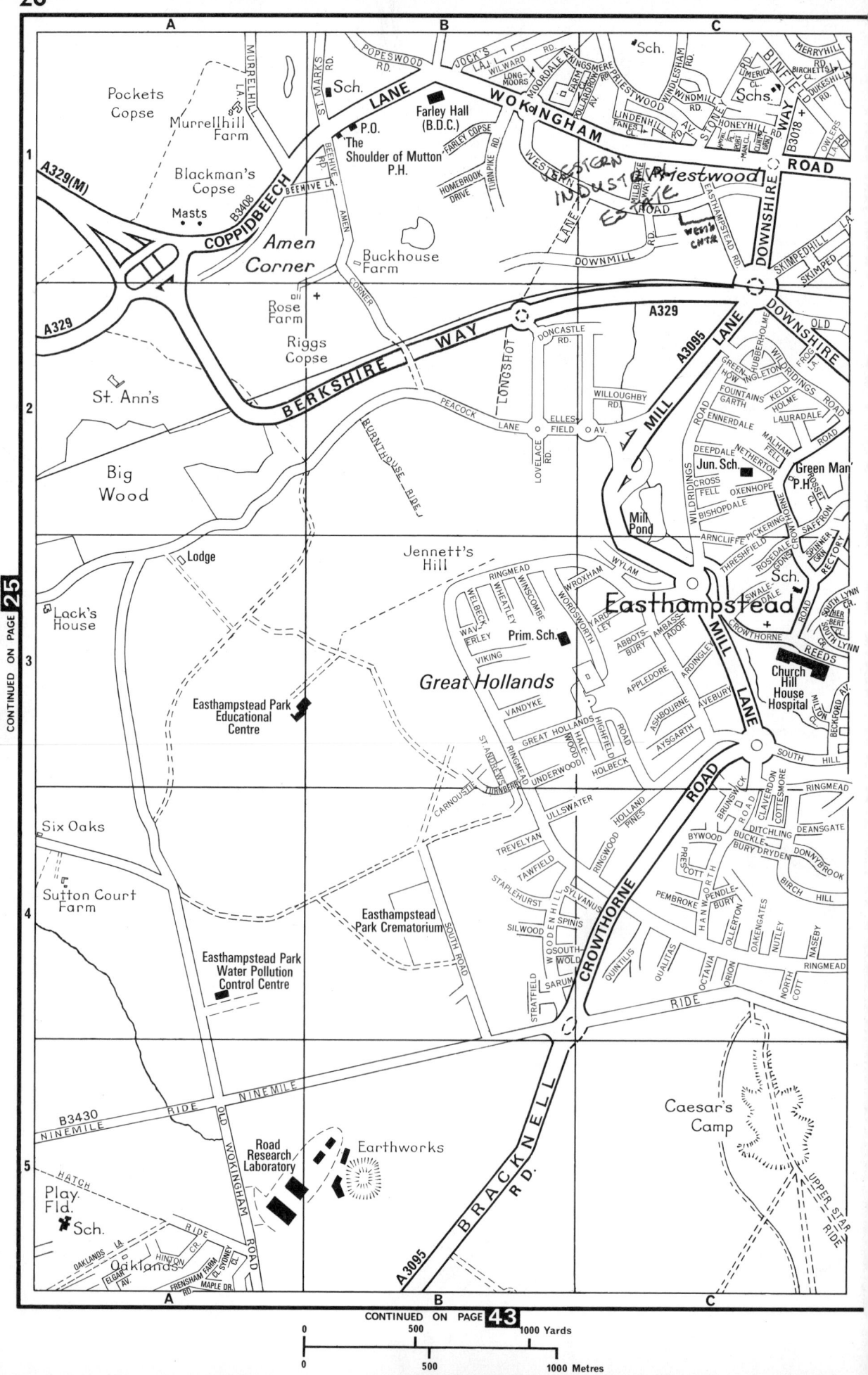

CONTINUED ON PAGE 25

A329(M)

A329

Pockets
Copse

Murrellhill
Farm

Blackman's
Copse

Masts

B3408

COPPIDBEECH

Amen
Corner

Rose
Farm

Riggs
Copse

St. Ann's

Big
Wood

Lodge

Lack's
House

Six Oaks

Sutton Court
Farm

MURRELLHILL LA.

ST MARKS RD.

BEEHIVE RD.

BEEHIVE LA.

AMEN

CORNER

POPESWOOD RD.

LANE

Sch.

P.O.

The Shoulder of Mutton
P.H.

Farley Hall
(B.D.C.)

Buckhouse
Farm

JOCK'S LA.

WILWARD RD.

LONG-MOORS

MOORDALE AV.

KINGSMERE

PRIESTWOOD AV.

FARLEY COPSE

HOMEBROOK DRIVE

TURNPIKE RD.

WOKINGHAM

WESTERN

LANE

LANE

WESTERN INDUSTRIAL ESTATE

WEST CNTR.

DOWNMILL

DOWNMILL RD.

A329

BERKSHIRE

WAY

PEACOCK

LANE

BURNTHOUSE

RIDE

LONGSHOT

LANE

DONCASTLE RD.

ELLES FIELD

LOVELACE RD.

WILLOUGHBY RD.

A3095

MILL

LANE

Sch.

Schs.

BINFIELD

WAY

MERRYHILL RD.

BIRCHETTS

DUKESHILL

LIMERICK

B3018

ROAD

DOWNSHIRE

DOWNSHIRE

SKIMPEDHILL

SKIMPED

OLD

WAY

LINDENHILL RD.

HONEYHILL RD.

LA.

WINDLSHAM RD.

WINDMILL AV.

WINDMILL

PRIESTWOOD

EASTHAMPSTEAD RD.

Jun. Sch.

DEEPDALE

CROSS
FELL

WILDRIDINGS

ROAD

WILDRIDINGS

GREAT
HOLLANDS

Jennett's
Hill

Great Hollands

Easthampstead Park
Educational
Centre

RINGMEAD

WELBECK

WAV

ERLEY

VIKING

WHEATLEY

WINSCOMBE

WROXHAM

WORDSWORTH

WYLAM

YARD
LEY

Prim. Sch.

ABBOTS
BURY

AMBASS
ADOR

Easthampstead

Sch.

Church Hill
House Hospital

REEDS

VANDYKE

CARNOUSTIE

ST ANDREW'S

TURNBERRY

RINGMEAD

UNDERWOOD

GREAT HOLLANDS

HALE
WOOD

HIGHFIELD

ROAD

HOLBECK

APPLEDORE

ASHBOURNE

ARDINGLEY

AYSGARTH

AVEBURY

SOUTH
HILL

Easthampstead
Park Crematorium

Easthampstead Park
Water Pollution
Control Centre

ULLSWATER

TREVELYAN

TAWFIELD

STAPLEHURST

SILWOOD

WOODENHILL

SOUTH
WOLD

SPINIS

SYLVANUS

STRATFIELD

SARUM

QUINTILIS

QUALITAS

OCTAVIA

ORION

NORTH
COTT

HOLLAND
PINES

RINGWOOD

PEMBROKE

HANWORTH

PENDLE-
BURY

OLLERTON

OAKENGATES

NUTLEY

NASEBY

RINGMEAD

BIRCH
HILL

DONKYBROOK

BYWOOD

BUCKLE

BURY

DRYDEN

PRES
COTT

BRUNSWICK

CLAVERDON

COTTESMORE

DITCHLING

DEANSGATE

ROAD

CROWTHORNE

ROAD

RIDE

Caesar's
Camp

UPPER STAR RIDE

Road Research
Laboratory

Earthworks

Play.
Fld.

Sch.

Oaklands

B3430

NINEMILE

RIDE

NINEMILE

RIDE

HATCH

OLD WOKINGHAM ROAD

SOUTH ROAD

BRACKNELL RD.

A3095

OAKLANDS LA.

HINTON

FRENSHAM FARM

SYDNEY

MAPLE DR.

CR.

CL.

ELGAR AV.

RD.

CONTINUED ON PAGE 43

0     500     1000 Yards

0     500     1000 Metres

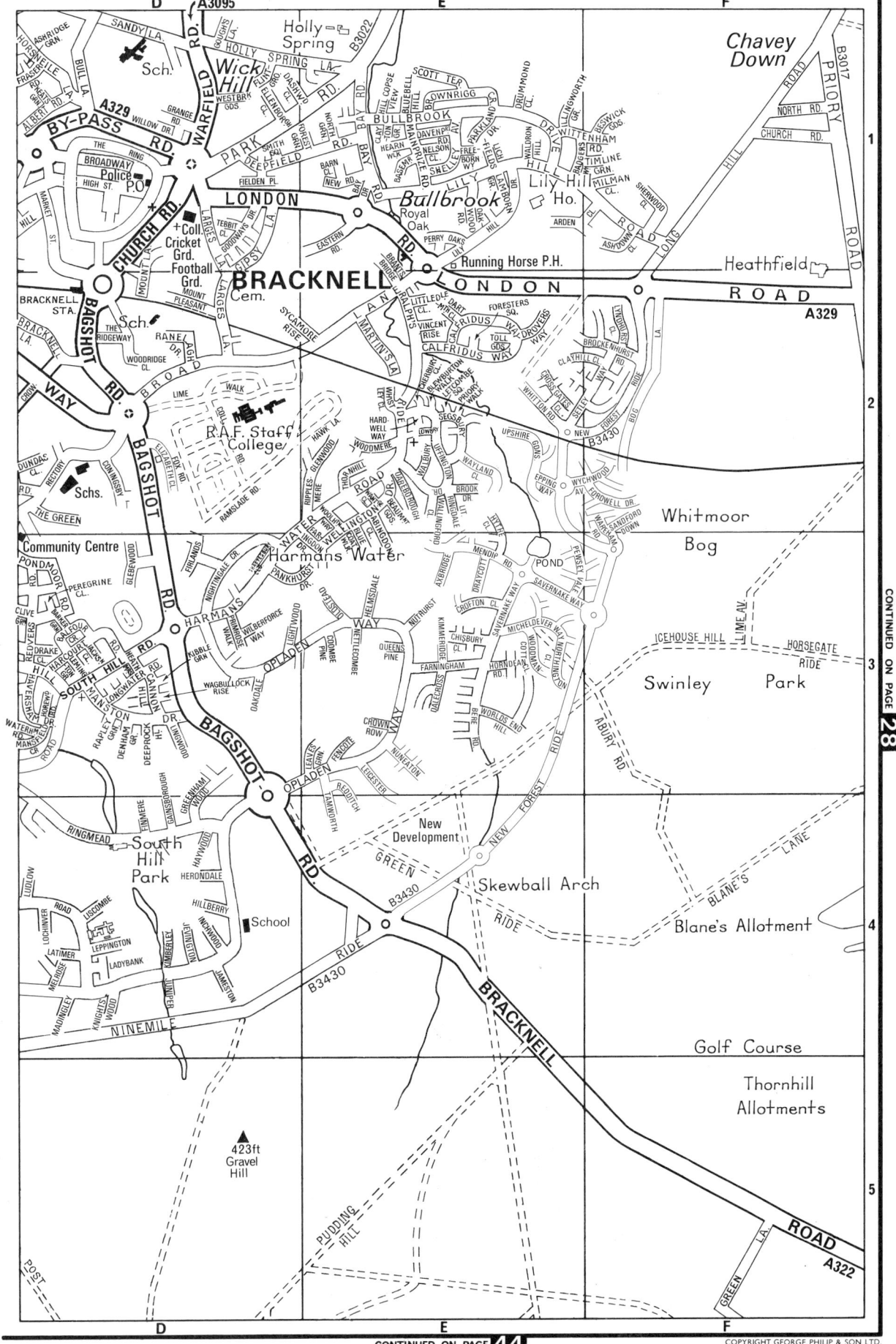

A     B     C

CONTINUED ON PAGE 27

THE GROVE
MILL
RIDE
KING EDWARD'S RISE
KENNEL WD.
KENNEL RIDE
A332
A330
WINKFIELD ROAD

Sch.
SCHOOL LA.
KING'S RIDE
JUBILEE AV.
BURLEIGH
KENNEL AV.
Rec. Grd.
Farm

ASHER DR.
FERRARD
WELAGH CR.
LEIGH WOOD
BRACKEN
WARREN ROW
PRINCE ANDREW RD.
HERON PL.
GOLD CUP LA.
NEW MEADOW
Burleigh Lodge
Ascot Heath

Ascot Priory

FERNBANK
BANK
CRES.
DARWELL DR.
MANSFIELD PL.
Blackmoor Stream
LANGDALE
NASH
Golf Course
COURSE RD.
RACE
NEW MILE RD.

Football Grd.
GOATERS RD.
Blackmoor Wood
PLACE
WENTWORTH AV.
WENTWORTH WAY
SUTHERLAND CHASE
VERNON DR.
BLYTHEWOOD
BURLEIGH LANE
ASCOT
Grand Stand
Grange Car Park

Playing Fld.
THE CLOSE
FERNBANK RD.
GANSBOROUGH DR.
HALLEY DR.
AUDLEY WAY
WINDSOR RD.
HIGH STREET
LONDON ROAD
LA.
CARBERY

A329
LONDON
RD.
O
Pol. S.
P.O. Fire Sta.
WELLS LA.

B3017
RIDE
FOREST RD.
Heatherwood Hosp.
P.C.
ST. GEORGE'S LA.
ST. GEORGE'S
Sch.

Englemere Pond
Nurses' Home
Ascot

SWINLEY ROAD
Englemere
ASCOT STA.
LYNDHURST RD.

Kingside
PRINCE CONSORT DR.
PRINCE ALBERT DRIVE
CARROLL CRES.
BOULDISH FARM RD.
ALL SOULS RD.
OLIVER RD.
SPRING GDS.
ROAD
CROMWELL RD.
FRANCIS CHICHESTER CL.
LOWER GRANGE

KING'S ROAD
SWINLEY ROAD
Sch.
CHURCH RD.
VICTORIA RD.
ELIZABETH GARDENS
BROCKENHURST
WOOD END DRIVE
TRUSS HILL RD.
CARDWELL CR.
COOMBE

Passmore's Plantation
WHYNSTONES RD.
RAVENSDALE RD.
South Ascot
ROAD
A330
ST. MARY'S HILL
Armitage Court

WOODLANDS
RIDE
HURST WOOD
FRIARY
MONKS DR.
REGENT'S WALK
LLANVAIR DR.
WOODLANDS CL.
LLANVAIR CL.
HORSEGATES RIDE
MONKS CL.
ST. MARY'S RD.
The Knoll

Kingside
DRIVE
St. Mary's Convent
ST. MARY'S RD.
THE COVERT
Broadlands

CORONATION DRIVE
Sch.
FARLEYDENE

But/steep Allotment
BOWDENS RIDE

Golf Course
RIDE
BOWDENS
Winklands Allotment
BAGSHOT ROAD
B3020
Berkshire Boundary
Surrey Boundary
Windlesham Hall

Club House
Fernhill Allotment
Golf Course
SUNNINGHILL RD.
'The Windmill' (P.H.)
RD.

P.C.
A322
A332
Dukeshill Allotment
HOLLYBUSH RD.
Windlesham Moor
Cricket Gd.
A30
LONDON ROAD
SNOW'S RIDE
CHESTER LA.
SNOW'S PADDOCK

A     B     C

CONTINUED ON PAGE 45

0   500   1000 Yards

0   500   1000 Metres

D E F

Johnson's Pond

Lower Farm

Cheapside

New Golden Gates

Pemberton Lodge

Sch.

HILLTOP CL.

WATERSPLASH

SUNNINGHILL LANE

PUMP LA.

RD. B383

Buckhurst Park

ROSY BOTTOM

BUCKHURST MILL

ROAD

SILWOOD CL.

Tetworth

The Cedars

Ashurst Lodge

CHURCH PATH

CHURCH LA.

Silwood Park

Harewood Lodge

Titness Park

The Oaks

Silwood Park

BUCKHURST LA.

VIRGINIA WATER

Blacknest Gate

LANE

Frostfarm Plantation

Car Pk.

BLACKNEST RD. A329

CHEAPSIDE LANE

LONDON ROAD

LONDON ROAD

SILWOOD RD.

AVENUE

Tittenhurst

SILWOOD ROAD

Coworth Park

Belvedere Fort

BEECH GROVE RD.

GWYNNE CL.

KINGSWICK CL.

KINGSWICK DR.

ORIENTAL RD.

Council Offices

Sch.

Schs.

Sunninghill

VILLAGE RD.

UPP. VILLAGE

HIGH ST.

KING'S RD.

QUEEN'S RD.

HIGH CLERE

THE SPINNEY

Sunningdale Park

HEATHFIELD AV.

LARCH RD.

KILN LANE

DALE RD.

SANDY LA.

COWORTH RD.

WHITMORE RD.

CHURCH LANE

The Red Lion (P.H.)

A30

Sunningdale

BOWDEN RD.

TRUSS HILL RD.

FOX COVERT LANE

BRIDGE RD.

CHARTERS COTTS.

HANCOCKS MT.

Works

BAGSHOT RD. B3020

Charters

HIGHFIELD RD.

PARK CRES.

PARK DR.

LYNDWOOD CR.

BEECH HILL RD.

RISE RD.

DRY ARCH RD.

STATION RD. B383

Schs.

CHURCH RD.

PARKSIDE RD.

SIDBURY RD.

TRYON

BEDFORD LANE

ROAD

Broomhall Farm

BROOMHALL LANE

P.O.

LONDON ROAD

CHOBHAM

WORPLE RD.

CROWN RD.

DAWSON WAY

REDWOOD DRIVE

BROOMFIELD PARK

SHRUBBS HILL LANE

SHEPLEY DR.

KEEPERS END

The Red Lion

RUNNYMEDE SURREY HEATH

DEVENISH

King's Beeches

CHARTERS RD.

Sch.

Sch.

Sunning Sch.

FIREBALL HILL

HAMILTON DR.

DEVENISH LA.

CHARTERS AVENUE

BALLENCRIEFF RD.

PINECOTES DR.

KNOLE WOOD DR.

GREENWAYS

Berkshire Boundary

Surrey Boundary

LADY MARGARET RD.

CHARTERS RD.

Level Crossing

Sunningdale STA.

CEDAR RD.

PRIORY RD.

P.H.

P.H.

NICOLLS CT.

BRIDGE VIEW

RICHMOND WOOD

ONSLOW RD.

HEATHER DR.

Broomhall

Old Windsor Bog

Thankerton House

LONDON ROAD

WESTWOOD LA.

Nurseries

Nurseries

WOODHALL LA.

Sunning Ho.

Wood Hall

CROSS RD.

Ridge Mount

RIDGE RD.

MOUNT RD.

KINGTON RD.

Sunningdale Golf Club Ho.

Hills End

FISHERS WOOD

TITLARKS HILL RD.

Monument

Little Arm

Sunningdale Golf Course

B

Long Down

CHOBHAM COMMON

B

B383

Windlesham Court

CONTINUED ON PAGE 30

1

2

3

4

5

D E F

CONTINUED ON PAGE 12

A     B     C

1

CONTINUED ON PAGE 29

Totem Pole

Wood Lee

The Dell

Berkshire Boundary
Surrey Boundary

VIRGINIA    WATER

Car Park

HILL CALLOW

HOLLOW   LANE

Virginia Beeches

Merlewood

Frostfarm Plantation

Wheatsheaf Hotel

B389

CHRISTCHURCH

WOODSIDE WAY

Christ Ch.+

GORSE HILL RD.

PIPERS END

2

BLACKNEST

A329

Waterfall

WATERFALL CL.

ROAD

WAVERLEY

STUART WAY

Sch.

DRIVE

CALLOW

WOODLANDS RD W

WOODLANDS RD.

WOODLANDS RD E.

MORELLA CL.

GORSE HEATH RD.

GORSE HILL RD.

HEATH CL.

STA. PARADE

RD.

SPRING WOODS

Wentworth Farm

PINEWOOD

STAYNE END

LINDALE

CHESTNUT AV.

LAKE RD.

LAKE

ABBEY RD.

ABBOTTS DR.

DRIVE

MONKS

AVENUE

ROAD

WALK

FRIARS RD.

Virginia Water

3

LONDON

A30

MEADOW RD.

DRIVE

SHERBOURNE DR.

PORTNALL

PORTNALL RD.

Wentworth Golf Course

WENTWORTH

Wentworth Club

WELLINGTON

ABBOTS

WELLINGTON

Wellington Bridge

DRIVE

BROADWAY

VIRGINIA

VIRGINIA

BADGERS HILL

RD.

AVENUE

OAKWOOD

NUNS

KEEPERS WLK.

THIS CLOSE

+ Bourne

BEECH BOURNE RD.

MINT

CABRERA AV.

TRUMPSGREEN AV.

Golf Course

NORTH WENTWORTH

RD.

FAIRWOOD

NORTH DR.

PORTNALL GOLF COURSE

HARPESFORD

L

SUNDON CR.

HILLSIDE AV.

CROWN

CAB. CL.

TRUMPSGREEN

RD.

THE MOUNT

CROWN LA.

Wentworth Golf Course

RISE

Wentworth Golf Course

HEATHERSIDE DR.

GOLF DRIVE

WEST

DRIVE

BOURNESIDE

DRIVE EAST

FAIRWAYS

AVENUE

Knowlehill

Stag & Hounds P.H.

SABY WAY

OAK TREE CL.

SURVIVAL

PER.

4

Wentworth Golf Course

Three Gables

Great Wood

MERESIDE PL.

BEECHWOOD

SOUTH

RD.

LANE

KITSMEAD

TRUMPSGREEN

Longcross Bridge

KNOWLE HILL

CORRIE GDNS.

KNOBLE GROVE CL.

KNOWLE GROVE

Little Arm

LONGCROSS STA.

5

Ship Hill

Long Arm

CHOBHAM

COMMON

B

RUNNYMEDE
SURREY HEATH

BURMA RD.

CHOBHAM

M3

HOLT

ANGLEWOOD CL.

ALBURY

LONGCROSS

Longcross House

Barrowhills

LANE

P.O.

ROAD

Old School Cafe

Flutters Hill

B386

A     B     C

0    500    1000 Yards

0    500    1000 Metres

D E F

Great
Fosters

Whitehall
Farm

Luddington
Ho.

STROUDE RD.

BLACK
LAKE CL.

HURST LA.

STROUDE AV.

LUDDINGTON AV.

Stroude
Farm

Stroude

THE LANE

WHITEHALL FM. LA.

1

Crabtree
Corner

Thorpe
Industrial
Est.

DELTA
WAY

CLANDIR AV.

THORPE
LEA
RD.

WARWICK AV.

LONGSIDE
CL.

B388

BOSCOMBE AV.

THORPE
BYPASS

CRABTREE DR.

GREEN

Cemᵞ

Eastly
End

THE
ROSARY

NORLANDS
LA.

AYMER CL.

MOORFIELD
CL.

WEIR PL.

PEKET
WAY

CLIVE
WAY

AYMER

ACRE
RD.

GILES
TRAVERS
CL.

COLD-
HARBOUR
LANE

LANE

LANE

Eastlyend
House

The
Grange

Car
Park

2

Corse
Hill

COTSWORTH

Royal
Holloway
Sanatorium

Hurst Farm

Thorpe
Green

B

STROUDE RD.

THE LANE

Cricket
Grd.

SANDY LA.

CHRISTCHURCH SANDHILLS

STROUDE

THORPE
ORD.

WESTERN
AV.

MIDWAY
THE

ROSEMARY

BENCE

THE
GOWER

FLEET
WAY

BOURNE
MEADOW
LANE

COTT. PAK
PARK WAY

VILLAGE

COLDHARBOUR

P.O.

TREES

YEW

St. Mary's
Ch.

Thorpe

MILL
LANE

'MILL HOUSE LANE

The

Bourne

THORPE

M3

M25

GREEN
LANE

B389

'Rose & Crown'
P.H.

P.O.

P

VIRGINIA
WATA

STA.

TRUMPSGREEN
RD.

ORCHARD

Sch.

SANDHILLS
CT.

THE DRIVE

TRUMPS
MILL
LANE

Works

Works

**2** (M3)

**12** (M25)

St Ann's Hill
(Public Park)

South
Wood

St Ann's Hill

Twynersh

ST. ANNS
HILL

B388
ROAD

ST.
ANNS RD.

Sch.

PYRCRFT RD.

The Grange

Sch.

3

BRIDGE
LANE

LYNE
ROAD

LYNE

LYNE

LYNE
CL.

HARROW
BOTTOM
RD.

Lyne Farm

FARM
CROSSING

RUXBURY

ALMNERS
RD.

DIANTHUS
CL.

RUTHERBANYK
OLDBURY
RD.

4

Trumps
Farm

Lyne Place

LYNE
RD.

The Brooks

Alm'ners Barn
Farm

HARDWICK
RD.

RD.

Lyne
Copse

Rec. Grd.

P.O.

Hersham Grove

Lyne

ALMNERS

Cockcrow Hill

A320

5

Hersham
Farm

Fan Court
School

Fan Court
Farm

LONGCROSS

(TRYS HILL)

ROAD

LANE

B386

France
Farm

Fan Grove

Sch.

Holy Trinity
Ch.

Silverlands

Botleys

STONEHILL RD.

HOLLOWAY

White Lodge
Centre

HILL

St Peter's
Hospital

Hardwick Court
Farm

A320

GUILDFORD

RD.

GREEN LA.

Sch.

BRET-
LANDS

ELM TREE

GREEN LANE

SANDALWO

FERNDALE
AV.

LITTLE GREEN LA.

LYNDHURST
WAY

HILLCRST
AV.

WAVERLEY
DRIVE

FERNLDS
CLOSE

CONTINUED ON PAGE **32**

CONTINUED ON PAGE 14

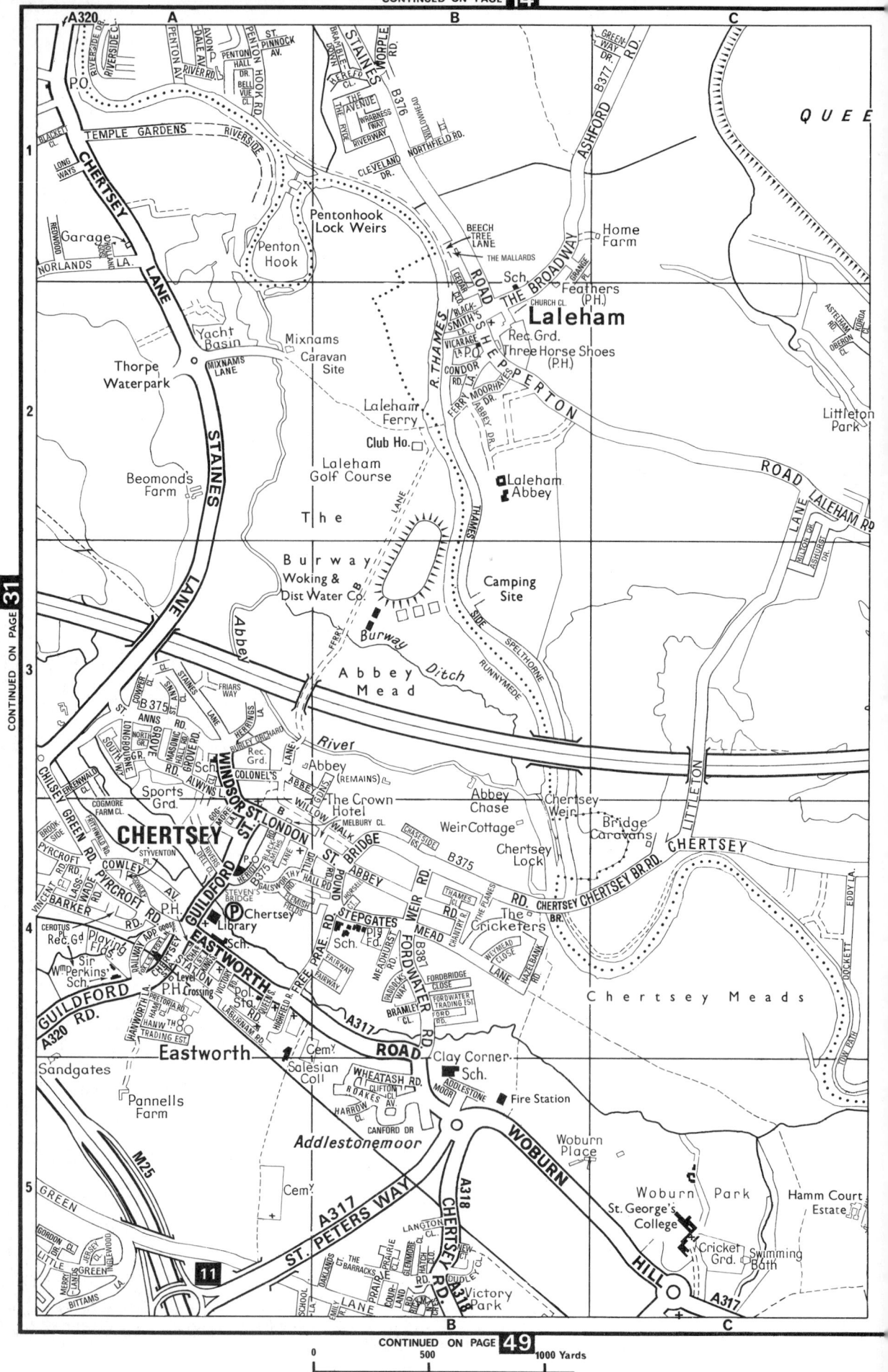

CONTINUED ON PAGE 31

CONTINUED ON PAGE 49

0     500     1000 Yards

0     500     1000 Metres

CONTINUED ON PAGE 15

D E F

**Sailing Area**

**N MARY RESERVOIR**

*Bird Sanctuary*

WINDMILL CL.
BROOKLANDS CL.
MILLFIELD
LINCOLN WY
CRAYONNE
Sch.
WEST DOLPHIN RD.
NORTH
SOUTH
HARRIS WAY
CYPRESS RD.
HOMEWATER
BEVERLEY RD.
RAVENS RD.
Sch.
Sch.
UPPER HALLIFORD STA.
NURSERY
EVELYN RD.
EVELYN CR.
NURSERY GDNS.
SUTHERLAND AV.
LAYTON'S LANE
STRATTON
RACING
GDNS.
FALCON WAY
PEREGRINE ROAD
Sch.

*Charlton*

ASHFORD RD.
SPELTHORNE LA.
OLD MARY RD.
CHARLTON RD.
HETHERINGTON RD.
HARROW
LODGE FIRE RD.
ALMOND
WALNUT TREE RD.
CROSS WELL CL.
GENEVA
WINDMILL RD.
HASLETT RD.
BIRCH GRO.
VINCENT RD.
Sch.

**Littleton** NEW RD.

Sch.
STUDIOS RD.
RECTORY RD.
GODDARD CL.
MAGDALENE RD.
HITCHCOMBE
WILDCROFT
Sch.
STEWART AV.
PETTS LA.
FRANCIS CL.

*River* Ash
BRIDGE
CRANWELL GR.
REC. GRD.
WINCHSTONE
HORNE RD.
SQUIRE'S RD.
HERMITAGE
GLOS.
YEW
BARTON
FORD
MONK
BAREFORD
**Shepperton Green**

**LALEHAM**
BRAVING TON
FAIRVIEW
CLOSE
ROSEWOOD
BRIAR RD.
BUSTY
BRIAR
THORN HILL WAY
JESSIMAN TER.
Sch.
ACACIA AV.
PRESTON AV.
GREENLOW CR.
PENTLAND AV.
PO.
Bull Inn
B.376
YANGTZE AV.
WALK
WATERSPLASH

**Refuse Incinerator**

The Bugle B.H.
HALLIFORD CL.
BLACK-BERRY CL.
CHERRY WAY
BRAMBLE CL.
HAW HORSE CL.
WALLER RD.
ANDERSON
PO.
UPPER HALLIFORD RD.
**Upper Halliford**
SCHOOL WALK
ROAD
HOLMBK. ORCH.
CHERTSEY FLD.
HALLIFORD GRN.
THE FOLD
HALLIFORD HO.
MINSTERLY AV.
CHESTNUT GRO.
**HALLIFORD**
HIGHFIELD
RADNOR RD.

*Halliford House*

Grange Farm Caravan Site

**UPP. HALLIFORD BYPASS**
**BRIDGE RD**
**GASTON RD**
**UPP. HALLIFORD RD**
A244

LOIS DR.
CRESCENT RD.
LINDEN RD.
BARBARA
LOIS DR.
CRESCENT WAY
CATLIN CRES.
GASTON WAY
B3366 DUPPAS
SHEPPERTON STA.
STANDS RD.
COTETT AV.
RUSSING-TON RD.
WESTERN AV.
NEIL
FARRELL
DRIVEWAY
WEST RD.
GORDON RD.
LINDSAY DR.
Gaston Bri.
CUCKOO POUND
PINHOE
GASTON BRI.
ROXFORD RD.

**GREEN**
CRESCENT
SHEPPERTON CT. DR.
MANOR FM. HERE
PEARMAIN PL.
MARION AV.
BARTON
MANOR FM. RD.
HIGH STREET
BRUCE AV.
KILMISTON
THURL STONE CL.
GROVE
COPTHORNE CL.
GLEBELAND GS.
MANYGATE
MEADOW VIEW
Sch.
REC. GRD.
MILLER
GORDON DR.

**Shepperton**
Sch.
B 375 WAY
RENFREE
FARM
ST. NICHOLAS DR.
Cem.
MANOR HO. CT.
Cricket Grd.
ORANGE WAY
GRANGE CL.
**CHURCH ROAD**
Anchor Hotel
CH. SQ. FERRY
PO.
Ferry
SHEEP WALK

**RUSSELL**
**WALTON LANE**
**FORDBRIDGE ROAD**
**GASTON ROAD**
**WALTON BR. RD.**
B 376
**Lower Halliford**
FELIX LA.
Sand & Ballast Pits
Ferry
HILL RISE
ELEY RD.
MANOR RD.
RIVERSIDE
THAMES ST.
RIVER MT.
MT. FELIX
PENNY LA.
RIDGEWAY
GATEWAY
HEPWORTH WAY
BRIDGE

Spelthorne
ELMBRIDGE RD.
Riverside Farm
Res.
Res.
**Football Ground**
WALTON LANE
R. THAMES
WALTON BR.
**NEW ZEALAND AV.**
A3050
A244
**DRIVE**
ASHLEY RD.
ASHLEY CL.
SANDY
Town Hall

**Shepperton Lock**
Pharaoh's I.
Weir
FERRY LANE
Hamhaugh I.
Thames Lock
Weir
DORNEY RD.
WALTON LANE
**OATLANDS DRIVE**
TOWER GR.
THE MOUNT
ASHLEY PARK
LINDEN GR.
SILVER DALE AV.
ASHLEY RD.
IRETON AV.
HIGHMOUNT
ORCHARD END
LAKESIDE

MOAT
WEY RD.
ROUND OAK RD.
WESSAMY RD.
BEALE'S LA.
RADNOR R.
GLEN
COE
HANWAY
ST. ALBANS
THE WILLOWS
CONVENT
GROTTO
GREENSIDE RD.
GREENLDS RD.
BONDETTE RD.
TUDOR WK.
**Portmore Park**
Greenlands Farm
Dairy Fm.
MALLARDS REACH
OATLANDS MERE
FARRINGTON ACRES
TEMPLEMERE
BEECHCROFT
**A3050**
BERKELEY
BEVERLEY CL.
BRYNFORD
CRICKET WAY
WEST DENE WAY
Cricket Grd.
THE PADDOCKS
SILVERDALE AV.
MARROWELLS
**OATLANDS CASTLE ROAD**
**CHASE**
B365
ASHLEY RD.

**Broad Water**
Oatlands Park Hotel
**Oatlands Park**
Swimming Pool
FINNART
MARLBOROUGH DR.
MEADOWS LEIGH
OLD PALACE
APEX RD.
VICTORIA RD.
KINGSTON
SARUM RD.
VALE RD.
OATLANDS DR.

CONTINUED ON PAGE 50

CONTINUED ON PAGE 34

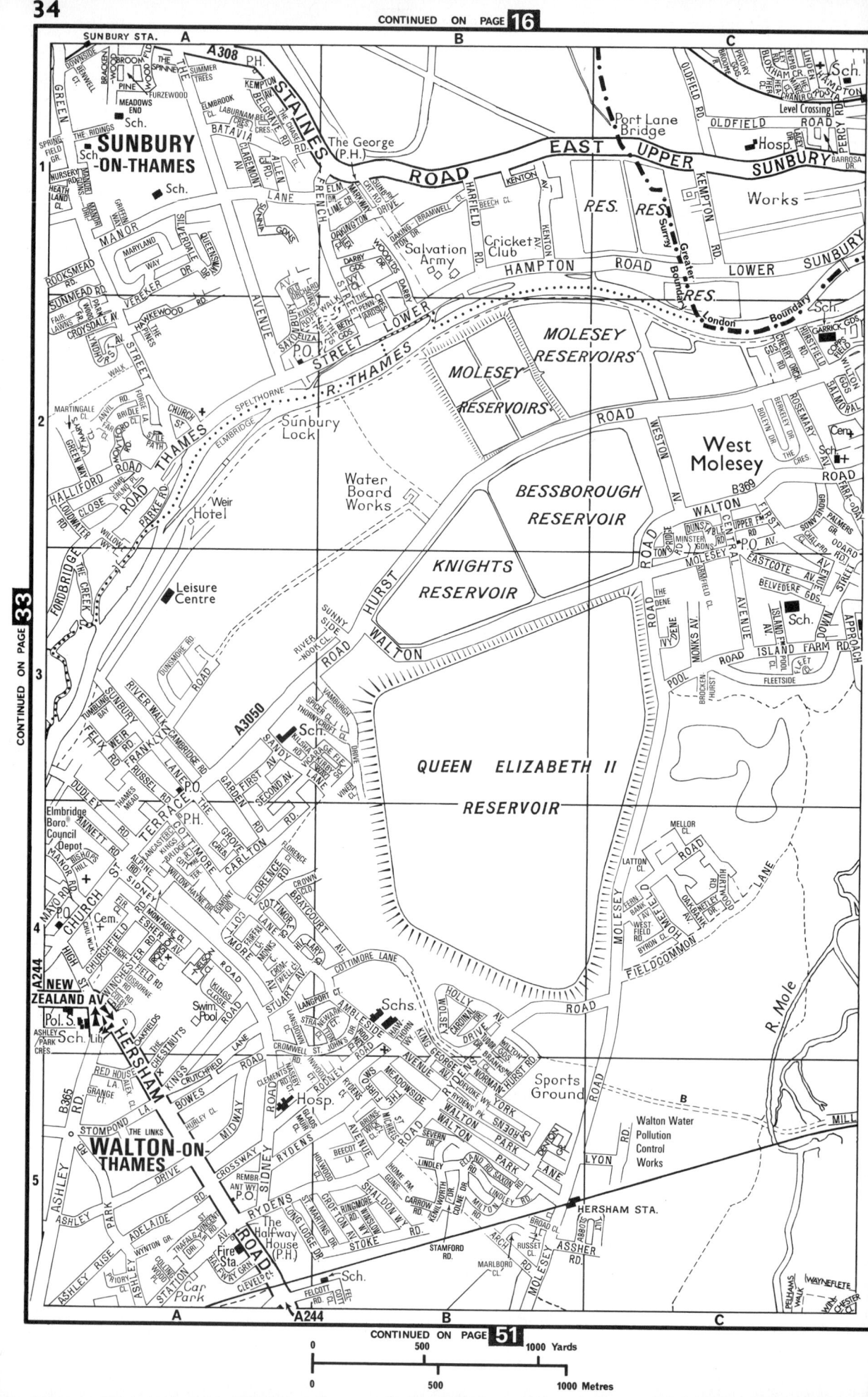

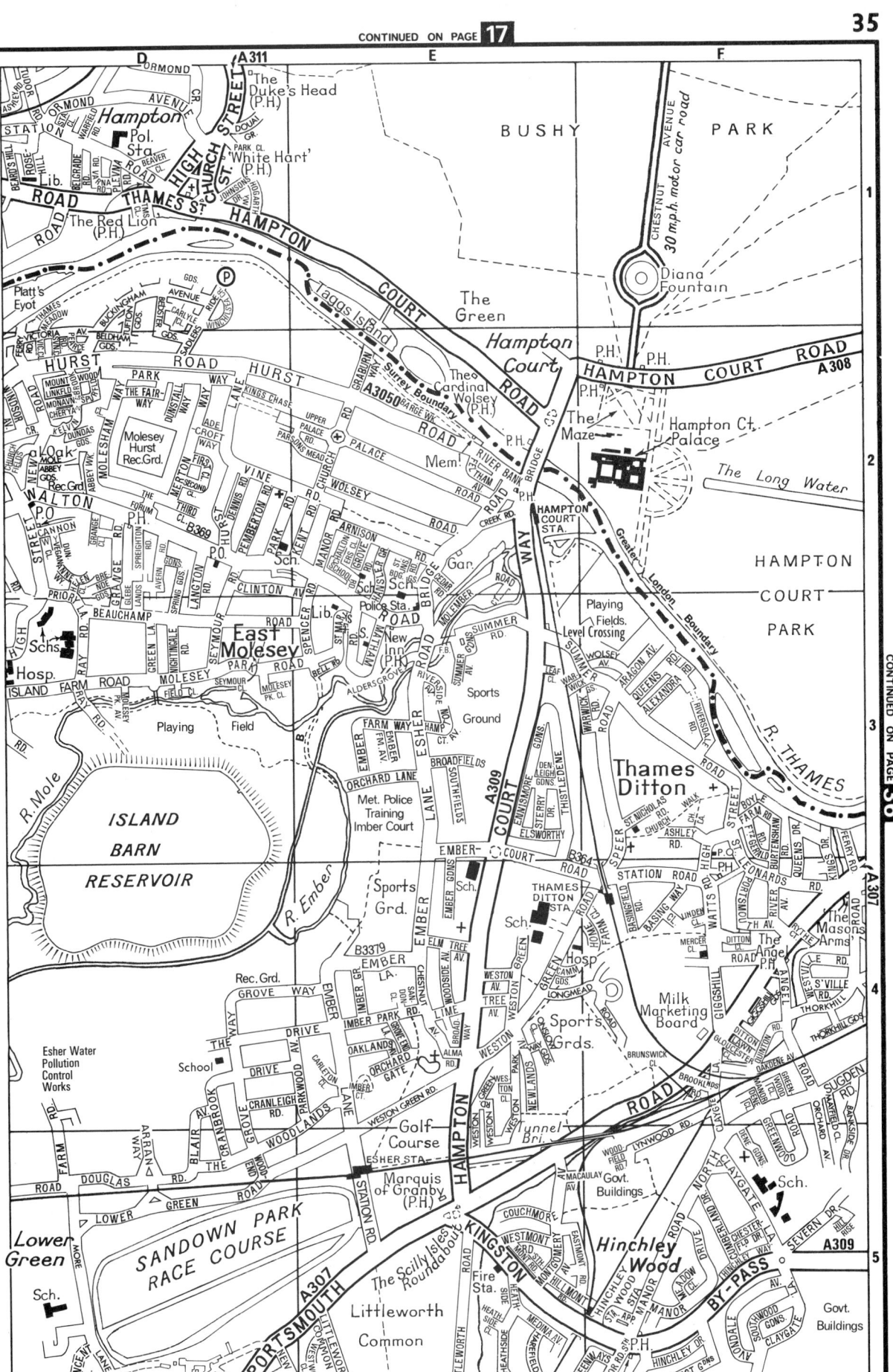

CONTINUED ON PAGE 18

Hampton Wick

The Long Water

Raven's Ait

Golf Course

Club Ho.

See page 159 for detailed plan of KINGSTON centre

KINGSTON-UPON-THAMES

■ Crematorium

Kingston Hospital

COOMBE RD.

SURBITON

Long Ditton

Southborough

UPPER BRIGHTON ROAD

Tolworth

CONTINUED ON PAGE 35

A309 KINGSTON BY-PASS

HOOK

KINGSTON BY-PASS

0    500    1000 Yards

0    500    1000 Metres

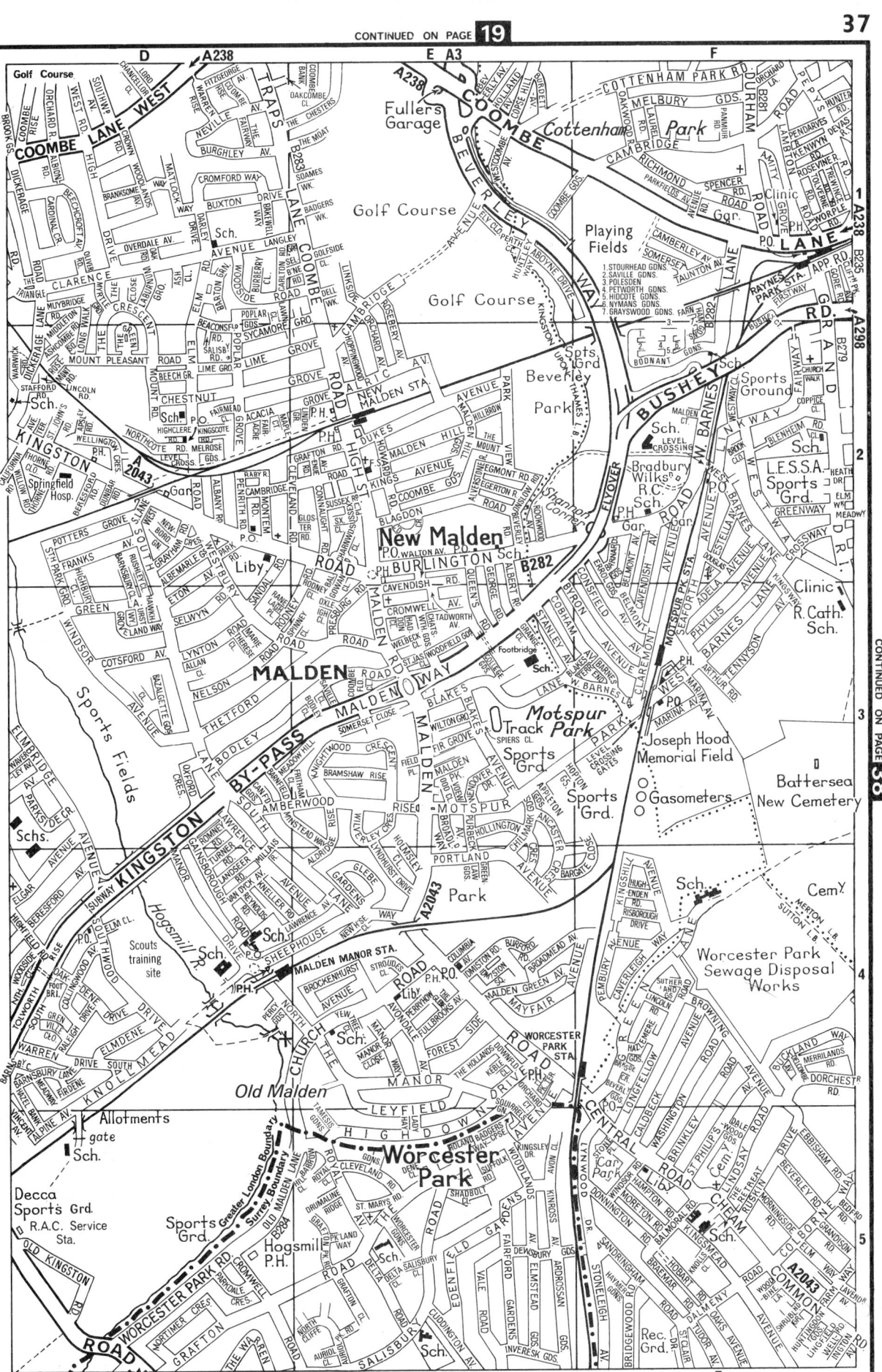

CONTINUED ON PAGE **20**

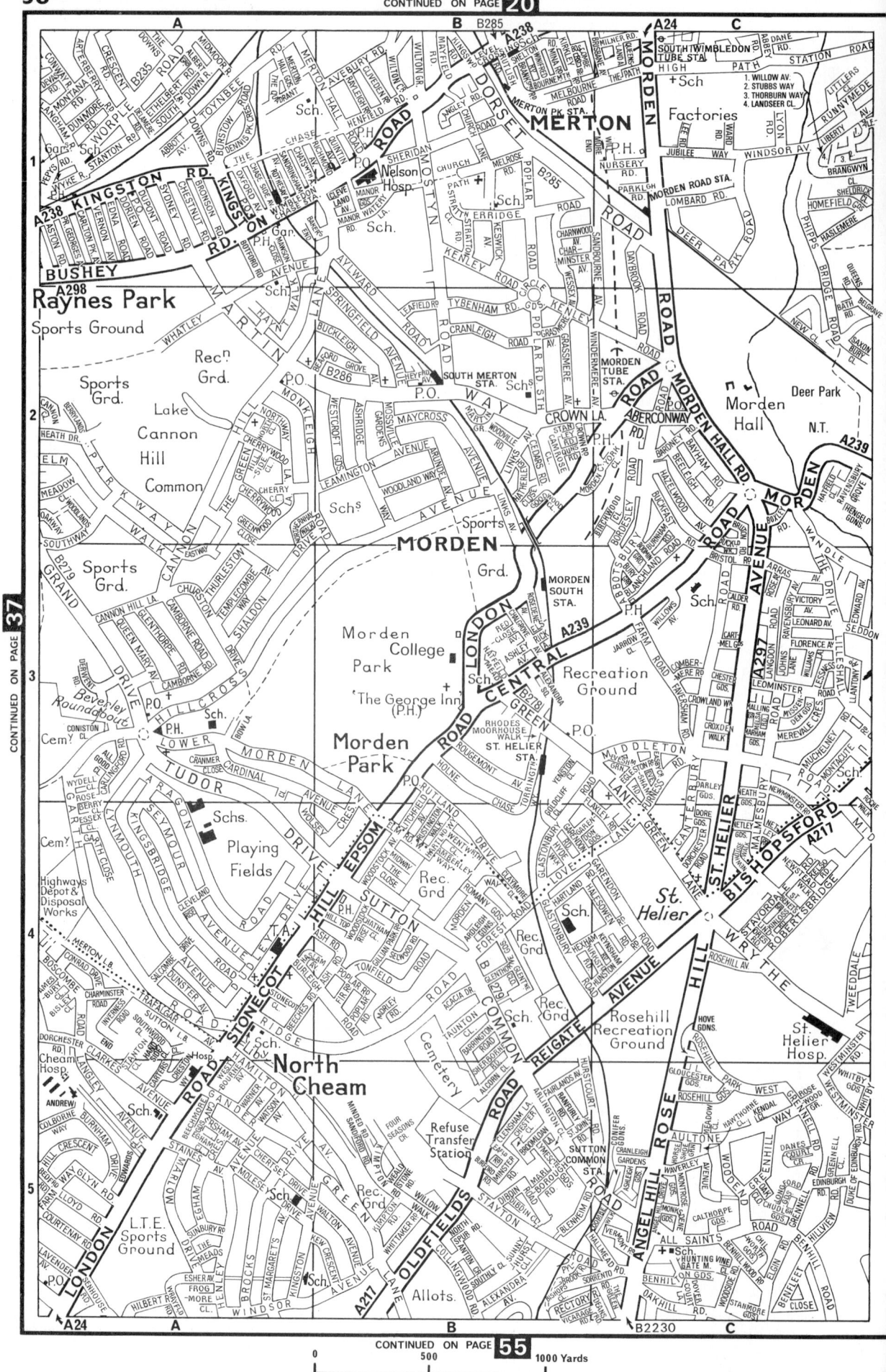

CONTINUED ON PAGE **37**

CONTINUED ON PAGE **55**

0          500          1000 Yards

0          500          1000 Metres

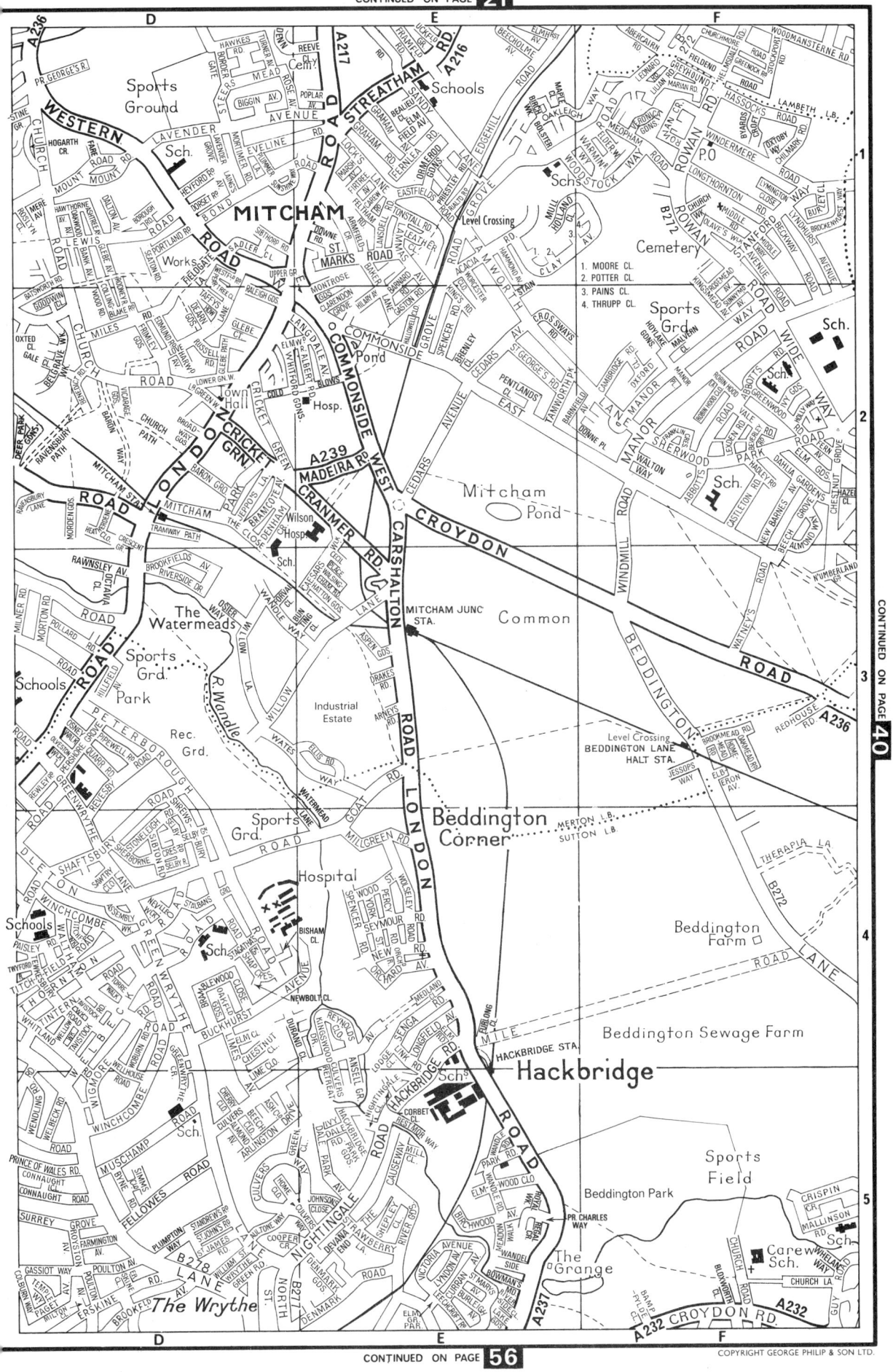

CONTINUED ON PAGE **40**

COPYRIGHT GEORGE PHILIP & SON LTD.

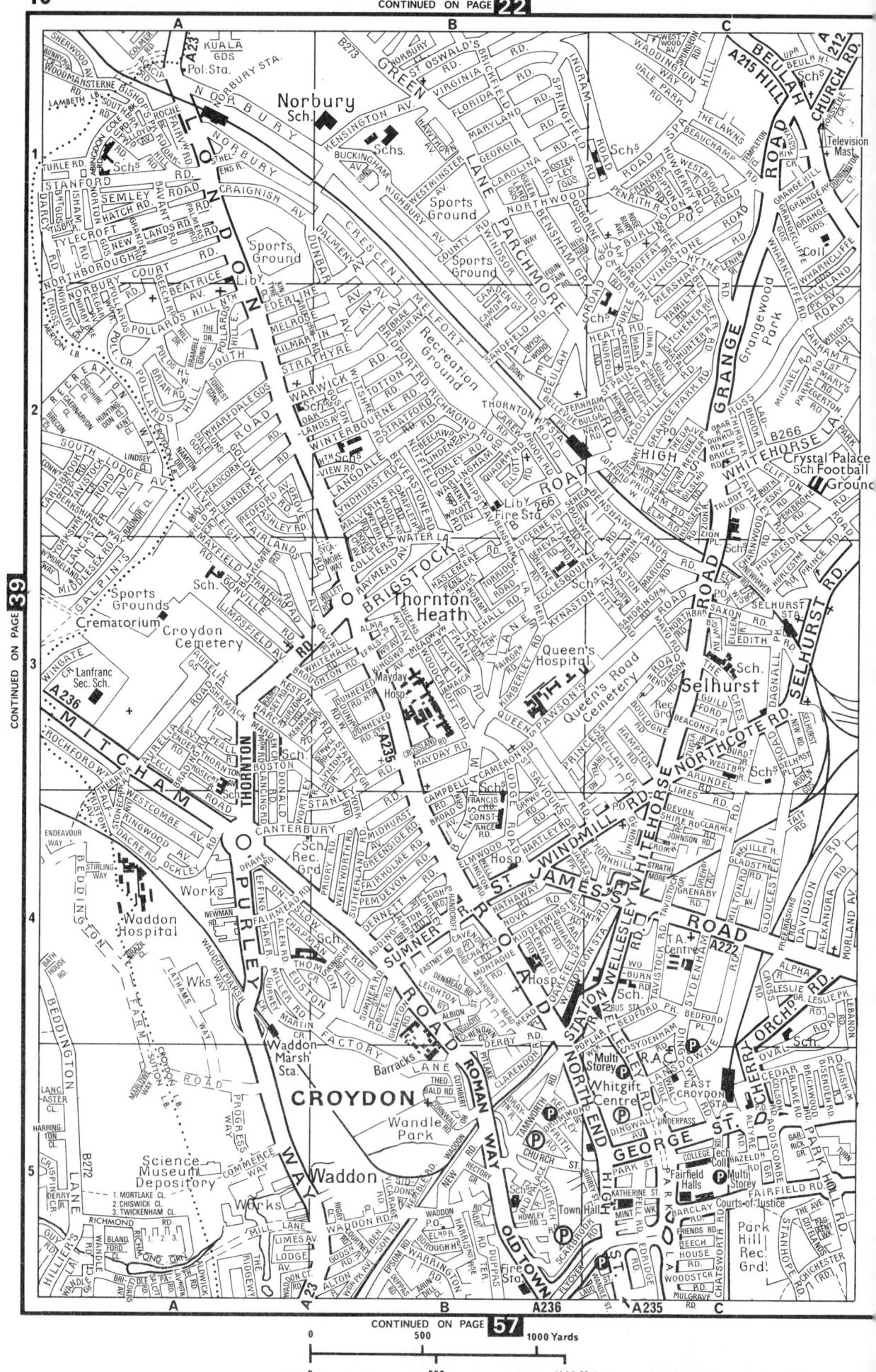

CONTINUED ON PAGE 22

CONTINUED ON PAGE 39

Norbury

Thornton Heath

Selhurst

CROYDON

Waddon

CONTINUED ON PAGE 57

0        500        1000 Yards

0        500        1000 Metres

CONTINUED ON PAGE **42**

Playing Fields

Orchard Playing Field

Sth Norwood Lake

Anerley

Betts Park

ANERLEY RD.

CROYDON

ELMERS

END

ROAD

BECKENHAM

HIGH ST.

Kent House Sta.

Kings Hall

Clock House

Electricity Works

Elmers End

Beckenham Crematorium

Elmers End Sta.

Sewage Works

UPPER ELMERS END R.

Sports Grounds

Sth Norwood

WHITEHORSE

NORWOOD HILL

Sth.

SELHURST RD.

HIGH ST.

PENGE RD.

PORTLAND

South Norwood Rec. Grd.

CROYDON

LANE

LANE

Long La. Wood

Woodside

Woodside Sta.

WOODSIDE RD.

SPRING LA.

LONG

ROAD

Ashburton Park

Ashburton Playing Fields

Woodmere

Mere End

School Playing Fld.

Parkfield Recn Grd.

LWR ADDISCOMBE

ADDISCOMBE

Addiscombe

Rec. Grd.

SHIRLEY

ROAD

A215

A232

WICKHAM ROAD

Hospital

Playing Field

Trinity Sch.

Shirley Park Golf Course

John Ruskin Sch.

Shirley

Rec Grd

Playing Field

CHICHESTER RD.

CONTINUED ON PAGE 24

CONTINUED ON PAGE 41

# BECKENHAM

Golf Course
Bromley Park

Shortlands

Town Hall

Beckenham Hospital

BROMLEY ROAD

BECKENHAM LA.

Eden Park

Maternity Hosp.

Elgood Playing Field

Kelsey Park

HAYES

Hayes

Langley Court

Parklangley

WESTMORELAND

PICKHURST

Upper Elmers End

UPR. ELMERS END RD.

Bethlem Royal Hospital

Park Farm

Sports Ground

Langley Park

Golf Course

Golf Club Ho.

WEST WICKHAM STA.

WICKHAM ROAD

HIGH ST.

GLEBE WAY

CROYDON RD.

Spring Park Wood

Spring Pk. Primy. Sch.

Cheyne Hosp.

Playing Field

West Wickham

W. Wickham Common

ADDINGTON RD.

Hayes Down Sch.

HAYES STA.

Sports Ground

Blake Rec. Grd.

Eden Park Sta.

LINKS WAY

SOUTH EDEN PARK ROAD

BECKENHAM RD.

STATION RD.

HAWES LANE

THE PICKHURST

LANGLEY WAY

A232

A234

A222

A2015

A21

A222

A232

A20/2

CONTINUED ON PAGE 59

0     500     1000 Yards

0     500     1000 Metres

CONTINUED ON PAGE **44**

GREENWOOD
KEATS
CELL
PUR
PURL
BUTLER AV.
GRANGE
RD.
EVEREST
BELMONT
HILLARY DR.
FRESHAM
CORONATION DR.
OLD SAWMILL LA.

WILTSHIRE
WESTBURY
THE
GOSSIAM WAY
CORSHAM
AVENUE
LYNC
THORN
BURY
LARKSWOOD DR.
CIRCLE HILL RD.
Sch.
P.O.

OLD WOKINGHAM RD.
WOOD
PINE
ROAD
LYON RD.

BRACKNELL

A3095 ROAD

THE DEVIL'S HIGHWAY
ROMAN ROAD

ELLIS RD.
WOKINGHAM RD.
NEW RD.
AVENUE
A3095

DUKE'S
RIDE
ALBERT RD.
HEATH HILL RD.
PINE FIELDS
CHURCH HILL RD.
NAPIER RD.
FIRE H. CL.

WATERLOO RD.
LANE END WAY
CHURCH STREET
CAMBRIDGE RD.
WELLINGTON RD.

Crowthorne

HIGH ST.
LOWER BROADMOOR ROAD
ADDISCOMBE
CHAUCER RD.
GOLDSMITH WAY
SHAW PK.
PINEHILL RD.
GRANT RD.
GORDON RD.

BROADMOOR
BROOKERS ROW
BROOKERS CORNER
BROADMOOR
ROAD

CHAPLAINS RD.
Lodge Hills
Cricket Grd.

The Prince Alfred (P.H.)

Broadmoor Hospital

Sch.
ROAD
GORDON RD.

SANDHURST RD.
BYRON CL.
KINGSLEY CL.
ARENAL DR.
Pine Hill

SOUTH BROADMOOR

Broadmoor Farm

Poppy Hills

Wellington College

A3095 ROAD

Wildmoor Bottom

moor Bottom

STRAW ROAD
LINDALE RD.
WAY
FEKENHAM LI.

Playing Field

Playing Field
LONGDOWN
LAPWING
MICKLE
OAKTREE WAY
MICKLE
LONG
HARTS LEAP CL.
HEARTS LEAP RD.
SPRING WOODS
BEECH RIDE
RUBIN LA.
ROBIN
THIBET RD.
PRIM
ROSE
GREENWAYS
BROOM ACRES

Sandhurst
WELLINGTON
ST. HELENS RD.
WILLOWS
THE BROADWAY
ALBION RD.
PARK
BROOKSIDE
GREEN LA.
WOODBINE CL.

ABINGDON RD.
BRAYE CL.
APPLE WAY
ACACIA
WHITMORE DR.
WAR GROVE
EVENLODE
SISS
RACK WAY

OAK AVENUE
CAMBRIDGE ROAD
CHURCH RD.
MINS
ROOKWOOD WAY
VICTORIA RD.
BROOK

Owlsmoor

OXFORD
HARVARD RD.
YALE
WADHAM
MERTON CL.
MAGDALEN RD.
PETERHOUSE CL.

Sch.

YEOVIL RD.
SILVER HILL
ROAD
COLLEGE CRES.

Sch.
ELTERN CL.
BLACKBIRD CL.
BLACKCAP PL.
BLUETHROAT
AVOCET
Sch.
BULL FINCH
CHAKE CRES.
RICHMOND RD.
THE CLOSE

Ranges

Ryl. Military College Hosp.

Hosp.

YORKTOWN
CROWTHORNE
A321
New Inn
SANDHURST STA.
The White Swan (P.H.)
WARREN RD.
YORK RD.
COMPTON
THE
ALBION RD.
P.O.
ROAD

VULCAN WAY

Works

MARSHALL ROAD

SWAN LANE
DARBY GREEN LA.
WINCHESTER WAY
LYNDHURST RD.
ANDOVER RD.
HEARSLEY GDNS.
BEECHNUT DR.
COMPTON CL.
ROSEMARY
LYON CL.
CHURCH
BEAULIEU GDNS.
CRICKET HILL LA.

Berkshire Boundary
Hampshire Boundary

YORKTOWN
DEVON CL.
FLORENCE RD.
BROOKSOME
BACON
BURNE JONES DR.
REYNOLDS GRN.
NEW LOWRY CL.
TURNER PL.
MUNNINGS DR.
BERRY BANK
CONSTABLE CL.
ROAD
WESTBOURNE RD.
Oak Gr. Spts Grd.

Sports Grounds

Racquets Cts.

Royal Military Academy

Lower Lake

St. Michael

R. Blackwater

WHITE RD.
HAIG
ROBERT'S RD.
KING'S WALK
ALLENBY RD.
STAFF COLLEGE RD.
Surrey Boundary

York Town

READING RD. A327
Darby Grn.
DARBY GREEN ROAD
GLOBE FARM
OLDE FARM CLO.
HARTLEY LA.
BRAMLEY CL.
FROGMORE
BEAULIEU
FROGMORE ROAD
WOODBRIDGE RD.
P.O.
BINNS LA.
BRINN'S LA.
BELL
FOXLEY LANE
ASJIT CL.
ROSEMARY GARDEN
HAMBLE LANE
TICH BORNE LA.
HOLLY LANE
MEADOW WAY
KINGSWAY

LAUNDRY LA.
THE TERRACE
SULLIVAN RD.
Victoria RD.
STANHOPE RD.
LONDON A30
EDWARD AV.
ALEXANDRA AV.
FRIMLEY RD. B3411
A30 ROAD
HARCT.
PLANTATN. ROW

| | |
|---|---|
| 1 | DURHAM RD. |
| 2 | FRODSHAM WAY |
| 3 | KEEBLE WAY |
| 4 | NUFFIELD DR. |
| 5 | BIRKBECK PL. |
| 6 | GIRTON CL. |
| 7 | DOVEDALE CL. |
| 8 | TOTTENHAM WK. |
| 9 | HORNBEAM CL. |
| 10 | MAGNOLIA CL. |
| 11 | MAY CL. |
| 12 | SHRIVENHAM CL. |
| 13 | ATREBATTI RD. |
| 14 | COOKHAM CL. |
| 15 | FARINGDON CL. |
| 16 | FARCROSSE CL. |
| 17 | HUNGERFORD CL. |
| 18 | SEVERN CL. |
| 19 | HUMBER WAY |
| 20 | BURGHEAD CL. |
| 21 | INVERNESS WAY |
| 22 | FORTROSE CL. |

0    500    1000 Yards

0    500    1000 Metres

CONTINUED ON PAGE **27**

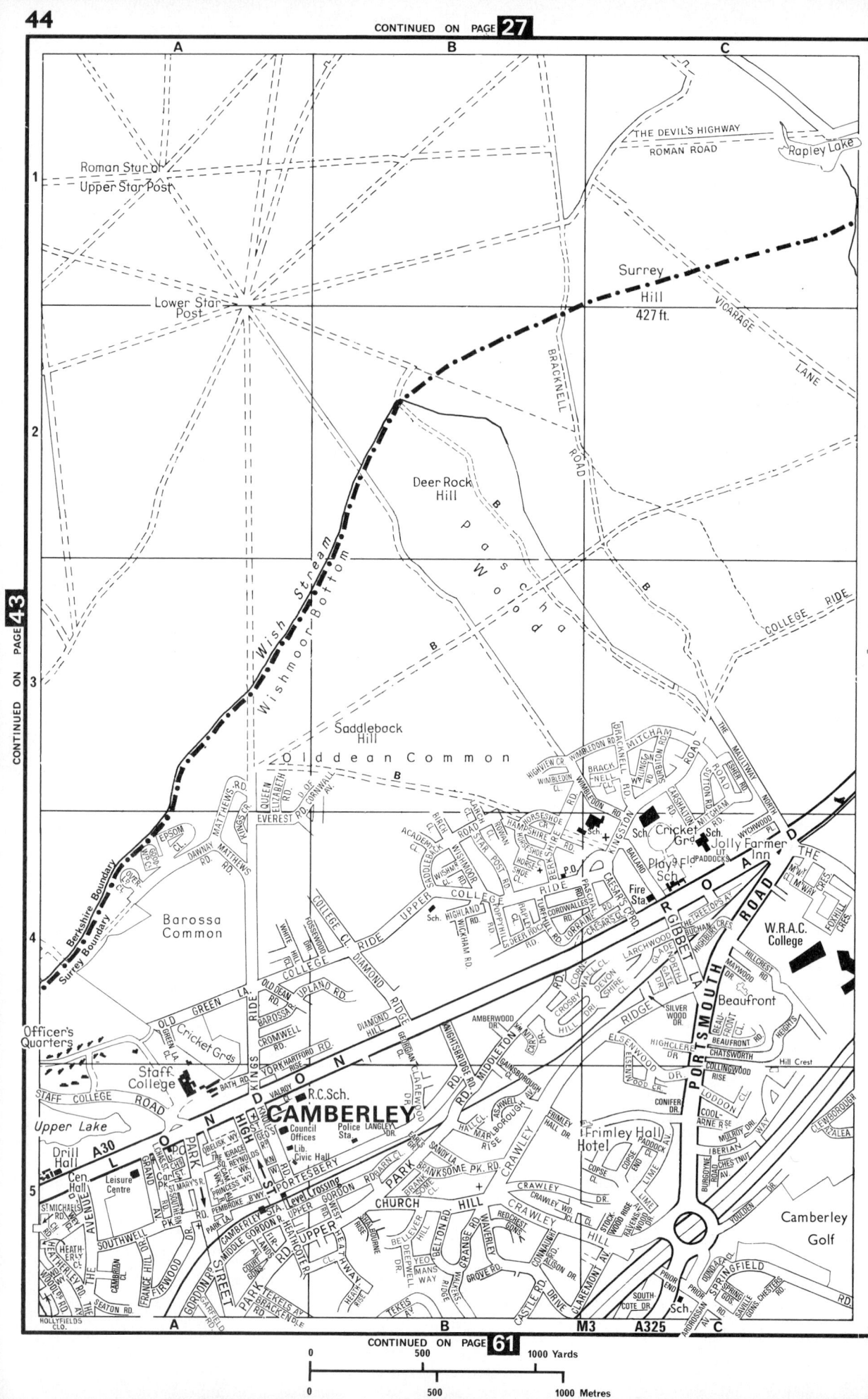

CONTINUED ON PAGE **43**

CONTINUED ON PAGE **61**

| 0 | 500 | 1000 Yards |
| 0 | 500 | 1000 Metres |

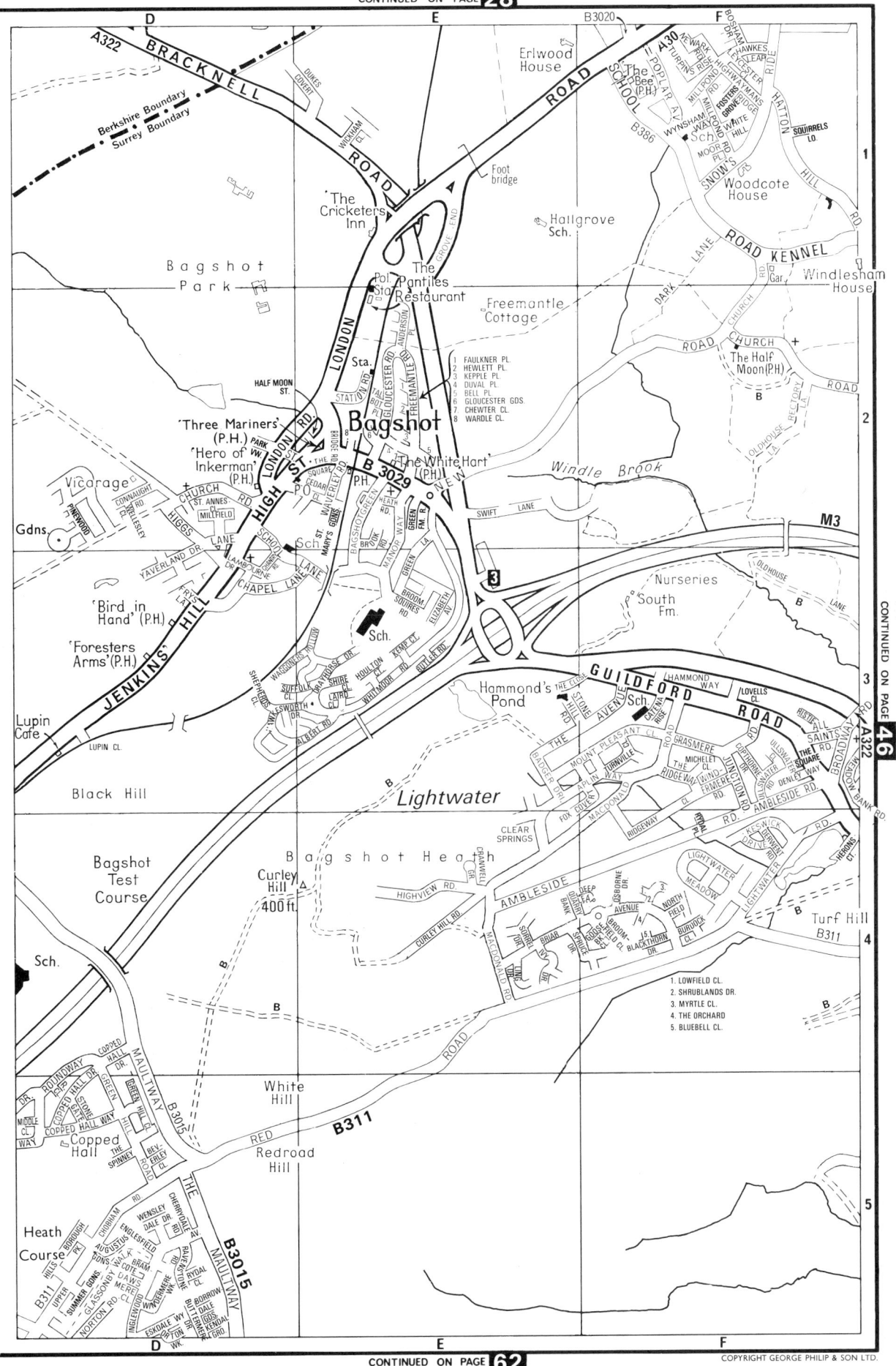

CONTINUED ON PAGE **29**

A B383
B386

B
B

Westwood
Lodge
Updown Hill
House
'Brickmakers
Arms' (P.H.)
ROAD
Valley End
House

1

Convent of
the Good Shepherd
Pond

WESTWOOD
Gunners

**Windlesham**
LANE
Valley
End

ROAD
CHESTNUT
LA.

KINGS RD.
CALDWELL RD.
HIGHAMS
END
SPARROW
ROW
LANE

UPDOWN HILL
CHERTSEY
The Surrey
Cricketers'
(P.H.)
Oak
Wood
VALLEY
Chobham
Place

FINNEY DR.
Heathpark
Wood
B

The
Sun (P.H.)
Westcroft
Park
WOODCOCK LA.
STEEP
HILL
WOOD-
COCK DR.

THORNDOWN LA.
BRADLEY GREEN
WOODLANDS
WINDLESHAM
2
POUND LA.
ROAD
ORCHARD
HILL
Windlesham
Park
LANE

M3
Twelve
Oaks
RYE
GROVE
LANE
B
ROAD

HOOK
MILL
LANE
SCOTLEY
Clappers Brook
FORD BR.

Broadway
Green Farm
Manor Farm
Shrubb's Farm

3
BROADWAY
OLDHOUSE LANE
RYE GROVE
BLIND LANE
B
Halebourne
WATER

A322
Hale Bourne
HALEBOURNE
Ford

BIRCHWOOD DR.
GLEBE CL.
RIVERSIDE
WYCHELM
MARSHWOOD
FARNHAM
WEST RD.
BURNT
POLLARD
LANE
BLACKSTROUD
EAST
HOOKSTONE
Green
LANE
ROAD
BAGSHOT
ROAD
CLAPPERS
BEGGARS LA.

SPRING
FIELD
B
B
B
Pankhurst
Farm
Brook Place
LANE

GUILDFORD
RD.
COLDHARBOUR LA.

B311
A 319
BAGSHOT
West End
Malthouse
Farm
BENNER

4
RED
ROAD
The
Gordon
Boys' Sch.
WINDLESHAM RD.
CHURCH RD.
BENNER LANE
Sch.
FAIRFIELD LA.
Sch.
The
Oaks
LOVELANDS

B
B
B
BIRCH
STREETS
OLD ACRE
HEATH
MEADOW
MALTHOUSE LA.
JENNER DR.
BARNES
PT.

Cuckoo
Hill
ASHLEY
BROAD ST.
CUCKOO VALE
WAY
ORCHARD CL.
REVESBY
The
Wheatsheaf
(P.H.)
HIGH ST.
P.O.
BANK
BOLDING ISE LA.
COMMONFIELDS
SEFTON LA.
BELDAM
SCOTTS GRD.
GROVE
Ford

BRENTMOOR
PENN'S
ROAD
BRENTMOOR
RD.
BIRCH
PLATT
ROUND LA.
FELLOW
GRN.
SCH.
RD.
WILLOW GRN.
BRIDGE RD.
PENNYPOT
LANE
Beldam Bri.
SCOTT'S

**Donkey Town**
GUILDFORD
KINGS
The
Bourne
LANE
ROAD
OLDHOUSE
B
LANE
BURYANS

5
B
Lucas Green
Manor
GREEN
ROAD
A322
FORD
RD.
LUCAS

A B
C

CONTINUED ON PAGE **63**

0        500        1000 Yards

0        500        1000 Metres

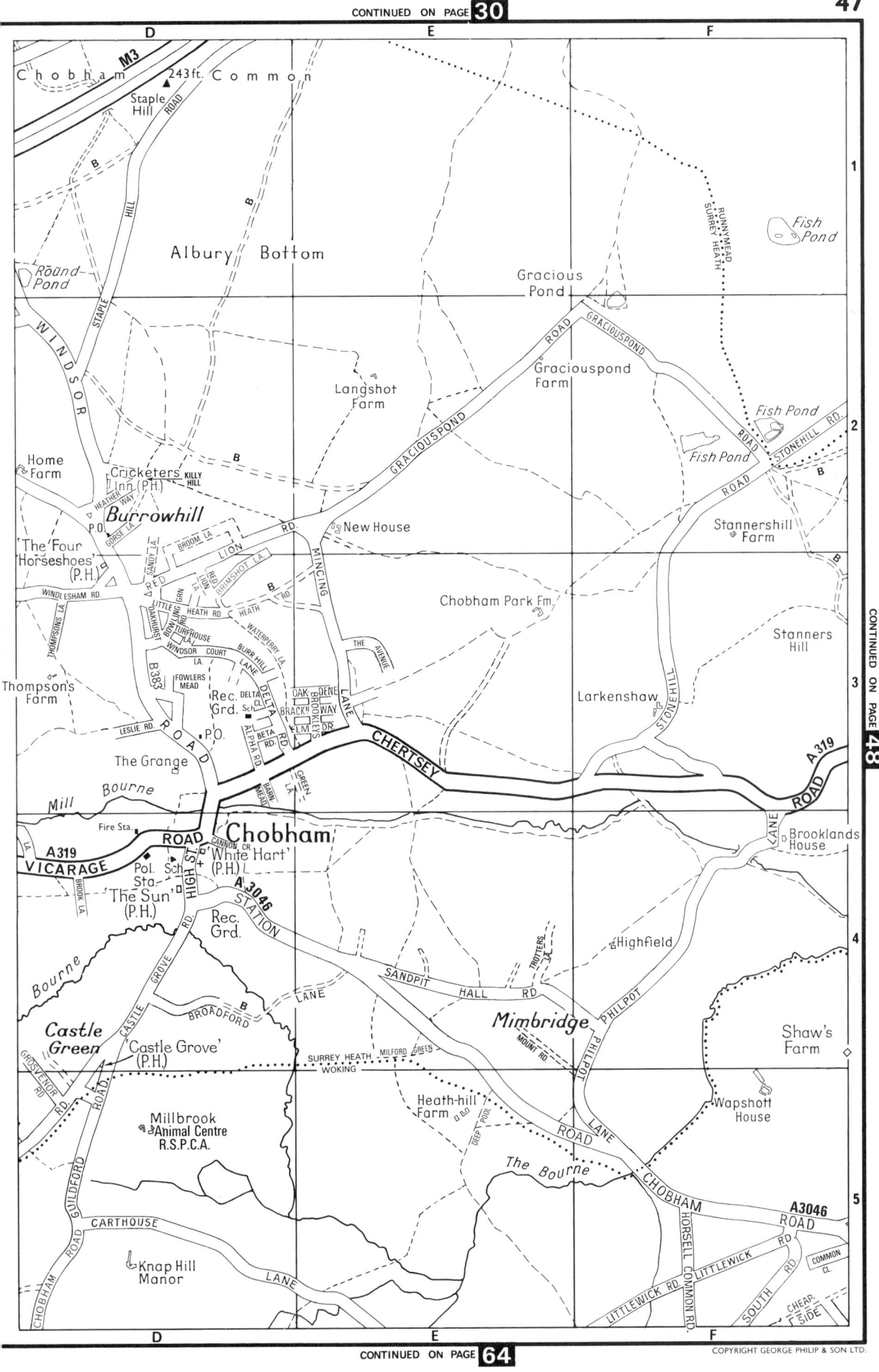

CONTINUED ON PAGE **48**

CONTINUED ON PAGE **31**

CONTINUED ON PAGE **47**

Foxhills

ACCOMODATION ROAD

STONEHILL ROAD

FOXHILLS ROAD

Botleys Park Hospital

Pond

ST. PETER'S WAY A320

RD. A320

BITTAMS

HILLCREST AV.

FERNDALE

Stone Hill

STONEHILL ROAD

Rec. Grd.

FOXHILLS ROAD

COTTAGE

**Ottershaw**

GUILDFORD ROAD

Amb. Sta.

TRINGHAM CLN.

MURRAY ROAD

P

BROX

P.O.

Farm

B3121

FIRSDENE CL.

SPRATIS LA.

The Farm

Queenwood

CHOBHAM ROAD

CROSS

FLOWER

THE

COACH RD.

CHOBHAM LA.

BEECH

CHAWOR

Sch.

SLADE

ROAD

ROAD

COLEBROOK

ROUSLEY RISE

FLETCHER

Sch.

Stanners Hill

HOME FARM CL.

Tulk House

The Common

CROFTON CL.

TRELAWN CL.

DUFFINS

ORCHARD

SOUTHWOOD AV.

BROX

CRISPIN'S WAY

LANE

BROX

Ottershaw Park

BROX

GREATWOOD CL.

CHERTSEY ROAD

A319

Main Entrance

SURREY HEATH

Great Blackmole Pond

WOOD-LANDS CL.

GUILDFORD ROAD

Anningsley Park

Fair Oaks Aerodrome

YOUNGSTROAT LANE

Bonsey's Bri.

WOKING

Dunford Br.

Hoyt Common

Bonsey's Farm

Scotchers Farm

Shaw Farm

MARTYR'S

Anthony's

'The Bleak House' P.H.

Golf Course

Club Ho. B385

WOODHAM

SHEERWATER

LANE

RD.

PRIORY CL.

BROADWATER

LYNWOOD

Horsell Common

A3046

A245

ROAD

Six Cross Roads Roundabout

CHERTSEY RD.

A320

MONUMENT RD.

WOODHAM ROAD

All Saints Ch.

A245

WOODHAM WAYE

THE GATEWAY

Woking Athletic Ground

*Basingstoke Canal*

**Sheerwater**

Sch.

Sch.

LAUREL

DEVONSHIRE AV.

DARTMOUTH AV.

ST. MICHAELS RD.

ALBERT

SHORES

KETTLEWELL HILL

GRANGE RD.

MULBERRY

SUMMER-HAYES CL.

GRANGE PARK

MYLOR CL.

PENHURST CL.

CASTLE RD.

WOODHAM

LITTLE ORCHARD

CHERTSEY RD.

THE RIDING

WOODHAM WAYE

BLACKMORE CR.

BUNYARD

ST. MICHAELS WAY

SHANBURY PATH

DRIVE

0     500     1000 Yards

0     500     1000 Metres

CONTINUED ON PAGE 32

A318  A319  A317  WEYBRIDGE RD.

Trading Estate

Addlestone

St. Pauls Sch.

Police Sta.

Library

Civic Cen.

Ham Moor

Level Crossing

SPINNEY

Rowhill

Row Town

Hillside Gdns.

B3121

HARE LANE

CHURCH HILL

ONGAR ROAD

Coombelands

Works

M25

Black Horse (P.H.)

Moated Farm

NEW HAW ROAD

BYFLEET ROAD

Crockford Bridge

Mill Pond

Level Crossing

White Hart' (P.H.)

New Haw

Wey Manor Farm

MANOR ROAD

Hall's Farm

Holme Farm

Rose Park

The Bourne

Min. of Agriculture Central Veterinary Laboratory

River Wey Navigation

Byfleet & New Haw Sta.

BROOKLANDS

Works

Woodham

Woodham Lodge

WOODHAM LANE

HOLLY LANE

SELBOURNE AVENUE

WOODHAM PARK

Heathervale Mun. Caravan Park

Rec. Grd.

Scotland Bridge

PARK AVENUE

DARTNELL AVENUE

Sch.

OYSTER LANE

A245 RD.

Byfleet

PARVIS ROAD

HIGH RD.

SHEERWATER AVENUE

West Byfleet Golf Course

Club Ho.

Sheerwater Bri.

West Byfleet Sta.

CLAREMONT ROAD

CAMPHILL ROAD

Camphill Court

PARVIS ROAD

West Hall

West Byfleet

WOKING ROAD

ELMSTEAD ROAD

Murray's Bridge

CHURCH ROAD

RECTORY

HART ROAD

Woking Guildford

DODD'S LANE

COPYRIGHT GEORGE PHILIP & SON LTD.

CONTINUED ON PAGE 50

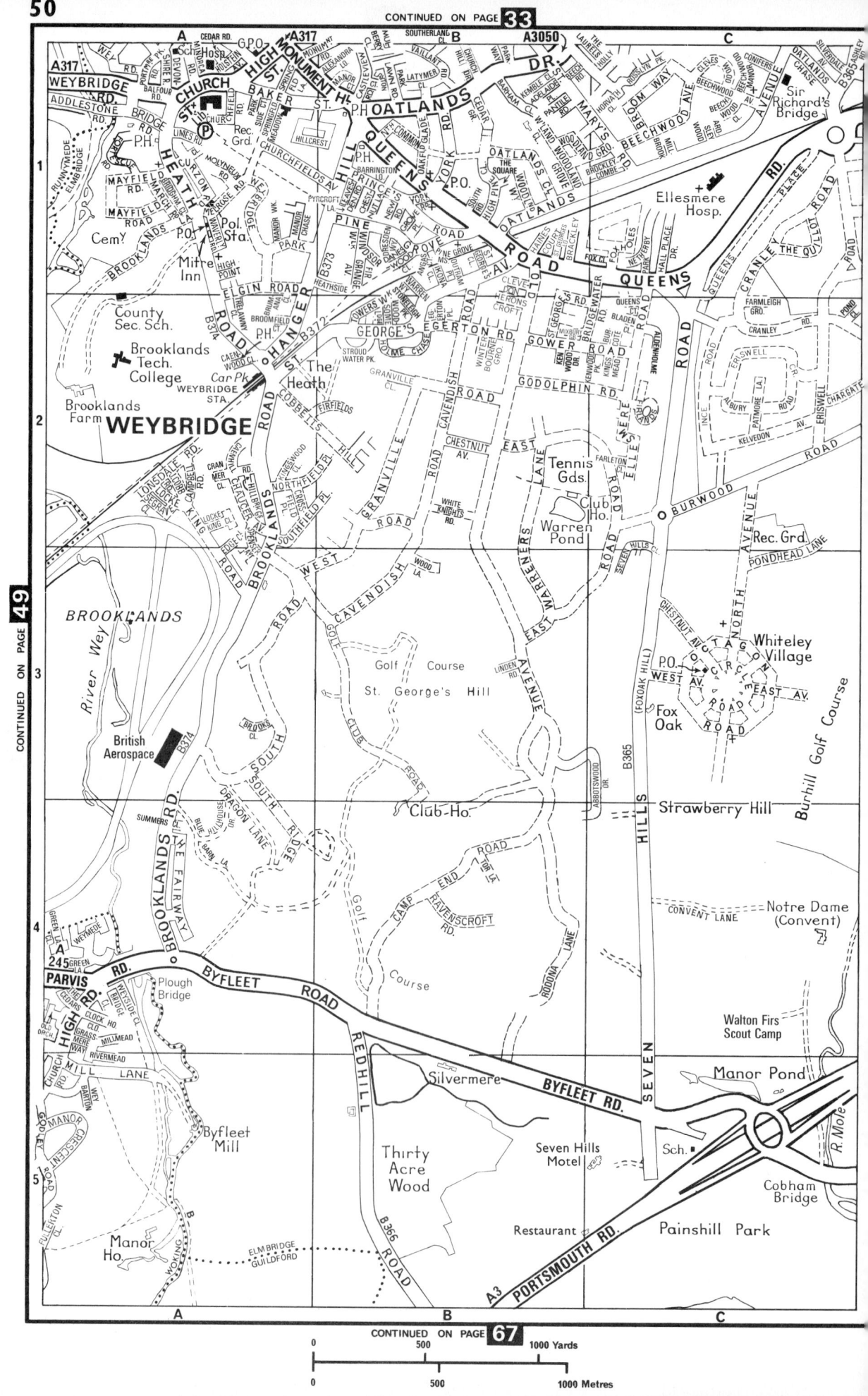

CONTINUED ON PAGE 33

CONTINUED ON PAGE 49

CONTINUED ON PAGE 67

0          500          1000 Yards

0          500          1000 Metres

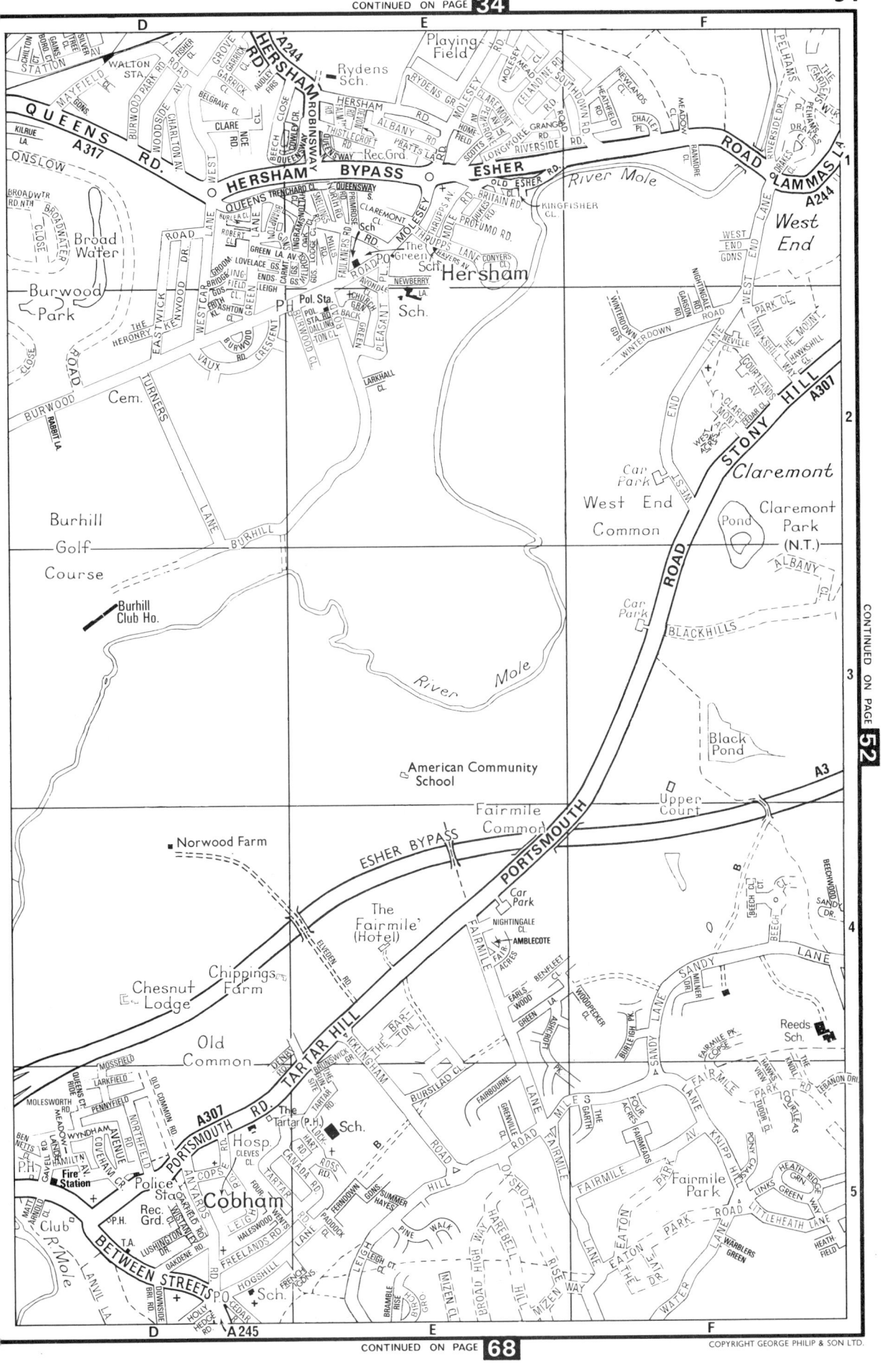

CONTINUED ON PAGE **52**

CONTINUED ON PAGE 35

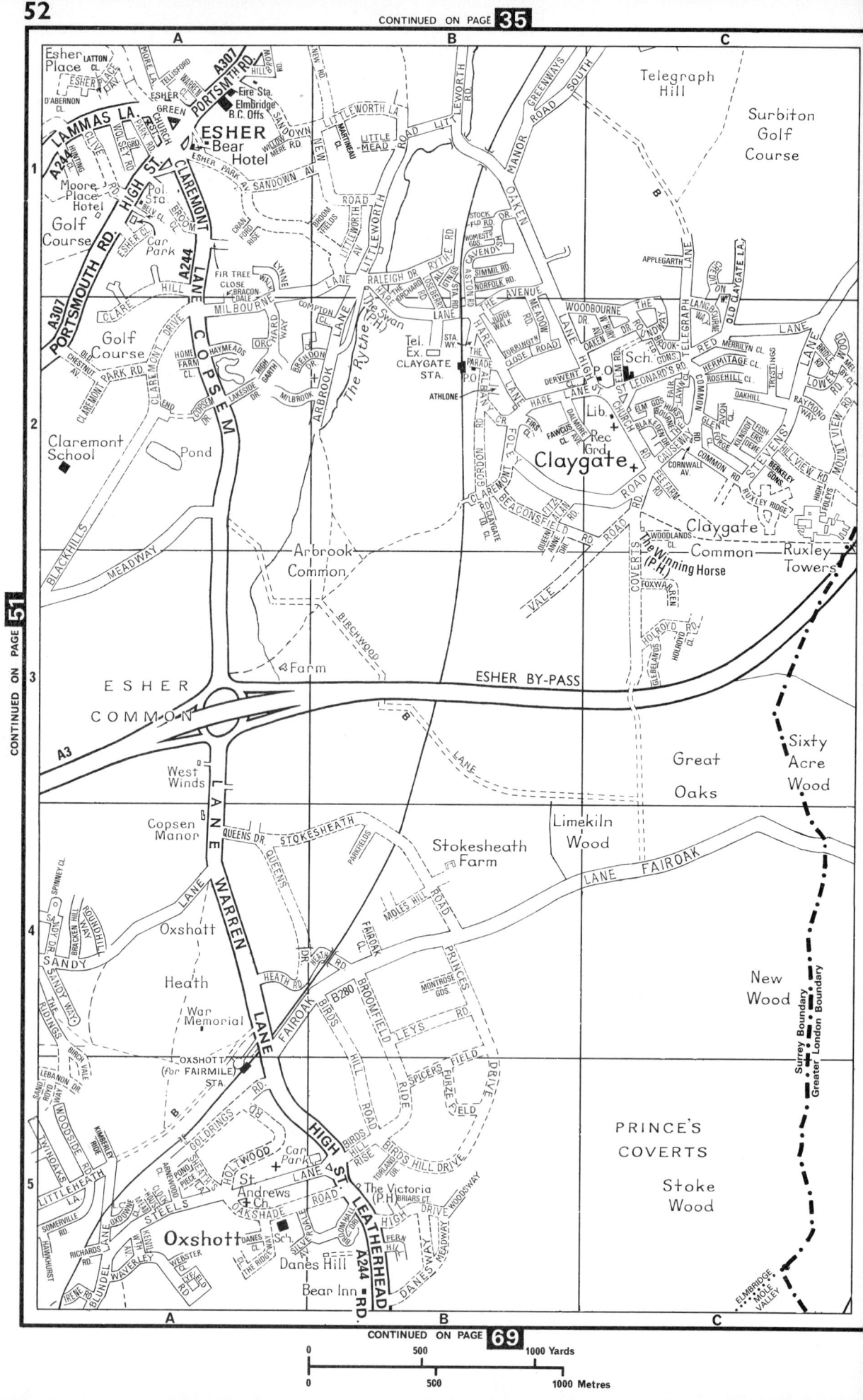

CONTINUED ON PAGE 69

CONTINUED ON PAGE 51

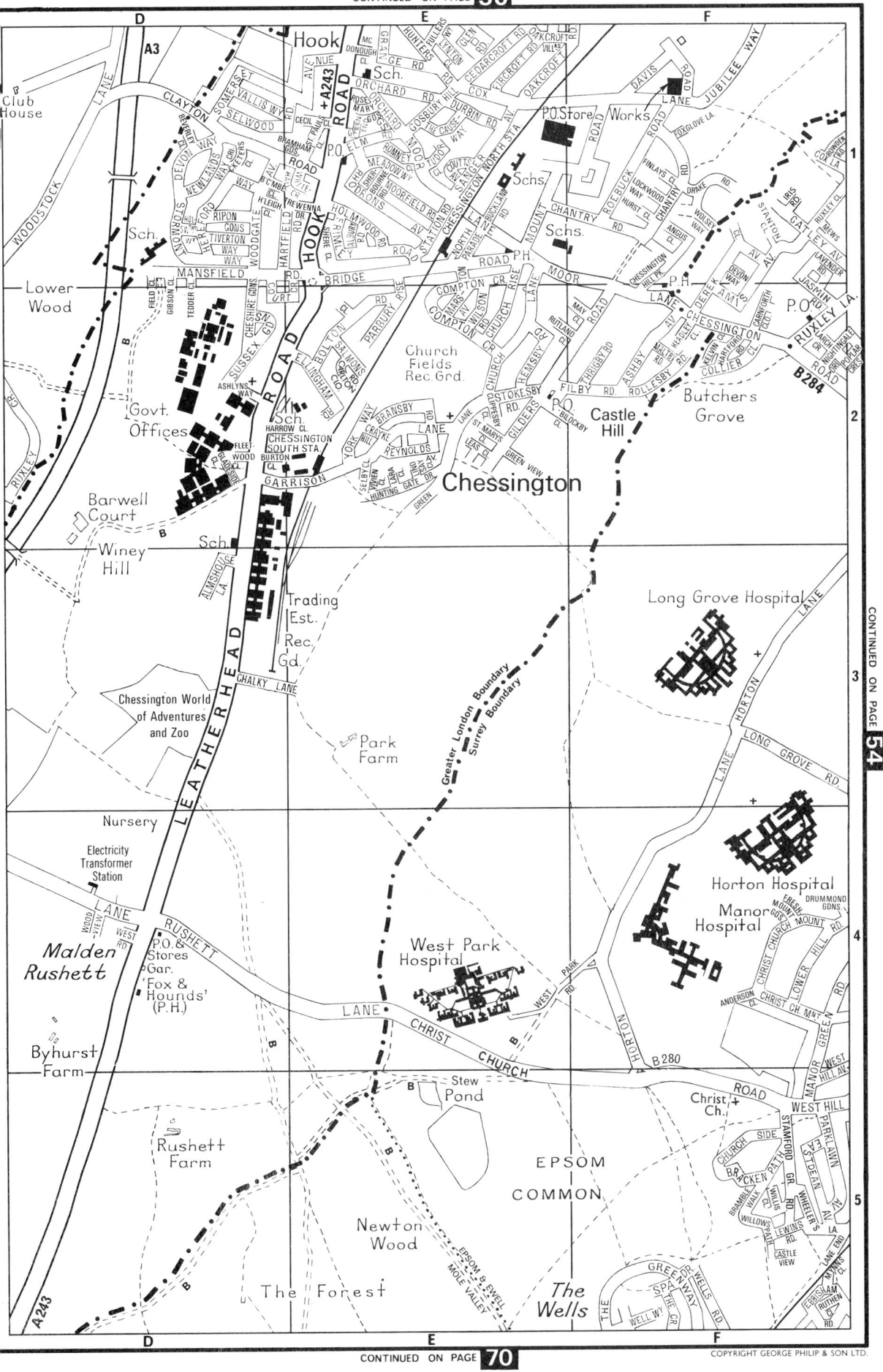

CONTINUED ON PAGE **54**

Chessington

Hook

Club House

Lower Wood

Govt. Offices

Barwell Court

Winey Hill

Chessington World of Adventures and Zoo

Park Farm

Trading Est.
Rec. Gd.

Nursery

Electricity Transformer Station

Malden Rushett

P.O. & Stores
Gar.
'Fox & Hounds' (P.H.)

Byhurst Farm

Rushett Farm

Church Fields Rec. Grd.

Castle Hill

Butchers Grove

Long Grove Hospital

Horton Hospital

Manor Hospital

West Park Hospital

Stew Pond

Christ Ch.

Epsom Common

Newton Wood

The Forest

The Wells

West Hill

LEATHERHEAD ROAD

HOOK ROAD

CHRIST CHURCH ROAD

Greater London Boundary
Surrey Boundary

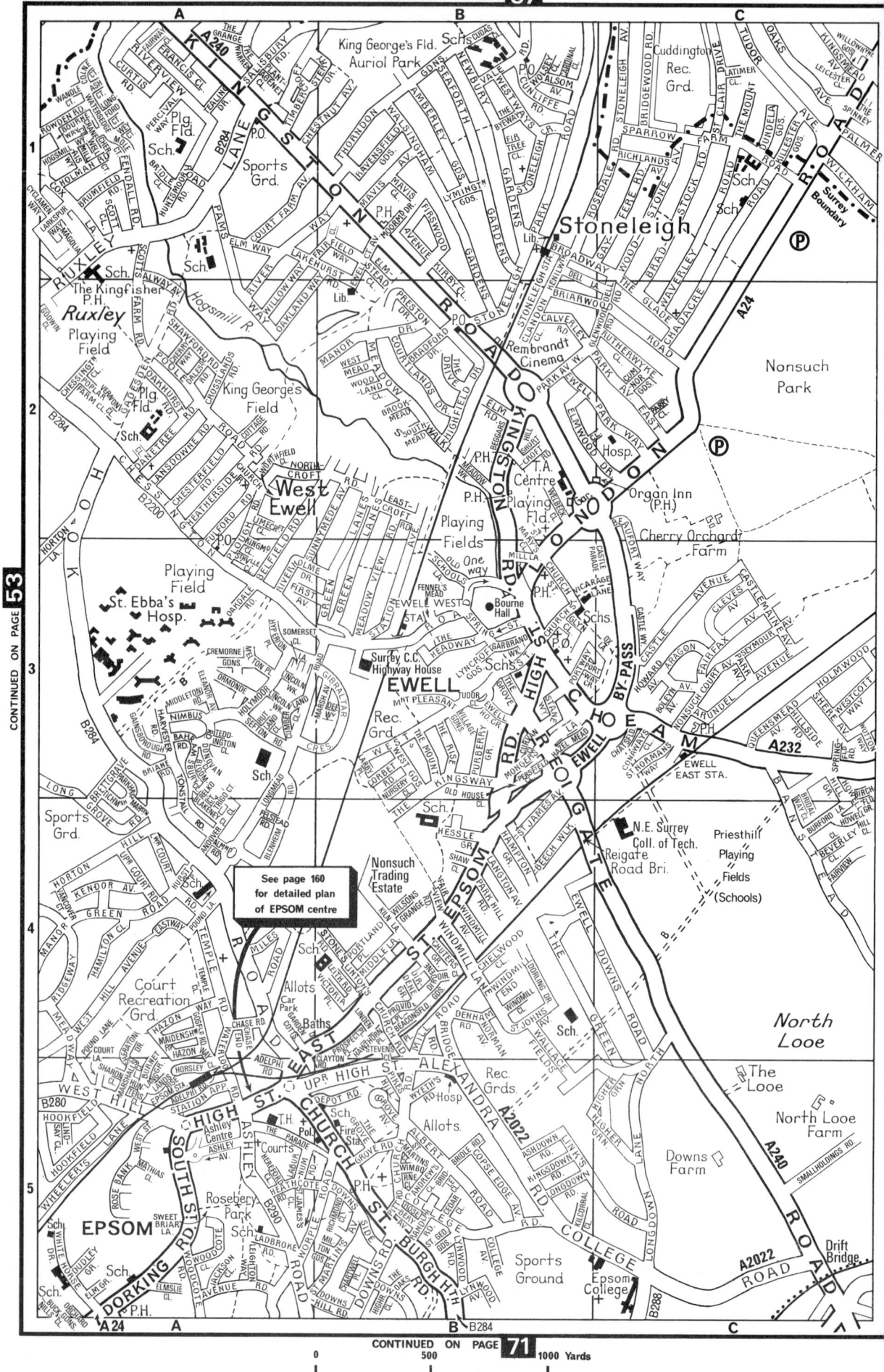

CONTINUED ON PAGE **37**

CONTINUED ON PAGE **53**

See page 160 for detailed plan of EPSOM centre

CONTINUED ON PAGE **71**

0        500        1000 Yards

0        500        1000 Metres

CONTINUED ON PAGE 38

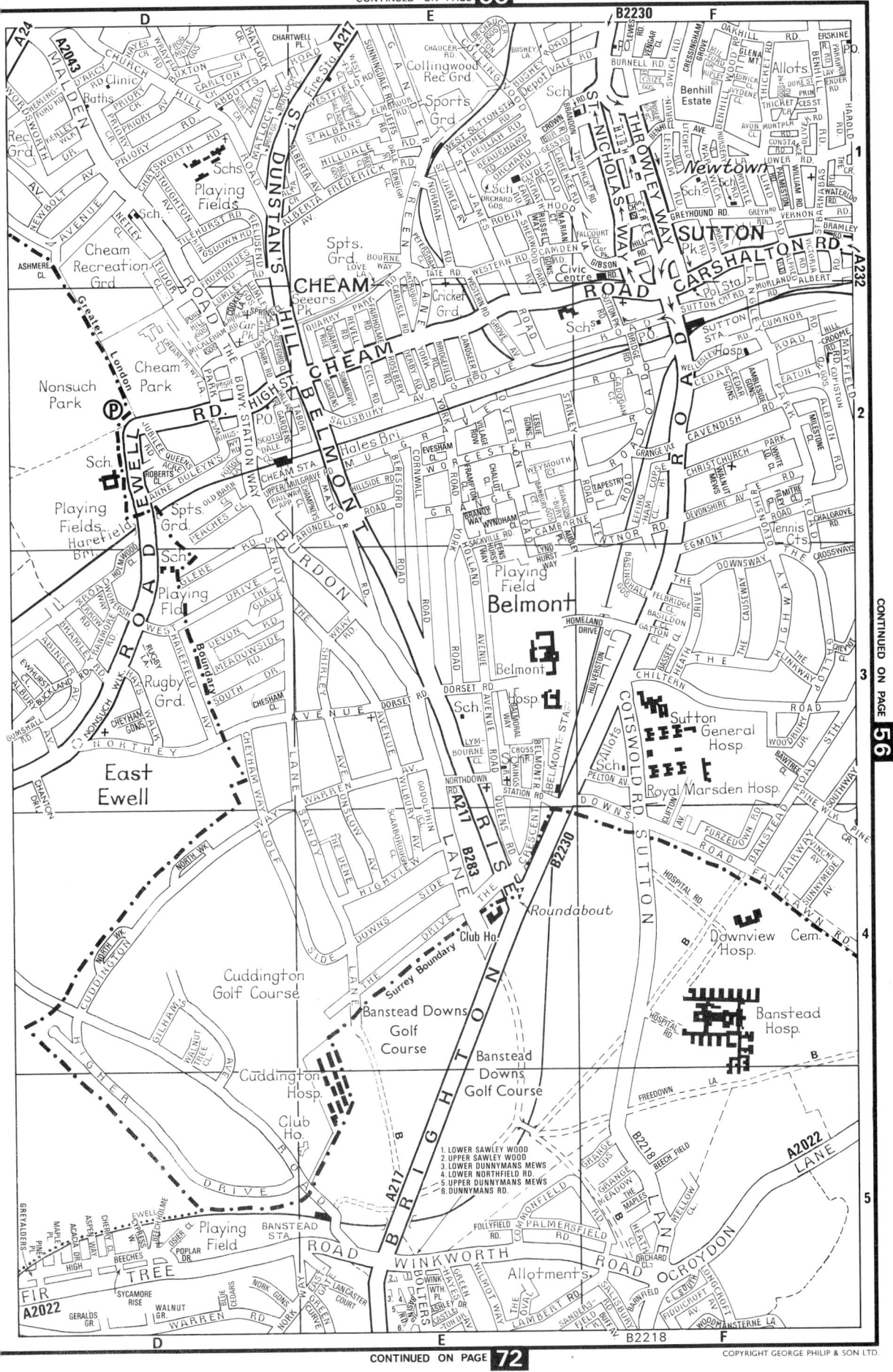

CONTINUED ON PAGE 56

CONTINUED ON PAGE 72

CONTINUED ON PAGE 39

B277    B    A237    A232    C

**CARSHALTON**

**WALLINGTON**

**BEDDINGTON**

CROYDON RD.

MANOR RD.

HIGH ST.   ACRE LA.

WOODCOTE

Leisure Centre The Grove

Playing Fields

Carshalton Sta.

Carshalton House

Carshalton Park

War Memorial Hosp.

Fire Sta.

Pol. Sta.

Allotments

Cemy.

**Carshalton on the Hill**

Stanley Park

Carshalton Beeches

**Carshalton Beeches**

**South Beddington**

Sports Grd.

Stanley Pk. Rd.

Wallington Sta.

Beddington Sta.

**Woodcote Green**

Medical Research Council

B.I.B.R.A.

Queen Mary's Hospital for Children

Cricket Grd.

**Woodcote**

Oaks Sports Centre Golf Course

The Oaks Park

Little Woodcote Estate

*Little Woodcote*

LITTLE   WOODCOTE   LA.

SMITHAMBOTTOM   LA.

FOXLEY   LANE

Nursery

WOODMANSTERNE   LANE

FAIRLAWN   Greater   London   Surrey   ROAD

A2022 CROYDON

The Oaks Farm

Barn Grove

Nurseries

Playing Field

Ruffett

Big Wood

Pondfield Shaw

Woodcote Grove Ho.

Woodcote Pk. Golf Club

Playing Field

Rec. Grd.

Golf Course

Rec. Grd.

B278

A2030 SMITHAM

WOODCOTE GRO. RD.

A237

THE CHASE

WARWICK RD.

HOWARD RD.

CONTINUED ON PAGE 73

CONTINUED ON PAGE 55

0   500   1000 Yards

0   500   1000 Metres

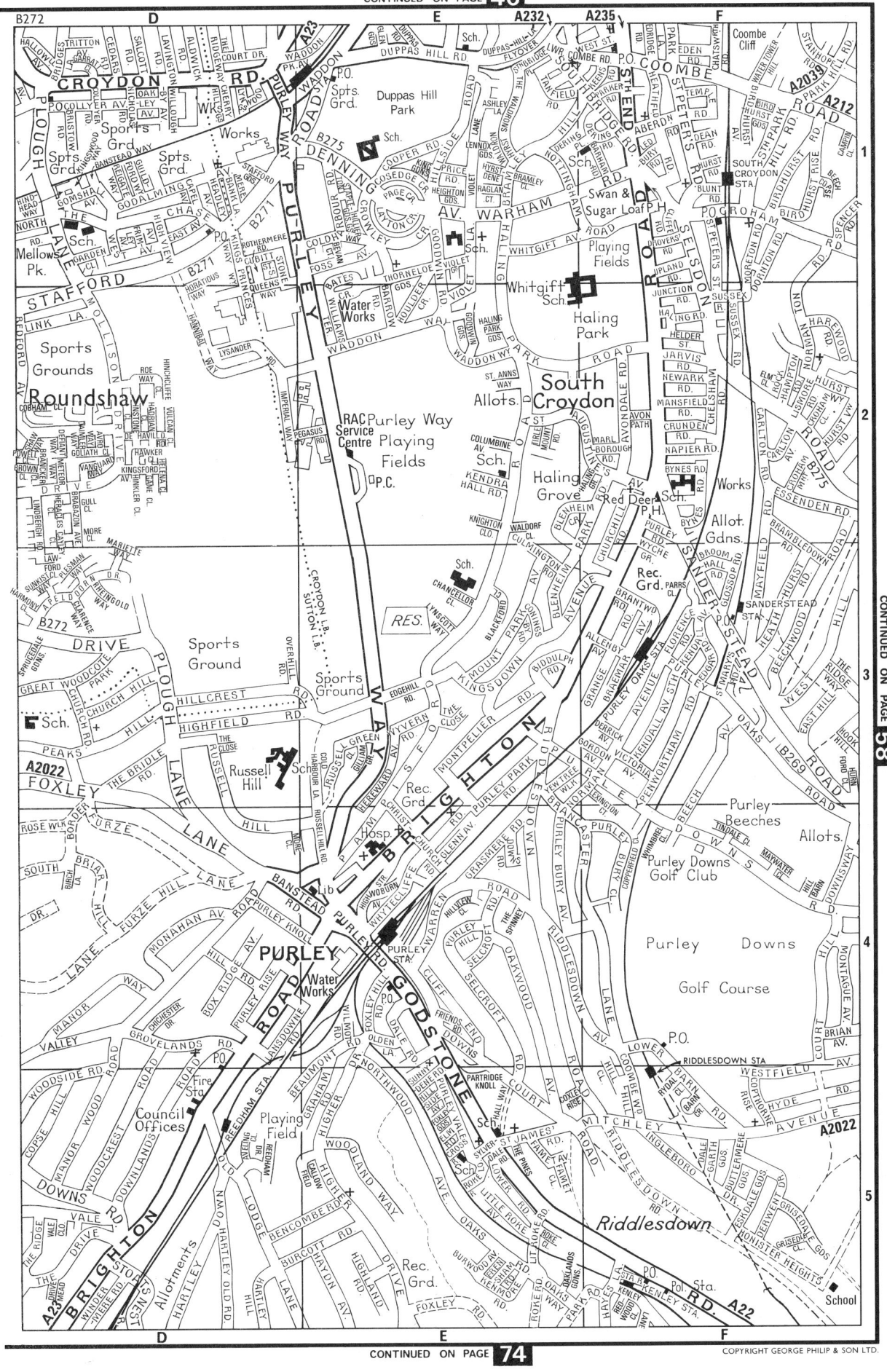

CONTINUED ON PAGE **58**

CONTINUED ON PAGE 41

CONTINUED ON PAGE 57

A    B    C

Upper Shirley

THE DENE
SANDPITS RD.
SANDROCK PL.
BADGER'S HOLE
SPRUCEDALE GDNS.
Club Ho.

Addington Golf Course

Lloyd Park
Coombe Farm
Coombe Park
Coombe Road
Addington Hills

BROWNLOW
LEIGHTON GDNS.
RUSH MEAD CL.
RUTLAND GDNS.
WAY
LLOYD PK.
BLOSSOM CL.
A212
Sch.
OAKS ROAD
COOMBE ROAD
SHIRLEY HILLS
BIRCH HILL
PINE COOMBE
ABBOTS GRN.

COOMBE RD.
CROHAM PARK AV.
CAMPDEN RD.
CASTLEMAINE AV.
BALLATER RD.
MELVILLE AV.
PILGRIMS WAY
Playing Fields
CONDUIT LANE
Coombe Wood
SHIRLEY LANE
GRAVEL HILL
Walk
Bishops
Addington Palace Golf Course
Addington Palace (Music Sch.)
A212
Club Ho.

1

CROHAM ROAD
MANOR WAY
SEY RISE
MANOR GDNS.
BANKSIDE
Sports Grd.
Swimming Pool
Schools
Hospital
Heathfield
BALLARDS FARM RD.
HOLLINGSWORTH RD.
CHAPEL WAY
CROSSWAYS
GREEN WALK
RAWLINS CL.

2

HURST WAY
RD.
HIGH BEECH
Croham Hurst Golf Club
Croham Hurst Golf Course
Croham Hurst
Breakneck Hill
LYTCHGATE CL.
FARLEY ROAD
BALLARDS WAY
CROHAM VALLEY ROAD
THE RUFFETTS
CHEST RD.
RUFFETTS CL.
VIEW
CHESTNUT GR.
THE GALLOP
Bramley Bank
BROADCOOMBE
WARREN
SHEPHERDS WAY
LEDDER
EDGECOOMBE
FREELANDS
FARNBOROUGH AV.
COPSE VIEW
HEATHFIELD VALE
Gilbert Scott Primary Sch.
Sch.
John Newnham Sch.
A2022 ROAD
PO.
HOLMBURY GRO.

Littleheath
Littleheath Woods
Sch.
SELSDON ROAD
FARNBRGH. CR.
SELSDON PARK
HEATHER WAY
PENNY CROFT
MIDDLEFIELD
FLOWERSWOOD
BECKER RD.
Sch.
NEWLANDS WAY
BARDOLPH
YEWTREE WAY

UPPER SELSDON ROAD
WEST HILL
SANDS CL.
ELMHURST CL.
WISBOROUGH RD.
B275
Hooks Hill
THE RIDGE WAY
HOOK HILL
BARNFIELD RD.
KIRKLEN BRIDGE WAY
MUIR CL.
RIDGE
LANGLEY AV.
ARUNDEL AV.
ARUNDEL RD.
COURTLANDS
NORFOLK AV.
QUEENHILL ROAD
BYRON CL.
BRENT RD.
FOX EARTH RD.
THE RUSH
FOXEARTH SPUR
Sch.
INGHAM ROAD
RONGHAM
SELSDON ROAD
LANGLEY AV.
BRUCE DR.
DULVERTON RD.
KINGSWAY
ABBEY RD.
YORK RD.
YORK RD.
DALE VIEW
HERON CL.
THOROLD CL.
SORREL BANK
LINTON GLADE
HART'S CROFT
BROOK'S CROFT
CASCADES

3

SOUTHCOTE RD.
DAYS ACRE
MORLEY RD.
ARKWRIGHT RD.
LANGLEY OAKS AV.
SYLVAN CL.
MOUNT WOOD
The Hooks
Lib
Sch.
SUNDALE AV.
PARK GDNS.
BENHURST AV.
GREVILLE AV.
LINTON GLADE
SELSDON
OSPREY GDNS.
WAGTAIL
GOLDFINCH
LAPWING RD.
QUAIL GDNS.

4

SANDERSTEAD
Lib
Farm Fields
OVERSTONE RD.
THE WINDINGS
THE WOODFIELDS
PURLEY DOWNS
NORTH
GLEBE
HYRST DOWN
HARBLE DOWN RD.
JORDAN CL.
CHURCH WAY
ADDINGTON ROAD
A2022
Club Ho.
Selsdon Park Hotel
Selsdon Hill
Selsdon Park Golf Course
Golf Course
RAVENSMEAD CL.
WOODM...
HAWTHORN CR.
LYNNE CL.
REDWING RD.
BIRDWOOD CL.
CURLEW CL.
SANDPIPER
COVE
ARLEIGH WAY
SUFFIELD CL.
KERSEY DRIVE
BORDON
Steven's Larch
Selsdon Wood
Broom Wood
Broom Shaw

5

BRIAN AV.
WESTFIELD
HYDE RD.
RECTORY
A2022
Playing Field
Sch.
BORROWDALE CL.
MITCHLEY AV.
CRANLEIGH GDNS.
STANLEY GDNS.
BALFONT CL.
BLACKSMITHS HILL
Spts. Grd.
Fire Sta.
Mitchley Wood
Ragged Grove
Barnfield Shaw
Sch.
HOLMWOOD AV.
TANDRIDGE GDNS.
MITCHLEY VIEW
BRIAR GR.
LIME MEADOW AV.
HAZELW...
SANDERSTEAD COURT
LEIGHTON GDNS.
ORCHARD RISE
B269
WENTWORTH WAY
Kings Wood
KINGSWOOD WAY
KINGSWOOD
BEECH WAY
ABERCROMBIE CL.
ALBATROSS
Elm Farm
Hogcroft Shaw

Farleigh

CONTINUED ON PAGE 75

0    500    1000 Yards

0    500    1000 Metres

A    B    C

Shirley
Heath

PALACE
VIEW

Spring
Park

Threehalfpenny
Wood

Wickham
Court
(Coloma
College)

Well
Wood

CHURCH RD.

ADDINGTON

A2022 RD.

Fox Hill

The Larches

Long
Shaw

Cooper's
Wood

Addington
Park
Rec. Grd.

GATE Addington

Police
Station

Sch.

Bradmanshill
Wood

KENT

Schs.

Castle
Hill Sch.

R.C.

Bushfield
Shaw

Fire
Sta.

New
Addington

Rowdown
Wood

Huntingfield

St. Francis
Centre

Club Ho.

Sch.

WESTCOTT
CL.

WOLSEY

ALDRICH CR.

SHAXTON CR.

GRENVILLE RD.

BOTHWELL RD.

HENEAGE RD.

Lib. SALCOT

P.O.

Swim.
Baths

Sch.

Works

Sch.

Greyhound
Training
Kennels

Addington
Court
Golf
Course

Playing
Field

Sch.

Hall

Recreation Grd.

UVEDALE
CRES.

Frith Wood

Haggler's
Dean

Frylands
Wood

Farleigh
Dean

Hutchinsons
Bank

Boundary

Surrey Boundary

Schools

Playing
Fields

SHEEPBARN
LA.

Crab
Wood

Chapel
Hill

Coldblow
Shaw

Beechfield
Wood

Fairchildes
House

Fairchildes
Farm

Sch.

Limekiln
Shaw

White
Bear (P.H.)

Fickleshole
Farm

Fickleshole

FARLEIGH

Farleigh Court

Great Park Wood

Little Farleigh
Green Farm

Little
Farleigh
Green

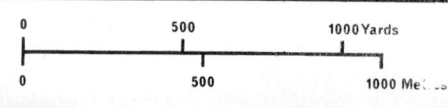

CONTINUED ON PAGE 62

CONTINUED ON PAGE **45**

CONTINUED ON PAGE **61**

**A**     **B**     **C**

REDMAYNE CL.

LANGDON CL.
TREMAYNE CL.
KESWICK RD.
INGLEWOOD AV.
CUMBERLAND
COPELANDS
ROAD
BUTTERMERE

BROWNING
GOLDNEY
ROAD

ARUNDEL

FOLBOROUGH

BELLINGHAM
CHESTON
BRANDON CL.
RED
WOOD
YOXLEY
SHILDON
CLOSE
WAY

HEATHER
RIDGE ARC.

Sch.

PENDRAGON

MARTINDALE
RONY
BECK

Chobham Ridges

THE MAULTWAY

BYRON AV.
HASLEMERE CL.
SILVER
PL.
HERRICK
WALKER
ROAD
LOWES
WATER
WK.
DALSTON CL.

WENDOVER DR.
EDGEMOOR

PATTERSON CL.

**Brompton Hospital**

Dean's
Bottom

CHRYSTALE DR.
WINGFIELD
CONS.

OLD

BISLEY

ROAD

THE ROAD

1. MARSHALL CL.
2. MYERS WAY
3. HARBERSHON DR.
4. GOSWELL CL.

Colony Gate

**Frith
Hill**

FRITH
HILL RD.

VALLEY RD.

B3015

ROAD

ABERDEENT

SOMME RD.

MINDRN RD.

AISNE RD.

THIEPVAL RD.

**Alma/Dettingen
Barracks**

MARNE RD.

NEWFOUNDLAND RD.

WOOD END RD.

BRIDGE ROAD

MAINSTONE CL.

BLACKDOWN
RIDGE
MOUNT

ALFRISTON RD.

FERNLEIGH RISE

*Deepcut*

LAKE RD.

BRUNSWICK
ROAD

**Blackdown
Barracks**

Narrow
bridge

DEEPCUT

B3012

**W e s t e n d   C o m m o n**

Strawberry Bottom

**C o l o n y   B o g**

Mainstone
Bottom

FIELD

FIRING
RANGE

SURREY HEATH
GUILDFORD

Mainstone
Hill

**Pirbright   Ranges**

JEFFERSON RD.

**Pirbright
Camp**

BEECH

**P i r b r i g h t   C o m m o n**

GREENWOOD RD.
RADAIR WK.

ROAD

BRUNSWICK
ROAD

Lodge
Hill

*Basingstoke Canal*

GUILDFORD RD. GAPEMOUTH ROAD GAPEMOUTH ROAD

Gapemouth
Plantation

OLD
GUILDFORD ROAD

Car Parking
Space

GRANGE

B

ROAD

**Rifle Ranges**

TUNNEL
HILL

Tunnel
Hill

**A**     **B**     **C**

1

2

3

4

5

CONTINUED ON PAGE **79**

0    500    1000 Yards

0    500    1000 Metres

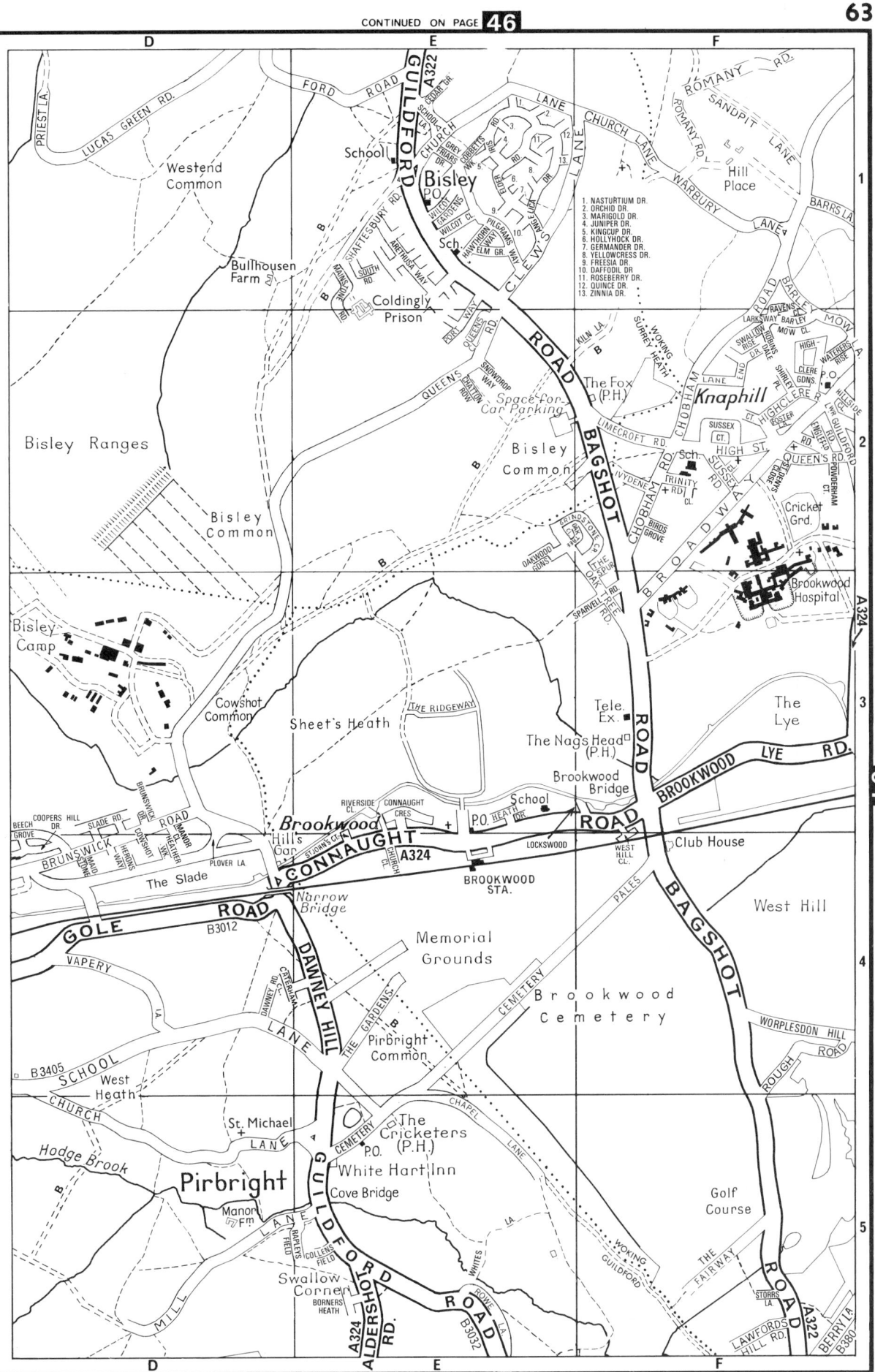

CONTINUED ON PAGE **64**

CONTINUED ON PAGE **63**

A324

A B C

1

Knaphill Nursery

Whitfield Court

Parley Brook
CARTHOUSE
ROAD
LITTLEWICK LANE

Parley Bridge

Cricketers Inn (P.H.)

HORSELL BIRCH

**Horsell**
Industrial Estate

**Goldsworth Park**

School

Lake

CHEAPSIDE
HORSE LANE

HIGH STREET
SOUTH MEADWAY
SOUTH CL.

CHURCH HILL

P.O.

Sch.
Sch.

Barrs Lane

2

ANCHOR HILL
BARNBY RD.
ROBIN HOOD WAY

VICTORIA RD.
INKERMAN RD.

Military Prison

Overthorpe Close

Winston Churchill Sch.

Sch.

LOWER GUILDFORD RD.

BARRACK PATH

Robin Hood
Copse Rd.

**ST. JOHN'S ROAD**

RD.

**GOLDSWORTH**

KINGSWAY

Schs.

3

HERMITAGE

Crematorium

LANSDOWN CL.

Football Ground

Basingstoke Canal (disused)

St. John's
Lye

JACKMAN'S LANE

ST. JOHN'S HILL ROAD

FAIRWAY CL.
GOLF CLUB RD.

Comeragh Court

**Hook Heath**

The Grange

D POND
MILE

HOOK HEATH AV.

St. Catherine's

Star (P.H.)

COLLEGE LA.

BLACKBRIDGE

Orchard Mains

WYCH HILL

WYCH HILL WAY

**ROAD**

CAVENDISH

YORK RD.

WEST HILL

Woking Golf Course

West Hill Golf Course

4

HOOK HEATH ROAD

SAUNDERS

Fishers Hill

HEATH

HOOK HILL LANE

MOUNT RD.

GOOSE LANE

EGLEY ROAD

**Mayford**

Bird in Hand (P.H.) P.O.

Mayford Bri.

WESTFIELD

Club House

Worplesdon Golf Course

Crastock Farm

LANE SMARTS

Nurseries

SMARTS HEATH

Smarts Heath

Mayford Centre

Dangart House

GUILDFORD ROAD

5

BERRY

Bridley Manor

Kemishford Bri.

PREY HEATH ROAD

WORPLESDON STA.

PREY HEATH CL.

Pyle Hill

B380

A320

0        500        1000 Yards

0        500        1000 Metres

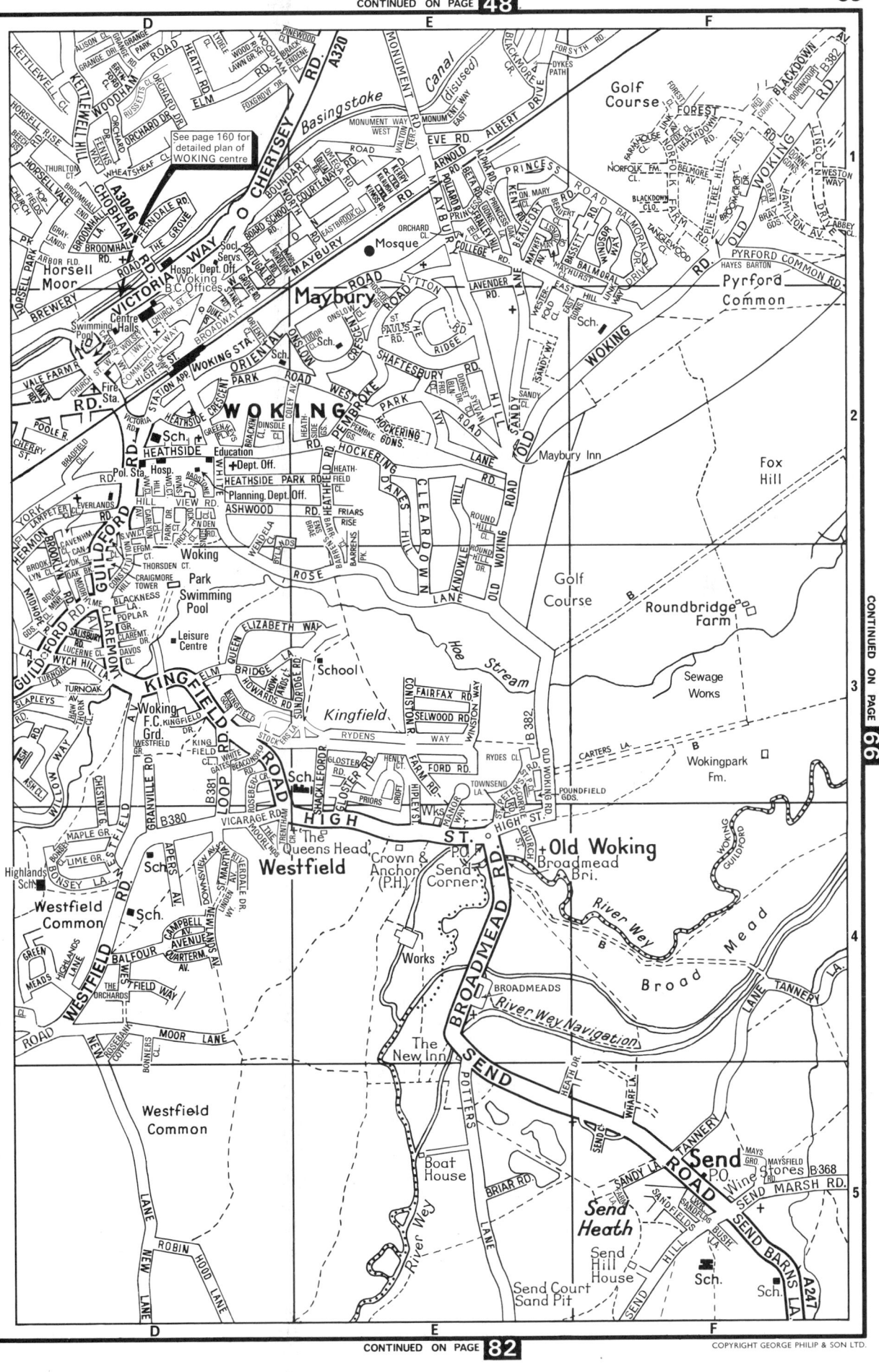

See page 160 for detailed plan of WOKING centre

**WOKING**

**Maybury**

**Pyrford Common**

Golf Course

FOREST

Fox Hill

Golf Course

Roundbridge Farm

Sewage Works

Wokingpark Fm.

Horsell Moor

Westfield

Kingfield

**Old Woking**

Broadmead Bri.

River Wey

Broad Mead

Westfield Common

The New Inn

River Wey Navigation

BROADMEADS

Westfield Common

Boat House

**Send**

Send Heath

Send Hill House

Send Court Sand Pit

CONTINUED ON PAGE **66**

CONTINUED ON PAGE **49**

A · B · C

CONTINUED ON PAGE **65**

Coldharbour

HARE HILL CL.
RIDGWAY
RIDGWAY
Ridgway
ROMANS WAY
PEATMORE
PEATMORE CL.
ENGLIFF LA.
FLOYD'S LA.
Lees Fm.
ROSEBRIAR CL.
WEXFENNE GDNS.

Woking
Guildford

Wisley

WISLEY LANE

The Anchor P.H.

WEY BANK SQUARE

Pyrford Lock

The Decoy

Townslow Meadow

River Wey

Royal Horticultural Society's Gdns.

Old Woking Rd.
PYRFORD WOODS
ORCHARD LEA CL.
CROSS ACRES
WESTON WAY
WESTON GDNS.
ABBEY CL.
NICHOLAS GDS.
TEGG'S LA.
MANOR CL.
ONSLOW W.
PYRFORD HTH.

COLDHARBOUR RD.
UPSHOT LANE
PYRFORD COMMON RD.
CHURCH HILL
SANDY LANE
B 367

The Rowley Bristow Orthopaedic Hospital

ELVEDEN CL.
Green Fm.

LOWER PYRFORD ROAD

LOCK ROAD

Pyrford Court

Pyrford

WARREN LANE
WARREN LANE

The Bourne
NEWARK LANE

River Wey Navigation

WHARF LA.

Ockham Court

Mill
MILL LA.

Battleston Hill

B 2215
B 2039

OCKHAM

Abbey Stream Bri.
Newark Priory (ruins)
Weir
Mill

Woking Guildford

Ockham Mill Stream

Dunsborough House

Ripley Green

Antiques

'The Half Moon' (P.H.)

'Talbot Hotel' (P.H.)

Ripley

HIGH ST.

Lock
NEWARK CL.
NEWARK CRES.
GEORGELANDS
WENTWORTH CL.
B367
NEWARK ROAD

P.O.
Sch.
ROSE
WHITE HART MEADOWS
RYDE CL.
Sch. Ripley Court

Pol. Sta.

Ockham Park

Papercourt Fm.
TANNERY LANE
Papercourt Sand Pit
POLESDON LANE

Toby Cottage

Ben Turner (Tractors)

Nurseries

Garage

MILESTONE CL.
GROVE HEATH NTH.

RIPLEY BYPASS

ROSE LANE

GUILESHILL LANE

Green
Sendmarsh
THE RIDINGS
MANOR RD.
'The Saddlers Arms' (P.H.)
'Jovial Sailor' (P.H.)

Send
B 368
MARSH LANE
GREEN DR.
MEADOW DR.
TUCKEY GROVE
STRINGHAMS
BIRNAM
GROVE CL.
FIR PL.
FULLERS RD.
HAWTHORN RD.
BRAMBLE WAY
WILLOW DR.
BEECH DR.
MAPLE
BOUGHTON HALL AV.
HAZEL DR.
LINDEN CL.
CHESTNUT CL.

GROVE HEATH
Garage
Grove Heath
Groveheath

PORTSMOUTH ROAD

KILN LANE
A3
GAMBLES LANE

HUNGRY HILL LANE

Hungry Hill

Ryde Farm

B 2215

CONTINUED ON PAGE **83**

0 · 500 · 1000 Yards

0 · 500 · 1000 Metres

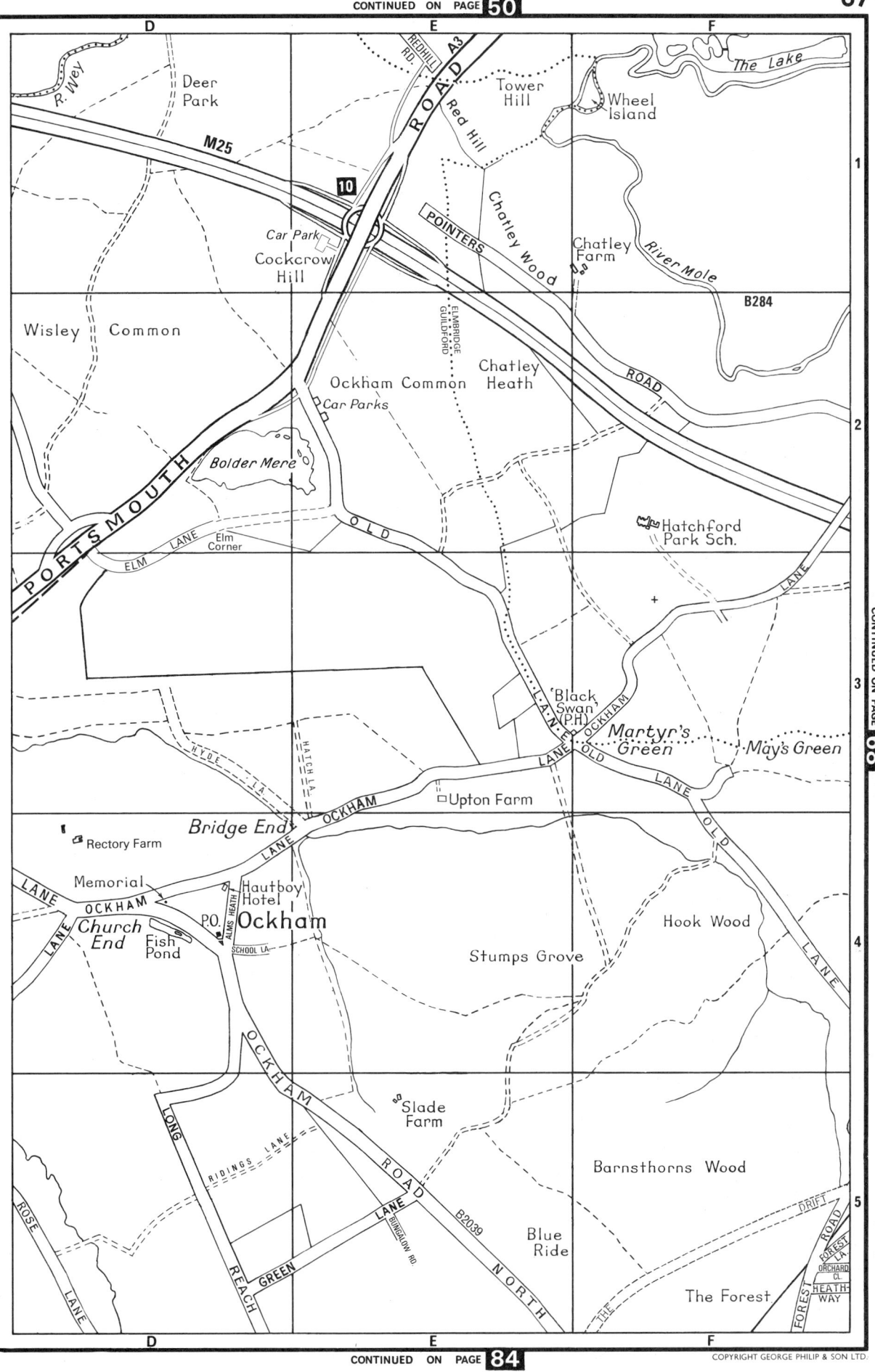

CONTINUED ON PAGE **68**

CONTINUED ON PAGE 51

A     B     C

R. Mole

ANVIL LA.

A245

HIGH ST.

ST. ANDREWS WK.

DOWNSIDE BR. RD.

CHURCH ST.

SPENCER RD.

CEDAR RD.

AV.

MILL RD.

LEIGH PL.

LEIGH HILL

BRAMBLE BOWSPRIT RISE

MIZEN CL.

WAY

WOOD END

BROOK FARM RD.

OAK ROAD

FOXSHOTT WAY

FAIRMILE LANE

WATER LA.

BROOK LANDS

Knowle Hill Park

CLOSE

FOGO

EVELYN WAY

BLUNDEL LANE

STOKE CL.

ASPEN DL.

KNOWLE PK.

RIVERHILL

1

Cobham Court

Downside Bridge

STOKE

Lower Cobham Tilt

ELM GROVE RD.

DOWN VIEW

ASHFORD GDNS.

AVENUE RD.

TILT MEADOW

MILL HEDGE

TILT RD.

D'ABERNON DR.

VINCENT RD.

STATION RD.

WINSTON DR.

Sch.

Plough Inn

STOKE CL.

The Running Mare (P.H.)

Cobham Cemetery

Upper Cobham Tilt

COBHAM & STOKE D'ABERNON STA.

Spts. Fld.

Lower Farm

DRIFT LANE

Stoke D'Abernon

PLOUGH LANE

Cobham Park

PARK WOOD

DOWNSIDE LANE

Inn

Cobham Stud Farm

Water Wheel & Weir

Mill Race

Upper Farm

Sports Grd.

COBHAM ROAD

Pav.

2

Halfpenny Cross

Cossins

CHILBROOK Farm

CHILBROOK FARM RD.

Parkside School

Ho.

St. Mary

R. Mole

HORSLEY RD.

COBHAM PARK RD.

Cricketers Sch.(P.H.)

Downside Common Inst.

Downside Farm

Downside

Stoke D'Abernon Bri.

COBHAM

Pondtail Farm

DOWNSIDE COMMON RD.

DEACON CL.

DOWNVIEW CL.

MIDDLETON RD.

GOOSE GREEN

New Barn Farm

BOOKHAM ROAD

Wrens Hill Wood

Muggeridge Wood

Yehudi Menuhin's Music Sch.

B

M25

STENTS LANE

The Grange

3

Down Wood

Old Oak Common

Chesmore Farm

4

Newmarsh Farm

New Barn Wood

ELMBRIDGE

Bank's Common

Little Bookham Common

Great Bookham Common

B

Brick Kiln Copse

Bushy Thicket

BANK'S LANE

B

COMMON ROAD

COMMONSIDE

Gallows Grove

OLD LANE

OLD LANE (GDNS.)

The Lord Howard (P.H.)

HOWARD RD.

LOW. PARK

SURREY GDNS.

FOREST RD.

EFFINGHAM JUNCTION STA.

Sewage Works

The Approach

The Grange Hotel

BOOKHAM STA.

MADDOX LANE

GUILDFORD

Mole Valley

MADDOX PARK

LEASIDE

MEADOW

CHURCH RD.

Works

CHURCH ROAD

EDENSIDE

5

Effingham Common

EFFINGHAM

Norwood Farm

LOWER FARM RD.

COMMON ROAD

ATWOOD

BURNHAMS RD.

T. BOOKHAM ST.

B

A     B     C

CONTINUED ON PAGE 67

CONTINUED ON PAGE 85

0    500    1000 Yards

0    500    1000 Metres

CONTINUED ON PAGE **70**

Surrey Boundary
'The Star' (P.H.)
CLAPNON CHASE
EPSOM GAP
KINGSTON ROAD
A243
A244
OLD FARMHOUSE DR.
WRENS HILL
NORTH COTE
HARDWICKE LANE
CHASE
RANDOLPH CL.
B
LANE
The Furze
Knott Park
BURN CL.
CHARLWOOD
THE MANOR WAY
DRIVE
Oxshott Flat
Horns Hill
ELMBRIDGE MOLE VALLEY
Leatherhead Golf Course
PATCHESHAM PARK
Pachesham Park
ASHTEAD GAP
1

WOODLANDS LANE
Woodlands Park
Old Parks
Woodlands Park
Woodlands Park
Queen Elizabeth's Training College for The Disabled
Oak Lawn
Leatherhead
OXSHOTT ROAD
PACHESHAM DR.
Oxshott Common
ROWHURST AVE.
Golf Course
ROAD
Club Ho.
TEAZLE WOOD PK.
Teazle Wood
Works
B2430
KINGSTON
RYEBRI.
WOODBRI.
RYE BROOK
WOODBRIDGE AV.
SANDES PL.
FAIRWAY
CLARE WD.
2

R. Mole
Slyfield Ho.
M25
Pachesham
Sewage Works
OAKLAWN
WOODLANDS ROAD
The Mounts
The Rye Brook
Central Electricity Research Labs.
Leatherhead Common
FAIRS RD.
ALBANY PARK RD.
DILSTON
Rec. Grd.
Sch.
CLARE CR.
MERTON WAY
CLARE
BROOKWAY
JAPERDELE
3

Little Wood
Bushy Copse
Sheepbell Farm
B. RIVER LA.
RANDALLS ROAD
Sch.
Electrical Research Assoc.
KELVIN AVENUE
GATESTON RD.
RANDALLS CR.
RANDALLS WAY
Dairies
The Plough (P.H.)
Gas Wks.
KINGSLEA
A245
A243
KINGST.RD.
WOODVIL.
Schs.

Ashspring Copse
MARK OAK LANE
LANGALLER LA.
Monksgreen Farm
Library
RIVERA RD.
OLD MILL RD.
Oldmill Footbridge
FRIARS ORCHARD
Randalls Park
Crematorium
Cemetery
Common Meadow
R. Mole
Printing Industry Res. Assoc.
BFMIRA
Leatherhead STA.
Pol. Sta.
Drill Hall
Kingston House Gdns.
MOLE BUSINESS PARK
INDUSTRIAL ESTATE
STATION RD. NTH.
BULL HL.
ROAD
PARK RISE
FAIRFIELD
LERET WAY
KINGSTON
CHURCH ST.
4

FETCHAM COMMON LA.
MONKS RD.
SHAMROCK
POUND CR.
HOME FIELD
COBHAM
ROUND OAK RD.
CANNON WAY
NUTCROFT GR.
GROVE
RAYMEAD CL.
CANNON
CANNONSIDE
RAYMEAD WAY
SYCAMORE CL.
ROAD
Mill Pond
Fire Sta.
MILL LA.
BRIDGE ST.
WATERWAY RD.
SUNMEAD
ELMER COTTS.
BELMONT RD.
Leisure Centre
Bus Garage
Thorncroft
Lib.
VICARAGE LA.
KINCH RD.

THE GLADE
THE COPSE
HILLEY FIELD LA.
COCK LANE
HAZEL
OSWALD RD.
COPPER BEECH
THE STREET
ORCHARD CL.
LODGE CL.
LODGE RD.
THE BALLANDS NTH.
SCHOOL LA.
THE BALLANDS STH.
THE DRIVE
ROAD
ARBOUR CL.
HAWKS HILL CL.
THE MOUNT
RD.
HAWKS HILL
5

SIDE
PARK
EASTWICK
MEADOW WAY
GREENWAY
WILLOW VALE
KENNEL LANE
BUSHY RD.
REVELL DR.
REVELL CL.
PENNYMEAD
HUMPHREY CL.
BICKNEY CL.
WARENE RD.
GATESDEN CL.
BELL LA.
LOWER
BADINGHAM DRI.
CEDAR DRI.
FETCHAM PK. DRI.
CHURCH RD.
DELL CL.
MONT CL.
Fetcham
WESTFIELD DR.
BARCLAY CL.
SPRINGFIELD DR.
RICHMOND WAY
VINCENT
WELLS
RIDGELANDS CL.
OAK LANDS
PARK
ROOKERY
RIDGEWAY
THE BERKELEYS
DRAYTON CL.
BOCKETTS
B
Hawk's Hill
A246

Southey Hall
Sch.
THE SPINNEY
PARK GREEN
PENACRES
EASTWICK PK. AV.
MURRELLS WALK
FERNLEA CL.
PARKLANDS WAY
DURLESTON PARK
KESWICK RD.
ORCHARD END
FOX COVERT
BARRETT RD.
THE GREEN
SUMNERS CL.
FARM WAY
GUILDFORD RD.
LEATHERHEAD (YOUNG ST.)
BY-PASS
B2122 A246
A246

CONTINUED ON PAGE 53

A       B       C

A243
Surrey Boundary
EPSOM GAP

Ashtead Common

THE CREST
THE GREENWAY
COMMON
EPSOM & EWELL
MOLE VALLEY
MARNEYS
WOODLANDS RD.
WELLS RD.
ROAD DORKING
CASTLE RD.
EBBISHAM WAY
WOODCOTE SIDE

1

WOODS ROAD
THE COMMON
ASHTEAD
The Rye Brook
Footbridge
Wood
Level Crossing
Field
ASHTEAD STA.
P.O.
BROADHURST
OVERDALE
CULVERHAY
OVERDALE
ST. STEPHEN'S AV.
CRADDOCKS
NEWTON WOOD
PETTERS RD.
CHAFFERS
MEAD END
BRAMLEY
DARCY
AVENUE
BAGOT CL.
FOREST CR.
ROAD FARM
Highfield Farm
HILDERS
Park Farm Ho.
WILMERHATCH

2

Swim Pool
LINKS
PRESTON GR.
FAIRHOLME
CRES.
WARWICK
TAYLOR RD.
READ RD.
WOODFIELD LANE
Sch.
MEADOW RD.
WALTERS MEAD
BROADMEAD
MARLD
HILLSIDE ROAD
BERRY
STONY CROFT
CRISPIN
EPSOM
Pond
ROOKERY HILL
Ashtead Park
PLEASURE PIT RD.
CHERRY ORCHARD

3

A243
Oil Depot
WEST FARM
Lower Ashtead
Barnett Wood
HARRIOT'S
AVENUE
GLADSTONE RD.
VIRGINIA CL.
HIGHFIELDS
PADDOCKS
Sch.
Ashtead
THE WARREN
City of London Freemens Sch.
RALLWOOD RD.
OAKEN COPPICE
GREENSIDE
PAUL'S

LEATHERHEAD
Poor's Allots
HAZELMERE
BARNETT
Waterfields
A245
Sch.
Sch.
UPLANDS
GRANGE
Stag Leys
Thirty Acres Barn
SHEPHERDS WK.

4

Sports Grd.
Playing Fld.
LINDEN PIT PATH
EPSOM
HIGH ST.
Hosp.
Sch.
B2033
Downsend (Sch.)
LEATHERHEAD BY-PASS
Lay-by A.A. area
See page 160 for detailed plan of LEATHERHEAD centre
LEATHERHEAD
M25
PEBBLE LANE
Street
Addlestead Wood

5

A245 CHURCH
GIMCRACK HILL
DORKING RD.
B2450
HIGHLANDS RD.
Royal Sch. for the Blind
Vale Lodge
Highland Park
Downside
Gar.
HEADLEY RD.
A24
Common Fields
Highlands Farm
THE DRIVE
Tyrrells Wood
Golf Club House
HEADLEY ROAD
Stane
Headley Court
Playing Field
CLAY LANE
LEE GREEN
REIGATE ROAD
B2033
LEATHERHEAD BY-PASS ROAD
A24 GARDEN CLOSE

CONTINUED ON PAGE 87

0     500    1000 Yards

0     500    1000 Metres

CONTINUED ON PAGE 69

CONTINUED ON PAGE 54

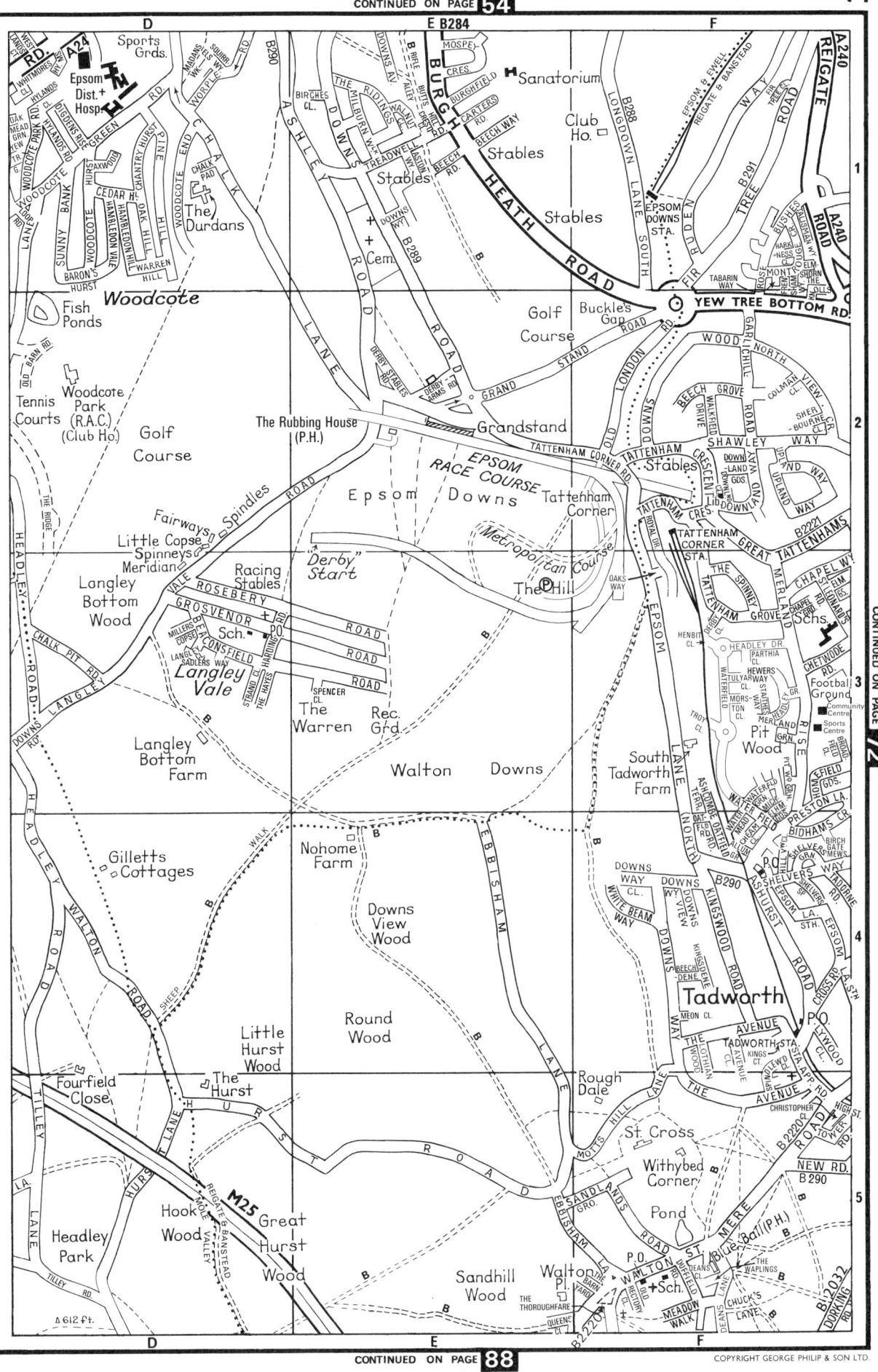

CONTINUED ON PAGE 72

CONTINUED ON PAGE 55

A217
B2217
WOODMANSTERNE RD
MANSTERNE
CUNNINGHAM RD.

WARREN MEAD
DRIFT WAY
ROUNDWOOD WAY
ROUNDWOOD VIEW
MEAD PARSONSFIELD
SHELLEY CL.
Sch.
BRIDGEFIELD
PARK
PARKWOOD ROAD
NORK RISE
NORK WAY
Nork
Park Wood
BEACON WAY
BUCKLES WAY
TUMBLEWOOD RD.
HILLSIDE CL.
TUDOR CL.
BURGH WOOD
HILLSIDE CL.
BURGH MOUNT
CHURCHYARD
WOODGAVIL
Fire Sta.
NORTH ACRE
GARRATTS LANE
A217
BOLTERS LA.
CASTLETON RD.
B2219
KINGSLEY AV.
GREENH'S GDS.
THE HORSESHOE
GREEN HAYES AV.
SANDERSFIELD GDS.
WILMOT WAY
GARDEN CLOSE
HIGH ST.
B2217
Sch.
THE ORCHARD
Lib.
Rec. Grd.
P.O.
Sch.
LANE
COLCOKES RD.
BANSTEAD
GREAT ELLSHAMS
Allots.
THE BEECHES
KENILWORTH CL.
RENILWORTH
PEMBROKE
WOODMANSTERNE LA.
CHEYNE CT.
VEN. AV.
JANOS
Rec. Grd.
Cricket Grd
ROSEHILL FARM MEADOW
Hosp.
Apsley
Hosp.
Banstead Place
MINT RD.
THE RACERY
ROAD

Tumble Beacon
Nork Park
TATTENHAM WAY
A240
Great Burgh
REIGATE ROAD
CLAREMOUNT GDNS.
HOMEFM.
SHAWLEY CR.
TATTENHAMS WAY
B2221
GREAT TATTENHAMS
ST. MONICAS WAY
CHETWOOD RD.
WEST DRIVE
CHURCH LANE
WATERER GDNS.
TANGIER WOOD
MEADOW WAY
TANGIER WAY
THE GARE
DICELAND RD.
FERNDALE RD.
GARRARD RD.
MONS. RD.
CHIPSTEAD RD.
POUND RD.
WELLESFORD CL.
STIRLING CLOSE
REGIS RD.
LYME REGIS RD.
THE LYME
CHIPSTEAD POUND
HOLLY LANE EAST
HOLLY LANE
CHALK PIT
Belvedere Ho.
Merton
New Place
Little Haugh
Park Downs
Council Depot.
The Queen Elizabeth Hospital for Children
Banstead Wood
Holly Hill

Council Offices
THE BRINDLES
PIQUETS WAY
Schs.
Tattenham Way Rec. Grd.
WOOD LANE
Wood Lodge
Canons Wood
Ruffett Wood
RUFFETTS WAY
CANONS RD.
DUNCAN RD.
GREEN LANE
BALLARDS GREEN
EGMONT WAY
MAYBURY CL.
OATLANDS RD.
WARREN HILL
Surrey Yeoman (P.H.) Gar.
Pond
Burgh Heath
Burgh Heath
READS REST LA.
Perrotts Farm
Lunch Wood
Fames Rough

BRIGHTON ROAD
CHETWODE RD.
MARBLES WAY
MERTON GDNS.
MORDEN CL.
School
HATCH GARDENS
LONGFIELD
HOMEFIELD GS.
CUDDINGTON CL.
PRESTON LANE
COPLEY WAY
VERNON WALK
COPTHILL LANE
COPLEIGH DR.
OAKDENE
THE RIDINGS
CEDAR WALK
FURZEHILL LANE
DOLUC DR.
Chipstead Bottom
Chiphouse Wood
GLADE SPUR
GLADE
DRIVE
THE CHASE
OUTWOOD LANE
LARCH CL.
Out Wood

CONTINUED ON PAGE 71

SHELVERS WAY
FLEETWOOD CL.
TRITTONS
MABBOTTS
WESSELS
CROFTETS
HUDSONS
NORTON
SAXONS
WATERHOUSE LANE
ALLCOCKS LANE
Garden Farm
P.O.
FURZE GROVE
FURZE FIELD
FINLAY
BALLANTINE DR.
Furze Hill
ST. MONICAS RD.
KINGSWOOD STA.
Kingswood
FOREST DRIVE
PINEHURST CL.
BEECHWOOD AV.
LILLEY DR.
BEECHWOOD
THE DELL
HAREWOOD
HARPURS
DELVES
KIPINGS
RADOLPHS
RUSSELS
BAYEAUX
HEATHCOTE
Tadworth Court Hosp.
'Red Ho. Arms' (P.H.)
'Kingswood Red Ho. Arms'
BRIGHTON ROAD
STREET
B2032
BONSOR DRIVE
WATERHOUSE LANE
WARREN WAY
WOODLAND WAY
BEECH DR.
BEARS DEN
HEATHER CL.
BEECHES WOOD
Kingswood Golf Course
Eyhurst Farm
Eyhurst Court
Longcroft Shaw
Farm

TADORNE RD.
CROSS RD.
EPSOM LANE STH.
OAKLANDS WAY
THE NORREYS
MEARE CL.
WATTS LA.
Sch.
Tunnel
STOKES RIDINGS
TADWORTH ROAD
CHAPEL RD.
HIGH ST.
NEW RD.
Blue Anchor (P.H.)
B290
DORKING RD.
B2032
Car Park
MILL RD.
Banstead Newton
THE WARREN
Tadorne
HEMLOCK CL.
VICARAGE CL.
NUT LODGE DR.
WALL
ACORN GROVE
GLEN SHAW
BIRCH GROVE
SILVER GROVE
EYHURST SPUR
EYHURST CLOSE
Kingswood Warren Res. Centre
Avalon
Club Ho.
Kingswood
BRIGHTON ROAD
A217
CHIPSTEAD LANE
PIGEONHOUSE LA.
MONKSWELL LANE
SOUTHERNS LA.
Morrey Shaw
Northfield Shaw
Westfield Shaw

CONTINUED ON PAGE 89

0   500   1000 Yards

0   500   1000 Metres

A237
A23

# Woodmansterne

Depot

Rec. Grd.
WOODMANSTERNE ST. P.O.
WOODMANSTERNE COURT
KENNETH RD.
BATIN CL.
KINGSCROFT RD.
BECKEN SHAW
GDS.
HEMPSTAW AV.
PRESTBY CR.
THE READENS
RECTORY LANE
MANOR HILL
B278
MANOR WAY
B2032
HATCH LANE
WHITETHORN
REDFORD
BEECHWOOD
RICHMOND RD.
FRY STON RD.
GROVE LA.
LYNWOOD AVE.
CLIFTON RD.
BRAMLEY
SOUTH
WOOD AVE.
JULIEN
THE GROVE
THE AVENUE
SOUTH WAY
WOODCOTE GRO. RD.
MALCOLM
Surrey Boundary
WINIFRED
NUTFIELD RD.
STOCK RD.
BRIG.
ALKAN
ROSE RD.
MEL.
WOODMANSTERNE RD.
WOODMAN RD.
LION GN. STATION
L/G APP.
VIC. RD.
SCH.
EDWARD RD.
LINDEN RD.
ST. ANDREW'S RD.
LYNDHURST
WOODMANSTERNE STA.
HILL
VALLEY
P.O.
Sch.
BARRIE CL.
CON.
VINCENT RD.
SHERWOOD RD.
ROAD
FOURTH DR.
Sch
P.O.
REDLANDS
B276
MARKT. LA.

SANDOWN RD.
HIGH BRIDGE
CHIPSTEAD
LANE
Sch
WESTLEIGH
CHIPSTEAD CL.
WOODLANDS GR.
RIDGEMOUNT AVE.
PARKSIDE GDNS.
PORTNALLS CLO.
PORTNALLS RISE
PORTNALLS ROAD
COULSDON SOUTH STA.

High Bridge
UPPER PINE
PINE WALK
COURT HILL
CHIPSTEAD WAY
ACKFORD ROAD
WALPOLE
HIGHFIELD ROAD
SOLOMS
COURT
Cane Hill Hosp.

How Hills
Golf Course
THE PINES
RICKMAN HILL RD.
BRIGHTON ROAD
REDDOWN RD.
DENE RD.
WESTWOOD RD.
MOORSOME WY.
ASBOURNE
CHARLTON GDNS.
Farthing
Downs

PARK ROAD
HOLLY LANE
B 2219
Lib.
P.O.
Car Park
LOWER PARK RD.
STATION APP.
CHIPSTEAD STA.
Chipstead Golf Cl.
BOUVERIE RD.
LISSOMS RD.
HIGH WOLD
RICKMAN HILL
HOLLYMEAK
WOODFIELD HILL
STARROCK HILL
WOODFELD RD.
THE NETHERLANDS
WOODPLACE LANE

HAZELWOOD LA.
OLD OAK
STAGBURY
STAGBURY HO.
AVE.
BOURKE HILL
HOLLYMEAD ROAD
How Green
YEW TREE CL.
COULSDON LANE
Starrock Green
WILHELMINA AV.
WOODPLACE TERRACE

BRIDGE WAY
CLEAVE PRIOR
Dene Farm
HAZELWOOD AVENUE
DOGHURST LA.
HIGH LANE
VINCENT GREEN
P.O.
VINCENT CL.
STARROCK LANE
Greater
London
Boundary
Woodplace Farm
DRIVE
WOODPLACE ROAD

Chipstead Bottom
High Br.
OUTWOOD LANE
CASTLE
White Hart (P.H.)
# Chipstead
*Hooley*
Star Bridge
Boxers Wood

Long Plantation
ROAD
ELMORE ROAD
Elmore Pond
Bowling Club
Farm
MAPLE WAY
CLOVER HILL
ROWAN GR.
MARG'S
P.O.
track
train track
Forge Bridge
PARK LA.
NETHERNE LANE

Church Green
Mem
STAR LANE
CHURCH LANE
LANE DR.
CHURCH LANE AV.
BRIGHTON ROAD
Netherne Wood
Netherne Hospital

Shabden Park Hospital
The Grove
HIGH HOGSCROSS LANE
Noke Farm
BROAD WALK
GARDEN WALK
Fast train
DEAN LANE
DEAN LA. PARK

WHITE LANE
RUFFETS END
Sch.
MARKEDGE LA.
BROAD WALK ESTATE
Cafe
A23
Coldroast Shaw
Tunnel
Tunnel

GLEBE RD.
M23
7

CONTINUED ON PAGE 74
CONTINUED ON PAGE 90

CONTINUED ON PAGE 57

A23 BRIGHTON RD.

C A 22

GODSTONE RD.

CONTINUED ON PAGE 73

KENLEY

Coulsdon Court (Golf Club)

Golf Course

Kenley Park Ho.

Kenley Ho.

Kenley Common

Betts Mead Rec. Grd.

Bradmore Green

COULSDON

Kenley Aerodrome

Old Coulsdon

Welcome Tea Rooms

Parson's Pightle

Devilsden Wood

Coulsdon Common

Sisters Pond

Fox (P.H.)

Figgs Wood

Dean Hill

Caterham Barracks

Sports Grd.

Broad Wood

Piles Wood

St. Lawrence's Hosp.

Westway Common

Court Farm

Glebe Ho.

Furzefield Wood

Alderstead Heath

Chaldon

Chaldon Mead Hostel

Fryern Farm

Queen's

Playing Field

A 2031

0    500    1000 Yards

0    500    1000 Metres

CONTINUED ON PAGE **58**

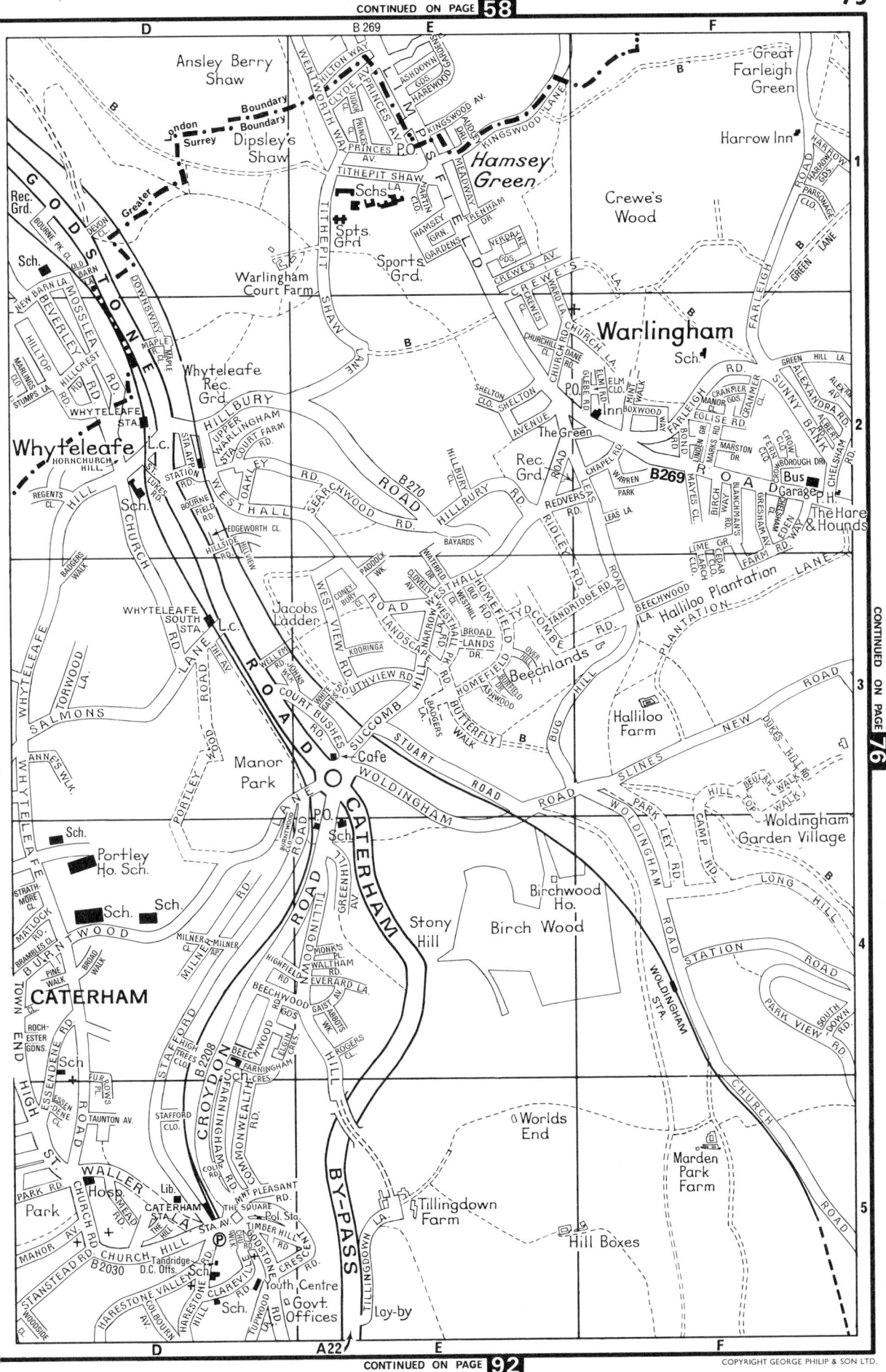

CONTINUED ON PAGE **76**

CONTINUED ON PAGE **92**

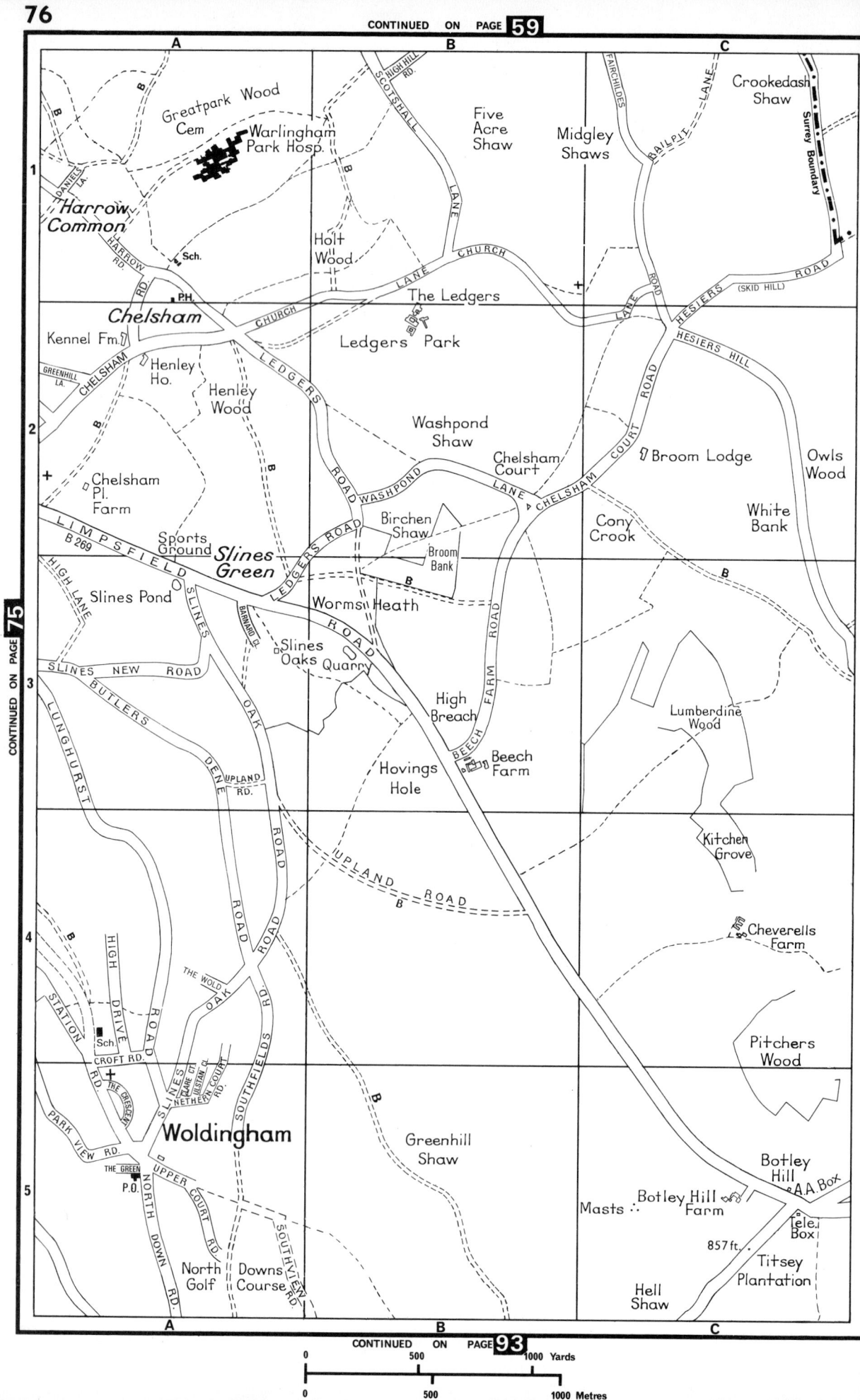

**76**

CONTINUED ON PAGE **59**

A            B            C

Greatpark Wood

Cem

Warlingham
Park Hosp.

Five
Acre
Shaw

Midgley
Shaws

Crookedash
Shaw

HIGH HILL RD.

SCOTSHALL LANE

FAIRCHILDES LANE

BAILPIT LANE

Surrey Boundary

**1**

Harrow
Common

HARROW RD.

DANIELS LA.

Holt
Wood

CHURCH LANE

Sch.

The Ledgers

(SKID HILL)

HESIERS ROAD

P.H.

Chelsham

CHELSHAM ROAD

GREENHILL LA.

Kennel Fm.

Henley
Ho.

Henley
Wood

LEDGERS ROAD

Ledgers Park

Washpond
Shaw

Chelsham
Court

CHELSHAM COURT ROAD

HESIERS HILL

Broom Lodge

Owls
Wood

**2**

Chelsham
Pl.
Farm

Sports
Ground

Slines
Green

Slines Pond

LIMPSFIELD ROAD B 269

HIGH LANE

SLINES

WASHPOND LANE

Birchen
Shaw

Broom
Bank

Worms Heath

Slines
Oaks Quarry

LEDGERS ROAD

BEECH FARM ROAD

White
Bank

Cony
Crook

**3**

SLINES NEW ROAD

BUTLERS DENE ROAD

LUNGHURST ROAD

OAK ROAD

BARNARD CL.

UPLAND RD.

Hovings
Hole

High
Breach

Beech
Farm

Lumberdine
Wood

Kitchen
Grove

UPLAND ROAD

**4**

HIGH DRIVE

THE WOLD

OAK ROAD

SOUTHFIELDS RD.

STATION RD.

Sch.

CROFT RD.

Cheverells
Farm

Pitchers
Wood

**5**

Woldingham

SLINES RD.

CLARE CT.

NETHERN CT.

ULSTAN CL.

PARK VIEW RD.

THE CRESCENT

THE GREEN

P.O.

UPPER COURT RD.

NORTH DOWN RD.

SOUTHVIEW RD.

Greenhill
Shaw

North
Golf

Downs
Course

Botley
Hill

Botley Hill
Farm

A.A. Box

Masts

857 ft.

Tele.
Box

Hell
Shaw

Titsey
Plantation

CONTINUED ON PAGE **75**

A            B            C

CONTINUED ON PAGE **93**

0      500     1000 Yards

0      500     1000 Metres

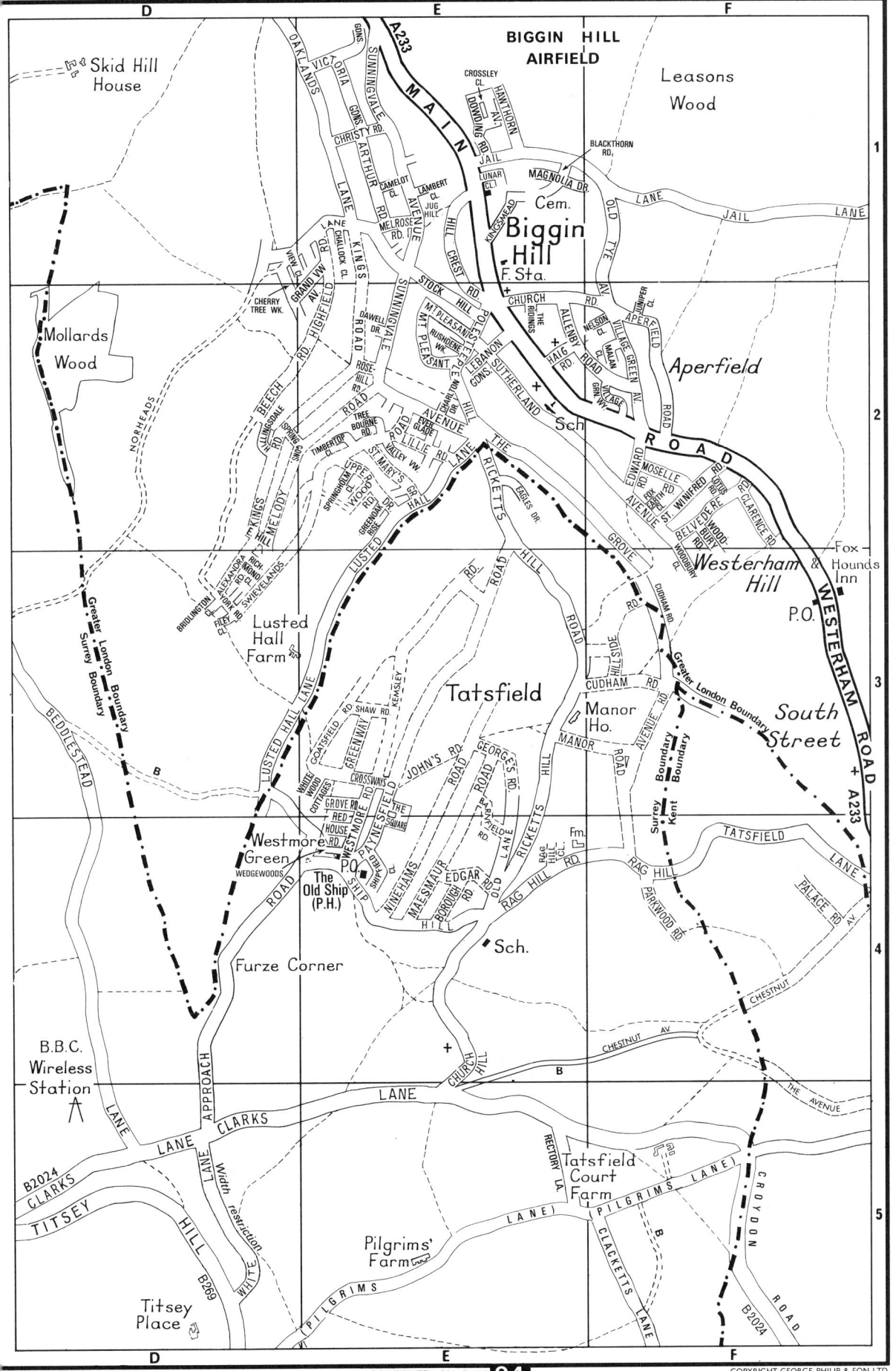

CONTINUED ON PAGE **61**

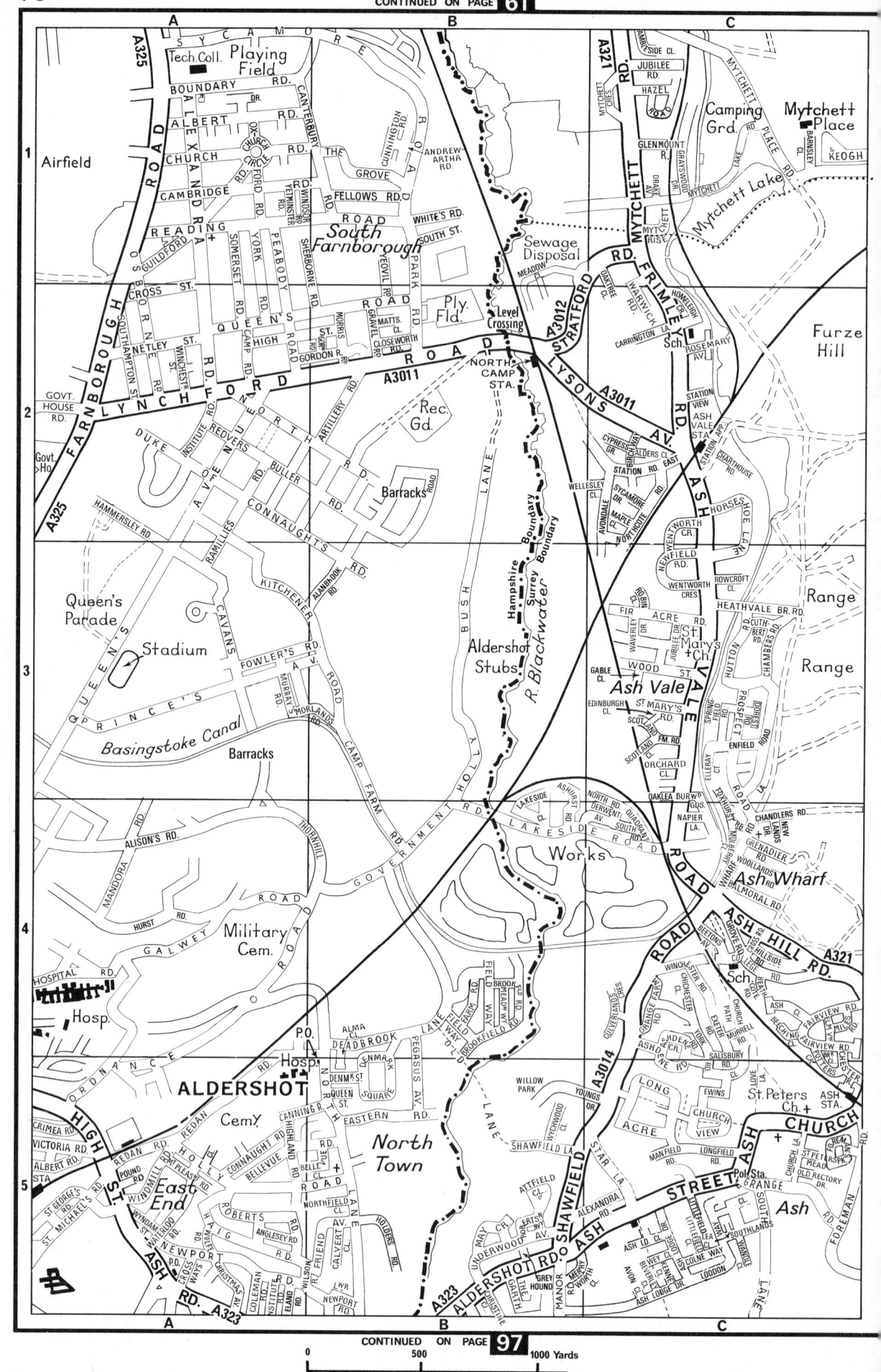

CONTINUED ON PAGE **97**

0        500        1000 Yards

0        500        1000 Metres

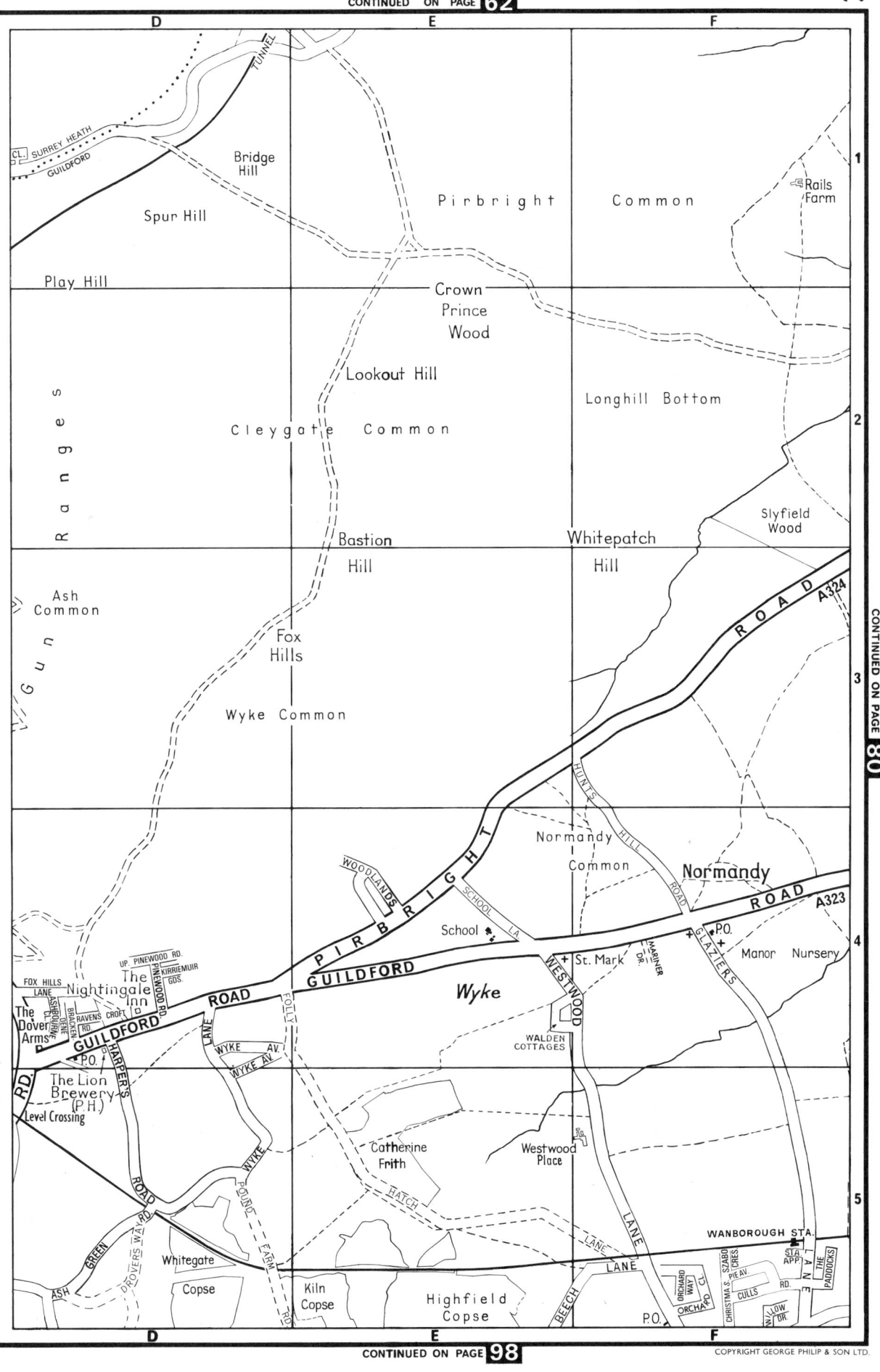

CL. SURREY HEATH
GUILDFORD

Bridge
Hill

Spur Hill

P i r b r i g h t    C o m m o n

Rails
Farm

**1**

Play Hill

Crown
Prince
Wood

Lookout Hill

Longhill Bottom

R a n g e s

C l e y g a t e   C o m m o n

**2**

Slyfield
Wood

Bastion
Hill

Whitepatch
Hill

Ash
Common

Fox
Hills

G u n

Wyke Common

ROAD

A324

**3**

Normandy
Common

**Normandy**

ROAD

A323

WOODLANDS

SCHOOL LA.

PIRBRIGHT

HUNT'S HILL ROAD

GLAZIERS

P.O.

Manor  Nursery

**4**

School

St. Mark

MARINER DR.

UP. PINEWOOD RD.
KIRRIEMUIR GDS.
The
Nightingale
Inn
PINEWOOD RD.

FOX HILLS
LANE

ROAD

GUILDFORD

ROAD

*Wyke*

WESTWOOD

ASHBOURNE
BRACKEN

The
Dover
Arms

RAVENS
CROFT

BOURNE RD.

P.O.

HARPER'S

WYKE AV.

WYKE AV.

WALDEN
COTTAGES

RD.

GUILDFORD

LANE

FOLLY

The Lion
Brewery
(P.H.)
Level Crossing

WYKE

Catherine
Frith

Westwood
Place

**5**

ROAD

POUND

FARM RD.

HATCH

LANE

WANBOROUGH STA.

STA. APP.

THE PADDOCKS

GREEN

DROVERS WAY

Whitegate

Kiln
Copse

Highfield
Copse

BEECH  LANE

LANE

ORCHARD
WAY
ORCHARD CL.

CHRISTMAS

SZABO CRES.

PIE AV.

CULLS

WILLOW DR.

LANE

ASH
Copse

P.O.

CONTINUED ON PAGE **80**

CONTINUED ON PAGE **63**

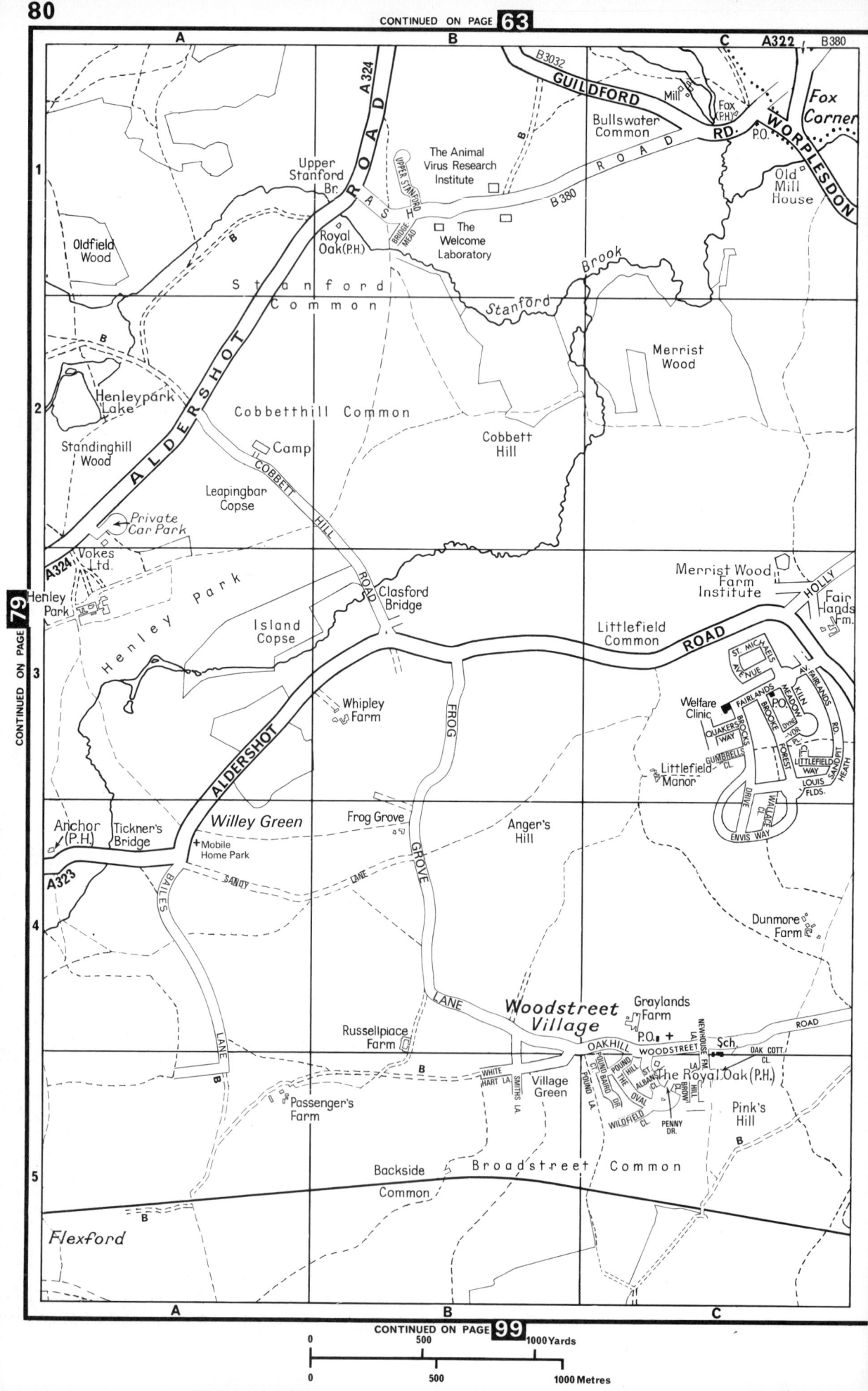

CONTINUED ON PAGE 79

CONTINUED ON PAGE **99**

| | | | |
|---|---|---|---|
| 0 | 500 | 1000 | Yards |
| 0 | 500 | 1000 | Metres |

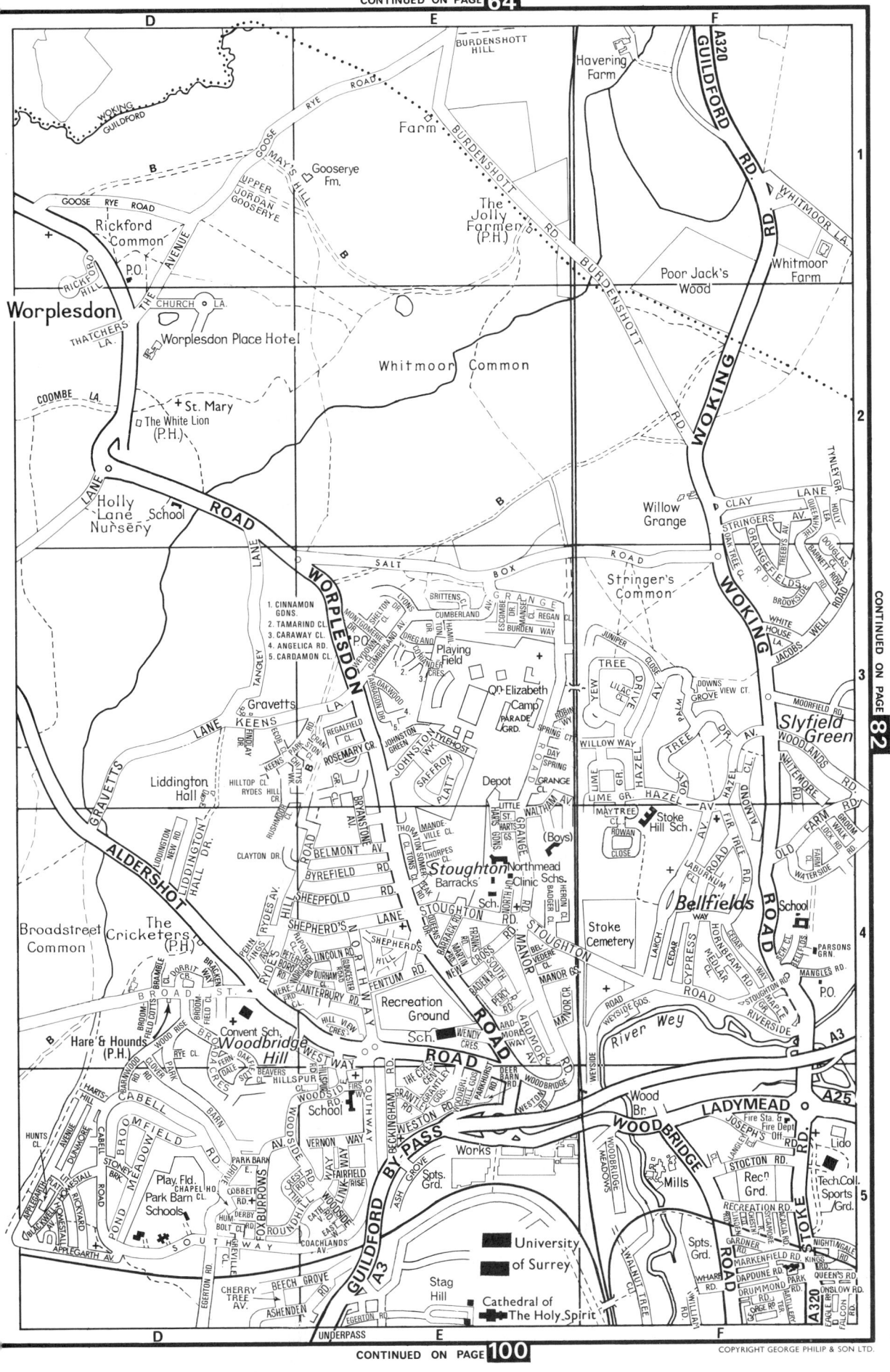

CONTINUED ON PAGE **82**

COPYRIGHT GEORGE PHILIP & SON LTD.

CONTINUED ON PAGE **65**

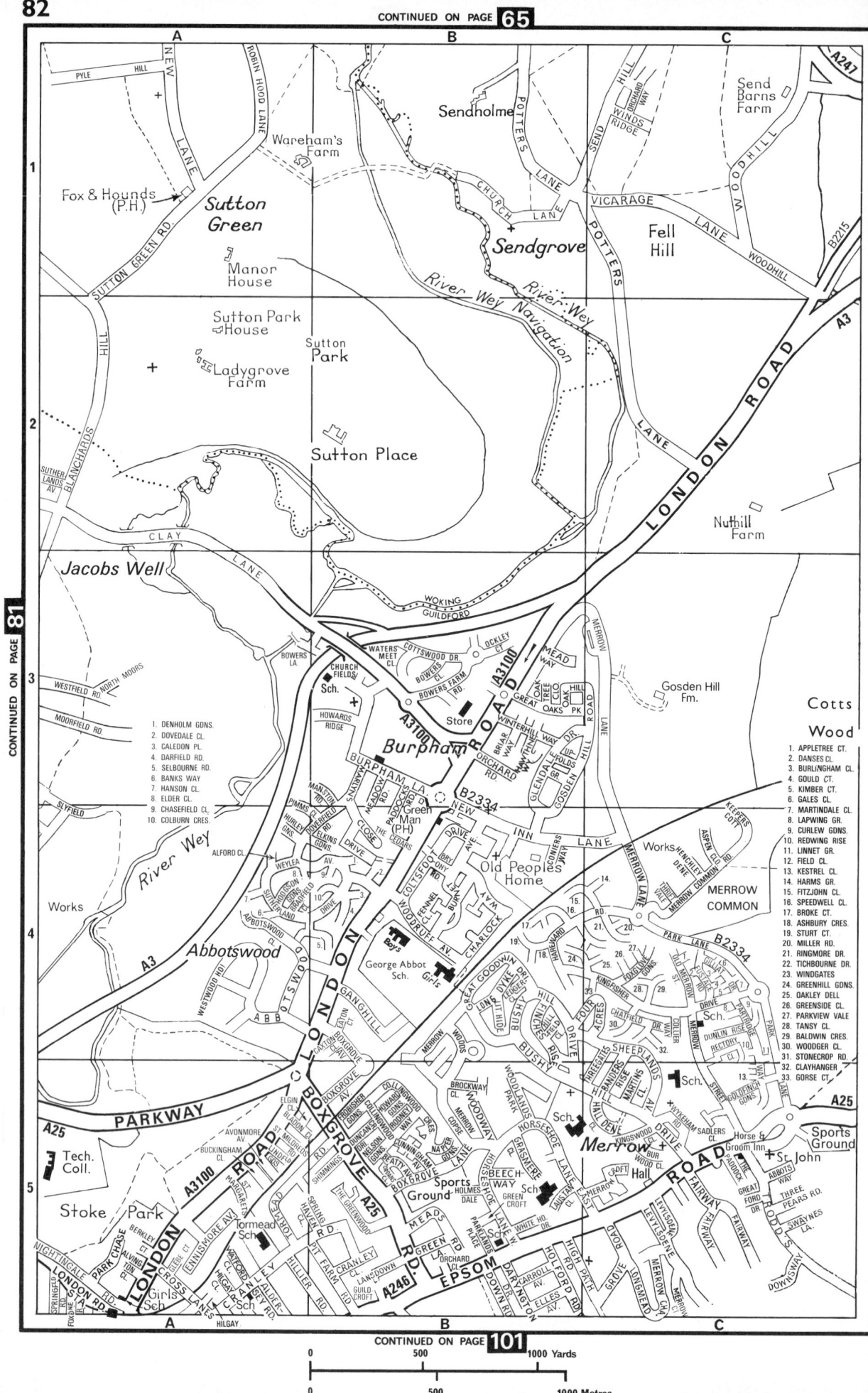

CONTINUED ON PAGE **81**

A      B      C

PYLE HILL

Fox & Hounds (P.H.)

Sutton Green

Wareham's Farm

Sendholme

Send Barns Farm

Sendgrove

Fell Hill

Manor House

Sutton Park House

Ladygrove Farm

Sutton Park

Nuthill Farm

Sutton Place

River Wey Navigation

River Wey

LONDON ROAD

Jacobs Well

CLAY LANE

Woking Guildford

Cotts Wood

1. DENHOLM GDNS.
2. DOVEDALE CL.
3. CALEDON PL.
4. DARFIELD RD.
5. SELBOURNE RD.
6. BANKS WAY
7. HANSON CL.
8. ELDER CL.
9. CHASEFIELD CL.
10. COLBURN CRES.

Burpham

Green Man (PH)

Old Peoples Home

Merrow Common

1. APPLETREE CT.
2. DANSES CL.
3. BURLINGHAM CL.
4. GOULD CT.
5. KIMBER CT.
6. GALES CL.
7. MARTINDALE CL.
8. LAPWING GR.
9. CURLEW GDNS.
10. REDWING RISE
11. LINNET GR.
12. FIELD CL.
13. KESTREL CL.
14. HARMS GR.
15. FITZJOHN CL.
16. SPEEDWELL CL.
17. BROKE CT.
18. ASHBURY CRES.
19. STURT CT.
20. MILLER RD.
21. RINGMORE DR.
22. TICHBOURNE DR.
23. WINDGATES
24. GREENHILL GDNS.
25. OAKLEY DELL
26. GREENSIDE CL.
27. PARKVIEW VALE
28. TANSY CL.
29. BALDWIN CRES.
30. WOODGER CL.
31. STONECROP RD.
32. CLAYHANGER
33. GORSE CL.

River Wey

Works

Abbotswood

George Abbot Sch. Boys Girls

Merrow

Merrow Common

B2334

A3

A25 PARKWAY

Tech. Coll.

Stoke Park

Tormead Sch.

Sports Ground

Beechway Sch.

Merrow Hall

Horse & Groom Inn

St. John

Sports Ground

LONDON ROAD

BOXGROVE ROAD

EPSOM RD.

A246

A25

Girls Sch.

A       B       C

CONTINUED ON PAGE **101**

0     500     1000 Yards

0     500     1000 Metres

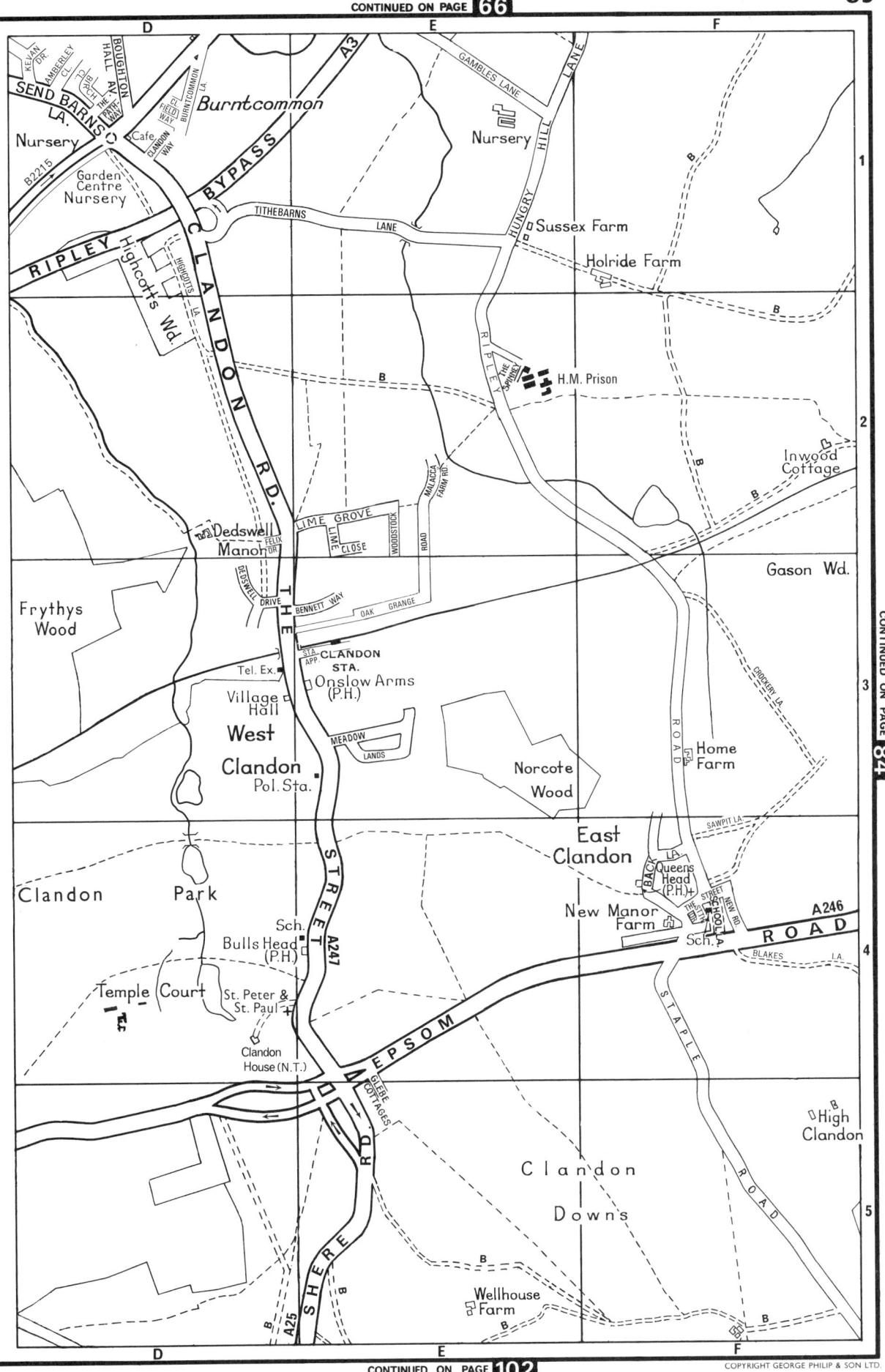

CONTINUED ON PAGE **84**

CONTINUED ON PAGE 83

A B C

1

GREEN LANE WEST

LONGREACH

NORTHCOTE CRESCENT

NIGHTINGALE CRESCENT
NIGHTINGALE AV.
Sch.
EDWIN RD.
NORTHCOTE RD.
HEATHERDENE
MEADOW WAY
HOWARD CL.

Manor Farm
FARLEYS CL.
WOODSIDE
GRETA BANK
EAST

B2039
OCKHAM ROAD NTH.
THE HIGHLANDS

WILDWOOD
PARKSIDE CL.
ROAD
FOREST RD.
HOOKE CL.
HEATH VIEW
NIGHTINGALE RD.
NORRELS RIDE
THE RIDINGS

HORSLEY STA.
COBHAM WAY
Horsley Hotel
STATION APP.
KINGSTON AV.
OCKHAM
THE RISE
STATION PAR.
THE CHASE
COBHAM WAY

NORRELS DRIVE

HIGH PARK AV.
HIGH PARK AVENUE

Jury Farm
B

Jury Cottages

RIPLEY

STREET

TOLLESWORTH LANE

P.O.
Rectory
OLD RECTORY LA.
THE BIRCHES
GLENDENE AV.

OAK WOOD DR. STH.
OAKWOOD CL.

FOWOODLAND DR.
WOODLAND DR.

Pennymead Lake

2

Hammonds Farm
B

Village Green
The Barley Mow (P.H.)

SILKMORE LANE
KITSONS LA.
TINTELLS LA.
KENYONS
LITTLE CRANMORE LA.

B

FRENCHLANDS HATCH
PARK CORNER DR.
PERYERS
W.R.
MANOR GR.
HIGHFIELDS

MEADOW BANK
PENNYMEAD RISE
PENNYMEAD DR.

LYNX RD.
PINE WALK

FARM CL.
Pond

Pond

THE STREET
THE LANE

Village Hall
FAIRWELL LA.
West Horsley
PINCOTT LA.
SCHOOL LA.
Sch.
MT. PLEASANT
CRANMORE LA.
P.O.
FEARN LA.

West Horsley Place

B2039
BISHOPS MEAD PAR.
Sch.
HOLMWOOD CL.
ST. MARTINS CL.
FORTIFIED GATE
Horsley Towers
GUILDFORD LODGE DRIVE

SOUTH

3

Great Wix Wood

BUTLERS HILL
Garage
Wix Farm

Nurseries

St. Mary
The Grove Fruit Farm
B

ROAD
War Memorial
St. Martins P.H.
Fortified Gate
East Horsley
GARAGE

WELLINGTON COTT.
Thatchers Restaurant
LONGHURST RD.

GUILDFORD
THE WARREN
ROWBARNS WAY

CHALK LANE

Hatchlands
EPSOM
A246
Lay-by
WIX HILL
SHERE RD.
JEFFRIES RD.
Chalk Pit

Western Wood

B

LARK RISE

GREEN DENE

4

BLAKES
FULLERS

B

The Sheepleas

Car Park

B

Car Park
B

Hillside

Mountain Wood

B

HONEYSUCKLE LANE

5

Barnet Wood

FARM ROAD
Fullers Farm
Hook Wood
Woodcote Lodge

B

SHERE ROAD
GREEN

B

BOTTOM

SHEEPWALK LANE

A B C

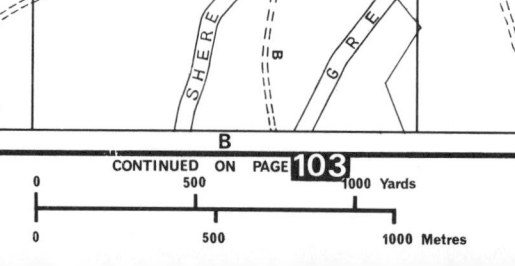

CONTINUED ON PAGE 103

0        500        1000 Yards

0        500        1000 Metres

CONTINUED ON PAGE **68**

D E F

Little Bookham

P.O.
FAIRLAWN
SOLE FARM
Indian Fm

Thornet Wood

Greatlee Wood

Lee Wood Farm

Littlelee Wood

Great Ridings Plantation

EFFINGHAM COMMON

Windsor Castle (P.H.)

CHILDS HALL
SOLE FARM
MIDDLEMEAD FARM
LONG MEADOW
ASHLEY CL.
THE GARSTONS
STONEHILL CL.
VICARAGE CL.
CHURCH RD.
SOLCOTE
THE MEAD
THE LORNE
GLEBE CL.
RD.

Great Bookham

Dunglass Farm

WATER LANE
SWANNS MEADOW
HAWKWOOD RISE
HAWKWOOD DELL

The Grange

MANORHOUSE LA.
RECTORY LANE

Ridings Wood

ROAD
LEEWOOD WAY
LOWER
'The Plough (P.H.)
Sch
Sch
The Lodge
Manor House

B

Orestan Farm
ORESTAN LANE

B

DIRTHAM LANE

CALVERT ROAD
CHESTER RD.

Park Wood

Ridings Wood

CHURCH ST.
YEW TREE WK.
BROWNS LA.
STREET
P.O.

Effingham

Rec. Grd.

GUILDFORD RD.
A246

ROAD

ORCHARD GDNS.
LONDON CL.
MT. PLEASANT
NORWOOD
NORWOOD RD.
MEAD WAY
STRATHCONA AV.
WOODLANDS RD.
CHALKPIT LANE

MANOR GDS.
BEECH
BEECH CL.

SALMONS ROAD

Club Ho.

Standard Hill

GUILDFORD ROAD

Warren Farm

Effingham Golf Course

Reservoir (Underground)

AVENUE
HIGH BARN ROAD
BEECH LANE

MOLE VALLEY (GUILDFORD)

Big High Grove

PARK HORSLEY

ROAD

DIRTHAM LANE

GREEN DENE

LONDON LANE

Rowbarns Grange

B

Oldlands Plantation

Black Bush Plantation

Oldlands Copse

Northfield Plantation

B

Six Acre Copse

Hazel Bucket

Chippens Copse

Burrows Wood

St. Teresa's Convent

Stars Wood

White Hill

High Barn

B

Stonyrock Copse

STONYROCK ROAD

Round Lions Copse

B

Yewtree Farm

B

Ranmore House Farm

Crocknorth Farm

B

CROCKNORTH ROAD

Birchetts Plantation

GUILDFORD MOLE VALLEY

Dunley Hill Farm

Dogkennel Green

CRITTEN LANE

RANMORE COMMON ROAD

Lillies Copse

D E F

CONTINUED ON PAGE **104**

CONTINUED ON PAGE **86**

1
2
3
4
5

CONTINUED ON PAGE 69

CONTINUED ON PAGE 85

B2122
YOUNG ST.
A246

Playing Field
DURLESTON PARK DR.
Eastwick
TEN ACRES
THE PARK
PARK VIEW
PARK DR.
EASTWICK RD.
DUNSHOTT
PINE WALK
FIFE WAY
CHURCH RD.
POSTHSE LA.
L.P.O.
Sch.
Car Pk.
P
BARBETT RD.
BROWNING RD.
HUNTSMAN CL.
BURNEY CL.
GREVILLE CT.
GILMAIS CL.
PRIORS MEAD
CAMILLA DR.
CHILMANS DR.
PINEDEAN
PROCTOR GDNS.
CANDY CROFT
GARRARDS
LOWER FIELD RD.
KESWICK AV.
LOWER RD.
HIGH ST.
FAIRFIELD RD.
SOUTHEY RD.
CLINTON RD.
MILTON CL.

LEATHERHEAD
A246
GROVE SIDE RD.
NEWNHAM RD.
LOWER FAIRFIELD RD.
BEALES RD.
STYLES END
WEST DOWN
DOWLANS RD.
KIDBOROUGH DOWN
DOWLANS CL.
HOWARD RD.
DAWNAY RD.
PELHAM WAY
ORKDALE
Sch.
KINGSTON AV.
DORKING RD.
ALLEN RD.
CRAB-TREE CL.
BLACKHORNE RD.
HILLTOP RISE
HALE PIT RD.
HAWKS HILL
DOWNSVIEW RD.
SHERB'NE DANS'R RD.
NORBURY WAY
DOWNS
BROCK CL.
ASHDALE
TIMBER CL.
OAK
Rec. Grd.

Roaringhouse Farm
Fetcham Downs
Updown Wood
Walnut Tree Clump
Norbury Park
Norbury Park
Swanworth Farm
MICKLEHAM

Denshire Hill
Bookham Wood
Druids Grove

ROAD
CHAPEL
POLESDEN LA.
ADMIRAL'S
Goldstone Farm
HOGDEN LA.
Connicut Wood
CONNICUT LANE
Phœnice Farm
BAGDEN HILL LANE
Preserve Copse
Polesden Lacey
(N.T.)
Polesden Farm
Chapelhill Wood
Freehold Wood
CHAPEL
Chapel Wood
Chapel Hill
Beechy Wood
CRABTREE
LANE
Chapel Farm
Camilla Lacey
CAMILLA DR.
Old Dene
ROAD
COMMON
Tanner's Hatch (Youth Hostel)
Bagden Wood
Long Bottom
Dorking Wood
Ashcombe Wood
Ashleigh
BURNEY RD.
ADLERS LA.
PILGRIMS
Gravel Pit Plantat'n
LANE
Bradley Farm
BRADLEY LA.
Fort (Dismantled)
Ranmore Common
RANMORE
COMMON RD.
ROAD
Denbies Farm
North Downs Way
Ranmore Common
St. Barnabas
Sch.
Denbies
Ranmore Roundabout The Spains
RANMORE
ROAD
KEPPEL RD.
YEW-TREE RD.
LIMEWAY TER.
MASON'S PADDOCK
CHALKPIT TER.
HILL RISE
FRASER GDNS.
ASHCOMBE
Sec. Sch.
A2003
River

CONTINUED ON PAGE 105

0 500 1000 Yards
0 500 1000 Metres

CONTINUED ON PAGE **70**

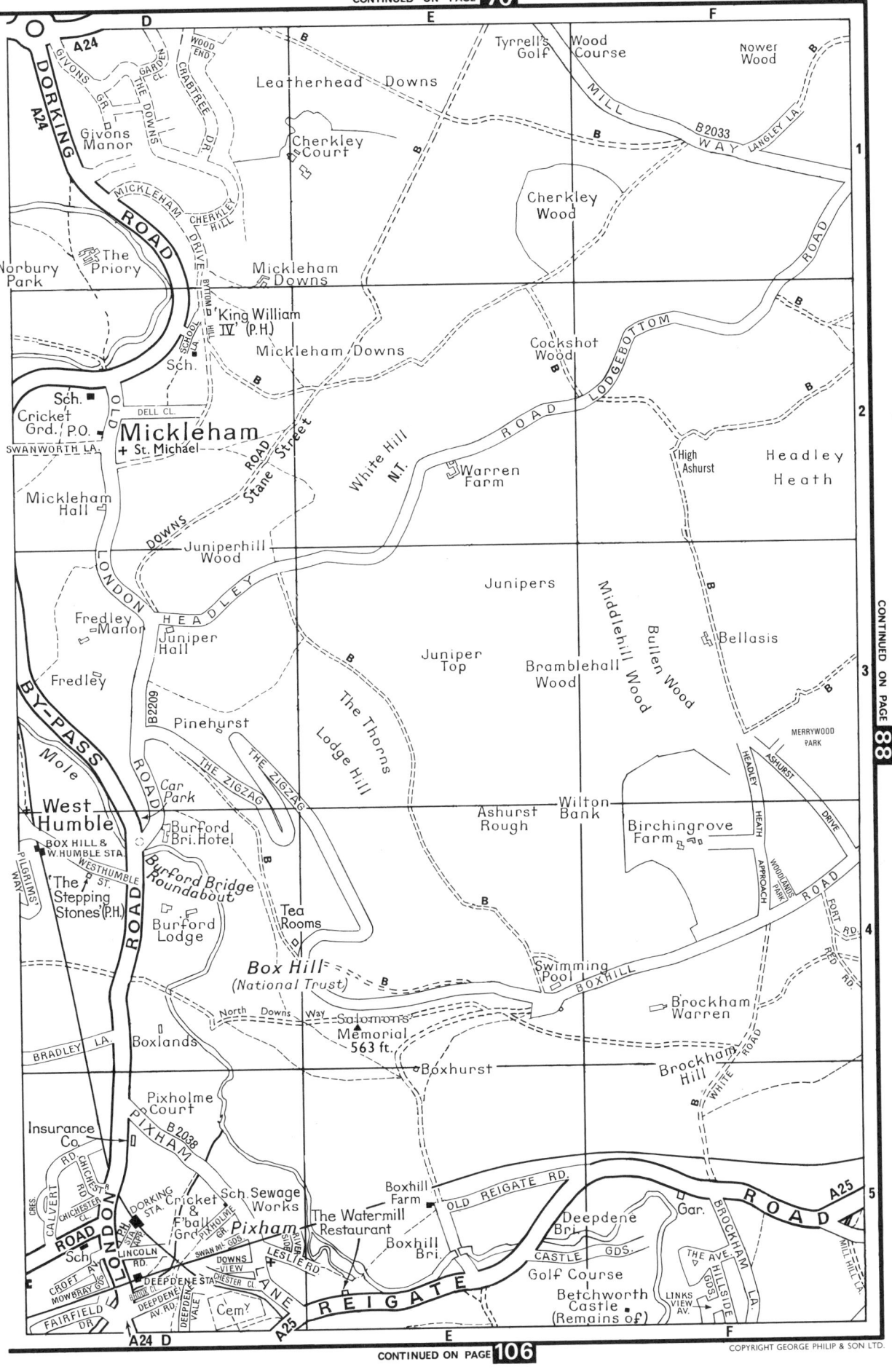

CONTINUED ON PAGE **88**

CONTINUED ON PAGE **106**

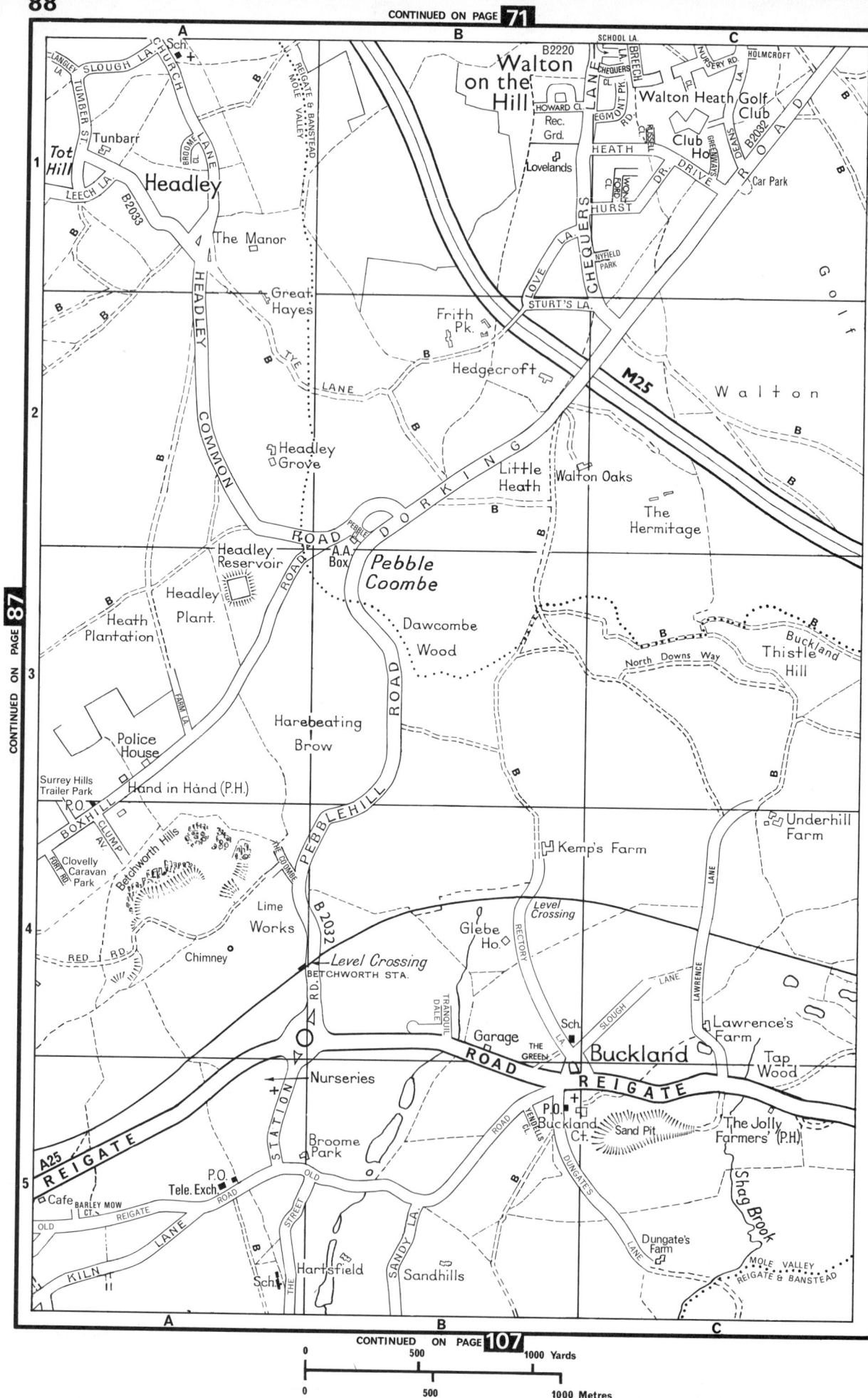

CONTINUED ON PAGE 71

CONTINUED ON PAGE 87

CONTINUED ON PAGE 107

Walton on the Hill

Walton Heath Golf Club

Club Ho.

Car Park

Golf

Walton

The Hermitage

Buckland Thistle Hill

North Downs Way

Underhill Farm

Kemp's Farm

Lawrence's Farm

Tap Wood

Buckland

Level Crossing

Glebe Ho.

Garage

THE GREEN

Sch.

P.O.

Buckland Ct.

Sand Pit

The Jolly Farmers' (P.H.)

Shag Brook

Dungate's Farm

MOLE VALLEY
REIGATE & BANSTEAD

REIGATE ROAD

Sandhills

Hartsfield

Sch.

Broome Park

Nurseries

Tele. Exch.

P.O.

Cafe
BARLEY MOW CT.

A25 REIGATE

KILN LANE

OLD REIGATE ROAD

STATION ROAD

Betchworth Sta.
Level Crossing
BETCHWORTH STA.

Lime Works

Chimney

RED RD.

Betchworth Hills

Clovelly Caravan Park

Surrey Hills Trailer Park

Police House

Hand in Hand (P.H.)

Harebeating Brow

PEBBLEHILL ROAD
B 2032

Pebble Coombe

Dawcombe Wood

Headley Reservoir
A.A. Box

Headley Plant.

Heath Plantation

FARM LA.

Headley Grove

Little Heath

Walton Oaks

Hedgecroft

Frith Pk.

Great Hayes

The Manor

Headley

Tunbarr

Tot Hill

Sch.

SLOUGH LA.
LANGLEY LA.
TUMBER ST.
CHURCH LANE
BROOME LANE

LEECH LA.
B2033

HEADLEY COMMON ROAD

TYE LANE

DORKING ROAD

STURT'S LA.

M25

B2220
SCHOOL LA.
CHEQUERS LA.
BRECH LA.
NURSERY RD.
HOLMCROFT
HOWARD CL.
Rec. Grd.
Lovelands
HEATH
HURST
CROSS
DRIVE
DEANS
GREEN
B2032
LOVE LANE
EGMONT RD.
RUSSELL CT.
NYFIELD PARK

LAWRENCE LANE
RECTORY LANE
SLOUGH LA.
DUNGATE'S LANE
YENDALS CL.
TRANQUIL DALE
CLUMP AV.
BOXHILL RD.
FORT RD.
THE COOMBE
SANDY LA.
THE STREET
OLD REIGATE LANE

CONTINUED ON PAGE 107

0        500        1000 Yards

0        500        1000 Metres

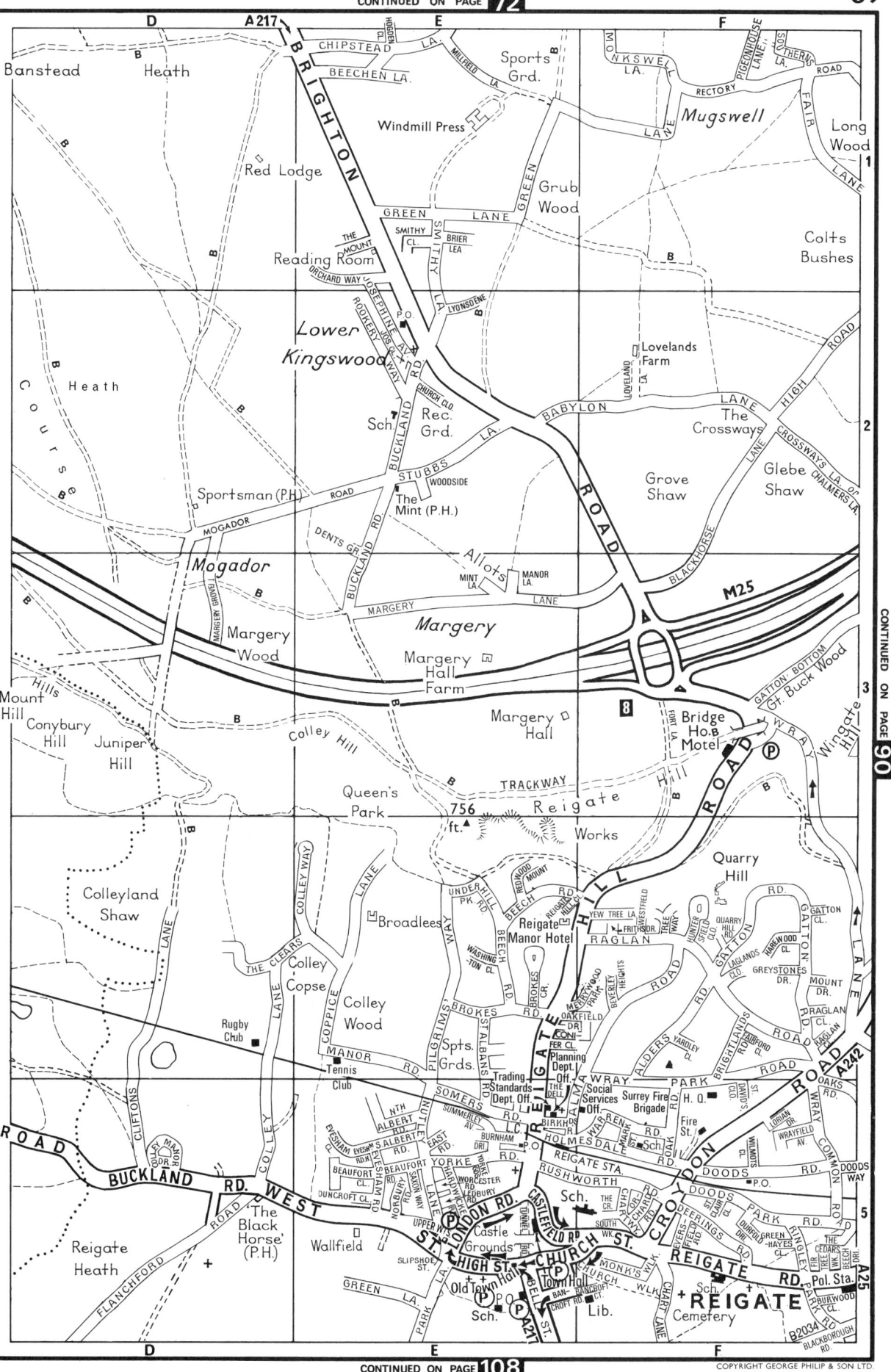

CONTINUED ON PAGE **73**

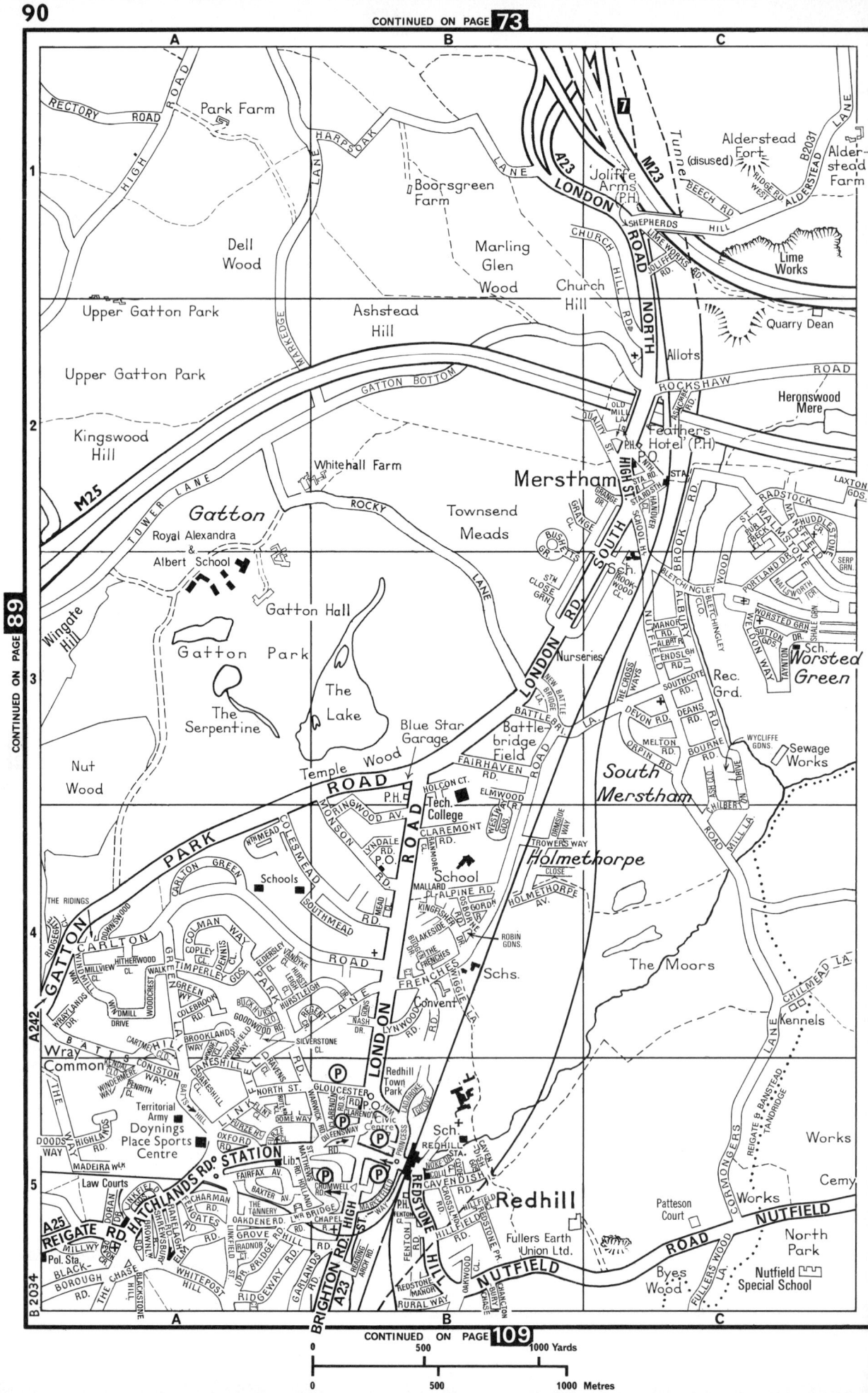

CONTINUED ON PAGE **109**

0    500    1000 Yards

0    500    1000 Metres

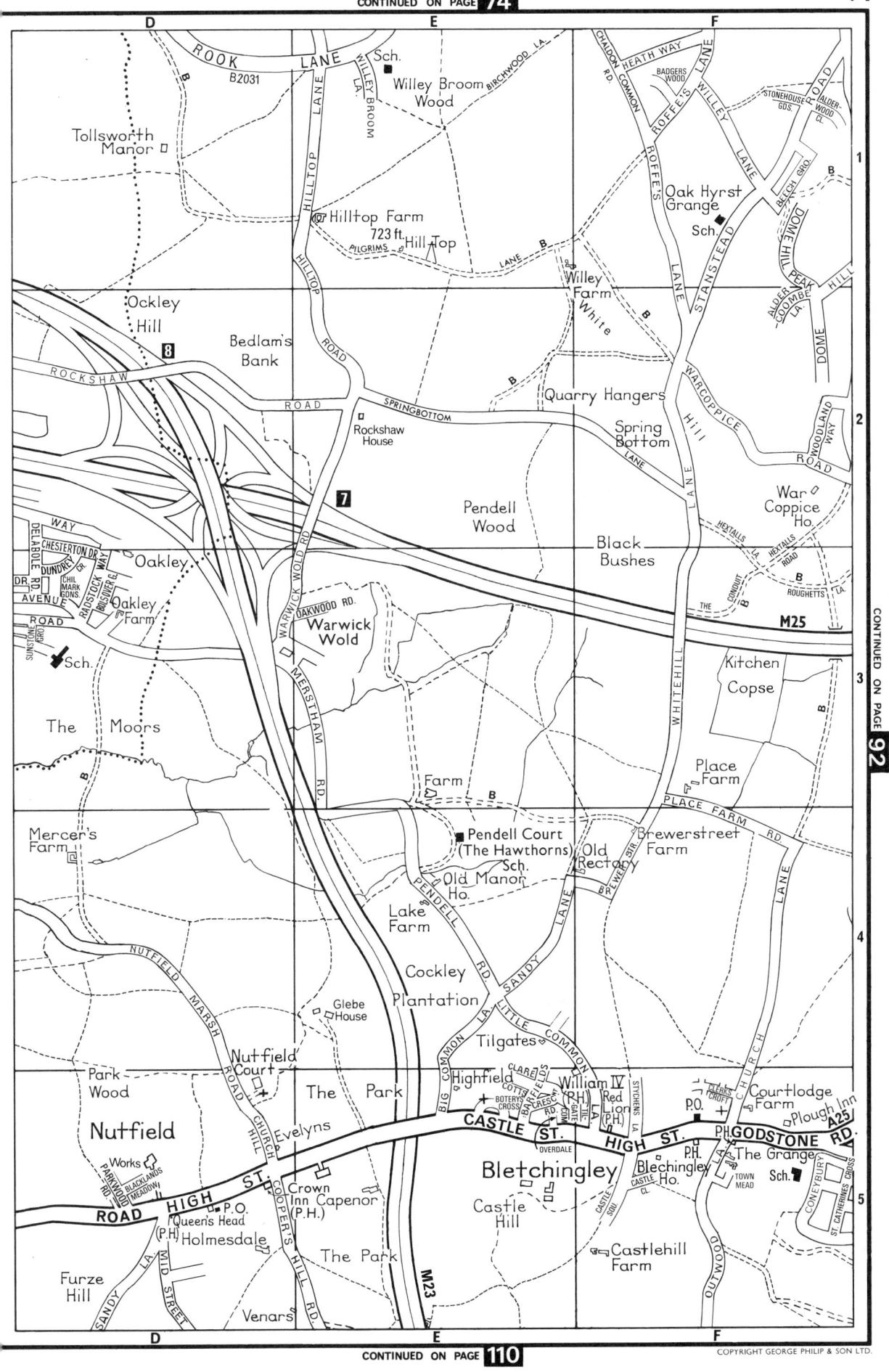

CONTINUED ON PAGE **92**

COPYRIGHT GEORGE PHILIP & SON LTD.

CONTINUED ON PAGE 75

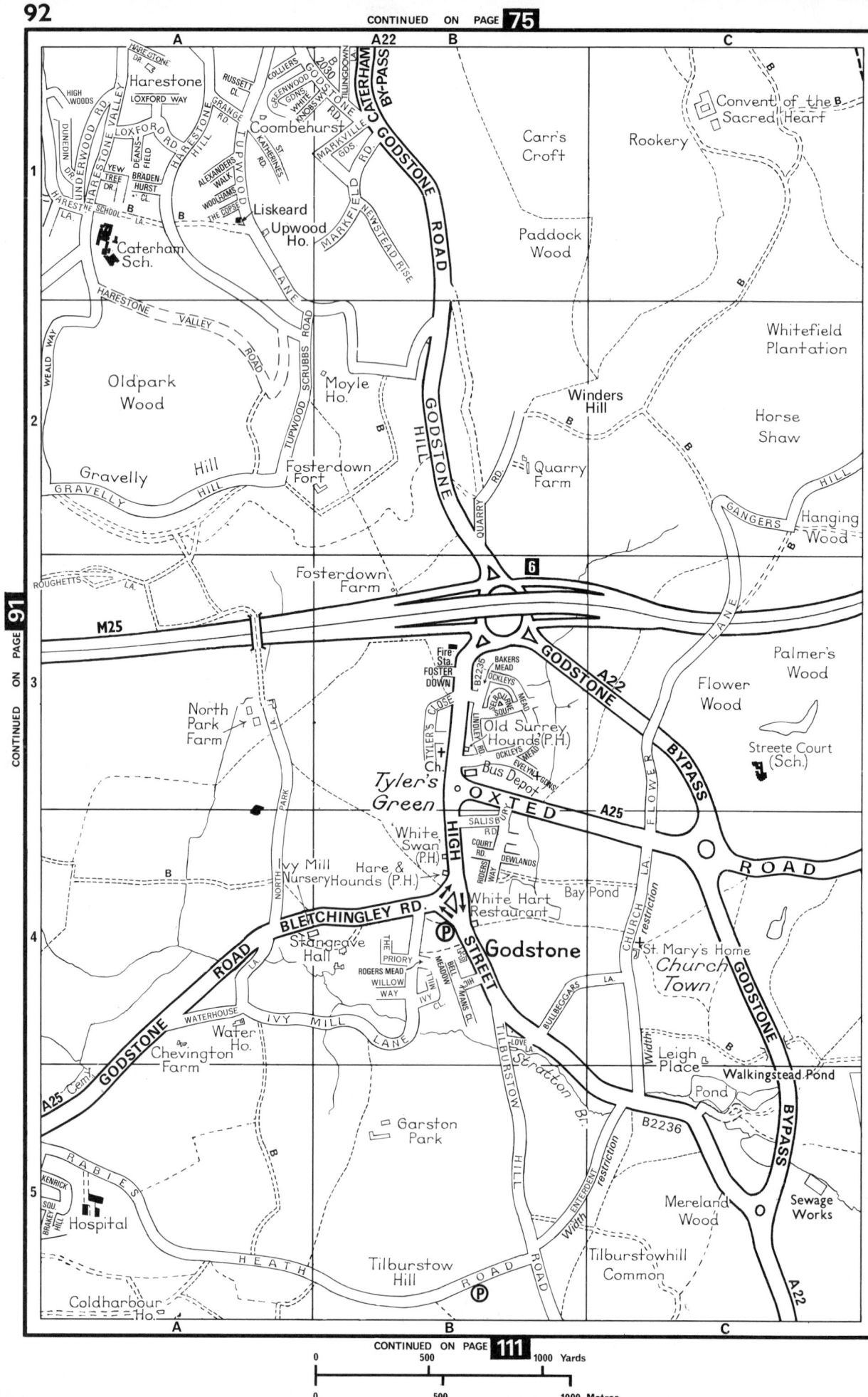

CONTINUED ON PAGE 91

CONTINUED ON PAGE 111

0      500      1000 Yards

0      500      1000 Metres

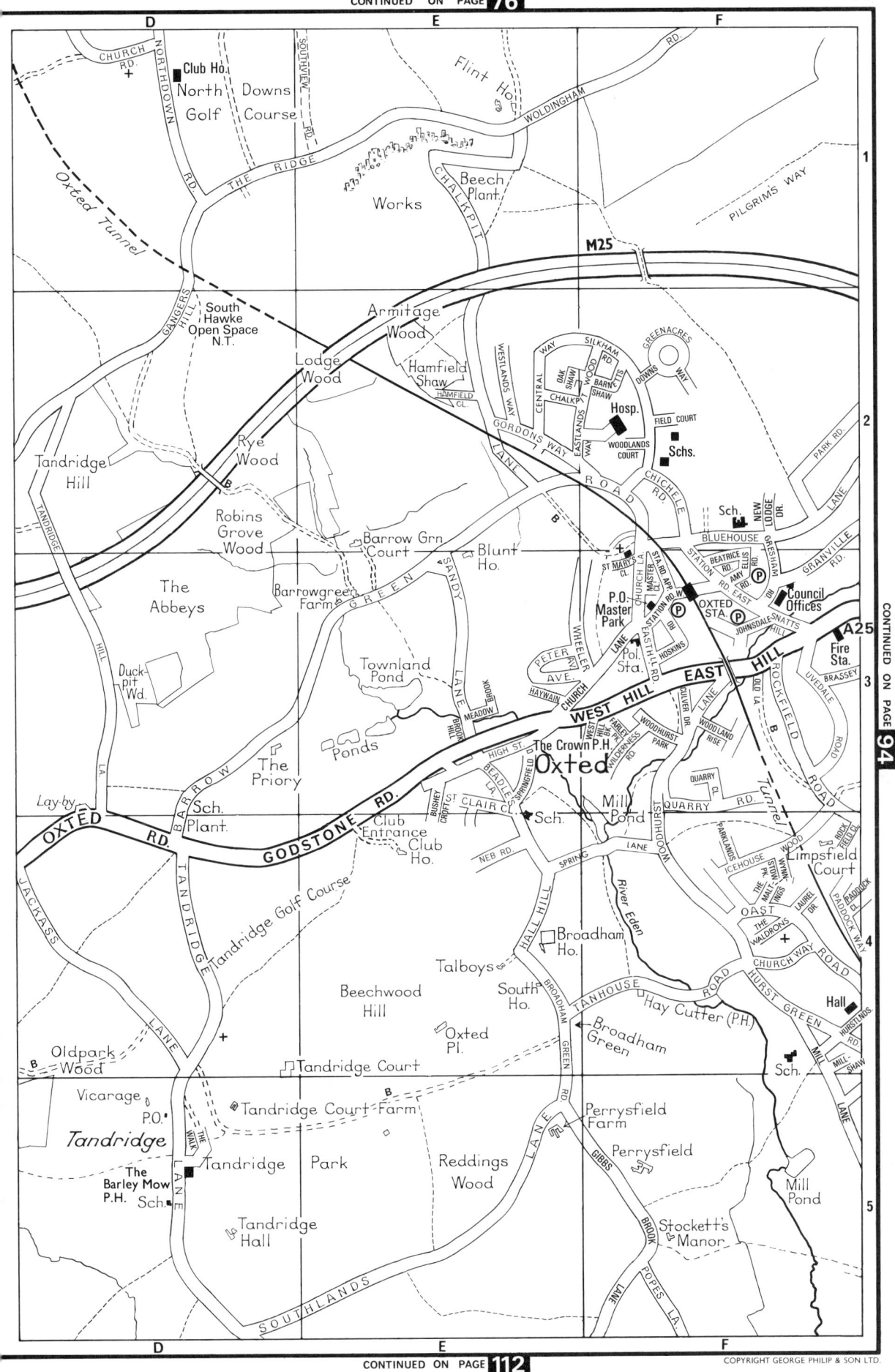

CONTINUED ON PAGE **77**

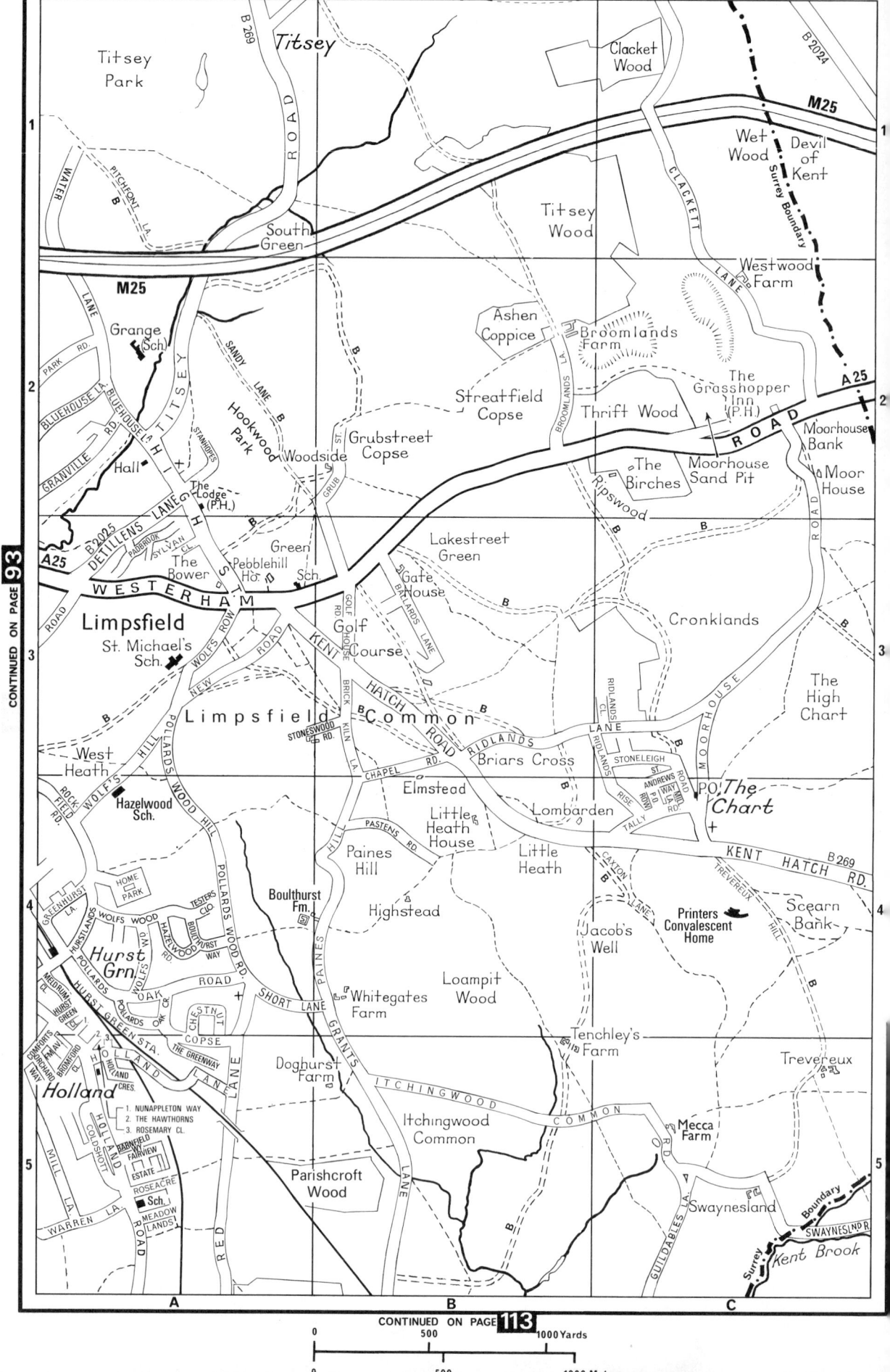

CONTINUED ON PAGE **93**

CONTINUED ON PAGE **113**

0          500          1000 Yards

0          500          1000 Metres

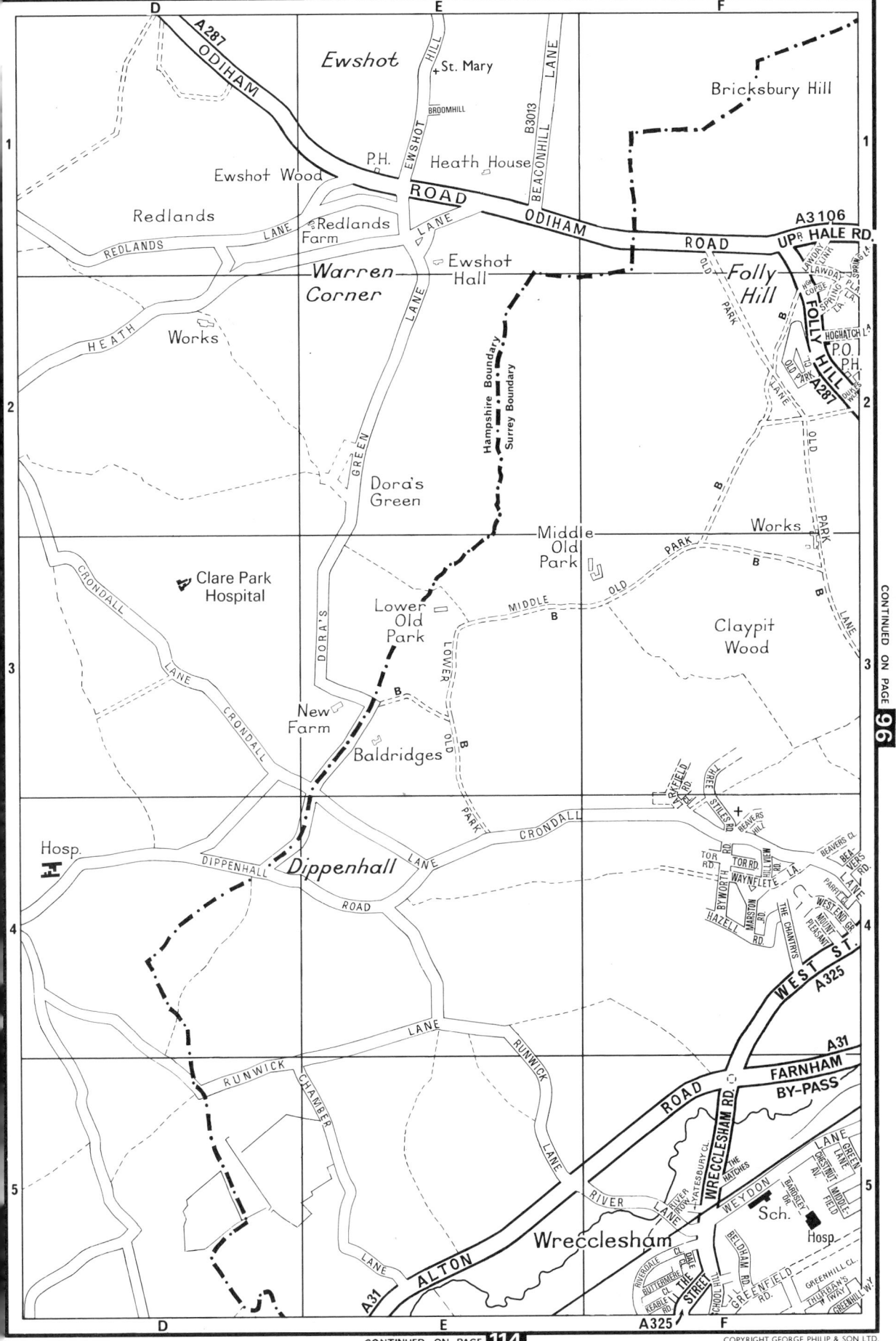

CONTINUED ON PAGE **96**

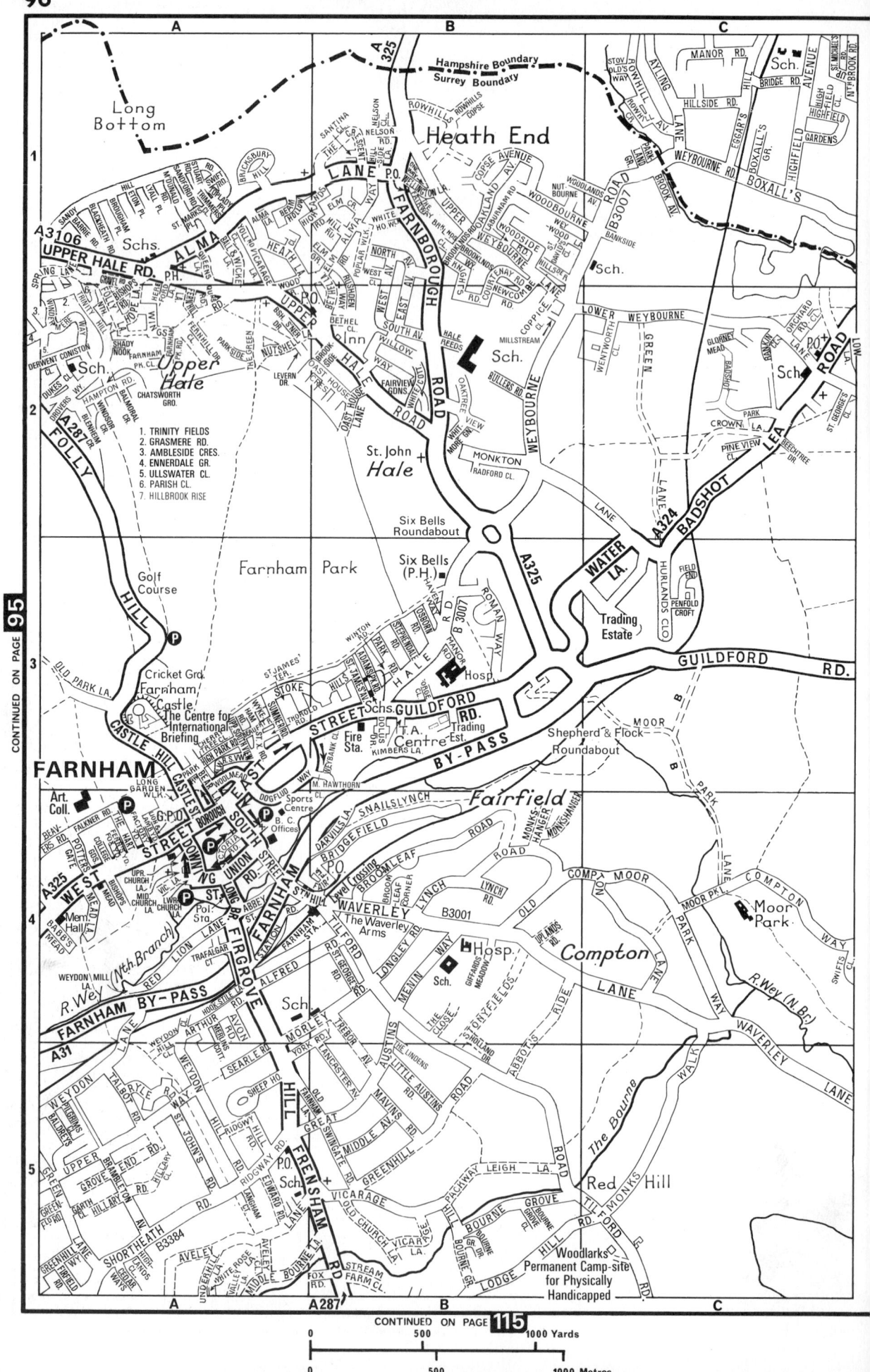

CONTINUED ON PAGE 95

CONTINUED ON PAGE 115

Long Bottom

Heath End

Hampshire Boundary
Surrey Boundary

MANOR RD.

Sch.

HILLSIDE RD.

WEYBOURNE RD.

BOXALL'S

HIGH HIGHFIELD GARDENS

A3106

UPPER HALE RD.

ALMA LANE

P.H.

Schs.

FARNBOROUGH ROAD

WEYBOURNE LANE

Sch.

Upper Hale

UPPER HALE ROAD

St. John
Hale

LOWER WEYBOURNE

GREEN

Sch.

BADSHOT LEA ROAD

1. TRINITY FIELDS
2. GRASMERE RD.
3. AMBLESIDE CRES.
4. ENNERDALE GR.
5. ULLSWATER CL.
6. PARISH CL.
7. HILLBROOK RISE

A3287

FOLLY HILL

Farnham Park

Six Bells Roundabout

Golf Course

Six Bells (P.H.)

A325

WATER LA.

A324

GUILDFORD RD.

Cricket Grd.
Farnham Castle
The Centre for International Briefing

Trading Estate

Shepherd & Flock Roundabout

MOOR

FARNHAM

STREET GUILDFORD RD.
The Centre

Hosp.

BY-PASS

Fairfield

Art. Coll.

WEST STREET

A325

Fire Sta.

Sports Centre

Compton

Moor Park

SOUTH STREET

UNION RD.

BOROUGH

DOWNING

Bridgefield

LYNCH RD.

COMPTON LANE

WAVERLEY WAY

Mem. Hall

Pol. Sta.

FIRGROVE

Waverley
The Waverley Arms

B3001

Hosp.

Sch.

R.Wey (N.Br.)

FARNHAM BY-PASS

A31

HILL FRENSHAM

Sch.

Red Hill

MONKS

Woodlarks Permanent Camp-site for Physically Handicapped

SHORTHEATH

B3384

Sch.

CONTINUED ON PAGE 115

0        500        1000 Yards

0        500        1000 Metres

# Explore your Local History with Ordnance Survey Historical County Guides

| | |
|---|---|
| **Surrey**<br>Derek Turner<br>March  Hardback<br>0 540 01135 5  **£9.95** | **Hampshire & the Isle of Wight**<br>David Hinton & A N Insole<br>March  Hardback<br>0 540 01137 1  **£9.95** |
| **Kent**<br>Felix Hull<br>February  Hardback<br>0 540 01134 7  **£9.95** | **Oxfordshire & Berkshire**<br>James Bond & Luke Over<br>February  Hardback<br>0 540 01136 3  **£9.95** |

A new series of county guides based on 19th century 1 inch to the
mile Ordnance Survey mapping. Each guide gives an historical
introduction to the county and shows through the comparison of 19th
and 20th century mapping and early and contemporary photographs,
how towns, villages and landscapes have changed over the last

# Featuring:

- Each county is shown complete on early series mapping.
- Many rare and previously unpublished Victorian photographs.
- Modern maps and photographs to highlight changes in town and county.
- Authoritative text written by a recognized authority explaining the development of each county.

There have been many changes over the last 100-150 years: the spread of industrial revolution, the development of railways and canals and the rise of major urban centres. The *Ordnance Survey Historical County Guides* highlight the differences, and sometimes surprising similarities, in the passage of time.

*Bracknell in 1905 and the present. The Bull Inn can be seen on the left in both photographs.*

**George Philip, 27a Floral Street, London WC2E 9DP**

- - - - - - - - - - - - - - - - - - - - - - - - -

# ORDER NOW

From all good booksellers or direct from George Philip Services, FREEPOST, Littlehampton, West Sussex, BN17 5BR (no stamp required in the UK).

Please send me the following: _____

_____

☐ I enclose a cheque (payable to George Philip Services) for £_____
Please add 15% to cover postage and packing.
☐ Please debit my Access/Visa/American Express account.

| | | | | | | | | | | | | | | | |
|--|--|--|--|--|--|--|--|--|--|--|--|--|--|--|--|

or phone your order (24hr answering service) with credit card no. to 0903 717453.

Name _____

Address _____

_____

Signature _____ Date _____ SSA/1/88

CONTINUED ON PAGE 78

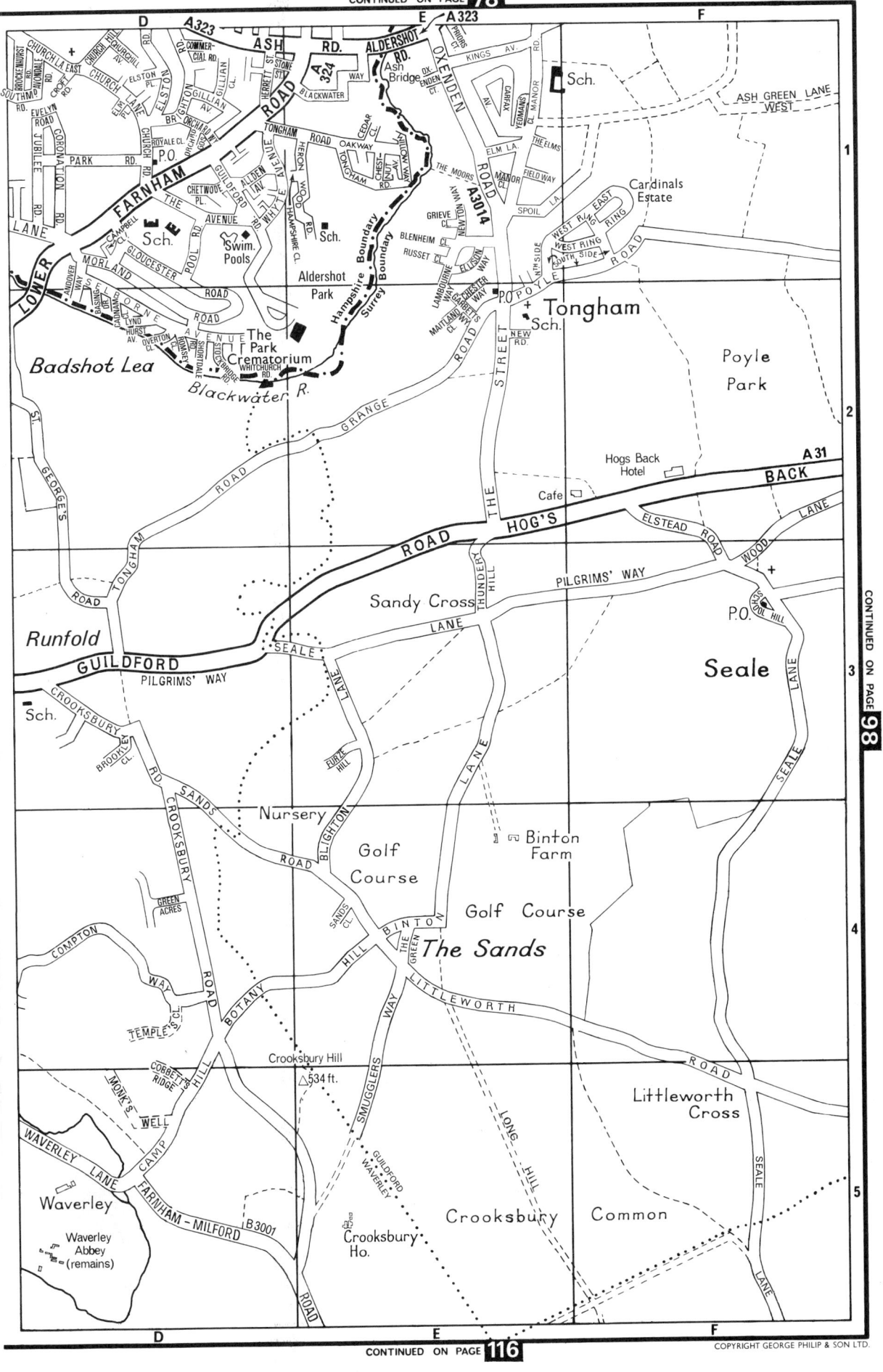

CONTINUED ON PAGE 98

**98**

CONTINUED ON PAGE **79**

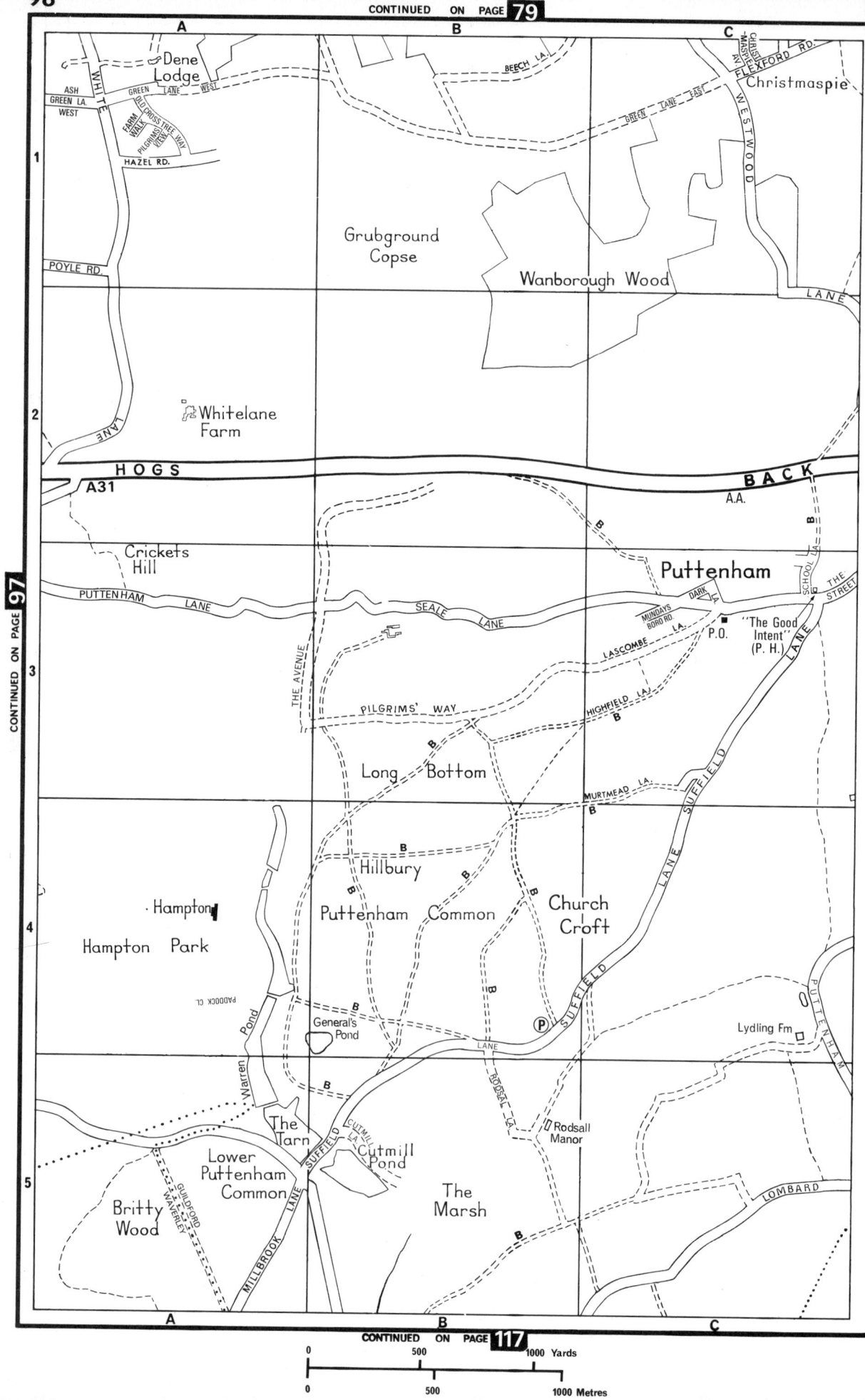

A          B          C

Dene Lodge

ASH GREEN LA. WEST

GREEN LANE WEST

FARM WALK CROSS TREE WAY

PILGRIMS' WAY

HAZEL RD.

BEECH LA.

Christmaspie

GREEN LANE EAST

WESTWOOD

CHRISTMAS MASPIE AV.

FLEXFORD RD.

1

POYLE RD.

Grubground Copse

Wanborough Wood

LANE

WHITE LANE

Whitelane Farm

2

LANE

H O G S          B A C K

A31          A.A.

Crickets Hill

PUTTENHAM LANE

SEALE LANE

Puttenham

B

SCHOOL LA.

THE STREET

PARK LA.

MUNDAYS BORO RD.

LASCOMBE LA.

P.O.

"The Good Intent" (P.H.)

3

THE AVENUE

PILGRIMS' WAY

HIGHFIELD LA.

B

B

Long   Bottom

MURTMEAD LA.

B

SUFFIELD LANE

LANE

B

Hillbury

B

B

Church Croft

Hampton

PADDOCK CL.

Hampton Park

Puttenham Common

B

B

B

SUFFIELD LANE

PUTTENHAM

4

Pond

General's Pond

P

LANE

RODSAL LA.

Lydling Fm

Warren Pond

The Tarn

SUFFIELD LA.

CUTMILL LA.

Cutmill Pond

Rodsall Manor

5

Lower Puttenham Common

GUILDFORD WAVERLEY

Britty Wood

MILLBROOK LANE

SUFFIELD LANE

The Marsh

B

LOMBARD

A          B          C

CONTINUED ON PAGE **117**

CONTINUED ON PAGE **97**

| 0 | 500 | 1000 Yards |
| 0 | 500 | 1000 Metres |

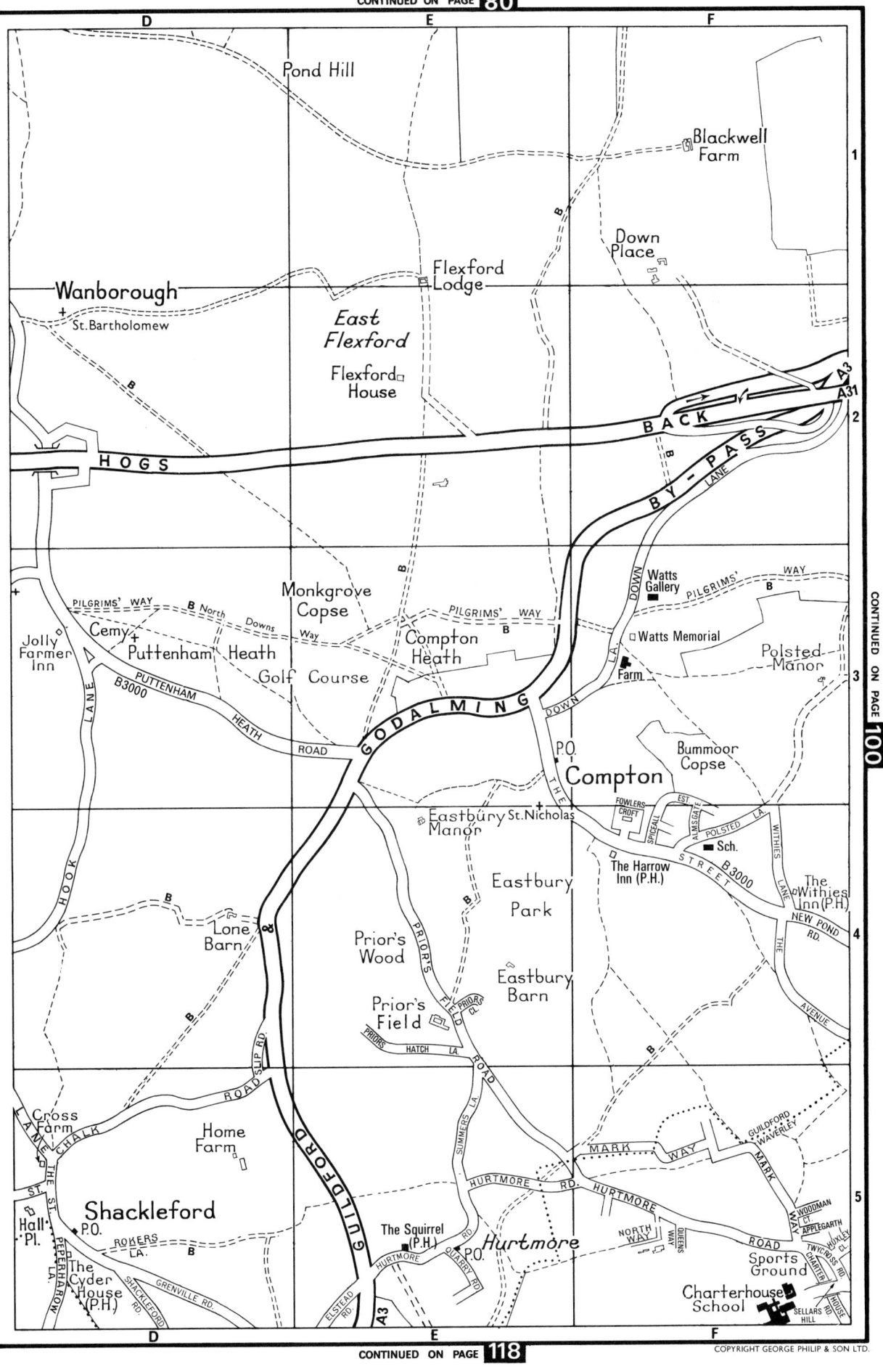

CONTINUED ON PAGE 81

CONTINUED ON PAGE 99

A     B     C    A320

**Onslow Village**

Manor Farm

Hospital

OCCAM RD. ALAN TURING RD. FRED RICK SANZER GILL AV. PRIESTLEY RD. ROSALIND FRANKLIN CL.

Sch.

Underpass to Cath. & Univ.

GUILDFORD & GODALMING BY-PASS

A3

ST. JOHNS' HEATH RD. RAYMOND CRES. QN. ELEANOR'S RD. WILDERNESS ELLIS AV.

ALRESFORD RD. OLD COURT THE OVAL

CATHEDRAL RIDGEMOUNT GUILDFORD PK. AV. EST.

Sports Centre

ARTILLERY RD. WOODBRIDGE LEAS RD. CHURCH RD. STOKE CHERTSEY YORK RD.

P

P

MAIN STA.

HIGH

MILLBROOK

Sch.

Castle

Hosp.

ROAD

WOODLAND AV.

PORTSMOUTH ROAD

PARK

Guildford B.C. Offs.

The Jolly Farmer (P.H.)

R. Wey

SHALFORD ROAD

1

Henley Fort (disused) School Camp 453 ft.

FARNHAM

BEECHCROFT DR. HIGH VIEW RD. MANOR ABBOT'S WAY FRIAR'S GATE

A3 A31 HOG'S BACK

**See page 159 for detailed plan of GUILDFORD centre.**

GUILDOWN UPR. GUILDOWN ROAD

Cem.

The Ship Inn

Rivermount

2

Sunnydown Sch.

B

ST. CATHERINE'S DRI. CHESTNUT AV.

LANE

PILGRIMS' WAY SANDY

North Downs Way

SOUTHFIELDS B PILGRIMS WAY

Coll. of Law (Braboeuf Manor)

THE FRIARY PINE RIDGE MUNSTEAD VIEW

THE RIDGES

Surrey County Police H.Q. Mount Browne

Shalford Jctn.

St. Mary

3

Orange Grove

**Orange Court Farm**

**Littleton**

Loseley House

LITTLETON

ROAD

PORTSMOUTH

ROAD

R. Wey

4

B3000 NEW POND ROAD

STAKESCORNER ROAD

A248 BROADFORD ROAD

The Parrot (P.H.) STONE BRIDGE FIELD Stone Bridge Wharf

UNSTEAD WOOD

OAKDENE RD. JAMES RD. MILL LA.

**Peasmarsh**

R. Wey

OLD PORTSMOUTH ROAD

**Binscombe**

WOODLAND VIEW

Sch.

BROAD ACRE

GUILDFORD WAVERLEY

**Northbourne**

DOWNERS MEADOW

Guildford Crematorium, Broadwater

Sch.

R. Wey Navigation

R. Wey

5

Allot. Gdns.

DAVIES CL. ROBIN HILL FARMCOMBE HILL

MEADOW MORE LANE HALL LA.

Level Crossing

FARNCOMBE STA.

P

Swimming Pool

Broadwater Park

Broad Water Lake

**Farncombe**

A3100 MEADROW

TILTHAMS CORNER RD. UNSTEAD LANE FARNBOROUGH HILL RD.

Level Crossing

A     B     C

CONTINUED ON PAGE 119

0   500   1000 Yards

0   500   1000 Metres

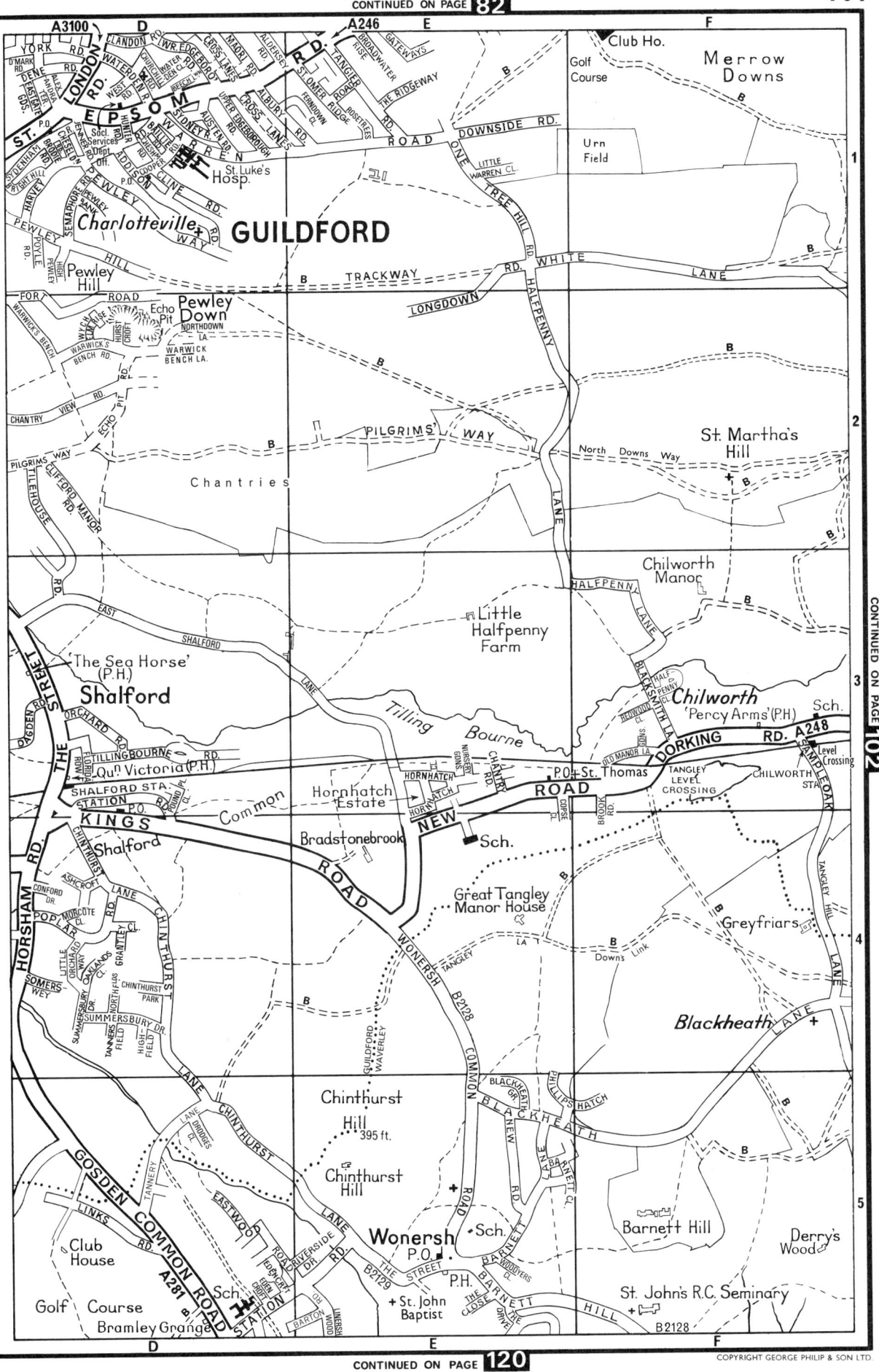

CONTINUED ON PAGE 82

CONTINUED ON PAGE 102

CONTINUED ON PAGE 120

CONTINUED ON PAGE 83

A        B        C

Car Parking Space
A25
Troods Lane
Car Park
Harrow Hill
Corgi Cafe
R.A.C. Box
The Barn Cafe
(Local beauty spot area)
Car Park
SHERE

**Netherlands**
New Scotland Farm
**Tickners Copse**

**West**

1

White Lane
Whitelane Cottage
GUILDFORD LANE
PILGRIMS' WAY
**Albury Downs**
WATER LANE
Silent Pool
P
ROAD

2

Dalton Hill
Waterloo Pond
MILL LA
GUILDFORD ROAD
PARKERS HILL
Drummond Arms' Inn
P.O.
THE STREET
**Albury**
WESTON FIELDS
WESTON YD
TUPPERS COURT
CHURCH LA
St. Peter & St. Paul
Catholic Apostolic Church
NEW ROAD
**Albury Park**

3

To Halfpenny La
A248
DORKING ROAD
ROSEACRE CAFE GDNS
PINE VIEW
Albury Warren
PARK RAILINGS
William IV (P.H.)
HEATH LANE

4

Lockner Holt
GUILDFORD WAVERLEY
The Villagers (P.H.)
P
**Blackheath**
BLACKHEATH
Albury Heath
**Brook**
LEVEL CROSSING
BROOK LA
DARK LANE
BROOK HILL
Foxholes Wood

5

Derry's Wood
LITTLEFORD LANE
The Hallams
SHOPHOUSE LANE
*Farley Green*
St. Michael

A        B        C

CONTINUED ON PAGE 121

0   500   1000 Yards
0   500   1000 Metres

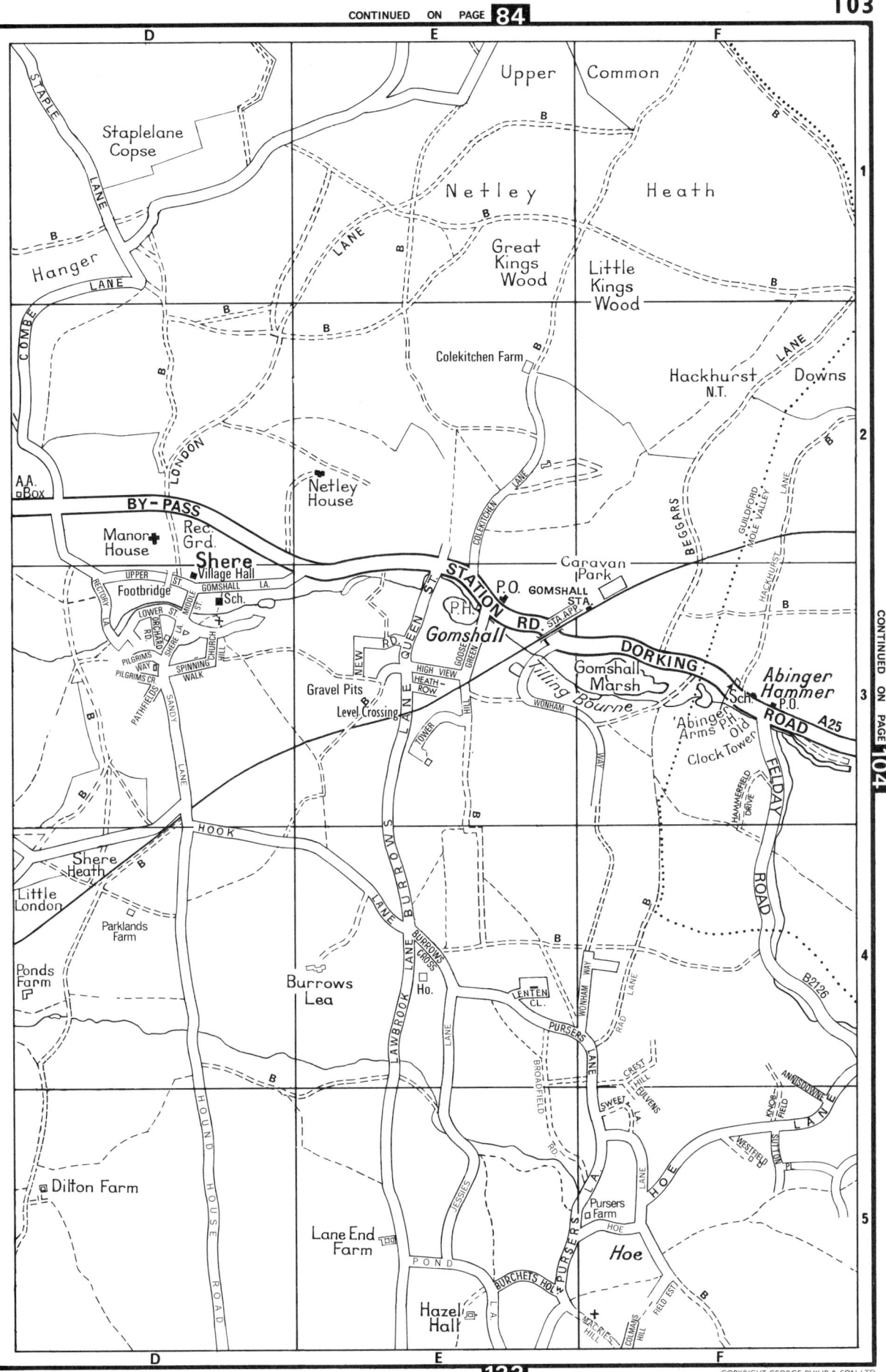

CONTINUED ON PAGE **122**

CONTINUED ON PAGE **104**

CONTINUED ON PAGE **85**

A                                B                                C

1

Effingham    Upper    Common

Great
Copse

B

B

Oaken Grove

B

GUILDFORD

MOLE VALLEY

B

SHEEPWALK LANE

B

B

B

Pickett's
Hole

Rifle Range

B

Coomb
Farm

Blindoak
Gate

Old Simm's
Copse

B

Dunley
Wood

North Downs Way

Coomb
Copse

B

WHITE    DOWN    LANE

2

New
Barn

Park
Farm

B

Rectory

COAST
HILL LANE

CONTINUED ON PAGE **103**

Leasers
Barn

B

Deerleap Wood

St. John's +
Ch.

COAST    HILL

The Rough

B

Evershed's
Rough

The Paddock

WEST  LANE

THE ROOKERY

Fish
Pond

Broomy Downs

B

Westlane
Barn

Wotton

B

Abinger
Hall

B

The Crossways

Sch.
The
Wotton
Hatch (P.H.)

3

A25

GUILDFORD          ROAD

Manor
Farm

Horsley
Copse

SHEEP
HOUSE
GRN

SHEEPHOUSE

Paddington
Farm

THE DENE

ABINGER  LANE

Abinger
Mill

Firtree
Plat

HOLLOW

Wotton House
(Fire Service
College)

Damphurst
Wood

Tilling  Bourne

BRICKYARD LA.

Townhurst
Wood

Whitings
Wood

Fish
Ponds

B

Ellix
Wood

Chandlers
Wood

4

High
Copse

Bushy
Wood

RAIKES

HOLLOW  RAIKES

Stone Age
Farm

Sch.
Abinger
Hatch (P.H.)

Mundies
Plantation

Kempslade
Farm

WATER LA.

Sutton

'The
Volunteer'
(P.H.)

St. James
+

Abinger

B

Millpond
Copse

Noons
Corner

HORSHAM

Suttonplace
Farm

Frolbury

Abinger
Manor
Farm

ABINGER  LANE

LANE

FRIDAY STREET

Friday
Street

5

WOODHOUSE LA.

SUTTON

MOLE VALLEY
GUILDFORD

ROAD  B2126

EVELYN
COTT.

GLEBE
LA.

B

B

Pasture  Wood

Abinger
Common

RADNOR  LA.

Youth
Hostel

A                                B                                C

CONTINUED  ON  PAGE **123**

| 0 | 500 | 1000 Yards |
|---|-----|------------|
| 0 | 500 | 1000 Metres |

CONTINUED ON PAGE **86**

D   E   F   A2003

Landbarn Farm

HARTLEYS COPSE

Pipp Brook

LIMEWAY TER.
FRASERS GDNS.
RANMORE RD.
CHALKPIT LA.

DORKING WEST STA.

Rec. Grd
Guildford & Dorking F.C.
H.P.O.
P.H.

See page 160 for detailed plan of DORKING centre

BEECH CL.
CURTIS RD.
PORTLAND RD.

**DORKING**

Holehill Copse
Bushy Plat
Springfield

Clay Copse

Milton Court

MILTONCOURT LANE

SONDES PL. DR.

SPRING GDS.
COMMERCE RD.
P.H.
CHURCH ST.
HIGH ST.
WEST ST.
F.STA.
MARL-BOROUGH RD.

A25

Rose Hill
1

Miltoncourt Farm
Milton Heath

Milton Heath

Sondes Place

WESTCOTT ROAD

WESTCOTT ROAD

Westcott House

Prince of Wales (P.H.)

SRINGFIELD RD.
ST. JOHN'S RD.
ASHLEY RD.
WATSON RD.
CHADHURST RD.
THE BURTHALL
NORTH
FURLONG RD.
LINCE LA.

NOWER RD.
HORSHAM RD.
VINCENT DR.
ARUNDEL RD.
VINCENT'S RD.
NORFOLK RD.
Sch.

VINCENT DR.
WESTBANK RD.
Bus Sta.

St. PAUL'S RD. WEST
Gen. Hosp.
CLIFTON RD.
SOUTH RD.
ROSE HILL
UPR. ROSE HL.
CEDAR

HORSHAM ROAD

2

GUILDFORD
THE PADDOCK
DEERLEAP RD.
SANDROCK RD.
BALCHINS LANE

P.O.
P. PARSONAGE LA.
STONES LA.
POINTERS HILL
SCHOOL LA.
MILTON ST.
SCHOOL AV.
STONESFIELD

Cricket & Football Grd.

Milton Heath

HAMPSTEAD LANE
LONGFIELD RD.
Sch.
Sch.

HARROWORD WEST
KNOLL
HARROW RD. E.
TOWER
HAMPSTEAD LANE

Mill Pond

**Westcott**

Holy Trinity Ch.
Westcott Heath

THE HILDENS

Bury Hill

The Nower
△ 399 ft.

RIDGEWAY
RIDGE WAY DR.
GREAT WAY
HAMP-STEAD
ORCHARD RD.
ELMHURST
ROMAN RD.

The Lake

Home Farm

Marley Rise

Rough Rew (S.E.E.B.)

A2003

OGMORE LANE

Durrants Wood

Milton Brook

The Grove

ROUGH REW ESTATE

3

CONTINUED ON PAGE **106**

Florence Cottages

Pipp Brook

Sylvanus Wood

Britt's Wood

Westlees Farm

Harelands Wood

Holmwood Farm

COLDHARBOUR LANE

A24

*Tillingbourne*

WOLVENS LANE

Chadhurst Farm

Chadhurst Moor

4

Stable Copse

Squire's Farm

BOAR HILL

The Rough

Horseman's Crag

REDLANDS LA.

Hovelfield Copse

Tilling

Fletchinghurst Barn

Fish Ponds

Squires Great Wood

Mag's Well Res'r.

COLDHARBOUR LANE

Bourne

Home Farm

Broadmoor

**A b i n g e r   F o r e s t**

Winterfold Wood

Redlands Wood

5

Upper Merriden Farm

D   E   F

CONTINUED ON PAGE **124**

CONTINUED ON PAGE 87

A · B · C

1

Mole Valley D.C.
Offs
REIGATE
HIGH ST.
Swimming Pool
Dorking Halls
Cotmandene
Sch.
Pol. Sta.
Liby
A24
A25
DEEPDENE RD.
OVER DALE
The Punch Bowl Motel
Nursery
SPITAL HEATH
Club Ho.
Park Copse
Park Farm
Deepdene House
Deepdene Wood

Betchworth Park
Golf Course

Brockham
R. Mole
Borough Bri.
BROCKHAM
P.O.
Sch.
HILLSIDE CL.
HILLSIDE GDNS.
LITTLE BORGH
BROCKHAM LA.
KILN
LANE
TANNERS HILL
WHEELERS LA.
THE SMITHERS
MIDDLE ST.
SCHOOL LA.
OLD

2

Hosp.
The Glory Wood
Denfield
Goodwyns Place
The Devils Den
TOWER HILL
MARTINEAU
CLAYGATE RD.
STUBBS CL.
RASHER MEAD
St. Paul's Sch.
Chart Park
Club Ho.
Deepdene
CHART LA.
NEW ROAD
Golf Course
Wet Grove
Tilehurst Farm
TILEHURST
Goldenlands Farm
Osierbed Copse

Field Plantation

Knight's Barn
Felton's Farm
Tanner's Brook
BUSHBURY
GLENFIELD
SILVERDALE CL.
BOXHILL WAY
RIDGE CL.
NINEDALE

3

Flint Hill
FLINT HILL RD.
GOODWYNS
Sch.
DEEPDENE
CHART LA. STH.
CHART DOWNS ESTATE
Royal Oak (P.H.)
CHADHURST CL.
WILDCROFT DR.
Stonebridge
LARKSPUR WAY
MAGNOLIA WAY
RUSSET WAY
Inholms Farm
LANE
LANE
LANE
PARKPALE
Bushbury Farm
Tweed Copse
PARK CL.
Bushbury
Roothill Wood
ROOTHILL LANE
Roothill
Eastman's Copse
HIGHRIDGE LANE
Penfold's Copse
A2003
A24
CONTINUED ON PAGE 105

4

St. John Sch.
Fire Sta.
North Holmwood
HARDY CL.
Bentsbrook
BENTSBROOK CL.
HOLMESDALE
INHOLMS
Cricket Grd.
Beldham's Farm
Lower Inholms Farm
Holmwood House
Black Brook
Blackbrook
Plough (P.H.)
Scammells Corner
Woodlands Park
Scammells Grove
RED LANE
BROCKHAMHURST LANE
Little Brockhamhurst Farm
Westwood Common
Jessies Rough
Pond

5

HORSHAM RD.
A24
OAK LA.
SWALLOW LA.
BONDS LA.
NORFOLK LA.
HOLMWOOD VIEW RD.
The Holmwood
N.T.
BLACKBROOK ROAD
Brook Lodge
Waterland Farm
Hither Hawesrew
The Old Croft
Fourwents Pond
Moorfield
Wymbleton House
Snellings Copse
Brookfield Copse
South Holmwood
MILL RD.
FOLLY LA.
WARWICK CL.
Holly & Laurel (P.H.)
Oakdale
Mill House
Holmwood Park Farm
HENFOLD LA.

A · B · C

0     500     1000 Yards

0     500     1000 Metres

CONTINUED ON PAGE **108**

D E F

1

2

3

4

5

NUTWOOD AV.

Betchworth

THE STREET

P.H.

More Place

WONHAM LANE

SANDY LANE

Wonham Manor

Wonham Mill

SANDY LANE

Betchworth Ho.

Betchworth Bri.

River Mole

SNOWERHILL ROAD

TRUMPETSHILL

FLANCHFORD ROAD

Wilderness Wood

MOLE VALLEY

REIGATE & BANSTEAD

Trumpets Hill

WHEELER'S PK RD.

DODDS PK RD.

BRENNE RD.

OAKDENE RD.

OAKDENE CL.

Snower Hill

Ricebridge Fm.

Snowerhill Farm

Rice Bri.

WELLHOUSE LANE

MIDDLE RD.

RD.

Duffle's Plantation

John's Copse

River Mole

Little Flanchford Farm

THE CLOSE

Strood Green

TWEED LA.

JUBILEE TERR.

Gadbrook Copse

ROAD

TAPNER'S ROAD

Gadbrook

ROAD

Little Abbots Farm

Gospel Hall

Gad Brook

Tapner's Bridge

Mark Mead Plantation

FLANCHFORD ROAD

Leigh Place

STREET

GADBROOK

(Research Labs)

Brockham Park

Hook Farm

'Seven Stars' (P.H.)

Dawesgreen

TAPNER'S ROAD

LEIGH PLACE ROAD

ROAD

Oak Pollard

Bunce Common

BUNCE COMMON ROAD

P.O.

Sch.

P.H.

Leigh

THE GLEBE

HARRINGTON CL.

Sch.

B

Buncecommon Fm.

Hook Copse

CHARMANS LA.

Brown's Copse

CLAY HILL CL.

Leigh Bri.

Cramps Farm

Swains Farm

SHELLWOOD ROAD

Twenty Acre Shaw

CLAYHILL LA.

Clayhill Farm

Hammer Bri.

Shellwood Pond

Profits Farm

Shellwood Manor

B

Kiln Copse

SMALL'S HILL ROAD

New Barn

BROAD LANE

Brook Farm

Shellwood Cross

Rigden Rough

Mynthurst

DEANOAK LA.

B

CONTINUED ON PAGE 89

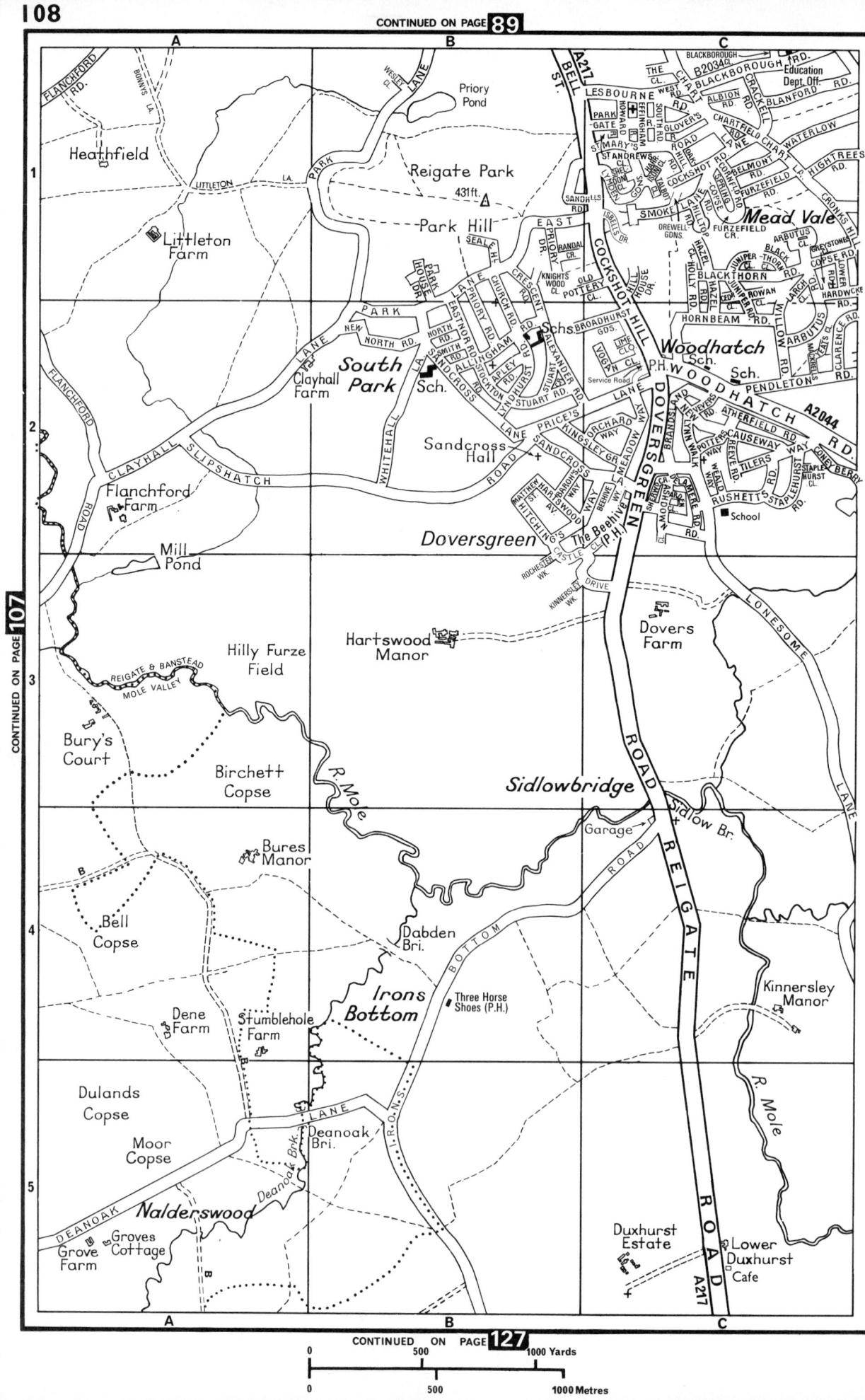

CONTINUED ON PAGE 107

CONTINUED ON PAGE 127

0        500        1000 Yards

0        500        1000 Metres

D · A23 · E · F

THE CHASE · RINGLEY PARK RD. · CHIDDSEX · OAK WAY · BLACK STONE LA.

Redhill Common

HIGHTREES RD. · MILL SANDPIT RD. · BRIGHTON RD. · HOOLEY · GARIBALDI ST. · P.H.

Dunottar Sch. for Girls · PENDLETON CL. · KING'S AV.

CRONKSHILL · FAIRLAWN · ST. JOHN'S RD. · THE CUTTING · EARLS WOOD · CHURCH RD.

St. John's Sch.

CRONKSHILL CL. · ROSEMEAD CL. · Redhill Amb. Sta. · MOUNTVIEW · ARDSHIEL DR. · FOUNTAIN RD.

SOMERSET RD. · CLARENCE W'K · THE CRESCENT · PENDLETON · UTTERTON WAY

Redhill General Hospital

Earlswood · Golf Course · Cricket Grd.

Common · Boating Lake · New Pond · Car Park · ASYLUM ARCH · Gate ARCH · PRINCE'S RD.

WOODHATCH · FELLAND WAY · Sewage Works · Council Depot · Allots Football Grd. · Nag's Head (P.H.)

Royal Earlswood Hospital

East Surrey Hospital

Garstons Ho.

THREE ARCH RD. · CANADA AV. · MAPLE RD.

Felland Copse

Petrol Station · HEATHFIELD DR. · HANWORTH RD. · TOLLGATE AV.

HORLEY · PETRIDGE RD. · WIMBOURNE AV. · SHIRLEY · HAMPTON RD. · DENTON · EDGE FIELD CL. · BUSHFIELD CL. · HAWTHORN CL. · FOXLEY CL. · GRANT WOOD CL. · AMBLE SIDE CL.

Hazelhurst Farm

Geals Copse

Petridgewood Common · DUNLIN CL. · Maple Manor · A2044 · MAPLE DR. · P.H. · MAYFIELD CL. · PR. ALBERT SQUARE · BROOKFIELD CLOSE · HILLFORD PL. · WOODSIDE WAY · COPSLEIGH CL. · THE BROW · SPENCER WAY · JASMIN CL. · JORDAN · GREENWOOD · LAVENDER CL. · YEOMANS WAY · IVYDENE CL.

Mayfield

Green · Benting Wood

Wyatts Farm · Lonesome Farm

Salfords · Salfords Br. · R.A.C. Box · The Mill House Hotel · P.O. · HONEYCROCK LA. · SOUTHERN AV. · WESTMEAD DR.

The General Napier (P.H.) · PARK AV. · PARK RD. · PARK VIEW

Dean Farm · JUNE LA. · Dairy Ho. · Farm · Oakfield · AXES LANE · PICKETTS

Elmersland Farm

SALFORDS STA. Industrial Estate · SALBROOK ROAD · S.P.D. Ltd. · Perry Wood · High Trees · Pickett's Farm

The Park · BEAUMONTS · LODGE · MONTFORT RISE · Horley Lodge · PEAR TREE HILL · WOOD

Saxley Hill · MEATHGREEN · LANE · BONEHURST ROAD

Meathgreen Bri. · BEECH WD VLS · EMPIRE VILLAS · A23 · CROSSOAK · Philips Research Laboratories

Mason's Br. · House · BRIDGE · ROAD · KING MILL LANE · HOGTROUGH LA. · BOWERHILL LANE

South Park · The Lake · FULLERS WD · CLAY · WAY

Queen's Ho. · Cemy. · HILLVIEW DR. · Gurney's Ho. · Gladstones Ho. · Ham Farm

Staplehurst Farm · TANDRIDGE REIGATE & BANSTEAD

Works · DUNRAVEN AV. · NEW HOUSE LANE · ST. GEORGE'S RD.

CONTINUED ON PAGE 110

D · E · F

# 110

CONTINUED ON PAGE **91**

**Sandhills**

**M23**

COOPER'S HILL RD.

SANDY LANE

BRAES MEAD

KENTWYNS RISE

MID STREET

Sch. Hall
Allot. Gdns.

Lyttel Hall
*(Brewing Industry
Research Foundation)*

Home Farm

**South
Nutfield**

TRINDLES RD.

HOLMESDALE RD.

NUTFIELD STA.
OAKWOOD CL.

MORRIS RD.

SHEARS PK.

BOXERHILL

NETHERLEIGH

CRICKET HILL

THE AVENUE

RIDGEGREEN

PHILPS CL.

KINGSCROSS

Ridgegreen House

KINGSCROSS

LANE

Kennels

Old Kiln

**Ridge
Green**

CRABHILL

Crabhill Ho.
(Winged Fellowship
Holiday Home)

Crabhill Farm

Henhaw Farm

**Bransland
Wood**

Poundhill
Wood

**Temple
Wood**

CONTINUED ON PAGE **109**

**Redhill
Aerodrome**

**Lawn
Hill**

Pond

LANE

MOATS LANE

LANE

MOATS

South Hale Farm

Burstow
Park

ROAD

**Furzefield
Wood**

GREEN

HATCH

LANE

PRINCE OF WALES ROAD

Harewoods

Shepheards
Hurst

The
Orchards

DYKERS

BRICKFIELD

Dog & Duck
(P.H.)

Rectory

Outwood
Common

SOUTWOOD ROAD

**Torycross
Shaw**

LANE

HATCH LANE

HATHERSHAM LANE

WASP GREEN LA.

**Outwood**

Cricket
Grd.

P.O.

Bell Inn
(P.H.)

Gay
Ho.

Windmill

GAYHOUSE

REIGATE & BANSTEAD
TANDRIDGE

ROOKERY HILL

MILLERS HILL

BELL WEATHER LA.

B.H.

LITTLE COLLINS

MILLERS COPSE

Lodge

Marl
Pond

SCOTT'S HILL

M23

CONTINUED ON PAGE **129**

0        500        1000 Yards

0        500        1000 Metres

CONTINUED ON PAGE **92**

D · E · F

A22

Coldharbour Farm

Moor's Wood

Tilburstowhill Farm

Orme House

Hart

Wonham House (Hotel)

Lodge

Fox & Hounds (P.H.)

1

HART'S LANE

Steadmanshill Wood

Eight Acre Shaw

Blackvent Wood

Underhills

Posterngate Farm

Hawksnest Ghyll

Ty Copse

Norbryght

Stansted Ho.

Cucksey's Farm

LAGHAM PARK

HAR- Sch.

COURT

HUNTERS CHASE

Bletchingley Tunnel

WOODLANDS DR.

OAKLANDS

WAY

FASTER

Furze Wood

ROAD

GODSTONE STA.

P.O.

Nursery

2

Seven Acre Wood

TERRACOTTA RD.

LAGHAM RD.

Four Acre Wood

Works

GRANGE COURT

Railway Hotel (P.H.)

RUSHTON AV.

The Park

La Bonne Auberge

Oakhurst Court

R.S.P.C.A. Centre

Lagham Manor

WATER

Cafe

LA.

Birchen Copse

South Godstone

B

3

Yewtree Farm

The Mount

Pond

South Park Farm

Eight Acre Shaw

DANEMORE LANE

Garden Centre

Ponds

Moat

Tanglewood

Osier Pit

ROAD

The Grange

Lodge Farm

Fidler's Grove

CARLTON

Putney Gill

Springfield

4

Hangdog Wood

Brookland Farm

FEATHERSTONE

Gayhouse Furzes

Tile Barn

Hookstile Ho.

LANE

ST. JOHN'S MEADOW

LANGSMEAD

Heath Grange

Sch.

Blindley Heath

COTTENHAMS

LANE

HORNECOURT HILL

Rowe Tye

BYERS

Blue Anchor Inn

P.O.

B2029

5

Hornecourt Wood

WHITEWOOD

(P.H.)

Jolly Farmer

Cricket Grd.

A22

D · E · F

CONTINUED ON PAGE **130**

CONTINUED ON PAGE **112**

CONTINUED ON PAGE 93

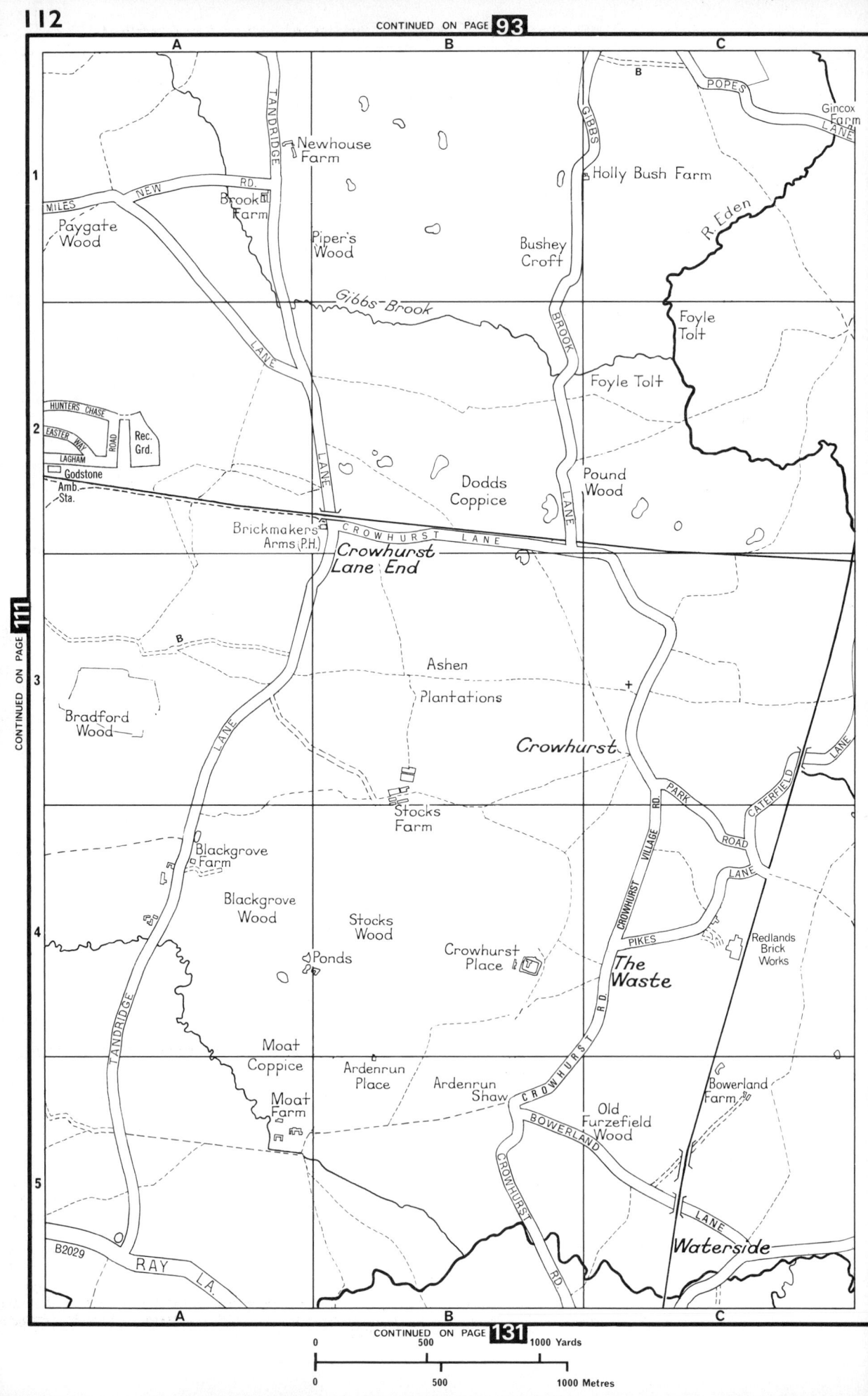

CONTINUED ON PAGE 111

CONTINUED ON PAGE 131

A          B          C

Newhouse Farm
Brook Farm
Paygate Wood
Piper's Wood
MILES NEW RD.
TANDRIDGE LANE
Holly Bush Farm
POPES
Gincox Farm LANE
GIBBS
R. Eden
Bushey Croft
Gibbs-Brook
BROOK
Foyle Tolt
Foyle Tolt
HUNTERS CHASE
EASTER WAY
LAGHAM
ROAD
Rec. Grd.
Godstone Amb. Sta.
Dodds Coppice
Pound Wood
LANE
Brickmakers Arms (P.H.)
CROWHURST LANE
Crowhurst Lane End
Ashen Plantations
Crowhurst
Bradford Wood
Stocks Farm
CATERFIELD LANE
PARK RD
Blackgrove Farm
Blackgrove Wood
Stocks Wood
Ponds
Crowhurst Place
CROWHURST VILLAGE LANE
ROAD
LANE
PIKES
The Waste
Redlands Brick Works
TANDRIDGE LANE
Moat Coppice
Ardenrun Place
Ardenrun Shaw
CROWHURST RD
BOWERLAND
Old Furzefield Wood
Bowerland Farm
Moat Farm
CROWHURST RD
BOWERLAND
LANE
Waterside
B2029 RAY LA.

0    500    1000 Yards
0    500    1000 Metres

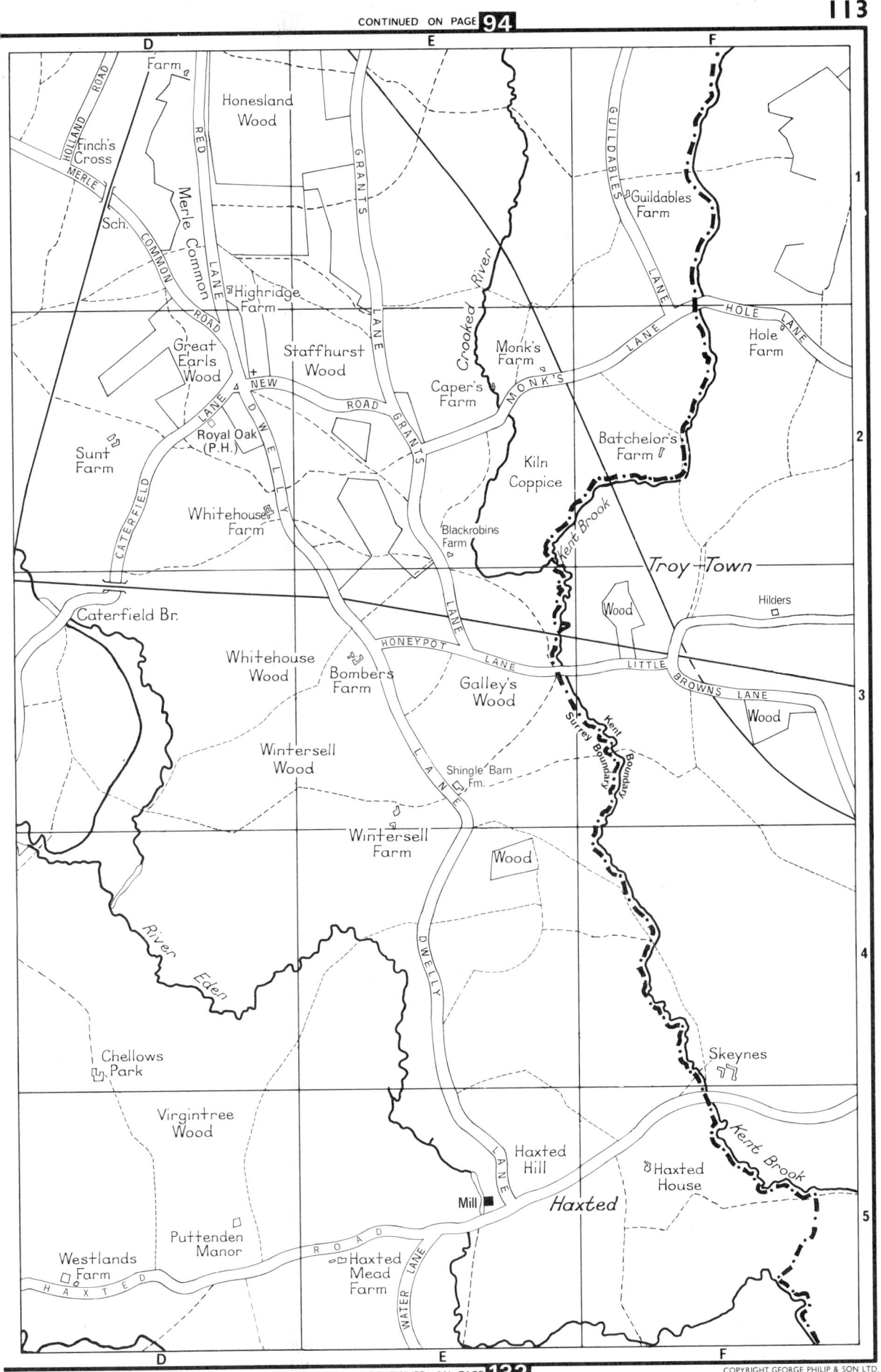

**114**

A31 A31

ALTON ROAD

CRONDALL RD.

R. Wey

HOLT POUND LANE

WRECCLESHAM HILL

Surrey
Hampshire

WESTFIELD LA.

THE STREET
A325

SCHOOL RD.

COBBETS WAY

BEALES LA.
GREEN
LIT. THURBARNS
LT. GREEN LA.

Sch.
P.O.
SHORT HEATH

KINGS LA.

COKENOR WOOD
LH. COPSE WAY
HILL CREST DR.
HEA THER CL.

QUENNELS HILL
BROADWELL RD.
WOODCUT RD.

COLE
SON
HILL RD.

POYDELL

BAT & BALL LA.
SUNNY LA.
WICKET HILL

BARN LA.

B3384

SANDROCK
HILL RD.

THE CHINE

BEACON
HILL RD.
BOWER RD.

BOUNDSTONE

LAUREL
VINE LANE

HOLLOWAY HILL

WOODCUT
Estate

ECHO

Rec.
Grd.

Forest Inn
(P.H.)

Holt
Pound

Allots

FULLERS

ROAD

Rowledge

MANLEY BRIDGE RD.

BROWNS WALK

ROSEMARY LA.

HIGH ST.

BELL LANE

CHAPEL RD.

BOUNDSTONE
CLANE MEAD
THE CLOSE

THORN
CL.

WHITEPOST
ROAD

SHRUBBS LA.

SWITCHBACK LA.

SWISS CL.

LINKS WOOD RD.

CLIFTON CL.

Holt Pound

Inclosure

Earlsfield
Braemar

RECREATION RD.

SCHOOL RD.

CHERRY TREE RD.

PROSPECT RD.

CHERRY TREE WLK.

THE HAWTHORN LA.

THE AVENUE

MAYFIELD RD.

ORCHARD
END

MEADOW
WAY

LONG

ORCHARD
LA.

PEARTREE
LA.

Sports
Grd.

Boundary Boundary

Boundary

Alice
Holt
Lodge

Lodge
Pond

Glenbervie

Inclosure

BOUNDARY

CHURCH
LA.

LICKFORDS

ROAD

THE

Frensham
Heights
School

FRENSHAM HEIGHTS RD.

ROAD

BROOMFIELD

ALICE HOLT FOREST

FARNHAM ROAD

Plain
Piece

Bucks
Horn
Oak

P.O.

Halfway
House
(P.H.)

WEST

END

LANE

SUMMERHILL

LANE

WOODHILL

B

Willow's Green

Inclosure

DOCKENFIELD

Bealeswood
Common

B

Goose
Green
Inclosure

A325 BORDON CAMP ROAD

Dockenfield

Batt's
Corner

GREEN LA.

DOCKENFIELD

P.O.

ABBOTTS COTT RD.

STREET

Farm

Abbotts Wood

Inclosure

0        500        1000 Yards

0        500        1000 Metres

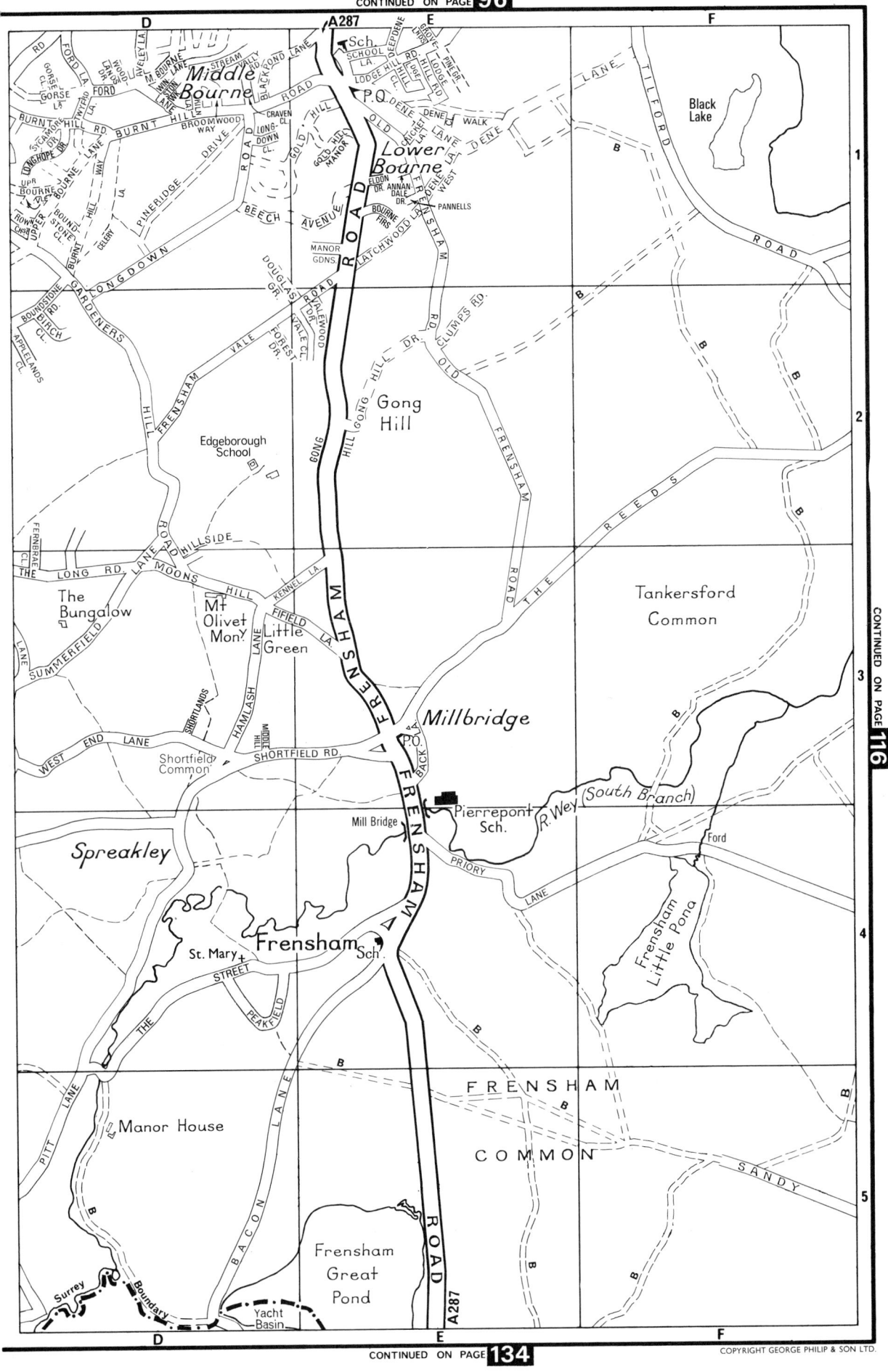

CONTINUED ON PAGE **116**

COPYRIGHT GEORGE PHILIP & SON LTD.

CONTINUED ON PAGE **97**

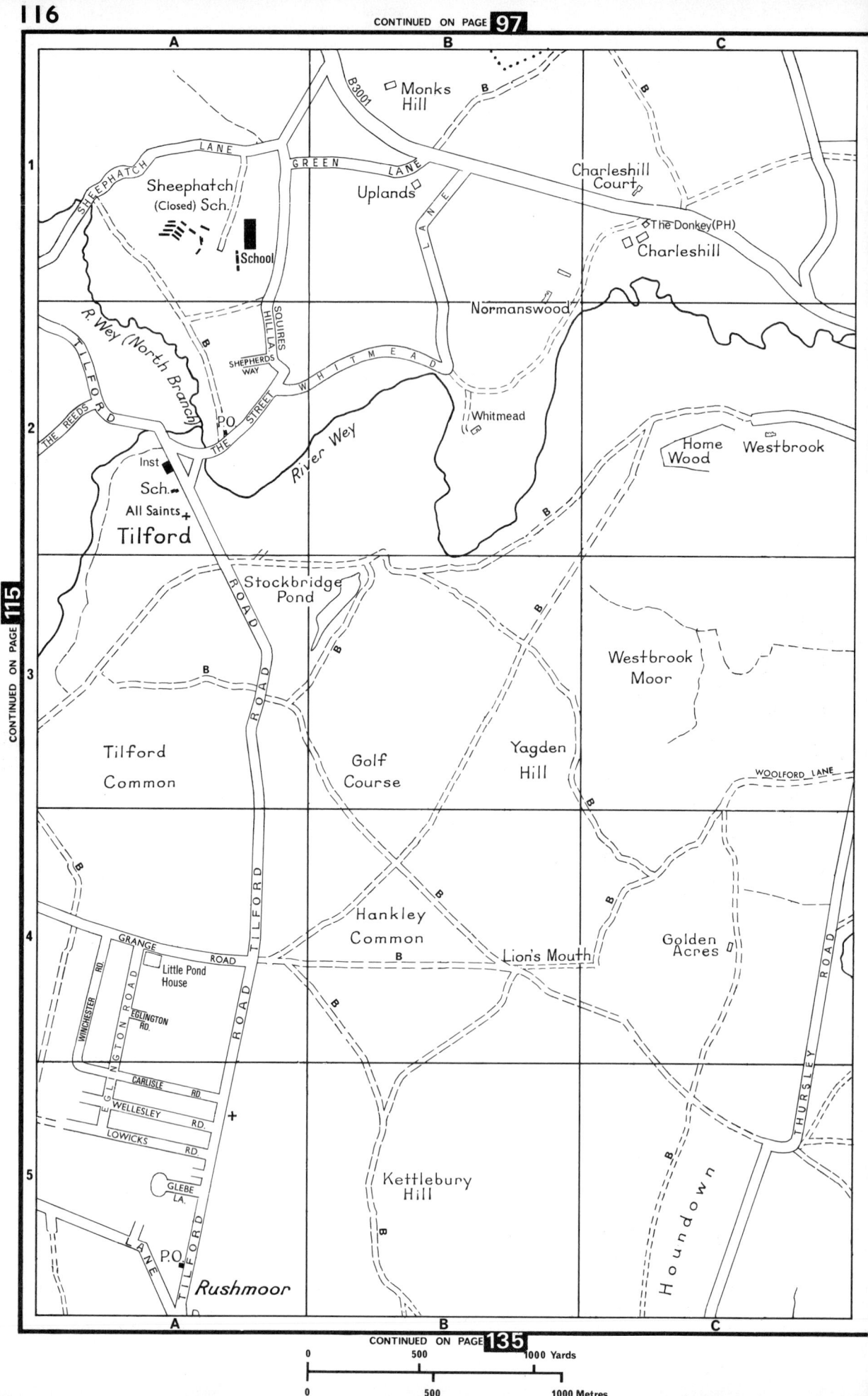

CONTINUED ON PAGE **135**

CONTINUED ON PAGE **115**

0        500        1000 Yards

0        500        1000 Metres

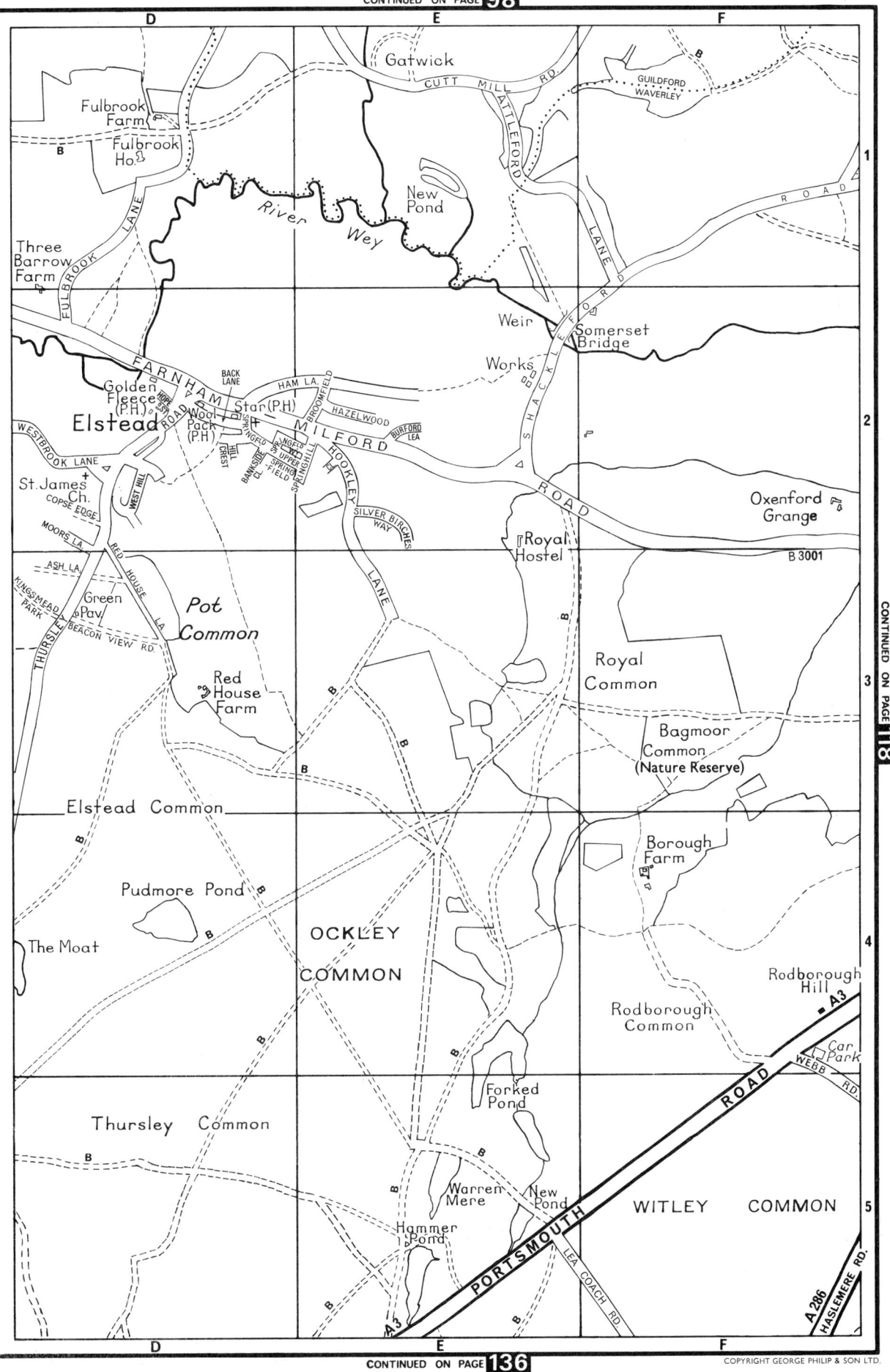

CONTINUED ON PAGE 98

CONTINUED ON PAGE 118

CONTINUED ON PAGE 136

CONTINUED ON PAGE 99

CONTINUED ON PAGE 117

Norney

Norney Grange

The Rough

The Farm

GRENVILLE RD.

ELSTEAD SCH. LA.

SHACKLEFORD RD.

Sch.

MORNY ROUGH

A3

BY-PASS

PEPERHAROW

Water Board Pumping Sta.

River Wey

WESTBROOK ROAD

Peper Harow

Park House Sch.

Peper Harow Park

Eashing

Eashing Bridge

THE DRIVE

LOWER EASHING RD.

Works

Eashing Bridge

THE HOLLOW

EASHING LANE

UPPER EASHING

Upper Eashing

Halfway House

HALFWAY LA.

Westbrook

GODALMING STA.

NEW WAY

OCKFORD RD.

GODALMING & GUILDFORD ROAD

B3001

Cuckoo Corner

MANOR FIELDS

AMBERLEY RD.

ELSTEAD ROAD

MANOR CL.

MANOR LEA

HURST LA.

CHAPEL CL.

CHAPEL CL.

GEORGE RD.

MIDLETON RD.

POTTERS CL.

MEADOW CL.

Eashing Park

Ockford Ridge

Cem.

GUILDFORD — WAVERLEY

BARGATE RISE

STONEY

HOLLY

ARBOUR RD.

EASHING LA.

FRANKLIN RD.

Sch.

AARONS HILL

OCKFORD RIDGE

MILTON CRES.

PRIMROSE RIDGE

HAWTHORN RD.

CLIFFE RD.

GODALMING RD.

COOPER RD.

CURTIS RD.

CLIFFE RISE

St. Hilary's Sch.

BRAEMAR

BRAEFAR

SHACKSTEAD LA.

Inn on the Lake

WINDY WOOD

COLLEGE HILL

FOXDENE

PALL MALL

PHIPPS RIDGE

Ashstead Farm

A3100 PORTSMOUTH ROAD

The Refectory

Milford House Hotel

Red Lion Hotel

Milford Hospital

LANE

Kennel Moor

Milford

'White Lion' (P.H.)

Moushill Down

LOWER MOUSHILL LA.

UPPER MANOR RD.

UPPR MANOR RD.

OAK TREE RD.

ELMSIDE

The Manor Sch.

The Lawns

P.O.

CHURCH RD.

DRY FIELDS

SPRING WOOD

STATION LANE

PORTSMOUTH ROAD

A3

SANDY LA.

MOUSHILL LA.

NEW RD.

CHERRY TREE RD.

GREEN LA.

THE GORDONS

LADY CROSS

Milford Heath

HIGH CROFT

MITFORD LODGE

BUSDENS WAY

BUSDENS GDNS

BUSDENS LA.

BUSDENS CL.

PETWORTH ROAD

Rodborough Sch.

RAKE

LANE

Level Crossing

Milford STA.

TUESLEY LANE

WATER LANE

OXTED GREEN

HEATH VIEW RD.

PECKHAMS LANE

MERRYACRES

KHARTOUM RD.

Waverley D.C. Depot

S.C.C. Depot

Fowl House

Wheeler Street

Large Enton Lake

Enton Green

Greystones

Club Ho.

HASLEMERE ROAD

A286

GASDEN COPSE

GASDEN LANE

YEW TREE RD.

CRAWHURST LANE

KESWICK RD.

WILDCROFT RD.

LITTLE LONDON

CROFT RD.

The Star (P.H.)

WHEELER LANE

SUNNY HILL

SUNNY LANE

WILLOW MEAD

BANISTER RD.

MALTHOUSE MEAD

ROKE LANE

CHICHESTER RD.

DORLECOTE

MIDDLEMARCH

MILL LANE

A283 ROAD

| 0 | 500 | 1000 Yards |
| 0 | 500 | 1000 Metres |

D · E · A3100 · F

**GODALMING**

Catteshall

The Ram

Unsted Park

Lodge

Catteshall Manor

Farm

Ambulance Station

Social Services Office

Waverley B.C. Offs.

Police Sta.

Holloway Hill

Crownpits

Heath Fm.

Munstead Heath

Combe Rise

Wood

Munstead Ho.

Combe Fm.

College

Allots.

Tuesley Court

Busbridge Park

Middle Lake

Lower Lake

Thorncombe Street

Oldwick's Copse

Car Park

Busbridge Park

Car Park

Winkworth Arboretum (N.T.)

South Munstead Farm

House in the Wood

Juniper Hill

Hare's Grove

Hydon Hill Cheshire Home

Hydestile

P.O.

King George V Hosp.

Hydon's Ball (N.T.)

Austen's Wood

High Barn

Winkworth Farm

Winkworth Hill

Whinfold

1

2

3

4

5

CONTINUED ON PAGE **120**

D · E · F

CONTINUED ON PAGE **101**

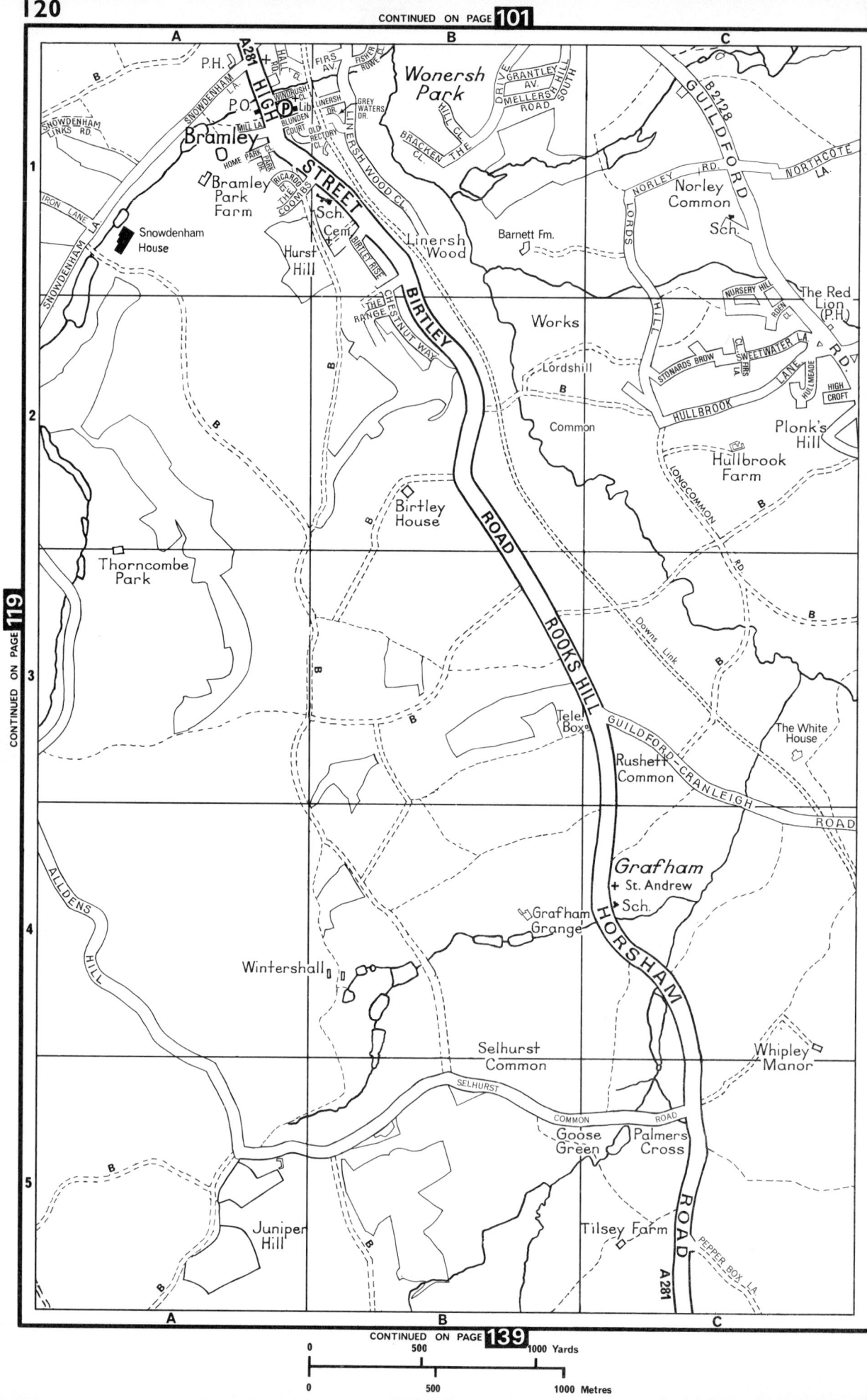

CONTINUED ON PAGE **119**

CONTINUED ON PAGE **139**

A     B     C

P.H.

A281 HIGH

Snowdenham
Links Rd.

P.O.

**Bramley**

Bramley
Park
Farm

Snowdenham
House

IRON LANE LA.

SNOWDENHAM LA.

STREET

Sch.
Cem.

Hurst
Hill

HALL

FIRS
AV.

FISHER
ROWE

WINDRUSH
CL.

MILL LA.

BLUNDEN
COURT

OLD
RECTORY

Lib.

Linersh
Dr.

GREY
WATERS
DR.

LINERSH WOOD CL.

Wonersh
Park

THE
DRIVE

GRANTLEY
AV.

MELLERS
ROAD

HILL

THE

BRACKEN
CL.

HILL CL.

Linersh
Wood

Barnett Fm.

Works

Lordshill

Common

THE
RANGE

CHESTNUT WAY

BIRTLEY RISE

BIRTLEY

ROAD

ROOKS HILL

GUILDFORD

B2128

NORLEY

RD.

NORTHCOTE
LA.

Norley
Common

Sch.

LORDS

NURSERY HILL

BODEN
CL.

The Red
Lion
(P.H.)

STONARDS BROW

CL. HRS
LA.

SWEETWATER LA.

HULLMEADE

HIGH
CROFT

HULLBROOK

LANE

RD.

Plonk's
Hill

LONG COMMON

Hullbrook
Farm

Downs Link

GUILDFORD-CRANLEIGH

ROAD

RD.

The White
House

Thorncombe
Park

Birtley
House

Tele.
Box

Rusheff
Common

ALLDENS

HILL

Wintershall

*Grafham*

+ St. Andrew

Sch.

Grafham
Grange

HORSHAM

Whipley
Manor

Selhurst
Common

SELHURST

COMMON ROAD

Goose
Green

Palmers
Cross

Juniper
Hill

Tilsey Farm

ROAD

A281

PEPPER BOX LA.

A     B     C

0    500    1000 Yards

0    500    1000 Metres

1

2

3

4

5

CONTINUED ON PAGE **102**

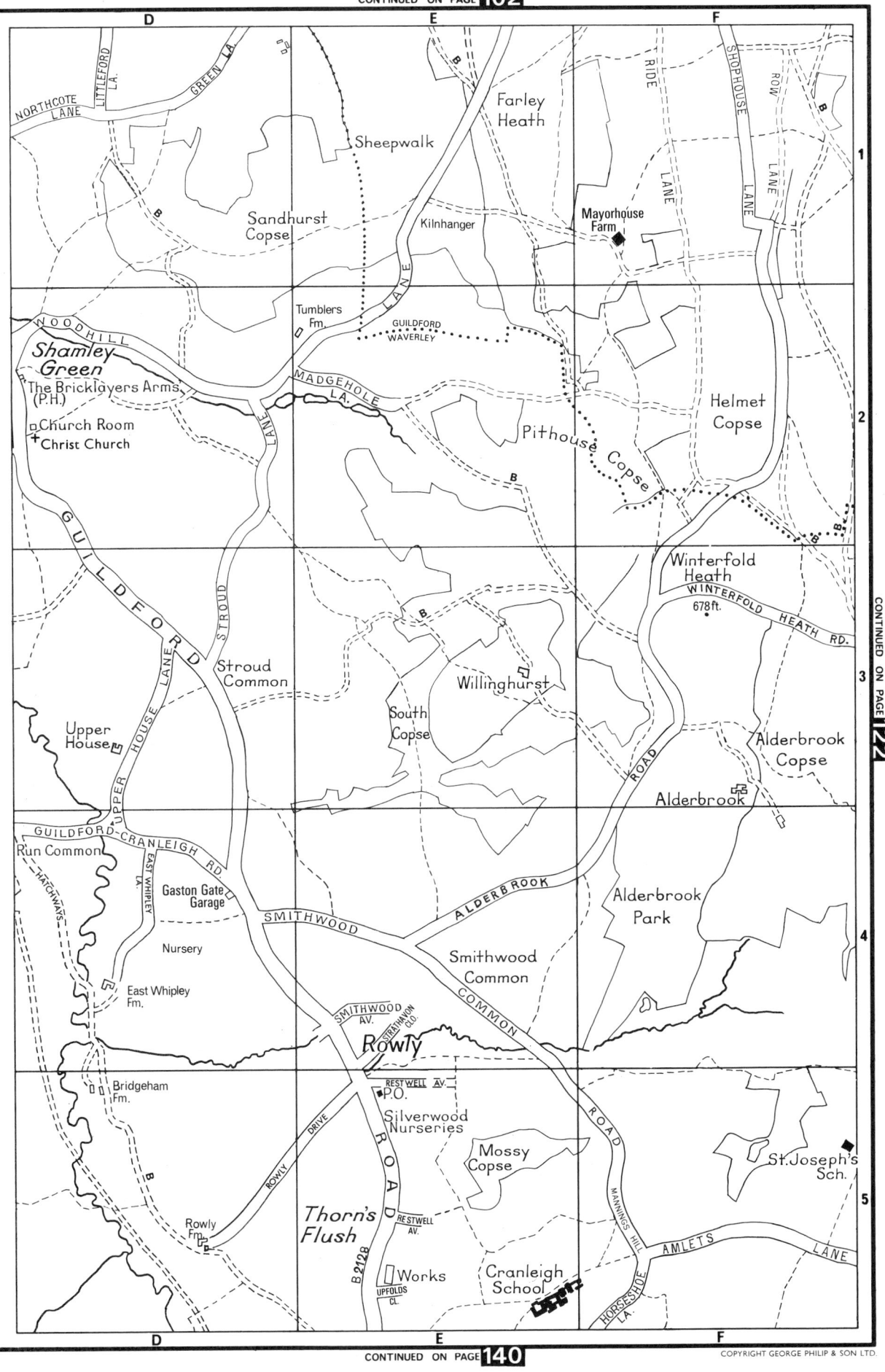

CONTINUED ON PAGE **122**

CONTINUED ON PAGE **140**

CONTINUED ON PAGE **103**

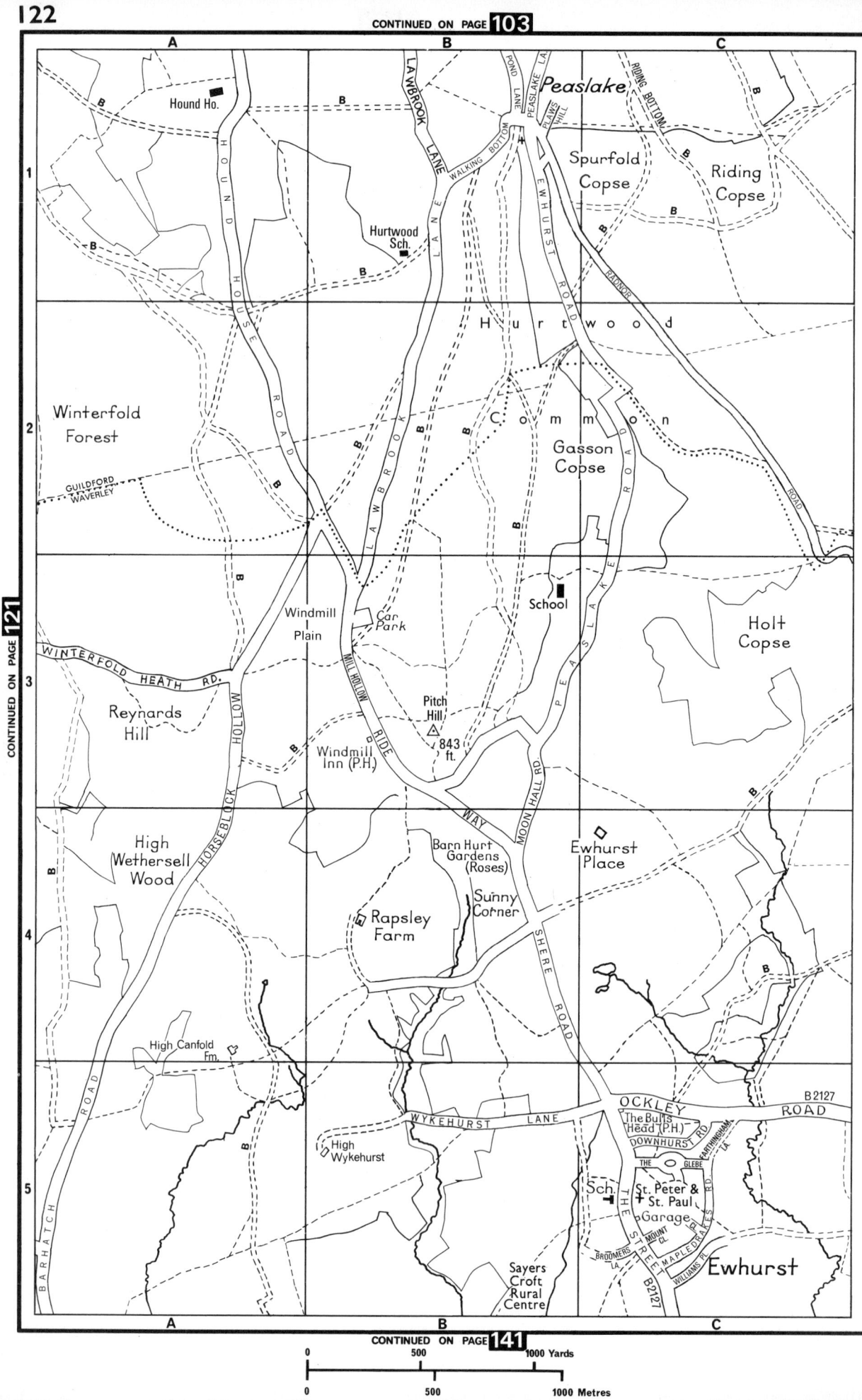

CONTINUED ON PAGE **121**

A    B    C

Peaslake

Hound Ho.

LAWBROOK LANE

POND LANE

PEASLAKE LA.

PLAWS HILL

RIDING BOTTOM

WALKING BOTTOM

EWHURST ROAD

Spurfold Copse

Riding Copse

Hurtwood Sch.

HOUND HOUSE ROAD

RADNOR ROAD

H u r t w o o d

Winterfold Forest

LAWBROOK LANE

C o m m o n

Gasson Copse

GUILDFORD WAVERLEY

PEASLAKE ROAD

School

Holt Copse

WINTERFOLD HEATH RD.

Windmill Plain

Car Park

MILL HOLLOW RIDE

Reynards Hill

HORSEBLOCK HOLLOW

Pitch Hill
△ 843 ft.

MOON HALL RD.

Windmill Inn (P.H.)

Ewhurst Place

High Wethersell Wood

WAY

Barn Hurt Gardens (Roses)

Sunny Corner

Rapsley Farm

SHERE ROAD

BARHATCH ROAD

High Canfold Fm.

OCKLEY ROAD

B 2127

WYKEHURST LANE

The Bulls Head (P.H.)

DOWNHURST RD.

FARTHINGHAM LA.

High Wykehurst

THE GLEBE

THE STREET

St. Peter & St. Paul

MAPLEDRAKES RD.

Sch.

Garage

MOUNT CL.

Ewhurst

BROOMERS LA.

WILLIAMS PL.

B 2127

Sayers Croft Rural Centre

A    B    C

CONTINUED ON PAGE **141**

0   500   1000 Yards

0   500   1000 Metres

CONTINUED ON PAGE **104**

D     E     F

Sch.

Weir

King Georges
Hill

Abinger
Bottom

Parkhurst

Leylands
Farm

1

*Felday*

Feldemore

*Holmbury
St. Mary*

**Wotton**

Hall

*Pitland
Street*

P.H.

P.O.

**Common**

Cricket
Grd.

Linholme

Hopedene

Highashes
Farm

2

Somerset
Cottage

Highashes
Wood

*Moxley*

Great
Foxmoor
Wood

Holmbury
Hill 857 ft.

Upfolds
Farm

Buildings
Copse

Hill
Fort

Moseley
Copse

Whitefield
Wood

Tanhurst

Joldwynds

*Hurtwood*

Holmbury

Polland
Corner

3

Radnor
Ho.

Birkett's
Farm

Leith
Hill
Wood

Pratsham
Grange

Lukyns

Pond

Holmbury
Ho.
Farm

Etherley Copse

4

*Prince
Hill*

Brookhurst
Farm

Wickland
Farm

Forest Green
Ho.

B 2126
ETHERLEY HILL

Gosterwood Manor

*Forest
Green*

Goster
Wood

OCKLEY   B 2127

ROAD

Parrot
(P.H.)

Artist's
Studio

Rishet's
Copse

Holy +
Trinity

Sports
Grd.
Gar.

Stubbetts
Corner

Woodland

Cobbett's
Farm

Waterland
Farm

NEW RD.

North Breache
Manor

Lyefield
Farm

Jordan's
Farm

5

Yard Farm

Rewfield
Copse

Bridgeham
Farm

D     E     F

CONTINUED ON PAGE **142**

CONTINUED ON PAGE **124**

A     B     C

Shootlands
Leylands

Upper
Warren

Waterden
Plantation

Southmoor
Copse

Redlands

1

CROCKERS LANE

COLDHARBOUR

Plough
Copse

ANSTIE LANE

Broadmoor Bottom

Wotton
Common

Whiteberry
Gate

Warren
Plantation

Coldharbour Sch.
Common

Crockers
Farm

P.O.

Anstiebury
Camp

Anstiebury
Farm

Anstie
Grange

MOORHURST

Moorhurst

Snakes
Hill

Old Schoolhouse

Coldharbour

Spring
Copse

LANE

2

Kitlands

Minnickwood
Farm

Leith Hill

The Landslip

Mosses    Wood

Gill Wood

Minnickfold

WOOD ROAD

Tower
965ft

Leith
Hill
Hotel

Cockshot
Farm

Bushy
Copse

Weir

HENHURST

MOSSES

Campfield
Place

Boathouse

Maryholm

Slittens
Copse

CROSS LANE

CONTINUED ON PAGE **123**

3

LEITH HILL

Farmhouse
Copse

Hooks
Copse

Broome
Hall

Fish
Pond

Beare
Gill

BROOMHALL

Leith Hill

Round
Copse

Hartshurst
Farm

ROAD

Church
Wood

BROOMHALL ROAD

Buckinghill
Farm

4

Landlane
Gate

EMERLEY HILL

OCKLEY

B2126

ROAD

Sheep
Green

BOGNOR

Highfield
Wood

Holmswood Gill

BURYWOOD HILL

High
Woods

Pond

LAKE

Jayes
Park

Youngs'
Farm

5

Volvens

MOLE STREET

Jayes   Park

P.O.

COLES

Weir

St. Margaret

Ockley
Court

OCKLEY
& CAPEL
STA.

'Kings Arms'
Gar. (P.H.)

LANE

SID
APP.

ROAD

STANE STREET

'Red Lion'
(P.H.)

Courtbottom
Wood

COLES LANE

WEARE ST.

The
Green

A29 Ockley

Church
Copse

WOODLANDS DR.

A     B     C

| 0 | 500 | 1000 Yards |
| 0 | 500 | 1000 Metres |

CONTINUED ON PAGE **126**

D

E

F

1

2

3

4

5

WARWICK RD.

NORFOLK RD.

BETCHETS GRN. RD.

BUCKINGHAM RD.

Subway

Holmwood Park

Works

Ewood Farm

Vicarage

Betchets Green

Holmwood Corner

Sch.

HORSHAM

A24

Vigo Farm

Holmwood Corner Common

Swires Farm

Petersfield Farm

HENFOLD LANE

West End Barn

Capel Leyse

B

B

Brook Copse

Farm

RD.

B

OLD HORSHAM RD.

STUBBLES GRN.

PADDOCK GREEN

HOLMWOOD STA.

MEREBANK

White Hart (P.H.)

Rabbits Copse

HENFOLD HILL

Reffolds Copse

Brookwood Farm

OAK CORNER

WILLOW RD.

LEITH RD.

CROSS WAY

OAK END

LEITH RD.

ANSTIEBURY CL.

WOODSIDE RD.

GROVE RD.

Gar.

Gar. Subway

Garstons Copse

B

Henfold

HENFOLD

B

HIGHLAND RD.

SPRINGWELL RD.

Beare Green

Duke's Head (P.H.)

Sch.

Trouts Farm

Arnolds

RD.

Palmersbeare Farm

Ratfield Wood

Brooklag Farm

PARKGATE RD.

BOGNOR

WIGMORE LANE

Surrey Hills Hotel

Melvill Ho.

VILLAGE ST.

LINDERHILL RD.

Sch.

Farm

Wigmore

Sprots Farm

Caravan Site

Thurbarns Hill

Works

Kingsland Copse

WINFIELD DR.

P.O.

Six Bells (P.H.)

Newdigate

RUSPER

Rugge Farm

HOYLE HILL

Hoyle Farm

Cafe

TRIG

STREET

North Lands

GREEN'S LANE

CAPEL BYPASS

SEAMAN'S GREEN RD.

Round Wood

B

Hillhouse Farm

Broomells

Birchy Copse

Green's Farm

ROAD

Ryersh Farm

Misbrooks Green

Broomell's Farm

Grass Copse

Tanhouse Farm

King's Hd. (P.H.)

OLD BARN DR.

Capel House Farm

Works

MORTIMER RD.

VICARAGE

LANE

TEMPLE LANE

B

St. John the Baptist

STREET

BROADWOOD COTTAGES

Aldhurst Farm

Crown Inn

Sch.

Friends Meeting House

Capel

P.O.

Bennett's Wood

BAKERS WAY.

NURSERY RD.

OLD CLAY DR.

OAK HALL WAY.

B

COLES LANE

B2126

THE STREET

BENNETT'S WOOD

Clarks Green Farm

Peter's Wood

A24

D

E

F

CONTINUED ON PAGE **107**

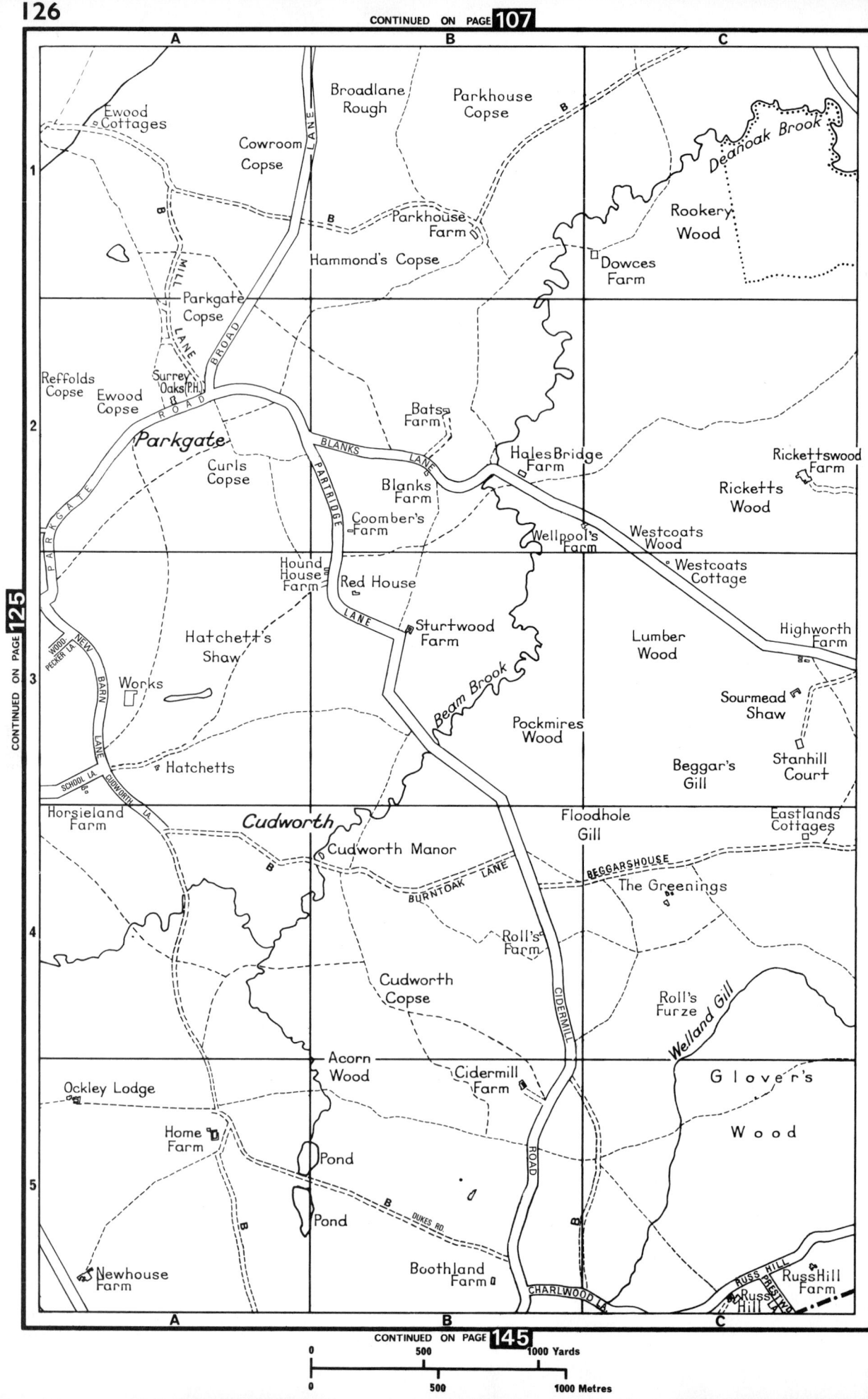

CONTINUED ON PAGE **125**

A · B · C

1

Ewood Cottages

Broadlane Rough

Parkhouse Copse

Deanoak Brook

Cowroom Copse

MILL LANE

Parkhouse Farm

Hammond's Copse

Rookery Wood

Dowces Farm

Parkgate Copse

2

Reffolds Copse

Ewood Copse

BROAD ROAD

Surrey Oaks (P.H.)

Parkgate

Curls Copse

PARKGATE

BLANKS LANE

Bats Farm

Blanks Farm

Coomber's Farm

Hales Bridge Farm

Wellpool's Farm

Westcoats Wood

Ricketts Wood

Rickettswood Farm

PARTRIDGE LANE

Hound House Farm

Red House

Sturtwood Farm

Westcoats Cottage

3

WOODPECKER LA.

NEW BARN LANE

Works

Hatchett's Shaw

LANE

Beam Brook

Pockmires Wood

Lumber Wood

Highworth Farm

Sourmead Shaw

SCHOOL LA.

CUDWORTH LA.

Hatchetts

Beggar's Gill

Stanhill Court

Horsieland Farm

Cudworth

Cudworth Manor

Floodhole Gill

Eastlands Cottages

BURNTOAK LANE

BEGGARSHOUSE

The Greenings

4

Roll's Farm

Cudworth Copse

CIDERMILL

Roll's Furze

Welland Gill

Glover's

Acorn Wood

Ockley Lodge

Cidermill Farm

Wood

Home Farm

Pond

ROAD

5

Pond

DUKES RD.

Newhouse Farm

Boothland Farm

CHARLWOOD LA.

RUSS HILL PRESTLEY

Russ Hill

RussHill Farm

A · B · C

0        500        1000 Yards

0        500        1000 Metres

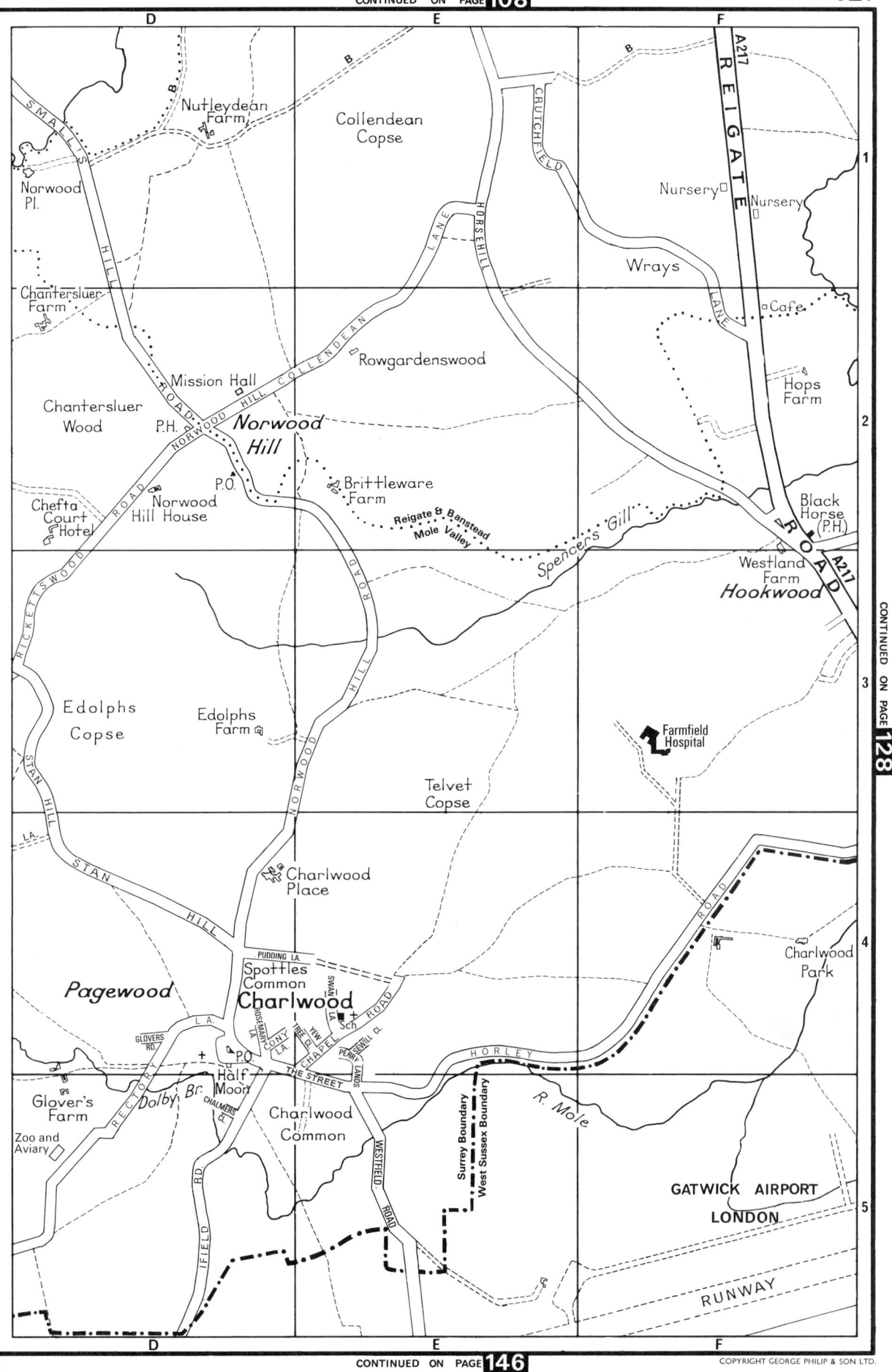

CONTINUED ON PAGE **128**

D      E      F

A217   REIGATE

1

Nursery   Nursery

Wrays

Cafe

Hops Farm

Nutleydean Farm

Collendean Copse

CRUTCHFIELD

HORSEHILL   LANE

Norwood Pl.

Chantersluer Farm

Rowgardenswood

Mission Hall

Chantersluer Wood

P.H.

COLLENDEAN HILL

Norwood Hill

2

Black Horse (P.H.)

ROAD   A217

P.O.

Chefta Court Hotel

Norwood Hill House

Brittleware Farm

Reigate & Banstead
Mole Valley

Spencers Gill

Westland Farm

Hookwood

NORWOOD HILL   ROAD

3

Farmfield Hospital

RICKETTSWOOD   ROAD

Edolphs Copse

Edolphs Farm

Telvet Copse

STAN HILL   LA.

STAN HILL

NORWOOD   HILL   ROAD

Charlwood Place

ROAD

Charlwood Park

4

PUDDING LA.

Spottles Common

Pagewood

LA.

GLOVERS RD.

CROSSMARY LA.

CONY LA.

SWAN LA.

YEW TREE CL.

**Charlwood**

Sch

CHAPEL   ROAD

HORLEY   ROAD

PERRY LANDS

SEWILL CL.

P.O.

Half Moon

THE STREET

R. Mole

Glover's Farm

Dolby Br.

CHALMERS CL.

Charlwood Common

RECTORY   RD.

IFIELD   RD.

WESTFIELD   ROAD

Zoo and Aviary

Surrey Boundary

West Sussex Boundary

**GATWICK AIRPORT**

**LONDON**

5

RUNWAY

CONTINUED ON PAGE 109

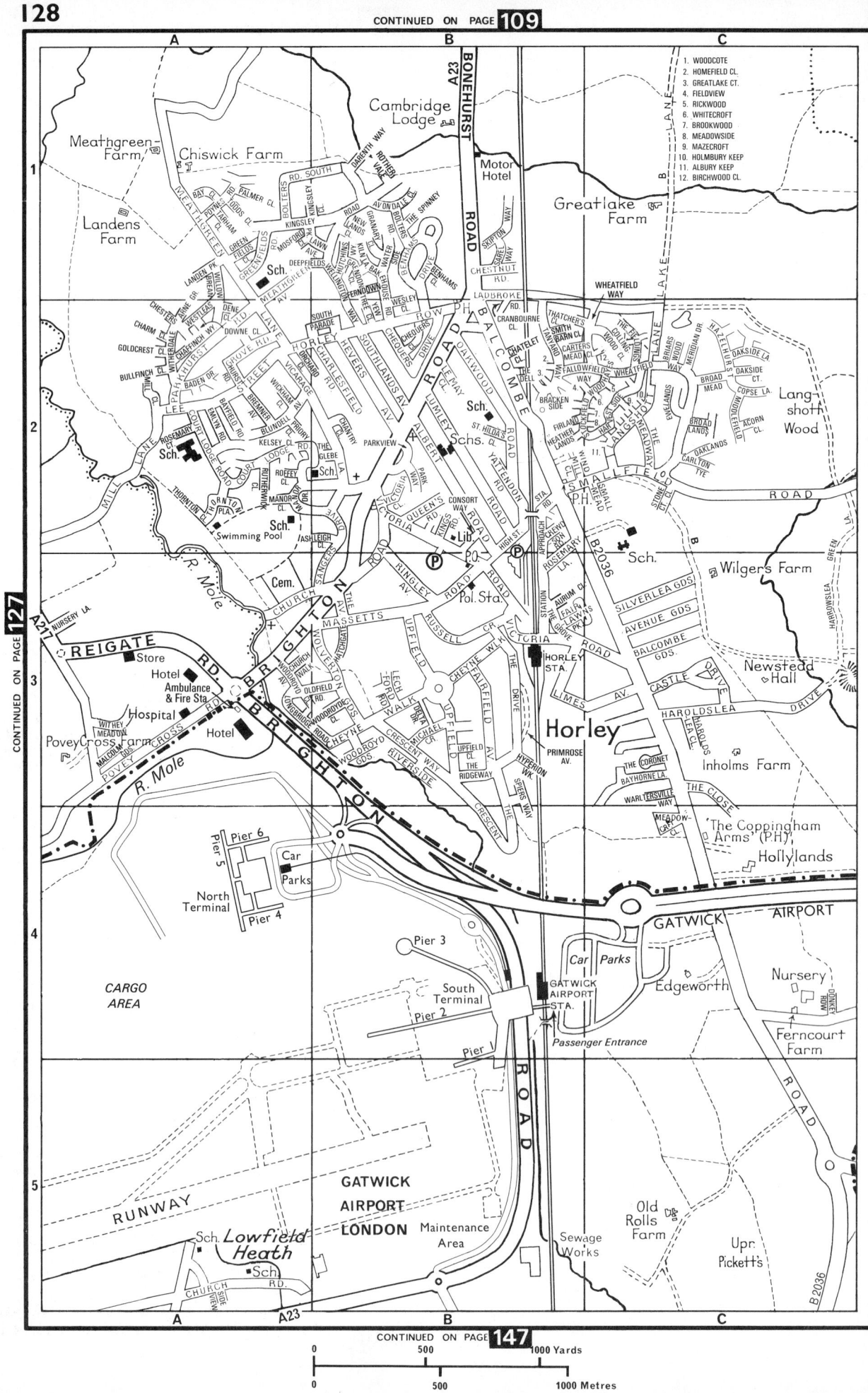

1. WOODCOTE
2. HOMEFIELD CL.
3. GREATLAKE CT.
4. FIELDVIEW
5. RICKWOOD
6. WHITECROFT
7. BROOKWOOD
8. MEADOWSIDE
9. MAZECROFT
10. HOLMBURY KEEP
11. ALBURY KEEP
12. BIRCHWOOD CL.

CONTINUED ON PAGE 127

HORLEY

GATWICK AIRPORT

GATWICK
AIRPORT
LONDON

CONTINUED ON PAGE 147

0        500        1000 Yards

0        500        1000 Metres

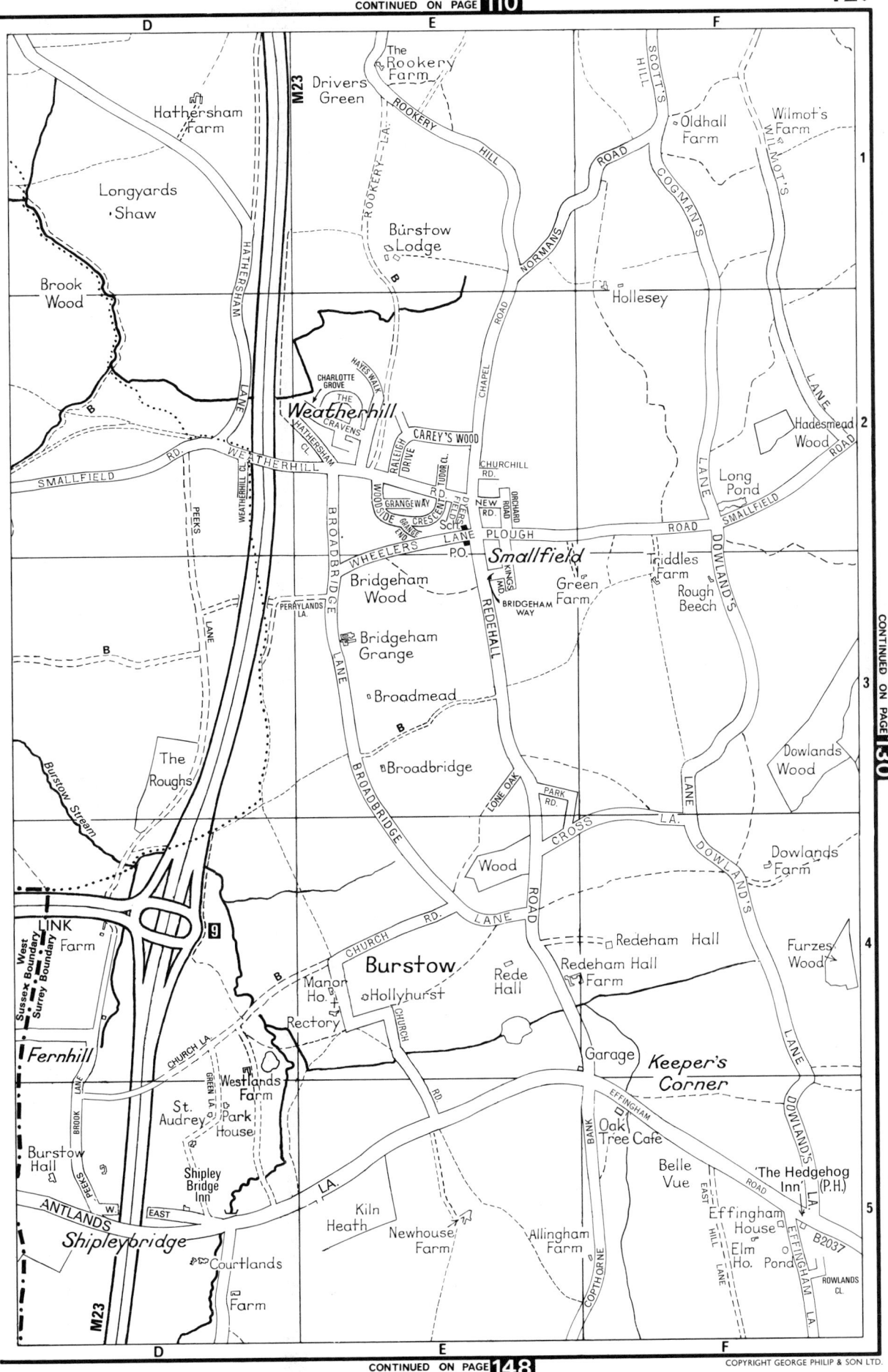

CONTINUED ON PAGE 111

A       B       C

Horncourt Hill

Hays Bridge Business Centre

WHITEWOOD ROAD

Horne Grange

**Horne**

Brickhouse Farm

Stanton's Hall

B

LANE

Church Farm

Sch.

Hornehouse Farm

CHURCH ROAD

CROYDONBARN LANE

BRICKHOUSE LANE

HARE LANE

Goulds Farm

Baron's Croft

B CROCKERS

Lay-by

EASTBOURNE ROAD A22

SMALLFIELD ROAD

BONES

Wood

Wood

East Bysshe Farm

Gate Ho. Farm

Bysshe Court

LANE

Highfield Farm

CLAY LANE

Horne Park

The Blacksmith's Head (PH)

High House Farm

CHITHURST

Roughbeech Wood

Hornepark Farm

BONES RD

Frogpit Heath

R.A.C. Box

Lowlands Farm

New chapel

Chithurst Farm

LANE

Nevergood Wood

Leighfurze Field

Kingswood Farm

PARK LANE

East Park

Yewtree Farm

Cricket Grd.

Mormon Temple

WEMBURY PARK

WIRE MILL

Eastpark Farm

Newchapel Stud Farm

Hobbs Barracks

Birchen Wood

Home Wood

The Plantation

STUB POND

Chapel Wood

WOODCOCK HILL

LANE

Brick Barn Wood

West Park

Bewkes

WEST

Moat

Hedgecourt Fm.

Eden Brook

Wood

B 2028

Newlake Gardens

OLD HERONS

MILL LANE

Park Farm

Prospect Ho.

B 2037

**Domewood**

Thorny Park

HERON'S CLOSE

LEA

Hedgecourt Pond

A264 COPTHORNE RD. A264

CONTINUED ON PAGE 129

CONTINUED ON PAGE 149

0     500     1000 Yards

0     500     1000 Metres

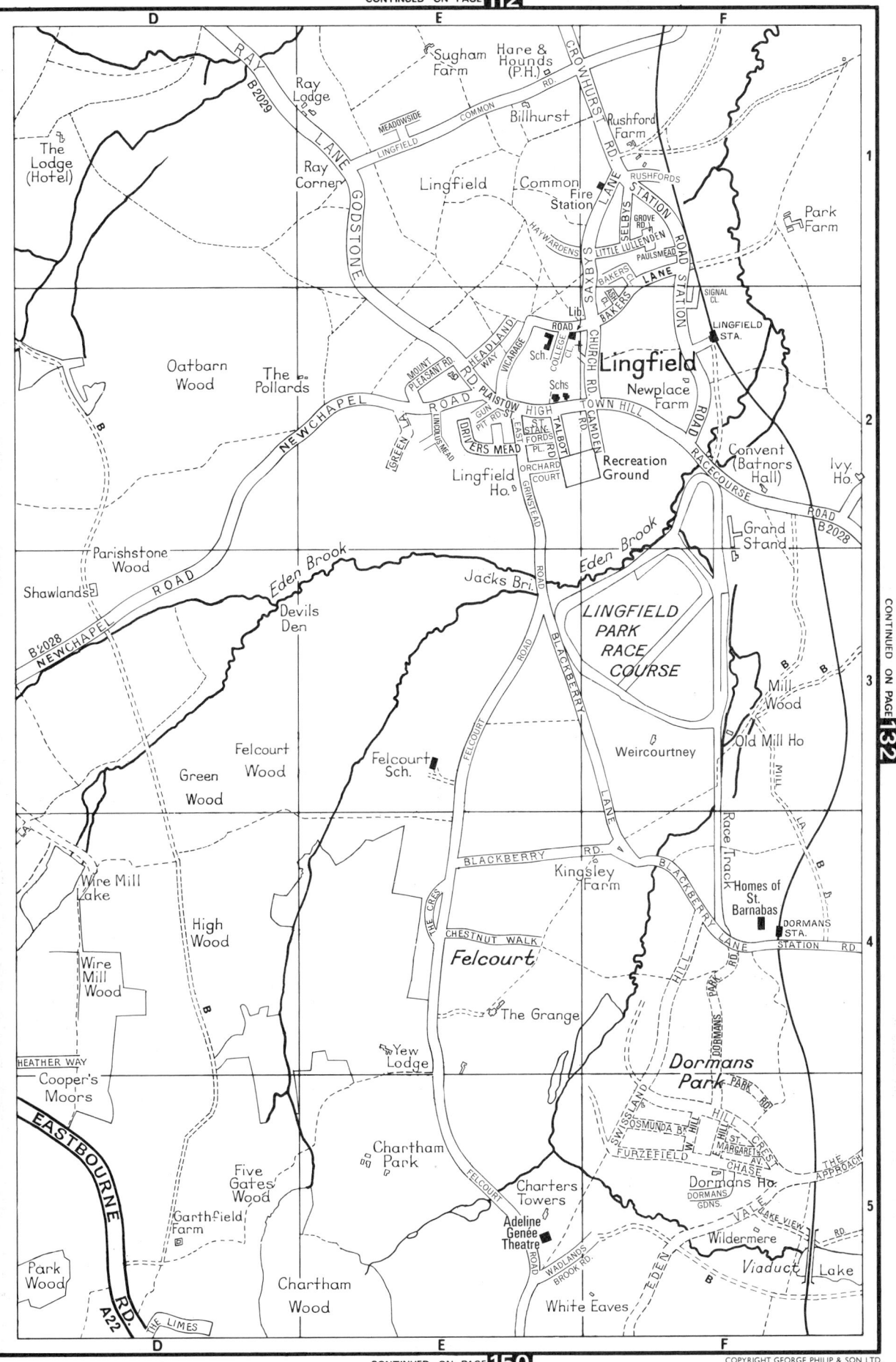

CONTINUED ON PAGE **132**

CONTINUED ON PAGE **113**

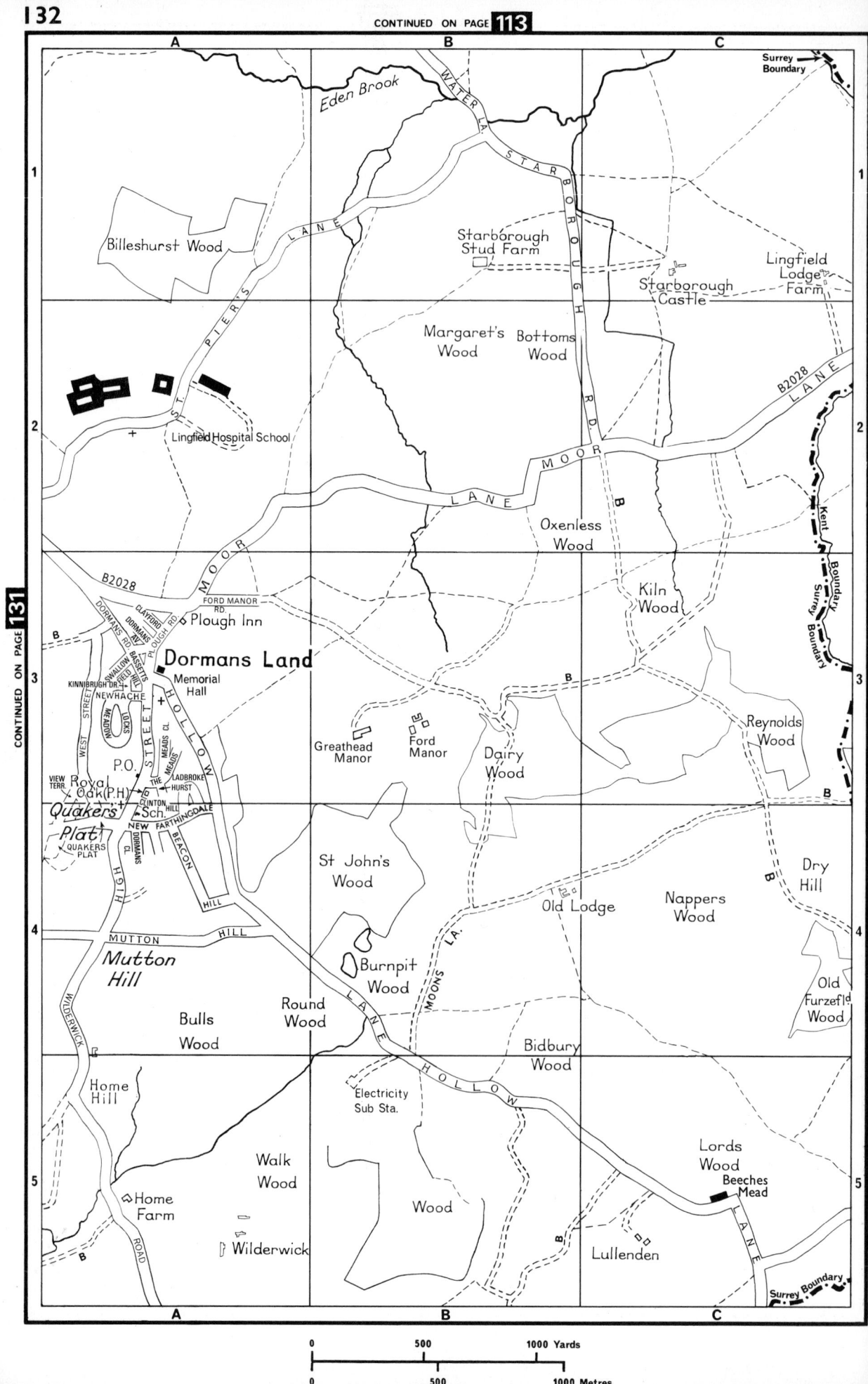

Surrey
Boundary

*Eden Brook*

WATER LA.

ST PIER'S LANE

STARBOROUGH RD

Billeshurst Wood

Starborough
Stud Farm

Starborough
Castle

Lingfield
Lodge
Farm

B2028 LANE

Margaret's
Wood

Bottoms
Wood

Lingfield Hospital School

MOOR LANE

Oxenless
Wood

Kent Boundary Surrey

Kiln
Wood

B2028

FORD MANOR RD.

Plough Inn

**Dormans Land**

CLAYFORD
DORMANS RD.
SWALLOW
REED HILL
BASSETS
NEWHACHE
PLOUGH RD.

KINNIBRUGH DR.

WEST STREET

MEADOW

P.O.

VIEW TERR.

Royal
Oak (P.H.)

*Quakers
Plat*

QUAKERS
PLAT

HIGH

NEW
DORMANS

CLINTON
HILL
Sch.

FARTHINGDALE

STREET HOLLOW

Memorial
Hall

THE MEADS

MEADS CL.

LADBROKE
HURST

Greathead
Manor

Ford
Manor

Dairy
Wood

Reynolds
Wood

St John's
Wood

BEACON

HILL

Old Lodge

MOONS LA.

Nappers
Wood

Dry
Hill

*Mutton
Hill*

MUTTON

HILL

Bulls
Wood

Round
Wood

LANE HOLLOW

Burnpit
Wood

Bidbury
Wood

Old
Furzef'ld
Wood

WILDERWICK

Home
Hill

Electricity
Sub Sta.

Lords
Wood

Beeches
Mead

Walk
Wood

Wood

Home
Farm

ROAD

Wilderwick

Lullenden

LANE

Surrey Boundary

CONTINUED ON PAGE **131**

| 0 | | 500 | | 1000 Yards |

| 0 | | 500 | | 1000 Metres |

D    E    F

1

Frithend Ho.

FRITHEND    ROAD

A325

ROAD

*Frithend*

Kites Hill

Manor Farm

R. Wey

St. Teresa's Convent

HEATH HILL

Surrey Boundary
Hampshire Boundary

Gum Hill

Grooms Farm

Baigent's Bri.

Heath Hill

R. Slea

Baigent's Hill

LANE

LANE    FRENSHAM    RD.    SMITHFIELD

LA.

2

B3004

CAMP

Trottsford Farm

TROTTSFORD

ROAD

WATERY

BULL'S HOLLOW

Pond

*Stream Forest*

LA.

New Inn (P.H.)

*Sleaford*

Headley Park

Fir Hanger

PICKETS    HILL

HOPPERY

Tignals

SPATS

LANE

BORDON

3

A325

Broxhead Common

Headleywood Farm

R.    Wey

RD.

HANGER

PROSPECT

HILL

LANE

The Oaks

HEARN LA.

THE MOUNT

4

Barracks

B3002

LINDFORD    ROAD

LIPHOOK    ROAD

FRENSHAM    ROAD

HEADLEY    ROAD

P.O.

Royal Exchange (P.H.)

CRAYSHOTT
LAURELS

FRENSHAM    ROAD    CURTIS

CHURCH    LA.

The Wheatsheaf P.H.

The Crown P.H.

BARLEY    MOW HILL

*Arford*

ARFORD COMMON

BEECH HILL

CHAPEL
GUNS
HEATHER

FIVEACRE CL.

CL.

CANES
LA.

LINDFORD
TREE

TAYLORS
LA.

WINDSOR    RD.
WINDSOR
WK.

*Lindford*

TURK
WINDSOR

BLUE
BELL    RD.

COOL-
GREANY    HILL

MILL

CHURCHFIELDS

OPEN
FRED
FARTHING
FIELDS

P.O.

HIGH    ST.

LONG    CROSS    HILL

Holly
Bush
Inn

*Headley*

Rec. Grn.

Sch.

ARFORD    ROAD

BOWCOT HILL

BEECH HILL RD.

HEADLEY    HILL    RD.

*FULLER'S*

B3002

VALE

PHILLIPS CR.    PHILLIPS
CL.

Deep Pond

CHASE    LA.

R. Wey

MADENE CR.

ELDEBERRY    RD.

MILL    LANE

Ellis's Mill

HEADLEY    FIELDS

GLEBE    RD.

THE PADDOCK

CRABTREE
LA.

HILLAND

CHURCHILL
CRES.

PERRY
WAY

CHESTNUT
END

Hilland Wood

5

*Alexandria Park*

Sch.

WATERSIDE CL.

*Deadwater*

GREEN
ACRES

WASHFORD

MILLCHASE

HAMILTON CL.

Ford

HOLLYWATER    ROAD

Sch.

STANDFORD    LANE

B3004

LIPHOOK

HURLAND

GENTLES    LANE

CHALET
VARNA RD.
ALMA RD.

HEATHCOT RD.

MEADOWVIEW

HILL
CANE
HOLLYBROOK
PARK

D    E    F

CONTINUED ON PAGE **134**

CONTINUED ON PAGE **115**

CONTINUED ON PAGE **133**

A     B     C

POND LANE

Frensham Pond Hotel & Restaurant

FARNHAM

A287

CHURT RD

CROSSWATER LANE

The Flashes

The De

Churt Common

JUMPS ROAD

JUMPS

ROAD

JUMPS

CRABTREE LANE

1

FRENSHAM LANE

BACON LANE

Surrey Boundary

B

Ford

LANE

STAR HILL

STAR HILL GR.

JUMPS LANE

KILN ROAD

OLD KILN CL

RECREATION

WISHANGER

Wishanger Pond

Wishanger Farm

SIMONDSTONE LA.

LAMPARD LANE

Redhearn Green

RED HEARN FIELDS

OLD KILN LANE

GREEN CROSS LANE

Green Cross

2

SMITHFIELD LANE

Hampshire Boundary

Churt

P.O.

HALE HOUSE LANE

THE MEADOWS

CUTT LA.

KUTTS

Sch.

BARFORD LA.

GREEN HANGAR

LANE

HANGER LANE

GREEN

ROAD

CHURT RD

SPATS LA.

ROAD

Elliot's Farm

Lower Hearn

3

CHURT ROAD

Land of Nod

HAMMER

WHITMOOR VALE

B

Hatch Hill

Golf Course

WHITMOOR VALE ROAD

CHURT ROAD

GLAYSHERS HILL

BIRCH RD.

KAY CR.

EMBLETON RD.

LARCH RD.

PINE VIEW

MILLE CR.

EDDY'S

GRAYSHOTT

LUDSHOTT GR.

DOWNING RD.

4

BEECH HILL RD.

SOUTH VIEW

HEADLEY HILL

BEECH HILL

B3002

HONEYSUCKLE LA.

FAIRVIEW RD.

WILSONS RD.

KENLEY RD.

LINDON RD.

HOLLY RD.

HOLLY CL.

ALMA RD.

WEST VIEW RD.

SEYMOUR SIDE RD.

CARLTON RD.

SEYMOUR RD.

ROAD

Whitmoor Vale Bottom

WHITMOOR VALE

Whitmoor Hanger

THE SPINNEY

WAGGONERS SWAN

SADLERS SCARP

THE PADDOCK

WHEELWRIGHTS LA.

Headley Down

FURZEVALE RD.

WITHER SLACK CL.

STONEHILL

FURLE HILL RD.

FURZE HILL RD.

KILN WAY

HEADLEY ROAD B3002

Grayshott Hall

SADLERS SCARP

BRIDLE CL.

5

GENTLES LA.

POND ROAD

Gentles Copse

Ludshott

Common

WAGGONERS WELLS LA.

ROAD

Convent

A     B     C

0    500    1000 Yards

0    500    1000 Metres

CONTINUED ON PAGE 116

D E F

vil's Jumps
N.T.
375 ft
256
THURSLEY ROAD
Pride of the Valley Hotel
ROAD THURSLEY LANE
Churt Place Farm
Pitch Place Fm.
Pitch Place
1

HALE HOUSE LANE
OLD BARN LANE
TILFORD ROAD
HYDE LANE
PITCH PLACE RD.
SAILORS LANE
RIDGEWAY FM. RD.
2

GREEN LANE
Hyde Hill
CONTINUED ON PAGE 136

TILFORD ROAD
Marchants Hill Camp
Highcomb Bottom
3

EIGHT ACRES
CHURT WYNDE
HEATH CL.
CLOVELLY DR.
DOWNSIDE
SANDHEATH RD.
Linkside
LINKSIDE NTH
LINKSIDE WEST
LINKSIDE STH
CLOVELLY RD.
HILL RD.
BEACON HILL
ROAD
P.O.
Pol. Sta.
Youth Hostel
Golf Club
GROVE RD.
GILL WES RD.
FAIRWAYS
STEEPWAYS
Beacon Hill Rec. Gd.
DERBY RD.
PARSONS GN. LANE
BEACON HILL
WOOD
GROVERS LGN.
DOWN LANE
ROAD
Hindhead
The Beacon
Hindhead Common
N.T.
PORTSMOUTH ROAD
A3
4

BOXALLS HILL
CHURT ROAD
HUTGARTH
RIDGEMOOR CL.
HINDHEAD BRAE
Woodcock Bottom
N.T.
DEVIL'S PUNCH BOWL
TILFORD RD.
TOWER RD.
MEAD RD.
5

Surrey Boundary
BEECH LA.
BEECH HANGER END
SCHOOLS ROAD
VALEWOOD LANE
GLEN RD.
AVENUE RD.
Sch. St. Luke
PH.
HEADLEY
CROSSWAYS
B3002
TARN RD.
BOUNDARY RD.
THE AVENUE
HAZELHURST
FOREST DALE
Fire Sta.
THE MOORINGS
Sch.
PINE BANK
TOWER RD.
MOORLAND CL.
HIGHF'LD CR.
ROCKVILLE GDNS.
LONDON
P.O. HEATHER WAY
HINDHEAD ROAD
TYNDALL'S BROOM SQUARES
P
The Devil's Punch Bowl Hotel
Hindhead Country Club
Grayshott
OLD LANE
STONEY BOTTOM HILL
PORTSMOUTH ROAD
A3
PORTSMOUTH ROAD
A287
Hindhead Common

D E F

CONTINUED ON PAGE 151

CONTINUED ON PAGE **117**

A          B          C

CONTINUED ON PAGE **135**

A 286

ROKE LA.

ROAD

PORTSMOUTH

ROAD A3

P.O. Vic.
Sch  DYEHOUSE RD.
**Thursley**
THE LANE
■ Police Sta
THE STREET
+
HIGHFIELD LA.

Milhanger

A3

FRENCH LANE

B

Fish Ponds

Cosford House

FRENCH LA.

Heath Hall

Thursley Lake   Stable Lake

Witley Park

Upper Lake

Gate Ho⁵

Estate Office

1

2

*Bowlhead Green*

BOWLHEAD GREEN RD.

B

BROOK HILL

Screw Corner

HASLEMERE ROAD

Pirrie Hall & Rec. Grd.

P.O.
Dog & Pheasant (P.H.)
Brook Farm
*Brook*

CHURCH LANE

Uplands Park

LANE

3

**Rutton Hill**

RUTTON HILL ROAD

**Halnacker Copse**

PARK LANE

PARK

*Copse*

Park

■ Black Hanger
Forestry Commission

BOUNDLESS ROAD

PARK

**Begley Copse**

□ Boundless Farm

4

□ Greedhole Farm
B

**Boundless Copse**

B

B

Gibbet Hill

▲ 894 ft.

W i t l e y    F o r e s t

**Hurthill Copse**

**Witley Farm**

**Holmen's Grove**

Upper Birtley

B

☐ Lower Birtley Farm

HASLEMERE ROAD

5

B

B

**Invall**

B

B

A 286

Stroud

A          B          C

CONTINUED ON PAGE **152**

0        500        1000 Yards

0        500        1000 Metres

CONTINUED ON PAGE **118**

ROKE LANE

Barrow Hills

NEWLANDS

NORTH FIELD

A283

Witley Manor

White Hart (P.H.)

Witley Ponds

Sch.

WATER

Enton Hall Nursing Home

Fish Pond

Parson's Hanger

*Culmer*

Sweetwater Pond

Byrony Hill

*Hambledon*

PETWORTH LANE

Foot Grd.

P.O.

*Wormley*

King Edward's Sch.

Nat. Inst. of Oceanography

GURDON'S

BROOK

Leybourne

The Hill

Sch.

Inst.

MALT HOUSE

PADDOCK CL

VANN LANE

BEECH HILL

*Sandhills*

WITLEY STA.

CAR PARK

The Wood Pigeon (P.H.)

NEW ROAD

Hambledon Common

LANES END

Cricket Ground

SANDHILLS

Sandhills Common

COMBE

ROAD

WORMLEY LANE

ROAD

Factory

Kiln Copse

PETWORTH

Red Lands

Minepit Copse

Hambledon Hurst

LANE

CONTINUED ON PAGE **138**

Winterton Arms (P.H.)

Combe Court

Fish Ponds

*Northbridge*

Mont Colline

ROAD

Granthams

Combe Court Farm

PINHURST

HART'S GROVE

Combe Common

COMBE VIEW

WOODSIDE

YEWENS

WOODSIDE CL

ROSNEATH DR

QUEEN'S MEAD

Sch.

*Chiddingfold*

POOK HILL

LANE

Langhurst House

RIDGELEY

STEPHEN'S FIELD

ROSACOMBE

OAK

BEECH

PATHFIELD CL

COXCOMBE

ROAD

Green

PLAISTOW RD.

The Knipp

PRESTWICK

Pook Hill Cottages

POCKFORD

Crown (P.H.)

Oaklands Park

Langhurst Manor

MILL LANE

PETWORTH

A283

Turners Mead

Prestwick

Little Prestwick Farm

CONTINUED ON PAGE 119

A     B     C

B213

Hascombe Court

HOE LA.

MARE LANE

Hascombe

Hydon Heath

B

B

MARKWICK

B

B

B

FEATHERCOMBE

Great House Farm

1

Merry Harriers (P.H.)

Stable Cottage N.T.

Holloways Heath

B

B

B

ROCK HILL RD.

HAMBLEDON RD.

Elliot's Upper Vann Farm

Upper Vann Fruit Farm

B

B

B

Gunter's Wood

WOODLANDS RD.

2

Burgate House

B

LANE

Woodlands

Pond

VANN

Vannmoor

Lower Farm

LANE

B

CONTINUED ON PAGE 137

Brick Works

Lower Vann

3

B

LANE

B

B

VANN

4

B

SKINNERS LANE

ROAD

White Beech

B

WHITE BEECH

B

POCKFORD

CHIDDINGFOLD LANE

5

Blacknest Farm

Birchen Copse

ROAD

Highstreet Green

A     B     C

CONTINUED ON PAGE 154

0   500   1000 Yards

0   500   1000 Metres

CONTINUED ON PAGE 120

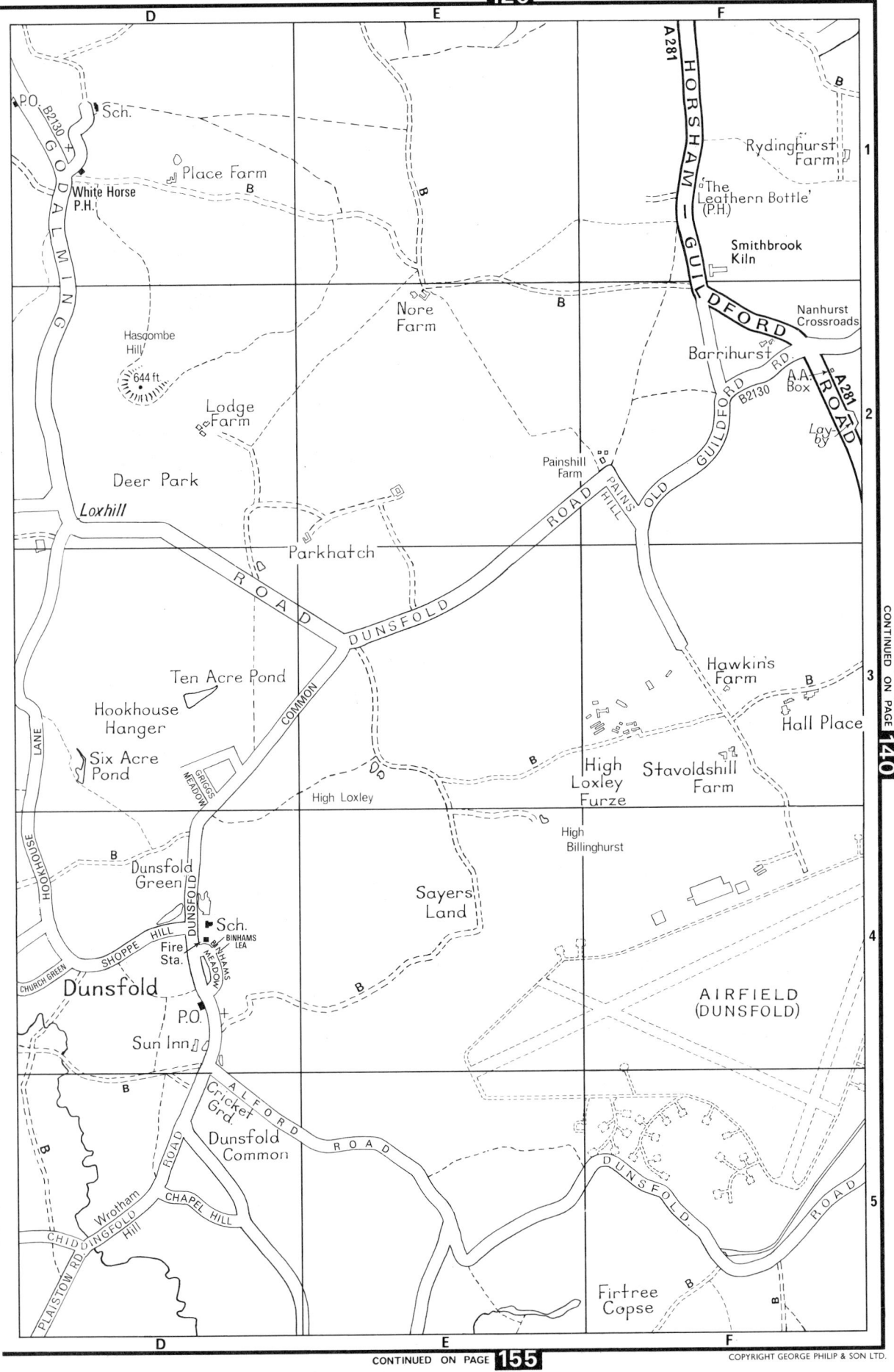

CONTINUED ON PAGE 140

CONTINUED ON PAGE 155

COPYRIGHT GEORGE PHILIP & SON LTD.

CONTINUED ON PAGE 121

A B C

CONTINUED ON PAGE 139

1

Elmslea

Cranleigh Sch. (Prep)

GUILDFORD

UPFOLD LANE

MANFIELD PARK

Ruffold Fm.

B2128

COMMON RD.

HORSESHOE LANE

EDGEFIELD

HORSESHOE LA.

Sports Field

The Cranley Hotel (P.H.)

LASHMERE

Cranleigh

Pond

Cranleigh Sch.

WYPHURST ROAD

THE RIDINGS RD.

THISTLEY LA.

GLEBE

PRECINCT

ST. NICOLAS CL.

PEREGRINE CL.

HARRIER CL.

WADDY RISE

SUMMERLANDS

MOWER

HARROW DENE

KILN COPSE

BARN FIELD

RD.

Rydinghurst

Sewage Works

ELM ROAD

Little Mead

ALFORD ROAD

STANTON CL.

WYNDHAM CRES.

PARK

Vine Works Industrial Estate

CARLYLE RD.

PARSONAGE

VICTORIA RD.

TYLERS CT.

Fire Sta.

Cem.

St. NICOLAS AV.

DEWLANDS

Sch.

Lib.

Cranleigh P.H.

NEW PARK RD.

WOODLAND

EWHURST RD.

B2130

ELMBRIDGE

ABBEY DRIVE

ESSEX CL.

Elmbridge Retirement Homes

HIGH ST.

P.O.

POL. STA.

Hosp.

Village Way Swimming Bath

WARRENS

MEAD

BRIDGE WALK

REDCROFT WALK

KINGS RD.

A281

2

Utworth Manor Farm

ALFORD ROAD

Knowle

Coldharbour

CHURCH

VILLAGE WAY

OVERFORD

Rec. Grd.

HITHERWOOD

BELL WYND

PELL WYND

MOUNT RD.

MOUNT

HORSHAM

THE MOUNT

THE DRIVE

ORCHARD GDNS.

AVENUE

WOODSTOCK RD.

RD.

Redhurst

AVEN

SHAW

NORTHDOWNS RD.

HERON

WAVERLEIGH RD.

NAPPER PL.

ELLERY CL.

NIGHTINGALE RD.

THURLOW WK.

FORTUNE DR.

CAMEDON CL.

ASH TREES

3

Wey & Arun Junc. Canal (disused)

Mill Farm

Lay-by

B

B

GUILDFORD

Mill Copse

ALFORD LANE

Holdhurst Farm

Bushy Copse

LION'S LANE

B

Snoxhall

Downs Link

B

VACHERY LANE

KNOWLE LANE

Water Br.

HAMMER LANE

4

A281

ROAD

FARNHURST LANE

Fast Br.

Flash Br.

B

Newhouse Farm

Birch Copse

KNOWLE LANE

Bookers Lee

Lay-by

WILDWOOD LANE

WILDWOOD ROAD

B

Three Compasses P.H.

DUNSFOLD ROAD

Laker's Green

GREEN LA.

5

Crossways Garage

Alfold Crossways

Gt. Wildwood Farm

Wildwood Copse

B

LOXWOOD RD.

B2133

CLAPPERS MEADOW

A281

ROAD

A B C

0 500 1000 Yards

0 500 1000 Metres

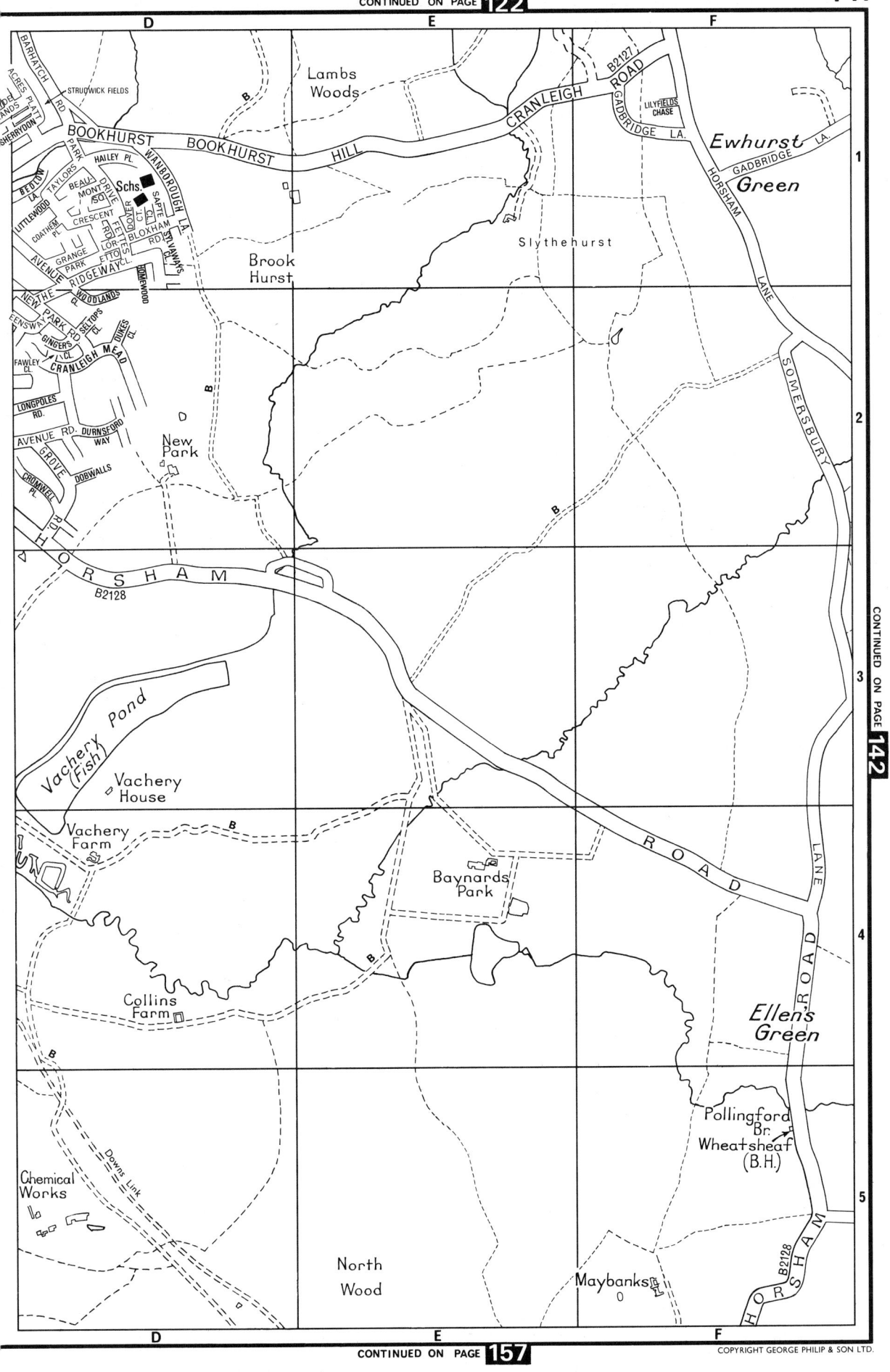

CONTINUED ON PAGE **142**

CONTINUED ON PAGE **123**

CONTINUED ON PAGE **141**

**A**    **B**    **C**

1

SWEETWATER LANE

Lowerbreach Farm

LOWERHOUSE

Spring Copse

FOREST GREEN

HOLDEN BROOK

Pisley Copse

GREEN LANE

Garrett's Gill

The Sturts

Mayes Green

Golf Course

Club Ho.

Gatton Manor

STANDON BROOK

Fir Copse

Hutchings Copse

2

HORSHAM LANE

Buildings

Wood

MOLE VALLEY WAVERLEY

LANE

Northlands

FROGETTS LANE

Walliswood Sch.

WALLISWOOD GREEN ROAD

CHAPEL LANE

Wallis Wood

Hunts Copse

TRAP LA.

STANDON

Radio Beacon Sta.

Works

Frogetts Farm

LAZENBY LA.

Scarlet Arms (P.H.)

Oakwoodland Wood

CHAPEL LA.

Oakwood Chapel

Chapel Copse

P.O.

OAKFIELDS

OAKWOODLAND

3

Somersbury Wood

Oakwoodhill

'Punch Bowl' (P.H.)

Exfold    Wood

Nags Wood

Works

SMOKEJACK

Smokejack Fm.

LANE

Woodhams Farm

ROAD

Wet Wood

Hillhouse Farm

Pound Farm

Ruckman's Farm

4

HONEYWOOD ROAD

SMOKEJACK HILL ROAD

Broadstone Farm

BROADSTONE

Monks

B

Pink Hurst

Pinkhurst Farm

Oakwood    Wood

Sansoms Copse

LANE

Honeywood Ho.

Birch Wood

5

*Ellen's Green* Sch.

FURZEN

ROAD

Surrey  Boundary

West Sussex Boundary

Ridge Farm

Ellen's Farm

Ridge Hanger

**A**    **B**    **C**

| 0 | 500 | 1000 Yards |
|---|-----|------------|

| 0 | 500 | 1000 Metres |
|---|-----|-------------|

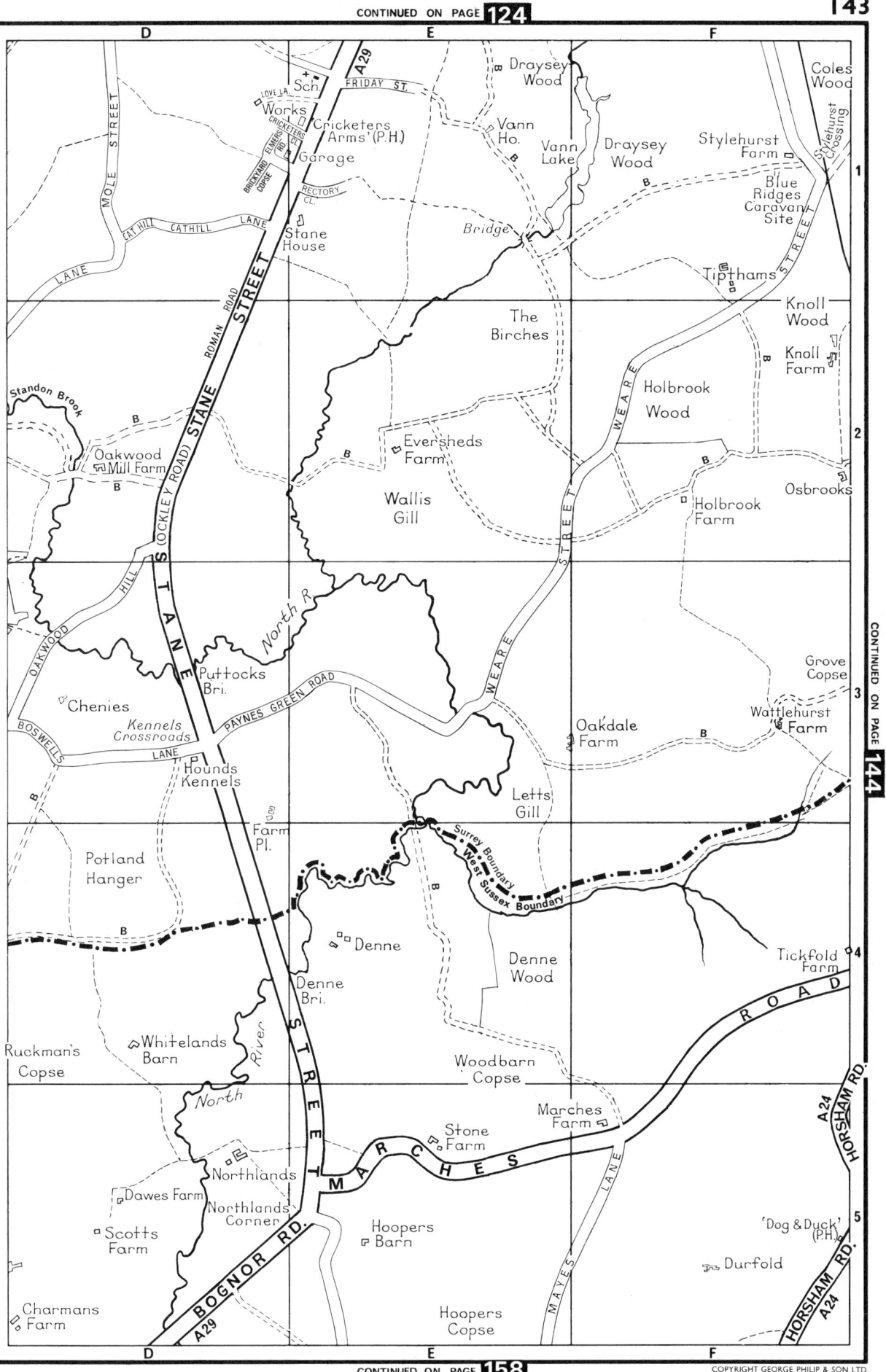

Coles
Wood

Draysey
Wood

FRIDAY ST.

A29

Sch.

LOVE LA.

Stylehurst
Crossing

Stylehurst
Farm

Vann
Ho.

Draysey
Wood

Works

CRICKETERS

ELMERS RD. CL.

Cricketers
Arms' (P.H.)

Vann
Lake

Garage

BRICKYARD COPSE

RECTORY CL.

Blue
Ridges
Caravan
Site

STREET

1

Tipthams

MOLE STREET LANE

CAT HILL CATHILL LANE

Stane
House

Bridge

Knoll
Wood

ROMAN ROAD

The
Birches

Knoll
Farm

Holbrook
Wood

STANE

Standon Brook

B

Oakwood
Mill Farm

B

Eversheds
Farm

WEARE STREET

2

Osbrooks

(OCKLEY ROAD)

B

Wallis
Gill

B

Holbrook
Farm

OAKWOOD HILL

STREET

North R.

Grove
Copse

BOSWELLS

Chenies

Puttocks
Bri.

PAYNES GREEN ROAD

WEARE

Oakdale
Farm

B

Wattlehurst
Farm

3

CONTINUED ON PAGE **144**

Kennels
Crossroads

LANE

Hounds
Kennels

Farm
Pl.

Letts
Gill

B

Potland
Hanger

B

Surrey Boundary

West Sussex Boundary

Denne

Denne
Wood

Tickfold
Farm

4

Ruckman's
Copse

River

Denne
Bri.

Whitelands
Barn

Woodbarn
Copse

ROAD

HORSHAM RD.

North

STREET

Stone
Farm

Marches
Farm

A24

Northlands

MARCHES

MAYES LANE

Dawes Farm

Northlands
Corner

Hoopers
Barn

'Dog & Duck'
(P.H.)

5

Scotts
Farm

Durfold

BOGNOR RD.

Charmans
Farm

A29

Hoopers
Copse

HORSHAM RD.

A24

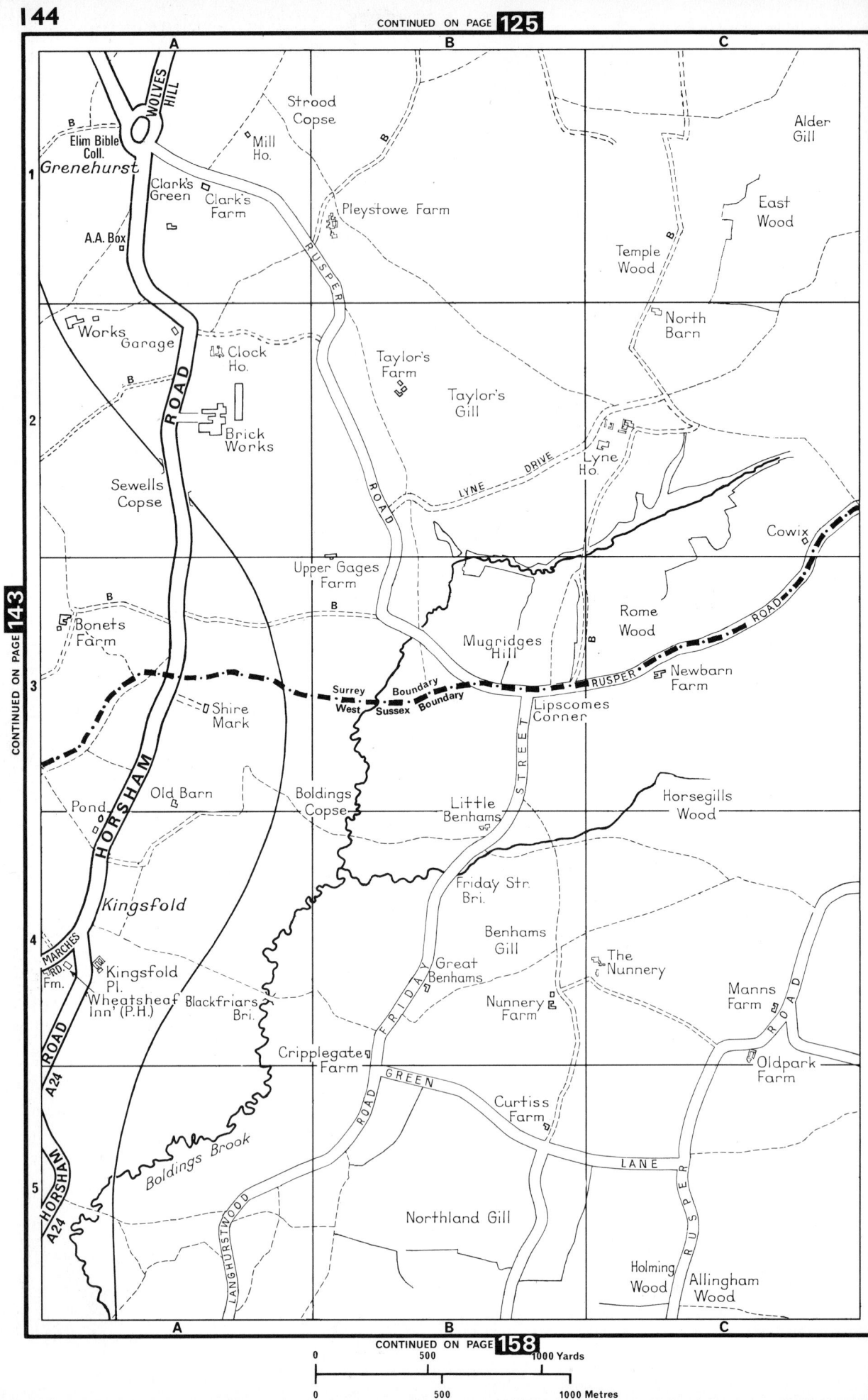

CONTINUED ON PAGE 125

A           B           C

CONTINUED ON PAGE 143

WOLVES HILL

Strood
Copse

Alder
Gill

Elim Bible
Coll.
*Grenehurst*

B

Mill
Ho.

East
Wood

1

Clark's
Green

Clark's
Farm

Pleystowe Farm

A.A. Box

Temple
Wood

B

North
Barn

Works
Garage

Clock
Ho.

Taylor's
Farm

Taylor's
Gill

Lyne
Ho.

LYNE DRIVE

2

Brick
Works

ROAD

Sewells
Copse

RUSPER

Cowix

Upper Gages
Farm

Mugridges
Hill

Rome
Wood

Bonets
Farm

B

B

B

Newbarn
Farm

RUSPER

3

Shire
Mark

Surrey Boundary
West Sussex Boundary

Lipscomes
Corner

ROAD

HORSHAM

Pond

Old Barn

Boldings
Copse

Little
Benhams

STREET

Horsegills
Wood

*Kingsfold*

Friday Str.
Bri.

Benhams
Gill

The
Nunnery

Manns
Farm

ROAD

4

MARCHES RD.

Fm.

Kingsfold
Pl.

Great
Benhams

FRIDAY

Nunnery
Farm

Wheatsheaf
Inn' (P.H.)

Blackfriars
Bri.

Oldpark
Farm

Cripplegate
Farm

Curtiss
Farm

ROAD

ROAD

A24

Boldings Brook

GREEN

LANE

RUSPER

5

HORSHAM

A24

LANGHURSTWOOD

Northland Gill

Holming
Wood

Allingham
Wood

A           B           C

CONTINUED ON PAGE 158

0     500     1000 Yards

0     500     1000 Metres

D     E     F

Melton
Hall

Oaklands'
Park

1

RUSPER ROAD

Scrag  Copse

The
Jordans

Jordans

ORLTON LANE

Orlton  Copse

PRESTWOOD LA.

2

Surrey Boundary

West Sussex Boundary

Shucketts
Copse

Tilgate

Peter's
Farm

Furzefield
Wood

Nine
Acre
Rew

Langhurst

Hill Ho.

The
Mount

COWIX ROAD

COPHATCH

Rusper
Ho.

Venters

Rutland
Lodge

Gate Inn

3

HIGH ST.

Gar.

Rusper

EAST  ST.

Sch.

The Star
P.H.

STEERS HILL

COOKS MEAD

GARDENERS
GREEN

SMUGGLERS
LANE

Stumbleholm
Farm

Lambs
Green

Lamb
Inn (P.H.)

Cow
Wood

Rusper
Valley
Vineries

Hyde
Hill

4

Rusper
Court

Axmas
Farm

B

Baldhorns
Park

Westons
Farm

Ruebens Gill

South
Wood

House
Copse

Upper
Bewbush

Burnt Stubbs

Kilnwood
Fm.

B

FAYGATE LANE

Kilnwood

5

Carylls

Deer
Park

Coombers
Farm

Kilnwood
Copse

Culross

Fay
Gate
Place

D     E     F

CONTINUED ON PAGE **146**

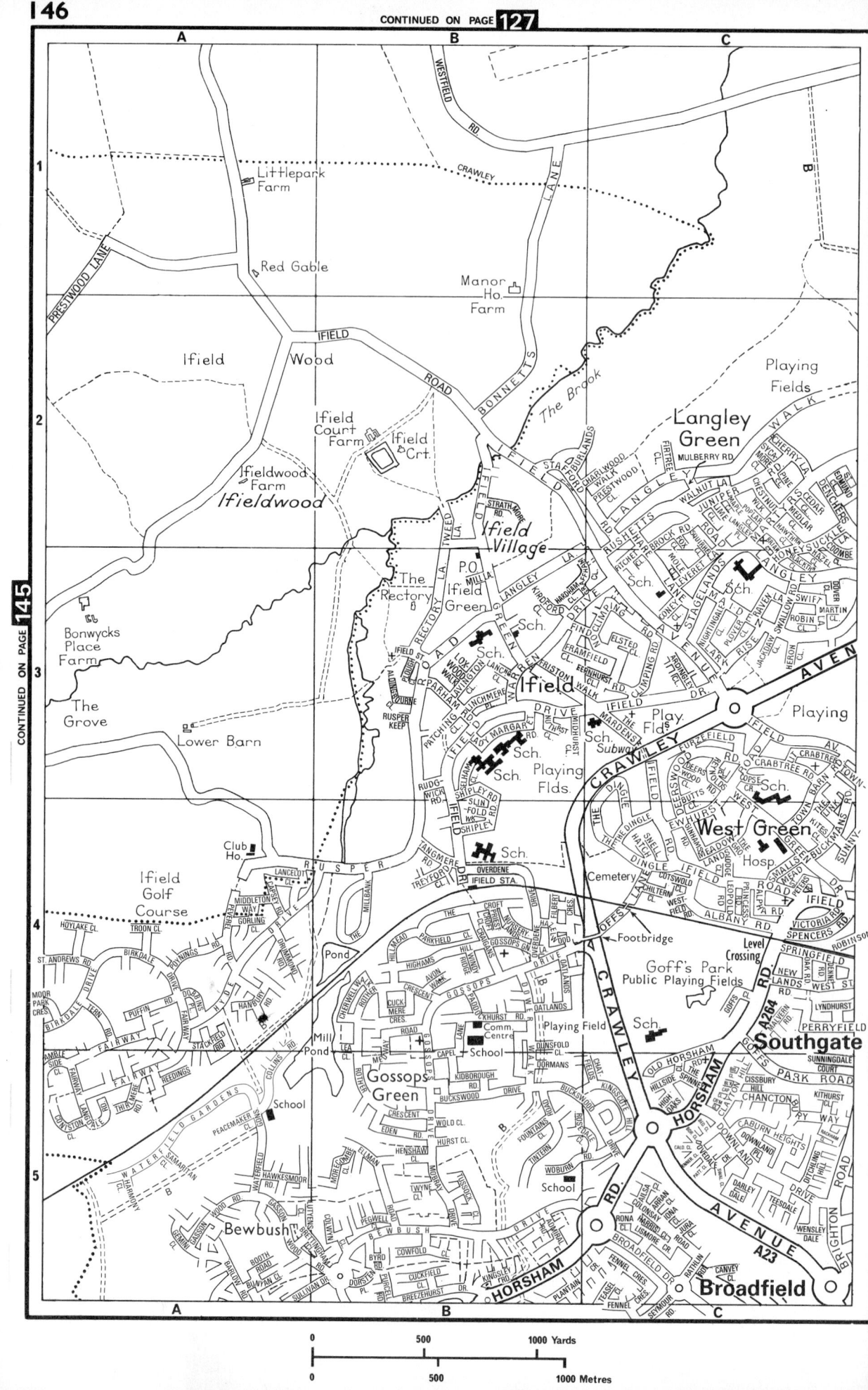

Lowfield Heath

Lovell Ho.

'The Greyhound' (P.H)

Gatwick Manor Hotel

Surrey & Sussex Crematorium

Forge Wood

Tinsley Green

County Oak

Industrial Estate

Sports Grd.

Sports Grd.

St. Hilda's Cl.

Playing Field

Northgate A2011

Playing Field

Sch.

Three Bridges

Playing Fields

Sch.

Sch.

Three Bridges Sta.

School

Fields

Fire Sta.

Town Hall

Tech. College

THREE BRIDGES

Mem. Gds.

Swimming Pool

Town Sports Centre

Paddling Pool

**CRAWLEY** Playing Fields

Furnace Green

Ford

Level Crossing

CRAWLEY STA.

EAST PARK

SOUTHGATE

Tilgate

CONTINUED ON PAGE **148**

CONTINUED ON PAGE **129**

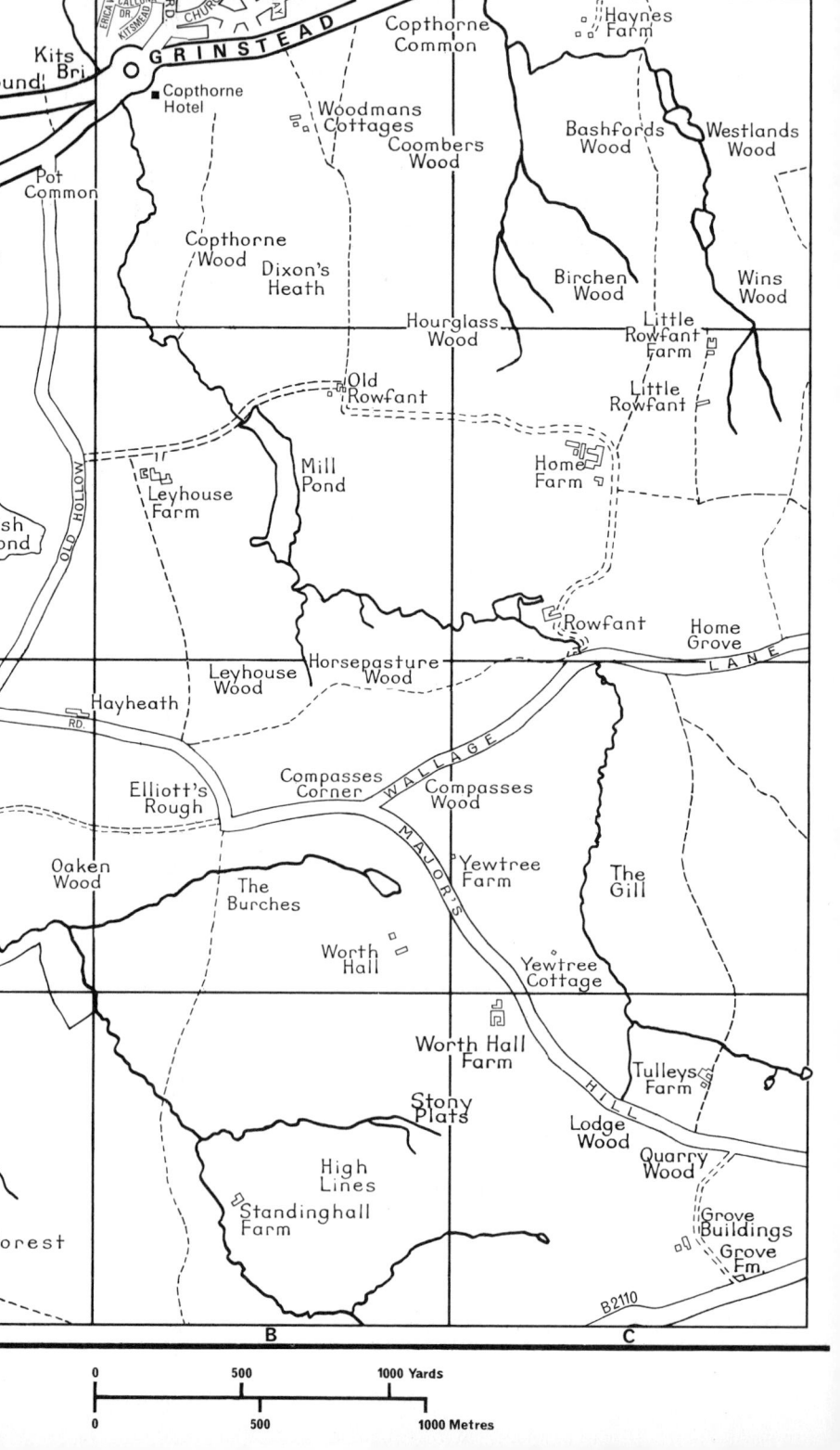

CONTINUED ON PAGE **147**

**Copthorne**

M23

SHIPLEYBRIDGE LANE

Prince Albert P.H.

Heathy Ground

Kits Bri

GRINSTEAD

Heathyground Pond

10 A264

Copthorne Hotel

Pot Common

Driver's Wood

A264 EAST

Stonelands Farm

Eiger Way
Roffeys Clo.
COPTHORNE BANK
P.O.
MEADOW
Sch.
BROOKHILL
WESTWAY
BROOKSIDE
P.O.
THE MEADOW
BRIDGELANDS CL.
BROOKVIEW
AKEHURST CL.
BROOKHILL CL.
ERICA WAY
CALLUNA DR.
KITSMEAD
CHURCH RD.
FAIRWAY
Sch.
BRAMB
NEW TOWN
CHURCH LANE
BEECHEY CL.
KNOWLE
KNOWLE
THE ELMS

Convent
BORERS ARMS RD.
Sch.
BEECHEY WAY
Golf Course
Club Ho.
THE DRIVE
DRIVE

P.H.
CLAY HALL LA.
Effingham Lodge
Roundabouts Farm
Sch.
Play Fld.
EAST HILL
EFFINGHAM
MILL

Surrey Boundary
West Sussex Boundary
Abergavenny Arms P.H.
ROAD
P.O.

Copthorne Common
Haynes Farm
Woodmans Cottages
Coombers Wood
Bashfords Wood
Westlands Wood

Copthorne Wood
Dixon's Heath
Hourglass Wood
Birchen Wood
Little Rowfant Farm
Wins Wood
Little Rowfant

Old Rowfant
Mill Pond
Home Farm

Leyhouse Farm

Fish Pond

Crabbet Park

OLD HOLLOW

THE GROOMS
STACE WAY
SHELLAND CL.
THE CANTER
BYERLEY WAY
THE SEDGEFIELD CL.
THE RIDINGS
LINGFIELD DR.
KELSO CL.
CHURCH RD.
THE RIDINGS
HEXHAM CL.
TURNERS
Sch.
HAZELHURST DR.
SALEHURST RD.

Leyhouse Wood
Horsepasture Wood
Rowfant
Home Grove
LANE

HILL
RD.
Hayheath
Elliott's Rough
Compasses Corner
Compasses Wood
WALLAGE
Yewtree Farm
The Gill

Worth
Street Hill

B
Worth Lodge
Oaken Wood
The Burches
Worth Hall
MAJOR'S
Yewtree Cottage

Worth Hall Farm
Stony Plats
Lodge Wood
HILL
Tulleys Farm
Quarry Wood
Grove Buildings
Grove Fm.

M23
B2036
Worthlodge Forest
High Lines
Standinghall Farm
B2110

| 0 | 500 | 1000 Yards |
|---|-----|------------|

| 0 | 500 | 1000 Metres |
|---|-----|-------------|

D    E    F

B2037   SNOW HILL   A264   A264   COPTHORNE

Effingham Park   GREEN LA.   CHESTER   Yewtree Farm   Nursery   TANGLEDAK MILL LA.

B2028   WEST PARK ROAD   CHAPEL LA.   FIELD CL.   Fellcot Farm   Nursery   RD.

Crkt. Grd.   LA.   The Bays   Little Frenches Farm   Furnace Wood   Miles's Farm   Surrey Boundary   TWITTEN LA.   ROWPLAT LA.   WARREN CL.   CRAWLEY DOWN RD.   Hall — 1

CRAWLEY ROAD   Great Frenches Park   Chestnut Lodge   Gibbshaven   FELBRIDGE   Thicket Cottage

P.H.   Furnace Pond   FURNACE FARM RD.   Furnace Fm.   HOPHURST HILL   Avenue Wood

Tel. Ex.   FELLCOTT LANE   LAKE VIEW   Waldenor   Smithfield Nurseries

Shepherd's Farm   Stubbits Wood   Cuttinglye Wood   ROAD   Gulledge Farm — 2

Fish Pond   CUTTINGLYE RD.   Park Fields Farm   Hophurst Farm   LANE   Gulledge Pit

Pescotts   Down Park Farm   Haven Farm   Gulledge Wood

Pescotts Wood   SANDY LANE   Crkt. Grd.   War Memorial   TILTWOOD DR.   Fish Ponds

RUFFWOOD   BUCKLEY PL.   STATION RD.   BOWERS PLACE RD.   LARCHS WAY   HAZEL WAY   Station Wd.   Rushetts Wood — 3

Crawley Down   Front Wood   SUNNY AV.   Sch.   VICARAGE   BURLEIGH WAY   WOODLAND DR.   Burleigh Wood

Huntsland   BEECH HOLME   KILN RD.   GRANGE ROAD   SANDHILL LANE

Swimming Pool   Bankton   Grange Farm   BURLEIGH LANE   Burleigh House Farm

WALLAGE LANE   Grange Hill   Sandhill   Fen Place Mill

Hundred Acres   Warren Wood   Medway River   Hurley Fm. — 4

Stone Croft   Clarke's Field   Home Wood   Moat Shaw   B2110

Miswell Wood   Burleigh Oaks Fm.   Mill Wood   Millwood Farm   Furze Field

MEDWAY   Fen Place   Furzewood Farm   Kingscote Nursery

NORTH ST.   Turners Hill   Fish Pond

Butcher's Wood   Rec. Grd.   P.O.   Fire Sta.   EAST ST.   Burleigh Farm   Tickeridge Farm   LANE

The Rayces   Sch.   The Crown (P.H.)   Spring Wood   Oak Lodge — 5

St. Leonard's Ch.   SELSFIELD RD.   B2028   Rashes Fm.   Rookery Wood   South Wood

Withypits   VOWEL   Stone Wood

Withypits Farm   Minepit Wood

D    E    F

CONTINUED ON PAGE 150

CONTINUED ON PAGE 131

CONTINUED ON PAGE 149

A       B       C

Felbridge Place
THE LIMES
St. John's Ch.
THE GLEBE
The Star P.H.
A264
COPTHORNE RD.
EASTBOURNE RD.
Sch.
CRAWLEY DN.
Felbridge
P.O.
Felbridge Court
Felbridge Hotel
FURZE LA.
PINE GR.
YEW LA.
STREAM PARK
LONDON RD.
A22
Baldwyns
Lowerbarn Farm
BUCKHURST MEAD
LOWDELL'S LANE
Spts. Grd. Sch.
LANE
FELCOVER
FURZEFIELD RD.
LOWDELLS DR.
SPRINGFIELD
HERMITAGE RD.
ELBRIDGE
Brown's Wood
VALE
BROWNS WOOD
MARLPIT CL.
EDEN
The Alders
ALDERS VIEW DRIVE
Surrey Boundary
Sussex Boundary
West
Queen Victoria Hospital
The Birches
IMBERHORNE WAY
HEATHCOTE DRIVE
Halsford Grn.
Rec. Grd.
SACKVILLE
KING GEORGE AV.
DORSET AV.
KNOLE GR.
WINDMILL LANE
HIGHFIELD RD.
DURMANS RD.
WILLOW RD.
DUNNINGS RD.
CHARWOODS
LINGFIELD RD.
HACKENDEN
Schs.
Convent
ELIZABETH AV.
GREENSTEDE AV.
HOLTYE RD.
A264
BLACKWELL FARM RD.
LYNTON PK. AV.
Blackwell
Mt. Noddy Cem.
Police H.Q.
Council Offices
EAST GRINSTEAD
Imberhorne Farm
FAIRLAWN CR.
OAKHURST GDNS.
MANOR RD.
LINDEN AV.
HALSFORD PARK RD.
MAYPOLE RD.
PARK
Sch.
CROSSWAYS
ST. EDWARDS
CAMPBELL CRES.
CHAPMANS LA.
FAIRLAWN DR.
MEADOW CROFT
PARKSIDE
LODGE
AVENUE
Lib.
St. AGNES RD.
SOUTH WICK
MOORE
GREEN HEDGES
ST. JOHN'S RD.
Play Fld.
Rec. Grd.
Fire Sta.
White Hart (P.H.)
Tower
SANDY LA.
BEECHING WAY
CRANSTON RD.
ESTLOTS DR.
Mem.
Imberhorne Farm
THE BLYTONS
BURNS WAY
BYRON
CHAUCER RD.
SHELLEY WAY
THE BRONTES
KIPLING CRES.
MILTON
Sta.
BROOKLANDS WAY
RAILWAY APP.
D P.O.
Swim. Pool
ORCHARD WAY
DALLAWAY GDNS.
QUEEN'S RD.
CHRISTOPHER DE LA WARR RD.
CANTELUPE RD.
CHEQUER RD.
HIGH ST.
CHURCH
LEWES RD.
OLD RD.
A22
Great Wood
Coles Wood
IMBERHORNE LANE
Barredale Court
Hill Place
Brook Ho.
Brooklands Park
WEST HILL ROAD
WEST HILL
WEST HURST
WEST HILL LA.
Cricket Grd.
HARVEST FARM
ACORN JCL.
KILDBRAVE RD.
ASHDOWN RD.
RIDGEWAY RD.
SOUTHLANDS RD.
STUART WAY
VICTORIA WAY
EDINBURGH WAY
CHESTNUT CL.
GARDEN HOUSE
PORTLAND RD.
HERONTYE DR.
LOWER MERE
MALLARD PL.
ARLFIELD RD.
Great Harwoods Farm
High Grove
Tilkhurst Farm
Crockshed Wood
TURNER'S HILL ROAD
SAINT HILL ROAD
COOMBE HILL ROAD
Hazleden Cross
Coombe Hall
Coombe Hall Farm
Bulrushes Farm
Sunnyside
NIGHTINGALE CL.
MILL WAY
PADDOCK GDNS.
STEPHENSON DRIVE
COLLINGWOOD CL.
FARADAY RD.
MORTON RD.
P.O.
CORONATION RD.
THE MEADS
FOREST VIEW RD.
STOCKWELL RD.
LISTER AV.
Rec. Grd.
River Medway
Hazleden
Fonthill Lodge
Imberley Lodge
Dunning's Wood
MEDWAY DR.
HOATHLY HILL
DUNNINGS ROAD
Boyles Farm
B2110
TURNER'S HILL
THE PLANTATION
Kingscote House
Swimming Bath
Fonthill
High Wood
Dunnings
Sunshine Home for Blind Babies
Rockingshill Wood
The Rough
Home Farm
Saint Hill Green
Saint Hill
Standen
Busses Farm
Ridge Hill Manor
Hen Robin Wood
Fish Pond
Cock Robin Wood
Hollybush Wood
Busses Wood
Weir Wood Reservoir

A       B       C

0    500    1000 Yards
0    500    1000 Metres

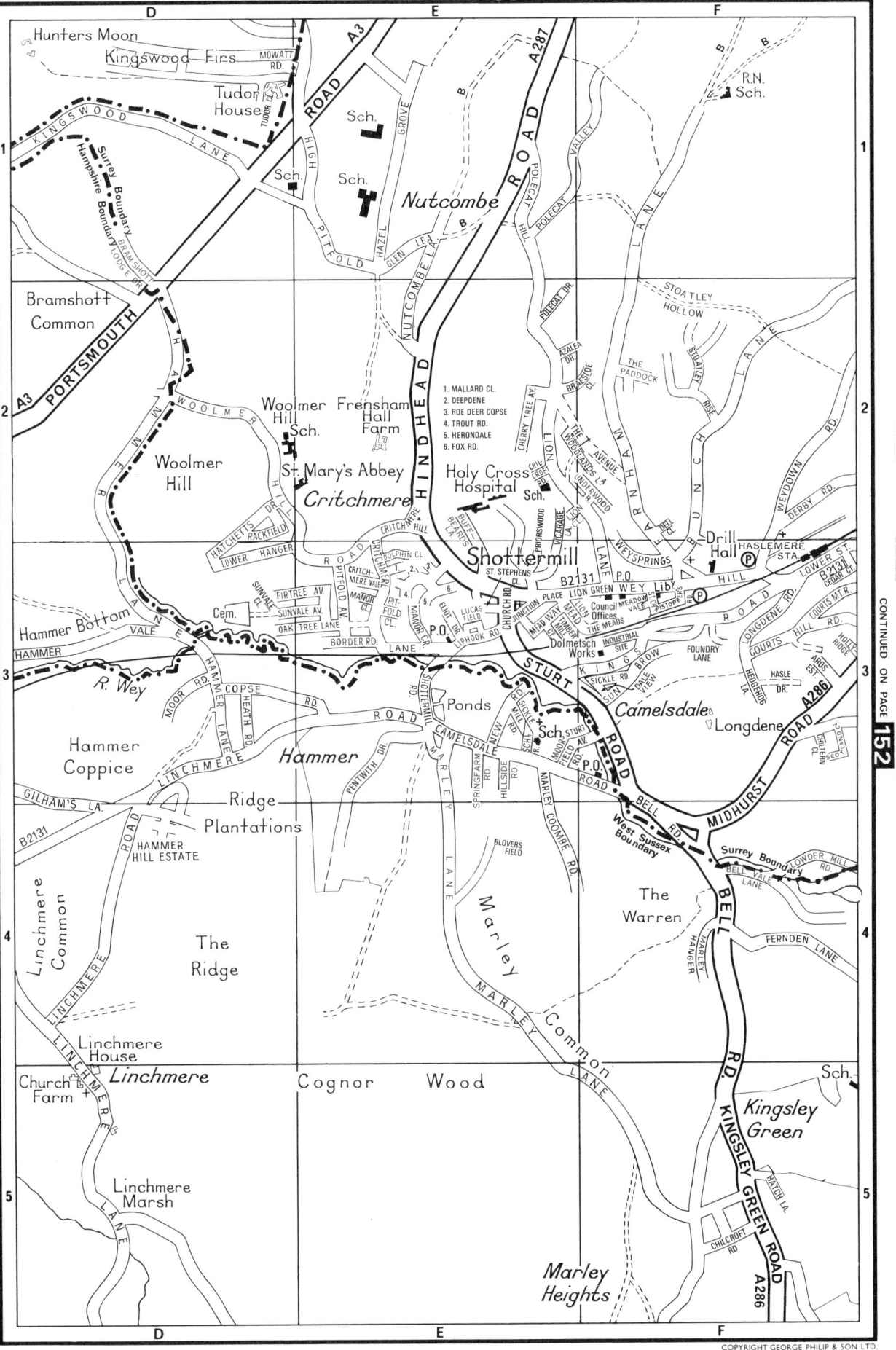

CONTINUED ON PAGE **152**

1. MALLARD CL.
2. DEEPDENE
3. ROE DEER COPSE
4. TROUT RD.
5. HERONDALE
6. FOX RD.

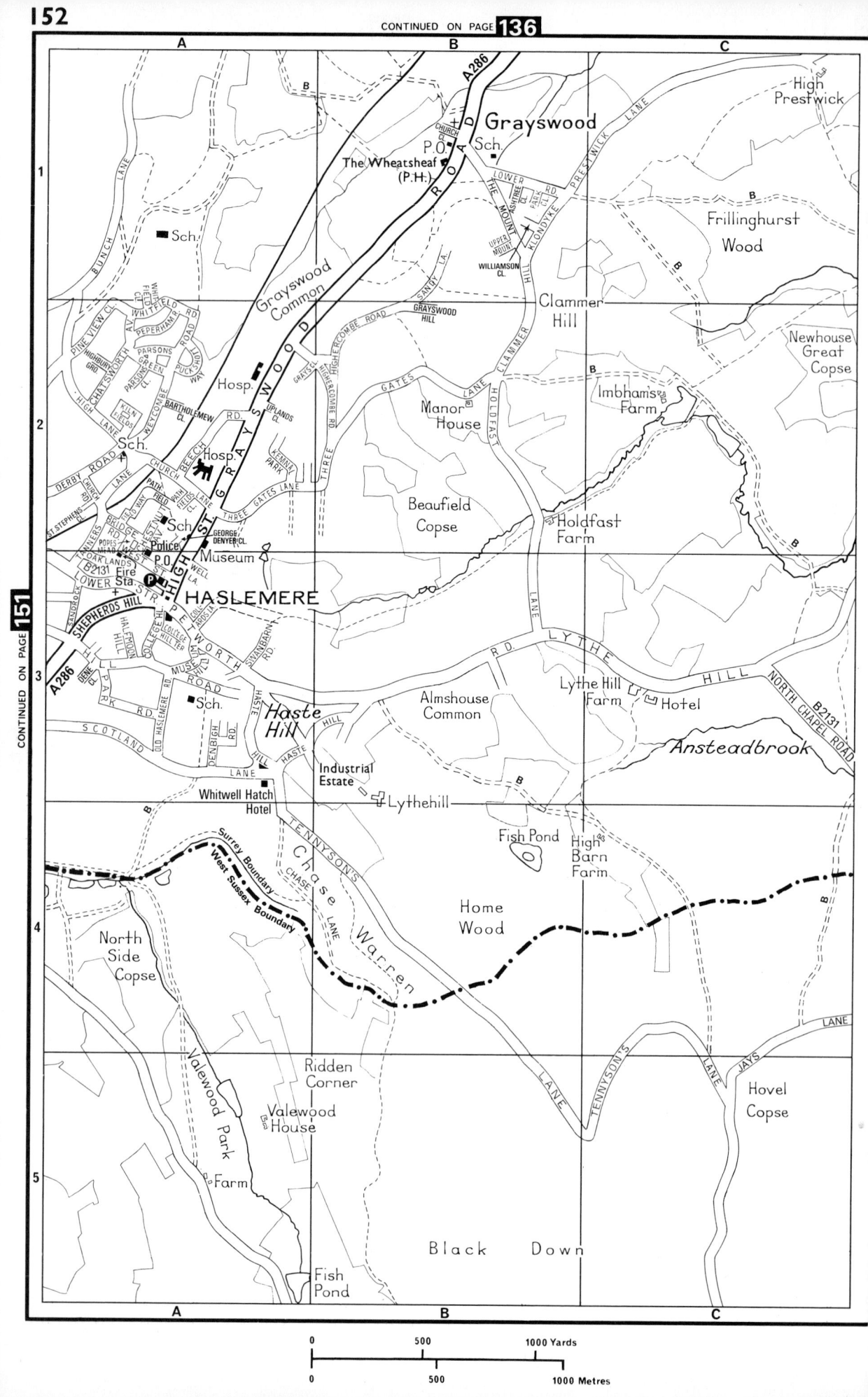

CONTINUED ON PAGE **136**

CONTINUED ON PAGE **151**

Grayswood

High
Prestwick

Frillinghurst
Wood

The Wheatsheaf
(P.H.)

Sch.

Clammer
Hill

Grayswood
Common

Grayswood
Hill

Newhouse
Great
Copse

Hosp.

Manor
House

Imbhams
Farm

Sch.

Hosp.

Beaufield
Copse

Holdfast
Farm

HASLEMERE

Museum

Police
P.O.
Fire Sta.

Haste
Hill

Almshouse
Common

Lythe Hill
Farm

Hotel

Ansteadbrook

Sch.

Whitwell Hatch
Hotel

Industrial
Estate

Lythehill

Fish Pond

High
Barn
Farm

Surrey Boundary
West Sussex Boundary

North
Side
Copse

Chase
Warren

Home
Wood

Hovel
Copse

Ridden
Corner

Valewood
House

Valewood Park

Farm

Black    Down

Fish
Pond

0        500        1000 Yards

0        500        1000 Metres

D     E     F

Sydenhurst

Birch Copse

Bethwins

A 283 ROAD

Frillinghurst Farm

ROUGH LA

Cherfold

Mill Farm

1

West End Farm

Great Copse

B

KILLINGHURST

COMBE LANE

WEST END LANE

FURNACE PLACE RD

CHIDDINGFOLD

2

Chaleshurst Copse

LANE

Gostrode Farm

Killinghurst Great Copse

Ramsnest Common

B

New Inn (P.H.)

B

Surrey Boundary

Fish Pond

B

B2131 LANE

RODGATE

West Sussex Boundary

CRIPPLECRUTCH HILL

Potlane Farm

B

3

Stilland Farm

Parkgate Farm

Fish Pond

LANE

SHILLINGLEE LANE

Dickhurst Great Copse

STILLAND

Newhouse Farm

CHAPEL ROAD

DICK

HURST LANE

Fisherstreet

The Tower

NORTH LANE

PETWORTH

Gospel Green

Eastland Farm

4

JAYS LANE

JOBSON'S

Jay's Copse

Frith Wood

Frith Hill

B

B

ROAD

A 283

5

JOBSON'S LANE

D     E     F

CONTINUED ON PAGE **154**

CONTINUED ON PAGE **138**

CONTINUED ON PAGE **153**

## A

PICKHURST ROAD

HIGH STREET

Botany Bay

Lagfold Copse

LANE PLAISTOW

B

Pickhurst

Tugley Farm

Oaken Wood

Canterbury Copse

The Hatchetts

BURNINGFOLD

Tugley Wood

Oak Wood

FISHER HILL

WHITES LANE

FISHER LANE

Fisherlane Farm

FISHER LANE

Durfold Hall Fm

Stick Factory

DURFOLD

Shillinglee Park

Downlands

Fisherlane Wood

Durfold Wood

Shortland Copse

SHORT'S WOOD

B

Surrey Boundary

West Sussex Boundary

SHILLINGLEE LANE

PLAISTOW

Newhouse Farm

Eastend Farm

Shorts Farm

ROAD

SHORT'S LANE

The Lake

Haymans Farm

Kingspark Wood

Mill Copse

Birchfold Copse

Dale's Farm

Chilsfold Farm

| 0 | | 500 | | 1000 Yards |
|---|---|---|---|---|

| 0 | | 500 | | 1000 Metres |
|---|---|---|---|---|

D

E

F

RD.

Fry's
Cross

RAMS LA.

KNIGHTONS LANE

HURLANDS LA.

Burningfold
Manor
Farm

B

Hurlands
Farm

Sprunks

Sedghurst
Wood

B

Sachel
Court

1

Knightons

B

Springbok
Farm

Hurlands
Copse

Ireland

Sydney Wood

B

Old
Knightons

Old
Lock
House

Velhurst
Farm

Priorswood
Farm

B

ROSEMARY LA.

Furzen
Farm

2

Tidy's
Copse

Le Barn

B

Upper
Ifold

B

B

B

Bonfire
Hanger

Oakhurst

Upper Ifold
Wood

B

Thirds
Copse

Sydney
Farm

B

Weald
Barkfold
Copse

B

Surrey Boundary
West Sussex Boundary

B

CONTINUED ON PAGE **156**

3

THE LANE

Hog Wood

Oakhurst

LANE

Ifold

B

HOGWOOD RD.

NORTH DRIVE

THE

Plaistow
Place

POUNDFIELD LA.

South
Wood

4

Pittsgate
Corner

ROAD

THE PLAISTOW CHALK

RIDE

Plaistow

Sch.

Inn

LOXWOOD

ROAD

DRIVE

ROAD

P.O.

Quennell
House

Chandlers
Farm

5

RICKMAN'S

LANE

Rumbolds
Farm

Foxbridge Farm

D

E

F

CONTINUED ON PAGE **140**

A    B    C

1

Park Farm
B2133 ROAD
LOXWOOD
Sch.
Alfold House Farm
A281
GUILDFORD
White Lea
Pallinghurst Farm
Males Farm
ROAD
HILLHOUSE LA.

ROSEMARY LANE
P.O.
P.H.
St. Nicholas
Alfold

2

Turtle Farm
Alfold Bars
Gar. P.H.
Loxwood Hall
Monkton Hook
Pallinghurst
B
Surrey Boundary
West Sussex Boundary
Tismans
HARNSFOLD LA.

CONTINUED ON PAGE **155**

Tokens Farm
LOXWOOD-GUILDFORD
Old Songhurst Farm

3

Merry Hills
Village Hall
Pephurst Wood

4

SPY LANE
Loxwood
Spy Farm
NICOLS FIELD WAY
BAKERS
BURY PLACE
P.O.
STATION RD.
ROAD
Loxwood Place Farm
LOXWOOD
Boardenhouse Farm
Jenkins's Wood
ROAD
Farm

Brewhurst Mill
Brewhurst Farm
St. John the Baptist

5

Headfoldswood Farm
Vicarage
PLAISTOW ROAD
Cricket Grd.
Flitchfold Farm
Hooklane Copse
DRUNGEWICK LANE
Drungewick Manor Ho.
Headfoldswood Common
SKIFF RD.
B2133
Lakers Lodge

A    B    C

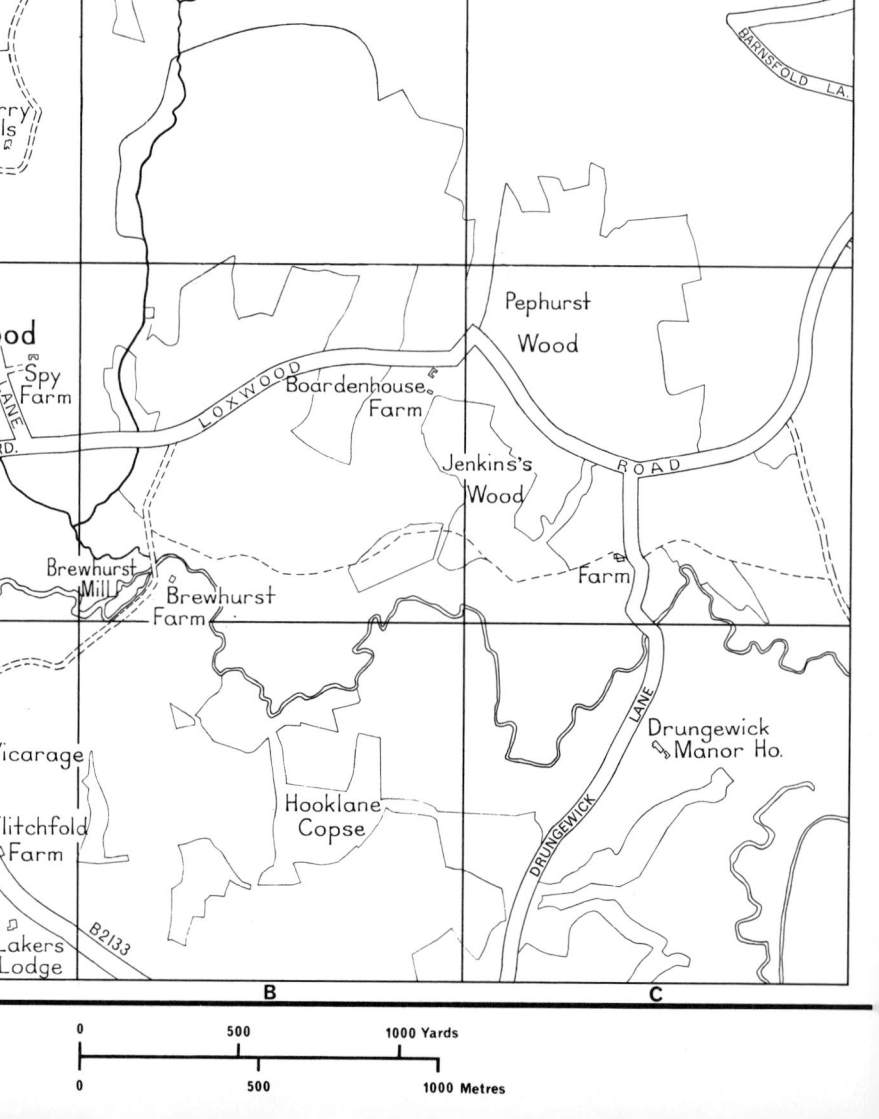

0    500    1000 Yards

0    500    1000 Metres

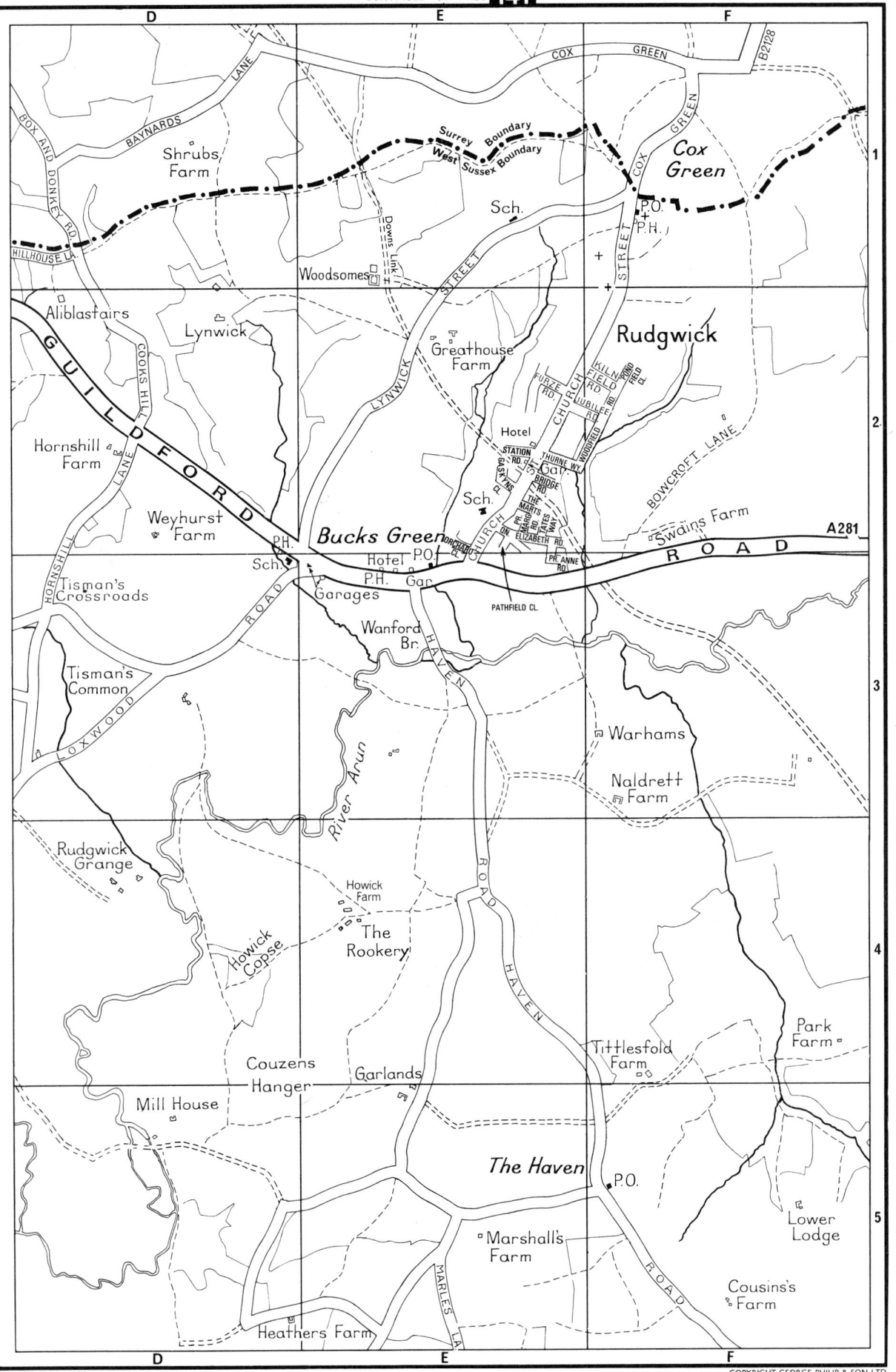

BAYNARDS LANE

BOX AND DONKEY RD.

HILLHOUSE LA.

Shrubs
Farm

Surrey   Boundary
West   Sussex   Boundary

Cox
Green

B2128

Sch.

COX   GREEN

STREET

COX   GREEN   STREET

P.O.
P.H.

Woodsomes

Downs Link

**Rudgwick**

Aliblastairs

Lynwick

LYNWICK   STREET

Greathouse
Farm

KILN
FIELD

POND
FIELD
CL.

JUBILEE

WOODFIELD

GUILDFORD

COOKS HILL LANE

Hornshill
Farm

Weyhurst
Farm

Hotel

STATION
RD.

THURNE WY.

BRIDGE
RD.

SWAN'S

FURZE
RD.

ST.
MARY'S

THE
MARTS

GATES WAY

ELIZABETH RD.

PR. ANNE
RD.

Sch.

Bucks Green

CHURCH

ROAD

HORNSHILL LANE

P.H.
Sch.

Hotel
P.H.
P.O.
Gar.

Garages

PATHFIELD CL.

Swains Farm

A 281
ROAD

BOWCROFT LANE

Tisman's
Crossroads

Wanford
Br.

HAVEN

Tisman's
Common

LOXWOOD ROAD

Warhams

Naldrett
Farm

River Arun

Rudgwick
Grange

Howick
Farm

Howick
Copse

The
Rookery

ROAD

HAVEN

Park
Farm

Couzens
Hanger

Garlands

Tittlesfold
Farm

Mill House

**The Haven**

P.O.

Lower
Lodge

MARLES LA.

Marshall's
Farm

ROAD

Cousins's
Farm

Heathers Farm

CONTINUED ON PAGES **143 & 144**

A    B    C

1

Graylands

Holbrook
Park

Little London Hill
A 24
B2199
KNOB HILL
DAUX
HILL
Warnham
BELL RD.
STATION
Restricted  times  of  access
WARNHAM
STA.
Level
Crossing
Boldings Brook
LANGHURSTWOOD
RAPELAND HILL
ROAD

2

Warnham Court
Sch.
Warnham Mill Pond
Millpond Plantation
COTTINGHAM
CAVENDISH AV.
LANE
LANE
GIBLETS LA.
NORTHLANDS

Deer
Park
ROBINHOOD
LANE
WARNHAM
Warnham
Mill Br.
Warnham Mill Pond
COOK
ROAD
HEATH
Channells Brook
PEARY CL.
FOX GLOVE AV.
BROOK
BEAVER CL.
COPSE CL.
GATEFORD DR.
CRES.
BADGERS CL.
Level
Crossing
ROUGH WY.
FARHALLS
FARM
RD.

3

HORSHAM BY-PASS
A24
WARNHAM RD.
AVE.
DRIVE
The Common
Sch.
AMUNDSEN RD.
POND TAIL
POND CL.
BROOME CL.
HEATH
ERICA WAY
NORTH HEATH
COLTSFOOT DR.
KESTREL
SORREL CL.
BLUEBELL CL.
SWALLOWTAIL
SERRIN
SISKIN
Little
Haven
TREADCROFT
SEARLES
OAK-LEIGH
LITTLE
HAVEN
MILLTHORPE RD.
ROAD
Sch.
Crawley
Forest Hosp.
COMPTONS
EARL'S WOOD CL.
HOWARD CL.
WINDMILL
COMPTS
BROW

4

HORSHAM
PARSONAGE
Level
Crossing
C.I.B.A.
Industrial
Estate
FOUNDRY
KING'S
Kingslea
School
A264
HARWOOD
ROAD
REDWING
REDKILN WAY
LINTOTT GDNS.
ST. GEORGE'S
GDNS.
ROAD
BUNTING
PATCHINGS
MILLAIS
Sch.
Sch.

5

A 281
GUILDFORD RD.
IRWIN DR.
Hills
Cemy
Hillside
The Crescent
BISHOPRIC
RD.
Sch.
High Sch.
Girls
WORTHING
RD.
EAST
ST.
CARFAX
QUEEN
ST.
BRIGHTON
RD.
A281
Town
Hall
Shopping
Precinct
Horsham
Football
Ground
ST. LEONARDS
ROAD
Oakhill
COMPTONS LA.
HERON
LANE
Sch.

A    B    C

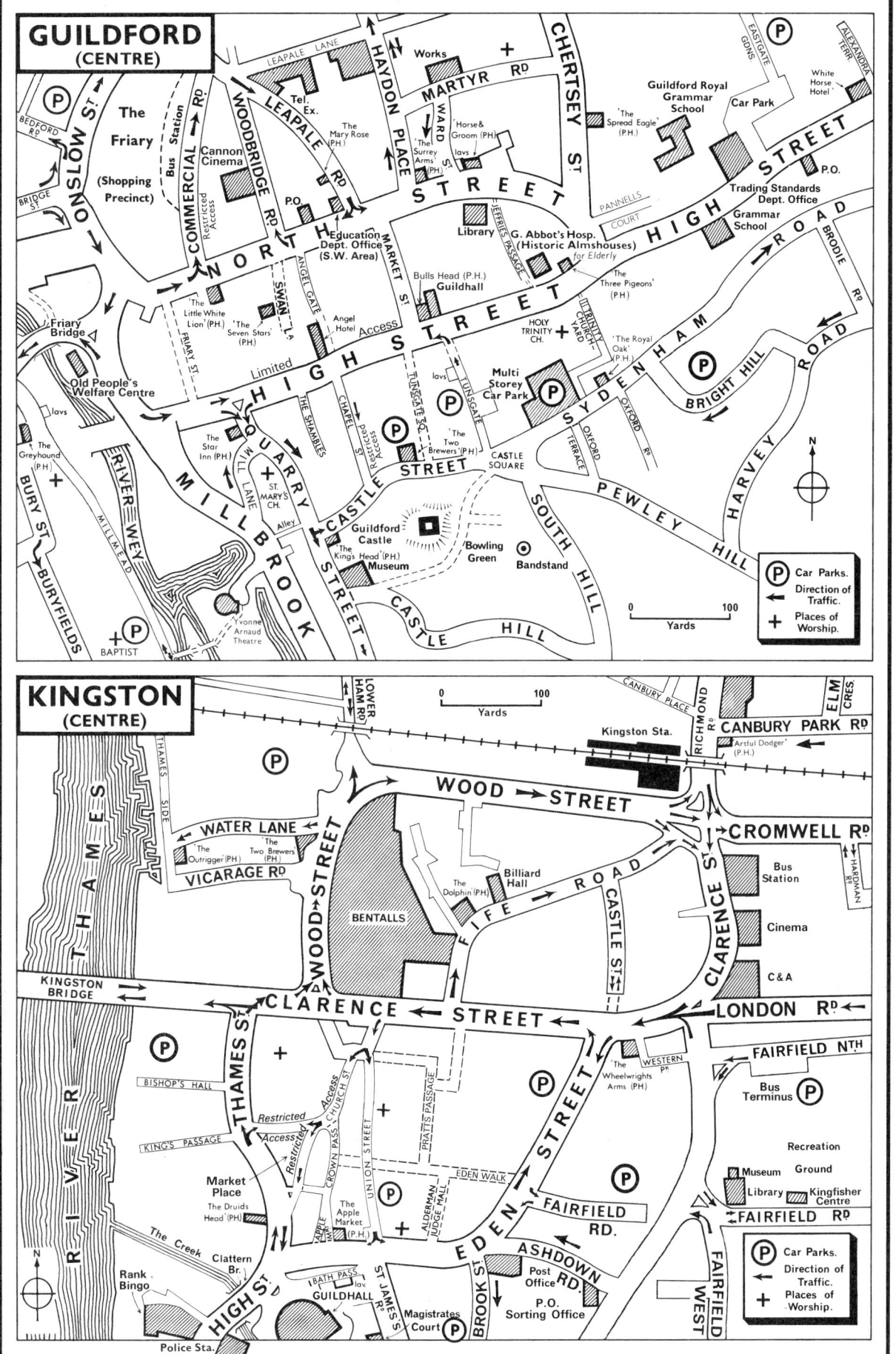

# GUILDFORD (CENTRE)

LEAPALE LANE
HAYDON PLACE
WARD ST
MARTYR RD
CHERTSEY ST
EASTGATE GDNS

Works

Tel. Ex.

The Mary Rose (P.H.)

'Horse & Groom (P.H.)
lavs
'The Surrey Arms' (P.H.)

'The Spread Eagle' (P.H.)

Guildford Royal Grammar School

Car Park

White Horse Hotel

BEDFORD RD
ONSLOW ST
The Friary
(Shopping Precinct)
Bus Station
COMMERCIAL RD
WOODBRIDGE RD
LEAPALE RD

Cannon Cinema

P.O.

Education Dept. Office (S.W. Area)

ANGEL GATE
MARKET ST
SWAN LA.

Library

Jeffries Passage
G. Abbot's Hosp. (Historic Almshouses) for Elderly

PANNELLS COURT

HIGH STREET

Trading Standards Dept. Office

P.O.

Grammar School

BRODIE RD

BRIDGE ST

'The Little White Lion' (P.H.)
'The Seven Stars' (P.H.)

Angel Hotel Access

Bulls Head (P.H.) Guildhall

HOLY TRINITY CH.
TRINITY CHURCH-YARD

'The Three Pigeons' (P.H.)

'The Royal Oak' (P.H.)

SYDENHAM ROAD

OXFORD RD

BRIGHT HILL

HARVEY ROAD

Friary Bridge

FRIARY ST

Old People's Welfare Centre

lavs

Limited Access

HIGH STREET

THE SHAMBLES
CHAPEL ST

lavs
TUNSGATE

Multi Storey Car Park

OXFORD TERRACE

The Greyhound (P.H.)

RIVER WEY
MILLMEAD

MILLBROOK
QUARRY STREET

MILL LANE
St. MARYS CH.

The Star Inn (P.H.)

'The Two Brewers' (P.H.)

STREET

CASTLE SQUARE

PEWLEY HILL
SOUTH HILL

N

BURY ST
BURYFIELDS

Alley

Guildford Castle
The King's Head (P.H.) Museum

Bowling Green

Bandstand

CASTLE HILL

0    100
Yards

P
BAPTIST

Yvonne Arnaud Theatre

P  Car Parks.
←  Direction of Traffic.
✝  Places of Worship.

# KINGSTON (CENTRE)

LOWER HAM RD
THAMES SIDE

0    100
Yards

CANBURY PLACE
RICHMOND RD
CANBURY PARK RD
ELM CRES.

Kingston Sta.

'Artful Dodger' (P.H.)

WOOD    STREET

CROMWELL RD

HARDMAN RD

WATER LANE

WOOD STREET

The Outrigger (P.H.)
The Two Brewers (P.H.)

VICARAGE RD

The Dolphin (P.H.)

BENTALLS

Billiard Hall

FIFE ROAD

CASTLE ST

Bus Station

Cinema

C & A

THAMES

KINGSTON BRIDGE

CLARENCE    STREET

LONDON RD

FAIRFIELD NTH

RIVER

THAMES ST

BISHOP'S HALL

KING'S PASSAGE

Restricted Access

CHURCH ST
Restricted Access

CROWN PASS

Restricted

UNION STREET

PRATTIS PASSAGE

EDEN WALK

'The Wheelwrights Arms' (P.H.)

WESTERN RD

EDEN STREET

Bus Terminus

Recreation Ground

Museum
Library

Kingfisher Centre

FAIRFIELD RD.

FAIRFIELD WEST

Market Place
The Druids Head (P.H.)

The Apple Market

ALDERMAN JUDGE MALL

The Creek

Clattern Br.

Rank Bingo

BATH PASS
lav
GUILDHALL
ST JAMES RD

HIGH ST.

Magistrates Court

FAIRFIELD RD.

BROOK ST
ASHDOWN RD.
Post Office
P.O. Sorting Office

P  Car Parks.
←  Direction of Traffic.
✝  Places of Worship.

Police Sta.

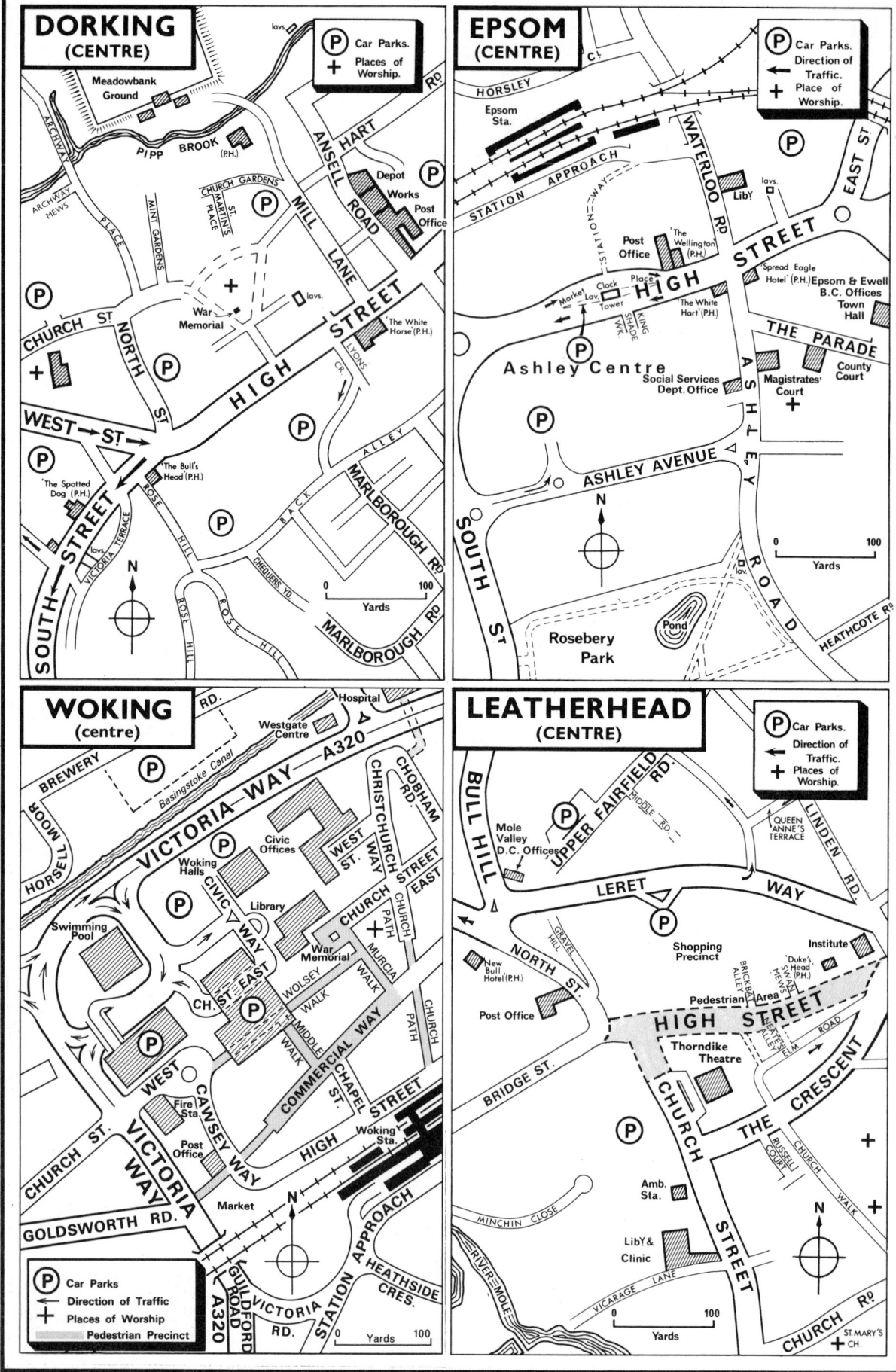

# DORKING (CENTRE)

Meadowbank Ground

PIPP BROOK (P.H.)

ARCHWAY

ARCHWAY MEWS

MINT GARDENS

CHURCH GARDENS
ST. MARTIN'S PLACE

PLACE

Depot Works

Post Office

HART LANE

ANSELL ROAD

MILL LANE

P

War Memorial

lavs.

CHURCH ST.

NORTH ST.

'The White Horse' (P.H.)

HIGH STREET

CR.

LYONS

WEST ST.

'The Bull's Head' (P.H.)

'The Spotted Dog' (P.H.)

SOUTH STREET

VICTORIA TERRACE

lavs.

ROSE HILL

CHEQUERS YD.

ROSE HILL

BACK ALLEY

MARLBOROUGH RD.

MARLBOROUGH RD.

N

0 Yards 100

Car Parks.
Places of Worship.

# EPSOM (CENTRE)

HORSLEY

Epsom Sta.

STATION APPROACH

STATION WAY

WATERLOO RD.

EAST ST.

Liby

lavs.

Post Office

'The Wellington' (P.H.)

Place

Market

Clock Tower

Lav.

KING SHADE WK.

HIGH STREET

'The White Hart' (P.H.)

Spread Eagle Hotel (P.H.)

Epsom & Ewell B.C. Offices
Town Hall

THE PARADE

County Court

Magistrates' Court

ASHLEY ROAD

Ashley Centre

Social Services Dept. Office

P

ASHLEY AVENUE

N

SOUTH ST.

Rosebery Park

Pond

HEATHCOTE RD.

0 Yards 100

Car Parks.
Direction of Traffic.
Place of Worship.

# WOKING (centre)

RD.

Hospital

Westgate Centre

BREWERY

HORSELL

VICTORIA WAY A320

Basingstoke Canal

CHOBHAM RD.

CHRISTCHURCH WAY

Civic Offices

Woking Halls

WEST ST.

CIVIC WAY

Library

Swimming Pool

CHURCH STREET EAST

CHURCH PATH

War Memorial

MURCIA WALK

WOLSEY WALK

CH. ST. EAST

MIDDLE WALK

CHAPEL ST.

COMMERCIAL WAY

CHURCH PATH

WEST

CAWSEY WAY

Fire Sta.

Post Office

HIGH STREET

Woking Sta.

VICTORIA WAY

Market

GOLDSWORTH RD.

GUILDFORD ROAD A320

STATION APPROACH

HEATHSIDE CRES.

N

0 Yards 100

Car Parks
Direction of Traffic
Places of Worship
Pedestrian Precinct

# LEATHERHEAD (CENTRE)

UPPER FAIRFIELD RD.

BULL HILL

Mole Valley D.C. Offices

PADDLE RD.

QUEEN ANNE'S TERRACE

LINDEN RD.

LERET WAY

Shopping Precinct

Institute

'Duke's Head' (P.H.)

BRICK ALLEY

SWAN MEWS

GATES ALLEY

ELM

New Bull Hotel (P.H.)

NORTH ST.

GRAVEL HILL

Pedestrian Area

HIGH STREET

ROAD

THE CRESCENT

Post Office

Thorndike Theatre

CHURCH STREET

CHURCH WALK

BRIDGE ST.

RUSSELL COURT

Amb. Sta.

MINCHIN CLOSE

RIVER MOLE

Liby & Clinic

VICARAGE LANE

N

0 Yards 100

CHURCH RD.

ST. MARY'S CH.

Car Parks.
Direction of Traffic.
Places of Worship.

# INDEX

## ABREVIATIONS

App.—Approach
Av.—Avenue
Cl.—Close
Cres.—Crescent
Ct.—Court
Dri.—Drive
Gdns.—Gardens
Gro.—Grove
Gt.—Great

La.—Lane
Pk.—Park
Pl.—Place
Rd.—Road
Sq.—Square
St.—Street, Saint
Ter.—Terrace
Wk.—Walk

1

| | | | |
|---|---|---|---|
| Branksmere Rd. | 1B 38 | Bridge Gdns., E. Molesey | 2E 35 |
| Branksome Cl., Camberley | 5B 44 | Bridge Gdns., Sunbury | 5E 15 |
| Branksome Cl., Walton-on- | 5B 34 | Bridge La., Vir. Water | 3D 31 |
| Thames | | Bridge Rd., Aldershot | 1C 96 |
| Branksome Park Rd. | 5B 44 | Bridge Rd., Bagshot | 2E 45 |
| Branksome Rd., Brixton | 1A 22 | Bridge Rd., Beckenham | 5A 24 |
| Branksome Hill Rd., York Tn. | 4E 43 | Bridge Rd., Camberley | 1D 61 |
| Branksome Way | 1D 37 | Bridge Rd., Chertsey | 4B 32 |
| Bransby Rd. | 2E 53 | Bridge Rd., Chessington | 1E 53 |
| Branston Rd., Deadwater | 5D 133 | Bridge Rd., Cobham | 1A 68 |
| Branston Rd., Kew | 4B 8 | Bridge Rd., Cove | 5C 60 |
| Brantridge Rd. | 5E 147 | Bridge Rd., Cranleigh | 2C 140 |
| Brants Bridge | 1E 27 | Bridge Rd., East Molesey | 3E 35 |
| Brantwood Cl. | 5D 49 | Bridge Rd., Epsom | 4B 54 |
| Brantwood Gdns. | 5D 49 | Bridge Rd., Godalming | 1D 119 |
| Brantwood Rd., Herne Hill | 1B 22 | Bridge Rd., Haslemere | 2A 152 |
| Brantwood Rd., Sanderstead | 3F 57 | Bridge Rd., Rudgwick | 2E 157 |
| Brassey La. | 3A 94 | Bridge Rd., Sunninghill | 3D 29 |
| Brassey Rd. | 3F 93 | Bridge Rd., Sutton | 2F 55 |
| Brathway Rd. | 2B 20 | Bridge Rd., Twickenham | 1A 18 |
| Bravington Cl. | 3D 33 | Bridge Rd., Wallington | 1C 56 |
| Braxted Park | 5A 22 | Bridge Rd., Weybridge | 1A 50 |
| Bray Gardens | 1F 65 | Bridge St., Colnbrook | 3A 7 |
| Bray Rd., Guildford | 1B 100 | Bridge St., Godalming | 2D 119 |
| Bray Rd., Stoke D'Aber. | 1C 68 | Bridge St., Guildford | 1C 100 |
| Braycourt Av. | 4A 34 | Bridge St., Leatherhead | 4F 69 |
| Braye Cl. | 3D 43 | Bridge St., Staines | 4F 13 |
| Braywood Av. | 5D 13 | Bridge St., Walton | 4F 33 |
| Brazier La. | 4A 10 | Bridge View | 4F 29 |
| Brazil Cl. | 4A 40 | Bridge Way, Chipstead | 3D 73 |
| Breakfield | 1A 74 | Bridge Way, Whitton | 2D 17 |
| Breamwater Gdns. | 3A 18 | Bridgefield | 4B 96 |
| Brecon Cl. | 2A 40 | Bridgefield Cl. | 1A 72 |
| Bredon Rd. | 4D 41 | Bridgefield Rd. | 2E 55 |
| Breech La. | 1C 88 | Bridgeham Cl. | 1A 50 |
| Breezehurst Dr. | 5B 146 | Bridgeham Way | 3E 129 |
| Bregsells Dr. | 2D 125 | Bridgelands Cl. | 1B 148 |
| Bremer Rd. | 3A 14 | Bridgeman Rd. | 5F 17 |
| Bremner Av. | 2A 128 | Bridgemead | 1B 80 |
| Brenchley Gdns. | 1E 23 | Bridges La. | 1D 57 |
| Brenda Rd. | 3D 21 | Bridgewater Rd. | 2B 50 |
| Brende Gdns. | 2D 35 | Bridgewood Rd., Stoneleigh | 1C 54 |
| Brendon Cl. | 2A 52 | Bridgewood Rd., Worcester Pk. | 5F 37 |
| Brendon Dr. | 2A 52 | Bridgham Cl. | 1A 50 |
| Brent Lea | 3A 8 | Bridgman Rd. | 1D 9 |
| Brent Rd., Brentford | 3A 8 | Bridle Cl., Epsom | 5B 54 |
| Brent Rd., Selsdon | 3B 58 | Bridle Cl., Grayshott | 5C 134 |
| Brentford | 2B 8 | Bridle Cl., Ruxley | 1A 54 |
| Brentmoor Rd. | 5C 44 | Bridle Cl., Sunbury | 2A 34 |
| Brentway | A3 8 | Bridle Rd. | 5A 42 |
| Brentwick Gdns. | 2B 8 | Bridle Rd., Claygate | 2C 52 |
| Bretharte Rd. | 2E 61 | Bridle Rd., Epsom | 5B 54 |
| Bretlands Cl. | 5F 31 | Bridle Road, The | 3D 57 |
| Brettgrave | 3A 54 | Bridle Way, Crawley | 3F 147 |
| Brewer Rd. | 5D 147 | Bridle Way, Croydon | 1D 59 |
| Brewer St. | 4F 91 | Bridle Way, The | 1C 56 |
| Brewery La. | 5F 49 | Bridlepath Way | 2F 15 |
| Brewery Rd. | 2C 65 | Bridport Rd. | 2B 40 |
| Brian Av. | 4A 58 | Brier Lea | 1E 89 |
| Briane Rd. | 3A 54 | Brierley | 2D 59 |
| Briar Av., Lightwater | 4E 45 | Bright Hill | 1D 101 |
| Briar Av., Norbury | 5A 22 | Brightfield Rd. | 1C 24 |
| Briar Banks | 3B 56 | Brightlands Rd. | 4F 89 |
| Briar Cl., Byfleet | 4E 49 | Brightling Rd. | 1A 24 |
| Briar Cl., Hanworth | 4C 16 | Brightman Rd. | 2C 20 |
| Briar Cl., Isleworth | 1F 17 | Brighton Cl. | 1E 49 |
| Briar Ct. | 2C 146 | Brighton Rd., Addlestone | 1E 49 |
| Briar Gr. | 5A 58 | Brighton Rd., Aldershot | 1D 97 |
| Briar Hill | 4D 57 | Brighton Rd., Burgh Heath | 3A 72 |
| Briar La., Addington | 1D 59 | Brighton Rd., Coulsdon | 2F 73 |
| Briar La., Woodcote Grn. | 3B 56 | Brighton Rd., Godalming | 2D 119 |
| Briar Rd., Norbury | 2A 40 | Brighton Rd., Hooley | 4E 73 |
| Briar Rd., Send | 5E 65 | Brighton Rd., Horley | 3A 128 |
| Briar Rd., Shepperton | 3D 33 | Brighton Rd., Horsham | 5B 158 |
| Briar Rd., Twickenham | 2E 17 | Brighton Rd., Kingswood | 1E 89 |
| Briar Way | 3B 82 | Brighton Rd., Purley | 5D 57 |
| Briar Wk. | 5F 9 | Brighton Rd., Redhill | 5B 90 |
| Briars Cl. | 5B 60 | Brighton Rd., Southgate | 5C 146 |
| Briars Ct. | 5B 52 | Brighton Rd., Surbiton | 3A 36 |
| Briars Wood | 2C 128 | Brightside Av. | 5B 14 |
| Briarwood Rd., Clapham | 1F 21 | Brightside Rd. | 1B 24 |
| Briarwood Rd., Brookwood | 3A 64 | Brightwell Cres. | 4D 21 |
| Briarwood Rd., Stoneleigh | 2B 54 | Brightwells Rd. | 3A 96 |
| Brick Kiln La. | 3B 94 | Brigstock Rd., Thornton Heath | 3B 40 |
| Brickbat Alley, Leatherhead | 160 | Brigstock Rd., Woodmansterne | 1E 73 |
| Brickfield Rd., Norbury | 1B 40 | Brimshot La. | 3D 47 |
| Brickfield Rd., Outwood | 4B 110 | Brindles, The | 2B 72 |
| Brickhouse La. | 1B 130 | Brinkley Rd. | 5F 37 |
| Bricksbury Hill | 1A 96 | Brinn's La. | 5D 43 |
| Brickwood Rd. | 5C 40 | Brisbane Av. | 1C 38 |
| Brickyard Copse | 1D 143 | Briscoe Rd. | 5D 21 |
| Brickyard La. | 3B 104 | Bristol Cl., Stanwell | 1C 14 |
| Bridalway Cl. | 3C 54 | Bristol Cl., Three Bridges | 2F 147 |
| Bridge Av. | 2F 9 | Bristol Gdns. | 2F 19 |
| Bridge Cl., Byfleet | 4A 50 | Bristol Rd. | 3C 38 |
| Bridge Cl., Horsell | 2C 64 | Bristow Cres. | 1D 61 |
| Bridge End | 1D 61 | Bristow Rd., Camberley | 1D 61 |

| | | | |
|---|---|---|---|
| Bristow Rd., Gypsy Hill | 4C 22 | Brockenhurst Rd., South Ascot | 3C 28 |
| Bristow Rd., Waddon | 1D 57 | Brockenhurst Way | 1F 39 |
| Britain Rd. | 1E 51 | Brockham | 1C 106 |
| Britannia Way | 2C 14 | Brockham Av. | 3A 74 |
| British Grove | 2E 9 | Brockham Cl. | 4B 20 |
| Briton Cres. | 4A 58 | Brockham Cres. | 2E 59 |
| Briton Hill Rd. | 3A 58 | Brockham Green | 1C 106 |
| Brittania Rd. | 3B 36 | Brockham Lane | 5F 87 |
| Brittens Cl. | 3E 81 | Brockham Rise | 4B 24 |
| Britton Cl. | 4A 58 | Brockhamhurst Rd. | 4C 106 |
| Brixton Hill | 2A 22 | Brocklebank Rd. | 2C 20 |
| Brixton Water La. | 1A 22 | Brockley Gro. | 1A 24 |
| Broad Acre | 5A 100 | Brockley Hal Rd. | 1F 23 |
| Broad Cl. | 5B 34 | Brockley Park | 2F 23 |
| Broad Green Av. | 4B 40 | Brockley Rise | 2F 23 |
| Broad High Way | 5E 51 | Brockley Rd. | 1F 23 |
| Broad La., Borough Green | 2D 27 | Brockley View | 2F 23 |
| Broad La., Hampton Hill | 5D 17 | Brockley Way | 1F 23 |
| Broad Lane, Parkgate | 2A 126 | Brockleycombe | 1C 50 |
| Broad Oaks Way | 3C 42 | Brocks Cl. | 1E 119 |
| Broad Ride | 1B 30 | Brocks Dr., Guildford | 3C 80 |
| Broad St., Donkey Town | 5A 46 | Brocks Dr., N. Cheam | 5A 38 |
| Broad St., Guildford | 4D 81 | Brocks Way | 3C 30 |
| Broad St., Wokingham | 2D 25 | Brockway | 2C 30 |
| Broad Walk, Burgh Heath | 3A 72 | Brockway Cl. | 5B 82 |
| Broad Walk, Camberley | 2E 61 | Brockwell Park Gdns. | 2B 22 |
| Broad Walk, Caterham | 4D 75 | Broderick Grove | 1A 86 |
| Broad Walk, Crawley | 4D 147 | Brodie Rd. | 1D 101 |
| Broad Walk, Hooley | 5E 73 | Brodrick Rd. | 3D 21 |
| Broadacre | 4A 14 | Broke Ct. | 4B 82 |
| Broadacres | 4D 81 | Brokes Cres. | 4E 89 |
| Broadbridge La. | 2E 129 | Brokes Rd. | 4E 89 |
| Broadcoombe | 2C 58 | Brokhill Cl. | 1B 148 |
| Broadfield Cl. | 3F 71 | Bromford Ct. | 5A 94 |
| Broadfield Dr. | 5C 146 | Bromley Av. | 5C 24 |
| Broadfield Rd., Catford | 2C 24 | Bromley Cres. | 2C 42 |
| Broadfield Rd., Hoe | 4E 103 | Bromley Gdns. | 2C 42 |
| Broadfields | 3E 35 | Bromley Gro. | 1B 42 |
| Broadford La. | 4D 47 | Bromley Hill | 5C 24 |
| Broadford Rd. | 4C 100 | Bromley Rd., Beckenham | 1B 42 |
| Broadham Green La. | 4E 93 | Bromley Rd., Lammas Park | 1A 8 |
| Broadhurst | 1B 70 | Brompton Cl. | 1C 16 |
| Broadhurst Gdns. | 2B 108 | Bronson Rd. | 1A 38 |
| Broadland Way | 3E 37 | Brontes, The | 2B 150 |
| Broadlands, Frimley | 3F 61 | Brook | 2C 136 |
| Broadlands, Horley | 2C 128 | Brook Av. | 1C 96 |
| Broadlands Av., Shepperton | 3E 33 | Brook Cl., Ash | 4C 78 |
| Broadlands Av., Streatham | 3A 22 | Brook Cl., Dorking | 5D 87 |
| Broadlands Dr. | 3E 75 | Brook Cl., Raynes Park | 2F 37 |
| Broadlands, The, | 3C 16 | Brook Cl., Sandhurst | 3E 43 |
| Broadley Grn. | 2A 46 | Brook Cl., West Bedfont | 2D 15 |
| Broadleys | 3D 15 | Brook Dr., Ashford | 5F 15 |
| Broadmead, Ashtead | 2B 70 | Brook Dr., Bracknell | 2E 27 |
| Broadmead, Bellingham | 3A 24 | Brook Farm Rd. | 1B 68 |
| Broadmead, Horley | 2C 128 | Brook Gdns. | 1D 37 |
| Broadmead Av. | 4E 37 | Brook Hill, Albury Heath | 4C 102 |
| Broadmead Rd. | 4E 65 | Brook Hill, Brook | 2C 136 |
| Broadmeads | 4E 65 | Brook Hill, Oxted | 3E 93 |
| Broadmoor Rd. | 1D 43 | Brook La., Brook | 4C 102 |
| Broadoaks Cres. | 5E 49 | Brook La., Chobham | 4D 47 |
| Broadstone Rd. | 4B 142 | Brook Lane North | 2A 8 |
| Broadview Rd. | 5F 21 | Brook Rd., Bagshot | 2E 45 |
| Broadwater Cl., Hersham | 1D 51 | Brook Rd., Brentford | 3C 8 |
| Broadwater Cl., West Byfleet | 4C 48 | Brook Rd., Camberley | 1C 60 |
| Broadwater Cl., Wraysbury | 2D 13 | Brook Rd., Chilworth | 4F 101 |
| Broadwater La. | 1E 119 | Brook Rd., Earlswood | 1E 109 |
| Broadwater Rise | 1E 101 | Brook Rd., Hook | 5B 36 |
| Broadwater Rd. | 4D 21 | Brook Rd., Horsham | 3C 158 |
| Broadwater Rd. North | 1D 51 | Brook Rd., Merstham | 3C 90 |
| Broadway, Bracknell | 1D 27 | Brook Rd., South | 3A 8 |
| Broadway, Brookwood | 3F 63 | Brook Rd., Thornton Heath | 2B 40 |
| Broadway, Hammersmith | 2F 9 | Brook Rd., Twickenham | 1F 17 |
| Broadway, Laleham | 2B 32 | Brook Rd., Wormley | 2E 137 |
| Broadway, Stoneleigh | 1B 54 | Brook St. | 1B 36 |
| Broadway, Tolworth | 4C 36 | Brookdale Rd. | 2A 24 |
| Broadway, Thames Ditton | 4E 35 | Brooke Forest | 3C 80 |
| Broadway, Virginia Water | 2C 30 | Brookers Cl. | 2A 70 |
| Broadway, Woking | 2D 65 | Brookers Corner | 1D 43 |
| Broadway Av., Richmond | 1A 18 | Brookers Row | 1D 43 |
| Broadway Av., Selhurst | 3C 40 | Brookfield Av., Carshalton | 1A 56 |
| Broadway Cl. | 5B 58 | Brookfield Av., The Wrythe | 5D 39 |
| Broadway Gdns. | 2D 39 | Brookfield Cl. | 3E 109 |
| Broadway Rd. | 3F 45 | Brookfield Dr. | 1B 64 |
| Broadway, The, Cheam | 2D 55 | Brookfield Gdns. | 2C 52 |
| Broadway, The, Crawley | 4D 147 | Brookfield Rd., Aldershot | 4B 78 |
| Broadway, The, Wimbledon | 5B 20 | Brookfield Rd., Bedford Park | 1D 9 |
| Broadway, The, Woodham | 3D 49 | Brookfield, Godalming | 5B 100 |
| Broadway, The, York Town | 4D 43 | Brookfields Av. | 3D 39 |
| Broadwell Rd. | 1C 114 | Brookhill Rd. | 1B 148 |
| Broadwood Cotts. | 5E 125 | Brookhouse Rd. | 5C 60 |
| Brock Rd. | 2C 146 | Brookhowse Rd. | 3A 24 |
| Brockenhurst | 3C 34 | Brookhurst Rd., Addlestone | 2E 49 |
| Brockenhurst Av. | 4E 37 | Brooklands Av. | 3C 20 |
| Brockenhurst Cl. | 5A 48 | Brooklands Cl., Heath End | 1B 96 |
| Brockenhurst Rd., Addiscombe | 4E 41 | Brooklands Cl., Sunbury | 1F 33 |
| Brockenhurst Rd., Aldershot | 1D 97 | Brooklands La. | 1A 50 |
| Brockenhurst Rd., Bracknell | 2F 27 | Brooklands Rds., Byfleet | 4A 50 |

| | | | | | | | |
|---|---|---|---|---|---|---|---|
| Bushey Way | 3B 42 | Cadley Ter. | 3E 23 | Cameron Cl. | 2C 140 | Cardinal Av., Kingston | 4B 18 |
| Bushfield Dr. | 3E 109 | Cadnam Cl. | 2D 97 | Cameron Rd., Bellingham | 3A 24 | Cardinal Av., Morden | 3A 38 |
| Bushnell Rd. | 3E 21 | Cadogan Cl. | 4E 17 | Cameron Rd., Thornton Heath | 3B 40 | Cardinal Cl., Morden | 3A 38 |
| Bushwood Rd. | 3C 8 | Cadogan Ct. | 2F 55 | Camilla Cl. | 1A 86 | Cardinal Cl., Stoneleigh | 1B 54 |
| Bushy Hill Dr. | 4B 82 | Cadogan Rd. | 3A 36 | Camilla Dr. | 3C 86 | Cardinal Cres. | 1D 37 |
| Bushy Park Gdns. | 4E 17 | Caen Wood Rd. | 2A 70 | Camlin Rd. | 4C 24 | Cardinal Dr. | 4B 34 |
| Bushy Park Rd. | 5A 18 | Caens Hill Rd. | 2A 50 | Camm Gdns. | 4E 35 | Cardinal Rd. | 2A 16 |
| Bushy Rd., Fetcham | 4D 69 | Caenwood Cl. | 2A 50 | Camp End Rd. | 4B 50 | Cardinals Wk. | 5D 17 |
| Bushy Rd., Teddington | 5E 17 | Caernarvon Cl., Frimley | 3F 61 | Camp Farm Rd. | 3B 78 | Cardingham | 2B 64 |
| Busk Cres. | 5C 60 | Caernarvon Cl., Mitcham | 2A 40 | Camp Hill | 5D 97 | Cardross St. | 1F 9 |
| Bute Av. | 3B 18 | Caesar's Camp Rd. | 4C 44 | Camp Rd., South Farnborough | 2A 78 | Cardwell Cres. | 3C 28 |
| Bute Gardens West | 1C 56 | Caesar's Close | 4C 44 | Camp Rd., Wimbledon | 4F 19 | Carew Cl. | 3B 74 |
| Bute Gdns. | 1C 56 | Caesar's Way | 3E 33 | Camp Rd., Woldingham | 4F 75 | Carew Rd., Ashford | 5E 15 |
| Bute Rd., Croydon | 4B 40 | Caesars Wk. | 3E 39 | Camp View | 4F 19 | Carew Rd., Beddington | 2C 56 |
| Bute Rd., Wallington | 1C 56 | Caffins Cl. | 3D 147 | Campbell Av. | 4D 65 | Carew Rd., Lammas Park | 1A 8 |
| Butler Rd., Bagshot | 3E 45 | Caillard Rd. | 4F 49 | Campbell Cl., Aldershot | 1D 97 | Carew Rd., Mitcham | 1E 39 |
| Butler Rd., Crowthorne | 1D 43 | Cains La. | 1F 15 | Campbell Cl., Twickenham | 2E 17 | Carew Thornton Heath | 2B 40 |
| Butlers Dene Rd. | 3A 76 | Cairn Cl. | 1F 61 | Campbell Cres. | 2B 150 | Carey Rd. | 2D 25 |
| Butlers Hill | 3A 84 | Caithness Rd. | 5E 21 | Campbell Rd., Caterham | 4C 74 | Carey's Wood | 2E 129 |
| Butter Hill | 1B 56 | Calbourne Rd. | 2E 21 | Campbell Rd., Croydon | 4B 40 | Carfax | 5B 158 |
| Butterfly Walk | 3E 75 | Caldbeck Av. | 5F 37 | Campbell Rd., Twickenham | 3E 17 | Carfax Av. | 1E 97 |
| Buttermere Cl., Feltham | 2F 15 | Calder Rd. | 3C 38 | Campbell Rd., Weybridge | 2A 50 | Cargill Rd. | 2C 20 |
| Buttermere Cl., Wrecclesham | 5F 95 | Calder Way | 5B 7 | Campden Rd. | 1A 58 | Cargreen Rd. | 2D 41 |
| Buttermere Dr. | 5D 45 | Calderdale Cl. | 5C 146 | Campen Cl. | 3A 20 | Carholme Rd. | 2A 24 |
| Buttermere Gdns. | 5F 57 | Caldervale Rd. | 1F 21 | Campfield Wk. | 1C 38 | Carisbrook Rd. | 2A 40 |
| Buttermoere Dr. | 1B 20 | Caldwell Rd. | 1A 46 | Camphill Ct. | 4E 49 | Carisbrooke | 3E 61 |
| Butts Cl. | 3C 146 | Caledon Rd. | 4B 82 | Camphill Rd. | 4D 49 | Carleton Av. | 3C 56 |
| Butts Cottages | 3C 16 | Caledonia Rd. | 2C 14 | Campin Cl. | 1F 57 | Carleton Cl. | 4E 35 |
| Butts Cres. | 3C 16 | Calfridus Way | 2E 27 | Campion Rd. | 1F 19 | Carlin Walk Dr. | 4B 44 |
| Butts, The, Brentford | 3A 8 | California Rd. | 2D 37 | Campshill Rd. | 1B 24 | Carlingford Rd. | 3A 38 |
| Butts, The, Sunbury-on-Thames | 2B 34 | Callander Rd. | 3B 24 | Camrobe Av. | 4A 16 | Carlisle Cl. | 1C 36 |
| Buxton Av. | 4C 74 | Calley Down Cres. | 3E 59 | Camrose Cl. | 2B 38 | Carlisle Rd. | 5A 116 |
| Buxton Cres. | 1D 55 | Callow Field | 5E 57 | Can Hatch | 2A 72 | Carlisle Rd., Cheam | 2E 55 |
| Buxton Dr. | 1D 37 | Callow Hill | 2C 30 | Canada Av. | 2E 109 | Carlisle Rd., Hampton Hill | 5D 17 |
| Buxton La. | 3C 74 | Calluna Dr. | 2B 148 | Canada Dr. | 2E 109 | Carlos St. | 2D 119 |
| Buxton Rd., Ashford | 4C 14 | Calmont Rd. | 5C 24 | Canada Rd., Byfleet | 4F 49 | Carlton Av., Hounslow | 1B 16 |
| Buxton Rd., Barnes | 5E 9 | Calonne Rd. | 4A 20 | Canada Rd., Cobham | 5D 51 | Carlton Av., Selsdon | 2F 57 |
| Buxton Rd., Thornton H'th | 3B 40 | Calthorpe Gdns. | 5C 38 | Canadian Av. | 2A 24 | Carlton Cl., Camberley | 1F 61 |
| By-pass Rd. | 1D 27 | Calton Av. | 1C 22 | Canbury Av. | 1B 36 | Carlton Cl., Chessington | 2E 53 |
| Byegrove Rd. | 5D 21 | Calverley Rd. | 2B 54 | Canbury Park Rd. | 1B 36 | Carlton Cl., Woking | 5A 48 |
| Byerley Way | 3A 148 | Calvert Cl. | 5B 78 | Canbury Pl. | 1B 36 | Carlton Cres. | 1D 55 |
| Byers La. | 5E 111 | Calvert Rd., Dorking | 5D 87 | Candy Croft | 1A 86 | Carlton Dr. | 1A 20 |
| Byeway, The, Mortlake | 5D 9 | Calvert Rd., Effingham | 2D 85 | Canes La. | 4D 133 | Carlton Green | 4A 90 |
| Byeway, The, Stoneleigh | 1B 54 | Calvin Cl. | 1F 61 | Canewdok Cl. | 3D 65 | Carlton Park Av. | 1A 38 |
| Byeways | 3D 17 | Camac Rd. | 2E 17 | Canford Dr. | 5B 32 | Carlton Rd., Acton Green | 1D 9 |
| Byeways, The | 2A 70 | Cambalt Rd. | 1A 20 | Canford Gdns. | 3D 37 | Carlton Rd., Brentford | 2A 8 |
| Byeways, The | 3C 36 | Camber Cl. | 4F 147 | Canford Rd. | 1E 21 | Carlton Rd., Godstone | 4F 111 |
| Byfleet | 4F 49 | Camberley | 5A 44 | Canham Rd., Bedford Park | 1D 9 | Carlton Rd., Headley Down | 5A 134 |
| Byfleet Corner | 5D 49 | Camberley Av. | 1F 37 | Canham Rd., South Norwood | 2C 40 | Carlton Rd., Kingston | 1D 37 |
| Byfleet Rd., Byfleet | 4A 50 | Camberwell | 1C 22 | Canmore Gdns. | 5F 21 | Carlton Rd., Redhill | 4A 90 |
| Byfleet Rd., New Haw | 2F 49 | Camborne Rd., Cheam | 2E 55 | Canning Rd., Addiscombe | 5D 41 | Carlton Rd., Selsdon | 2F 57 |
| Bygrove | 2D 59 | Camborne Rd., Morden | 3A 38 | Canning Rd., Aldershot | 5A 78 | Carlton Rd., Sheen | 5C 8 |
| Bylands | 3D 65 | Cambourne Av. | 1A 8 | Cannizaro Rd. | 4A 20 | Carlton Rd., Sunbury | 5F 15 |
| Byne Rd., Penge | 5E 23 | Cambourne Rd. | 2B 20 | Cannon Cl., Hampton Hill | 5D 17 | Carlton Rd., Walton | 4A 34 |
| Byne Rd., Sutton | 5D 39 | Cambray Rd. | 2F 21 | Cannon Cl., Raynes Park | 2A 38 | Carlton Rd., Woking | 5A 48 |
| Bynes Rd. | 2F 57 | Cambria Ct. | 2A 16 | Cannon Cr. | 4D 47 | Carlton Ter. | 3E 23 |
| Byrd Rd. | 5B 146 | Cambria Gdns. | 2C 14 | Cannon Gro. | 4E 69 | Carlton Tye | 2C 128 |
| Byrefield Rd. | 4E 81 | Cambrian Cl. | 5A 44 | Cannon Hill | 3D 27 | Carlwell St. | 4D 21 |
| Byron Av., Carshalton | 1A 56 | Cambrian Rd., Richmond | 1B 18 | Cannon Hill La. | 3A 38 | Carlyle Cl. | 1D 35 |
| Byron Av., Coulsdon | 1A 74 | Cambridge Av. | 2E 37 | Cannon Way, Fetcham | 4E 69 | Carlyle Rd., Addiscombe | 5D 41 |
| Byron Av., Heatherside | 1A 62 | Cambridge Cres. | 4F 17 | Cannon Way, W. Molesey | 2D 35 | Carlyle Rd., Cranleigh | 1C 140 |
| Byron Av., Motspur Park | 3F 37 | Cambridge Gdns. | 1C 36 | Cannonside | 4E 69 | Carlyle Rd., Staines | 5A 14 |
| Byron Cl., Crawley | 3F 147 | Cambridge Grove Rd. | 2C 36 | Canon's Hill | 2B 74 | Carlyon Av. | 2D 65 |
| Byron Cl., Hampton Hill | 4C 16 | Cambridge Pk. | 1A 18 | Canonbie Rd. | 2E 23 | Carlyon Cl., Mytchett | 5E 61 |
| Byron Cl., Knaphill | 2A 64 | Cambridge Rd., Anerley | 2E 41 | Canons La. | 2A 72 | Carlyon Cl., Woking | 2D 65 |
| Byron Cl., Walton-on-Thames | 4C 34 | Cambridge Rd., Barnes | 4E 9 | Canons Wk. | 5F 41 | Carlyon Rd. | 5D 61 |
| Byron Gdns. | 1A 56 | Cambridge Rd., Carshalton | 2A 56 | Canopus Way | 2C 14 | Carmarthen Cl. | 3C 60 |
| Byron Gro. | 2B 150 | Cambridge Rd., Cottenham Park | 1F 37 | Cansbury Av. | 1A 16 | Carmichael Rd. | 3D 41 |
| Byron Pl. | 4A 70 | Cambridge Rd., Crowthorne | 2D 43 | Cantelope Rd. | 2C 150 | Carminia Rd. | 3E 21 |
| Byron Rd., Selsdon | 3B 58 | Cambridge Rd., Hampton | 5C 16 | Canter, The | 3A 148 | Carmont Gdns. | 1D 51 |
| Byron Rd., Weybridge | 1F 49 | Cambridge Rd., Horsham | 5B 158 | Canterbury Cl. | 1A 42 | Carnac St. | 4C 22 |
| Byron Way | 1F 61 | Cambridge Rd., Kew | 3C 8 | Canterbury Gro. | 4B 22 | Carnforth Cl. | 2F 53 |
| Byton Rd. | 5E 21 | Cambridge Rd., Kingston | 1C 36 | Canterbury Rd., Croydon | 4A 40 | Carnforth Rd. | 5F 21 |
| Byttom Hill | 2D 87 | Cambridge Rd., Mitcham | 2F 39 | Canterbury Rd., Guildford | 4E 81 | Carnoustie | 4B 26 |
| Byward Av. | 1A 16 | Cambridge Rd., New Malden | 2D 37 | Canterbury Rd., Hanworth | 3C 16 | Carolina Rd. | 1B 40 |
| Byway, The, Carshalton | 3A 56 | Cambridge Rd., Owlsmoor | 3E 43 | Canterbury Rd., St. Helier | 4C 38 | Caroline Cl. | 5D 15 |
| Byway, The, Stoneleigh | 1B 54 | Cambridge Rd., Richmond | 1A 18 | Canterbury Rd., S. Farnborough | 1A 78 | Caroline Ct. | 2F 9 |
| Bywood | 4C 26 | Cambridge Rd., Sandhurst | 3E 43 | | | Caroline Dr. | 1D 25 |
| Bywood Av. | 3E 41 | Cambridge Rd., South Farnborough | 1A 78 | Cantley Cres. | 1D 25 | Caroline Rd. | 5B 20 |
| Bywood Cl. | 1B 74 | | | Cantley Gdns. | 1D 41 | Caroline Cl. | 2E 9 |
| Byworth Rd. | 4F 95 | Cambridge Rd., Sunbury | 5E 15 | Canvey Cl. | 5C 146 | Caroline Way | 2E 61 |
| | | Cambridge Rd., Teddington | 4F 17 | Capel | 5D 125 | Carolyn Cl. | 3A 64 |
| | | Cambridge Rd., Walton | 3A 34 | Capel Av. | 1D 57 | Carrington Av. | 1D 17 |
| | | Cambridge Wk. | 5A 44 | Capel Bypass | 5D 125 | Carrington La. | 2C 78 |
| **C** | | Cambury Promenade | 5B 18 | Capella | 4B 146 | Carrington Rd. | 5C 8 |
| | | Camden Av. | 2A 16 | Capri Rd. | 4D 41 | Carroll Av. | 5B 82 |
| | | Camden Gdns. | 2B 40 | Capsey Rd. | 4A 146 | Carroll Cres. | 2B 28 |
| Cabell Rd. | 5D 81 | Camden Hill Rd. | 5D 23 | Capstone Rd. | 4C 24 | Carrow Rd. | 5B 34 |
| Cabrera Av. | 3C 30 | Camden Rd., Carshalton | 1A 56 | Caradon Cl. | 2C 64 | Carshalton | 1A 56 |
| Cabrera Cl. | 3C 30 | Camden Rd., Cheam | 1E 55 | Caraway Cl. | 3E 81 | Carshalton Gro. | 1A 56 |
| Cabrol Rd. | 4C 60 | Camden Rd., Lingfield | 2F 131 | Carberry Av. | 1B 8 | Carshalton Park Rd. | 2A 56 |
| Caburn Heights | 5C 146 | Camden Way | 2B 40 | Carbery La. | 2C 28 | Carshalton Pl. | 1B 56 |
| Cadbury Cl. | 5F 15 | Camelia Pl. | 2D 17 | Cardamon Cl. | 3E 81 | Carshalton Rd., Camb. | 3C 44 |
| Cadbury Rd. | 5F 15 | Camelot Cl., Biggin Hill | 1E 77 | Cardigan Cl. | 2A 64 | Carshalton Rd., Carshalton | 1A 56 |
| Caddy Cl. | 4E 13 | Camelot Cl., Wimbledon | 4B 20 | Cardigan Rd., Barnes | 4E 9 | Carshalton Rd., Mitcham | 3E 39 |
| Cader Rd. | 1C 20 | Camelsdale Rd. | 3E 151 | Cardigan Rd., Richmond | 1B 18 | Carshalton Rd., Woodmansterne | 5A 56 |
| | | | | Cardigan Rd., Wimbledon | 5C 20 | Carslake Rd. | 1F 19 |

| | | | | | |
|---|---|---|---|---|---|
| Coolarne Rise | 5C 44 | Copse Rd., Woking | 2B 64 | Cottimore La. | 4A 34 | Coworth Cl. | 3F 29 |
| Coolgardie Rd. | 4E 15 | Copse Side | 4A 100 | Cottimore Ter. | 4A 34 | Coworth Rd. | 3E 29 |
| Coolgreany Hill | 4E 133 | Copse, The, Caterham | 1A 92 | Cottingham Av. | 2B 158 | Cowper Av. | 1A 56 |
| Coombe Av. | 1A 58 | Copse, The, Fetcham | 5D 69 | Cottingham Rd. | 5F 23 | Cowper Cl. | 3A 32 |
| Coombe Bank | 1E 37 | Copse View | 3C 58 | Cottington Rd. | 4B 16 | Cowper Gdns. | 2C 56 |
| Coombe Cl., Crawley | 3C 146 | Copse Way | 1C 114 | Cotton Hill | 4B 24 | Cowper Rd., Kingston | 4B 18 |
| Coombe Cl., Frimley | 3E 61 | Copsem Dr. | 2A 52 | Cottswood Dr. | 3B 82 | Cowper Rd., Wimbledon | 5C 20 |
| Coombe Cres. | 5C 16 | Copsem La. | 2A 52 | Couchmore Av. | 5E 35 | Cowshot | 4D 63 |
| Coombe Dr. | 2D 49 | Copsleigh Av. | 4E 109 | Coulsdon | 3A 74 | Cowslip La. | 5E 47 |
| Coombe End | 5D 19 | Copsleigh Cl. | 3E 109 | Coulsdon Court Rd. | 1A 74 | Cox Green | 1F 157 |
| Coombe Gdns., Cottenham Park | 1E 37 | Copsleigh Way | 3E 109 | Coulsdon La. | 3E 73 | Cox La. | 1F 53 |
| | | Copthall Gdns. | 2F 17 | Coulsdon Rise | 2A 74 | Coxcombe La. | 5F 137 |
| Coombe Gdns., New Malden | 2E 37 | Copthall Way | 3D 49 | Coulsdon Rd., Caterham | 4C 74 | Coxdean | 3A 72 |
| Coombe Hill Rd., East Grinstead | 3C 150 | Copthill La. | 3A 72 | Coulsdon Rd., Coulsdon | 1A 74 | Coxley Rise | 5E 57 |
| | | Copthorne | 1B 148 | Coulter Rd. | 1F 9 | Crab Hill | 5B 24 |
| Coombe Hill Rd., Kingston | 5E 19 | Copthorne Av. | 2F 21 | Country Way | 4A 16 | Crabbet Rd. | 3E 147 |
| Coombe House | 1D 37 | Copthorne Bank | 1B 148 | County Oak La. | 2D 147 | Crabhill La. | 2A 110 |
| Coombe La., Croydon | 1B 58 | Copthorne Cl. | 3E 33 | County Rd. | 1B 40 | Crabtree Cl. | 1A 86 |
| Coombe La., Raynes Park | 1E 37 | Copthorne Dr. | 3F 45 | Courland Rd. | 5B 32 | Crabtree Dr. | 1D 87 |
| Coombe La., Sunninghill | 2C 28 | Copthorne Rise | 5F 57 | Course Rd. | 2C 28 | Crabtree La., Bookham | 1A 86 |
| Coombe La., Worplesdon | 2D 81 | Copthorne Rd., Felbridge | 1F 149 | Court Av. | 3B 74 | Crabtree La., Churt | 2C 134 |
| Coombe Lane West | 5E 19 | Copthorne Rd., Leatherhead | 3A 70 | Court Bushes Rd. | 3D 75 | Crabtree La., Headley | 4F 133 |
| Coombe Neville | 5D 19 | Copyhold Rd. | 3B 150 | Court Cl., Beddington | 2C 56 | Crabtree Rd., Crawley | 3C 146 |
| Coombe Park | 4D 19 | Corbet Rd. | 3B 54 | Court Cl., Twickenham | 3D 17 | Crabtree Rd., Frimley | 2C 60 |
| Coombe Pine | 3E 27 | Corbetts Wk. | 1E 63 | Court Cl. Av. | 3D 17 | Crabtree Rd., Leatherhead | 5A 70 |
| Coombe Ridings | 4D 19 | Corby Dr. | 5C 12 | Court Cres. | 2D 53 | Crabtree Rd., Thorpe | 1E 31 |
| Coombe Rise | 1D 37 | Cordelia Gdns. | 2C 14 | Court Downs Rd. | 1A 42 | Crackell Rd. | 1C 108 |
| Coombe Rd., Chiswick | 2E 9 | Cordelia Rd. | 2C 14 | Court Dr., Carshalton | 1A 56 | Craddock Ac. | 2B 70 |
| Coombe Rd., Croydon | 1A 58 | Cordrey Gdns. | 1A 74 | Court Dr., Waddon | 1D 57 | Cradhurst Cl. | 2D 105 |
| Coombe Rd., Hampton | 5C 16 | Cordwalles Rd. | 4B 44 | Court Farm Av. | 1A 54 | Craig Rd. | 4A 18 |
| Coombe Rd., Kingston | 1C 36 | Corfe Gdns. | 2E 61 | Court Farm Rd. | 2D 75 | Craigen Av. | 4E 41 |
| Coombe Rd., Malden | 1E 37 | Coriander Cres. | 3E 81 | Court Gdns. | 5A 44 | Craigmore Tower | 3D 65 |
| Coombe Rd., Upper Sydenham | 4E 23 | Corinthian Way | 2C 14 | Court Green Heights | 3C 64 | Craignair Rd. | 2A 22 |
| Coombe Wk. | 5C 38 | Corkran Rd. | 4B 36 | Court Haw | 1D 73 | Craignish Av. | 1A 40 |
| Coombe Wood Hill | 5F 57 | Corkscrew Hill | 5B 42 | Court Hill, Chipstead | 2D 73 | Craigwell Av. | 3A 16 |
| Coombe Wood Rd. | 4D 19 | Cormongers La. | 5C 90 | Court Hill, Sanderstead | 4F 57 | Crail Cl. | 3D 25 |
| Coombe, The | 4A 88 | Cormorant Cl. | 4E 43 | Court La. | 2D 23 | Crake | 4E 43 |
| Coombefield Cl. | 3E 37 | Corney Rd. | 3E 9 | Court Lane Gdns. | 2D 23 | Cramhurst La. | 5A 118 |
| Coombelands La. | 2D 49 | Cornfields | 5B 100 | Court Lodge Rd. | 2A 128 | Crampshaw La. | 3B 70 |
| Coomber Way | 4F 39 | Cornfields Rd. | 1C 108 | Court Rd., Banstead | 1B 72 | Crampton Rd. | 5E 23 |
| Coombs, The | 1A 120 | Cornflower Cl. | 4F 41 | Court Rd., Caterham | 5C 74 | Cranborne Av. | 5C 36 |
| Cooper Cres. | 5D 39 | Cornford Gro. | 3E 21 | Court Rd., Godstone | 4B 92 | Cranborne Wk. | 5E 147 |
| Cooper Rd., Croydon | 1E 57 | Cornwall Av., Byfleet | 5F 49 | Court Rd., S. Norwood | 2D 41 | Cranbourne Cl. | 2B 128 |
| Cooper Rd., Guildford | 1D 101 | Cornwall Av., Claygate | 2C 52 | Court Way | 2F 17 | Cranbrook Dr., Esher | 5D 35 |
| Cooper Mill Rd. | 5A 7 | Cornwall Cl. | 4B 44 | Court Wood La. | 4D 59 | Cranbrook Dr., Whitton | 2D 17 |
| Cooper's Hill Rd. | 5D 91 | Cornwall Gro. | 2E 9 | Courtenay Rd., Cheam | 5A 38 | Cranbrook Rd., Beulah Hill | 1C 40 |
| Coopers Cl. | 4A 14 | Cornwall Rd., Cheam | 2E 55 | Courtenay Rd., Heath End | 2B 96 | Cranbrook Rd., Chiswick | 2E 9 |
| Coopers Hill Dr. | 4D 63 | Cornwall Rd., Croydon | 5B 40 | Courtenay Rd., Maybury | 1E 65 | Cranbrook Rd., Wimbledon | 5A 20 |
| Coopers Hill La. | 3C 12 | Cornwall Rd., Twickenham | 2F 17 | Courtenay Rd., Mitcham | 5D 21 | Crane Av. | 1F 17 |
| Coopers Rise | 2C 118 | Cornwall Way | 5F 13 | Courtfield Rise | 5B 42 | Crane Ct. | 1A 54 |
| Coopers Rd. | 2A 46 | Cornwell Rd. | 1B 12 | Courtfield Rd. | 5E 15 | Crane Park Rd. | 3D 17 |
| Cootes Av. | 4A 158 | Coronation Dr. | 1D 43 | Courthill Rd. | 1B 24 | Crane Rd., Hanworth | 3B 16 |
| Copelands Cl. | 1A 62 | Coronation Rd., Aldershot | 1D 97 | Courthorpe Rd. | 4A 20 | Crane Rd., Twickenham | 2E 17 |
| Copenhagen Way | 5A 34 | Coronation Rd., East Grinstead | 3C 150 | Courthorpe Villas Rd. | 5B 20 | Crane Way | 2D 17 |
| Copers Cope Rd. | 1A 42 | Coronation Rd., South Ascot | 4B 28 | Courtland Av. | 5A 22 | Craneford Cl. | 2F 17 |
| Cophatch Rd. | 3D 145 | Coronation Square | 2E 5 | Courtlands Av., Esher | 2F 51 | Craneford Way | 2F 17 |
| Copleigh Dr. | 3A 72 | Coronet, The | 3C 128 | Courtlands Av., Hampton | 5C 16 | Cranes Dr. | 2B 36 |
| Copley Cl., Reigate | 4A 90 | Corporation Rd. | 3E 41 | Courtlands Av., North Sheen | 4C 8 | Cranes Pk. | 2B 36 |
| Copley Cl., Woking | 3A 64 | Corrib Dr. | 1A 56 | Courtlands Av., West Wickham | 4C 42 | Cranes Park Av. | 2B 36 |
| Copley Park | 5A 22 | Corrie Gdns. | 4C 30 | Courtlands Cl. | 3A 58 | Cranes Park Cres. | 2B 36 |
| Copley Way | 3A 72 | Corrie Rd., Addlestone | 1F 49 | Courtlands Cres. | 1B 72 | Cranfield Rd. | 3B 56 |
| Copped Hall Dr. | 5D 45 | Corrie Rd., Old Woking | 3E 65 | Courtlands Dr. | 2B 54 | Cranford Av. | 2C 14 |
| Copped Hall Way | 5D 45 | Corrigan Av. | 5B 56 | Courtlands Rd. | 4C 36 | Cranford Cl., Stanwell | 2C 14 |
| Copper Beech Cl. | 4B 64 | Corry Rd. | 4D 135 | Courtleas | 5F 51 | Cranford Cl., Wimbledon | 5F 19 |
| Copper Mill La. | 4C 20 | Corsair Cl. | 2C 14 | Courtney Cres. | 2A 56 | Cranford Rise | 1A 52 |
| Copperfield | 4D 69 | Corsair Rd. | 2C 14 | Courtney Rd. | 5B 40 | Cranleigh | 1C 140 |
| Copperfield Cl. | 4F 57 | Corscombe Cl. | 4D 19 | Courtrai Rd. | 1F 23 | Cranleigh Cl. | 4A 58 |
| Copperfield Rise | 1D 49 | Corsehill St. | 5F 21 | Courts Hill Rd. | 3F 151 | Cranleigh Gdns., Kingston | 5B 18 |
| Coppermill Rd. | 1E 13 | Corsham Way | 1D 43 | Courts Mount Rd. | 3F 151 | Cranleigh Gdns., Rose Hill | 5C 38 |
| Coppice Cl., Hale | 2B 96 | Cortis Rd. | 1F 19 | Coutts Av. | 1E 53 | Cranleigh Gdns., Sanderstead | 4A 58 |
| Coppice Cl., Raynes Park | 2F 37 | Corunna Dr. | 5C 158 | Coval La. | 5C 8 | Cranleigh Mead | 2D 141 |
| Coppice Dr., Old Windsor | 2C 12 | Cosdach Av. | 2C 56 | Coval Rd. | 5C 8 | Cranleigh Rd., Esher | 4D 35 |
| Coppice Dr., Roehampton | 1F 19 | Cosedge Cres. | 1E 57 | Cove Rd. | 5B 60 | Cranleigh Rd., Ewhurst | 1E 141 |
| Coppice La. | 4E 89 | Coteford St. | 4E 21 | Coveham Cres. | 5D 51 | Cranleigh Rd., Felthamhill | 4F 15 |
| Coppice Wk. | 3A 147 | Cotelands | 5C 40 | Coventry Rd. | 2D 41 | Cranleigh Rd., S. Merton | 2B 38 |
| Coppidbeech La. | 1A 26 | Cotenham Dr. | 5F 19 | Coverack Cl. | 4F 41 | Cranley Cl. | 5B 82 |
| Coppins, The | 2E 59 | Cotford Rd. | 2C 40 | Coverdale Rd. | 1F 9 | Cranley Gdns. | 2C 56 |
| Copps Field | 2C 34 | Cotherstone Rd. | 2A 22 | Covert, The, Hawley | 3B 60 | Cranley Rd., Guildford | 5A 82 |
| Copse Av., Heath End | 1B 96 | Cotsford Av. | 3D 37 | Covert, The, S. Ascot | 4C 28 | Cranley Rd., Weybridge | 1C 50 |
| Copse Av., W. Wickham | 5A 42 | Cotswold Cl., Crawley | 4C 146 | Coverton Rd. | 4D 21 | Cranmer Av. | 1A 8 |
| Copse Cl., Ashtead | 2A 70 | Cotswold Cl., Hawley | 3B 60 | Coverts Rd. | 3C 52 | Cranmer Cl., Morden | 3A 38 |
| Copse Cl., Camberley | 5C 44 | Cotswold Cl., Kingston Hill | 5C 18 | Covey Cl. | 3C 60 | Cranmer Cl., Warlingham | 2F 75 |
| Copse Cl., Chilworth | 3E 101 | Cotswold Cl., Staines | 4A 14 | Covington Gdns. | 5B 22 | Cranmer Cl., Weybridge | 2A 50 |
| Copse Cl., Horsham | 3C 158 | Cotswold Rd. | 3F 55 | Covington Way | 5A 22 | Cranmer Gdns. | 2F 75 |
| Copse Cres. | 3C 146 | Cotswold St. | 4B 22 | Cow La. | 2D 119 | Cranmer Rd., Hampton Hill | 4D 17 |
| Copse Edge | 3D 117 | Cottage Cl. | 2B 48 | Cowden Rd. | 4A 24 | Cranmer Rd., Mitcham | 2E 39 |
| Copse Edge Av. | 5B 54 | Cottage Farm Way | 2E 31 | Cowdray Cl. | 4F 147 | Cranmer Ter. | 4D 21 |
| Copse End | 5C 44 | Cottage Gro. | 3A 36 | Cowey Cl. | 3C 146 | Cranmore La. | 3B 84 |
| Copse Glade | 4A 36 | Cottage Rd. | 2A 54 | Cowfold Cl. | 5B 146 | Cranmore Rd., Catford | 3C 24 |
| Copse Hill, Cottenham Park | 5F 19 | Cottenham Cl. | 5F 19 | Cowick Rd. | 4E 21 | Cranmore Rd., Mytchett | 5F 61 |
| Copse Hill, Purley | 5D 57 | Cottenham Park Rd. | 5F 19 | Cowix Rd. | 3D 143 | Cranston Cl., Guildford | 3E 81 |
| Copse Hill, Purley | 2F 55 | Cottenhams | 5A 111 | Cowleaze Rd. | 1B 36 | Cranston Rd., East Grinstead | 2C 150 |
| Copse La. | 2C 128 | Cotterill Rd. | 5B 36 | Cowley Av. | 4A 32 | Cranston Rd., Lewisham | 2F 23 |
| Copse Rd., Cobham | 5D 51 | Cottesbrook Cl. | 4A 7 | Cowley Cl., Selsdon | 3B 58 | Crantock Rd. | 3B 24 |
| Copse Rd., Hammer | 3D 151 | Cottesmore | 4C 26 | Cowley Cr., Hersham | 1E 51 | Cranwell Gr., Lightwater | 4E 45 |
| Copse Rd., Matthewsgreen | 1D 25 | Cottimore Av. | 4A 34 | Cowley La. | 4A 32 | Cranwell Gr., Littleton | 2D 33 |
| Copse Rd., Reigate | 1C 108 | Cottimore Cres. | 4A 34 | Cowley Rd. | 5D 9 | Craster Rd. | 2A 22 |

| Name | Ref | Name | Ref | Name | Ref | Name | Ref | Name | Ref |
|---|---|---|---|---|---|---|---|---|---|
| D'Abernon Cl. | 1A 52 | Darlaston Rd. | 5A 20 | Deepcut | 4A 62 | Dene Tye | 3F 147 | | |
| D'Abernon Dr. | 2B 68 | Darley Cl., Addlestone | 1E 49 | Deepcut Bridge Rd. | 4A 62 | Dene Wk. | 1E 115 | | |
| D'Arcy Av. | 1C 56 | Darley Cl., Croydon | 3F 41 | Deepdale, Bracknell | 2C 26 | Denefield Dr. | 1C 74 | | |
| D'Arcy Cl. | 2B 70 | Darley Dr. | 1D 37 | Deepdale, Wimbledon | 4A 20 | Denehurst Gdns., North Sheen | 5C 8 | | |
| D'Arcy Rd., Ashtead | 2B 70 | Darley Gdns. | 3C 38 | Deepdene, Lower Bourne | 1E 115 | Denehurst Gdns., | 2E 17 | | |
| D'Arcy Rd., Cheam | 1D 55 | Darleydale | 5C 146 | Deepdene, Shottermill | 2E 151 | Twickenham | | | |
| Dacre Rd. | 4A 40 | Darlington Rd. | 4B 22 | Deepdene Av., Croydon | 5D 41 | Denfield | 2A 106 | | |
| Dacres Rd. | 3F 23 | Darnley Pk. | 5D 33 | Deepdene Av., Dorking | 1A 106 | Denham Cres. | 2D 39 | | |
| Daffodil.Dr. | 1E 63 | Darrell Rd. | 1D 23 | Deepdene Avenue Rd. | 5D 87 | Denham Gro. | 3D 27 | | |
| Dafforne Rd. | 3E 21 | Dart Rd. | 4B 60 | Deepdene Dr. | 1A 106 | Denham Rd. | 2B 16 | | |
| Dagden Rd. | 3D 101 | Dartmouth Av. | 5C 48 | Deepdene Gdns., Dorking | 1A 106 | Denholm Gdns. | 4B 82 | | |
| Dagmar Rd. | 5C 18 | Dartmouth Cl. | 2E 27 | Deepdene Gdns., Tulse Hill | 2A 22 | Denison Rd. | 4F 15 | | |
| Dagnall Pk. | 3C 40 | Dartmouth Grn. | 5C 48 | Deepdene Park Rd. | 1A 106 | Denleigh Gdns. | 3E 35 | | |
| Dagnan Rd. | 1F 21 | Dartmouth Rd. | 3E 23 | Deepdene Vale | 5D 87 | Denley Way | 3F 45 | | |
| Dahlia Gdns. | 2F 39 | Dartnall Av. | 4E 49 | Deepdene Wood | 1A 106 | Denman Dr. | 5D 15 | | |
| Dahomey Rd. | 5F 21 | Dartnall Cl. | 4E 49 | Deepfield Rd. | 1D 27 | Denmark Av. | 5A 20 | | |
| Daimler Way | 2D 57 | Dartnall Cres. | 4E 49 | Deepfield Way | 1A 74 | Denmark Gdns. | 5E 39 | | |
| Dainford Cl. | 4B 24 | Dartnall Park Rd. | 4E 49 | Deepfields | 1B 128 | Denmark Rd., Guildford | 1D 101 | | |
| Dalberg Rd. | 1B 22 | Dartnall Pl. | 4E 49 | Deeprock Hill | 3D 27 | Denmark Rd., Hackbridge | 5E 39 | | |
| Dalcross | 3E 27 | Dartnall Rd. | 4D 41 | Deepwell Dr. | 5B 44 | Denmark Rd., Kingston | 2B 36 | | |
| Dale Cl., Addlestone | 1E 49 | Darvel Cl. | 1B 64 | Deer Barn Rd. | 5E 81 | Denmark Rd., Norwood | 3E 41 | | |
| Dale Cl., Horsham | 3C 158 | Darvills La. | 4B 96 | Deer Leap | 4F 45 | Denmark Rd., Twickenham | 3E 17 | | |
| Dale Cl., Sunningdale | 3E 29 | Darwell Dr. | 1A 28 | Deer Park Cl. | 5C 18 | Denmark Rd., Wimbledon | 5A 20 | | |
| Dale Park Av. | 5E 39 | Darwin Rd. | 2A 8 | Deer Park Gdns. | 2D 39 | Denmark Sq. | 5B 78 | | |
| Dale Park Rd. | 1C 40 | Daryngton Dr. | 5B 82 | Deer Park Rd. | 1C 38 | Denmark St., Aldershot | 5B 78 | | |
| Dale Rd., Cheam | 1E 55 | Dashwood Cl., Bracknell | 1D 27 | Deer Rock Rd. | 4B 44 | Denmark St., Wokingham | 2D 25 | | |
| Dale Rd., Purley | 4E 57 | Dashwood Cl., Byfleet | 4E 49 | Deerbrook Rd. | 2B 22 | Denmead Rd. | 4B 40 | | |
| Dale Rd., Sunbury | 5F 15 | Dassett Rd. | 4B 22 | Deerhurst Rd. | 4A 22 | Dennan Rd. | 4B 36 | | |
| Dale Rd., Sunningdale | 3E 29 | Datchet Rd. | 3A 24 | Deering Rd. | 5F 89 | Denne Parade | 5B 158 | | |
| Dale Rd., Walton | 4F 33 | Dault Rd. | 1C 20 | Deerleap Rd. | 2D 105 | Denne Rd., Horsham | 5B 158 | | |
| Dale St. | 2D 9 | Daux Hill | 2A 158 | Deerswood Cl. | 3C 146 | Denne Rd., West Green | 4C 146 | | |
| Dale View, Camelsdale | 3F 151 | Davell Cl. | 1B 64 | Deerswood Rd. | 3C 146 | Dennett Rd. | 4B 40 | | |
| Dale View, Headley Park | 5C 70 | Davenport Rd., Bullbrook | 1E 27 | Deeside Rd. | 3C 20 | Denning Av. | 1E 57 | | |
| Dale View, Woking | 2B 64 | Davenport Rd., Hither Grn. | 1B 24 | Defiant Way | 2D 57 | Denning Cl. | 4C 16 | | |
| Dalebury Rd. | 3D 21 | Daventry Cl. | 4B 7 | Defoe Av. | 3C 8 | Dennis Cl., Redhill | 4A 90 | | |
| Dalegarth Gdns. | 5F 57 | David Rd. | 4B 7 | Defrene Rd. | 4F 23 | Dennis Cl., Sunbury | 5E 15 | | |
| Daleham Av. | 5D 13 | Davids Rd. | 2E 23 | Dekker Rd. | 1C 22 | Dennis Park Cres. | 1A 38 | | |
| Dalekeith Rd. | 2C 22 | Davidson Rd. | 4D 41 | Delabole Rd. | 2D 91 | Dennis Rd. | 2D 35 | | |
| Daleside Rd., Ewell | 2A 54 | Davies Cl., Croydon | 3D 41 | Delamare Cres. | 3E 41 | Dennison Rd. | 5D 21 | | |
| Daleside Rd., Tooting Bec | 4E 21 | Davies Cl., Godalming | 5A 100 | Delamere Rd., Raynes Park | 1A 38 | Denton Cl. | 3E 109 | | |
| Dalewood Gdns. | 5F 37 | Davis Rd., Chessington | 1F 53 | Delamere Rd., Reigate | 2C 108 | Denton Gro. | 5B 34 | | |
| Dallas Rd., Cheam | 2D 55 | Davis Rd., Hammersmith | 1E 9 | Delara Way | 2C 64 | Denton Rd., Richmond | 1A 18 | | |
| Dallas Rd., Upper Sydenham | 3E 23 | Davisville Rd. | 1E 9 | Delcombe Av. | 4F 37 | Denton Rd., Wokingham | 2E 25 | | |
| Dallaway Gdns. | 2C 150 | Davos Cl. | 3D 65 | Delderfield | 4B 70 | Denton St. | 1C 20 | | |
| Dalling Rd. | 1F 9 | Dawell Dr. | 2E 77 | Delia St. | 2C 20 | Denton Way, Frimley | 2E 61 | | |
| Dallinger Rd. | 1C 24 | Dawley Ride | 4A 7 | Dell Cl., Fetcham | 5E 69 | Denton Way, Knaphill | 2B 64 | | |
| Dallington Cl. | 2E 51 | Dawlish Av. | 3C 20 | Dell Cl., Mickleham | 2D 87 | Dents Gr. | 2E 89 | | |
| Dalmain Rd. | 2F 23 | Dawnay Rd. | 3C 20 | Dell Cl., Shottermill | 2F 151 | Dents Rd. | 1D 21 | | |
| Dalmally Rd. | 4D 41 | Dawnay Rd., Camberley | 4A 44 | Dell Cl., Sutton | 1C 56 | Denvale Walk | 2B 64 | | |
| Dalmeny Av. | 1B 40 | Dawnay Rd., Gt. Bookham | 1A 86 | Dell La. | 1B 54 | Denzil Rd. | 1C 100 | | |
| Dalmeny Rd., Carshalton on the Hill | 2B 56 | Dawney Gdns. | 3C 20 | Dell Rd., Stoneleigh | 2C 54 | Depot Rd., Epsom | 5B 54 | | |
| | | Dawney Hill | 4E 63 | Dell, The, Feltham | 2A 16 | Depot Rd., Horsham | 5C 158 | | |
| Dalmeny Rd., Worc. Pk. | 5F 37 | Dawney Rd. | 4D 63 | Dell, The, Goldsworth | 3C 64 | Depot Rd., Northgate | 2D 147 | | |
| Dalmore Av. | 2B 52 | Dawsmere Cl. | 5D 45 | Dell, The, Horley | 2B 128 | Derby Arms Rd. | 2E 71 | | |
| Dalmore Rd. | 3C 22 | Dawson Rd., Byfleet | 4F 49 | Dell, The, Reigate | 5E 89 | Derby Cl. | 3F 71 | | |
| Dalston Cl. | 1A 62 | Dawson Rd., Kingston | 2B 36 | Dell, The, Tadworth | 4A 72 | Derby Hill | 3E 23 | | |
| Dalton Av. | 1D 39 | Day Spring | 3E 81 | Dell Walk | 1E 37 | Derby Hill Cres. | 3E 23 | | |
| Dan Ct. | 5D 49 | Day's Acre | 3A 58 | Dellbow Rd. | 1A 16 | Derby Rd., Cheam | 2E 55 | | |
| Danbrook Rd. | 5A 22 | Daybrook Rd. | 1C 38 | Delmey Cl. | 5D 41 | Derby Rd., Croydon | 4B 40 | | |
| Dancer Rd. | 5C 8 | Daylesford Av. | 5E 9 | Delta Cl., Chobham | 3D 47 | Derby Rd., Guildford | 5D 81 | | |
| Dane Rd., Ashford | 5E 15 | Daymerselea Ridge | 4A 70 | Delta Cl., Worcester Pk. | 5E 37 | Derby Rd., Haslemere | 2A 152 | | |
| Dane Rd., Warlingham | 2E 75 | Daysbrook Rd. | 2A 22 | Delta Dr. | 3B 128 | Derby Rd., North Sheen | 5C 8 | | |
| Dane Rd., Wimbledon | 1C 38 | Dayseys Hill | 5B 110 | Delta Rd., Chobham | 3D 47 | Derby Rd., Tolworth | 4C 36 | | |
| Danebury Av. | 1E 19 | De Burgh Pk. | 1C 72 | Delta Rd., Woking | 1E 65 | Derby Rd., Wimbledon | 5B 20 | | |
| Daneby Rd. | 3B 24 | De Haviland Way | 1C 14 | Delta Rd., Worcester Park | 5E 37 | Derby Stables Rd. | 2B 71 | | |
| Danecroft Rd. | 1C 22 | De Havilland Rd. | 2D 57 | Delta Way | 1F 31 | Derek Av., Ruxley | 2F 53 | | |
| Danehurst Cres. | 5C 158 | De La Mere Rd. | 1B 8 | Delves | 4A 72 | Derek Av., Wallington | 1B 56 | | |
| Danemore La. | 4F 111 | De La Warr Rd. | 2C 150 | Demesne Rd. | 1C 56 | Derek Cl. | 1F 53 | | |
| Danes La. | 5A 52 | De Montfort Rd. | 3A 22 | Dempster Cl. | 4A 36 | Deridene Cl. | 1C 14 | | |
| Danes Hill | 2E 65 | Deacon Cl., Downside | 3A 68 | Dempster Rd. | 1C 20 | Dering Pl. | 1E 57 | | |
| Danesbury | 2E 59 | Deacon Rd. | 1B 36 | Den Cl. | 2B 42 | Dering Rd. | 1F 57 | | |
| Danesbury Rd. | 2A 16 | Deadbrook La. | 4B 78 | Den Rd. | 2B 42 | Derinton Rd. | 4E 21 | | |
| Danescourt Cres. | 5C 38 | Deadwater Rd. | 5D 133 | Denham Rd., Egham | 4E 13 | Dermody Rd. | 1B 24 | | |
| Daneshill | 5A 90 | Deal Rd. | 5E 21 | Denham Rd., Epsom | 4B 54 | Deronda Rd. | 2B 22 | | |
| Daneshill Cl. | 5A 90 | Dean Cl., Woking | 1F 65 | Denbigh Cl. | 1E 55 | Derrick Av. | 3F 57 | | |
| Danesway | 5B 52 | Dean La. | 5F 73 | Denbigh Gdns. | 1B 18 | Derrick Rd. | 2F 41 | | |
| Daneswood Av. | 3B 24 | Dean Lane Pk. | 4F 73 | Denbigh Rd, | 3A 152 | Derry Rd., Hawley | 3C 60 | | |
| Daneswood Cl. | 1B 50 | Dean Rd., Croydon | 1F 57 | Denby Rd. | 5D 51 | Derry Rd., Waddon | 5A 40 | | |
| Danetree Cl. | 2B 54 | Dean Rd., Godalming | 1D 119 | Denchers Plat | 2C 146 | Derrydown | 4C 64 | | |
| Danetree Rd. | 2A 54 | Dean Rd., Hanworth | 4C 16 | Dene Cl., Hayes | 4C 42 | Derwent Av. | 4C 78 | | |
| Daniels La. | 1A 76 | Dean Rd., Whitton | 1D 17 | Dene Cl., Haslemere | 2A 152 | Derwent Av., Kingston | 4D 19 | | |
| Danses Cl. | 4C 82 | Dean Walk | 1A 86 | Dene Cl., Horley | 2C 128 | Derwent Av., W. H'th. | 5B 60 | | |
| Dapdune Rd. | 5F 81 | Deanery Rd. | 1D 119 | Dene Cl., Lower Bourne | 1E 115 | Derwent Cl., Addlestone | 1F 49 | | |
| Daphne St. | 1C 20 | Deanoak La. | 5A 108 | Dene Cl., Worcester Pk. | 5E 37 | Derwent Cl., Claygate | 2B 52 | | |
| Darby Cres. | 2B 34 | Deans Cl., Croydon | 5D 41 | Dene Gdns. | 5F 35 | Derwent Cl., Crawley | 4B 146 | | |
| Darby Gdns. | 1B 34 | Deans Cl., Tadworth | 4F 71 | Dene Lane | 1E 115 | Derwent Cl., Hook | 2F 15 | | |
| Darby Green La. | 5D 43 | Deans La. | 1C 88 | Dene Lane West | 1E 115 | Derwent Cl., Upper Hale | 2A 96 | | |
| Darcy Cl. | 3B 74 | Deans Rd., Merstham | 3C 90 | Dene Pl. | 2C 64 | Derwent Dr. | 5F 57 | | |
| Darcy Rd., Norbury | 1A 40 | Deans Rd., Sutton | 5C 38 | Dene Rd., Ashtead | 3B 70 | Derwent Quadrant | 4C 78 | | |
| Darell Rd. | 5C 8 | Dean's Walk | 2B 74 | Dene Rd., Farnborough | 5C 60 | Derwent Rd., Anerley | 1E 41 | | |
| Darenth Way | 2B 128 | Deansfield | 1A 92 | Dene Rd., Guildford | 1D 101 | Derwent Rd., Egham | 5E 13 | | |
| Darfield Rd., Guildford | 4B 82 | Dearn Gdns. | 2D 39 | Dene St. | 1A 106 | Derwent Rd., Lammas Park | 1A 8 | | |
| Darfield Rd., Lewisham | 1F 23 | Deburgh Rd. | 5C 20 | Dene Street Gdns. | 1A 106 | Derwent Rd., Lightwater | 4F 45 | | |
| Darfold Rd. | 1A 24 | Dedisham Cl. | 4E 147 | Dene, The, Abinger | 3A 104 | Derwent Rd., Whitton | 1D 17 | | |
| Dark La., Putenham | 3C 98 | Dedswell Dr. | 3D 83 | Dene, The, Belmont | 4E 55 | Desborough Cl. | 4D 33 | | |
| Dark La., Windlesham | 2F 45 | Dee Way | 3B 54 | Dene, The, Shirley | 1C 58 | Desenfans Rd. | 1C 22 | | |
| Darkhole Ride | 1C 10 | Deep Pool | 5E 47 | Dene, The, W. Molesey | 3C 34 | Desford Way | 3D 15 | | |

| Street | Ref | Street | Ref | Street | Ref | Street | Ref |
|---|---|---|---|---|---|---|---|
| Eglantine Rd. | 1C 20 | Elliott Rd., Turnham Green | 2D 9 | Elmfield Rd. | 3E 21 | Endlesham Rd. | 2E 21 |
| Egleston Rd. | 3C 38 | Ellis Av. | 1B 100 | Elmfield Way | 3A 58 | Endsleigh Cl. | 3B 58 |
| Egley Dr. | 4C 64 | Ellis Cl. | 3A 74 | Elmgate Ave. | 3A 16 | Endsleigh Gdns., Surbiton | 3A 36 |
| Egley Rd. | 4C 64 | Ellis Farm Cl. | 4C 64 | Elmgrove Cl. | 3A 64 | Endsleigh Gdns., Hersham | 1D 51 |
| Eglington Rd. | 5A 116 | Ellis Rd., Coulsdon | 3A 74 | Elmgrove Rd., Addiscombe | 4E 41 | Endsleigh Rd. | 3C 90 |
| Eglise Rd. | 2F 75 | Ellis Rd., Crowthorne | 1D 43 | Elmgrove Rd., Weybridge | 5D 33 | Endway | 4C 36 |
| Egmont Av. | 4C 36 | Ellis Rd., Oxted | 3F 93 | Elmhurst Av. | 5E 21 | Endymion Rd. | 1A 22 |
| Egmont Park Rd. | 1C 88 | Ellison Rd. | 5A 22 | Elmhurst Dr. | 2F 105 | Enelby Rd. | 4C 36 |
| Egmont Rd., New Malden | 2E 37 | Ellison Way | 1E 97 | Elmore Rd. | 4E 73 | Enerdals Cl. | 2F 15 |
| Egmont Rd., Sutton | 3F 55 | Ellman Rd. | 5B 146 | Elmpark Gdns. | 3B 58 | Enfield Rd., Acton | 1C 8 |
| Egmont Rd., Tolworth | 4C 36 | Ellora Rd. | 4F 21 | Elms Cres. | 1F 21 | Enfield Rd., Ash Vale | 3C 78 |
| Egmont Rd., Walton-on-Thames | 4A 34 | Elm Bridge La. | 3D 65 | Elms Rd., Clapham | 1F 21 | Enfield Rd., Brentford | 2A 8 |
| Egmont Way | 3A 72 | Elm Cl., Hackbridge | 4D 39 | Elms Rd., Wokingham | 2D 25 | Engadine St. | 2B 20 |
| Egremont Rd. | 3B 22 | Elm Cl., Horsell | 1C 64 | Elms, The | 1E 97 | Englefield Green | 4B 12 |
| Eight Acres | 3D 135 | Elm Cl., Leatherhead | 4A 70 | Elmscott Rd. | 4C 24 | Englefield Rd. | 2F 63 |
| Eileen Rd. | 3C 40 | Elm Cl., Sendmarsh | 5A 66 | Elmsgate | 4F 99 | Engleheart Rd. | 2B 24 |
| Eland Rd., Aldershot | 5A 78 | Elm Cl., South Croydon | 2F 57 | Elmshaw Rd. | 1F 19 | Englehurst | 5C 12 |
| Eland Rd., Waddon | 5B 40 | Elm Cl., Tolworth | 4D 37 | Elmshorn | 1F 71 | Englesfield | 5D 45 |
| Eland Rd., Walton-on-Thames | 5B 34 | Elm Cl., Twickenham | 3D 17 | Elmside | 2D 59 | Englewood Rd. | 1F 21 |
| Elberon Av. | 3F 39 | Elm Cl., Warlingham | 2F 75 | Elmside, Guildford | 1B 100 | Engliff La. | 1A 66 |
| Elborough St. | 2B 20 | Elm Cres., Heath End | 1B 96 | Elmside, Milford | 3B 118 | Enmore Gdns. | 1D 19 |
| Elbow Meadow | 4B 7 | Elm Cres., Kingston | 1B 36 | Elmsleigh Rd., Staines | 4A 14 | Enmore Rd. | 3D 41 |
| Elder Cl. | 4A 82 | Elm Dr., Chobham | 3D 47 | Elmsleigh Rd., Twickenham | 3E 17 | Ennerdale | 2C 26 |
| Elder Rd., Bisley | 1E 63 | Elm Dr., Leatherhead | 5A 70 | Elmslie Cl. | 5A 54 | Ennerdale Cl. | 5C 146 |
| Elder Rd., W. Norwood | 4C 22 | Elm Dr., Sunbury | 1B 34 | Elmstead Cl. | 1B 54 | Ennerdale Rd. | 4B 8 |
| Elder Way | 1F 39 | Elm Gdns., Burgh Heath | 3F 71 | Elmstead Gdns. | 5E 37 | Ennersdale Rd. | 1B 24 |
| Elderberry Rd., Ealing | 1B 8 | Elm Gdns., Claygate | 2C 52 | Elmstead Rd. | 5D 49 | Ennismore Av., Guildford | 5A 82 |
| Elderberry Rd., Lindford | 4E 133 | Elm Gdns., Mitcham | 2F 39 | Elmsway | 4D 15 | Ennismore Av., Turnham Green | 2E 9 |
| Eldersley | 4A 90 | Elm Gro., Bisley | 1E 63 | Elmswood | 5C 68 | |  |
| Elderslie Cl. | 3A 42 | Elm Gro., Caterham | 4C 74 | Elmtree Cl., Ashford | 4D 15 | Ennismore Gdns. | 3E 35 |
| Elderton Rd. | 4F 23 | Elm Gro., Horsham | 5C 158 | Elmtree Cl., Byfleet | 5F 49 | Ensign Cl. | 2C 14 |
| Eldon Av. | 5E 41 | Elm Gro., Sutton | 1F 55 | Elmtree Rd. | 4E 17 | Ensign Way | 2C 14 |
| Eldon Dr. | 1E 115 | Elm Gro., Wimbledon | 5A 20 | Elmwood Av. | 3A 16 | Enterdent | 5F 92 |
| Eldon Pk. | 2E 41 | Elm Grove Parade | 5E 39 | Elmwood Cl., Ashtead | 2B 70 | Envis Way | 4C 80 |
| Eldon Rd. | 4C 74 | Elm Grove Rd., Barnes | 4F 9 | Elmwood Cl., Hackbridge | 5E 39 | Epping Walk | 5E 147 |
| Eldridge Cl. | 2A 16 | Elm Grove Rd., Cobham | 1B 68 | Elmwood Dr. | 2B 54 | Epping Way | 2E 27 |
| Eleanor Av. | 3A 54 | Elm Grove Rd., North Farnborough | 5D 61 | Elmwood Gro. | 3C 22 | Epsom | 5A 54 |
| Eleanor Gro. | 5E 9 | | | Elmwood Rd., Brookwood | 3A 64 | Epsom Cl. | 4A 44 |
| Elers Rd. | 1A 8 | Elm Grove, Epsom | 5A 54 | Elmwood Rd., Camberwell | 1C 22 | Epsom Gap | 1F 69 |
| Elfindale Rd. | 1C 22 | Elm Grove, Farnham | 1B 96 | Elmwood Rd., Chiswick | 3D 9 | Epsom Lane North | 2F 71 |
| Elfrida Cres. | 4A 24 | Elm Grove Rd., South Ealing | 1B 8 | Elmwood Rd., Croydon | 4B 40 | Epsom Lane South | 4F 71 |
| Elgar Av., Brentford | 1B 8 | Elm La., Catford | 2A 24 | Elmwood Rd., Mitcham | 2D 39 | Epsom Rd., Ashtead | 2B 70 |
| Elgar Av., Crowthorne | 5A 26 | Elm La., Tongham | 1E 97 | Elmwood Rd., Redhill | 3B 90 | Epsom Rd., Crawley | 5E 147 |
| Elgar Av., Norbury | 2A 40 | Elm La., Wisley | 3D 67 | Elmworth Grove | 3C 22 | Epsom Rd., East Horsley | 3B 84 |
| Elgar Av., Tolworth | 4C 36 | Elm Pk., Brixton Hill | 1A 22 | Elsdon Rd. | 2B 64 | Epsom Rd., Ewell | 4B 54 |
| Elger Way | 1B 148 | Elm Pk., Cranleigh | 1A 140 | Elsenham St. | 2B 20 | Epsom Rd., Guildford | 1D 101 |
| Elgin Av. | 5E 15 | Elm Pk., South Norwood | 2D 41 | Elsenwood Cres. | 4C 44 | Epsom Rd., Leatherhead | 4A 70 |
| Elgin Cl. | 5A 82 | Elm Pl. | 1D 97 | Elsenwood Dr. | 4C 44 | Epsom Rd., Merrow | 5B 82 |
| Elgin Cres. | 4D 75 | Elm Rd., Beckenham | 1F 41 | Elsiemaud Rd. | 1A 24 | Epsom Rd., Morden Pk. | 4B 38 |
| Elgin Rd,. Addiscombe | 5D 41 | Elm Rd., Chessington | 1E 53 | Elsinore Av. | 2C 14 | Epsom Rd., Waddon | 5B 40 |
| Elgin Rd., Beddington | 2C 56 | Elm Rd., Claygate | 2C 52 | Elsinore Rd. | 2F 23 | Eresby Cr. | 4A 42 |
| Elgin Rd., Rose Hill | 5C 38 | Elm Rd., East Bedfont | 2E 15 | Elsley Cl. | 4E 61 | Erica Gdns. | 1D 59 |
| Elgin Rd., Weybridge | 1A 50 | Elm Rd., Ewell | 2B 54 | Elsrick Av. | 3B 38 | Erica Cl., Copthorne | 2B 148 |
| Eliot Bank | 3E 23 | Elm Rd., Farncombe | 5A 100 | Elstan Way | 4F 41 | Erica Way, Horsham | 3B 158 |
| Eliot Dr. | 3E 151 | Elm Rd., Goldsworth | 2C 64 | Elstead | 2D 117 | Eridge Cl. | 4F 147 |
| Elizabeth Av., Ashford | 5B 14 | Elm Rd., Hackbridge | 4E 39 | Elstead Rd., Milford | 3A 118 | Eriswell Cres. | 2C 50 |
| Elizabeth Av., Bagshot | 3E 45 | Elm Rd., Heath End | 1B 96 | Elstead Rd., Norney | 1A 118 | Eriswell Rd. | 2C 50 |
| Elizabeth Cl. | 2D 27 | Elm Rd., Kingston | 1B 36 | Elstead Rd., Seale | 2F 97 | Erkenwald Cl. | 3A 32 |
| Elizabeth Cres. | 1C 150 | Elm Rd., Leatherhead | 4A 70 | Elsted Cl. | 3C 146 | Ermyn Cl. | 4B 70 |
| Elizabeth Gdns., Ascot | 3C 28 | Elm Rd., Malden | 1D 37 | Elston Pl. | 1D 97 | Ermyn Way | 4B 70 |
| Elizabeth Gdns., Sunbury-on-Thames | 2B 34 | Elm Rd., Mortlake | 5D 9 | Elston Rd. | 1D 97 | Erncroft Way | 1F 17 |
| | | Elm Rd., Purley | 5E 57 | Elstree Hill | 5C 24 | Ernest Av. | 4B 22 |
| Elizabeth Gdns., Upper Norwood | 5C 22 | Elm Rd., Reigate | 5A 90 | Elsworthy | 3E 35 | Ernest Gdns. | 3C 8 |
| | | Elm Rd., Selhurst | 2C 40 | Elthruda Rd. | 1C 24 | Ernest Gro. | 3A 42 |
| Elizabeth Rd., Guildford | 5A 100 | Elm Rd., Warlingham | 2F 75 | Elton Cl. | 5A 18 | Ernest Rd. | 1C 36 |
| Elizabeth Rd., Wokingham | 2E 25 | Elm Rd., Woking | 1D 65 | Elton Rd., Kingston | 1C 36 | Ernie Rd. | 5F 19 |
| Elizabeth Way | 4B 16 | Elm Road West | 4B 38 | Elton Rd., Woodcote | 4C 56 | Erpingham Rd. | 5F 9 |
| Elizabethan Cl. | 2C 14 | Elm Tree Av. | 4E 35 | Elveden Cl. | 2B 66 | Erridge Rd. | 1B 38 |
| Elizabethan Way | 2C 14 | Elm Tree Cl., Botleys | 5F 31 | Elveden Rd. | 4D 51 | Errol Gdns. | 2F 37 |
| Elkins Gdns. | 4B 82 | Elm Treet Cl., Chertsey | 5A 32 | Elwell Cl. | 4E 13 | Erskine Cl. | 5D 39 |
| Ellenborough Cl. | 1D 27 | Elm View | 4C 78 | Elwill Way | 2B 42 | Erskine Rd., Carshalton | 1A 56 |
| Ellenbridge Way | 3A 58 | Elm Walk | 2A 38 | Ely Cl. | 1E 37 | Erskine Rd., The Wrythe | 5D 39 |
| Elleray Ct. | 3C 78 | Elm Way, Raynes Park | 5F 37 | Ely Rd. | 3C 40 | Erviston Gdns. | 5B 22 |
| Elleray Rd. | 5F 17 | Elm Way, Ruxley | 1A 54 | Elystan Cl. | 3C 56 | Esam Way | 4B 22 |
| Ellerdine Rd. | 1E 17 | Elmbank Av., Egham Wick | 5B 12 | Embankment, The, Runnymede | 2C 12 | Escombe Dr. | 3E 81 |
| Ellerker Gdns. | 1B 18 | Elmbank Av., Guildford | 1B 100 | Embankment, The, Twickenham | 2F 17 | Escott Pl. | 2C 48 |
| Ellerman Av. | 2C 16 | Elmbourne Rd. | 3E 21 | | | Escourt Rd. | 3E 41 |
| Ellerslie Sq. | 1A 22 | Elmbridge Av. | 3D 37 | Ember Cl. | 1F 49 | Esher | 1A 52 |
| Ellerton Rd., Surbiton | 5B 36 | Elmbridge Rd. | 1A 140 | Ember Farm Av. | 3E 35 | Esher Av., Cheam | 5A 38 |
| Ellerton Rd., Wandsworth | 2D 21 | Elmbrook Cl. | 1A 34 | Ember Farm Way | 3E 35 | Esher Av., Walton-on-Thames | 4A 34 |
| Ellerton Rd., Wimbledon | 5E 19 | Elmbrook Rd. | 1E 55 | Ember Gdns. | 4E 35 | Esher Cl. | 1A 52 |
| Ellery Cl. | 2C 140 | Elmcourt Rd. | 3B 22 | Ember La. | 4E 35 | Esher Gdns. | 3A 20 |
| Ellery Rd. | 5C 22 | Elmcroft Cl., Feltham | 1F 15 | Embercourt Rd. | 3E 35 | Esher Green | 1A 52 |
| Elles Av. | 5B 82 | Elmcroft Cl., Frimley | 3E 61 | Embleton Rd. | 4A 134 | Esher Park Av. | 1A 52 |
| Elles Rd. | 5C 60 | Elmcroft Cl., Hook | 5B 36 | Emerton Rd. | 1E 69 | Esher Place Av. | 1A 52 |
| Ellesfield Av. | 2B 26 | Elmcroft Dr., Ashford | 4D 15 | Emily Rd. | 5B 32 | Esher Rd., Camberley | 3C 44 |
| Ellesmere Dr. | 5B 58 | Elmcroft Dr., Hook | 5B 36 | Emilyn Rd. | 1E 9 | Esher Rd., East Molesey | 3E 35 |
| Ellesmere Rd., Chiswick | 3D 9 | Elmdene | 4D 37 | Emlyn La., Earlswood | 4F 69 | Esher Rd., Hersham | 1E 51 |
| Ellesmere Rd., Twickenham | 1A 18 | Elmdene Cl. | 3F 41 | Emlyn Rd., Earlswood | 1E 109 | Eskdale Gdns. | 5F 57 |
| Ellesmere Rd., Weybridge | 2C 50 | Elmer Cottages | 5F 69 | Emlyn Rd., Horley | 2A 128 | Eskdale Way | 5D 45 |
| Ellingham Rd., Chessington | 2E 53 | Elmer Rd. | 2B 24 | Emmanuel Rd. | 2F 21 | Eskmont Ridge | 5C 22 |
| Ellingham Rd., Shepherd's Bush | 1F 9 | Elmers Av. | 3B 36 | Empire Villas | 5E 109 | Esmond Rd. | 2D 9 |
| | | Elmers End Rd. | 1E 41 | Empress Av. | 4D 61 | Essenden Rd. | 2F 57 |
| Ellington Rd. | 4F 15 | Elmers Rd., Addiscombe | 4D 41 | Emsworth St. | 3A 22 | Essendene Cl. | 5D 75 |
| Elliot Gdns. | 2D 33 | Elmers Rd., Ockley | 1D 143 | Ena Rd. | 2A 40 | Essendene Rd. | 5D 75 |
| Elliott Rd., Thornton Heath | 2B 40 | Elmfield | 5C 68 | Endeavour Way | 4A 40 | Essex Cl., Addlestone | 1E 49 |
| | | Elmfield Av. | 4F 17 | Endeavour Way, Summerstown | 4C 20 | Essex Cl., Morden | 4A 38 |

| | | | | | | | |
|---|---|---|---|---|---|---|---|
| Fearsden Cl. | 2C 48 | Fernhill La., Upper Hale | 2A 96 | Finney Dr. | 2A 46 | Fleet Rd. | 5A 60 |
| Featherbed La. | 2D 59 | Fernhill Rd. | 2B 60 | Fiona Cl. | 5C 68 | Fleet Sq. | 2C 36 |
| Fearhercombe | 1A 138 | Fernholme Rd. | 1F 23 | Fir Acre Rd. | 3C 78 | Fleet Way | 2E 31 |
| Featherhead La | 2D 59 | Fernhurst Cl. | 3C 146 | Fir Cl. | 4A 34 | Fleetside | 3C 34 |
| Feathers La. | 3E 13 | Fernhurst Rd., Addiscombe | 4E 41 | Fir Dr. Blackwater | 1B 60 | Fleetwood Cl., Chessington | 2D 53 |
| Featherstone Av. | 3E 23 | Fernhurst Rd., Ashford | 4E 15 | Fir Grange Av. | 1B 50 | Fleetwood Cl., Tadworth | 4A 72 |
| Feathstone | 4E 111 | Ferniehurst Cl. | 1E 61 | Fir Gro., Malden | 3E 37 | Fleetwood Rd. | 2C 36 |
| Fee Farm Rd | 2C 52 | Fernlands Cl. | 5F 31 | Fir Grove, Woking | 3B 64 | Fleming Cl. | 4D 61 |
| Felbridge Av. | 3F 147 | Fernlea | 5D 69 | Fir Rd., Hanworth | 4B 16 | Fleming Mead | 5D 21 |
| Felbridge Cl., East Grinstead | 1B 150 | Fernlea Rd., Balham | 2E 21 | Fir Rd., North Cheam | 4B 38 | Fleming Way | 2D 147 |
| Felbridge Cl., Sutton | 3F 55 | Fernlea Rd., Mitcham | 1E 39 | Fir Tree Cl., Esher | 1A 52 | Flemish Fields | 4A 32 |
| Felbridge Cl., West Norwood | 4B 22 | Fernleigh Rise | 3A 62 | Fir Tree Cl., Stoneleigh | 1B 54 | Fletcher Cl. | 2C 48 |
| Felbridge Ct. | 1A 150 | Ferns Cl. | 3B 58 | Fir Tree Gdns., Addington | 1D 59 | Fletcher Rd., Ealing | 1D 9 |
| Felbridge Rd. | 1F 149 | Fernside Av. | 3A 16 | Fir Tree Gro. | 2B 56 | Fletcher Rd., Ottershaw | 2C 48 |
| Felcott Rd. | 5B 34 | Fernside Rd. | 2E 21 | Fir Tree Pl. | 4D 15 | Fletchers Cl. | 5C 158 |
| Felcott Rd., Crawley Down | 1E 149 | Fernthorpe Rd. | 5F 21 | Fir Tree Rd., Banstead | 5D 55 | Flexford Rd. | 1C 98 |
| Felcott Rd., Walton-on-Thames | 5A 34 | Fernwood Av. | 4F 21 | Fir Tree Rd., Bellfields | 4F 81 | Flint Cl., Leatherhead | 1A 86 |
| Felcourt | 4E 131 | Ferrard Cl. | 1A 28 | Fir Tree Rd., Epsom Downs | 1F 71 | Flint Cl., Redhill | 5A 90 |
| Felcourt Rd., Felbridge | 1B 150 | Ferrers Av. | 1C 56 | Fir Tree Rd., Highland Park | 5A 70 | Flint Gro. | 1D 27 |
| Felcourt Rd., Felcourt | 3E 131 | Ferrers Rd. | 4F 21 | Fir Tree Walk | 5F 89 | Flint Hill | 3A 106 |
| Felday Glade | 1D 123 | Ferriers Way | 3A 72 | Firbank Dr. | 3B 64 | Flint Hill Cl. | 3A 106 |
| Felday Rd., Abinger | 3F 103 | Ferris Av. | 5E 41 | Firbank La. | 3C 64 | Flintlock Cl. | 5B 7 |
| Felday Rd., Ladywell | 1A 24 | Ferry Av. | 5F 13 | Firbank Pl. | 5B 12 | Floral Ct. | 2A 70 |
| Feldwick Pl. | 5B 90 | Ferry La., Guildford | 2C 100 | Fircroft Cl. | 2D 65 | Florence Av., Morden | 3C 38 |
| Felix Dr. | 2D 83 | Ferry La., Hythe End | 3E 13 | Fircroft Rd., Chessington | 1E 53 | Florence Av., Woodham | 4D 49 |
| Felix La. | 3F 33 | Ferry La., Kew | 3B 8 | Fircroft Rd., Upper Tooting | 3D 21 | Florence Cl. | 4A 34 |
| Felix Rd. | 3A 34 | Ferry La., Laleham | 2B 32 | Firdene | 4D 37 | Florence Gdns. | 5B 14 |
| Fell Rd. | 5C 40 | Ferry La., Shepperton | 4D 33 | Fireball Hill | 4D 29 | Florence Rd., Feltham | 2A 16 |
| Felland Way | 2D 109 | Ferry Rd., Barnes | 3E 9 | Firfield Rd., Addlestone | 1E 49 | Florence Rd., Kingston | 5B 18 |
| Fellbridge | 1A 150 | Ferry Rd., Teddington | 4F 17 | Firfield Rd., Farnham | 5A 96 | Florence Rd., Sanderstead | 3F 57 |
| Fellbrigg Rd. | 1D 23 | Ferry Rd., Thames Dit'n | 3F 35 | Firfields | 2B 50 | Florence Rd., Walton-on-Thames | 4A 34 |
| Fellbrook | 3A 18 | Ferry Rd., West Molesey | 2D 35 | Firgrove Hill | 4A 96 | |  |
| Fellow Green Rd. | 5B 46 | Ferry Sq. | 4D 33 | Firhill Rd. | 4A 24 | Florence Rd., Wimbledon | 5B 20 |
| Fellowes Rd., The Wrythe | 5D 39 | Ferrymoor | 3A 18 | Firlands, Bracknell | 3D 27 | Florence Rd., York Town | 4E 43 |
| Fellows Rd., South Farnborough | 1B 78 | Fetcham | 5D 69 | Firlands, Horley | 2B 128 | Florian Av. | 1A 56 |
| Felmingham Rd. | 1E 41 | Fetcham Common La. | 4D 69 | Firlands, Weybridge | 2C 50 | Florida Rd. | 1B 40 |
| Felsberg Rd. | 1A 22 | Fetcham Park Dr. | 5E 69 | Firlands Av. | 5A 44 | Florida Row | 3D 101 |
| Felstead Rd. | 4A 54 | Fettes Rd. | 1D 141 | Firle Cl. | 3D 147 | Flower Cres. | 2B 48 |
| Feltham | 3A 16 | Fickleshole | 5F 59 | Firs Av. | 1B 120 | Flower House Est. | 4B 24 |
| Feltham Av. | 2E 35 | Fiddicroft Av. | 5F 55 | Firs Cl., Dorking | 2F 105 | Flower La. | 3C 92 |
| Feltham Hill Rd. | 4D 15 | Field Cl., Chessington | 1D 53 | Firs Cl., Esher | 2B 52 | Flower Wk. | 2C 100 |
| Feltham Rd., Ashford | 4D 15 | Field Cl., E. Moseley | 3D 35 | Firs Cl., Lewisham | 2F 23 | Floyd's La. | 1A 66 |
| Feltham Rd., Mitcham | 1E 39 | Field Cl., Merrow | 5C 82 | Firs Cl., Merrow | 5C 82 | Foley Rd. | 2B 52 |
| Feltham Rd., Reigate | 3D 109 | Field Ct., Sanderstead | 5B 58 | Firs La. | 2C 120 | Follet Cl. | 1B 12 |
| Feltham Wk. | 3D 109 | Field Ct. | 2F 93 | Firs Rd. | 1B 74 | Folly Hill | 2A 96 |
| Felthambrook Way | 4A 16 | Field End, Coulsdon | 5C 56 | Firs, The | 2B 100 | Folly La., Farnham | 2A 96 |
| Felthamhill Rd. | 4A 16 | Field End, Farnham | 3C 96 | Firs Way | 5F 81 | Folly La., South Holmwood | 5A 106 |
| Fencote | 3E 27 | Field End, Twickenham | 4F 17 | Firsby Av. | 4F 41 | Follyfield Rd. | 5E 55 |
| Fendall Rd. | 1A 54 | Field End, West End | 5B 46 | First Av., Epsom | 3A 54 | Follyhatch La. | 5E 79 |
| Fengates Rd. | 5A 90 | Field La., Brentford | 3A 8 | First Av., Mortlake | 5E 9 | Fontaine Rd. | 5A 22 |
| Fennel Cl. | 4B 82 | Field La., Frimley | 2E 61 | First Av., Walton | 3A 34 | Fontenoy Rd. | 3F 21 |
| Fennel Cres. | 5C 146 | Field Pl. | 3E 37 | First Av., West Molesey | 2C 34 | Fontley Way | 2E 19 |
| Fennel's Mead | 3B 54 | Field Rd., Feltham | 1A 16 | First Cl. | 2D 35 | Fontmell Cl. | 4D 15 |
| Fenns La. | 5A 46 | Field Rd., Hawley | 2C 60 | First Cross Rd. | 3E 17 | Fontmell Pk. | 4D 15 |
| Fenns Way | 1D 65 | Field View, Egham | 4F 13 | First Rd. | 2A 40 | Ford Cl., Ashford | 5C 14 |
| Fenn's Yard | 4A 96 | Field View, Feltham | 4E 15 | First Slip | 2F 69 | Ford Cl., Shepperton Grn. | 3D 33 |
| Fenton Av. | 5B 14 | Field Way, Addington | 2D 59 | Firstway | 1F 37 | Ford La. | 1D 115 |
| Fenton Cl. | 5B 90 | Field Way, Burntcommon | 1D 83 | Firswood Av. | 1B 54 | Ford Manor Rd. | 3A 132 |
| Fenton Rd. | 5B 90 | Field Way, Haslemere | 2A 152 | Firtree Av., Mitcham | 1E 39 | Ford Rd., Ashford | 4C 14 |
| Fentum Rd. | 4E 81 | Fieldcommon La. | 4C 34 | Firtree Av., Shottermill | 3D 151 | Ford Rd., Bisley | 1E 63 |
| Fenwick Cl. | 2B 64 | Fielden Pl. | 1D 27 | Firtree Cl., Epsom Downs | 1F 71 | Ford Rd., Chertsey | 4B 32 |
| Ferguson Av. | 3B 36 | Fieldhouse Rd. | 2F 21 | Firtree Cl., Langley Green | 2C 146 | Ford Rd., Chobham | 3C 46 |
| Fermor Rd. | 2F 23 | Fieldhurst Cl. | 1E 49 | Firtree Cl., Leatherhead | 5A 70 | Ford Rd., Old Woking | 3E 65 |
| Fern Av. | 2F 39 | Fielding Av. | 3D 17 | Firwood Cl. | 3A 64 | Fordbridge Cl. | 4B 32 |
| Fern Bank Rd. | 1E 49 | Fielding Cl. | 1D 27 | Firwood Dr. | 5A 44 | Fordbridge Rd., Ashford | 4D 15 |
| Fern Cl. Camberley | 1F 61 | Fielding Rd., Bedford Park | 1D 9 | Firwood Rd. | 3A 30 | Fordbridge Rd., Lower Halliford | 3F 33 |
| Fern Cl. Warlingham | 2F 75 | Fielding Rd., Streatham Vale | 1F 39 | Fisher Cl., Crawley | 5D 147 | |  |
| Fern Gro. | 2A 16 | Fieldings, The, Forest Hill | 2E 23 | Fisher Cl., Weybridge | 1D 51 | Fordel Rd. | 2B 24 |
| Fern Hill | 5B 52 | Fieldings, The, Horley | 2C 128 | Fisher La. | 2A 154 | Fordingbridge Cl. | 5B 158 |
| Fern Hill La. | 3C 64 | Fieldsend Rd. | 1D 55 | Fisher Rowe Cl. | 1B 120 | Fordmill Rd. | 3A 24 |
| Fern Hill Pk. | 3C 64 | Fieldside Rd. | 4B 24 | Fisherman Cl. | 4A 18 | Fordwater Rd. | 4B 32 |
| Fern Rd. | 1D 119 | Fieldview, Earlsfield | 2C 20 | Fisher's La. | 2D 9 | Fordwater Reading Estate | 4B 32 |
| Fern Walk | 4C 14 | Fieldview, Horley | 2B 128 | Fishers Wood | 4F 29 | Fordwell Rd. | 2F 27 |
| Fern Way | 3B 158 | Fieldway, Aldershot | 4B 78 | Fishersdene | 2C 52 | Fordyce Rd. | 1B 24 |
| Fernbank Cres. | 1A 28 | Fife Rd., East Sheen | 1D 19 | Fishponds Rd., Tooting | 4D 21 | Foremans Pk. | 5C 78 |
| Fernbank Place | 1A 28 | Fife Rd., Kingston | 1B 36 | Fishponds Rd., Wokingham | 3D 25 | Foreman's Rd. | 5C 78 |
| Fernbank Rd. | 1A 28 | Fife Way | 1A 86 | Fitchet Cl. | 3C 146 | Forest Cl., Ascot Heath | 2A 28 |
| Fernbrae Cl. | 2D 115 | Fifehead Cl. | 5C 14 | Fitzalan Rd., Claygate | 2B 52 | Forest Cl., Horsley | 1C 84 |
| Fernbrook Rd. | 1C 24 | Fifield La. | 3D 115 | Fitzalan Rd., Horsham | 4C 158 | Forest Cl., Woking | 1F 65 |
| Ferndale | 4D 81 | Fifth Cross Rd. | 3E 17 | Fitzgeorge Av. | 1D 37 | Forest Cres. | 1C 70 |
| Ferndale Av. | 5F 31 | Filbert Cres. | 4B 146 | Fitzgerald Rd. | 3F 35 | Forest Dale | 5E 135 |
| Ferndale Rd., Banstead | 2B 72 | Filby Rd. | 2F 53 | Fitzgerard Av. | 5E 9 | Forest Dr., Farnham | 2D 115 |
| Ferndale Rd., Staines | 4C 14 | Filey Cl., Biggin Hill | 3D 77 | Fitzhugh Gro. | 1D 21 | Forest Dr., Kingswood | 4B 72 |
| Ferndale Rd., Woking | 1D 65 | Filey Cl., Sutton | 2F 55 | Fitzjames Av. | 5D 41 | Forest Green | 1E 27 |
| Ferndale Rd., Woodside | 3E 41 | Filmer Gro. | 1D 119 | Fitzjohn Cl. | 4B 82 | Forest Gren. | 4F 123 |
| Fernden La. | 4F 151 | Finborough Rd. | 5E 21 | Fitzroy Gdns. | 5D 23 | Forest Hill Rd. | 1E 23 |
| Ferndown | 1B 128 | Finch Av. | 4C 22 | Fitzwilliam Av. | 4B 8 | Forest Hills | 1D 61 |
| Ferndown Cl. | 1E 101 | Finch Dr. | 2B 16 | Five Acres | 3D 147 | Forest La. | 5F 67 |
| Fernery, The | 4F 13 | Finchampstead Rd. | 4D 25 | Five Oaks Cl., Addlestone | 2D 49 | Forest Ridge | 2A 42 |
| Ferney Rd. | 4F 49 | Finches Rise | 4B 82 | Five Oaks Cl., Woking | 3A 64 | Forest Rd., Ascot | 5B 10 |
| Fernham Rd. | 2B 40 | Findlay Dr. | 3D 81 | Flanchford Farm La. | 3E 107 | Forest Rd., Crowthorne | 1D 43 |
| Fernhill Cl., Woking | 3C 64 | Findon Rd., Hammersmith | 1F 9 | Flanchford Rd., Bedford Park | 1E 9 | Forest Rd., Effingham Junction | 5F 67 |
| Fernhill Cl., Hawley | 2B 60 | Findon Rd., Ifield | 3C 146 | Flanchford Rd., Reigate | 5D 89 | Forest Rd., Feltham | 3A 16 |
| Fernhill Dr. | 2A 96 | Finlay Gdns. | 1E 49 | Flanders Rd. | 2E 9 | Forest Rd., Horsley | 2C 84 |
| Fernhill Gdns. | 4B 18 | Finlays Cl. | 1F 53 | Flaxley Rd. | 4C 38 | Forest Rd., Kew | 3C 8 |
| Fernhill La., Hawley | 2B 60 | Finmere | 4D 27 | Fleece Rd. | 4A 36 | Forest Rd., St. Helier | 4B 38 |
| | | Finnart Cl. | 5E 33 | Fleet Cl. | 3C 34 | Forest Rd., Woking | 1F 65 |

| | | | | | | | |
|---|---|---|---|---|---|---|---|
| Forest Side | 4E 37 | Foxearth Spur | 3B 58 | Freshford St. | 3C 20 | Furlong Cl. | 4E 39 |
| Forest View | 5E 147 | Foxes Dale | 2B 42 | Freshmount Gdns. | 4F 53 | Furlong Rd. | 2D 105 |
| Forest View Rd. | 3C 150 | Foxglove Gdns. | 4C 82 | Freshwater Cl. | 5E 21 | Furmage St. | 2C 20 |
| Forest Way | 2C 70 | Foxglove La. | 1F 53 | Freshwater Rd. | 5E 21 | Furnace Dr. | 5E 147 |
| Forester Rd. | 5D 147 | Foxgrove Av. | 5B 24 | Frewin Rd. | 2D 21 | Furnace Farm Rd., Snowhill | 1E 149 |
| Foresters Cl., Beddington | 2C 56 | Foxgrove Dr. | 1D 65 | Friars Av. | 3E 19 | Furnace Farm Rd., Tilgate | 5E 147 |
| Foresters Cl., Woking | 2A 64 | Foxgrove Rd. | 5A 24 | Friar's Gate | 1B 100 | Furnace Parade | 5E 147 |
| Foresters Dr. | 2C 56 | Foxhill Cres. | 4C 44 | Friars La. | 1A 18 | Furnace Pl. | 5E 147 |
| Foresters Sq. | 2E 27 | Foxhills Cl. | 2B 48 | Friars Orchard | 4E 69 | Furnace Place Rd. | 2D 153 |
| Forestfield, Crawley | 5E 147 | Foxhills Rd. | 1B 48 | Friars Rise | 2E 65 | Furneaux Av. | 4B 22 |
| Forestfield, Horsham | 4C 158 | Foxholes | 1C 50 | Friars Rd. | 2C 30 | Furness Rd. | 3C 38 |
| Forge Av. | 3B 74 | Foxhurst Rd. | 4C 78 | Friars Rookery | 4D 147 | Furnival Cl. | 3C 30 |
| Forge Cl., Claygate | 2C 52 | Foxlake Rd. | 4F 49 | Friars Stile Rd. | 1B 18 | Furrows Pl. | 5D 75 |
| Forge Cl., Farnham | 3B 96 | Foxley Cl., Blackwater | 5D 43 | Friars Way | 3A 32 | Furrows, The | 5B 34 |
| Forge La., Cheam | 2D 55 | Foxley Cl., Salfords | 3E 109 | Friarswood | 3C 58 | Further Green Rd. | 2C 24 |
| Forge La., Hanworth | 4B 16 | Foxley Gdns. | 5E 57 | Friary Rd., S. Ascot | 3C 28 | Furze Cl. | 5A 90 |
| Forge La., Sunbury-on-Thames | 2A 34 | Foxley Hill Rd. | 4E 57 | Friary Rd., Wraysbury | 1C 12 | Furze Field | 5B 52 |
| Forge La., Three Bridges | 3E 147 | Foxley La. | 3D 57 | Friary St., Guildford | 159 | Furze Gro. | 4B 72 |
| Forge Rd. | 3E 147 | Foxley Rd., Kenley | 5E 57 | Friary, The | 1C 12 | Furze Hill | 4D 57 |
| Forrest Gdns. | 2A 40 | Foxley Rd., Thornton H'th. | 2B 40 | Friday Rd. | 5D 21 | Furze Hill Cres. | 2D 43 |
| Forster Rd., Brixton Hill | 2A 22 | Foxon Cl. | 4C 74 | Friday Street, Abinger | 5B 104 | Furze Hill Rd. | 5A 134 |
| Forster Rd., Elmers End | 2F 41 | Foxon La. | 4C 74 | Friday St., Ockley | 1E 143 | Furze Hill, Kingswood | 3B 72 |
| Forsyth Path | 5C 48 | Foxon Lane Gdns. | 4C 74 | Friday Street, Kingsfold | 4B 144 | Furze Hill, Redhill | 5A 90 |
| Forsyth Rd. | 5C 48 | Foxwarren | 3C 52 | Friday Street | 5C 104 | Furze Hill, Sandy Cross | 3E 97 |
| Forsythe Cres. | 1C 40 | Foxwood Cl. | 3A 16 | Friend Av. | 5B 78 | Furze La., Farncombe | 5A 100 |
| Fort La. | 3F 89 | Frailey Cl. | 1E 65 | Friends Rd., E. Croydon | 5C 40 | Furze La., Felbridge | 1A 150 |
| Fort Rd., Guildford | 2D 101 | Frailey Hill | 1E 65 | Friends Rd., Purley | 4E 57 | Furze La., Purley | 4D 57 |
| Fort Rd., West Humble | 4F 87 | Framfield Cl. | 3B 146 | Friern Rd. | 2D 23 | Furze Rd., Addlestone | 2D 49 |
| Fortescue Av. | 3D 17 | Framfield Rd. | 1E 39 | Frimley | 3E 61 | Furze Rd., Rudgwick | 2E 157 |
| Fortescue Rd., Mitcham | 5D 21 | Frampton Cl. | 2E 55 | Frimley Av. | 1D 57 | Furze Rd., Thornton Heath | 2C 40 |
| Fortescue Rd., Weybridge | 1A 50 | France Hill Dr. | 5A 44 | Frimley Cl. | 2E 59 | Furzedown Dr. | 4E 21 |
| Forth Cl. | 4B 60 | Francemary Rd. | 1A 24 | Frimley Cres. | 2E 59 | Furzedown Rd., Belmont | 4F 55 |
| Fortrose Cl. | 4E 43 | Franche Court Rd. | 3C 20 | Frimley Gdns. | 2D 39 | Furzedown Rd., Tooting Bec | 4E 21 |
| Fortune Dr. | 2C 140 | Francis Av. | 3A 16 | Frimley Green Rd. | 3E 61 | Furzefield | 3C 146 |
| Fortyfoot Rd. | 4A 70 | Francis Chichester Cl. | 3C 28 | Frimley Grove Gdns. | 2E 61 | Furzefield Chase | 5F 131 |
| Forum, The | 2D 35 | Francis Cl., Ewell | 1A 54 | Frimley Hall Dr. | 5B 44 | Furzefield Cres. | 1C 108 |
| Foss Av. | 1E 57 | Francis Cl., Littleton | 2D 33 | Frimley High St. | 3D 61 | Furzefield Rd., Felcourt | 1B 150 |
| Foss Rd. | 4C 20 | Francis Rd., Beddington | 2C 56 | Frimley Rd., Ash Vale | 1C 78 | Furzefield Rd., Mead Vale | 1C 108 |
| Fossewood Dr. | 4B 44 | Francis Rd., Caterham | 4C 74 | Frimley Rd., Camberley | 5F 43 | Furzen La. | 5A 142 |
| Foster Down | 3B 92 | Francis Rd., Croydon | 4B 40 | Frimley Rd., Chessington | 1E 53 | Furzevale Rd. | 5A 134 |
| Foster La. | 2F 63 | Franciscan Rd. | 4D 21 | Frinton Rd. | 5E 21 | Furzewood | 1A 34 |
| Foster Rd. | 2D 9 | Franconia Rd. | 1F 21 | Friston Wk. | 3B 146 | Fydlers Cl. | 5C 10 |
| Fosters Green | 1F 45 | Frank Cl. | 2C 36 | Frith Hill Rd., Frimley | 2F 61 | Fyles Cl. | 4A 158 |
| Fosters Grove | 1F 45 | Frank Dixon Way | 2C 22 | Frith Hill Rd., Godalming | 1D 119 | | |
| Foulser Rd. | 3E 21 | Frank's Field Estate | 5F 103 | Frith Knoll | 1D 51 | | |
| Foulsham Rd. | 2C 40 | Frankfurt Rd. | 1C 22 | Frith Pk. | 1C 150 | | |
| Foundary Cl. | 4C 158 | Franklands Dr. | 2D 49 | Frith Rd. | 5B 40 | G | |
| Foundary La. | 4C 158 | Franklin Cres. | 2F 39 | Frithend Rd. | 1D 133 | | |
| Foundry La. | 3F 151 | Franklin Rd. | 3A 34 | Friths Dr. | 4F 89 | Gable Cl. | 3C 78 |
| Fountain Cl. | 5B 146 | Franklyn Rd., Ockford Ridge | 2C 118 | Frithwald Rd. | 4A 32 | Gables Av. | 4D 15 |
| Fountain Cl. | 4D 23 | | | Frobisher Cl. | 2C 74 | Gables, The | 2B 72 |
| Fountain Rd., Mitcham | 1D 39 | Franklyn Rd., Penge | 5E 23 | Frobisher Cres. | 2C 14 | Gabriel St. | 2F 23 |
| Fountain Rd., Norbury | 1B 40 | Franks Av. | 2D 37 | Frobisher Gdns. | 5B 82 | Gadbrook Rd. | 3D 107 |
| Fountain Rd., Redhill | 1D 109 | Franks Rd. | 4E 81 | Frodsham Way | 3E 43 | Gadesden Rd. | 2A 54 |
| Fountain Rd., Tooting | 4D 21 | Fransfield Gro. | 3E 23 | Frog Grove La. | 3B 80 | Gainsborough | 4D 27 |
| Fountains Av. | 3C 16 | Frant Rd. | 3B 40 | Frog La. | 2C 26 | Gainsborough Cl., Beckenham | 5A 24 |
| Fountains Cl. | 3C 16 | Fraser Gdns. | 5C 86 | Frogetts La. | 2B 142 | Gainsborough Cl., Camberley | 5B 44 |
| Fountains Garth | 2C 26 | Fraser Rd. | 1D 27 | Froghall Dr. | 2F 25 | Gainsborough Ct. | 1D 51 |
| Four Acres, Merrow | 4B 82 | Fraser St. | 2D 9 | Frogmore | 1B 20 | Gainsborough Dr., Ascot | 1A 28 |
| Four Acres, Oxshott | 5F 51 | Frasers Gdns. | 1F 105 | Frogmore Cl. | 5A 38 | Gainsborough Dr., Sanderstead | 5B 58 |
| Four Seasons Cres. | 5B 38 | Frederick Cl. | 1E 55 | Frogmore Gdns. | 1D 55 | Gainsborough Gdns. | 1E 17 |
| Four Wents | 5D 51 | Frederick Gdns. | 1E 55 | Frogmore Green | 1A 60 | Gainsborough Rd., Crawley | 5D 147 |
| Fourth Cross Rd. | 3E 17 | Frederick Pl. | 2D 25 | Frogmore Park Dr. | 1B 60 | Gainsborough Rd., Ewell | 3A 54 |
| Fourth Dr. | 1F 73 | Frederick Rd. | 1E 55 | Frogmore Rd. | 1A 60 | Gainsborough Rd., Kew | 4B 8 |
| Fowler Rd. | 5C 60 | Frederick Sanyer Rd. | 1A 100 | Frome Cl. | 4B 60 | Gainsborough Rd., Malden Manor | 4D 37 |
| Fowler's Rd. | 3A 78 | Free Prae Rd. | 4A 32 | Fromondes Rd. | 1D 55 | | |
| Fowlers Croft | 4F 99 | Freeborn Way | 1E 27 | Fruen Rd. | 2F 15 | Gainsborough Rd., Turnham Green | 2E 9 |
| Fowlers La. | 1C 26 | Freedown La. | 5F 55 | Fry Rd. | 4C 14 | | |
| Fowlers Mead | 3D 47 | Freelands Av. | 3C 58 | Fry's La. | 3D 45 | Gaist Av. | 4E 75 |
| Fox Cl., Crawley | 2C 146 | Freelands Rd. | 5D 51 | Fryern Wood | 5C 74 | Galatia Rd. | 3E 9 |
| Fox Cl., Oatlands Pk. | 1C 50 | Freemantle Rd. | 2E 45 | Fryston Av., Addiscombe | 5E 41 | Gale Cres. | 2B 72 |
| Fox Cl., Woking | 1F 65 | Freemasons Rd. | 4C 40 | Fryston Av., Woodmansterne | 1E 73 | Gales Cl. | 4C 82 |
| Fox Covert, Fetcham | 5E 69 | Freesia Dr. | 1E 63 | Fulbrook Av. | 4D 49 | Gales Dr. | 4D 147 |
| Fox Covert, Lightwater | 3F 45 | French Av. | 1E 49 | Fulbrook La. | 2D 117 | Gales Pl. | 4E 147 |
| Fox Covert La. | 3D 29 | French Gdns., Blackwater | 1B 60 | Fulford Rd., Caterham | 4C 74 | Gallery Rd. | 2C 22 |
| Fox Glove Av. | 3C 158 | French Gdns., Cobham | 5E 51 | Fulford Rd., W. Ewell | 3A 54 | Galleymead Rd. | 4B 7 |
| Fox Hill | 5A 23 | French La. | 2B 136 | Fullbrooks Av. | 4E 37 | Gallop, The, Bramley Bank | 2B 58 |
| Fox Hill Gdns. | 5D 23 | French St. | 1B 34 | Fullers Av. | 5B 36 | Gallop, The, Sutton | 3F 55 |
| Fox Hills La. | 4D 79 | French's Wells | 2B 64 | Fullers Farm Rd. | 4A 84 | Gallop, The, Windsor Great Park | 2F 11 |
| Fox Lane, Caterham | 4B 74 | Frencham Heights Rd. | 3C 114 | Fullers Rd. | 2B 114 | | |
| Fox La., Lit. Bookham | 5C 68 | Frenches Av. | 1E 49 | Fuller's Vale | 4F 133 | Galpin's Rd. | 3A 40 |
| Fox Lane North | 4A 32 | Frenches Ct. | 4B 90 | Fullers Way | 5B 36 | Galsworthy Rd., Chertsey | 4A 32 |
| Fox Lane South | 4A 32 | Frenches Rd. | 4B 90 | Fuller's Wood | 1D 59 | Galsworthy Rd., Kingston | 1C 36 |
| Fox Rd., Bracknell | 2D 27 | Frenchlands Hatch | 2C 84 | Fullers Wood La. | 1F 109 | Galveston Rd. | 1B 20 |
| Fox Rd., Farnham | 5B 96 | Frensham | 4E 115 | Fullerton Cl. | 5A 50 | Galwey Rd. | 4A 78 |
| Fox Rd., Shottermill | 2E 151 | Frensham Dr., New Addington | 2E 59 | Fullerton Dr. | 5F 49 | Gambles La., Sendmarsh | 5B 66 |
| Fox Yard | 4A 96 | Frensham Dr., Roehampton Vale | 3E 19 | Fullerton Rd., Addiscombe | 4D 41 | Gamble Rd. | 4D 21 |
| Foxborough Gdns. | 1A 24 | | | Fullerton Rd., Byfleet | 5F 49 | Gander Green La. | 1E 55 |
| Foxborough Hill | 1F 119 | Frensham La. | 1A 134 | Fullerton Rd., Carshalton | 3A 56 | Gane Cl. | 2D 57 |
| Foxborough Hill Rd. | 5C 100 | Frensham Rd., Crowthorne | 1D 43 | Fullerton Rd., Wandsworth | 1C 20 | Gangers Hill | 2C 92 |
| Foxbourne Rd. | 3E 21 | Frensham Rd., Farnham | 5A 96 | Fullerton Way | 5F 49 | Ganghill | 4B 82 |
| Foxburrows Av. | 5D 81 | Frensham Rd., Frensham | 4E 115 | Fullmer Way | 3D 49 | Gap Rd. | 4B 20 |
| Foxcombe | 2E 59 | Frensham Rd., Headley | 4E 133 | Fulmer Cl. | 4C 16 | Gapemouth Rd. | 4A 62 |
| Foxdene | 3C 118 | Frensham Rd., Hearn | 2F 133 | Fulvens | 5F 103 | Garbetts Way | 2E 97 |
| Foxdene Rd. | 5A 82 | Frensham Rd., Kenley | 5E 57 | Fulwell Park Av. | 3D 17 | Garbrand Wk. | 3B 54 |
| Foxearth Cl. | 2F 77 | Frensham Vale Rd. | 2D 115 | Fulwell Rd. | 4E 17 | Garden Av. | 5E 21 |
| Foxearth Rd. | 3B 58 | Frensham Way | 1F 71 | Fulwood Gdns. | 1F 17 | | |

| | |
|---|---|
| Garden Cl., Addlestone | 1F 49 |
| Garden Cl., Ashford | 5E 15 |
| Garden Cl., Banstead | 1B 72 |
| Garden Cl., Hanworth | 4C 16 |
| Garden Cl., Leatherhead | 5A 70 |
| Garden Cl., Roehampton | 2F 19 |
| Garden Cl., Shamley Grn. | 2C 120 |
| Garden Cl., Waddon | 1D 57 |
| Garden Cottages | 4A 54 |
| Garden House La. | 3C 150 |
| Garden La. | 2A 22 |
| Garden Rd., Anerley | 1E 41 |
| Garden Rd., Walton-on-Thames | 3A 34 |
| Garden Wk. | 5E 73 |
| Garden Wood Rd. | 2B 150 |
| Gardeners Green | 4D 145 |
| Gardeners Hill Rd. | 1D 115 |
| Gardeners Wk. | 1A 86 |
| Gardens, The, E. Bedfont | 1E 15 |
| Gardens, The, Eden Park | 1B 42 |
| Gardens, The, Esher | 1F 51 |
| Gardens, The, Pirbright | 4E 63 |
| Gardenwood La. | 2B 150 |
| Gardner Rd., Guildford | 5F 81 |
| Gardner Rd., Hanworth | 3C 16 |
| Garendon Gdns. | 4B 38 |
| Garendon Rd. | 4B 38 |
| Garfield La. | 1E 49 |
| Garfield Rd., Addlestone | 1E 49 |
| Garfield Rd., Camberley | 5A 44 |
| Garfield Rd., Twickenham | 2F 17 |
| Garfield Rd., Wimbledon | 4C 20 |
| Garibaldi Rd. | 1D 109 |
| Garland Rd. | 2B 150 |
| Garland Way | 4C 74 |
| Garlands Rd., Leatherhead | 4A 70 |
| Garlands Rd., Redhill | 5A 90 |
| Garlichill Road | 2F 71 |
| Garlies Rd. | 3F 23 |
| Garnet Rd. | 2C 40 |
| Garrads Rd. | 3F 21 |
| Garrard Rd. | 1B 72 |
| Garratt La. | 1D 57 |
| Garratt La. | 1C 20 |
| Garratt Ter. | 4D 21 |
| Garratts La. | 1B 72 |
| Garrick Cl., Hersham | 1D 51 |
| Garrick Cl., Staines | 5A 14 |
| Garrick Ct. | 5D 35 |
| Garrick Gdns., N. Sheen | 4C 8 |
| Garrick Gdns., W. Moseley | 2C 34 |
| Garrick Gr. | 5C 40 |
| Garrick Wk. | 5D 147 |
| Garrick Way | 3E 61 |
| Garrison La. | 2D 53 |
| Garside Cl. | 5D 17 |
| Garson La. | 2C 12 |
| Garson Rd. | 2F 51 |
| Garston La. | 1C 74 |
| Garstons, The | 1F 85 |
| Garth Cl., Cheam | 4A 38 |
| Garth Cl., Farnham | 5A 96 |
| Garth Rd., Kingston | 4B 18 |
| Garth Rd., North Cheam | 4A 38 |
| Garth, The, Ash | 5B 78 |
| Garth, The, Hampton Hill | 5D 17 |
| Garth, The, Oxshott | 5F 51 |
| Garthorne Rd. | 2F 23 |
| Gartmoor Gdns. | 2B 20 |
| Gascoigne Rd., New Addington | 3E 59 |
| Gascoigne Rd., Weybridge | 5D 33 |
| Gasden Copse | 5A 118 |
| Gasden La. | 5A 118 |
| Gaskarth Rd. | 1E 21 |
| Gaskyns Cl. | 2E 157 |
| Gassiot Rd. | 4E 21 |
| Gassiot Way | 5D 39 |
| Gasson Wood Rd. | 5A 146 |
| Gaston Bridge Rd. | 3F 33 |
| Gaston Rd. | 2E 39 |
| Gaston Way | 3E 33 |
| Gate Rd. | 5E 33 |
| Gateford Dr. | 3C 158 |
| Gatehouse Cl. | 5D 19 |
| Gates Green Rd. | 5C 42 |
| Gatesden Rd,. | 5E 69 |
| Gateside Rd. | 3D 21 |
| Gatestone Rd. | 5C 22 |
| Gateway | 5E 33 |
| Gateway, The | 5B 48 |
| Gateways | 1E 101 |
| Gatfield Gro. | 3C 16 |
| Gatley Av. | 1F 53 |
| Gatton | 2A 90 |
| Gatton Cl., Belmont | 3F 55 |
| Gatton Cl., Reigate | 4F 89 |
| Gatton Park Rd. | 4A 90 |
| Gatton Rd., Reigate | 4F 89 |
| Gatton Rd., Tooting | 4D 21 |
| Gatwick Rd., Crawley | 2E 147 |
| Gatwick Rd., Southfields | 2B 20 |
| Gauntlet Cres. | 3C 74 |
| Gauntlett Rd. | 1A 56 |
| Gavell Rd. | 5D 51 |
| Gaveston Cl. | 5F 49 |
| Gaveston Rd. | 3F 69 |
| Gayfere Rd. | 1C 54 |
| Gayford Rd. | 1E 9 |
| Gayhouse La. | 5C 110 |
| Gaynesford Rd., Carshalton on the Hill | 2A 56 |
| Gaynesford Rd., Forest Hill | 3F 23 |
| Gayville Rd. | 1E 21 |
| Gaywood Ct. | 2D 22 |
| Gaywood Rd. | 2B 70 |
| Gemini Cl. | 5A 146 |
| Geneva Cl. | 1F 33 |
| Geneva Rd., Kingston | 2B 36 |
| Geneva Rd., Thornton Heath | 3B 40 |
| Genoa Av | 1A 20 |
| Genoa Rd. | 1E 41 |
| Gentles La. | 5F 133 |
| George La. | 1B 24 |
| George Denyer Cl. | 2A 152 |
| George Rd., Farncombe | 5A 100 |
| George Rd., Guildford | 5F 81 |
| George Rd., Kingston Hill | 5C 18 |
| George Rd., Malden | 2E 37 |
| George Rd., Milford | 3B 118 |
| George St., Croydon | 5C 40 |
| George St., Richmond | 1B 18 |
| George St., Staines | 4A 14 |
| George St., Sutton | 1F 55 |
| Georgelands | 4B 66 |
| George's Rd. | 3E 77 |
| Georges Terr. | 4C 74 |
| Georgia Rd. | 1B 40 |
| Georgian Cl., Camberley | 4B 44 |
| Georgian Cl., Staines | 4B 14 |
| Geraldine Rd., Brentford | 3C 8 |
| Geraldine Rd., Wandsworth | 1C 20 |
| Geralds Gr. | 5D 55 |
| Gerard Av. | 2C 16 |
| Gerard Rd. | 4E 9 |
| Germander Dr. | 1E 63 |
| Gerotus Pl. | 4A 32 |
| Ghent St. | 3A 24 |
| Gibbet La. | 4C 44 |
| Gibbon Rd. | 1B 36 |
| Gibbs Av. | 4C 22 |
| Gibbs Brook La. | 1C 112 |
| Giblets La. | 2C 158 |
| Gibraltar Cres. | 3B 54 |
| Gibson Cl. | 1D 53 |
| Gibson Pl. | 1B 14 |
| Gibson Rd. | 1F 55 |
| Gibsons Hill | 5B 22 |
| Gidd Hill | 1E 73 |
| Giffard Rd. | 4C 60 |
| Giggshill Gdns. | 4F 35 |
| Giggshill Rd. | 4F 35 |
| Gilbert Rd., Frimley | 2D 61 |
| Gilbert Rd., Wimbledon | 5C 20 |
| Gilbey Rd. | 4D 21 |
| Gilders Rd. | 2E 53 |
| Giles Cop | 4D 23 |
| Giles Travers Cl. | 2E 31 |
| Gilham's Av. | 4D 55 |
| Gilham's La. | 3D 151 |
| Gilkes Cres. | 1C 22 |
| Gill Av. | 1A 100 |
| Gillett Rd. | 2C 40 |
| Gilliam Gr. | 3E 57 |
| Gillian Av. | 1D 97 |
| Gillian Cl. | 1D 97 |
| Gillian Dr. | 4C 82 |
| Gillian Park Rd. | 4B 38 |
| Gillian St. | 1A 24 |
| Gilliat Dr. | 4C 82 |
| Gilmais | 1A 86 |
| Gilmore Cres. | 4D 15 |
| Gilpin Av. | 5D 9 |
| Gilpin Cres. | 2D 17 |
| Gilsland Rd. | 2C 40 |
| Gilton Rd. | 3C 24 |
| Gimcrack Hill | 4A 70 |
| Gingers Cl. | 2D 141 |
| Ginhams Rd. | 4C 146 |
| Gipsy La., Bracknell | 1D 27 |
| Gipsy La., Wokingham | 3E 25 |
| Gipsy Rd. | 4C 22 |
| Gipsy Road Gdns. | 4C 22 |
| Girdwood Rd. | 2A 20 |
| Girton Cl. | 3E 43 |
| Girton Gdns. | 5A 42 |
| Girton Rd. | 4F 23 |
| Givons Gro. | 1D 87 |
| Glade Spur | 4C 72 |
| Glade, The, East Ewell | 3D 55 |
| Glade, The, Fetcham | 4D 69 |
| Glade, The, Furnace Green | 5E 147 |
| Glade, The, Kingswood | 4B 72 |
| Glade, The, Monks Orchard | 3F 41 |
| Glade, The, Old Coulsdon | 3B 74 |
| Glade, The, Staines | 5B 14 |
| Glade, The, Stoneleigh | 2C 54 |
| Glade, The, West Wickham | 5B 42 |
| Gladeside | 3F 41 |
| Gladeside Cl. | 2D 53 |
| Gladsmuir Cl. | 5A 34 |
| Gladstone Av. Feltham | 1A 16 |
| Gladstone Av. Twickenham | 2E 17 |
| Gladstone Rd., Acton Green | 1D 9 |
| Gladstone Rd., Ashtead | 2B 70 |
| Gladstone Rd., Croydon | 4C 40 |
| Gladstone Rd., Hook | 5B 36 |
| Gladstone Rd., Horsham | 4B 158 |
| Gladstone Rd., Kingston | 2C 36 |
| Gladstone Rd., Wimbledon | 5B 20 |
| Glamis Cl. | 3F 61 |
| Glamorgan Rd. | 5A 18 |
| Glanfield Rd. | 2A 42 |
| Glanty | 4E 13 |
| Glanty, The | 4E 13 |
| Glanville Rd. | 1A 22 |
| Glasbrook Av. | 2C 16 |
| Glasford St. | 5E 21 |
| Glassonby Wk. | 5D 45 |
| Glastonbury Rd. | 4B 38 |
| Glayshers Hill | 4A 134 |
| Glazebrook Cl. | 3C 22 |
| Glazebrook Rd. | 5E 17 |
| Glazier Rd. | 4A 134 |
| Glaziers La. | 4F 79 |
| Glebe Av. | 1D 39 |
| Glebe Cl., Crawley | 3D 147 |
| Glebe Cl., Gt. Bookham | 1F 85 |
| Glebe Cl., Lightwater | 3A 46 |
| Glebe Cottages | 5E 83 |
| Glebe Ct., Guildford | 5A 82 |
| Glebe Ct., Mitcham | 2D 39 |
| Glebe Gdns., Byfleet | 5F 49 |
| Glebe Gdns., Malden | 4E 37 |
| Glebe Hyrst | 4A 58 |
| Glebe La., Abinger | 5B 104 |
| Glebe La., Rushmoor | 5A 116 |
| Glebe Path | 2D 39 |
| Glebe Rd., Arford | 4F 133 |
| Glebe Rd., Ashtead | 2B 70 |
| Glebe Rd., Barnes | 4E 9 |
| Glebe Rd., Carshalton | 2B 56 |
| Glebe Rd., Cranleigh | 1C 140 |
| Glebe Rd., Dorking | 1F 105 |
| Glebe Rd., East Ewell | 3D 55 |
| Glebe Rd., Egham | 5F 13 |
| Glebe Rd., Hooley | 5E 73 |
| Glebe Rd., Old Windsor | 1B 12 |
| Glebe Rd., Staines | 4B 14 |
| Glebe Rd., Warlingham | 2F 75 |
| Glebe Rd., West Heath | 4C 60 |
| Glebe St., Chiswick | 2D 9 |
| Glebe St., Twickenham | 1F 17 |
| Glebe, The, Blackwater | 1B 60 |
| Glebe, The, Ewhurst | 5C 122 |
| Glebe, The, Horley | 2B 128 |
| Glebe, The, Leigh | 4F 107 |
| Glebe, The, Malden | 4E 37 |
| Glebe Way, Hanworth | 3C 16 |
| Glebe Way, Sanderstead | 4A 58 |
| Glebe Way, W. Wickham | 5B 42 |
| Glebelands/ Claygate | 3C 52 |
| Glebelands, East Molesey | 2D 35 |
| Glebelands Gdns. | 3E 33 |
| Glebelands Rd., Camberley | 1C 60 |
| Glebelands Rd., Feltham | 2A 16 |
| Glebelands Rd., Wokingham | 1D 25 |
| Glebewood | 3D 27 |
| Gledhow Wood | 4C 72 |
| Glen Albyn Rd. | 3A 20 |
| Glen Av. | 4D 15 |
| Glen Cl., Hindhead | 4D 135 |
| Glen Cl., Kingswood | 5A 72 |
| Glen Cl., Littleton | 2D 33 |
| Glen Gdns. | 1E 57 |
| Glen Lea | 1E 151 |
| Glen Rd., Grayshott | 5D 135 |
| Glen Rd., Hindhead | 4D 135 |
| Glen Rd., Hook | 1E 53 |
| Glen Road End | 3B 56 |
| Glen, The, Addlestone | 1D 49 |
| Glen, The, Shirley | 5F 41 |
| Glen Vue | 2C 150 |
| Glena Mount | 1F 55 |
| Glenavon Cl. | 2C 52 |
| Glenbow Rd. | 5C 24 |
| Glenbuck Rd. | 3B 36 |
| Glenburnie Rd. | 3D 21 |
| Glencairn Rd. | 5A 22 |
| Glenco Cl. | 3F 61 |
| Glencoe | 3F 61 |
| Glencoe Rd. | 5D 33 |
| Glendale Cl. | 2C 64 |
| Glendale Dr., Burpham | 3B 82 |
| Glendale Dr., Wimbledon | 4B 20 |
| Glendale Gro. | 3B 82 |
| Glendale Rd. | 1B 74 |
| Glendene Av. | 1C 84 |
| Glendower Rd. | 5D 9 |
| Gleneagle Rd. | 4F 21 |
| Gleneagles Cl. | 1B 14 |
| Gleneagles Dr. | 5A 60 |
| Gleneldon Rd. | 4A 22 |
| Glenelg Rd. | 1A 22 |
| Glenfarg Rd. | 2B 24 |
| Glenfield | 1A 8 |
| Glenfield Cl. | 2C 106 |
| Glenfield Rd., Banstead | 1B 72 |
| Glenfield Rd., Strood Grn. | 2C 106 |
| Glenfield Rd., Streatham | 2F 21 |
| Glenfield Rd., Sunbury | 5E 15 |
| Glengarry Rd. | 1D 23 |
| Glenheadon Rise | 5B 70 |
| Glenhurst | 3F 45 |
| Glenhurst Rise | 5C 22 |
| Glenhurst Rd. | 3A 8 |
| Glenister Park Rd. | 5F 21 |
| Glenmore Cl. | 5B 32 |
| Glenmount Rd. | 1C 78 |
| Glenn Av. | 4E 57 |
| Glennie Rd. | 3B 22 |
| Glentham Rd. | 3F 9 |
| Glenthorne Av. | 4E 41 |
| Glenthorne Cl. | 4B 38 |
| Glenthorne Gdns. | 4B 38 |
| Glenthorne Rd., Hammersmith | 2F 9 |
| Glenthorne Rd., Kingston | 2B 36 |
| Glenthorpe Rd. | 3A 38 |
| Glenville Gdns. | 5E 135 |
| Glenville Rd. | 1C 36 |
| Glenwood, Bracknell | 2E 27 |
| Glenwood, Dorking | 2A 106 |
| Glenwood Rd., Catford | 2A 24 |
| Glenwood Rd., Ewell | 2B 54 |
| Globe Path | 5D 43 |
| Glory Mead | 3A 106 |
| Glossop Rd. | 3F 57 |
| Gloster Rd., Malden | 2E 37 |
| Gloster Rd., Woking | 3E 65 |
| Gloucester Cl., Frimley | 3E 61 |
| Gloucester Cl., Thames Ditton | 4F 35 |
| Gloucester Ct. | 3C 8 |
| Gloucester Cres. | 5C 14 |
| Gloucester Dr. | 3F 13 |
| Gloucester Gdns., Bagshot | 2E 45 |
| Gloucester Gdns., Sutton | 5C 38 |
| Gloucester Rd., Aldershot | 1D 97 |
| Gloucester Rd., Bagshot | 2E 45 |
| Gloucester Rd., Croydon | 4C 40 |
| Gloucester Rd., Feltham | 2B 16 |
| Gloucester Rd., Hampton Hill | 5D 17 |
| Gloucester Rd., Kew | 3C 8 |
| Gloucester Rd., Kingston | 2C 36 |
| Gloucester Rd., Lammas Park | 1A 8 |
| Gloucester Rd., Redhill | 5B 90 |
| Gloucester Rd., Twickenham | 4E 17 |
| Gloucester Rd., Whitton | 2D 17 |
| Gloucester Rd., Woodbridge Hill | 4E 81 |
| Glovers Field | 3E 151 |
| Glovers Rd., Charlwood | 4D 127 |
| Glover's Rd., Reigate | 1C 108 |
| Glyn Cl. | 3B 54 |
| Glyn Rd. | 5A 38 |
| Glynswood, Camberley | 1E 61 |
| Glynswood, Upper Bourne | 2C 114 |
| Goat Rd. | 4E 39 |
| Goaters Rd. | 1A 28 |
| Goatsfield Rd. | 3E 77 |
| Godalming | 1D 119 |
| Godalming Av. | 1D 57 |
| Godalming Rd. | 1D 139 |
| Goddard Cl. | 2D 33 |
| Goddard Rd. | 2F 41 |
| Goddards La. | 1D 61 |
| Godden Cres. | 5C 60 |
| Godfrey Av. | 2E 17 |
| Godfrey Way | 2C 16 |

| Street | Ref. |
|---|---|
| Godley Rd., Byfleet | 5A 50 |
| Godley Rd., Earlsfield | 2C 20 |
| Godolphin Cl. | 3E 55 |
| Godolphin Rd., Hammersmith | 1F 9 |
| Godolphin Rd., Weybridge | 2B 50 |
| Godric Cres. | 3E 59 |
| Godson Rd. | 5B 40 |
| Godstone | 4B 92 |
| Godstone Bypass | 3B 92 |
| Godstone Hill | 2B 92 |
| Godstone Rd., Bletchingley | 5F 91 |
| Godstone Rd., Caterham | 5D 75 |
| Godstone Rd., Kenley | 1C 74 |
| Godstone Rd., Lingfield | 1E 131 |
| Godstone Rd., Oxted | 4D 93 |
| Godstone Rd., Purley | 4E 57 |
| Godstone Rd., Sutton | 1F 55 |
| Godstone Rd., Twickenham | 1F 17 |
| Godstone Rd., Whyteleafe | 1D 75 |
| Godwin Cl. | 2B 54 |
| Goff's Rd. | 5E 15 |
| Goffs Cl. | 4C 146 |
| Goffs Lane | 4C 146 |
| Goffs Park Rd. | 5C 146 |
| Gogmore La. | 4A 32 |
| Goidel Cl. | 1C 56 |
| Gold Cup La. | 1A 28 |
| Gold Hill | 1E 115 |
| Gold Hill Manor | 1E 115 |
| Goldcliff Cl. | 4B 37 |
| Goldcrest Cl. | 2A 128 |
| Goldcrest Way, New Addington | 2E 59 |
| Goldcrest Way, Woodcote | 3C 56 |
| Goldfinch Cl. | 3D 147 |
| Goldfinch Gdns. | 5C 82 |
| Goldfinch Rd. | 3C 58 |
| Goldhawk Rd. | 2E 9 |
| Goldney Rd. | 1F 61 |
| Goldrings Rd. | 5A 52 |
| Goldsworth Orchard | 2B 64 |
| Goldsmith Way | 2D 43 |
| Goldsworth Rd. | 2C 64 |
| Goldwell Rd. | 2A 40 |
| Gole Rd. | 4D 63 |
| Golf Cl. | 5D 49 |
| Golf Club Dr. | 5D 19 |
| Golf Club Rd., Weybridge | 3B 50 |
| Golf Club Rd., Woking | 3B 64 |
| Golf Dr. | 1F 61 |
| Golf House Rd., Limpsfield | 3B 94 |
| Golf Links Av. | 4D 135 |
| Golf Rd., Kenley | 2C 74 |
| Golf Side, Belmont | 4D 55 |
| Golf Side, Twickenham | 3E 17 |
| Golfside Cl. | 1E 37 |
| Goliath Cl. | 2D 57 |
| Gomer Gdns. | 5F 17 |
| Gomer Pl. | 5F 17 |
| Gomshall | 3E 103 |
| Gomshall Av. | 1D 57 |
| Gomshall Gdns. | 1C 74 |
| Gomshall La. | 3D 103 |
| Gomshall Rd. | 3D 55 |
| Gong Hill | 2E 115 |
| Gong Hill Dr. | 2E 115 |
| Gonville Rd. | 3A 40 |
| Goodchild Rd. | 2E 25 |
| Goodenough Cl. | 3A 74 |
| Goodenough Rd. | 5B 20 |
| Goodenough Way | 3A 74 |
| Goodhart Way | 4C 42 |
| Goodhew Rd. | 3D 41 |
| Goodings Grn. | 2F 25 |
| Goodman Pl. | 4A 14 |
| Goodrich Rd. | 1D 23 |
| Goodways Dr. | 1D 27 |
| Goodwin Gdns. | 2E 57 |
| Goodwin Rd., Hammersmith | 1F 9 |
| Goodwin Rd., South Croydon | 1E 57 |
| Goodwood Cl., Camberley | 4A 44 |
| Goodwood Rd., Morden | 2B 38 |
| Goodwood Close, Tilgate | 5E 147 |
| Goodwood Rd. | 4A 90 |
| Goodwyns Rd. | 3A 106 |
| Goose Bank Cl. | 4F 45 |
| Goose Grn., Downside | 3A 68 |
| Goose Grn., Gomshall | 3E 103 |
| Goose La. | 4B 64 |
| Goose Pl. | 4A 32 |
| Goose Rye Rd. | 1D 81 |
| Gordon Av., Camberley | 1D 61 |
| Gordon Av., East Sheen | 5D 9 |
| Gordon Av., Purley | 3F 57 |
| Gordon Av., Richmond | 1F 17 |
| Gordon Cl. | 4B 14 |
| Gordon Cres. | 1D 61 |
| Gordon Dr., Chertsey | 5A 32 |
| Gordon Dr., Shepperton | 4E 33 |
| Gordon Rd., Ashford | 3C 14 |
| Gordon Rd., Camberley | 5A 44 |
| Gordon Rd., Carshalton Beeches | 2A 56 |
| Gordon Rd., Caterham | 4C 74 |
| Gordon Rd., Chiswick | 3C 8 |
| Gordon Rd., Claygate | 2B 52 |
| Gordon Rd., Crowthorne | 2E 43 |
| Gordon Rd., Eden Park | 2A 42 |
| Gordon Rd., Egham | 4E 13 |
| Gordon Rd., Elmers End | 2F 41 |
| Gordon Rd., Horsham | 4B 158 |
| Gordon Rd., Kingston | 1B 36 |
| Gordon Rd., Lower Halliford | 3E 33 |
| Gordon Rd., North Sheen | 4C 8 |
| Gordon Rd., Redhill | 4B 90 |
| Gordon Rd., S. Farnboro' | 2B 78 |
| Gordon Rd., Surbiton | 4B 36 |
| Gordonbrook Rd. | 1A 24 |
| Gordondale | 3B 20 |
| Gordons Way | 2E 93 |
| Gore Rd. | 1F 37 |
| Goring Rd. | 4F 13 |
| Goring Sq. | 4A 14 |
| Gorings Mead | 5B 158 |
| Gorling Cl. | 4A 146 |
| Gorringe Park Av. | 5E 21 |
| Gorse Cl. | 1D 115 |
| Gorse Ct. | 4C 82 |
| Gorse End | 3B 158 |
| Gorse Hill | 2D 31 |
| Gorse Hill Rd. | 2C 30 |
| Gorse La., Chobham | 2D 47 |
| Gorse La., Farnham | 1D 115 |
| Gorse Rise | 4E 21 |
| Gorse Rd., Frimley | 2E 61 |
| Gorse Rd., Shirley | 5A 42 |
| Gorselands Cl. | 4E 49 |
| Gorsewood Rd. | 3A 64 |
| Gorst Rd. | 1D 21 |
| Gosburton Rd. | 2E 21 |
| Gosbury Hill | 1E 53 |
| Gosden Cl., Bramley | 5D 101 |
| Gosden Cl., Crawley | 4E 147 |
| Gosden Common Rd. | 5D 101 |
| Gosden Hill Rd. | 3B 82 |
| Gosden Rd. | 5B 46 |
| Gosfield Rd. | 4A 54 |
| Gossops Dr. | 4B 146 |
| Gossops Green La. | 4B 146 |
| Gostling Rd. | 2D 17 |
| Goston Gdns. | 2B 40 |
| Gothic Rd. | 3E 17 |
| Goudhurst Rd. | 4C 24 |
| Gough's La. | 1D 27 |
| Goughs Meadow | 4D 43 |
| Gould Ct. | 4C 82 |
| Gould Rd., East Bedfont | 2F 15 |
| Gould Rd., Twickenham | 2E 17 |
| Government Ho. Rd. | 2A 78 |
| Government Rd. | 4B 78 |
| Govett Av. | 3E 33 |
| Govett Gr. | 1A 46 |
| Gower Rd. | 2B 50 |
| Gower, The, | 2E 31 |
| Graburn Way | 2E 35 |
| Grace Reynolds Wk | 5A 44 |
| Gracedale Rd. | 4E 21 |
| Gracefield Gdns. | 3A 22 |
| Graciouspond Rd. | 2E 47 |
| Graemesdyke Rd. | 5C 8 |
| Graffham Cl. | 3B 146 |
| Grafton Cl., W. Byfleet | 5D 49 |
| Grafton Cl., Whitton | 2C 16 |
| Grafton Cl., Worcester Park | 5E 37 |
| Grafton Park Rd. | 5E 37 |
| Grafton Rd., Croydon | 4B 40 |
| Grafton Rd., New Malden | 2E 37 |
| Grafton Rd., Worcester Park | 5D 37 |
| Graham Av., Lammas Park | 1A 8 |
| Graham Av., Mitcham | 1E 39 |
| Graham Cl. | 5A 42 |
| Graham Gdns. | 4B 36 |
| Graham Rd., Acton | 1D 9 |
| Graham Rd., Hampton | 4C 16 |
| Graham Rd., Mitcham | 1E 39 |
| Graham Rd., Purley | 5E 57 |
| Graham Rd., Wimbledon | 5B 20 |
| Graigans | 4B 146 |
| Granada St. | 4D 21 |
| Granard Av. | 1F 19 |
| Granard Rd. | 2D 21 |
| Granary Cl. | 1B 128 |
| Granary Way | 5A 158 |
| Grand Av., Camberley | 5A 44 |
| Grand Av., Surbiton | 3C 36 |
| Grand Dr. | 3A 38 |
| Grand Stand Rd. | 2E 71 |
| Grand View Av. | 2E 77 |
| Granden Rd. | 1A 40 |
| Grandford Rd. | 5B 158 |
| Grandison Rd., Clapham | 1E 21 |
| Grandison Rd., N. Cheam | 5F 37 |
| Grange Av., Beulah Hill | 1C 40 |
| Grange Av., Crowthorne | 1D 43 |
| Grange Av., Surbiton | 3C 36 |
| Grange Av., Twickenham | 3E 17 |
| Grange Cl., Ashtead | 3A 70 |
| Grange Cl., Bellfields | 3E 81 |
| Grange Cl., Malden | 3E 37 |
| Grange Cl., Merstham | 2B 90 |
| Grange Cl., Three Bridges | 3E 147 |
| Grange Cl., Wimbledon | 1E 119 |
| Grange Cl., Wraysbury | 1D 13 |
| Grange Court, S. Godstone | 2F 111 |
| Grange Ct., Walton | 5A 34 |
| Grange Dr., Merstham | 2C 90 |
| Grange Dr., Woking | 1D 65 |
| Grange End | 2E 129 |
| Grange Farm Rd. | 4C 78 |
| Grange Gdns., Banstead | 5F 55 |
| Grange Gdns., Norwood | 1C 40 |
| Grange Hill | 1C 40 |
| Grange La. | 3D 23 |
| Grange Meadow | 5F 55 |
| Grange Mill Way | 3A 24 |
| Grange Mount | 3A 70 |
| Grange Park Rd. | 2C 40 |
| Grange Park, Cranleigh | 1D 141 |
| Grange Park, Woking | 1D 65 |
| Grange Park Cl. | 5E 19 |
| Grange Pl. | 1B 32 |
| Grange Rd., Ash | 5C 78 |
| Grange Rd., Ashtead | 3A 70 |
| Grange Rd., Barnes | 4E 9 |
| Grange Rd., Bellfields | 4E 81 |
| Grange Rd., Beulah Hill | 2C 40 |
| Grange Rd., Bracknell | 1D 27 |
| Grange Rd., Camberley | 5B 44 |
| Grange Rd., Caterham | 1A 92 |
| Grange Rd., Cheam | 2E 55 |
| Grange Rd., Chiswick | 2C 8 |
| Grange Rd., Crawley Down | 3D 149 |
| Grange Rd., Egham | 4D 13 |
| Grange Rd., Farnborough Green | 3D 61 |
| Grange Rd., Hersham | 1E 51 |
| Grange Rd., Hook | 1E 53 |
| Grange Rd., Kingston | 2B 36 |
| Grange Rd., Molesey | 3D 35 |
| Grange Rd., Pirbright | 5B 62 |
| Grange Rd., Sanderstead | 3F 57 |
| Grange Rd., Tilford | 4A 116 |
| Grange Rd., Tongham | 2E 97 |
| Grange Rd., Woking | 5A 48 |
| Grange Rd., Woodham | 3D 49 |
| Grange, The, Redhill | 4B 90 |
| Grange, The, Shirley | 3F 41 |
| Grange, The, Wimbledon | 5A 20 |
| Grange, The, Worc. Pk. | 1A 54 |
| Grange Vale | 2F 55 |
| Grangecliffe Gdns. | 1C 40 |
| Grangefields Rd. | 2F 81 |
| Grangemill Rd. | 3A 24 |
| Grangeway | 2E 129 |
| Grant Cl. | 3E 33 |
| Grant Pl. | 4D 41 |
| Grant Rd., Addiscombe | 4D 41 |
| Grant Rd., Crowthorne | 2D 43 |
| Grantham Rd. | 3D 9 |
| Grantley Av. | 1B 120 |
| Grantley Cl. | 4D 101 |
| Grantley Gdns. | 5E 81 |
| Grantley Rd. | 5E 81 |
| Granton Rd. | 5F 21 |
| Grants La. | 4B 94 |
| Grantwood Cl. | 3E 109 |
| Granville Av., Feltham | 3A 16 |
| Granville Av., Hounslow | 1C 16 |
| Granville Cl. | 2B 50 |
| Granville Gdns. | 5A 22 |
| Granville Rd., New Oxted | 3F 93 |
| Granville Rd., Southfields | 2B 20 |
| Granville Rd., Weybridge | 2B 50 |
| Granville Rd., Woking | 4D 65 |
| Grasmere Av., Cove | 5B 60 |
| Grasmere Av., Kingston Vale | 4D 19 |
| Grasmere Av., Morden | 2B 38 |
| Grasmere Av., Whitton | 1D 17 |
| Grasmere Cl., East Bedfont | 2F 15 |
| Grasmere Cl., Guildford | 5B 82 |
| Grasmere Rd., Lightwater | 3F 45 |
| Grasmere Rd., Purley | 4E 57 |
| Grasmere Rd., Streatham | 4A 22 |
| Grasmere Rd., Woodside | 3E 41 |
| Grass Mount | 3E 23 |
| Grass Way | 1C 56 |
| Grassmere Way | 4A 50 |
| Grassmount | 3C 56 |
| Grattons Dr. | 3F 147 |
| Gravel Hill, Addington | 2C 58 |
| Gravel Hill, Leatherhead | 4F 69 |
| Gravel Rd., South Farnborough | 2B 78 |
| Gravel Rd., Twickenham | 2E 17 |
| Gravel Rd., Upper Hale | 1A 96 |
| Gravelley Ride | 4F 19 |
| Gravelly Hill | 2A 92 |
| Graveney Gr. | 5E 23 |
| Graveney Rd. | 4D 21 |
| Gravetts La. | 3D 81 |
| Gravetye Cl. | 5E 147 |
| Grayham Rd. | 2D 37 |
| Graylands | 1D 65 |
| Grays Cl. | 2A 152 |
| Grays La., Ashford | 4D 15 |
| Grays La., Ashtead | 3C 70 |
| Grays Rd. | 5A 100 |
| Grayshot Dr. | 5D 43 |
| Grayshott | 5D 135 |
| Grayshott Laurels | 4E 133 |
| Grayshott Rd. | 4A 134 |
| Grayswood | 1B 152 |
| Grayswood Dr. | 1C 78 |
| Grayswood Gdns. | 2F 37 |
| Grayswood Hill | 2B 152 |
| Grayswood Rd. | 2A 152 |
| Great Austins | 5B 96 |
| Great Bookham | 1F 85 |
| Great Chertsey Rd. Hanworth | 3C 16 |
| Great Chertsey Rd., Grove Park | 4D 9 |
| Great Ellshams | 1B 72 |
| Great George St. | 2D 119 |
| Great Goodwin Dr. | 4B 82 |
| Great Hollands Rd. | 3B 26 |
| Great Oaks Pk. | 3B 82 |
| Great Quarry | 2C 100 |
| Great South-West Rd. | 1E 15 |
| Great Tattenhams | 2F 71 |
| Great West Rd., Brentford | 3A 8 |
| Great West Rd., Chiswick | 3E 9 |
| Great Woodcote Pk. | 3D 57 |
| Greatfield Rd. | 3C 60 |
| Greatford Dr. | 5C 82 |
| Greathearst End | 5C 68 |
| Greatlake Ct. | 2B 128 |
| Greatwood Cl. | 3B 48 |
| Greaves Pl. | 4D 21 |
| Grebe Cl. | 3B 158 |
| Grecias Crescent | 5B 22 |
| Green Acres, Deadwater | 5D 133 |
| Green Acres, The Sands | 4D 97 |
| Green Av. | 1A 8 |
| Green Cl., Hanworth | 4B 16 |
| Green Cl., Shortlands | 2C 42 |
| Green Cl., The Wrythe | 5D 39 |
| Green Croft | 5B 82 |
| Green Curve | 5E 55 |
| Green Dale | 1C 22 |
| Green Dene | 4C 84 |
| Green Dragon La. | 2B 8 |
| Green Dr., Sendmarsh | 5A 66 |
| Green Dr., Wokingham | 3E 25 |
| Green End | 1E 53 |
| Green Farm Rd. | 2E 45 |
| Green Hangar | 3C 134 |
| Green Hedges Av. | 2C 150 |
| Green Hill Cl., Camberley | 5D 45 |
| Green Hill La. | 2F 75 |
| Green Hill Rd., Camberley | 5D 45 |
| Green Hill Way | 1C 114 |
| Green La., Alford Crossways | 5A 140 |
| Green La., Ash | 1A 98 |
| Green La., Bagshot | 3E 45 |
| Green La., Binscombe | 4A 100 |
| Green La., Blackwater | 1B 60 |
| Green La., Byfleet | 4A 50 |
| Green La., Caterham | 4B 74 |
| Green La., Cheapside | 1D 29 |
| Green La., Chertsey | 5F 31 |
| Green La., Chessington | 3E 53 |
| Green La., Chobham | 3E 47 |
| Green La., Churt | 3C 134 |
| Green La., Cobham | 4E 51 |
| Green La., Dockenfield | 5B 114 |
| Green La., East Molesey | 3D 35 |
| Green La., Egham | 4E 13 |
| Green La., Farnham | 2C 96 |
| Green La., Forest Green | 1C 142 |

| Name | Ref |
|---|---|
| Hatch Rd. | 1A 40 |
| Hatches, The | 4D 61 |
| Hatchet La. | 4C 10 |
| Hatchett | 2E 15 |
| Hatchetts Dr. | 3D 151 |
| Hatchfield Rd. | 3B 70 |
| Hatchgate | 3B 128 |
| Hatchlands Rd. | 5A 90 |
| Hatchways | 4D 121 |
| Hatfield Cl. | 2C 37 |
| Hatfield Mead | 3B 38 |
| Hatfield Rd., Ashtead | 3B 70 |
| Hatfield Rd., Ealing | 1D 9 |
| Hathaway Rd. | 4B 40 |
| Hatherleigh Cl. | 2B 38 |
| Hatherley Rd. | 4B 8 |
| Hatherop Rd. | 5C 16 |
| Hathersham Cl. | 2E 129 |
| Hathersham La. | 5A 110 |
| Hathersham Rd. | 1D 129 |
| Hatherwood | 4B 70 |
| Hathesham Cl. | 2E 129 |
| Hatton Gdns. | 3E 39 |
| Hatton Hill Rd. | 1F 45 |
| Hatton Rd. | 2E 15 |
| Havana Rd. | 3B 20 |
| Harvard Rd. | 3E 43 |
| Havelock Rd., Addiscombe | 5D 41 |
| Havelock Rd., Wimbledon | 4C 20 |
| Havelock Rd., Wokingham | 2D 25 |
| Haven Gate | 3C 158 |
| Haven Rd., Ashford | 4D 15 |
| Haven Rd., Bucks Green | 3E 157 |
| Haven, The | 5C 8 |
| Haven Way | 3B 96 |
| Haverfield Rd. | 3C 8 |
| Haverhill Rd. | 2F 21 |
| Havers Av. | 1E 51 |
| Haversham Cl. | 1B 18 |
| Haversham Dr. | 3D 27 |
| Hawarden Gro. | 2B 22 |
| Hawarden Rd. | 4B 74 |
| Hawes Lane | 4B 42 |
| Hawk La. | 2E 27 |
| Hawke Rise | 1F 85 |
| Hawke Rd. | 5C 22 |
| Hawker Cl. | 2D 57 |
| Hawkes Leap | 1F 45 |
| Hawkes Rd. | 1D 39 |
| Hawkesbourne Rd. | 3C 158 |
| Hawkesbury Rd. | 1F 19 |
| Hawkesfield Rd. | 3F 23 |
| Hawkesley Cl. | 4F 17 |
| Hawkesmoor Rd. | 5A 146 |
| Hawkeswood Rd. | 2A 34 |
| Hawkesworth Dr. | 3D 45 |
| Hawkhirst Rd. | 1C 74 |
| Hawkhurst | 5A 52 |
| Hawkhurst Way, Malden | 3D 37 |
| Hawkhurst Way, W. Wickham | 5A 42 |
| Hawkins Rd. | 5D 147 |
| Hawks Hill | 5F 69 |
| Hawks Hill Cl. | 5F 69 |
| Hawks Rd. | 1B 36 |
| Hawks Way | 3A 14 |
| Hawkshill Cl. | 2F 51 |
| Hawkshill Way | 2F 51 |
| Hawkslade Rd. | 1F 23 |
| Hawksview | 5F 51 |
| Hawkswell Cl. | 1A 64 |
| Hawkswell Path | 2A 64 |
| Hawkswood Av. | 2E 61 |
| Hawkswood Dell | 1F 85 |
| Hawkswood Rise | 1F 85 |
| Hawkswood Rd. | 2A 34 |
| Hawley | 2C 60 |
| Hawley Cl. | 5C 16 |
| Hawley La. | 2C 60 |
| Hawley Rd. | 1B 60 |
| Hawley Way | 4D 15 |
| Haws La. | 1A 14 |
| Hawstead Rd. | 1A 24 |
| Hawth Av. | 5D 147 |
| Hawth Cl. | 5D 147 |
| Hawthorn Av., Biggin Hill | 1E 77 |
| Hawthorn Av., Carshalton on the Hill | 2B 56 |
| Hawthorn Av., Norbury | 1B 40 |
| Hawthorn Cl., Crawley | 2C 146 |
| Hawthorn Cl., Hanworth | 4C 16 |
| Hawthorn Cl., Salfords | 3E 109 |
| Hawthorn Cl., Woking | 3D 65 |
| Hawthorn Cres., Blackwater | 1B 60 |
| Hawthorn Cres., Selsdon | 4B 58 |
| Hawthorn Dr. | 1F 59 |
| Hawthorn Gdns. | 1B 8 |
| Hawthorn Green | 1E 41 |

| Name | Ref |
|---|---|
| Hawthorn Hatch | 3A 8 |
| Hawthorn La. | 2C 114 |
| Hawthorn Pl. | 4B 54 |
| Hawthorn Rd., Brentford | 3A 8 |
| Hawthorn Rd., Carshalton | 2A 56 |
| Hawthorn Rd., Frimley | 2E 61 |
| Hawthorn Rd., Glantly | 4E 13 |
| Hawthorn Rd., Ockford Ridge | 3C 118 |
| Hawthorn Rd., Sendmarsh | 5A 66 |
| Hawthorn Rd., Woking | 3C 64 |
| Hawthorn Way, Bisley | 1E 63 |
| Hawthorn Way, Earlswood | 1F 109 |
| Hawthorn Way, New Haw | 3E 49 |
| Hawthorn Way, Shepperton | 2E 33 |
| Hawthorn Way, Upper Halliford | 2E 33 |
| Hawthorn Way, Walton on Thames | 4B 34 |
| Hawthorne Av. | 1D 39 |
| Hawthorne Cl. | 5C 38 |
| Hawthorne Cres., Selsdon | 4B 58 |
| Hawthorne Way, Burpham | 3B 82 |
| Hawthorns | 5A 94 |
| Hawthorns, The | 4B 7 |
| Haxted | 5E 113 |
| Haxted Rd. | 5D 113 |
| Haycroft Cl. | 3B 74 |
| Haycroft Rd., Brixton Hill | 1A 22 |
| Haycroft Rd., Hook | 5B 36 |
| Haydn Av. | 1B 74 |
| Haydn Park Rd. | 1E 9 |
| Haydon Ct. | 4E 49 |
| Haydon Pl. | 1C 100 |
| Haydon Park Rd. | 4B 20 |
| Haydons Rd. | 4C 20 |
| Hayes Barton | 1F 65 |
| Hayes Chase | 3C 42 |
| Hayes Cres. | 1D 55 |
| Hayes Hill | 4C 42 |
| Hayes Hill Rd. | 4C 42 |
| Hayes La., Kenley | 1B 74 |
| Hayes La., Parklangley | 2B 42 |
| Hayes Mead | 4C 42 |
| Hayes Rd. | 1B 74 |
| Hayes, The | 3D 71 |
| Hayes Walk | 2E 129 |
| Hayes Way | 2B 42 |
| Hayesford Park Dr. | 3C 42 |
| Hayling Av. | 3A 16 |
| Haymeads | 2A 52 |
| Haymer Gdns. | 5F 37 |
| Hayne Rd. | 1A 42 |
| Haynt Wk. | 2A 38 |
| Hays Walk | 3D 55 |
| Haysleigh Gdns. | 1D 41 |
| Hayter Rd. | 1A 22 |
| Haywain | 3E 93 |
| Haywardens | 1E 131 |
| Haywards | 2F 147 |
| Haywards Gdns. | 1A 20 |
| Haywood | 4D 27 |
| Hazel Av. | 3F 81 |
| Hazel Bank | 4D 37 |
| Hazel Cl., Brentford | 3A 8 |
| Hazel Cl., Englefield Green | 5B 12 |
| Hazel Cl., Langley Green | 3C 146 |
| Hazel Cl., Reigate | 1C 108 |
| Hazel Cl., Whitton | 2E 17 |
| Hazel Dr., Sendmarsh | 5A 66 |
| Hazel Gro., Nutcombe | 1E 151 |
| Hazel Gro., Staines | 5B 14 |
| Hazel Gro., Sydenham | 4F 23 |
| Hazel La. | 3B 18 |
| Hazel Mead | 3B 54 |
| Hazel Rd., Ash | 1A 98 |
| Hazel Rd., Mychett | 1C 78 |
| Hazel Rd., West Byfleet | 5D 49 |
| Hazel Rd., Woodhatch | 1C 108 |
| Hazel Walk | 3A 106 |
| Hazel Way, Crawley Down | 3E 149 |
| Hazel Way, Fetcham | 4D 69 |
| Hazelbank Rd., Catford | 3C 24 |
| Hazelbank Rd., Chertsey | 4B 32 |
| Hazelbourne Rd. | 1E 21 |
| Hazeldean Rd. | 5C 40 |
| Hazeldene | 1E 49 |
| Hazeldene Ct. | 1C 74 |
| Hazeldene Rd. | 3D 9 |
| Hazeldon Rd. | 1F 23 |
| Hazelhurst | 1B 42 |
| Hazelhurst Rd. | 4C 20 |
| Hazell Rd. | 4F 95 |
| Hazelmere Cl., East Bedfont | 1F 15 |
| Hazelmere Cl., Leatherhead | 3A 70 |
| Hazelthorne Rd. | 4F 23 |
| Hazelwell Rd. | 1A 20 |
| Hazelwick Av. | 3E 147 |

| Name | Ref |
|---|---|
| Hazelwick Mill La. | 3E 147 |
| Hazelwick Rd. | 3E 147 |
| Hazelwood, Crawley | 4B 146 |
| Hazelwood, Elstead | 2E 117 |
| Hazelwood Av. | 2C 38 |
| Hazelwood Cl. | 3B 36 |
| Hazelwood Gro. | 5B 58 |
| Hazelwood Lane | 2D 73 |
| Hazelwood Rd., Brookw'd | 2A 64 |
| Hazelwood Rd., Hurst Grn. | 4A 94 |
| Hazlemere Gdns. | 4F 37 |
| Hazlewell Rd. | 1F 19 |
| Hazon Way | 4A 54 |
| Headcorn Rd. | 2A 40 |
| Headington Dr. | 1E 25 |
| Headington Rd. | 2C 20 |
| Headlam Rd. | 1F 21 |
| Headland Way | 2E 131 |
| Headley | 4E 133 |
| Headley | 1A 88 |
| Headley Av. | 1D 57 |
| Headley Cl. | 2F 53 |
| Headley Common Rd. | 1A 88 |
| Headley Dr., New Addington | 2D 59 |
| Headley Dr., Tadworth | 3F 71 |
| Headley Fields | 4E 133 |
| Headley Heath App. | 3F 87 |
| Headley Hill Rd. | 4F 133 |
| Headley Rd., Deadwater | 5D 133 |
| Headley Rd., Epsom | 3D 71 |
| Headley Rd., Grayshott | 5C 134 |
| Headley Rd., Lindford | 4E 133 |
| Headley Rd., Leatherhead | 4A 70 |
| Headley Rd., Mickleham | 3D 87 |
| Headley View | 3F 71 |
| Headway Cl. | 4A 18 |
| Headway, The | 3B 54 |
| Hearn La. | 3F 133 |
| Hearn Wk. | 1E 27 |
| Hearne Rd. | 3C 8 |
| Hearnville Rd. | 2E 21 |
| Hearsley Gdns. | 5D 43 |
| Heath Cl., Banstead | 5F 55 |
| Heath Cl., Heath End | 1A 96 |
| Heath Cl., Hindhead | 3D 135 |
| Heath Cl., Stanwell | 1B 14 |
| Heath Cl., Virginia Water | 2C 30 |
| Heath Cl., Wokingham | 3D 25 |
| Heath Dr., Brookwood | 3E 63 |
| Heath Dr., Raynes Pk. | 2A 38 |
| Heath Dr., Send | 5E 65 |
| Heath Dr., Sutton | 3F 55 |
| Heath Dr., Walton on the Hill | 1C 88 |
| Heath End | 1B 96 |
| Heath Gdns. | 2F 17 |
| Heath Gro. | 5F 15 |
| Heath Grove Est. | 1B 24 |
| Heath Hill | 1A 106 |
| Heath Hill La. | 1E 133 |
| Heath Hill Rd. | 1D 43 |
| Heath House Rd. | 4F 63 |
| Heath Hurst Rd. | 3F 57 |
| Heath La., Brook | 4C 102 |
| Heath La., Ewshot | 2D 95 |
| Heath La., Heath End | 1A 96 |
| Heath La., Munstead Heath | 3E 119 |
| Heath Moors | 3D 27 |
| Heath Park Dr. | 2A 46 |
| Heath Ridge Green | 5F 51 |
| Heath Rise, Sendmarsh | 5B 66 |
| Heath Rise, Virginia Water | 2C 30 |
| Heath Rise, West Hill | 1A 20 |
| Heath Rise, Westcroft | 2D 105 |
| Heath Rd., Bagshot | 2E 45 |
| Heath Rd., Caterham | 5C 74 |
| Heath Rd., Chobham | 3D 47 |
| Heath Rd., Hammer | 3D 151 |
| Heath Rd., Munstead Heath | 3E 119 |
| Heath Rd., Oxshott | 4A 52 |
| Heath Rd., Thornton H'th | 2C 40 |
| Heath Rd., Twickenham | 2F 17 |
| Heath Rd., Weybridge | 1A 50 |
| Heath Rd., Woking | 1D 65 |
| Heath, The | 5C 74 |
| Heath View | 1C 84 |
| Heath Way, Caterham | 1F 91 |
| Heath Way, Horsham | 3B 158 |
| Heatham Pk. | 2F 17 |
| Heathcot Rd. | 5D 133 |
| Heathcote | 4A 72 |
| Heathcote Cl. | 4C 78 |
| Heathcote Dr. | 2B 150 |
| Heathcote Rd., Ash Wharf | 4C 78 |
| Heathcote Rd., Camberley | 5A 44 |
| Heathcote Rd., Epsom | 5A 54 |
| Heathcote Rd., Richmond | 1A 18 |
| Heathcroft Av. | 5F 15 |

| Name | Ref |
|---|---|
| Heathdene Rd., Norbury | 5A 22 |
| Heathdene Rd., South Beddington | 2B 56 |
| Heathdown Rd. | 1F 65 |
| Heather Cl., Farnham | 1C 114 |
| Heather Cl., Hampton | 1C 34 |
| Heather Cl., Horsham | 3B 158 |
| Heather Cl., Kingswood | 4A 72 |
| Heather Cl., Horsham | 3B 158 |
| Heather Cl., Woking | 1C 64 |
| Heather Cl., Woodham | 3E 49 |
| Heather Dr., Broomhall | 4F 29 |
| Heather Dr., Lindford | 4D 133 |
| Heather Mead | 2F 59 |
| Heather Ridge Arcade | 1A 62 |
| Heather Walk | 4D 63 |
| Heather Way, Chobham | 2D 47 |
| Heather Way, Hindhead | 5E 135 |
| Heather Way, New Chap. | 4D 131 |
| Heather Way, Selsdon | 3C 58 |
| Heatherdale Cl. | 5C 18 |
| Heatherdale Rd. | 1D 61 |
| Heatherdene | 1B 84 |
| Heatherdene Cl. | 2D 39 |
| Heatherfields Rd. | 2F 95 |
| Heatherlands, Horley | 2B 128 |
| Heatherlands, Sunbury | 5A 16 |
| Heatherley Cl. | 5A 44 |
| Heatherley Rd. | 5A 44 |
| Heathers, The | 2C 14 |
| Heatherset Gdns. | 5A 22 |
| Heatherside Dr. | 3B 30 |
| Heatherside Rd. | 2A 54 |
| Heathersland | 3A 106 |
| Heathervale Rd. | 3E 49 |
| Heathfield, Cobham | 5F 51 |
| Heathfield, Three Bridges | 2F 147 |
| Heathfield Av. | 3D 29 |
| Heathfield Cl., Godalming | 3D 119 |
| Heathfield Cl., Woking | 2E 65 |
| Heathfield Dr. | 3D 109 |
| Heathfield Gdns. | 2D 9 |
| Heathfield North | 2F 17 |
| Heathfield Rd., Acton | 1C 8 |
| Heathfield Rd., Bromley Park | 5C 24 |
| Heathfield Rd., Hersham | 1F 51 |
| Heathfield Rd., S. Croydon | 1F 57 |
| Heathfield Rd., Wandsworth | 1C 20 |
| Heathfield Rd., Woking | 2E 65 |
| Heathfield South | 2F 17 |
| Heathfield Squ. | 2C 20 |
| Heathfield Ter. | 2D 9 |
| Heathfield Vale | 3C 58 |
| Heathland Cl. | 1A 34 |
| Heathlands Rd. | 4F 25 |
| Heathrise, Camberley | 5B 44 |
| Heathrow | 3E 103 |
| Heathrow Cl. | 4C 7 |
| Heathside, Hinchley Wood | 5E 35 |
| Heathside, Whitton | 2C 16 |
| Heathside Cl. | 5E 35 |
| Heathside Cres. | 2D 65 |
| Heathside Gdns. | 2E 65 |
| Heathside La. | 4D 135 |
| Heathside Park Rd. | 2D 65 |
| Heathside Rd. | 2D 65 |
| Heathside, Weybridge | 1A 50 |
| Heathvale Bridge Rd. | 3C 78 |
| Heathview Gdns. | 2F 19 |
| Heathview Rd., Milford | 4A 118 |
| Heathview Rd., Thornton Heath | 2B 40 |
| Heathway, Camberley | 5B 44 |
| Heathway, Effingham Junction | 5F 67 |
| Heathway, Shirley | 5A 42 |
| Heathway Cl. | 5B 44 |
| Heaton Rd. | 5E 21 |
| Hebdon Rd. | 3D 21 |
| Heber Rd. | 1D 23 |
| Hebron Rd. | 1F 9 |
| Hedgehog La. | 3F 151 |
| Hedgeway | 1B 100 |
| Hedgley St. | 1C 24 |
| Hedgerley Ct. | 2C 64 |
| Hedley Rd. | 2C 16 |
| Heenan Cl. | 3E 61 |
| Heighton Gdns. | 1E 57 |
| Heights Cl., Banstead | 2A 72 |
| Heights Cl., Wimbledon | 5F 19 |
| Helby Rd. | 1F 21 |
| Helder Gro. | 2C 24 |
| Helder St. | 2F 57 |
| Helen Av. | 2A 16 |
| Helen Cl. | 2D 35 |
| Helena Cl. | 2D 57 |
| Helgiford Gdns | 5F 15 |

| Name | Ref. |
|---|---|
| Inkerman Rd. | 2A 64 |
| Inman Rd. | 2C 20 |
| Inner Park Rd. | 2A 20 |
| Innes Gdns. | 1F 19 |
| Innes Rd. | 4C 158 |
| Institute Rd., Aldershot | 5A 78 |
| Institute Rd., S. Farnboro | 2A 78 |
| Institute Rd., Westcott | 2D 105 |
| Instone Cl. | 2D 57 |
| Inveresk Gdns. | 5E 37 |
| Inverness Rd. | 4A 38 |
| Inverness Way | 4E 43 |
| Invincible Rd. | 5C 60 |
| Inwood Av. | 3B 74 |
| Inwood Cl. | 5F 41 |
| Inwood Ct. | 5A 34 |
| Iona Cl., Catford | 2A 24 |
| Iona Cl., Crawley | 5C 146 |
| Ipswich Rd. | 5E 21 |
| Irene Rd. | 5A 52 |
| Ireton Av. | 5F 33 |
| Iris Rd., Bisley | 1E 63 |
| Iris Rd., Ruxley | 1F 53 |
| Iron La. | 1F 119 |
| Irons Bottom Rd. | 5B 108 |
| Irvine Dr. | 3B 60 |
| Irwin Dr. | 4A 158 |
| Irwin Rd. | 1B 100 |
| Isbells Rd. | 1C 108 |
| Isham Rd. | 1A 40 |
| Isis Way | 4E 43 |
| Island Cl. | 4F 13 |
| Island Farm Av. | 3C 34 |
| Island Farm Rd. | 3C 34 |
| Island Rd. | 5D 21 |
| Itchingwood Common Rd. | 5C 94 |
| Iveagh Rd., Guildford | 1B 100 |
| Iveagh Rd., Woking | 2A 64 |
| Ively Dr. | 5B 60 |
| Iverna Gdns. | 1F 15 |
| Ivers Way | 2D 59 |
| Ivy Cl. | 1B 34 |
| Ivy Cres. | 2C 8 |
| Ivy Dr. | 4E 45 |
| Ivy Gdns. | 2F 39 |
| Ivy La. | 2E 65 |
| Ivy Mill Cl. | 4B 92 |
| Ivy Mill La. | 4A 92 |
| Ivy Pl. | 3B 36 |
| Ivy Rd. | 4C 36 |
| Ivydale Rd., Hackbridge | 5E 39 |
| Ivydale Rd., Nunhead | 1F 23 |
| Ivyday Gro. | 3A 22 |
| Ivydene Cl., Salfords | 3E 109 |
| Ivydene Cl., Sutton | 1F 55 |
| Ivydene, Knaphill | 2F 63 |
| Ivydene, W. Molesey | 3C 34 |
| Ivymount Rd. | 3B 22 |

**J**

| Name | Ref. |
|---|---|
| Jackass La. | 4D 93 |
| Jackdaw Cl. | 3C 146 |
| Jackdaw La. | 3C 158 |
| Jackman's La. | 3B 64 |
| Jacks Bridge Rd. | 2E 131 |
| Jackson Cl., Bracknell | 3D 27 |
| Jackson Cl., Epsom | 5A 54 |
| Jacob Rd. | 4F 43 |
| Jacobs Well Rd. | 2A 82 |
| Jail La. | 1F 77 |
| Jamaica Rd. | 3B 40 |
| James Rd., Frimley | 2D 61 |
| James Rd., Peasmarsh | 4C 100 |
| James Way | 2D 61 |
| Jameston | 4D 27 |
| Jamnagar Cl. | 5A 14 |
| Jannoway Hill | 2C 64 |
| Japonica Cl. | 2C 64 |
| Jarrow Cl. | 3C 37 |
| Jarvis Rd. | 2F 57 |
| Jasmin Cl. | 3E 109 |
| Jasmin Gdns. | 5A 42 |
| Jasmin Rd. | 2F 53 |
| Jasmine Cl. | 1A 64 |
| Jasmine Green | 1E 41 |
| Jason Cl. | 3D 109 |
| Jasper Rd. | 4D 23 |
| Jebb Av. | 1A 22 |
| Jeddo Rd. | 1E 9 |
| Jefferson Rd. | 4C 62 |
| Jeffries Passage, Guildford | 159 |
| Jeffries Rd. | 4B 84 |
| Jeffs Rd. | 1E 55 |
| Jelf Rd. | 1B 22 |
| Jengar Cl. | 1F 55 |
| Jenkins' Hill | 3D 45 |
| Jenner Dr. | 4B 46 |
| Jenner Rd. | 1D 101 |
| Jennings Rd. | 1D 23 |
| Jenson Way | 5D 23 |
| Jephtha Rd. | 1B 20 |
| Jeppo's La. | 2D 39 |
| Jersey Cl., Chertsey | 4A 32 |
| Jersey Cl., Farnborough | 5C 60 |
| Jersey Rd. | 5E 21 |
| Jesmond Rd. | 4D 41 |
| Jessamy Rd. | 5D 33 |
| Jessica Rd. | 1C 20 |
| Jessies La. | 5E 103 |
| Jessiman Terr. | 3D 33 |
| Jessops Way | 3F 39 |
| Jevington | 4D 27 |
| Jews Wk. | 4E 23 |
| Jeypore Rd. | 2C 20 |
| Jillian Cl. | 5C 16 |
| Jobson's La. | 5D 153 |
| Jocelyn Rd. | 5B 8 |
| Jock's La. | 1B 26 |
| Jockey Mead | 5A 158 |
| John Cobb Rd. | 2A 50 |
| John St. | 2D 41 |
| John's Rd. | 3E 77 |
| Johns Cl. | 4E 15 |
| Johns La. | 3C 38 |
| Johns Walk | 3D 75 |
| Johnsdale | 3F 93 |
| Johnson Dr. | 1D 35 |
| Johnson Rd. | 4C 40 |
| Johnson Wk. | 5D 147 |
| Johnsons Cl. | 5E 39 |
| Johnston Green | 3E 81 |
| Johnston Wk. | 3E 81 |
| Joliffe Rd. | 1C 90 |
| Jordan Cl., Salfords | 3E 109 |
| Jordan Cl., Sanderstead | 4A 58 |
| Jordans Cl., Crawley | 3D 147 |
| Jordan's Cl., Guildford | 5B 82 |
| Jordans Cl., Stanwell | 2B 14 |
| Jordans Cres. | 3D 147 |
| Jordans, The | 3C 150 |
| Joseph's Rd. | 5F 81 |
| Josephine Av., Lwr. Kingswood | 2E 89 |
| Josephine Av., Tulse Hill | 1A 22 |
| Josephine Cl. | 2E 89 |
| Jubilee Av., Ascot | 1B 28 |
| Jubilee Av., Whitton | 2D 17 |
| Jubilee Av., Wokingham | 1D 25 |
| Jubilee Cl. | 2B 14 |
| Jubilee Cres. | 1F 49 |
| Jubilee Dr. | 3C 78 |
| Jubilee Hall Rd. | 4D 61 |
| Jubilee La. | 2C 114 |
| Jubilee Rd., Aldershot | 1D 97 |
| Jubilee Rd., Cheam | 2D 55 |
| Jubilee Rd., Mytchett | 1C 78 |
| Jubilee Rd., Rudgwick | 2F 157 |
| Jubilee Ter., Dorking | 1A 106 |
| Jubilee Ter., Grayshott | 5D 135 |
| Jubilee Terr., Strood Green | 2D 107 |
| Jubilee Way, Merton | 1C 38 |
| Jubilee Way, Tolworth | 5C 36 |
| Jug Hill | 1E 77 |
| Julian Cl. | 2C 64 |
| Julien Rd., South Ealing | 2A 8 |
| Julien Rd., Woodmansterne | 1F 73 |
| Jumps Rd. | 1B 134 |
| Junction Pl. | 3E 151 |
| Junction Rd., Ashford | 4E 15 |
| Junction Rd., Dorking | 1F 105 |
| Junction Rd., Lightwater | 3F 45 |
| Junction Rd., Little Ealing | 2A 8 |
| Junction Rd., S. Croydon | 2F 57 |
| June Cl., Coulsdon | 5B 56 |
| June Cl., Salfords | 4F 109 |
| Junewood Cl. | 4D 49 |
| Juniper | 4D 27 |
| Juniper Cl., Biggin Hill | 2F 77 |
| Juniper Cl., Guildford | 3F 81 |
| Juniper Cl., Reigate | 1C 108 |
| Juniper Dr. | 1E 63 |
| Juniper Rd., Crawley | 2C 146 |
| Juniper Rd., Reigate | 1C 108 |
| Jura Cl. | 5C 146 |
| Jutland Rd. | 2B 24 |
| Juxon Cl. | 5B 146 |

**K**

| Name | Ref. |
|---|---|
| Kangley Bridge Rd. | 4A 24 |
| Kashmir Ct. | 3F 49 |
| Katherine Cl. | 1D 49 |
| Katherine St. | 5C 40 |
| Kay Cres. | 4A 134 |
| Kayemoor Rd. | 2A 56 |
| Keable Rd. | 5F 95 |
| Kearton Cl. | 2C 74 |
| Keats Green | 1D 27 |
| Keats Way, Crowthorne | 1D 43 |
| Keats Way, Shirley | 3E 41 |
| Keble Cl., Old Malden | 4E 37 |
| Keble Cl., Three Bridges | 2F 147 |
| Keble St. | 3C 20 |
| Keeble Way | 3E 43 |
| Keedonwood Rd. | 4C 24 |
| Keeley Rd. | 5A 40 |
| Keens Lane | 3D 81 |
| Keens Park Rd. | 3D 81 |
| Keens Rd. | 1F 57 |
| Keep Hatch Rd. | 1E 25 |
| Keep, The | 5B 18 |
| Keepers Cott. | 4C 82 |
| Keepers Wk. | 3C 30 |
| Keevil Dr. | 2A 20 |
| Keldholme | 2C 26 |
| Kellerton Rd. | 1C 24 |
| Kellino St. | 4D 21 |
| Kelmscott Rd. | 1D 21 |
| Kelsey Cl. | 2A 128 |
| Kelsey La. | 1A 42 |
| Kelsey Park Av. | 2A 42 |
| Kelsey Way | 2A 42 |
| Kelso Cl. | 3A 148 |
| Kelso Rd. | 4C 38 |
| Kelvedon Av. | 2C 50 |
| Kelvedon Cl. | 5C 18 |
| Kelvin Av., Leatherhead | 3F 69 |
| Kelvin Av., Teddington | 5E 17 |
| Kelvin Cl. | 2F 53 |
| Kelvin Gro., Hook | 5B 36 |
| Kelvin Gro., Upper Sydenham | 3E 23 |
| Kelvin La. | 2D 147 |
| Kelvin Way | 2D 147 |
| Kelvinbrook | 2D 35 |
| Kelvington Cl. | 4F 41 |
| Kelvington Rd. | 1F 23 |
| Kemara Cl. | 2E 147 |
| Kemble Cl. | 1B 50 |
| Kemble Rd., Croydon | 5B 40 |
| Kemble Rd., Forest Hill | 2F 23 |
| Kemerton Rd., Addiscombe | 4D 41 |
| Kemerton Rd., Beckenham | 1B 42 |
| Kemishford La. | 5B 64 |
| Kemnal Pk. | 2A 152 |
| Kemp Ct. | 3E 45 |
| Kempshott Rd., Horsham | 4A 158 |
| Kempshott Rd., Streatham Vale | 5A 22 |
| Kempton Av. | 1A 34 |
| Kemsley Cl. | 3E 77 |
| Kemton Rd. | 1C 34 |
| Kemton Walk | 3F 41 |
| Kendal Cl. | 5C 37 |
| Kendal Cl. | 5A 90 |
| Kendal Gro. | 5D 45 |
| Kendale Rd. | 4C 24 |
| Kendall Av., Elmers End | 1F 41 |
| Kendall Av., Sanderstead | 3F 57 |
| Kendall Avenue South | 3F 57 |
| Kendall Rd. | 1F 41 |
| Kendor Av. | 4A 54 |
| Kendra Hall Rd. | 2E 57 |
| Kendrey Gdns. | 2E 17 |
| Kenilworth Av., Oxshott | 5A 52 |
| Kenilworth Av., Wimbledon | 4B 20 |
| Kenilworth Cl. | 1C 72 |
| Kenilworth Dr. | 5B 34 |
| Kenilworth Gdns. | 4B 14 |
| Kenilworth Rd., Kent House | 1F 41 |
| Kenilworth Rd., Staines | 3C 14 |
| Kenilworth Rd., Stoneleigh | 2B 54 |
| Kenilworth Rd., West Heath | 4A 60 |
| Kenley | 1C 74 |
| Kenley Cl. | 3C 74 |
| Kenley Gdns. | 2B 40 |
| Kenley La. | 1C 74 |
| Kenley Rd., Headley Down | 4A 134 |
| Kenley Rd., Kingston | 1C 36 |
| Kenley Rd., Morden | 1B 38 |
| Kenley Rd., Twickenham | 1F 17 |
| Kenley Wk. | 1D 55 |
| Kenlor Rd. | 4D 21 |
| Kenmara Cl. | 2E 147 |
| Kenmare Rd. | 3A 40 |
| Kenmore Cl. | 3E 61 |
| Kenmore Rd. | 5E 57 |
| Kennedy Av. | 1B 150 |
| Kennedy Rd. | 5B 158 |
| Kennel Av. | 1B 28 |
| Kennel Cl., Ascot Heath | 5B 10 |
| Kennel Cl., Fetcham | 5D 69 |
| Kennel La., Fetcham | 5D 69 |
| Kennel La., Millbridge | 3D 115 |
| Kennel La., Windlesham | 1F 45 |
| Kennel Ride | 5B 10 |
| Kennel Wood | 1B 28 |
| Kennel Wood Cres. | 4E 59 |
| Kennet Cl. | 5C 78 |
| Kennet Rd. | 1D 73 |
| Kenrick Squ. | 5A 92 |
| Kensington Av. | 1B 40 |
| Kenston Rd. | 3A 40 |
| Kent Cl., Mitcham | 2A 40 |
| Kent Cl., Staines | 5C 14 |
| Kent Dr. | 4E 17 |
| Kent Gate Way | 2D 59 |
| Kent Hatch Rd. | 3B 94 |
| Kent House La. | 5F 23 |
| Kent House Rd. | 4F 23 |
| Kent Rd., Ackton Green | 1D 9 |
| Kent Rd., East Molesey | 2E 35 |
| Kent Rd., Kew | 3C 8 |
| Kent Rd., West Wickham | 4B 42 |
| Kent Rd., Windlesham | 1A 46 |
| Kent Rd., Woking | 1E 65 |
| Kent Way | 5B 36 |
| Kenton Av. | 1B 34 |
| Kenton Cl. | 1F 61 |
| Kenton Way | 2A 64 |
| Kentwyns Rise | 1A 110 |
| Kenwood Dr., Beckenham | 2B 42 |
| Kenwood Dr., Hersham | 2D 51 |
| Kenwood Dr., Sunbury | 5A 16 |
| Kenwood Dr., Weybridge | 2B 50 |
| Kenwood Park | 2B 50 |
| Kenwyn Rd. | 1F 37 |
| Kenyngton Ct. | 4A 16 |
| Kenyngton Dr. | 4A 16 |
| Kenyons | 2B 84 |
| Keogh Cl. | 1C 78 |
| Keppel Rd. | 5C 86 |
| Keppel Spur | 2B 12 |
| Kepple Pl. | 2E 45 |
| Kerrill Av. | 3B 74 |
| Kerry Ter. | 1E 65 |
| Kersey Dr. | 4C 58 |
| Kersfield Rd. | 1A 20 |
| Keston Av., Old Coulsdon | 3B 74 |
| Keston Av., Woodham | 4D 49 |
| Kestrel Av., Herne Hill | 1B 22 |
| Kestrel Av., Staines | 4A 14 |
| Kestrel Cl., Guildford | 5C 82 |
| Kestrel Cl., Horsham | 3C 158 |
| Kestrel Way | 4E 59 |
| Keswick Av., Coombe | 4D 19 |
| Keswick Av., Merton | 1B 38 |
| Keswick Cl., Camberley | 1A 62 |
| Keswick Cl., Sutton | 1F 55 |
| Keswick Rd., Fetcham | 5E 69 |
| Keswick Rd., Lightwater | 4F 45 |
| Keswick Rd., Milford | 5A 118 |
| Keswick Rd., West Hill | 1A 20 |
| Keswick Rd., West Wickham | 5C 42 |
| Keswick Rd., Whitton | 1D 17 |
| Kettering St. | 5F 21 |
| Kettlewell Cl. | 1D 65 |
| Kettlewell Dr. | 5A 48 |
| Kettlewell Hill | 5A 48 |
| Kevan Dr. | 1D 83 |
| Kew | 3C 8 |
| Kew Bridge Rd. | 3B 8 |
| Kew Cres. | 5B 38 |
| Kew Foot Rd. | 5B 8 |
| Kew Gardens Rd. | 3C 8 |
| Kew Rd. | 5B 8 |
| Keymer Rd. | 3A 22 |
| Khama Rd. | 4D 21 |
| Khartoum Rd., Tooting | 4D 21 |
| Khartoum Rd., Wheeler St. | 5A 118 |
| Kibble Green | 3D 27 |
| Kidborough | 5B 146 |
| Kidborough Down | 2A 86 |
| Kidderminster Rd. | 4B 40 |
| Kidmans Cl. | 3C 158 |
| Kielder Walk | 1A 62 |
| Kilcorral Cl. | 5B 54 |
| Kildoran Rd. | 1A 22 |
| Kilgour Rd. | 1F 23 |
| Killarne Rd. | 1C 20 |
| Killearn Rd. | 2B 24 |
| Killester Gdns. | 1C 54 |
| Killieser Av. | 3A 22 |
| Killinghurst La. | 2D 153 |
| Killy Hill | 2D 47 |

## L

| Street | Ref |
|---|---|
| Little London | 5A 118 |
| Little London Hill | 1A 158 |
| Little Lullenden | 1F 131 |
| Little Mead | 1B 140 |
| Little Orchard, Woodham | 4D 49 |
| Little Orchard, Woking | 5B 48 |
| Little Orchard Way | 4D 101 |
| Little Paddocks | 4C 44 |
| Little Park Dr. | 3B 16 |
| Little Platt | 5D 81 |
| Little Queen's Rd. | 5F 17 |
| Little Ringdale | 2E 27 |
| Little Roke Av. | 5E 57 |
| Little Roke Rd. | 5E 57 |
| Little St. | 4E 81 |
| Little Thurbans Cl. | 1C 114 |
| Little Tunners Ct. | 1D 119 |
| Little Warren Cl. | 1E 101 |
| Little Woodcote La. | 4B 56 |
| Littlecote Cl. | 2A 20 |
| Littlecroft Rd. | 4D 13 |
| Littledale Cl. | 2E 27 |
| Littlefield Cl., Ash | 5C 78 |
| Littlefield Cl., Guildford | 3C 80 |
| Littlefield Gdns. | 5C 78 |
| Littlefield Way | 3C 80 |
| Littleford La. | 5A 102 |
| Littleheath La. | 5A 52 |
| Littleheath Rd. | 2B 58 |
| Littlemead | 1B 52 |
| Littlers Cl. | 1C 38 |
| Littleton | 2D 33 |
| Littleton La., Laleham | 4C 32 |
| Littleton La., Littleton | 4B 100 |
| Littleton La., Reigate | 1A 108 |
| Littleton Rd. | 5E 15 |
| Littleton St. | 3C 20 |
| Littlewick Rd. | 5F 47 |
| Littlewood | 1D 141 |
| Littlewood Rd. | 1B 24 |
| Littleworth Av. | 1B 52 |
| Littleworth Common Rd. | 5E 35 |
| Littleworth La. | 1B 52 |
| Littleworth Rd., Esher | 2B 52 |
| Littleworth Rd., The Sands | 4E 97 |
| Liverpool Rd., Brentford | 1B 8 |
| Liverpool Rd., Kingston | 5C 18 |
| Liverpool Rd., Selhurst | 2C 40 |
| Livingstone Rd. | 4C 74 |
| Livingstone Rd., Beulah Hill | 1C 40 |
| Livingstone Rd., Crawley | 5D 147 |
| Livingstone Rd., Horsham | 5B 158 |
| Llanaway Cl. | 1D 119 |
| Llanaway Rd. | 1D 119 |
| Llantony Rd. | 3C 38 |
| Llanvair Cl. | 3B 28 |
| Llanvair Dr. | 3B 28 |
| Lloyd Av., Norbury | 1A 40 |
| Lloyd Av., Woodmansterne | 5B 56 |
| Lloyd Park Av. | 1A 58 |
| Lloyd Rd. | 5A 38 |
| Lloyds Way | 3F 41 |
| Loats Rd. | 1A 22 |
| Lochinver | 4D 27 |
| Lock La. | 1B 66 |
| Lock Rd., Guildford | 4F 81 |
| Lock Rd., Ham | 4A 18 |
| Lock's La. | 1E 39 |
| Locke King Rd. | 2A 50 |
| Lockfield Rd. | 2B 64 |
| Lockhart Rd. | 5E 51 |
| Locks Meadow | 3A 132 |
| Locks Ride | 5A 10 |
| Locksmeade Rd. | 4A 18 |
| Lockswood | 3F 63 |
| Lockwood Cl., Fox Lane | 3B 60 |
| Lockwood Cl., Lwr. Sydenham | 4F 23 |
| Lockwood Path | 5C 48 |
| Lockwood Way | 1F 53 |
| Loddon Cl., Camberley | 5C 44 |
| Loddon Cl., West Heath | 4B 60 |
| Loddon Way | 5C 78 |
| Loder Cl. | 5C 48 |
| Lodge Av. | 5A 40 |
| Lodge Cl., Dorking | 3A 106 |
| Lodge Cl., East Grinstead | 2B 150 |
| Lodge Cl., Englefield Grn. | 4C 12 |
| Lodge Cl., Fetcham | 4E 69 |
| Lodge Cl., Hackridge | 4E 39 |
| Lodge Cl., Stoke D'Aber. | 1C 68 |
| Lodge Cl., West Green | 4C 146 |
| Lodge Gdns. | 3A 42 |
| Lodge Hill | 1B 74 |
| Lodge Hill Cl. | 1E 115 |
| Lodge Hill Rd. | 5B 96 |
| Lodge La., Addington | 2D 59 |
| Lodge La., Salfords | 5D 109 |
| Lodge Rd., Fetcham | 4E 69 |
| Lodge Rd., Wallington | 1B 56 |
| Lodge Way, Ashford | 3C 14 |
| Lodge Way, Charlton | 2E 33 |
| Lodgebottom Rd. | 2F 87 |
| Logmore La. | 2D 105 |
| Lois Dr. | 3E 33 |
| Lollesworth La. | 1B 84 |
| Loman Rd. | 5F 61 |
| Lombard Rd. | 1C 38 |
| Lombard St. | 5C 98 |
| Loncin Mead Av. | 3E 49 |
| London La., Bromley | 5C 24 |
| London La., Shere | 2D 103 |
| London Rd., Ascot | 2A 28 |
| London Rd., Bagshot | 1E 45 |
| London Rd., Blackwater | 1A 60 |
| London Rd., Bracknell | 1D 27 |
| London Rd., Brentford | 3A 8 |
| London Rd., Burpham | 4A 82 |
| London Rd., Camberley | 5A 44 |
| London Rd., Caterham | 5C 74 |
| London Rd., Dorking | 1A 106 |
| London Rd., East Grinstead | 1A 150 |
| London Rd., Ewell | 3B 54 |
| London Rd., Forest Hill | 2E 23 |
| London Rd., Guildford | 1D 101 |
| London Rd., Hackbridge | 3E 39 |
| London Rd., Hindhead | 5F 135 |
| London Rd., Horsham | 5B 158 |
| London Rd., Kingston | 1B 36 |
| London Rd., Mitcham | 2D 39 |
| London Rd., Morden | 3B 38 |
| London Rd., Norbury | 1A 40 |
| London Rd., North Cheam | 5A 38 |
| London Rd., Northgate | 2D 147 |
| London Rd., Redhill | 5B 90 |
| London Rd., Reigate | 5E 89 |
| London Rd., Shortlands | 1C 42 |
| London Rd., Staines | 4A 14 |
| London Rd., Sunningdale | 3F 29 |
| London Rd., Sunninghill | 2D 29 |
| London Rd., Tooting | 5E 2 |
| London Rd., Twickenham | 2F 17 |
| London Rd., Wallington | 1B 56 |
| London Rd., Wokingham | 2E 25 |
| London Rd., York Town | 5F 43 |
| London Rd. N., Merstham | 1B 90 |
| London Rd. S., Merstham | 3B 90 |
| London St. | 4A 32 |
| Lone Acre | 2A 46 |
| Lone Oak | 3E 129 |
| Lonesome La. | 3C 108 |
| Long Acre | 5C 78 |
| Long Acre Rd. | 2B 56 |
| Long Bourne Green | 5A 100 |
| Long Bridge | 4A 96 |
| Long Cl. | 4F 147 |
| Long Copse Cl. | 5D 69 |
| Long Cross Hill | 4F 133 |
| Long Ditton | 4A 36 |
| Long Dyke | 4B 82 |
| Long Garden Walk | 4A 96 |
| Long Gore | 4A 100 |
| Long Grove Rd. | 3F 53 |
| Long Hill Rd., Bracknell | 1F 27 |
| Long Hill, The Sands | 5E 97 |
| Long Hill, Woldingham | 4F 75 |
| Long La., Ashford | 3C 14 |
| Long La., Woodside | 3E 41 |
| Long Lodge Dr. | 5A 34 |
| Long Meadow | 1F 85 |
| Long Mickle | 3D 43 |
| Long Reach | 5D 67 |
| Long Rd., The | 2C 114 |
| Long Shaw | 3F 69 |
| Long Wk., Burgh Heath | 3A 72 |
| Long Wk., New Malden | 2D 37 |
| Long Wk., West Horsley | 3A 84 |
| Long Walk, The | 2A 12 |
| Longbeech Dr. | 5A 60 |
| Longbourne Way | 3A 32 |
| Longbridge Rd. | 3A 128 |
| Longbridge Way | 1B 24 |
| Longcommon Rd. | 2C 120 |
| Longcroft Av. | 5F 55 |
| Longcross Rd., | 5B 30 |
| Longdene Rd. | 3F 151 |
| Longdown Cl. | 1D 115 |
| Longdown La. North | 5C 54 |
| Longdown La. South | 1F 71 |
| Longdown Rd., Bellingham | 4A 24 |
| Longdown Rd., Epsom | 5B 54 |
| Longdown Rd., Guildford | 2E 101 |
| Longdown Rd., Lower Bourne | 1D 115 |
| Longdown Rd., Sandhurst | 3D 43 |
| Longfellow Rd. | 4F 37 |
| Longfield | 1C 42 |
| Longfield Av. | 4E 39 |
| Longfield Cl. | 3C 60 |
| Longfield Cres., Sydenham | 3E 23 |
| Longfield Cres., Tadworth | 3A 72 |
| Longfield Rd., Ash | 5C 78 |
| Longfield Rd., Dorking | 2F 105 |
| Longfield Rd., Horsham | 5A 158 |
| Longfield St. | 2B 20 |
| Longford | 4C 7 |
| Longford Av., Feltham | 1F 15 |
| Longford Av., Stanwell | 2C 14 |
| Longford Cl., Camberley | 1E 61 |
| Longford Cl., Hampton | 4C 16 |
| Longford Ct. | 1A 54 |
| Longford Gdns. | 5C 38 |
| Longford Rd. | 2D 17 |
| Longford Way | 2C 14 |
| Longheath Gdns. | 3E 41 |
| Longhill Rd., Catford | 3B 24 |
| Longhope Dr. | 1D 115 |
| Longhurst Gdns. | 3E 41 |
| Longhurst Rd., E. Horsley | 3C 84 |
| Longhurst Rd., Hither Green | 1C 24 |
| Longlands Av. | 5B 56 |
| Longleat Way | 2E 15 |
| Longley Rd., Croydon | 4B 40 |
| Longley Rd., Farnham | 4B 96 |
| Longley Rd., Tooting | 5D 21 |
| Longmead | 5C 82 |
| Longmead Cl. | 4C 74 |
| Longmead Rd. | 4D 21 |
| Longmead Rd., Epsom | 4A 54 |
| Longmead Rd., Esher | 4E 35 |
| Longmeadow | 1E 61 |
| Longmere Gdns. | 3A 72 |
| Longmoors | 1B 26 |
| Longmore Rd. | 1E 51 |
| Longpoles Rd. | 2D 141 |
| Longreach | 1A 84 |
| Long's Cl. | 1A 66 |
| Longs Way, Wokingham | 1E 25 |
| Longshot La. | 2B 26 |
| Longside Cl. | 1E 31 |
| Longstaff Cres. | 1B 20 |
| Longstaff Rd. | 1B 20 |
| Longstone Rd. | 4E 21 |
| Longthornton Rd. | 1F 39 |
| Longton Av. | 4D 23 |
| Longton Gro. | 4E 23 |
| Longwater Rd. | 3D 27 |
| Longways | 1A 32 |
| Longwood Dr. | 1F 19 |
| Longwood Rd. | 1C 74 |
| Longwood View | 5E 147 |
| Lonsdale Gdns. | 2A 40 |
| Lonsdale Rd., Barnes | 4E 9 |
| Lonsdale Rd., Dorking | 1A 106 |
| Lonsdale Rd., Norwood | 2E 41 |
| Lonsdale Rd., Turnham Green | 2E 9 |
| Lonsdale Rd., Weybridge | 2A 50 |
| Loop Rd., Epsom | 1D 71 |
| Loop Rd., Westfield | 4D 65 |
| Loppets Rd. | 5D 147 |
| Loraine Gdns. | 2B 70 |
| Loraine Rd. | 3C 8 |
| Lord Chancellor Cl. | 1D 37 |
| Lord Knyvetts Cl. | 1C 14 |
| Lords Cl., Feltham | 3C 16 |
| Lords Cl., Tulse Hill | 3C 22 |
| Lords Hill | 1C 120 |
| Lordsbury Field | 3C 56 |
| Lordship La. | 1D 23 |
| Loretto Cl. | 1D 141 |
| Lorian Dr. | 5F 89 |
| Lorne Av. | 4F 41 |
| Lorne Gdns. | 4F 41 |
| Lorne Rd. | 1F 85 |
| Lorraine Rd. | 4B 44 |
| Loseberry Rd. | 1B 52 |
| Loseley Rd. | 5A 100 |
| Lothair Rd. | 1A 8 |
| Lothian Wood | 4F 71 |
| Lotus Rd. | 2F 77 |
| Loubet St. | 5E 21 |
| Loudwater Cl. | 2A 34 |
| Loudwater Rd. | 2A 34 |
| Louis Fields | 3C 80 |
| Louisville Rd. | 3E 21 |
| Love La., Ash | 5C 78 |
| Love La., Cheam | 2D 55 |
| Love La., Godstone | 4B 92 |
| Love La., Long Ditton | 5A 36 |
| Love La., Mitcham | 2D 39 |
| Love La., Ockley | 1D 143 |
| Love La., St. Helier | 4B 38 |
| Love La., S. Norwood | 2E 41 |
| Love La., Walton on the Hill | 1B 88 |
| Loveday Rd. | 1A 8 |
| Lovel La. | 4C 10 |
| Lovelace Cl. | 5A 68 |
| Lovelace Dr. | 1A 66 |
| Lovelace Gdns., Hersham | 1D 51 |
| Lovelace Gdns., Surbiton | 4A 36 |
| Lovelace Rd., Bracknell | 2B 26 |
| Lovelace Rd., Surbiton | 4A 36 |
| Lovelace Rd., Tulse Hill | 3B 22 |
| Loveland La. | 2F 89 |
| Lovelands La. | 5C 46 |
| Lovell Rd., Ham | 3A 18 |
| Lovell Rd., Woodside | 4B 10 |
| Lovells Cl. | 3F 45 |
| Lovett Rd. | 4E 13 |
| Low La. | 2C 96 |
| Lowbury | 2E 27 |
| Lowburys | 3F 105 |
| Lowcross La. | 3D 23 |
| Lowdells Dr. | 1B 150 |
| Lowdell's La. | 1B 150 |
| Lowder Mill Rd. | 5F 151 |
| Lower Addiscombe Rd. | 4D 41 |
| Lower Barn La. | 3C 158 |
| Lower Barn Rd. | 4F 57 |
| Lower Bridge Rd. | 5A 90 |
| Lower Broadmoor Rd. | 2D 43 |
| Lower Charles St. | 5A 44 |
| Lower Church La. | 4A 96 |
| Lower Common South | 5F 9 |
| Lower Coombe Rd. | 1F 57 |
| Lower Court Rd. | 4A 54 |
| Lower Downs Rd. | 1A 38 |
| Lower Dunnymans Mews | 5E 55 |
| Lower Eashing La. | 2B 118 |
| Lower Edgeboro' Rd. | 1D 101 |
| Lower Farm Rd. | 5A 68 |
| Lower Farnham Rd. | 1D 97 |
| Lower Green West | 2D 39 |
| Lower Green Rd. | 5D 35 |
| Lower Grove Rd. | 1C 18 |
| Lower Guildford Rd. | 2F 63 |
| Lower Halliford | 3F 33 |
| Lower Ham Rd. | 1B 36 |
| Lower Hampton Rd. | 2B 34 |
| Lower Hanger | 3D 151 |
| Lower Hill Rd. | 4F 53 |
| Lower Kingswood | 2E 89 |
| Lower Mall | 2F 9 |
| Lower Manor Rd. | 1D 119 |
| Lower Marsh La. | 2B 36 |
| Lower Mere | 3C 150 |
| Lower Morden La. | 3A 38 |
| Lower Mortlake Rd. | 5B 8 |
| Lower Moushill Lane | 3A 118 |
| Lower Newport Rd. | 5B 78 |
| Lower Northfield Rd. | 5E 55 |
| Lower Oak Tree Rd. | 3B 118 |
| Lower Old Pk. | 3E 95 |
| Lower Peryers | 2C 84 |
| Lower Pillory Downs | 5B 56 |
| Lower Pyrford Rd. | 2B 66 |
| Lower Richmond Rd., Barnes | 5F 9 |
| Lower Richmond Rd., N. Sheen | 5C 8 |
| Lower Rd., Effingham | 2E 85 |
| Lower Rd., Fetcham | 5D 69 |
| Lower Rd., Grayswood | 1B 152 |
| Lower Rd., Mead Vale | 1C 108 |
| Lower Rd., Purley | 5E 57 |
| Lower Rd., Sutton | 1F 55 |
| Lower St. Haslemere | 3A 152 |
| Lower St., Shere | 3D 103 |
| Lower Sandfields | 5F 65 |
| Lower Sawley Wood | 5E 55 |
| Lower Shott | 1A 86 |
| Lower South View | 3A 96 |
| Lower Sunbury Rd. | 1C 34 |
| Lower Teddington Rd. | 1A 36 |
| Lower Village Rd. | 3C 28 |
| Lower Weybourne La. | 2C 96 |
| Lower Wood Rd. | 2C 52 |
| Lowerhouse La. | 1A 142 |
| Loweswater Wk. | 1A 62 |
| Lowfield Cl. | 4F 45 |
| Lowicks Rd. | 5A 116 |
| Lowlands Rd. | 1A 60 |
| Lowry Cl. | 5E 43 |
| Lowther Hill | 2F 23 |
| Lowther Rd., Barnes | 4E 9 |
| Lowther Rd., Kingston | 1B 36 |
| Loxford Rd. | 1A 92 |
| Loxford Way | 1A 92 |
| Loxhill Rd. | 5E 119 |
| Loxley Rd., Hanworth | 4C 16 |
| Loxley Rd., Wandsworth | 2D 21 |
| Loxton Rd. | 3E 23 |

| | | | | | | | |
|---|---|---|---|---|---|---|---|
| Manor Rd., Walton | 4F 33 | Marham Gdns., Wandsworth | 2D 21 | Marshall's Rd. | 1F 55 | Maybury Hill | 1E 65 |
| Manor Rd., West Wickham | 5A 42 | Marian Ct. | 1E 55 | Marshals Cl. | 5A 54 | Maybury Rd. | 1E 65 |
| Manor Rd. North | 4F 35 | Marian Rd. | 1F 39 | Marshwood Dr. | 4A 46 | Maybury St. | 4D 21 |
| Manor Rd. South | 1B 52 | Marie Therese Cl. | 3D 37 | Marston Av. | 2E 53 | Maycross Av. | 2B 38 |
| Manor Royal | 2D 147 | Marigold Dr. | 1E 63 | Marston Dr., Farnborough | 3D 61 | Mayday Rd. | 3B 40 |
| Manor, The, Milford | 3B 118 | Marigold Way | 4F 41 | Green | | Mayes Cl. | 2F 75 |
| Manor Vale | 2A 8 | Marina Av. | 3F 37 | Marston Dr., Warlingham | 2F 75 | Mayes La. | 5E 143 |
| Manor Walk | 1A 50 | Marina Way | 5A 18 | Marston Rd., Farnham | 4F 95 | Mayfair Av., Whitton | 2D 17 |
| Manor Way, Bagshot | 3E 45 | Mariner Dr. | 4F 79 | Marston Rd., Teddington | 4A 18 | Mayfair Av., Worcester Park | 4E 37 |
| Manor Way, Beckham | 1A 42 | Mariner Gdns. | 3A 18 | Marston Rd., Woking | 2B 64 | Mayfair Cl., Beckenham | 1A 42 |
| Manor Way, Egham | 5D 13 | Marion Av. | 3E 33 | Marston Way | 5B 22 | Mayfair Cl., Surbiton | 4B 36 |
| Manor Way, Mitcham | 2F 39 | Marion Rd., Crawley | 5E 147 | Martell Rd. | 3C 22 | Mayfield, Boundstone | 2C 114 |
| Manor Way, Old Woking | 4E 65 | Marion Rd., Thorn.H'th | 3C 40 | Martin Cl., Crawley | 3C 146 | Mayfield, Three Bridges | 4F 147 |
| Manor Way, Onslow Vill. | 2A 100 | Marius Rd. | 3E 21 | Martin Cl., Hamsey Grn. | 1E 75 | Mayfield Av., Turnham Green | 2E 9 |
| Manor Way, Oxshott | 1D 69 | Mark Oak La. | 4D 69 | Martin Cl., Selsdon | 4C 58 | Mayfield Ave., Woodham | 3E 49 |
| Manor Way, Purley | 4D 57 | Mark St. | 5F 89 | Martin Cres. | 4A 40 | Mayfield Cl., Ashford | 5D 15 |
| Manor Way, Selsdon | 4A 58 | Mark Way | 5F 99 | Martin Gro. | 2B 38 | Mayfield Cl., Esher | 4F 35 |
| Manor Way, Woodmansterne | 1D 73 | Markedge La., Chipstead | 5D 73 | Martin Rd. | 4E 81 | Mayfield Cl., Woodham | 3E 49 |
| Manor Way, Worcester Pk. | 4E 37 | Markedge La., Gatton | 2B 90 | Martin Way, Frimley | 2E 61 | Mayfield Cres. | 2A 40 |
| Manor Way, The | 1C 56 | Markenfield Rd. | 5F 81 | Martin Way, Morden | 2A 38 | Mayfield Gdns., Hersham | 1D 51 |
| Manor Wood Rd. | 5D 57 | Markfield | 4D 59 | Martin Way, Woking | 3B 64 | Mayfield Gdns., Hythe | 5A 14 |
| Manorcroft Rd., | 5E 13 | Markfield Rd. | 1B 92 | Martindale Av. | 1A 62 | Mayfield Rd., Ash | 5C 78 |
| Manordene Cl. | 4F 35 | Marketfield Rd. | 5B 90 | Martindale Cl. | 4C 82 | Mayfield Rd., Carshalton | 2A 56 |
| Manorhouse La. | 1F 85 | Marketfield Way | 5B 90 | Martindale Rd. | 2B 64 | Beeches | |
| Manorlea Rd. | 3A 118 | Markham Cl. | 5C 16 | Martineau Cl. | 1B 52 | Mayfield Rd., Frimley | 2D 61 |
| Mansel Cl. | 3E 81 | Markfield | 4D 59 | Martineau Dr. | 2A 106 | Mayfield Rd., Hawley | 3C 60 |
| Mansel Rd. | 5B 20 | Markville Gdns. | 1B 92 | Martingale Cl. | 2A 34 | Mayfield Rd., Merton | 1B 38 |
| Mansell Rd. | 1D 9 | Markway | 1B 34 | Martingales Cl. | 3A 18 | Mayfield Rd., Mitcham | 2A 40 |
| Mansfield Cres. | 3D 27 | Marwick La. | 1E 138 | Martins Cl., Blackwater | 1B 60 | Mayfield Rd., Sanderstead | 3F 57 |
| Mansfield Dr. | 2C 90 | Marlborough Cl. | 5B 34 | Martins Cl., Guildford | 5C 82 | Mayfield Rd., Walton | 1D 51 |
| Mansfield Pl. | 1A 28 | Marlborough Cres. | 1D 9 | Martins Dr. | 1D 25 | Mayfield Rd., Weybridge | 1A 50 |
| Mansfield Rd., Chessington | 1D 53 | Marlborough Dr. | 5E 33 | Martin's La. | 2E 27 | Mayford Cl. | 4C 64 |
| Mansfield Rd., South Croydon | 2F 57 | Marlborough Hill | 1A 106 | Martin's Rd. | 1C 42 | Mayford Rd. | 2E 21 |
| Manship Rd. | 5E 21 | Marlborough Rise | 5B 44 | Martlets, The | 4D 147 | Mayhurst Av. | 1E 65 |
| Mansion Hill | 2E 91 | Marlborough Rd., Ashford | 4C 14 | Marts, The | 2E 157 | Mayhurst Cl. | 1E 65 |
| Manston Cl. | 1E 41 | Marlborough Rd., Chiswick | 2D 9 | Martyr Rd. | 1C 100 | Mayhurst Cres. | 1E 65 |
| Manston Dr. | 3D 27 | Marlborough Rd., Colliers | 5D 21 | Martyrs Av. | 2C 146 | Mayle Way | 4A 134 |
| Manston Rd. | 3B 82 | Wood | | Martyr's Grn. | 3F 67 | Mayo Rd., Selhurst | 3C 40 |
| Mantilla Rd. | 4E 21 | Marlborough Rd., Cotmandene | 1A 106 | Martyr's La. | 4B 48 | Mayo Rd., Walton-on-Thames | 4A 34 |
| Manville Rd. | 3E 21 | Marlborough Rd., Gunnersbury | 1B 8 | Marvell Cl. | 3F 147 | Mayow Rd. | 4F 23 |
| Manwood Rd. | 1A 24 | Marlborough Rd., Hampton | 5C 16 | Mary Rd. | 1C 100 | Maypole Rd. | 2B 150 |
| Manygate La. | 4E 33 | Marlborough Rd., Hanworth | 3B 16 | Maryland Rd. | 1B 40 | Mayroyd Av. | 5C 36 |
| Maori Rd. | 1D 101 | Marlborough Rd., Maybury | 1D 65 | Maryland Way | 1A 34 | Mays Gro. | 5F 65 |
| Maple Cl., Ash Vale | 2C 78 | Marlborough Rd., Richmond | 1B 18 | Marys Ter. | 2F 17 | May's Hill | 1D 81 |
| Maple Cl., Clapham | 1F 21 | Marlborough Rd., South | 2F 57 | Maryvale | 3D 119 | Mays Hill Rd. | 1C 42 |
| Maple Cl., Langley Green | 2C 146 | Croydon | | Masefield Rd. | 4C 16 | Mays Rd., Twick'm. | 4E 17 |
| Maple Cl., Mitcham | 1E 39 | Marlborough Rd., Sutton | 5B 38 | Maskall Cl. | 2B 22 | Mays Rd., Wokingham | 2F 25 |
| Maple Cl., Whyteleafe | 2D 75 | Marlbrook Rd. | 5F 9 | Maskell Rd. | 3C 20 | Maysfield Rd. | 5F 65 |
| Maple Ct., Englefield Green | 5B 12 | Marld, The | 2B 70 | Mason Rd., Crawley | 5D 147 | Maywater Cl. | 4F 57 |
| Maple Ct., New Malden | 2D 37 | Marler Rd. | 2F 23 | Mason Rd., Farnborough | 4B 60 | Maywood Cl. | 5A 24 |
| Maple Dr., Crowthorne | 5A 26 | Marles La. | 5E 157 | Mason's Bridge Rd. | 3E 109 | Maywood Dr. | 4C 44 |
| Maple Dr., Salfords | 3D 109 | Marlets Cl. | 3B 158 | Mason's Paddock | 5C 86 | Maze Rd. | 3C 8 |
| Maple Gro., Bellfields | 4F 81 | Marley Cl. | 2D 49 | Masonic Hall Rd. | 3A 32 | Mazecroft | 2C 128 |
| Maple Gro., Brentford | 3A 8 | Marley Commbe Rd. | 3E 151 | Massets Rd. | 3B 128 | McDonough Cl. | 1E 53 |
| Maple Gro., Lammas Park | 1A 8 | Marley Hanger | 4F 151 | Master Cl. | 3F 93 | McIndoe Rd. | 1C 150 |
| Maple Gro., Westfield | 4D 65 | Marley La. | 4E 151 | Maswell Park Cres. | 1D 17 | McKay Rd. | 5F 19 |
| Maple Hatch Cl. | 3D 119 | Marley Rise | 3F 105 | Maswell Park Rd. | 1D 17 | Mead Av. | 4E 109 |
| Maple Leaf Cl. | 5C 60 | Marlingdene Cl. | 5C 16 | Matham Rd. | 3E 35 | Mead Cl., Cranleigh | 2C 140 |
| Maple Pl. | 5D 55 | Marlings Cl. | 2D 75 | Mathias Cl. | 5A 54 | Mead Cl., Egham | 5E 13 |
| Maple Rd., Anerley | 1E 41 | Marlow Cl. | 2E 41 | Mathison Way | 4B 7 | Mead Cl., Redhill | 4B 90 |
| Maple Rd., Bellfields | 3B 70 | Marlow Ct. | 3D 147 | Matlock Cres. | 1D 55 | Mead Cres., Bookham | 1F 85 |
| Maple Rd., Earlswood | 2D 109 | Marlow Cres. | 1F 17 | Matlock Gdns. | 1D 55 | Mead Cres., Carshalton | 1A 56 |
| Maple Rd., Penge | 5E 23 | Marlow Dr. | 5A 38 | Matlock Pl. | 1D 55 | Mead End | 2B 70 |
| Maple Rd., Sendmarsh | 5A 66 | Marlow Rd. | 2E 41 | Matlock Rd. | 4D 75 | Mead La., Chertsey | 4B 32 |
| Maple Rd., Surbiton | 3A 36 | Marlowe Way | 5A 40 | Matlock Way | 1D 37 | Mead Lane, Farnham | 4A 96 |
| Maple Rd., Whyteleafe | 2D 75 | Marlyns Cl. | 3B 82 | Matthew Arnold Cl. | 5D 51 | Mead Pl. | 4B 40 |
| Maple Way, Feltham | 3A 16 | Marlyns Dr. | 4B 82 | Matthew St. | 2B 108 | Mead Rd., Caterham | 5D 75 |
| Maple Way, Hooley | 4E 73 | Marmora Rd. | 1E 23 | Matthews Cl. | 2B 78 | Mead Rd., Cranleigh | 1C 140 |
| Mapledale Av. | 5D 41 | Marne Rd. | 3A 62 | Matthews Rd. | 4A 44 | Mead Rd., Crawley | 3D 147 |
| Mapledrakes Cl. | 5C 122 | Marneys Cl. | 1C 70 | Matthewsgreen Rd. | 1D 25 | Mead Rd., Ham | 3A 18 |
| Mapledrakes Rd. | 5C 122 | Marnock Rd. | 1F 23 | Matthey Pl. | 2F 147 | Mead Rd., Hersham | 1E 51 |
| Maples, The, Banstead | 5F 55 | Maroons Way | 4A 24 | Mauleverer Rd. | 1A 22 | Mead Rd., Hindhead | 5E 135 |
| Maples, The, Ottershaw | 2B 48 | Marpit Av. | 2A 74 | Maultway Cl. | 4C 44 | Mead, The Ashtead | 3B 70 |
| Maplestead Rd. | 2A 22 | Marpit Cl. | 1C 150 | Maultway Cres. | 4C 44 | Mead, The, Beckenham | 1B 42 |
| Maplethorpe Rd. | 2B 40 | Marpit La. | 2A 74 | Maultway, The | 3C 44 | Mead, The, Beddington | 2C 56 |
| Mapleton Rd. | 1C 20 | Marlyns Cl. | 3B 82 | Maurice Av. | 4C 74 | Mead, The, Farnborough | 5D 61 |
| Marble Hill Cl. | 2A 18 | Marlyns Dr. | 4B 82 | Maurice Av. | | Mead, The, West Wickham | 4B 42 |
| Marble Hill Gdns. | 2A 18 | Marmora Rd. | 1E 23 | Mavins Rd. | 5B 96 | Mead Way, Burpham | 3B 82 |
| Marbles Way | 3A 72 | Marne Rd. | 3A 62 | Mavis Av. | 1B 54 | Mead Way, Coulsdon | 2A 74 |
| March Rd., Twickenham | 2F 17 | Marneys Cl. | 1C 70 | Mavis Cl. | 1B 54 | Mead Way, Effingham | 2F 85 |
| March Rd., Weybridge | 1A 50 | Marnock Rd. | 1F 23 | Mawbey Rd. | 2C 48 | Mead Way, Parklangley | 3C 42 |
| Marches Rd. | 5E 143 | Maroons Way | 4A 24 | Mawson Cl. | 1A 38 | Mead Way, Raynes Park | 2F 37 |
| Marchmont Rd., Beddington | 2C 56 | Marriot Cl. | 1F 15 | Maxwell Dr. | 4E 49 | Mead Way, Shirley | 5E 41 |
| Marchmont Rd., Richmond | 1B 18 | Marriot Lodge Cl. | 1E 49 | Maxwell Rd. | 5E 15 | Mead Way, Shottermill | 3E 151 |
| Marco Rd. | 1F 9 | Marrow Brook La. | 5C 60 | Maxwell Way | 2E 147 | Mead Way Cl. | 5A 14 |
| Mardell Rd. | 3F 41 | Marrow Brook Rd. | 5C 60 | May Cl., Chessington | 2F 53 | Meadcourt | 1A 64 |
| Marden Cres. | 3A 40 | Marrowells | 5F 33 | May Cl., Ockford Ridge | 3C 118 | Meadhurst Rd. | 4B 32 |
| Marden Rd. | 3A 40 | Marryat Rd. | 4A 20 | May Cl., Sandhurst | 4E 43 | Meadlands Dr. | 3A 18 |
| Mardens, The | 3C 146 | Marsh Av., Ewell | 3B 54 | May Cres. | 5D 78 | Meadow Approach | 1B 148 |
| Mare La. | 1B 138 | Marsh Av., Mitcham | 1E 39 | May Rd. | 2E 17 | Meadow Bank, East Horsley | 2C 84 |
| Mareschal Rd. | 1C 100 | Marsh Farm Rd. | 2E 17 | May Tree Cl. | 4F 81 | Meadow Bank, Surbiton | 3B 36 |
| Margaret Rd. | 1C 100 | Marsh La. | 1E 49 | Maybelle Cl. | 2D 125 | Meadow Bank Rd. | 3F 45 |
| Margate Rd. | 1A 22 | Marshall Cl., Heatherside | 2A 62 | Mayberry Cl. | 4B 36 | Meadow Brook | 3E 93 |
| Margery Gr. | 3D 89 | Marshall Cl., Isleworth | 1C 16 | Maybourne Cl. | 4E 23 | Meadow Cl., Blackwater | 1B 60 |
| Margery La. | 3E 89 | Marshall Parade | 1A 66 | Maybourne Rise | 5C 64 | Meadow Cl., Cannon Hill | 2A 38 |
| Margin Dr. | 4A 20 | Marshall Rd., Godalming | 1D 119 | Maybury | 2E 65 | Meadow Cl., Esher | 1F 51 |
| Marham Gdns., Morden | 3C 38 | Marshall Rd., Sandhurst | 5E 43 | Maybury Cl., Burgh Heath | 3A 72 | Meadow Cl., Farncombe | 5A 100 |
| | | | | Maybury Cl., Frimley | 3D 61 | | |

| | | | |
|---|---|---|---|
| Meadow Cl., Hinchley Wood | 5F 35 | Medlake Rd. | 5E 13 |
| Meadow Cl., Milford | 3B 118 | Medland Cl. | 4E 39 |
| Meadow Cl., Mytchett | 1B 78 | Medlar Cl., Crawley | 2C 146 |
| Meadow Cl., Old Windsor | 1B 12 | Medlar Cl., Guildford | 4F 81 |
| Meadow Cl., Purley | 5C 56 | Medusa Rd. | 1A 24 |
| Meadow Cl., Rose Hill | 5C 38 | Medway | 4D 149 |
| Meadow Cl., Whitton | 1C 16 | Medway Dr., E. Grinstead | 4C 150 |
| Meadow Ct. | 3F 13 | Medway Dr., W. Heath | 3B 60 |
| Meadow Dr. | 5A 66 | Medway Rd. | 4B 146 |
| Meadow Gdns. | 4F 13 | Melbourne Gro. | 1D 23 |
| Meadow Hill, Malden | 3D 37 | Melbourne Rd., Kingston | 5A 18 |
| Meadow Hill, Woodcote | 5C 56 | Melbourne Rd., Merton | 1B 38 |
| Meadow Lands, Oxted | 5A 94 | Melbourne Rd., Wallington | 1C 56 |
| Meadow Lands Rd. | 3E 83 | Melbury Cl., Chertsey | 4B 32 |
| Meadow La., Fetcham | 4E 69 | Melbury Cl., Claygate | 2C 52 |
| Meadow Rise | 5C 56 | Melbury Cl., W. Byfleet | 5D 49 |
| Meadow Rd., Ashford | 4E 15 | Melbury Gdns. | 1F 37 |
| Meadow Rd., Ashtead | 2B 70 | Meldrum Cl. | 4A 94 |
| Meadow Rd., Burpham | 3B 82 | Melford Rd. | 2D 23 |
| Meadow Rd., Carshalton | 1A 56 | Melfort Rd. | 2B 40 |
| Meadow Rd., Claygate | 2B 52 | Melina Rd. | 1F 9 |
| Meadow Rd., Hanworth | 3B 16 | Meliot Rd. | 3C 24 |
| Meadow Rd., Hawley | 3C 60 | Mellersh Hill Rd. South | 1B 120 |
| Meadow Rd., Shortlands | 1C 42 | Mellison Rd. | 4D 21 |
| Meadow Rd., South Wimbledon | 5C 20 | Mellor Cl. | 4C 34 |
| | | Mellow Cl. | 5F 55 |
| Meadow Rd., Wentworth | 3A 30 | Mellows Rd. | 1C 56 |
| Meadow Rd., Wokingham | 2D 25 | Melody Rd., Biggin Hill | 2D 77 |
| Meadow Vale | 3F 151 | Melody Rd., Wandsworth | 1C 20 |
| Meadow View, Shepperton | 4E 33 | Melrose | 4D 27 |
| Meadow View, Thornton Heath | 3B 40 | Melrose Av., Mitcham | 5E 21 |
| Meadow View Rd. | 3B 54 | Melrose Av., Norbury | 2A 40 |
| Meadow Wk., Hackbridge | 5E 39 | Melrose Av., West Heath | 5A 60 |
| Meadow Wk., Stoneleigh | 2B 54 | Melrose Av., Whitton | 2D 17 |
| Meadow Wk., Walton on the Hill | 5F 71 | Melrose Av., Wimbledon Park | 3B 20 |
| | | Melrose Gdns. | 1A 50 |
| Meadow Way, Addlestone | 1E 49 | Melrose Gdns., Hammersmith | 1F 9 |
| Meadow Way, Aldershot | 4B 78 | Melrose Gdns., Malden | 2D 37 |
| Meadow Way, Blackwater | 5D 43 | Melrose Rd., Biggin Hill | 1E 77 |
| Meadow Way, Burgh Heath | 2A 72 | Melrose Rd., Merton | 1B 38 |
| Meadow Way, Chessington | 1E 53 | Melrose Rd., West Hill | 1B 20 |
| Meadow Way, Fetcham | 5D 69 | Melrose Rd., Weybridge | 1A 50 |
| Meadow Way, Horsley | 1B 84 | Melrose Rd., Woodmansterne | 1E 73 |
| Meadow Way, Old Windsor | 1B 12 | Melrose Ter. | 1F 9 |
| Meadow Way, West End | 4B 46 | Melsa Rd. | 3C 38 |
| Meadow Way, Wokingham | 2D 25 | Melton Pl. | 3A 54 |
| Meadow Way, Woodhatch | 2C 108 | Melton Rd. | 3C 90 |
| Meadowbrook Cl. | 4B 7 | Melville Av., Cottenham Park | 5E 19 |
| Meadowbrook Rd. | 1F 105 | Melville Av., Frimley | 2F 61 |
| Meadowcroft Cl., East Grinstead | 2B 150 | Melville Av., South Croydon | 1A 58 |
| | | Melville Rd. | 4E 9 |
| Meadowcroft Cl., Horley | 4C 128 | Melvin Rd. | 1E 41 |
| Meadowlands, Cobham | 5D 51 | Melvin Shaw | 4A 70 |
| Meadowlands, Crawley | 4C 146 | Membury Wk. | 2E 27 |
| Meadows End | 1A 34 | Mendip Rd. | 3E 27 |
| Meadows Leigh Cl. | 5E 33 | Menin Way | 4B 96 |
| Meadows, The, Churt | 2C 134 | Menlo Gdns. | 5C 22 |
| Meadows, The, Guildford | 2C 100 | Meon Cl. | 4F 71 |
| Meadowside, Bookham | 5C 68 | Meon Rd. | 1D 9 |
| Meadowside, Horley | 2C 128 | Meopham Rd. | 1F 39 |
| Meadowside, Lingfield | 1E 131 | Mercer Cl. | 4F 35 |
| Meadowside, Walton | 5B 34 | Mercia Way | 2D 65 |
| Meadowside Rd. | 3D 55 | Mercier Rd. | 1A 20 |
| Meadowview | 5D 133 | Mercury Rd. | 2A 8 |
| Meadowview Cl. | 4A 24 | Mere End | 4F 41 |
| Meadowview Rd. | 4A 24 | Mere Rd., Portmore Park | 5E 33 |
| Meadrow, Farncombe | 5B 100 | Mere Rd., Shepperton | 3E 33 |
| Meadrow, Godalming | 1D 119 | Mere Rd., Tadworth | 5F 71 |
| Meads Cl. | 3A 132 | Merebank | 2D 125 |
| Meads Rd. | 5B 82 | Merebank La. | 1D 57 |
| Meads, The, Dormans Land | 3A 132 | Meredyth Rd. | 4E 9 |
| Meads, The, East Grinstead | 3C 150 | Merefield | 5E 69 |
| Meads, The, Haslemere | 3F 151 | Merefield Gdns. | 3A 72 |
| Meads, The, North Cheam | 5A 38 | Mereside Pl. | 4B 30 |
| Meadvale Rd. | 4D 41 | Merevale Cres. | 3C 38 |
| Meadway, Ashford | 4D 15 | Mereway Rd. | 2E 17 |
| Meadway, Beckenham | 1B 42 | Mereworth Cl. | 3C 42 |
| Meadway, Epsom | 4A 54 | Mereworth Rd. | 3D 147 |
| Meadway, Esher | 3A 52 | Meridan Grove | 2C 128 |
| Meadway, Frimley | 2E 61 | Merland Green | 3F 71 |
| Meadway, Hamsey Green | 1E 75 | Merland Rise | 3F 71 |
| Meadway, Oxshott | 5B 52 | Merle Common Rd. | 1D 113 |
| Meadway, Staines | 5A 14 | Merlewood Cl. | 4C 74 |
| Meadway, The | 2C 128 | Merlin Gro. | 2A 42 |
| Meadway, Tolworth | 4D 37 | Merlins Cl. | 2D 75 |
| Meadway, Twickenham | 2E 17 | Merriland Rd. | 4F 37 |
| Meadway Cl. | 3E 41 | Merrilands Rd. | 4F 37 |
| Meadway Dr., Horsell | 1C 64 | Merrilyn Cl. | 2C 52 |
| Meadway Dr., New Haw | 2E 49 | Merritt Rd. | 1A 24 |
| Mears Cl. | 5A 72 | Merrivale Gdns. | 2C 64 |
| Meathgreen Av. | 1A 128 | Merrow | 5C 82 |
| Meathgreen La., Lee St. | 1A 128 | Merrow Chase | 5C 82 |
| Meathgreen La., Salfords | 5D 109 | Merrow Common | 4C 82 |
| Mede Cl. | 2C 12 | Merrow Copse | 5B 82 |
| Mede Field | 5E 69 | Merrow Cpse. | 5C 82 |
| Medfield St. | 2F 19 | Merrow Croft | 5C 82 |
| Medina Av. | 5E 35 | Merrow La. | 3C 82 |

| | | | |
|---|---|---|---|
| Merrow Rd. | 3D 55 | Midleton Rd. | 5E 81 |
| Merrow St. | 4C 82 | Midmoor Rd., Balham | 2F 21 |
| Merrow Way | 2E 59 | Midmoor Rd., Wimbledon | 1A 38 |
| Merrow Woods | 4B 82 | Midway, Cheam | 4B 38 |
| Merryacres | 5A 118 | Midway, Walton-on-Thames | 5A 34 |
| Merryfield Dr. | 4A 158 | Midway Av. | 2E 31 |
| Merryhill Rd. | 1C 26 | Miena Way | 2A 70 |
| Merrylands | 5A 32 | Mike Hawthorn Dr. | 3B 96 |
| Merrylands Rd. | 5C 68 | Milbanke Way | 1C 26 |
| Merrymeet | 5A 56 | Milborough Cres. | 1C 24 |
| Merrywood Pk., Box Hill | 3F 87 | Milbourne La. | 2A 52 |
| Merrywood Pk., Heatherside | 1F 61 | Milbourne Rd. | 4C 16 |
| Merrywood Pk., Reigate | 4E 89 | Milbrook, Esher | 2A 52 |
| Merryworth Cl. | 5B 78 | Milburn Wk. | 1E 71 |
| Mersham Rd. | 2C 40 | Milcombe Cl. | 2C 64 |
| Merstham | 2C 90 | Milden Gdns. | 4F 61 |
| Merstham Rd. | 3E 91 | Mile Path | 3B 64 |
| Merthyr Ter. | 3F 9 | Mile Rd. | 4E 39 |
| Merton | 1B 38 | Mile's Hill | 2E 123 |
| Merton Av. | 2E 9 | Miles La., Crowhurst | 1A 112 |
| Merton Cl. | 3F 43 | Miles La., Oxshott | 5F 51 |
| Merton Gdns. | 3A 72 | Miles New Rd. | 1F 111 |
| Merton Hall Gdns. | 1A 38 | Miles Pl. | 2B 36 |
| Merton Hall Rd. | 1A 38 | Miles Rd., Ash Wharf | 4C 78 |
| Merton Rd., South Wimbledon | 5C 20 | Miles Rd., Epsom | 4A 54 |
| | | Milestone Cl., Ripley | 4B 66 |
| Merton Rd., Southfields | 1B 20 | Milestone Cl., Sutton | 2F 55 |
| Merton Rd., Woodside | 3D 41 | Milestone Rd. | 5D 23 |
| Merton Way, East Molesey | 2D 35 | Milford | 3A 118 |
| Merton Way, Leatherhead Common | 3F 69 | Milford Grn. | 4E 47 |
| | | Milford Gro. | 1F 55 |
| Mervyn Rd. | 4E 33 | Milford Lodge | 4B 118 |
| Metcalf Rd. | 4D 15 | Milkwood Rd. | 1B 22 |
| Meteor Way | 2D 57 | Mill Bay La., Horsham | 5A 158 |
| Meudon Rd. | 5D 61 | Mill Cl., Bookham | 5C 68 |
| Mexfield Rd. | 1B 20 | Mill Cl., East Grinstead | 3C 150 |
| Michael Cres. | 3B 128 | Mill Cl., Hackbridge | 5E 39 |
| Michael Rd. | 2C 40 | Mill Cl., Horley | 2A 128 |
| Micheldever Rd. | 1C 24 | Mill Farm Av. | 5F 15 |
| Micheldever Way | 3F 27 | Mill Farm Cres. | 2C 16 |
| Michelet Cl. | 3F 45 | Mill Hedge Cl. | 1B 68 |
| Michelham Gdns. | 3F 71 | Mill Hill Gro. | 1C 8 |
| Michell Cl. | 5A 158 | Mill Hill La. | 5F 87 |
| Michels Row | 5B 8 | Mill Hill Rd., Acton | 1C 8 |
| Mickle Hill | 3D 43 | Mill Hill Rd., Barnes | 4E 9 |
| Mickleham | 2D 87 | Mill Hollow | 3B 122 |
| Mickleham By-Pass | 2C 86 | Mill House La. | 2E 31 |
| Mickleham Dr. | 1D 87 | Mill La., Bramley | 1A 120 |
| Mickleham Gdns. | 2D 55 | Mill La., Byfleet | 5A 50 |
| Mickleham Way | 2E 59 | Mill La., Chiddingfold | 5F 137 |
| Mid St. | 5D 91 | Mill La., Chilworth | 3A 102 |
| Middle Av. | 5B 96 | Mill La., Domewood | 1C 148 |
| Middle Bourne | 1D 115 | Mill La., Dorking | 1F 105 |
| Middle Bourne La. | 5A 96 | Mill La., Easthampstead | 2C 26 |
| Middle Church La. | 4A 96 | Mill La., Ewell | 3B 54 |
| Middle Cl., Camberley | 5D 45 | Mill La., Felbridge | 1F 149 |
| Middle Cl., Coulsdon | 3A 74 | Mill La., Godalming | 2C 118 |
| Middle Gordon Rd. | 5A 44 | Mill La., Guildford | 159 |
| Middle Green | 5C 14 | Mill La., Headley | 4E 133 |
| Middle Hill, Egham | 4C 12 | Mill La., Holland | 5A 95 |
| Middle Hill, Millbridge | 3D 115 | Mill La., Ifield Village | 3B 146 |
| Middle La., Epsom | 4B 54 | Mill La., Leatherhead | 4F 69 |
| Middle La., Teddington | 5F 17 | Mill La., Lee Street | 2A 128 |
| Middle Old Pk. | 3E 95 | Mill La., Lingfield | 3F 131 |
| Middle Rd., Leatherhead | 160 | Mill La., Parkgate | 1A 126 |
| Middle Rd., Mitcham | 1F 39 | Mill La., Peasmarsh | 4C 100 |
| Middle St., Brockham | 1C 106 | Mill La., Pirbright | 5D 63 |
| Middle St., Shere | 3D 103 | Mill La., Ripley | 3C 66 |
| Middle St., Strood Green | 2D 107 | Mill La., South Merstham | 4C 90 |
| Middle Wk. | 2D 65 | Mill La., The Chart | 4C 94 |
| Middle Way | 1F 39 | Mill La., Thorpe | 2E 31 |
| Middlefield, Horley | 2C 128 | Mill La., Virginia Water | 1E 29 |
| Middlefield, Selsdon | 3C 58 | Mill La., Waddon | 5A 40 |
| Middlefield, Wrecclesham | 5F 95 | Mill La., Wheeler Street | 5B 118 |
| Middlemarch | 5B 118 | Mill Pl. | 2B 36 |
| Middlemead Cl. | 1F 85 | Mill Ride | 1A 28 |
| Middlemeads Rd. | 1F 85 | Mill Rd., Banstead Newton | 5A 72 |
| Middlemoor Cl. | 3E 61 | Mill Rd., Cobham | 1A 68 |
| Middlemoor Rd. | 3E 61 | Mill Rd., Epsom | 4B 54 |
| Middlesex Rd. | 3A 40 | Mill Rd., Hersham | 5C 34 |
| Middleton Cl. | 3B 118 | Mill Rd., South Holmwood | 5A 106 |
| Middleton Rd., Camberley | 5B 44 | Mill Rd., South Wimbledon | 5C 20 |
| Middleton Rd., Downside | 3A 68 | Mill Rd., Three Bridges | 3E 147 |
| Middleton Rd., Ewell | 3A 54 | Mill Rd., Twickenham | 3D 17 |
| Middleton Rd., Horsham | 5A 158 | Mill Stream | 2B 96 |
| Middleton Rd., Morden | 3C 38 | Mill St., Colnbrook | 3A 7 |
| Middleton Way | 4A 146 | Mill St., Kingston | 2B 36 |
| Midgeley Rd. | 3D 147 | Mill St., Redhill | 1D 109 |
| Midholm Rd. | 5F 41 | Mill Vale | 1C 42 |
| Midhope Cl. | 3D 65 | Mill View Gdns. | 5E 41 |
| Midhope Gdns. | 3D 65 | Mill Way, East Grinstead | 3C 150 |
| Midhope Rd. | 3D 65 | Mill Way, Feltham | 1A 16 |
| Midhurst Av. | 4B 40 | Mill Way, Headley | 1F 87 |
| Midhurst Cl. | 3B 146 | Mill Way, Tyrell's Wood | 5B 70 |
| Midhurst Rd. | 4F 151 | Millais | 4C 158 |
| Midleton Cl. | 3B 118 | Millais Rd. | 4D 37 |
| Midleton Gdns. | 4B 60 | Millais Way | 1A 54 |

| Name | Ref | Name | Ref | Name | Ref | Name | Ref |
|---|---|---|---|---|---|---|---|
| Millbank, The | 4B 146 | Mint La. | 3E 89 | Montacute Rd., Morden | 3C 36 | More Rd. | 5A 100 |
| Millbrook, Guildford | 1C 100 | Mint Rd., Banstead | 1C 72 | Montacute Rd., New | 3E 59 | Morecambe Cl. | 5B 146 |
| Millbrook, Weybridge | 1C 50 | Mint Rd., Wallington | 1B 56 | Addington | | Moreland Av. | 3A 7 |
| Millbrook La. | 5A 98 | Mint St. | 2D 119 | Montagu Gdns. | 1C 56 | Morella Cl. | 2C 30 |
| Millchase | 5D 133 | Mint Walk, Croydon | 5C 40 | Montague Av. | 4F 57 | Morella Rd. | 2D 21 |
| Millen Cl. | 3E 49 | Mint Walk, Warlingham | 2F 75 | Montague Cl. | 4A 34 | Moremead Rd. | 4A 24 |
| Miller Rd., Croydon | 4A 40 | Missenden Gdns. | 3C 38 | Montague Rd., Croydon | 4B 40 | Morena St. | 2A 24 |
| Miller Rd., Guildford | 4C 82 | Mitcham | 1D 39 | Montague Rd., Richmond | 1B 18 | Moresby Av. | 4C 36 |
| Miller Rd., Tooting | 5F 21 | Mitcham La. | 5F 21 | Montague Rd., Wimbledon | 5B 20 | Moretaine Rd. | 3C 14 |
| Millers Copse, Langley Vale | 3D 71 | Mitcham Pk. | 2D 39 | Montana Cl. | 3F 57 | Moreton Rd., South Croydon | 1F 57 |
| Millers Copse, Outwood | 5B 110 | Mitcham Rd., Camberley | 3C 44 | Montana Rd., Tooting Bec | 3E 21 | Moreton Rd., Worcester Park | 5F 37 |
| Miller's La. | 5B 110 | Mitcham Rd., Croydon | 3A 40 | Montana Rd., Wimbledon | 1A 38 | Moring Rd. | 4E 21 |
| Millfield, Bagshot | 2D 45 | Mitcham Rd., Tooting | 4D 21 | Montegal Cl. | 2D 119 | Morkyns Walk | 3C 22 |
| Millfield, Sunbury | 1F 33 | Mitchells Rd. | 4D 147 | Montem Rd., Lewisham | 2F 23 | Morland Av. | 4C 40 |
| Millfield La. | 1E 89 | Mitchley Av. | 5F 57 | Montem Rd., New Malden | 2D 37 | Morland Cl. | 4C 16 |
| Millfield Rd. | 2C 16 | Mitchley Green | 5A 58 | Montford Rd. | 2A 34 | Morland Rd., Addiscombe | 4D 41 |
| Millgreen Rd. | 4E 39 | Mitchley Hill | 5A 58 | Montfort Rise | 5D 109 | Morland Rd., Aldershot | 1D 97 |
| Millins | 3E 43 | Mitchley View | 5A 58 | Montgomerie Dr. | 3E 81 | Morland Rd., Penge | 5F 23 |
| Millmead, Byfleet | 4A 50 | Mitre Cl. | 2F 55 | Montgomery Av. | 5E 35 | Morland Rd., Sutton | 2F 55 |
| Millmead, Guildford | 1C 100 | Mixbury Gr. | 2B 50 | Montgomery Rd. | 2D 9 | Morlands Rd. | 3A 78 |
| Millmead, Staines | 4A 14 | Mixnams La. | 2A 32 | Montholme Rd. | 1D 21 | Morley Rd., Farnham | 4A 96 |
| Millmead Terrace | 1C 100 | Mizen Cl. | 1B 68 | Montpelier Rd., Purley | 3E 57 | Morley Rd., Hither Green | 1B 24 |
| Millmeads | 3B 158 | Mizen Way | 5E 51 | Montpelier Rd., Sutton | 1F 55 | Morley Rd., Richmond | 1A 18 |
| Millpond Rd. | 1F 45 | Moat Ct. | 2B 70 | Montpelier Row | 2A 18 | Morley Rd., Selsdon | 3A 58 |
| Mills Rd., Chiswick | 2D 9 | Moat Rd. | 2C 150 | Montrell Rd. | 2A 22 | Morley Rd., St. Helier | 4B 38 |
| Mills Rd., Hersham | 1E 51 | Moat Side | 4B 16 | Montrose Av. | 2D 17 | Morney Rough | 1B 118 |
| Mills Spur | 2B 12 | Moat, The | 1E 37 | Montrose Cl., Ashford | 5E 15 | Morningside Rd. | 5F 37 |
| Millshaw | 4F 93 | Moat Walk | 3F 147 | Montrose Cl., Frimley | 2E 61 | Mornington Rd. | 4E 15 |
| Millthorpe Rd. | 4C 158 | Moats Lane | 3A 110 | Montrose Gdns., Mitcham | 2E 39 | Mornington Walk | 4A 18 |
| Millview Cl. | 4A 90 | Moffat Rd., Beulah Hill | 1C 40 | Montrose Gdns., Oxshott | 4B 52 | Morrel Ave. | 3C 158 |
| Millway | 5A 90 | Moffats Dr. | 4D 43 | Montrose Gdns., Rose Hill | 5C 38 | Morris Gdns. | 2B 20 |
| Millwood Rd. | 1D 17 | Moffatt Rd., Colliers W'd. | 4D 21 | Montrose Rd. | 1E 15 | Morris Rd., S. Farnborough | 2B 78 |
| Milman Cl. | 1F 27 | Mogador Rd. | 2D 89 | Montrose Walk | 5D 33 | Morris Rd., S. Nutfield | 1A 110 |
| Milne Park East | 4E 59 | Mogden La. | 1E 17 | Montrouge Cres. | 1F 71 | Morrish Rd. | 2A 22 |
| Milne Park West | 4E 59 | Moir Cl. | 3A 58 | Monument Hill | 1A 50 | Morston Cl. | 3F 71 |
| Milner Approach | 4D 75 | Mole Abbey Gdns. | 2D 35 | Monument Rd., Maybury | 5B 48 | Morten Cl. | 1F 21 |
| Milner Close | 4D 75 | Mole Cl., Crawley | 3C 146 | Monument Rd., Portmore Park | 5E 33 | Mortimer Cl. | 3F 21 |
| Milner Dr., Cobham | 4F 51 | Mole Cl., West Heath | 4B 60 | Monument Way East And West | 1E 65 | Mortimer Cres. | 5D 37 |
| Milner Dr., Whitton | 2E 17 | Mole Ct. | 1A 54 | Moon Hall Rd. | 3B 122 | Mortimer Rd., Capel | 5D 125 |
| Milner Pl. | 1B 56 | Mole Rd., Fetcham | 4E 69 | Moons Hill | 3D 115 | Mortimer Rd., Mitcham | 1D 39 |
| Milner Rd., Caterham | 4D 75 | Mole Rd., Hersham | 1E 51 | Moons La., Dormans Land | 4B 132 | Mortlake Cl. | 5A 40 |
| Milner Rd., Kingston | 2B 36 | Mole St., Ockley | 5A 124 | Moons La., Horsham | 5C 158 | Mortlake High St. | 4D 9 |
| Milner Rd., Merton | 1C 38 | Mole Valley Pl. | 3B 70 | Moor Cl. | 2C 16 | Mortlake Rd. | 3C 8 |
| Milner Rd., Mitcham | 3D 39 | Molember Rd. | 3E 35 | Moor La., Chessington | 1E 53 | Morton | 4A 72 |
| Milnthorpe Rd. | 3D 9 | Moles Hill | 4B 52 | Moor La., Dorman's Land | 3A 132 | Morton Cl. | 3E 61 |
| Milnwood Rd. | 4B 158 | Molesey Av. | 3C 34 | Moor La., Harmondsworth | 3C 7 | Morton Gdns. | 1C 56 |
| Milo Rd. | 1D 23 | Molesey Cl. | 1E 51 | Moor La., Poyle | 5A 7 | Morton Rd., East Grinstead | 3C 150 |
| Milton Av., Carshalton | 1A 56 | Molesey Dr. | 5A 38 | Moor La., Staines | 3F 13 | Morton Rd., Mitcham | 3D 39 |
| Milton Av., Croydon | 4C 40 | Molesey Pk. Av. | 3D 35 | Moor La., Westfield | 4D 65 | Morton Rd., Woking | 1C 64 |
| Milton Av., Westcott | 2E 105 | Molesey Pk. Cl. | 3D 35 | Moor Mead Rd. | 1F 17 | Morval Rd. | 1B 22 |
| Milton Cl., Easthampstead | 3C 26 | Molesey Park Rd. | 3D 35 | Moor Park Cres. | 4F 145 | Moselle Rd. | 2F 77 |
| Milton Cl., Feltham | 1A 16 | Molesey Rd. | 5B 34 | Moor Park La. | 3C 96 | Mosford Cl. | 1A 128 |
| Milton Cl., The Wrythe | 5D 39 | Molesham Cl. | 2D 35 | Moor Park Way | 4C 96 | Mospey Cres. | 1E 71 |
| Milton Cres. | 2B 150 | Molesham Way | 2D 35 | Moor Pl. | 2B 150 | Moss La. | 2D 119 |
| Milton Dr. | 3C 32 | Molesworth Rd. | 5D 51 | Moor Rd., Frimley | 3E 61 | Mosses Wood Rd. | 3A 124 |
| Milton Gdns., Epsom | 5B 54 | Mollison Dr. | 2D 57 | Moor Rd., Hammer | 3D 151 | Mossfield | 5D 51 |
| Milton Gdns., Wokingham | 1D 25 | Molly Miller's La. | 3D 25 | Moor Rd., Hawley | 3C 60 | Mosslea Rd., Penge | 5E 23 |
| Milton Mount Av. | 3F 147 | Molyneaux Rd., Farncombe | 5A 100 | Moordale Av. | 1B 26 | Mosslea Rd., Whyteleafe | 2D 75 |
| Milton Rd., Beddington | 2C 56 | Molyneaux Rd., Weybridge | 1A 50 | Moore Cl. | 1E 49 | Mossville Gdns. | 2B 38 |
| Milton Rd., Caterham | 4C 74 | Monahan Av. | 4D 57 | Moore Grove Cres. | 5D 13 | Mostyn Rd. | 1B 38 |
| Milton Rd., Cheam | 1E 55 | Monarch Cl., Crawley | 5B 146 | Moore Rd., Brookwood | 4C 62 | Mostyn Ter. | 1E 109 |
| Milton Rd., Croydon | 4C 40 | Monarch Cl., E. Bedfont | 2F 15 | Moore Rd., Upper Norwood | 5B 22 | Motspur Pk. | 3E 37 |
| Milton Rd., Egham | 4D 13 | Monarch Cl., W. Wickham | 1F 59 | Moores Rd. | 1A 106 | Motts Hill La. | 5F 71 |
| Milton Rd., Hampton | 5D 17 | Monarch Rd. | 2F 15 | Moorfield Cl. | 1F 31 | Mount Adon Pk. | 2D 23 |
| Milton Rd., Herne Hill | 1B 22 | Monaveen Gdns. | 2D 35 | Moorfield Rd., Camelsdale | 3E 151 | Mount Angelus Rd. | 2E 19 |
| Milton Rd., Mortlake | 5D 9 | Money Av. | 4C 74 | Moorfield Rd., Chessington | 1E 53 | Mount Ararate Rd. | 1B 18 |
| Milton Rd., Pound Hill | 3F 147 | Money Rd. | 4C 74 | Moorfield Rd., Guildford | 3A 82 | Mount Ash Rd. | 3E 23 |
| Milton Rd., Row Town | 2D 49 | Mongers La. | 3B 54 | Moorhayes Dr. | 2B 32 | Mount Av. | 5B 74 |
| Milton Rd., Tooting | 5E 21 | Monk Leigh Rd. | 2A 38 | Moorholme | 3D 65 | Mount Cl., Carshalton | 3B 56 |
| Milton Rd., Walton on | 5B 34 | Monks Av. | 3C 34 | Moorhouse Rd. | 3C 94 | Mount Cl., Ewhurst | 5C 122 |
| Thames | | Monks Cl., Farnborough | 5D 61 | Moorhurst Rd. | 2C 124 | Mount Cl., Fetcham | 5E 69 |
| Milton Rd., Wimbledon | 5C 20 | Monks Cl., Sunninghill | 3B 13 | Moorings, The | 5E 135 | Mount Cl., Kenley | 1C 74 |
| Milton Rd., Wokingham | 1D 25 | Monks Cl., Walton-on-Thames | 4A 34 | Moorland Cl. | 5E 135 | Mount Cl., Mayford | 4C 64 |
| Milton St. | 2E 105 | Monks Dr. | 3D 28 | Moorlands Rd. | 1C 60 | Mount Cl., Pound Hill | 3F 147 |
| Milton Way | 1A 86 | Monks Green | 4E 69 | Moorlands, The | 4D 65 | Mount Cl., West Wickham | 5C 42 |
| Miltoncourt La. | 1E 105 | Monk's La. | 2E 113 | Moormead Dr. | 1B 54 | Mount Dr. | 4F 89 |
| Miltons Cres. | 3C 118 | Monks Orchard Rd. | 4A 42 | Moormede Cres. | 4A 14 | Mount Ephraim La. | 3F 21 |
| Miltons Yd. | 1E 137 | Monk's Place | 4E 75 | Moors La. | 2D 117 | Mount Ephraim Rd. | 3F 21 |
| Mina Rd. | 1B 38 | Monks Rd., Banstead | 2B 72 | Moors, The | 1E 97 | Mount Felix | 4F 33 |
| Minard Rd. | 2C 24 | Monks Rd., Virginia Water | 2C 30 | Moorside La. | 2C 60 | Mount Hermon Cl. | 2D 65 |
| Minchin Cl. | 4F 69 | Monk's Well | 5D 97 | Moorside Rd. | 3C 24 | Mount Hermon Rd. | 3C 64 |
| Mincing La. | 3E 47 | Monk's Wk., Reigate | 5F 89 | Moorsome Way | 2F 73 | Mount La. | 1D 27 |
| Minden Rd. | 1E 41 | Monk's Wk., Farnham | 5C 96 | Moray Ave. | 4E 43 | Mount Lee | 4D 13 |
| Mindeo Rd. | 5B 38 | Monks Walk, S. Ascot | 3C 28 | Morcoombe Cl. | 5C 18 | Mount Nod Rd. | 3A 22 |
| Minehead Rd. | 4A 22 | Monks Way, Eden Park | 3A 42 | Morcote Cl. | 4D 101 | Mount Pk. | 3B 56 |
| Minerva Rd. | 1B 36 | Monks Way, Staines | 5C 14 | Morden | 2B 38 | Mount Park Av. | 3E 57 |
| Minley Rd. | 3A 60 | Monksdene Gdns. | 5C 38 | Morden Cl. | 3A 72 | Mount Park Cl. | 3B 56 |
| Minniedale | 3B 36 | Monksfield | 4D 147 | Morden Ct. | 2B 38 | Mount Pleasant, Biggin Hill | 2E 77 |
| Minorca Rd., Frimley | 2A 62 | Monkshanger | 4B 96 | Morden Gdns. | 2D 39 | Mount Pleasant, Effingham | 2F 85 |
| Minorca Rd., Weybridge | 1A 50 | Monkswell La. | 5C 72 | Morden Hall Rd. | 2C 38 | Mount Pleasant, Ewell | 3B 54 |
| Minstead Gdns. | 2E 19 | Monkton La. | 3B 96 | Morden Rd. | 1C 38 | Mount Pleasant, Farnham | 4F 95 |
| Minstead Way | 3D 37 | Monmouth Av. | 5A 18 | Morden Way | 4B 38 | Mount Pleasant, Guildford | 1C 100 |
| Minster Gdns. | 3C 34 | Monmow Ter. | 3B 64 | Mordred Rd. | 3C 24 | Mount Pleasant, Portmore Park | 5D 33 |
| Minster Rd., Godalming | 3D 119 | Mono La. | 3A 16 | More Cl., Croydon | 4D 57 | Mount Pleasant, W. Horsley | 3B 84 |
| Minster Rd., Sutton | 5B 38 | Monsell Gdns. | 4F 13 | More Cl., Sutton | 2D 57 | Mount Pleasant, Wokingham | 2D 25 |
| Minsterley Av. | 2F 33 | Monson Rd. | 4B 90 | More La., Esher | 1A 52 | Mount Pleasant Cl. | 3F 45 |
| Mint Gdns. | 1F 105 | Montacute Rd., Catford | 2A 24 | More La., Lower Green | 5D 35 | Mount Pleasant Rd., Aldershot | 5A 78 |

| | | |
|---|---|---|
| Nimrod Rd. | 5E 21 |
| Ninehams Cl. | 3C 74 |
| Ninehams Gdns. | 3C 74 |
| Ninehams Rd., Caterham | 4C 74 |
| Ninehams Rd., Tatsfield | 4E 77 |
| Ninemile Ride | 5A 26 |
| Niton Rd. | 5C 8 |
| Nobles Way | 5D 13 |
| Noke Dr. | 5B 90 |
| Nonsuch Court Av. | 3C 54 |
| Nonsuch Wk. | 3D 55 |
| Noons Corner | 5C 104 |
| Norbiton Av. | 1C 36 |
| Norbiton Common Rd. | 2C 36 |
| Norbury Av. | 1A 40 |
| Norbury Cl. | 1B 40 |
| Norbury Court Rd. | 2A 40 |
| Norbury Cres. | 1A 40 |
| Norbury Cross | 2A 40 |
| Norbury Hill | 5B 22 |
| Norbury Rise | 2A 40 |
| Norbury Rd., Reigate | 5E 89 |
| Norbury Rd., Thornton Heath | 1C 40 |
| Norbury Way | 1B 86 |
| Norcutt Rd. | 2E 17 |
| Norfolk Av. | 3A 58 |
| Norfolk Farm Cl. | 1F 65 |
| Norfolk Farm Rd. | 1F 65 |
| Norfolk House Rd. | 3A 22 |
| Norfolk La. | 4A 106 |
| Norfolk Rd., Claygate | 1B 52 |
| Norfolk Rd., Colliers W'd | 5D 21 |
| Norfolk Rd., Dorking | 1F 105 |
| Norfolk Rd., Feltham | 2B 16 |
| Norfolk Rd., Holmwood | 1D 125 |
| Norfolk Rd., Horsham | 5B 158 |
| Norfolk Rd., Thornton Heath | 2C 40 |
| Norheads La. | 2D 77 |
| Norhyrst Av. | 2D 41 |
| Nork | 1A 72 |
| Nork Gdns. | 5D 55 |
| Nork Rise | 1A 72 |
| Nork Way | 1A 72 |
| Norlands La. | 2F 31 |
| Norley View | 2F 92 |
| Norman Av., Epsom | 4B 54 |
| Norman Av., Feltham | 3C 16 |
| Norman Av., Purley | 3E 57 |
| Norman Av., Richmond | 2A 18 |
| Norman Rd., Cheam | 1E 55 |
| Norman Rd., South Wimbledon | 5C 20 |
| Norman Rd., Thornton Heath | 3B 40 |
| Normandy | 4F 79 |
| Normandy Gdns., Horsham | 5B 158 |
| Normanhurst | 4D 15 |
| Normanhurst Dr. | 1F 17 |
| Normanhurst Rd. | 5B 34 |
| Normans Rd. | 1E 129 |
| Normansfield Av. | 5A 18 |
| Normanton Av. | 3B 20 |
| Normanton Rd. | 2F 57 |
| Normanton St. | 3F 23 |
| Norrels Dr. | 1C 84 |
| Norrels Ride | 1C 84 |
| Norreys Av. | 2E 25 |
| Norris Rd. | 4A 14 |
| Norstead Pl. | 3E 19 |
| North Acre | 1B 72 |
| North Albert Rd. | 5E 89 |
| North Av., Carlshalton | 2B 56 |
| North Av., Heath End | 1B 96 |
| North Av., Whiteley Village | 3C 50 |
| North Brook La., Aldershot | 1C 96 |
| North Chapel Rd. | 4D 153 |
| North Cheam | 5A 38 |
| North Cliffe Cl. | 4E 37 |
| North Cl., Cannon Hill | 2A 38 |
| North Cl., Dorking | 3A 106 |
| North Cl., East Bedfont | 1E 15 |
| North Cl., Hawley | 3C 60 |
| North Cl., Horsham | 3B 158 |
| North Common | 1B 50 |
| North Cott. | 4C 26 |
| North Cross Rd. | 1D 23 |
| North Down | 4A 58 |
| North Downs Cres. | 3E 59 |
| North Downs Rd. | 3E 59 |
| North Dr., Ifold | 4F 155 |
| North Dr., Streatham | 4F 21 |
| North Dr., Virginia Water | 3A 30 |
| North Farm Rd. | 3C 60 |
| North Green | 1E 27 |
| North Gro. | 3A 32 |
| North Heath La. | 3B 158 |
| North Holmwood | 4A 106 |
| North La., Aldershot | 5B 78 |
| North La., Teddington | 5F 17 |

| | | |
|---|---|---|
| North Mead, Crawley | 3D 147 |
| North Mead, Redhill | 4A 90 |
| North Moors | 3A 82 |
| North Parade, Chess'ton | 1E 53 |
| North Parade, Horsham | 4B 158 |
| North Park | 1A 7 |
| North Park La. | 4A 92 |
| North Pl., Guildford | 1C 100 |
| North Pl., Mitcham | 5D 21 |
| North Pole La. | 2F 59 |
| North Rd., Ash Vale | 3C 78 |
| North Rd., Bracknell | 1F 27 |
| North Rd., Brentford | 3B 8 |
| North Rd., East Bedfont | 1E 15 |
| North Rd., Hersham | 1E 51 |
| North Rd., Lammas Park | 1A 8 |
| North Rd., North Sheen | 5C 8 |
| North Rd., South Farnborough | 2A 78 |
| North Rd., South Park | 2B 108 |
| North Rd., Stoughton | 4E 81 |
| North Rd., Surbiton | 3B 36 |
| North Rd., Three Bridges | 3E 147 |
| North Rd., Waddon | 1D 57 |
| North Rd., West Wickham | 4B 42 |
| North Rd., Wimbledon | 5C 20 |
| North Rd., Woking | 1D 65 |
| North Side, Tongham | 1E 97 |
| North Side, Wandsworth | 1C 20 |
| North Spur Rd. | 5B 37 |
| North St., Carshalton | 1B 56 |
| North St., Dorking | 1F 105 |
| North St., Egham | 4D 13 |
| North St., Farncombe | 5A 100 |
| North St., Guildford | 1C 100 |
| North St., Horsham | 5B 158 |
| North St., Leatherhead | 4F 69 |
| North St., Redhill | 5A 90 |
| North St., Turners Hill | 5D 149 |
| North St., Westcott | 2D 105 |
| North St., Winkfield | 4B 10 |
| North View | 4F 19 |
| North View Cres. | 2F 71 |
| North Wk., Addington | 2E 59 |
| North Walk, Belmont | 4D 55 |
| North Way, Godalming | 5F 99 |
| North Way, Wallington | 1C 56 |
| North Worple Way | 5D 9 |
| Northampton Rd. | 5D 41 |
| Northanger Rd. | 5A 22 |
| Northborough Rd. | 1A 40 |
| Northbrook Rd., Hither Green | 1C 24 |
| Northbrook Rd., Selhurst | 3C 40 |
| Northcote | 1F 49 |
| Northcote Av., Tolworth | 4C 36 |
| Northcote Av., Twickenham | 1F 17 |
| Northcote Cl. | 1B 84 |
| Northcote Cres. | 1B 84 |
| Northcote La. | 1C 120 |
| Northcote Rd., Ash Vale | 2C 78 |
| Northcote Rd., Horsley | 1B 84 |
| Northcote Rd., New Malden | 2D 37 |
| Northcote Rd., Selhurst | 3C 40 |
| Northcote Rd., Twickenham | 1F 17 |
| Northcote Rd., Wandsworth | 1D 21 |
| Northcote Rd., West Heath | 4B 60 |
| Northcroft Cl. | 4B 12 |
| Northcroft Gdns. | 4C 12 |
| Northcroft Rd. | 1A 8 |
| Northcroft Rd., Englefield Green | 4B 12 |
| Northcroft Rd., West Ewell | 2A 54 |
| Northcroft Villas | 4B 12 |
| Northdown Cl. | 4C 158 |
| Northdown La. | 2D 101 |
| Northdown Rd., Belmont | 3E 55 |
| Northdown Rd., Woldingham | 5A 76 |
| Northdowns | 2C 140 |
| Northenhay Wk. | 2A 38 |
| Northey Av. | 3D 55 |
| Northfield, Lightwater | 4F 45 |
| Northfield, Witley | 1E 137 |
| Northfield Av. | 1A 8 |
| Northfield Cl. | 5B 78 |
| Northfield Cres. | 1D 55 |
| Northfield Pl. | 2A 50 |
| Northfield Rd., Cobham | 5D 51 |
| Northfield Rd., Laleham | 1B 32 |
| Northfields, Ashtead | 3B 70 |
| Northfields, Shalford | 4D 101 |
| Northgate Av. | 3E 147 |
| Northgate Dr. | 4C 44 |
| Northgate Pl. | 3D 147 |
| Northgate Rd. | 4D 147 |
| Northington Cl. | 3F 27 |
| Northlands Rd. | 2C 158 |
| Northover | 3C 24 |
| Northstead Rd. | 3B 22 |

| | | |
|---|---|---|
| Northumberland Cl. | 1C 14 |
| Northumberland Cres. | 1F 15 |
| Northumberland Gdns. | 3F 39 |
| Northway, Cannon Hill | 2A 38 |
| Northway, Guildford | 4E 81 |
| Northway Rd. | 3D 41 |
| Northwood Av., Purley | 5E 57 |
| Northwood Av., Woking | 2A 64 |
| Northwood Rd., Carshalton | 2B 56 |
| Northwood Rd., Lewisham | 2F 23 |
| Northwood Rd., Norbury | 1B 40 |
| Norton Av. | 4C 36 |
| Norton Gdns. | 1A 40 |
| Norton Rd., Camberley | 5D 45 |
| Norton Rd., Wokingham | 2D 25 |
| Norwich Av. | 1E 61 |
| Norwich Rd., Crawley | 5E 147 |
| Norwich Rd., Thorn. H'th. | 2C 40 |
| Norwood Cl. | 2E 85 |
| Norwood High St. | 2B 22 |
| Norwood Hill | 2D 127 |
| Norwood Hill Rd. | 3E 127 |
| Norwood Park Rd. | 4C 22 |
| Norwood Rd., Effingham | 2E 85 |
| Norwood Rd., Tulse Hill | 3B 22 |
| Nottingham Cl. | 2A 64 |
| Nottingham Rd., Waddon | 1E 57 |
| Nottingham Rd., Wandsworth | 2D 21 |
| Nova Rd. | 4B 40 |
| Nowell Rd. | 3E 9 |
| Nower Rd. | 1F 105 |
| Noyna Rd. | 3E 21 |
| Nuffield Dr. | 3E 43 |
| Nugent Rd. | 2D 41 |
| Nunappleton Way | 4A 94 |
| Nuneaton | 3E 27 |
| Nuns Wk. | 3C 30 |
| Nursery Av. | 5F 41 |
| Nursery Cl. Capel | 5D 125 |
| Nursery Cl., Ewell | 3B 54 |
| Nursery Cl., Feltham | 2A 16 |
| Nursery Cl., Frimley | 3E 61 |
| Nursery Cl., Horsell | 1C 64 |
| Nursery Cl., Shirley | 5F 41 |
| Nursery Cl., Walton-on-the-Hill | 1C 88 |
| Nursery Cl., Woodham | 3D 49 |
| Nursery Gdns., Chilworth | 3E 101 |
| Nursery Gdns., Staines | 5B 14 |
| Nursery Gdns., Upp. Halliford | 1F 33 |
| Nursery Hill | 1C 120 |
| Nursery La. | 3A 128 |
| Nursery Rd., Farncombe | 5B 100 |
| Nursery Rd., Merton | 1C 38 |
| Nursery Rd., Mitcham | 2D 39 |
| Nursery Rd., Sunbury | 1F 33 |
| Nursery Rd., Sutton | 1F 55 |
| Nursery Rd., Walton-on-the-Hill | 1C 88 |
| Nursery Rd., Woking | 2A 64 |
| Nursery Way | 1C 12 |
| Nurserylands | 4B 146 |
| Nutbourne | 1B 96 |
| Nutcombe | 2E 151 |
| Nutcombe La. | 1F 105 |
| Nutcroft Gro. | 4E 69 |
| Nutfield | 5D 91 |
| Nutfield Marsh Rd. | 4D 91 |
| Nutfield Rd., Redhill | 5B 90 |
| Nutfield Rd., South Merstham | 5B 90 |
| Nutfield Rd., Thornton Heath | 2B 40 |
| Nutfield Rd., Woodmansterne | 1E 73 |
| Nuthurst | 3E 27 |
| Nuthurst Av., Cranleigh | 1C 140 |
| Nuthurst Av., Streatham | 3A 22 |
| Nuthurst Cl. | 3B 146 |
| Nutley | 4C 26 |
| Nutley La. | 5E 89 |
| Nutshell La. | 2A 96 |
| Nutty La. | 2E 33 |
| Nutwell St. | 4D 21 |
| Nutwood Av. | 1D 107 |
| Nutwood Cl. | 1D 107 |
| Nyefield Park Cl. | 1C 88 |
| Nylands Av. | 4C 8 |
| Nymans Gdns. | 1F 37 |
| Nyon Gro. | 3F 23 |

**O**

| | | |
|---|---|---|
| O'Connor Rd. | 2B 78 |
| Oak Av., Crowthorne | 3E 43 |
| Oak Av., Hanworth | 4C 16 |
| Oak Av., Shirley | 5A 42 |

| | | |
|---|---|---|
| Oak Av., Thorpe Lea | 5F 13 |
| Oak Bank | 3D 65 |
| Oak Cl., Chiddingfold | 5E 137 |
| Oak Cl., Northbourne | 5A 90 |
| Oak Cl., Copthorne | 1B 148 |
| Oak Cl., Morden | 5C 38 |
| Oak Corner | 2D 125 |
| Oak Cottage Cl. | 5C 80 |
| Oak Dell | 3F 147 |
| Oak End | 2D 125 |
| Oak End Way | 4D 49 |
| Oak Farm Cl. | 5D 43 |
| Oak Gdns. | 5A 42 |
| Oak Grange Rd. | 3E 83 |
| Oak Gro., Sunbury-on-Thames | 5A 16 |
| Oak Gro., W. Wickham | 5B 42 |
| Oak Grove Rd. | 1E 41 |
| Oak Hill, Burpham | 3B 82 |
| Oak Hill, Woodcote | 1D 71 |
| Oak Lands | 5E 69 |
| Oak La., Englefield Green | 3C 12 |
| Oak La., S. Holmwood | 5A 106 |
| Oak La., Twickenham | 2F 17 |
| Oak La., Woking | 1E 65 |
| Oak Lodge Cl. | 1E 51 |
| Oak Lodge Dr., Salfords | 4E 109 |
| Oak Lodge Dr., W. Wickham | 4B 42 |
| Oak Mead | 5A 100 |
| Oak Park | 5C 48 |
| Oak Ridge | 3A 106 |
| Oak Rd., Caterham | 4C 74 |
| Oak Rd., Cobham | 1B 68 |
| Oak Rd., Farnborough Pk. | 5D 61 |
| Oak Rd., Leatherhead Common | 2F 69 |
| Oak Rd., New Malden | 1D 37 |
| Oak Rd., Reigate | 5F 89 |
| Oak Rd., West Green | 4C 146 |
| Oak Row | 1F 39 |
| Oak Shaw | 2E 93 |
| Oak Tree Cl., Bisley Common | 2F 63 |
| Oak Tree Cl., Burpham | 3B 82 |
| Oak Tree Cl., Frimley | 4C 30 |
| Oak Tree Cl., Slyfield Green | 2F 81 |
| Oak Tree Dr., Englefield Grn. | 4C 12 |
| Oak Tree Dr., Guildford | 3F 81 |
| Oak Tree La. | 3D 151 |
| Oak Tree Rd., Bisley | 3F 63 |
| Oak Tree Rd., Milford | 3B 118 |
| Oak Way, Ashtead | 1C 70 |
| Oak Way, East Bedfont | 2F 15 |
| Oak Way, Northgate | 3D 147 |
| Oak Way, Reigate | 1D 109 |
| Oak Way, Southborough | 4A 36 |
| Oakbank | 2E 59 |
| Oakbank Av. | 4C 34 |
| Oakcombe Cl. | 1D 37 |
| Oakcroft Cl. | 5D 49 |
| Oakcroft Rd., Hook | 1E 53 |
| Oakcroft Rd., W. Byfleet | 5D 49 |
| Oakcroft Villas | 1E 53 |
| Oakdale | 3D 27 |
| Oakdale Rd., Ewell | 3A 54 |
| Oakdale Rd., Streatham | 4A 22 |
| Oakdale Rd., Weybridge | 5D 33 |
| Oakdene, Burgh H'th | 3A 72 |
| Oakdene, Chobham | 3E 47 |
| Oakdene Av. | 4F 35 |
| Oakdene Cl., Brockham | 1D 107 |
| Oakdene Cl., Gt. Bookham | 2A 86 |
| Oakdene Dr., | 4D 37 |
| Oakdene Rd., Brockham | 2D 107 |
| Oakdene Rd., Cobham | 5D 51 |
| Oakdene Rd., Holloway Hill | 2D 119 |
| Oakdene Rd., Lt. Bookham | 5C 68 |
| Oakdene Rd., Peasmarsh | 4C 100 |
| Oakdene Rd., Redhill | 5A 90 |
| Oaken Copse Cres. | 3D 61 |
| Oaken Coppice | 3C 70 |
| Oaken Dr. | 2C 52 |
| Oaken Lane | 1B 52 |
| Oakengates | 4C 26 |
| Oakfield | 2A 64 |
| Oakfield Dr., Reigate | 4E 89 |
| Oakfield Dr., Wimbledon | 3A 20 |
| Oakfield Gdns., Eden Park | 3A 42 |
| Oakfield Gdns., St. Helier | 4D 39 |
| Oakfield Glade | 1B 50 |
| Oakfield Rd., Ashford | 4D 15 |
| Oakfield Rd., Ashtead | 2B 70 |
| Oakfield Rd., Blackwater | 1B 60 |
| Oakfield Rd., Cobham | 5D 51 |
| Oakfield Rd., Croydon | 4B 40 |
| Oakfield Rd., Penge | 5E 23 |
| Oakfield Way | 1C 150 |
| Oakfields, Crawley | 3F 147 |
| Oakfields, Guildford | 4D 81 |
| Oakfields, Oakwoodhill | 3B 142 |

| | | | | | | |
|---|---|---|---|---|---|
| Oakfields, Walton-on-Thames | 4A 34 | Oakwood Av., Mitcham | 1D 39 | Old Farleigh Rd. | 4B 58 | Oliver Green | 2D 41 |
| Oakhall Dr. | 4F 15 | Oakwood Av., Purley | 4E 57 | Old Farm Rd., Guildford | 4F 81 | Oliver Rd., Ascot | 2C 28 |
| Oakham Dr. | 2C 42 | Oakwood Cl., E. Horsley | 2C 84 | Old Farm Rd., Hampton | 5C 16 | Oliver Rd., Horsham | 5A 158 |
| Oakhill, Claygate | 2C 52 | Oakwood Cl., Redhill | 5B 90 | Old Farnham La. | 5B 96 | Oliver Rd., New Malden | 1D 37 |
| Oakhill, Woodstreet Village | 4C 80 | Oakwood Cl., S. Nutfield | 1A 110 | Old Ferry Dr. | 1C 12 | Oliver Rd., Sutton | 1F 55 |
| Oakhill Cl. | 2A 70 | Oakwood Dr. | 2C 84 | Old Forge Cres. | 3E 33 | Ollerton | 4C 26 |
| Oakhill Cres. | 4B 36 | Oakwood Gdns., Bagshot | 2E 45 | Old Fox Cl. | 4B 74 | Olveston Wk. | 3D 39 |
| Oakhill Dr. | 4B 36 | Oakwood Gdns., Knaphill | 2E 63 | Old Frensham Rd. | 1E 115 | Omega Rd. | 1E 65 |
| Oakhill Gro. | 3B 36 | Oakwood Hill | 3D 143 | Old Green La. | 4A 44 | One Tree Hill Rd. | 1E 101 |
| Oakhill Path | 3B 36 | Oakwood Rd., Bracknell | 1E 27 | Old Guildford Rd., Frimley | 4F 61 | Onetree Cl. | 1E 23 |
| Oakhill Rd., Beckenham | 1B 42 | Oakwood Rd., Brookwood | 3A 64 | Old Guildford Rd., West | 2F 139 | Ongar Cl. | 2D 49 |
| Oakhill Rd., Horsham | 5C 158 | Oakwood Rd., Cottenham Park | 1F 37 | Cranleigh | | Ongar Hill | 2D 49 |
| Oakhill Rd., Lower Ashtead | 2A 70 | Oakwood Rd., Horley | 2B 128 | Old Haslemere Rd. | 3A 152 | Ongar Pl. | 2D 49 |
| Oakhill Rd., Mead Vale | 1C 108 | Oakwood Rd., Virginia Water | 3C 30 | Old Heron's Lea | 5A 130 | Ongar Rd. | 1D 49 |
| Oakhill Rd., Norbury | 1A 40 | Oakwood Rd., Warwick Fold | 3E 91 | Old Hill Rd. | 3C 64 | Onslow Av., Cheam | 3E 55 |
| Oakhill Rd., Rowhill | 2D 49 | Oakwood Rd., Windlesham | 2A 46 | Old Hollow | 3A 148 | Onslow Av., Richmond | 1B 18 |
| Oakhill Rd., Surbiton | 3B 36 | Oakwoodhill | 3C 142 | Old Horsham Rd., Beare Green | 2D 125 | Onslow Cl., Hinchley Wood | 4E 35 |
| Oakhill Rd., Sutton | 1F 55 | Oakwoodland La. | 3C 142 | Old Horsham Rd., Crawley | 5C 146 | Onslow Cl., Woking | 2E 65 |
| Oakhill Rd., Wandsworth | 1B 20 | Oareborough | 2E 27 | Old House Cl. | 3B 54 | Onslow Cres. | 2E 65 |
| Oakhurst, Burrowhill | 3D 47 | Oast House Cl. | 2D 13 | Old Kiln Rd. | 2B 134 | Onslow Gdns., Sanderstead | 4A 58 |
| Oakhurst Gdns. | 2B 150 | Oast House Cres. | 2B 96 | Old Kingston Rd. | 5D 37 | Onslow Gdns., Thames Ditton | 4E 35 |
| Oakhurst Rise | 3A 56 | Oast House La. | 2B 96 | Old La., Aldershot | 5B 78 | Onslow Gdns., Wallington | 2C 56 |
| Oakhurst Rd. | 2A 54 | Oast Rd. | 4F 93 | Old La., Grayshott | 5D 135 | Onslow Rd., Burwood Pk. | 1D 51 |
| Oakington Dr. | 1B 34 | Oates Wk. | 5D 147 | Old La., Martyr's Green | 2E 67 | Onslow Rd., Guildford | 5F 81 |
| Oakland Av. | 1B 96 | Oatfield Rd. | 4F 71 | Old La., Oxted | 3F 93 | Onslow Rd., New Malden | 2E 37 |
| Oakland Way | 2A 54 | Oatlands | 4B 146 | Old La., Tatsfield | 4E 77 | Onslow Rd., Richmond | 1B 18 |
| Oaklands, Haslemere | 3A 152 | Oatlands Av. | 1B 50 | Old Lane Gdns. | 4A 68 | Onslow Rd., Sanderstead | 4A 40 |
| Oaklands, Horley | 2C 128 | Oatlands Chase | 5F 33 | Old Lodge Cl. | 2C 118 | Onslow Rd., Sunningdale | 4F 29 |
| Oaklands, Kenley | 1B 74 | Oatlands Cl. | 1B 50 | Old Lodge La. | 1B 74 | Onslow St. | 1C 100 |
| Oaklands, S. Godstone | 2F 111 | Oatlands Dr. | 5E 33 | Old London Rd., Epsom Downs | 2F 71 | Onslow Way | 1A 66 |
| Oaklands Av., Esher | 4E 35 | Oatlands Grn. | 5E 33 | Old London Rd., Mickleham | 2D 87 | Openfields | 4E 133 |
| Oaklands Av., Thornton Heath | 2A 40 | Oatlands Mere | 5E 33 | Old Malden La. | 5D 37 | Openview | 2C 20 |
| Oaklands Av., West Wickham | 5A 42 | Oatlands Park | 5F 33 | Old Malt Way | 2C 64 | Opladen Way | 3E 27 |
| Oaklands Cl., Ascot | 5B 10 | Oatlands Rd. | 3A 72 | Old Manor Gdns. | 3F 101 | Orchard Av., East Bedfont | 1E 15 |
| Oaklands Cl., Shalford | 4D 101 | Oban Rd. | 2C 40 | Old Manor Drive | 1E 17 | Orchard Av., New Malden | 2E 37 |
| Oaklands Ct. | 5B 32 | Obelisk Way | 5A 44 | Old Manor La. | 3F 101 | Orchard Av., Ashford | 5E 15 |
| Oaklands Dr., Ascot | 5B 10 | Observatory Rd. | 5D 9 | Old Merrow St. | 4C 82 | Orchard Av., Hackbridge | 4E 39 |
| Oaklands Dr., Earlswood | 1E 109 | Oceansgate | 4C 26 | Old Mill La. | 2C 90 | Orchard Av., Long Ditton | 4F 35 |
| Oaklands Dr., Wokingham | 2D 25 | Occupation La., Ealing | 2A 8 | Old Oak Av. | 3D 73 | Orchard Av., Shirley | 4F 41 |
| Oaklands Gdns. | 5E 57 | Ockenden Cl. | 2D 65 | Old Orchard, Byfleet | 4A 50 | Orchard Av., Woodham | 4D 49 |
| Oaklands La., Biggin Hill | 1E 77 | Ockenden Gdns. | 2D 65 | Old Orchard, Sunbury | 1A 34 | Orchard Cl., Ash Vale | 3C 78 |
| Oaklands La., Oaklands | 5A 26 | Ockenden Rd. | 2D 65 | Old Palace La. | 1A 18 | Orchard Cl., Ashford | 5E 15 |
| Oaklands Rd. | 5C 24 | Ockfields | 4B 118 | Old Palace Rd., Croydon | 5B 40 | Orchard Cl., Banstead | 5F 55 |
| Oaklands Way | 4A 72 | Ockford Dr. | 2C 118 | Old Palace Rd., Guildford | 1B 100 | Orchard Cl., Bucks Green | 2E 157 |
| Oaklawn Rd. | 2E 69 | Ockford Ridge | 2C 118 | Old Palace Rd., Weybridge | 5D 33 | Orchard Cl., Effingham Com. | 5F 67 |
| Oaklea | 3C 78 | Ockford Rd. | 2C 118 | Old Park Av. | 1E 21 | Orchard Cl., Egham | 4E 13 |
| Oakleigh Av. | 4C 36 | Ockham | 4D 67 | Old Park Cl. | 2F 95 | Orchard Cl., Farnham | 2C 96 |
| Oakleigh Rd. | 3C 158 | Ockham La. | 3C 66 | Old Park La. | 1F 95 | Orchard Cl., Fetcham | 4E 69 |
| Oakleigh Way | 1E 39 | Ockham Road North | 4D 67 | Old Pasture Rd. | 2E 61 | Orchard Cl., Hawley | 2C 60 |
| Oakley Av. | 1D 57 | Ockham Road South | 1C 84 | Old Pond Cl. | 2D 61 | Orchard Cl., Horley | 2A 12 |
| Oakley Cl. | 1E 49 | Ockley | 5B 124 | Old Portsmouth Rd. | 4C 100 | Orchard Cl., Long Ditton | 4A 36 |
| Oakley Dell | 4C 82 | Ockley Ct. | 3B 82 | Old Pottery Cl. | 1B 108 | Orchard Cl., West End | 5A 46 |
| Oakley Gdns. | 1C 72 | Ockley Rd., Croydon | 4A 40 | Old Rectory Cl., Bramley | 1A 120 | Orchard Cl., Woking | 1E 65 |
| Oakley Ho. | 5A 100 | Ockley Rd., Ewhurst | 5C 122 | Old Rectory Cl., Walton-on- | 5F 71 | Orchard Ct. | 4E 37 |
| Oakley Rd., Camberley | 1D 61 | Ockley Rd., Ockley | 4A 124 | the-Hill | | Orchard Dr., Ashtead | 3A 70 |
| Oakley Rd., Whyteleafe | 2D 75 | Ockley Rd., Streatham | 4A 22 | Old Rectory Dr. | 5C 78 | Orchard Dr., Woking | 1D 65 |
| Oakley Rd., Woodside | 3E 41 | Ockleys Mead | 3B 92 | Old Rectory Gdns., | 5D 61 | Orchard End, Boundstone | 2C 11 |
| Oakmead Rd., Balham | 2E 21 | Octagon Rd. | 3C 50 | Farnborough | | Orchard End, Fetcham | 5E 69 |
| Oakmead Rd., Beddington | 3F 39 | Octavia | 4C 26 | Old Rectory Gdns., Godalming | 3E 119 | Orchard End, Walton-on- | 5F 33 |
| Oakridge Rd. | 4C 24 | Octavia Way | 5A 14 | Old Rectory La., E. Hors. | 2C 84 | Thames | |
| Oak Rd., Farnborough Pk. | 5D 61 | Odak Dell | 3F 147 | Old Redstone Dr. | 1E 109 | Orchard Field Rd. | 5A 10 |
| Oak Rd., West Green | 4C 146 | Odakdale Rd. | 4A 22 | Old Reigate Rd., Dorking | 5E 87 | Orchard Gate | 4E 35 |
| Oaks Av., Gypsy Hill | 4C 22 | Odakdene Dr. | 4D 37 | Old Reigate Rd., Dorking | 5A 88 | Orchard Gdns., Aldershot | 1D 97 |
| Oaks Av., Hanworth | 3B 16 | Odard Rd. | 2C 34 | Old Road, Buckland | 5B 88 | Orchard Gdns., Cheam | 1E 55 |
| Oaks Av., Stoneleigh | 1C 54 | Odiham Rd. | 1E 95 | Old Rd., East Grinstead | 2C 150 | Orchard Gdns., Chessington | 1E 53 |
| Oaks Av., Worcester Park | 5F 37 | Okeburn Rd. | 4E 21 | Old Rd., Row Town | 2D 49 | Orchard Gdns., Cranleigh | 2C 14 |
| Oaks Cl. | 4F 69 | Olave's Wk. | 1F 39 | Old Sawmill La. | 1D 43 | Orchard Gdns., Effingham | 2F 85 |
| Oaks La. | 5E 41 | Old Acre, W. Byfleet | 5D 49 | Old School La. | 2C 106 | Orchard Gdns., Epsom | 5A 54 |
| Oaks Rd., Purley | 5E 57 | Old Acre, West End | 4B 46 | Old Schools La. | 3B 54 | Orchard Hill, Carlshalton | 1B 56 |
| Oaks Rd., Reigate | 5F 89 | Old Av., Sheerwater | 5C 48 | Old Slade La. | 1B 7 | Orchard Hill, Windlesham | 2A 46 |
| Oaks Rd., Stanwell | 1C 14 | Old Av., West Byfleet | 5C 48 | Old Station La. | 1D 13 | Orchard La., East Molesey | 3E 35 |
| Oaks Rd., Upper Shirley | 1B 58 | Old Av., Weybridge | 1B 50 | Old Station Way | 1D 119 | Orchard La., Raynes Park | 1F 37 |
| Oaks Rd., Woking | 2D 65 | Old Avenue Cl. | 5C 48 | Old Town | 5B 40 | Orchard Lea Cl. | 1A 66 |
| Oaks, The, West Byfleet | 5E 49 | Old Barn Cl. | 2D 55 | Old Tye Av. | 1F 77 | Orchard Mains | 3C 64 |
| Oaks, The, Epsom | 5B 54 | Old Barn Dr. | 5D 125 | Old Westhall Cl. | 3E 75 | Orchard Rise, N. Sheen | 5C 8 |
| Oaks Way, Carshalton Beeches | 2A 56 | Old Barn La., Hindhead | 2D 135 | Old Westhill Ct. | 3E 75 | Orchard Rise, New Malden | 1D 37 |
| Oaks Way, Epsom | 3F 71 | Old Barn La., Kenley | 1D 75 | Old Windsor | 1B 12 | Orchard Rise, Shirley | 4F 41 |
| Oaks Way, Purley | 5E 57 | Old Barn Rd. | 2D 71 | Old Woking | 4E 65 | Orchard Rd., Badshot Lea | 2C 96 |
| Oaksford Av. | 3E 23 | Old Bisley Rd. | 2F 61 | Old Woking Rd. | 2E 65 | Orchard Rd., Brentford | 3A 8 |
| Oakshade Rd., Oxshott | 5A 52 | Old Bracknell La. | 2C 26 | Old Wokingham Rd. | 5A 26 | Orchard Rd., Burpham | 3B 82 |
| Oakshade Rd., Southend | 4C 24 | Old Bromley Rd. | 4B 24 | Oldbury Cl. | 3E 61 | Orchard Rd., Cheam | 1E 55 |
| Oakshaw Rd. | 2C 20 | Old Building St. | 1A 36 | Oldbury Rd. | 4F 31 | Orchard Rd., Chessington | 1E 53 |
| Oakside Ct. | 2C 128 | Old Charlton Rd. | 3E 33 | Olde Farm Cl. | 5D 43 | Orchard Rd., Cranleigh | 2C 140 |
| Oakside La. | 2C 128 | Old Chertsey La. | 4F 13 | Olden La. | 4E 57 | Orchard Rd., Dorking | 2F 105 |
| Oaktree Cl., | 1C 78 | Old Chestnut Av. | 2A 52 | Oldfield Gdns. | 3B 70 | Orchard Rd., East Bedfont | 1E 15 |
| Oaktree View | 2B 96 | Old Church La. | 5B 96 | Oldfield Rd., Hampton | 1C 34 | Orchard Rd., Hackbridge | 4E 39 |
| Oaktree Way | 3D 43 | Old Claygate La. | 2C 52 | Oldfield Rd., Horley | 3A 128 | Orchard Rd., Hampton | 5C 16 |
| Oakview Green | 4F 41 | Old Common Rd. | 5D 51 | Oldfields Rd. | 5B 38 | Orchard Rd., Horsham | 5C 158 |
| Oakview Rd. | 4A 24 | Old Compton La. | 49 96 | Oldham Ter. | 1D 9 | Orchard Rd., Kingston | 1B 36 |
| Oakway, Aldershot | 1E 97 | Old Ct. | 3B 70 | Oldhouse La., Bisley | 5B 46 | Orchard Rd., North | 5C 60 |
| Oakway, Beckenham | 1B 42 | Old Court Rd. | 1B 100 | Oldhouse La., Windlesham | 2F 45 | Farnborough | |
| Oakway, Raynes Park | 2A 38 | Old Cross Tree Way | 1A 98 | Oldridge Rd. | 2E 21 | Orchard Rd., North Sheen | 5C 8 |
| Oakway Dr. | 2E 61 | Old Dean Rd. | 4A 44 | Oldstead | 3E 27 | Orchard Rd., Old Windsor | 1B 12 |
| Oakwood, Carshalton | 3B 56 | Old Deer Park Gdns. | 5B 8 | Oldstead Rd. | 4B 24 | Orchard Rd., Onslow Village | 1B 100 |
| Oakwood, Guildford | 3E 81 | Old Devonshire Rd. | 2E 21 | Olive Rd. | 1A 8 | Orchard Rd., Reigate | 5F 89 |
| Oakwood Av. Beckenham | 1B 42 | Old Dock Cl. | 3C 8 | Oliver Av. | 2D 41 | Orchard Rd., Richmond | 1F 17 |
| | | Old Esher Rd. | 1E 51 | Oliver Cl. | 1E 49 | Orchard Rd., Sanderstead | 5B 58 |

| | |
|---|---|
| Orchard Rd., Shalford | 3D 101 |
| Orchard Rd., Shere | 3D 103 |
| Orchard Rd., Smallfield | 2E 129 |
| Orchard Rd., Sunbury | 5A 16 |
| Orchard Rd., Whitton | 1C 16 |
| Orchard Rd., Cl. | 2C 96 |
| Orchard St. | 4D 147 |
| Orchard, The, Bedford Pk. | 2D 9 |
| Orchard, The, Dorking | 3A 106 |
| Orchard, The, Esher | 1B 52 |
| Orchard, The, Lightwater | 4F 45 |
| Orchard, The, Virginia Water | 3D 31 |
| Orchard Way, Addlestone | 2E 49 |
| Orchard Way, Aldershot | 1D 97 |
| Orchard Way, Camberley | 2C 60 |
| Orchard Way, Carshalton | 1A 56 |
| Orchard Way, East Grinstead | 2C 150 |
| Orchard Way, Esher | 2A 52 |
| Orchard Way, Lwr. Kingswood | 1E 89 |
| Orchard Way, Monks Orchard | 4F 41 |
| Orchard Way, Oxted | 5A 94 |
| Orchard Way, Sendgrove | 1C 82 |
| Orchard Way, Staines | 3D 15 |
| Orchard Way, Wanborough | 5F 79 |
| Orchard Way, Woodhatch | 2C 108 |
| Orchardleigh | 4A 70 |
| Orchid Dr. | 1E 63 |
| Orde Cl. | 2F 147 |
| Ordnance Cl. | 3A 16 |
| Ordnance Rd. | 4A 78 |
| Oregano Way | 3E 81 |
| Orena Rd. | 5B 8 |
| Orestan La. | 2D 85 |
| Orewell Gdns. | 1C 108 |
| Orford Gdns. | 3F 17 |
| Oriel Hill | 1E 61 |
| Oriental Cl. | 2D 65 |
| Oriental Rd., Sunninghill | 2D 29 |
| Oriental Rd., Woking | 2D 65 |
| Orion | 4C 26 |
| Orleans Rd., Twickenham | 2A 18 |
| Orleans Rd., Upper Norwood | 5C 22 |
| Orlton La. | 2E 143 |
| Ormanton Rd. | 4E 23 |
| Orme Rd. | 1C 36 |
| Ormeley Rd. | 2E 21 |
| Ormond Av. | 1D 35 |
| Ormond Cres. | 1D 35 |
| Ormond Dr. | 5D 17 |
| Ormond Rd., Richmond | 1B 18 |
| Ormonde Av. | 3A 54 |
| Ormonde Rd., Godalming | 1D 119 |
| Ormonde Rd., Horsell | 1C 64 |
| Ormonde Rd., Mortlake | 5D 9 |
| Ormonde Rd., Wokingham | 2D 25 |
| Ormside Way | 4B 90 |
| Orpin Rd. | 3C 90 |
| Orton Wk. | 5D 45 |
| Orwell Cl. | 3B 60 |
| Osborn Rd., Farnham | 3B 96 |
| Osborne Cl., Elmers End | 2F 41 |
| Osborne Cl., Frimley | 3E 61 |
| Osborne Cl., Hanworth | 4B 16 |
| Osborne Dr. | 4F 45 |
| Osborne Gdns. | 1C 40 |
| Osborne Rd., Acton | 1C 8 |
| Osborne Rd., Egham | 5D 13 |
| Osborne Rd., Kingston | 5B 18 |
| Osborne Rd., Norbury | 1B 40 |
| Osborne Rd., Redhill | 4B 90 |
| Osborne Rd., South Farnborough | 2A 78 |
| Osborne Rd., Walton | 4A 34 |
| Osborne Rd., Wokingham | 2E 25 |
| Osbourne Av. | 2C 14 |
| Osbourne Cl. | 4B 16 |
| Osier Cl. | 5D 55 |
| Oslac Rd. | 4B 24 |
| Osmond Gdns. | 1C 56 |
| Osmunda Bank | 5F 131 |
| Osney Wk. | 3D 39 |
| Osprey Gdns. | 3C 58 |
| Ostade Rd. | 2A 22 |
| Osterley Cl. | 2F 25 |
| Osterley Gdns. | 1B 40 |
| Oswald Cl. | 4D 69 |
| Oswald Rd. | 4D 69 |
| Osward | 3D 59 |
| Osward Rd. | 3E 21 |
| Otford Cres. | 1F 23 |
| Otter Cl. | 2B 48 |
| Otter Mead La. | 2C 48 |
| Otterburn St. | 5E 2 |
| Otterden St. | 4A 24 |
| Ottershaw | 2B 48 |
| Otto Cl. | 3E 23 |
| Ottway's La. | 3A 70 |

| | |
|---|---|
| Ottways Av. | 3B 70 |
| Ouseley Rd., Balham | 2E 21 |
| Ouseley Rd., Wraysbury | 2C 12 |
| Outram Pl. | 1B 50 |
| Outram Rd. | 5D 41 |
| Outwood | 5C 110 |
| Outwood La., Bletchingley | 5F 91 |
| Outwood La., Chipstead | 4D 73 |
| Outwood Rd. | 1C 110 |
| Oval Rd. | 5C 40 |
| Oval, The, Banstead | 5E 55 |
| Oval, The, Farncombe | 5A 100 |
| Oval, The, Guildford | 1B 100 |
| Oval, The, West End | 4B 46 |
| Oval, The, Woodstreet Village | 5C 80 |
| Overbrae | 5A 24 |
| Overbrook, Godalming | 1E 119 |
| Overbrook, W. Horsley | 3B 84 |
| Overbury Av. | 2B 42 |
| Overbury Cres. | 3E 59 |
| Overdale, Ashtead | 1B 70 |
| Overdale, Bletchingley | 5B 91 |
| Overdale, Dorking | 1A 106 |
| Overdale, Goldsworth | 2B 64 |
| Overdale Av. | 1D 37 |
| Overdale Rise | 1E 61 |
| Overdale Rd. | 1A 8 |
| Overdene Dr. | 4B 146 |
| Overdown Rd. | 4A 24 |
| Overford Cl. | 2C 140 |
| Overford Dr. | 2C 140 |
| Overhill | 3E 75 |
| Overhill Rd., Dulwich | 2D 23 |
| Overhill Rd., Purley | 3D 57 |
| Overhill Way | 3B 42 |
| Overland Cl. | 4A 44 |
| Oversland Cl. | 3A 42 |
| Overstone Gdns. | 4F 41 |
| Overstone Rd. | 2F 9 |
| Overthorpe Cl. | 2A 64 |
| Overton Cl. | 2D 97 |
| Overton Rd. | 2E 55 |
| Overton Way | 1A 86 |
| Ovington Ct. | 1A 64 |
| Owen Rd. | 1A 46 |
| Owen St. | 1D 119 |
| Owlcastle Cl. | 3B 158 |
| Owlsmoor Rd. | 4E 43 |
| Owlstead Gdns. | 4A 58 |
| Ownsted Hill | 3E 59 |
| Ox La. | 3C 54 |
| Oxdowne Cl. | 5A 52 |
| Oxenden Ct. | 1E 97 |
| Oxenden Rd. | 1E 97 |
| Oxenhope | 2C 26 |
| Oxford Av. | 1A 38 |
| Oxford Cl. | 5E 15 |
| Oxford Cl. | 2F 39 |
| Oxford Cottages | 3F 15 |
| Oxford Cl. | 4B 16 |
| Oxford Cres. | 3D 37 |
| Oxford Gdns. | 3C 8 |
| Oxford Rd., Carshalton Beeches | 2A 56 |
| Oxford Rd., Fulwell | 4E 17 |
| Oxford Rd., Guildford | 1C 100 |
| Oxford Rd., Gunnersbury | 2C 8 |
| Oxford Rd., Horsham | 5B 158 |
| Oxford Rd., Norwood | 5C 22 |
| Oxford Rd., Redhill | 5A 90 |
| Oxford Rd., South Farnborough | 1A 78 |
| Oxford Rd., Wokingham | 1D 25 |
| Oxford Ter. | 1C 100 |
| Oxshott | 5A 52 |
| Oxshott Rise | 5E 51 |
| Oxshott Rd. | 1F 69 |
| Oxshott Way | 1B 68 |
| Oxted | 3F 93 |
| Oxted Green | 4A 118 |
| Oxted Rd. | 3B 92 |
| Oyster La. | 4F 49 |

**P**

| | |
|---|---|
| Pachesham Dr. | 1F 69 |
| Packway Leigh La. | 5B 96 |
| Paddenswick Rd. | 1F 9 |
| Padbrook | 2F 94 |
| Paddock Cl., Camberley | 5C 44 |
| Paddock Cl., Cobham | 5E 51 |
| Paddock Cl., Hambledon | 2F 137 |
| Paddock Cl., Oxted | 4F 93 |
| Paddock Gdns. | 3C 150 |

| | |
|---|---|
| Paddock Grn. | 2D 125 |
| Paddock Grn. Cl. | 2D 125 |
| Paddock Gr., | 2D 125 |
| Paddock, The, Grayshott | 5C 134 |
| Paddock, The, Headley | 4F 133 |
| Paddock, The, Merrow | 5C 82 |
| Paddock, The, Shottermill | 2F 151 |
| Paddock, The, Westcott | 2D 105 |
| Paddock Wk. | 3E 75 |
| Paddock Way, Oxted | 4F 93 |
| Paddock Way, Sheerwater | 5B 48 |
| Paddockhurst Rd. | 4B 146 |
| Paddocks Cl. | 2B 70 |
| Paddocks Mead | 1A 64 |
| Paddocks Rd. | 4B 82 |
| Paddocks, The, Addington | 2D 59 |
| Paddocks, The, Flexford | 5F 79 |
| Paddocks, The, Gt. Bookham | 1A 86 |
| Paddocks, The, Weybridge | 5F 33 |
| Paddocks Way, Ashtead | 3B 70 |
| Paddocks Way, Chertsey | 4B 32 |
| Padua Rd. | 1E 41 |
| Padwich Rd. | 4C 158 |
| Page Cres. | 1E 57 |
| Page Rd. | 1F 15 |
| Pageant Walk | 5C 40 |
| Pagehurst Rd. | 4E 41 |
| Pages Croft | 2F 25 |
| Paget Av. | 5D 39 |
| Paget Cl. | 4E 17 |
| Pagoda Av. | 5B 8 |
| Paines Hill | 2F 139 |
| Paines Hill Rd. | 4B 94 |
| Paisley Rd. | 4D 39 |
| Palace Dr. | 5E 33 |
| Palace Green | 2D 59 |
| Palace Rd., Crystal Palace | 5D 23 |
| Palace Rd., E. Molesey | 2E 35 |
| Palace Rd., Kingston | 2B 36 |
| Palace Rd., Tulse Hill | 2A 22 |
| Palace Sq. | 5D 23 |
| Palace View | 1D 59 |
| Palestine Gro. | 1C 38 |
| Palewell Common Dr. | 1D 19 |
| Palewell Pk. | 1D 19 |
| Palgrave Rd. | 1E 9 |
| Palm Gro. | 3F 81 |
| Palmer Av. | 1C 54 |
| Palmer Cl., Earlswood | 1E 109 |
| Palmer Cl., Horley | 1A 128 |
| Palmer Cres., Kingston | 2B 36 |
| Palmer Cr., Ottershaw | 2C 48 |
| Palmers Gr. | 2C 34 |
| Palmers Rd. | 1A 40 |
| Palmersfield Rd. | 5E 55 |
| Palmerston Cl. | 5A 48 |
| Palmerston Rd., Acton Grn. | 1D 9 |
| Palmerston Rd., Carshalton | 1B 56 |
| Palmerston Rd., East Sheen | 5D 9 |
| Palmerston Rd., Sutton | 1F 55 |
| Palmerston Rd., Twickenham | 1E 17 |
| Palmerston Rd., Wimbledon | 5B 20 |
| Pampisford Rd. | 4E 57 |
| Pams Way | 1A 54 |
| Pankhurst Dr. | 3D 27 |
| Panmuir Rd. | 1F 37 |
| Panmure Rd. | 3E 23 |
| Pannell Cl. | 2C 150 |
| Pannells | 1E 115 |
| Pannells Ct., Guildford | 159 |
| Pantile Rd. | 1B 50 |
| Pantiles | 2B 64 |
| Papercourt La. | 4A 66 |
| Papworth Way | 2B 22 |
| Parade Rd. | 3A 62 |
| Parade, The, Claygate | 2B 52 |
| Parade, The, Epsom | 5A 54 |
| Paradise Rd. | 1B 18 |
| Paragon Gro. | 3B 36 |
| Parbury Rd. | 1F 23 |
| Parbury Rise | 2E 53 |
| Parchmore Rd. | 1B 40 |
| Parchmore Way | 1B 40 |
| Pares Cl. | 1C 64 |
| Parfour Dr. | 2B 74 |
| Parham Rd. | 3B 146 |
| Parish Cl. | 2A 96 |
| Parish La. | 5F 23 |
| Park Av., Bromley Hill | 5C 24 |
| Park Av., Camberley | 1D 61 |
| Park Av., Carshalton | 2B 56 |
| Park Av., Caterham | 5C 74 |
| Park Av., East Sheen | 5D 9 |
| Park Av., Salfords | 4E 109 |
| Park Av., Staines | 5A 14 |
| Park Av., Thorpe Lea | 5E 13 |
| Park Av., Tooting | 5E 21 |

| | |
|---|---|
| Park Av., West Wickham | 5B 42 |
| Park Av., Whitton | 1D 17 |
| Park Av., Windsor | 1C 12 |
| Park Av., Wokingham | 2D 25 |
| Park Avenue East | 2C 54 |
| Park Avenue West | 2B 54 |
| Park Barn Dr. | 5D 81 |
| Park Chase, Godalming | 3D 119 |
| Park Chase, Guildford | 5A 82 |
| Park Cl., Carshalton | 2B 56 |
| Park Cl., Claremont | 2F 51 |
| Park Cl., Fetcham | 5E 69 |
| Park Cl., Grayswood | 1B 152 |
| Park Cl., Hampton | 1D 35 |
| Park Cl., Isleworth | 1D 17 |
| Park Cl., Strood Green | 3C 106 |
| Park Cl., Walton | 5F 33 |
| Park Cl., Woodham | 3E 49 |
| Park Copse | 1A 106 |
| Park Corner Dr. | 2C 84 |
| Park Ct., Hampton Wick | 1A 36 |
| Park Ct., Hanworth | 4B 16 |
| Park Ct., Woking | 2D 65 |
| Park Cres., Sunningdale | 3E 29 |
| Park Cres., Whitton | 2E 17 |
| Park Dr., Ashtead | 2C 70 |
| Park Dr., Bramley | 1A 120 |
| Park Dr., Bromley | 3C 42 |
| Park Dr., Cranleigh | 1D 141 |
| Park Dr., East Sheen | 5D 9 |
| Park Dr., Sunningdale | 3E 29 |
| Park Dr., Woking | 2D 65 |
| Park Dr., Acton | 1C 8 |
| Park End | 1C 42 |
| Park Farm Rd. | 5B 18 |
| Park Gdns. | 4C 18 |
| Park Green Dr. | 5D 69 |
| Park Hall Rd. | 3C 22 |
| Park Hill, Carshalton Beeches | 2A 56 |
| Park Hill, Clapham | 1F 21 |
| Park Hill, Richmond | 1B 18 |
| Park Hill Cl., Blackwater | 1B 60 |
| Park Hill Cl., Carshalton Beeches | 2A 56 |
| Park Hill Rise | 5D 41 |
| Park Hill Rd., Croydon | 5C 40 |
| Park Hill Rd., Carshalton | 2B 56 |
| Park Hill Rd., Epsom | 4B 54 |
| Park Hill Rd., Shortlands | 1C 42 |
| Park Hill Rd., South Croydon | 1F 57 |
| Park Horsley | 3D 85 |
| Park House Dr. | 1B 108 |
| Park House Gdns. | 1A 18 |
| Park La., Ashtead | 2C 70 |
| Park La., Brook | 3A 136 |
| Park La., Camberley | 5A 44 |
| Park La., Carshalton | 1B 56 |
| Park La., Cheam | 2D 55 |
| Park La., Croydon | 5C 40 |
| Park La., Hooley | 4F 73 |
| Park La., Merrow | 4C 82 |
| Park La., Reigate | 5E 89 |
| Park La., Richmond | 5A 8 |
| Park La., South Croydon | 1F 57 |
| Park La., South Park | 1B 108 |
| Park La., Teddington | 5F 17 |
| Park La., W. Wickham | 4A 42 |
| Park Lane East | 2B 108 |
| Park Lawn Av., Horley | 2B 128 |
| Park Lawn Rd. | 1B 50 |
| Park Leigh Rd. | 1C 38 |
| Park Ley Rd. | 3F 75 |
| Park Pl., Farnborough Pk. | 5D 61 |
| Park Pl., Gunnersbury | 2C 8 |
| Park Pl., Hampton | 5D 17 |
| Park Railings | 3C 102 |
| Park Rise, Horsham | 4A 158 |
| Park Rise, Leatherhead | 4F 69 |
| Park Rise Cl. | 4F 69 |
| Park Rd., Aldershot | 1D 97 |
| Park Rd., Ashford | 4E 15 |
| Park Rd., Ashtead | 3B 70 |
| Park Rd. Banstead | 1C 72 |
| Park Rd., Beckenham | 5A 24 |
| Park Rd., Bracknell | 1D 27 |
| Park Rd., Burstow | 3E 129 |
| Park Rd., Camberley | 5A 44 |
| Park Rd., Caterham | 5C 74 |
| Park Rd., Cheam | 2D 55 |
| Park Rd., Chipstead | 2D 73 |
| Park Rd., Chiswick | 3D 9 |
| Park Rd., Crowhurst | 3C 112 |
| Park Rd., Dormans Park | 5F 131 |
| Park Rd., East Grinstead | 2B 150 |
| Park Rd., East Molesey | 2D 35 |
| Park Rd., Egham | 4D 13 |
| Park Rd., Esher | 1A 52 |

| | | | | | | | | |
|---|---|---|---|---|---|---|---|---|
| Park Rd., Farnham | 3B 96 | Parklands, Guildford | 5B 82 | Patten Ash Dr. | 1E 25 | Pendleton Rd. | 2C 108 |
| Park Rd., Fickleshole | 5F 59 | Parklands, Oxted | 4F 93 | Patten Rd. | 2D 21 | Pendragon Rd. | 3C 24 |
| Park Rd., Godalming | 3D 119 | Parklands, Surbiton | 3B 36 | Pattenden Rd. | 2A 24 | Pendragon Way | 1A 62 |
| Park Rd., Guildford | 5F 81 | Parklands Pl. | 5B 82 | Patterdale Cl. | 5C 146 | Penerley Rd. | 2A 24 |
| Park Rd., Hampton Wick | 1A 36 | Parklands Rd. | 4E 21 | Patterson Cl. | 1A 62 | Penge | 5E 23 |
| Park Rd., Hanworth | 4B 16 | Parklawn Av., Epsom | 5F 53 | Patterson Rd. | 5D 23 | Penge La. | 5E 23 |
| Park Rd., Haslemere | 3A 152 | Parkleys | 4B 18 | Paul Gdns. | 5D 41 | Penge Rd. | 2D 41 |
| Park Rd., Isleworth | 4A 8 | Parkmead | 1F 19 | Paul's Pl. | 3C 70 | Penhurst | 5A 48 |
| Park Rd., Kempton Park | 5A 16 | Parkpale La. | 3C 106 | Pauline Cres. | 2D 17 | Peninsula Cl. | 1F 15 |
| Park Rd., Kenley | 1B 74 | Parkshot | 5B 8 | Paulsmead | 1F 131 | Penistone Rd. | 5A 22 |
| Park Rd., Kingston | 1C 36 | Parkside, Cheam | 2D 55 | Pavement, The | 4D 147 | Pennard Rd. | 1F 9 |
| Park Rd., New Malden | 2D 37 | Parkside, Crawley | 4D 147 | Pavilion Gdns. | 5B 14 | Pennards, The | 2B 34 |
| Park Rd., New Oxted | 2A 94 | Parkside, East Grinstead | 2B 150 | Pawlyne Rd. | 5E 23 | Pennine Way | 3B 60 |
| Park Rd., Redhill | 4A 90 | Parkside, Hampton | 4E 17 | Pawson's Rd. | 3B 40 | Pennings Av. | 4D 81 |
| Park Rd., Richmond | 1B 18 | Parkside Av. | 4A 20 | Paxton Gdns. | 4C 48 | Pennington Dr. | 5F 33 |
| Park Rd., S. Norwood | 2C 40 | Parkside Cl. | 1C 84 | Paxton Rd. | 3D 9 | Penny Croft | 3C 58 |
| Park Rd., Sandhurst | 4D 43 | Parkside Ct. | 1A 50 | Paynes Green Rd. | 3D 143 | Penny Dr. | 5C 80 |
| Park Rd., Shepperton | 4D 33 | Parkside Cres. | 3D 37 | Paynesfield Rd. | 4E 77 | Penny La. | 4F 33 |
| Park Rd., South Farnborough | 1B 78 | Parkside Gdns., Chipstead | 2E 73 | Peabody Estate | 2B 22 | Pennyfield | 5D 51 |
| Park Rd., Stanwell | 1B 14 | Parkside Gdns., Wimbledon | 4A 20 | Peabody Rd. | 1A 78 | Pennymead Dr. | 2C 84 |
| Park Rd., Surbiton | 3B 36 | Parkside Pl. | 1C 84 | Peacemaker Cl. | 5A 146 | Pennymead Rise | 2C 84 |
| Park Rd., Teddington | 5F 17 | Parkside Rd., Hounslow | 1D 17 | Peach St. | 2E 25 | Pennypot La. | 5C 46 |
| Park Rd., Tooting | 5D 21 | Parkside Rd., Sunningdale | 3E 29 | Peaches Cl. | 2D 55 | Penrhyn Rd. | 2B 36 |
| Park Rd., Twickenham | 1A 18 | Parkstead Rd. | 1F 19 | Peacock Av. | 2E 15 | Penrith Cl., Putney | 1A 20 |
| Park Rd., Wallington | 1B 56 | Parkstone Dr. | 1D 61 | Peacock Gdns. | 3C 58 | Penrith Cl., Redhill | 5A 90 |
| Park Rd., West | 2D 65 | Parkthorne Rd. | 2F 21 | Peacock La. | 2B 26 | Penrith Rd., Beulah Hill | 1C 40 |
| Park Rd., Whitton | 1D 17 | Parkview Rd. | 4D 41 | Peak Hill | 4E 23 | Penrith Rd., New Malden | 2D 37 |
| Park Rd., Wimbledon | 4B 20 | Parkview Vale | 4C 82 | Peak Rd. | 4E 81 | Penrith St. | 5F 21 |
| Park Rd., Woking | 2E 65 | Parkway, Abbotswood | 5A 82 | Peak, The | 3E 23 | Penrose Rd. | 4D 69 |
| Park Rd., Wokingham | 2D 25 | Parkway, Camberley | 1D 61 | Peakfield | 4D 115 | Pensfold Av | 4C 8 |
| Park Road East, Gunnersbury | 1C 8 | Parkway, Cannon Hill | 2A 38 | Peaks Hill | 3C 56 | Penshurst | 3E 27 |
| Park Road East, Ham | 4B 18 | Parkway, Dorking | 1F 105 | Peall Rd. | 3A 40 | Penshurst Grn. | 3C 42 |
| Park Road North | 1C 8 | Parkway, Horley | 2B 128 | Pear Tree Cl., Lindford | 4D 133 | Penshurst Rise | 3F 61 |
| Park Road West | 4B 18 | Parkway, New Addington | 3E 59 | Pear Tree Cl., Mitcham | 1D 39 | Penshurst Rd. | 3B 40 |
| Park Row | 3A 96 | Parkway, Pound Hill | 3F 147 | Pear Tree Hill | 4E 109 | Penshurst Way | 3E 55 |
| Park Side | 3E 49 | Parkway, Weybridge | 1B 50 | Pear Tree Rd., Addlest. | 1D 49 | Pentland Av. | 3D 33 |
| Park St., Bagshot | 2D 45 | Parkwood Av. | 4E 35 | Pear Tree Rd., Ashford | 4E 15 | Pentland St. | 1C 20 |
| Park St., Camberley | 5A 44 | Parkwood Cl. | 1A 72 | Pearce Rd. | 2D 35 | Pentlow St. | 4F 9 |
| Park St., Croydon | 5C 40 | Parkwood Gro. | 2A 34 | Pearfield Rd. | 3F 23 | Pentney Rd. | 2F 21 |
| Park St., Guildford | 1C 100 | Parkwood Rd., Banstead | 1A 72 | Pearl Ct. | 1A 64 | Penton Av. | 5A 14 |
| Park St., Horsham | 5B 158 | Parkwood Rd., Nutfield | 5D 91 | Pearmain Cl. | 3E 33 | Penton Hall Dr. | 1A 32 |
| Park St., Poyle | 3A 7 | Parkwood Rd., Tatsfield | 4F 77 | Pearson Rd. | 4F 147 | Penton Hook Rd. | 5A 14 |
| Park St., Teddington | 5E 17 | Parkwood Rd., Wimbledon | 4B 20 | Peartree La. | 2C 114 | Penton Rd. | 5A 14 |
| Park Ter. | 4E 37 | Parley Dr. | 2C 64 | Peary Cl. | 3B 158 | Pentreath Av. | 1B 100 |
| Park Terrace East | 5B 158 | Parr Av. | 3C 54 | Peaslake La. | 1A 122 | Pentwith | 3E 151 |
| Park Terrace West | 5B 158 | Parr Cl., Leatherhead | 3F 69 | Peaslake La. | 1B 122 | Penwith Rd. | 3B 20 |
| Park, The, Carlshalton | 1B 56 | Parr Ct. | 4B 16 | Peaslake Rd. | 3B 122 | Penwood End | 4B 64 |
| Park, The, Eastwick | 1A 86 | Parr Dr. | 2C 70 | Peatmore Av. | 1A 66 | Penwortham Rd., Sanderstead | 3F 57 |
| Park View, Bagshot | 2D 45 | Parris Croft | 2A 106 | Peatmore Cl. | 1A 66 | Penwortham Rd., Streatham | 5F 21 |
| Park View, Eastwick | 1A 86 | Parrs Cl. | 3F 57 | Pebble Coombe | 3B 88 | Vale | |
| Park View, Horley | 2B 128 | Parry Cl. | 2C 54 | Pebble La. | 4C 70 | Peperham La. | 2A 152 |
| Park View, New Malden | 2E 37 | Parry Rd. | 2C 40 | Pebblehill Rd. | 4A 88 | Peperharow La. | 5D 99 |
| Park View Rd., Salfords | 4E 109 | Parson's Mead | 4B 40 | Peckarmans Wood | 3D 23 | Peperharow Rd. | 1C 118 |
| Park View Rd., Woldingham | 4F 75 | Parsonage Cl. | 1F 75 | Peckham Rye | 1E 23 | Pepper Box La. | 5C 120 |
| Park View Ter. | 5B 158 | Parsonage La. | 2D 105 | Peckhams | 4A 118 | Pepys Cl. | 2C 70 |
| Park Way, East Molesey | 2D 35 | Parsonage Rd., Cranleigh | 1C 140 | Peek Cres. | 4A 20 | Pepys Rd. | 1A 38 |
| Park Way, Feltham | 2A 16 | Parsonage Rd., Englefield | 4C 12 | Peeks Brook La. | 5D 129 | Percival Rd., Feltham | 3F 15 |
| Park Way, Fetcham | 5D 69 | Green | | Peel Av. | 3F 61 | Percival Rd., Mortlake | 5D 9 |
| Park Wood View | 1A 72 | Parsonage Rd., Horsham | 4B 158 | Pegasus Av. | 5B 78 | Percival Way | 1A 54 |
| Parkcroft Rd. | 2C 24 | Parsonfield Cl. | 1A 72 | Pegasus Rd. | 2E 57 | Percy Av. | 4D 15 |
| Parkdale Cres. | 5D 37 | Parsonfield Rd. | 1A 72 | Pegwell Cl. | 5B 146 | Percy Bryant Rd. | 5F 15 |
| Parke Rd., Barnes | 4E 9 | Parsons Cl. | 2A 152 | Peket Cl. | 1F 31 | Percy Gdns. | 4D 37 |
| Parke Rd., Sunbury-on-Thames | 2A 34 | Parsons Grn., Guildford | 4F 81 | Pelham Rd., Elmers End | 1E 41 | Percy Rd., Anerley | 1E 41 |
| Parker Rd. | 1F 57 | Parsons Green, Haslemere | 2A 152 | Peleham Rd., Wimbledon | 5B 20 | Percy Rd., Guildford | 4E 81 |
| Parker's Cl. | 3B 70 | Parsons La. | 4D 135 | Pelham Way | 1A 86 | Percy Rd., Hackbridge | 4E 39 |
| Parker's Hill | 3B 70 | Parsons Mead | 2E 35 | Pelhams Cl. | 1F 51 | Percy Rd., Hammersmith | 1E 9 |
| Parker's La. | 3B 70 | Parsons Rd. | 4F 81 | Pelhams Wk. | 5C 34 | Percy Rd., Hampton | 5C 16 |
| Parkers Hill | 3B 102 | Parthia Cl. | 3F 71 | Pelinore Rd. | 3C 24 | Percy Rd., Horsham | 4A 158 |
| Parkfield, Godalming | 3D 119 | Partridge Cl. | 2E 61 | Pellatt Rd. | 1D 23 | Percy Rd., Whitton | 2D 17 |
| Parkfield, Ham | 4B 18 | Partridge Knoll | 5E 57 | Pelling Hill | 2B 12 | Percy Rd., Woodside | 3D 41 |
| Parkfield, Horsham | 4B 158 | Partridge La. | 2B 125 | Pelton Av. | 3F 55 | Percy Way | 2D 17 |
| Parkfield Av., Feltham | 3A 16 | Partridge Mead | 1A 72 | Pemberton Rd. | 2D 35 | Peregrine Cl., Bracknell | 3D 27 |
| Parkfield Av., Mortlake | 5D 9 | Partridge Rd. | 5C 16 | Pembroke | 4C 26 | Peregrine Cl., Cranleigh | 1C 140 |
| Parkfield Cres. | 3A 16 | Partridge Way | 5C 82 | Pembroke Av., Hersham | 1E 51 | Peregrine Rd. | 1F 33 |
| Parkfield Rd. | 3A 16 | Partrington Cl. | 5B 146 | Pembroke Av., Surbiton | 3C 36 | Perkins Ct. | 4C 14 |
| Parkfields, Barnes | 5F 9 | Parvis Rd. | 5E 49 | Pembroke Broadway | 5A 44 | Perran Rd. | 3B 22 |
| Parkfields, Crawley | 4B 146 | Paschal Rd. | 4C 44 | Pembroke Cl. | 2C 72 | Perrin Cl. | 4C 14 |
| Parkfields, Oxshott | 4B 52 | Pascoe Rd. | 1B 24 | Pembroke Gdns. | 2E 65 | Perring Av. | 3B 60 |
| Parkfields Cl. | 4B 18 | Pastens Rd. | 4B 94 | Pembroke Rd., Crawley | 2F 147 | Perrings | 3D 23 |
| Parkgate | 2A 126 | Pasture Rd. | 2C 24 | Pembroke Rd., Thorn. H. | 2C 40 | Perrior Rd. | 5A 100 |
| Parkgate Gdns. | 1D 19 | Pasture Wood Rd. | 1E 123 | Pembroke Rd., Woking | 2E 65 | Perry Av. | 1C 150 |
| Parkgate Rd., Parkgate | 2A 126 | Pasture, The | 4F 147 | Pembroke Villas | 5A 8 | Perry Cl. | 1E 119 |
| Parkgate Rd., Reigate | 1C 108 | Patchesham Pk. | 1F 69 | Pembury Av. | 4F 37 | Perry Hill | 3A 24 |
| Parkgate Rd., Wallington | 1B 56 | Patching Cl. | 3B 146 | Pembury Cl., Coulsdon | 5B 56 | Perry Oaks, Bracknell | 1E 27 |
| Parkhill Rd., Blackwater | 1B 60 | Patchings | 4C 158 | Pembury Cl., Hayes | 4C 42 | Perry Rise | 3F 23 |
| Parkhurst | 3A 54 | Paterson Rd. | 4C 14 | Pembury Rd. | 2D 41 | Perry Vale | 3E 23 |
| Parkhurst Fields | 2C 134 | Path Fields Cl. | 2A 152 | Pemdevon Rd. | 4B 40 | Perry Way | 5F 133 |
| Parkhurst Rd., Guildford | 5E 81 | Path, The | 1C 38 | Penberth Rd. | 2B 24 | Perryfield Rd. | 4C 146 |
| Parkhurst Rd., Lee Street | 2A 128 | Pathfield | 5F 137 | Pendarves Rd. | 1F 37 | Perryfield Way | 3A 18 |
| Parkhurst Rd., Sutton | 1F 55 | Pathfield Cl., Bucks | 2E 157 | Pendell Rd. | 4E 91 | Perryhow | 4E 37 |
| Parkland Dr. | 1E 27 | Green | | Pendennis Cl. | 5D 49 | Perryland La. | 3D 129 |
| Parkland Gro., Ashford | 4D 15 | Pathfield Cl., Chiddingfold | 5F 137 | Pendennis Rd. | 4A 22 | Perrylands | 5E 127 |
| Parkland Gro., Heath End | 1C 96 | Pathfield Rd. | 5A 22 | Penderel Rd. | 1C 16 | Persant Rd. | 3C 24 |
| Parkland Rd. | 4D 15 | Pathfields | 2A 152 | Penderry Rise | 3B 24 | Persfield Rd. | 3B 54 |
| Parkland Way | 5E 37 | Pathway, The, | 1D 83 | Pendle Rd. | 5E 21 | Pershore Gro. | 3D 39 |
| Parklands, Addlestone | 1E 49 | Patmore La. | 2C 50 | Pendlebury | 4C 26 | Perth Cl. | 1E 37 |
| Parklands, Fetcham | 5D 69 | Patrol Cl. | 1F 21 | Pendleton Cl. | 1D 109 | Perth Rd. | 1B 42 |

| | | | | | | | |
|---|---|---|---|---|---|---|---|
| Revesby Rd. | 3D 39 | Ridge Way, The, Sanderstead | 3F 57 | Ripley | 4B 66 | Roberts Cl., Cheam | 2D 55 |
| Rewley Rd. | 3D 39 | Ridge Way, The, Waddon | 5A 40 | Ripley Av. | 5D 13 | Roberts Cl., Stanwell | 1B 14 |
| Rex Av. | 4D 15 | Ridgegate Cl., | 4A 90 | Ripley Bypass | 1D 83 | Roberts Rd., Aldershot | 5A 78 |
| Reynolds Av. | 2E 53 | Ridgegreen Cl. | 2A 110 | Ripley Cl. | 2E 59 | Roberts' Rd., Camberley | 5F 43 |
| Reynolds Cl. | 4E 39 | Ridgehurst | 5A 158 | Ripley Gdns., Mortlake | 5D 9 | Roberts Way | 5C 12 |
| Reynolds Grn. | 5E 43 | Ridgelands | 5E 69 | Ripley Gdns., Sutton | 1F 55 | Robertsbridge Rd. | 4C 38 |
| Reynolds Pl. | 3C 146 | Ridgeley Rd. | 5E 137 | Ripley La. | 1A 84 | Robertson Way | 5B 78 |
| Reynolds Rd., Crawley | 3C 146 | Ridgemead Rd. | 3B 12 | Ripley Rd., East Clandon | 2E 83 | Robin Cl., Addlestone | 1F 49 |
| Reynolds Rd., Malden Manor | 4D 37 | Ridgemoor Cl. | 4E 135 | Ripley Rd., Hampton | 5C 16 | Robin Cl., Ash Vale | 3C 78 |
| Rhine Banks | 4B 60 | Ridgemount, Guildford | 1B 100 | Ripley Way | 4C 16 | Robin Cl., Crawley | 3C 146 |
| Rhodes Moorhouse Wk. | 3B 38 | Ridgemount, Walton-on-Thames | 5F 33 | Ripon Cl., Camberley | 1A 62 | Robin Gdns. | 4B 90 |
| Rhodes Way | 5D 147 | Ridgemount Av., Chipstead | 2E 73 | Ripon Cl., Guildford | 4D 81 | Robin Gr. | 3A 8 |
| Rhododendron Ride | 4A 12 | Ridgemount Av., Shirley | 5F 41 | Ripon Gdns. | 1D 53 | Robin Hill | 5A 100 |
| Rhododendron Rd. | 3F 61 | Ridgemount Cl. | 3A 62 | Ripplesmere | 2E 27 | Robin Hill Dr. | 1F 61 |
| Rhodrons Av. | 1E 53 | Ridges, The | 3C 100 | Ripston Rd. | 4E 15 | Robin Hood Cl., Hawley | 3C 60 |
| Rialto Rd. | 1E 39 | Ridgeside | 4D 147 | Risborough Dr. | 4F 37 | Robin Hood Cl., Mitcham | 2F 39 |
| Ribble Pl. | 3B 60 | Ridgeway, East Grinstead | 3C 150 | Rise Rd. | 3E 29 | Robin Hood Cl., Woking | 2B 64 |
| Ribblesdale Rd. | 5E 21 | Ridgeway, Epsom | 4A 54 | Rise, The, E. Grinstead | 3C 150 | Robin Hood Cres. | 2A 64 |
| Ricardo Ct. | 1A 120 | Ridgeway, Wimbledon | 5A 20 | Rise, The, Ewell | 3B 54 | Robin Hood La., Cheam | 1E 55 |
| Ricardo Rd. | 1B 12 | Ridgeway, Woking | 1C 64 | Rise, The, Horsley | 1C 84 | Robin Hood La., Guildford | 1A 82 |
| Richards Rd. | 5A 52 | Ridgeway Cl., Dorking | 2F 105 | Rise, The, Pound Hill | 4F 147 | Robin Hood La., Kingston Vale | 4E 19 |
| Richbell Cl. | 2A 70 | Ridgeway Cl., Lightwater | 4F 45 | Rise, The, Selsdon | 3B 58 | Robin Hood La., Mitcham | 2F 39 |
| Richford St. | 1F 9 | Ridgeway Cl., Oxshott | 5A 52 | Riseldine Rd. | 1F 23 | Robin Hood Rd., Wimbledon | 4F 19 |
| Richings Park | 1B 7 | Ridgeway Cl., Woking | 1C 64 | Ritchie Rd. | 3E 41 | Robin Hood Rd., Woking | 2A 64 |
| Richings Way | 1B 7 | Ridgeway Dr. | 3F 105 | Ritherdon Rd. | 3E 21 | Robin Hood Way | 5E 19 |
| Richland Av. | 5B 56 | Ridgeway Farm Rd. | 2F 135 | River Av. | 4F 35 | Robin La. | 4D 43 |
| Richlands Av. | 1C 54 | Ridgeway Gdns. | 5A 20 | River Bank | 2E 35 | Robin Way, Guildford | 3E 81 |
| Richmond Av., East Bedfont | 1F 15 | Ridgeway Rd., Dorking | 2F 105 | River Court Rd. | 2F 9 | Robin Way, Staines | 3A 14 |
| Richmond Av., Merton | 1B 38 | Ridgeway Rd., Farnham | 5A 96 | River Gdns., Feltham | 1A 16 | Robin Wood Pl. | 4D 19 |
| Richmond Cl., Biggin Hill | 3D 77 | Ridgeway Rd., Redhill | 5A 90 | River Gdns., Hackbridge | 5E 39 | Robin's Row | 1D 61 |
| Richmond Cl., Epsom | 5B 54 | Ridgeway, The, Acton | 1C 8 | River La., Leatherhead | 4F 69 | Robinhood La., Warnham | 3A 158 |
| Richmond Cl., Fetcham | 5D 69 | Ridgeway, The, Bracknell | 2D 27 | River La., Richmond | 2B 18 | Robinson Rd., Crawley | 4C 146 |
| Richmond Cl., Frimley | 2F 61 | Ridgeway, The, Carshalton Beeches | 2A 56 | River La., Wrecclesham | 5F 95 | Robinson Rd., Tooting | 5D 21 |
| Richmond Cres. | 4A 14 | Ridgeway, The, Cranleigh | 2D 141 | River Meads Av. | 3D 17 | Robinsway | 1E 51 |
| Richmond Dr. | 3E 33 | Ridgeway, The, Guildford | 1E 101 | River Mount | 4F 33 | Robson Rd. | 3B 22 |
| Richmond Green | 5A 50 | Ridgeway, The, Horley | 3B 128 | River Park Av. | 4F 13 | Rochdale Rd. | 1D 27 |
| Richmond Gro. | 3B 36 | Ridgeway, The, Horsley | 1C 84 | River Park Gdns. | 5B 24 | Roche Rd. | 1A 40 |
| Richmond Hill | 1B 18 | Ridgeway, The, Lightwater | 3F 45 | River Reach | 4A 18 | Roche Wk. | 3C 38 |
| Richmond Park Rd., East Sheen | 5D 9 | Ridgeway, The, Oxshott | 5A 52 | River Rd | 1A 32 | Rochester Av. | 3A 16 |
| Richmond Park Rd., Kingston | 5B 18 | Ridgeway, Walton on Thames | 4F 33 | River Row | 5F 95 | Rochester Gdns. | 4D 75 |
| Richmond Rd., Cottenham Park | 1F 37 | Ridgway Hill Rd. | 5A 96 | River Wk. | 3A 34 | Rochester Rd. | 1B 56 |
| | | Ridgway Pl. | 5A 20 | River Way, Twickenham | 3D 17 | Rochester Walk | 3B 108 |
| Richmond Rd., Godalming | 1D 119 | Ridgway Rd., Ridgway | 1A 66 | River Way, West Ewell | 2A 54 | Rochford Way | 3A 40 |
| Richmond Rd., Gunnersbury | 1B 8 | Ridgway, The, Brookwood | 4B 63 | Riverdale | 1A 18 | Rock Av. | 5D 9 |
| Richmond Rd., Horsham | 4B 158 | Riding Bottom | 1C 122 | Riverdale Cl. | 5F 95 | Rock Hill, Hambledon | 2A 138 |
| Richmond Rd., Kingston | 5B 18 | Riding Hill | 5A 58 | Riverdale Dr. | 4D 65 | Rock Hill, Sydenham | 4D 23 |
| Richmond Rd., Richmond | 1A 18 | Riding, The, Maybury | 5B 48 | Riverdale Rd., Hanworth | 4C 16 | Rock La. | 1C 114 |
| Richmond Rd., Staines | 4A 14 | Ridings La. | 5D 67 | Riverdale Rd., Richmond | 1A 18 | Rockbourne Rd. | 2F 23 |
| Richmond Rd., Thornton Heath | 2B 40 | Ridings, The, Ashtead | 2A 70 | Riverford Rd. | 5A 14 | Rockfield Cl. | 4F 93 |
| | | Ridings, The, Biggin Hill | 2E 77 | Riverholme Dr. | 3A 54 | Rockfield Rd. | 3F 93 |
| Richmond Rd., Waddon | 5A 40 | Ridings, The, Burgh H'th | 3B 72 | Rivermead, Byfleet | 5A 50 | Rockhampton Rd., South Croydon | 2F 57 |
| Richmond Rd., Woodmansterne | 1E 73 | Ridings, The, Camberley | 1F 61 | Rivermead, Horsham | 5A 158 | |
| | | Ridings, The, Cobham | 5A 52 | Rivermead Cl., Ham | 4A 18 | Rockhampton Rd., West Norwood | 4B 22 |
| Richmond Rd., York Town | 4E 43 | Ridings, The, Cranleigh | 1C 140 | Rivermead Cl., New Haw | 2E 49 | |
| Richmond Way | 5D 69 | Ridings, The, Crawley | 3F 147 | Rivermead Rd. | 2C 60 | Rockmount Rd. | 5C 22 |
| Richmond Wood | 4F 29 | Ridings, The, Epsom | 1E 71 | Rivermount Gdns | 2C 100 | Rocks La. | 5E 9 |
| Richmond-upon-Thames | 1A 18 | Ridings, The, Horsley | 1C 84 | Rivernook Cl. | 3A 34 | Rockshaw Rd. | 2C 90 |
| Rickards Cl. | 4B 36 | Ridings, The, Redhill | 4A 90 | Riversdale Rd. | 3F 35 | Rocky La. | 2B 90 |
| Ricketts Hill | 4E 77 | Ridings, The, Rowhill | 2D 49 | Riversdell Cl. | 4A 32 | Roden Gdns. | 3C 40 |
| Ricketts Hill Rd. | 2E 77 | Ridings, The, Sendmarsh | 5A 66 | Riverside, Bellfields | 4F 81 | Rodenhurst Rd. | 1F 21 |
| Rickettswood Rd. | 3D 127 | Ridings, The, Sunbury | 1A 34 | Riverside, Horley | 3B 128 | Rodgate La. | 3D 153 |
| Rickfield | 4B 146 | Ridings, The, Surbiton | 3C 36 | Riverside, Lower Halliford | 4F 33 | Rodney Cl., Malden | 3E 37 |
| Rickford Hill | 2D 81 | Ridings, The, Three Bridges | 3A 148 | Riverside, Old Windsor | 2C 12 | Rodney Cl., Walton-on-Thames | 4B 34 |
| Rickman Cres. | 5B 32 | Ridlands Cl. | 3C 94 | Riverside, Pixham | 5D 87 | Rodney Rd., Malden | 3D 37 |
| Rickman Hill Rd. | 2E 73 | Ridlands La. | 3B 94 | Riverside, Runnymede | 3E 13 | Rodney Rd., Mitcham | 1D 39 |
| Rickman Rd. | 2E 73 | Ridlands Rise | 4C 94 | Riverside, Twickenham | 2F 17 | Rodney Rd., Walton-on-Thames | 5B 34 |
| Rickman's La. | 5D 155 | Ridley Rd., Lammas Pk. | 1A 8 | Riverside Av., E. Molesey | 3E 35 | |
| Rickson's La. | 2B 84 | Ridley Rd., Warlingham | 2E 75 | Riverside Av., Lightwater | 3A 46 | Rodney Way, Guildford | 5B 82 |
| Rickwood | 2C 128 | Ridley Rd., Wimbledon | 5C 20 | Riverside Cl., Brookwood | 3E 63 | Rodney Way, Poyle | 4B 7 |
| Rickyard | 5D 81 | Ridsdale Rd., Penge | 5E 23 | Riverside Cl., Chertsey | 4A 32 | Rodona La. | 4B 50 |
| Riddlesdown Av. | 4E 47 | Ridsdale Rd., Woking | 2B 64 | Riverside Cl., Staines | 1A 32 | Rodsal La. | 5B 98 |
| Riddlesdown Rd., Purley | 3E 57 | Rifle Butts Alley | 1E 71 | Riverside Cl., Farnborough | 4C 60 | Rodway Rd. | 2F 19 |
| Ride La. | 1F 121 | Rigby Cl. | 5B 40 | Riverside Cl., Hackbridge | 5E 39 | Rodwell Rd. | 1D 23 |
| Ride, The, Brentford | 2A 8 | Riggindale Rd. | 4F 21 | Riverside Cl., Kingston | 2B 36 | Roe Deer Copse | 2E 151 |
| Ride, The, Ifold | 5F 155 | Rillside | 5E 147 | Riverside Dr., Chiswick | 3D 9 | Roe Way | 2D 57 |
| Ride Way | 3B 122 | Ring, The | 1D 27 | Riverside Dr., Ham | 3A 18 | Roebuck Cl. | 3A 16 |
| Riders Way | 4B 92 | Ringford Rd. | 1B 20 | Riverside Dr., Hythe | 4A 14 | Roebuck Rd. | 1F 53 |
| Rideway Cl. | 1D 61 | Ringley Av. | 3B 128 | Riverside Dr., Mitcham | 3D 39 | Roedean Cres. | 1E 19 |
| Ridge Cl., Brockham | 2C 106 | Ringley Oak | 4C 158 | Riverside Dr., Staines | 1A 32 | Roehampton | 2F 19 |
| Ridge Cl., Woking | 4C 64 | Ringley Park Av. | 1D 109 | Riverside Dr., West End | 1F 51 | Roehampton Cl. | 5E 9 |
| Ridge Langley | 3A 58 | Ringley Park Rd. | 5F 89 | Riverside Dr., Wonersh | 5E 101 | Roehampton Gate | 1E 19 |
| Ridge Mount Rd. | 4E 29 | Ringmead, Bracknell | 3B 26 | Riverside Pl. | 1C 14 | Roehampton High St. | 2F 19 |
| Ridge Pk. | 3C 56 | Ringmore Dr. | 4C 82 | Riverside Rd., Hersham | 1E 51 | Roehampton La. | 1E 19 |
| Ridge Rd., North Cheam | 4A 38 | Ringmore Rise | 2E 23 | Riverside Rd., Staines | 5A 14 | Roehampton Vale | 3E 19 |
| Ridge Rd., Tooting | 5E 21 | Ringmore Rd. | 5B 34 | Riverside Rd., Stanwell | 1C 14 | Roffe's La. | 5C 74 |
| Ridge Road West | 1C 90 | Ringstead Rd., Carshalton | 1A 56 | Riverview Gdns., Barnes | 3F 9 | Roffey Cl., Horley | 2A 128 |
| Ridge, The, Epsom | 2D 71 | Ringstead Rd., Catford | 2B 24 | Riverview Gdns., Twickenham | 3F 17 | Roffey Cl., Kenley | 1B 74 |
| Ridge, The, Fetcham | 5E 69 | Ringwold Cl. | 5F 23 | Riverview Gro. | 3C 8 | Roffeys Cl., Copthorne | 1B 148 |
| Ridge, The, Reedham | 5D 57 | Ringwood | 3C 26 | Riverview Pk. | 3A 24 | Rogers Cl., Caterham | 4E 75 |
| Ridge, The, Surbiton | 3C 36 | Ringwood Av., Croydon | 4A 40 | Riverview Rd., Chiswick | 3C 8 | Rogers Cl., Coulston | 2B 74 |
| Ridge, The, Whitton | 2E 17 | Ringwood Av., Redhill | 4B 90 | Riverview Rd., Ruxley | 1A 54 | Rogers Mead | 4B 92 |
| Ridge, The, Woking | 2E 65 | Ringwood Cl. | 5D 147 | Riverway, Laleham | 1B 32 | Rogers Rd. | 4D 21 |
| Ridge, The, Woldingham | 1D 93 | Ringwood Gdns. | 2F 19 | Rivey Cl. | 5D 49 | Rojack Rd. | 2F 23 |
| Ridge, The, Woodcote | 3C 56 | Ringwood Rd., Blackwater | 5D 43 | Roakes Av. | 5B 32 | Roke Cl., Purley | 5E 57 |
| Ridge Way, Hanworth | 3B 16 | Ringwood Rd., Farnbro' | 3D 61 | Robert Cl., Hersham | 1D 51 | Roke Cl., Wheeler Street | 5A 118 |
| Ridge Way, Horsham | 4A 158 | Ringwood Way | 4C 16 | Robert Way | 5E 61 | Roke La. | 5A 118 |
| | | | | | | Roke Rd. | 1B 74 |

| Street | Ref |
|---|---|
| Rokelo Rd. | 5E 57 |
| Rokers Hill | 5D 99 |
| Rokers La. | 5D 99 |
| Roland Way | 5E 37 |
| Rollesby Rd. | 2F 53 |
| Rollit Cres. | 1D 17 |
| Rollscourt Av. | 1B 22 |
| Roman Gdns. | 4B 38 |
| Roman Rise | 5C 22 |
| Roman Rd., Dorking | 2F 105 |
| Roman Rd., Turnham Green | 2E 9 |
| Roman Way, Croydon | 5B 40 |
| Roman Way, Farnham | 3B 96 |
| Romanhurst Av. | 2C 42 |
| Romanhurst Gdns. | 2C 42 |
| Romans Way | 1A 66 |
| Romany Rd. | 5C 46 |
| Romayne Cl. | 4C 60 |
| Romborough Way | 1B 24 |
| Romburgh Rd. | 3E 21 |
| Romeyn Rd. | 3A 22 |
| Rommany Rd. | 4C 22 |
| Romney Cl., Ashford | 4E 15 |
| Romney Cl., Chessington | 1E 53 |
| Romney Rd. | 3D 37 |
| Romola Rd. | 2B 22 |
| Romsey Cl., Badshot Lea | 2D 97 |
| Romsey Cl., Blackwater | 5D 43 |
| Romsey Cl., Hampton | 5C 16 |
| Rona Cl. | 5C 146 |
| Ronald Cl. | 2A 42 |
| Ronce La. | 5A 46 |
| Ronelean Rd. | 5B 36 |
| Ronneby Cl. | 5F 33 |
| Ronson Way | 4F 69 |
| Ronver Rd. | 2C 24 |
| Rook La. | 5B 74 |
| Rook Way | 3C 158 |
| Rookeries Cl. | 3A 16 |
| Rookery Cl. | 5E 69 |
| Rookery Dr. | 2C 104 |
| Rookery Hill, Ashtead | 2C 70 |
| Rookery Hill, Outwood | 5B 110 |
| Rookery La. | 1E 129 |
| Rookery Rd. | 4B 14 |
| Rookery, The | 3C 104 |
| Rookery Way | 2E 89 |
| Rooks Hill | 3B 120 |
| Rooksmead Rd. | 1A 34 |
| Rookstone Rd. | 4D 21 |
| Rookwood Av., New Malden | 2E 37 |
| Rookwood Av.,Sandhurst | 3E 43 |
| Rookwood Av., Wallington | 1C 56 |
| Rookwood Cl. | 3C 90 |
| Roothill La. | 3C 106 |
| Rope Wk. | 2A 34 |
| Rorkes Drift | 5F 61 |
| Rosa Av. | 4D 15 |
| Rosalind Franklin Cl. | 1A 100 |
| Rosamund Rd. | 5E 147 |
| Rosary Gdns. | 4D 15 |
| Rosary, The, Croydon | 3E 41 |
| Rosary, The, Thorpe | 1F 31 |
| Roscoe Rd. | 2E 65 |
| Rose Av., Morden | 3C 38 |
| Rose Ave., Mitcham | 1D 39 |
| Rose Bank | 5A 54 |
| Rose Briars | 3C 74 |
| Rose Bushes | 1F 71 |
| Rose Croft Gdns. | 2E 17 |
| Rose Dale | 5C 74 |
| Rose End | 4E 38 |
| Rose Gdns., Brentford | 1B 8 |
| Rose Gdns., Feltham | 3A 16 |
| Rose Gdns., S. Ealing | 1B 8 |
| Rose Heath Rd. | 1C 16 |
| Rose Hill, Dorking | 1F 105 |
| Rose Hill, Rose Hill | 5C 38 |
| Rose La. | 4B 66 |
| Rose Park | 3D 49 |
| Rose St. | 2E 25 |
| Rose Wk., Purley | 4D 57 |
| Rose Wk., Surbiton | 3C 36 |
| Rose Wk., West Wickham | 5B 42 |
| Roseacre | 5A 94 |
| Roseacre Cl. | 3D 33 |
| Roseacre Gdns. | 3A 102 |
| Rosebank | 5E 23 |
| Rosebank Cottages | 4D 65 |
| Roseberry Av., New Malden | 2E 37 |
| Roseberry Av., Norwood | 1C 40 |
| Roseberry Cl. | 3A 38 |
| Roseberry Dr. | 1E 63 |
| Roseberry Gdns. | 1F 55 |
| Roseberry Rd., Brixton | 1A 22 |
| Roseberry Rd., Cheam | 2E 55 |
| Roseberry Rd., Isleworth | 1E 17 |

| Street | Ref |
|---|---|
| Roseberry Rd., Kingston | 1C 36 |
| Rosebery Av. | 5B 54 |
| Rosebery Cres. | 4D 65 |
| Rosebery Rd. | 3D 71 |
| Rosebine Av. | 2E 17 |
| Rosebriar Cl. | 1B 66 |
| Rosecourt Rd. | 3A 40 |
| Rosedale | 2A 70 |
| Rosedale Cres. | 5B 146 |
| Rosedale Gdns. | 3C 26 |
| Rosedale Rd., Richmond | 5B 8 |
| Rosedale Rd., Stoneleigh | 1B 54 |
| Rosedene Av., Morden | 3B 38 |
| Rosedene Av., Streatham | 3A 22 |
| Rosefield Gdns. | 2C 48 |
| Rosefield Rd. | 4A 14 |
| Rosehill, Hampton | 1D 35 |
| Rosehill Av., St. Helier | 4C 38 |
| Rosehill Av., Woking | 1C 64 |
| Rosehill Cl. | 2C 52 |
| Rosehill Gdns., Feltham | 5C 38 |
| Rosehill Park West | 4C 38 |
| Rosehill Rd., Biggin Hill | 2E 77 |
| Rosehill Rd., Wandsworth | 1C 20 |
| Rosehill Farm Meadow | 1C 72 |
| Roseleigh Cl. | 1A 18 |
| Rosemary Av., Ash Vale | 2C 78 |
| Rosemary Av., West Molesey | 2C 34 |
| Rosemary Cl., Holland | 5A 94 |
| Rosemary Cl., West Heath | 5B 60 |
| Rosemary Court | 2A 128 |
| Rosemary Cres. | 3E 81 |
| Rosemary Gdns. | 5E 43 |
| Rosemary La., Alford | 2A 156 |
| Rosemary La., Blackwater | 5D 43 |
| Rosemary La., Charlwood | 4D 127 |
| Rosemary La., Farnham | 2C 114 |
| Rosemary La., Horley | 3B 128 |
| Rosemary La., Thorpe | 2E 31 |
| Rosemead Av., Feltham | 3F 15 |
| Rosemead Av., Mitcham | 1F 39 |
| Rosemead Cl. | 1D 109 |
| Rosemont Av. | 5D 49 |
| Rosemont Rd., New Malden | 2D 37 |
| Rosemount Rd., Richmond | 1B 18 |
| Rosendale Rd. | 2B 22 |
| Rosenheath Dr. | 5F 137 |
| Rosenheath Rd. | 1E 21 |
| Rosenthal Rd. | 1B 24 |
| Rosenthorpe Rd. | 1F 23 |
| Rosetrees | 1E 101 |
| Roseville Av. | 1C 16 |
| Rosevine Rd. | 1F 37 |
| Rosewarne Cl. | 2B 64 |
| Roseway | 1C 22 |
| Rosewood Dr. | 3D 33 |
| Rosewood Green | 5C 38 |
| Roslin Rd. | 1C 8 |
| Roslyn Cl. | 1D 39 |
| Ross Cl. | 5D 147 |
| Ross Parade | 2C 56 |
| Ross Rd., Beddington | 2C 56 |
| Ross Rd., Cobham | 5E 51 |
| Ross Rd., South Norwood | 2C 40 |
| Ross Wood Gdns. | 2C 56 |
| Rossdale | 1A 56 |
| Rosset Cl. | 2C 26 |
| Rossindel Rd. | 1C 16 |
| Rossiter Rd. | 2E 21 |
| Rosslyn Av., Barnes | 5E 9 |
| Rosslyn Av., Feltham | 1A 16 |
| Rosslyn Park | 1C 50 |
| Rosslyn Rd. | 1A 18 |
| Rostella Rd. | 4D 21 |
| Rostrevor Rd. | 4B 20 |
| Rosy Bottom | 1E 29 |
| Rothby Walk | 1A 62 |
| Rother Cres. | 4B 146 |
| Rother Rd. | 3B 60 |
| Rother Vale | 1B 128 |
| Rotherfield Av. | 1D 25 |
| Rotherfield Rd. | 1B 56 |
| Rothermere Rd. | 1D 57 |
| Rothes Rd. | 1A 106 |
| Rothesay Av., N. Sheen | 5C 8 |
| Rothesay Av., Wimbledon Chase | 1A 38 |
| Rothesay Rd. | 2C 40 |
| Rothschild St. | 4B 22 |
| Rougemont Av. | 3B 38 |
| Rough Field | 1B 150 |
| Rough La. | 1D 153 |
| Rough Rd. | 4F 63 |
| Rough Rew Estate | 3F 105 |
| Rough, The, | 1B 84 |
| Rough Way | 3C 158 |
| Roughetts La. | 3A 92 |

| Street | Ref |
|---|---|
| Round Gr. | 4F 41 |
| Round Hill | 3E 23 |
| Round Oak Rd. | 5D 33 |
| Roundhill Cl. | 3E 65 |
| Roundhill Dr. | 2E 65 |
| Roundhill Way, Chobham | 4A 52 |
| Roundhill Way, Woodbridge Hill | 5D 81 |
| Roundshaw | 2D 57 |
| Roundtable Rd. | 3C 24 |
| Roundthorn Way | 1A 64 |
| Roundway, Camberley | 5D 45 |
| Roundway, Egham | 4F 13 |
| Roundway Cl. | 5D 45 |
| Roundway, The | 2C 52 |
| Roundwood View | 1A 72 |
| Roundwood Way | 1A 72 |
| Roupell Rd. | 2A 22 |
| Rouse Gdns. | 4E 22 |
| Routh Rd. | 2D 21 |
| Row La. | 1F 121 |
| Row Town | 2D 49 |
| Rowan Av. | 4E 13 |
| Rowan Chase | 1D 115 |
| Rowan Cl., Camberley | 4B 44 |
| Rowan Cl., Ealing | 1B 8 |
| Rowan Cl., Guildford | 4D 81 |
| Rowan Cl., Mead Vale | 1C 108 |
| Rowan Cl., Crawley | 4D 147 |
| Rowan Cl., Feltham | 1A 16 |
| Rowan Cres. | 1F 39 |
| Rowan Gro. | 4E 73 |
| Rowan Rd., Brentford | 3A 8 |
| Rowan Rd., Mitcham | 1F 39 |
| Rowan Tree Rd. | 2E 17 |
| Rowans Cl. | 3B 60 |
| Rowans, The | 4F 15 |
| Rowbarns Way | 3C 84 |
| Rowbury | 5B 100 |
| Rowcroft Cl. | 3C 78 |
| Rowden Rd., Beckenham | 1F 41 |
| Rowden Rd., Ruxley | 1F 53 |
| Rowdown Cres. | 3F 59 |
| Rowe La. | 5E 63 |
| Rowfant Rd. | 2E 21 |
| Rowhill | 2D 49 |
| Rowhill Av. | 1C 96 |
| Rowhill Cres. | 1C 96 |
| Rowhills | 1B 96 |
| Rowhills Copse | 1B 96 |
| Rowhurst Av., Addlestone | 2E 49 |
| Rowhurst Av., Leatherhead | 2F 69 |
| Rowland Cres. | 4E 23 |
| Rowland Rd. | 1C 140 |
| Rowland Way | 5E 15 |
| Rowlands Cl. | 5F 129 |
| Rowledge | 2C 114 |
| Rowlls Rd. | 2C 36 |
| Rowly | 4E 121 |
| Rowly Dr. | 5D 121 |
| Rowplat La. | 1F 149 |
| Rowtown | 2D 49 |
| Roxborough Cl. | 1A 62 |
| Roxburgh Rd. | 4B 22 |
| Roxeth Ct. | 4D 15 |
| Roxford Cl. | 3F 33 |
| Roxley Rd. | 1B 24 |
| Roxton Gdns. | 1D 59 |
| Roxwell Rd. | 1E 9 |
| Roy Grove | 5D 17 |
| Royal Av. | 5E 37 |
| Royal Circus | 3B 22 |
| Royal Cl. | 5E 37 |
| Royal Dr. | 2F 71 |
| Royal Oak Rd. | 2C 64 |
| Royal Rd. | 4E 17 |
| Royal Wk. | 5E 39 |
| Royale Cl. | 1D 97 |
| Royston Av. | 4F 49 |
| Royston Av., The Wrythe | 5D 39 |
| Royston Av., Wallington | 1C 56 |
| Royston Cl., Crawley | 2E 147 |
| Royston Cl., Walton-on-Thames | 4A 34 |
| Royston Rd., Beckenham | 1F 41 |
| Royston Rd., Byfleet | 4F 49 |
| Royston Rd., Richmond | 1B 18 |
| Roystons, The | 3C 36 |
| Rozeldene | 5E 135 |
| Rubens St. | 3A 24 |
| Rudd Hall Rise | 1E 61 |
| Ruden Way | 1F 71 |
| Rudge Rd. | 1D 49 |
| Rudgwick Rd. | 3B 146 |
| Rudloe Rd. | 2F 21 |
| Ruffets Cl. | 2B 58 |
| Ruffets End | 5D 73 |

| Street | Ref |
|---|---|
| Ruffets, The | 2B 58 |
| Ruffetts Way | 2A 72 |
| Ruffwood | 3D 149 |
| Rugby La. | 3D 55 |
| Rugby Rd. | 1E 17 |
| Ruggles Brise Rd. | 4C 14 |
| Ruislip St. | 4D 21 |
| Runnemede Rd. | 4D 13 |
| Runnymede | 3D 13 |
| Runnymede Bridge | 4E 13 |
| Runnymede Cl. | 2D 17 |
| Runnymede Ct. | 4E 13 |
| Runnymede Cres. | 1A 40 |
| Runnymede Gdns. | 2D 17 |
| Runnymede Rd., Merton | 1C 38 |
| Runnymede Rd., Whitton | 1D 17 |
| Runwick La. | 5D 95 |
| Rupert Rd., Guildford | 1C 100 |
| Rupert Rd., Turnham Green | 1E 9 |
| Rural Way, Mitcham | 5F 21 |
| Rural Way, Redhill | 5B 90 |
| Ruscombe Way | 2F 15 |
| Rush Croft | 5B 100 |
| Rusham Park Av. | 5D 13 |
| Rusham Rd., Egham | 5D 13 |
| Rusham Rd., Wandsworth | 1E 21 |
| Rushams Rd. | 4A 158 |
| Rushden Cl. | 5C 22 |
| Rushden Way | 2B 96 |
| Rushdene Walk | 2E 77 |
| Rushett Cl. | 4A 36 |
| Rushett Dr. | 3A 106 |
| Rushett La. | 4D 53 |
| Rushett Rd. | 4A 36 |
| Rushetts Rd., Crawley | 2C 146 |
| Rushetts Rd., Woodhatch | 2C 108 |
| Rushey Green | 2A 24 |
| Rushey Mead | 1A 24 |
| Rushford Rd. | 1A 24 |
| Rushfords | 1F 131 |
| Rushley Cl. | 3D 37 |
| Rushmead Cl. | 1A 58 |
| Rusholme Gr. | 4D 23 |
| Rusholme Rd. | 1A 20 |
| Rushtall Av. | 2D 9 |
| Rushton Av. | 2F 111 |
| Rushworth Rd. | 5E 89 |
| Ruskin Av., East Bedfont | 1F 15 |
| Ruskin Av., Kew | 3C 8 |
| Ruskin Cl. | 3F 147 |
| Ruskin Dr. | 5F 37 |
| Ruskin Rd., Carshalton | 1B 56 |
| Ruskin Rd., Staines | 5A 14 |
| Ruskin Wk. | 1C 22 |
| Rusper Keep | 3B 146 |
| Rusper Rd., Capel | 1A 144 |
| Rusper Rd., Gossops Green | 4B 146 |
| Rusper Rd., Horsham | 4C 158 |
| Rusper Rd., Newdigate | 4F 125 |
| Russ Hill | 5C 126 |
| Russell Cl., Beckenham | 2B 42 |
| Russell Cl., Horsell | 1C 64 |
| Russell Cl., Walton | 1C 88 |
| Russell Ct. | 4A 70 |
| Russell Dr. | 1C 14 |
| Russell Green Cl. | 3E 57 |
| Russell Hill | 3D 57 |
| Russell Hill Rd. | 3E 57 |
| Russell Rd., Horsell | 1C 64 |
| Russell Rd., Shepperton | 4E 33 |
| Russell Rd., The Wrythe | 2D 39 |
| Russell Rd., Walton | 3A 34 |
| Russell Rd., Wimbledon | 5B 20 |
| Russell Way, Crawley | 4E 147 |
| Russell Way, Sutton | 1E 55 |
| Russells Cres. | 3B 128 |
| Russels | 4A 72 |
| Russet Cl., Stanwellmoor | 1A 14 |
| Russet Cl., Walton-on-Thames | 4B 34 |
| Russet Way | 3A 106 |
| Russett Cl., Caterham | 1A 92 |
| Russett Cl., Tongham | 1E 97 |
| Russett Gdns. | 1E 61 |
| Russington Rd. | 3E 33 |
| Russley Green | 4D 45 |
| Rusthall Cl. | 3E 41 |
| Rustic Av. | 5F 21 |
| Rustington Wk. | 4D 38 |
| Ruston Av. | 4C 36 |
| Rutford Rd. | 4A 22 |
| Ruthen Cl. | 5F 53 |
| Rutherford Way | 1E 147 |
| Rutherwick Cl. | 2A 128 |
| Rutherwick Rise | 2A 74 |
| Rutherwyck Cl. | 2C 54 |
| Rutherwyke Rd. | 4F 31 |

Rutland Cl., Ewell 3A 54
Rutland Cl., Chessington 2E 53
Rutland Cl., Redhill 5A 90
Rutland Dr. 3B 38
Rutland Gdns. 1A 58
Rutland Gro. 2F 9
Rutland Park 3A 24
Rutland Rd. 3E 17
Rutland Wk. 3A 24
Rutlish Rd. 1B 38
Rutson Rd. 5F 49
Rutton Hill Rd. 3B 136
Ruxbury Rd. 3F 31
Ruxley Cl. 1F 53
Ruxley Cres. 2D 53
Ruxley La. 2F 53
Ruxley Mews 1F 53
Ruxley Ridge 2C 52
Rycroft Av. 2D 17
Rycroft Rd., Lewisham 1B 24
Rycroft Rd., Streatham 5B 22
Rydal Cl., Camberley 5D 45
Rydal Cl., Purley 5F 57
Rydal Gdns. Coombe 4E 19
Rydal Gdns., Whitton 1D 17
Rydal Pl. 4F 45
Rydal Rd. 4F 21
Ryde Cl. 4B 66
Ryde Heron 2A 64
Ryde Vale Rd. 3E 21
Ryde, The 1B 32
Rydelands 1D 141
Rydens Av. 4D 81
Rydens Av. 5A 34
Rydens Cl. 5B 34
Rydens Gro. 1E 51
Rydens Pk. 5B 34
Rydens Rd. 5A 34
Rydens Way 3E 65
Rydes Cl. 3E 65
Rydes Hill Cres. 3D 81
Ryde's Hill Rd. 4D 81
Rydevale Rd. 3F 21
Rydon's La. 3B 74
Rydons Wood Cl. 3C 74
Rye Ash 3E 147
Rye Brook Rd. 2F 69
Rye Cl., Guildford 4D 81
Rye Cl., West Heath 3B 60
Rye Gro. 2B 46
Ryebridge Cl. 2F 69
Ryecroft Dr. 4A 158
Ryecrxoft Gdns. 1B 60
Ryedale 1E 23
Ryefield Rd., Norwood 5C 22
Ryefield Rd., Selsdon 5B 58
Ryelands 4B 146
Ryfold Rd. 3B 20
Ryland Cl. 4F 15
Rylandes Rd. 3B 58
Rylands Cl. 4C 74
Ryle Rd. 5A 96
Rylett Cres. 1E 9
Rylett Rd. 1E 9
Rymer Rd. 4D 41
Rymer St. 1B 22
Rythe Ct. 4F 35
Rythe Rd. 1B 52


S


Sackville Gdns. 1B 150
Sackville La. 1B 150
Sackville Rd. 2E 55
Saddleback Rd. 4B 44
Saddlewood 1D 61
Sadler Cl. 1D 39
Sadler Row 5D 147
Sadlers Cl. 5C 82
Sadlers Ridge 2D 35
Sadlers Scarp 5C 134
Sadlers Way 3D 71
Saffron Platt 3E 81
Saffron Rd. 2C 26
Saffron Way 4A 36
Sailors La. 2F 135
Sainfoin Rd. 3E 21
Sainsbury Rd. 4C 22
St. Agatha Dr. 5B 18
St. Agatha's Green 4D 39
St. Agbury Cl. 3D 73
St. Agnes Rd. 2C 150
St. Aidans Rd., Camberwell 1E 23
St. Aidans Rd., Ealing 1A 8
St. Albans Av., Acton 1D 9
St. Albans Av., Hanworth 4B 16
St. Albans Av., Weybridge 5D 33
St. Albans Cl. 5C 80
St. Alban's Gdns. 4F 17
St. Albans Gro. 4D 39
St. Albans Rd., Cheam 1E 55
St. Albans Rd., Kingston 5B 18
St. Albans Rd., Reigate 4E 89
St. Andrews 3B 26
St. Andrews Cl., Mead Vale 1C 108
St. Andrew's Cl., Old Windsor 1B 12
St. Andrew's Cl., Upper Halliford 2F 33
St. Andrew's Rd., Crawley 4A 146
St. Andrews Rd., Surbiton 3B 36
St. Andrews Rd., The Wrythe 5D 39
St. Andrew's Rd., Woodmansterne 1E 73
St. Andrew's Sq. 3A 36
St. Andrews Walk 1A 68
St. Andrews Way, Frimley 3E 61
St. Andrews Way, Limpsfield 3C 94
St. Anne's Av. 2C 14
St. Anne's Cl. 2D 45
St. Anne's Rd. 1E 119
St. Anns Cl. 3A 32
St. Ann's Cres. 1C 20
St. Ann's Hill 1C 20
St. Anns Hill Rd. 3F 31
St. Anns Rd. 3A 32
St. Anns Way 2E 57
St. Aubyn's Av., Whitton 1C 16
St. Aubyn's Av., Wimbledon 4B 20
St. Augustine's Av. 2E 57
St. Barnabas Rd., Sutton 1F 55
St. Barnabas Rd., Tooting 5E 21
St. Benet's Gro. 4C 38
St. Bredlade Cl. 1F 105
St. Catherines Cross 5F 91
St. Catherines Dr. 2C 100
St. Catherine's Estate 3C 64
St. Catherines Rd., Crawley 2F 147
St. Catherine's Rd., Frimley 2F 61
St. Christopher's Rd., Cove 5C 60
St. Christopher's Rd., Shottermill 3F 151
St. Clair Cl., Oxted 3E 93
St. Clair Cl., Reigate 5F 89
St. Clair Dr. 5F 37
St. Cloud Rd. 4C 22
St. Crispins Way 3C 48
St. Cross Rd., Frimley 3F 61
St. Davids 2A 74
St. Davids Cl., Hawley 3C 60
St. David's Cl., Heath End 1B 96
St. David's Cl., Reigate 5F 89
St. Davids Cl., W. Wickham 4A 42
St. Denis Rd. 4C 22
St. Denys Cl. 2F 63
St. Dunstan's Hill 1D 55
St. Dunstan's Rd., Feltham 3F 15
St. Dunstans Rd., South Norwood 2D 41
St. Edmund Cl. 2C 146
St. Edwards Cl. 2B 150
St. Elmo Rd. 1E 9
St. Fillans Rd. 2B 24
St. George's Av. 2A 50
St. George's Cl., Farnham 2C 96
St. George's Cl., Weybridge 1B 50
St. George's Gdns., Epsom 5B 54
St. George's Gdns., Horsham 4C 158
St. George's La. 2C 28
St. George's Lo. 1B 50
St. George's Rd., Addlestone 1E 49
St. Georges Rd., Beckenham 1A 42
St. George's Rd., Camberley 5A 44
St. George's Rd., East End 5A 78
St. George's Rd., Farnham 4B 96
St. George's Rd., Badshot Lea Rd., Farnham 2D 97
St. George's Rd., Hanworth 4B 16
St. Georges Rd., Kingston 5C 18
St. George's Rd., Mitcham 2E 39
St. Georges Rd., Richmond 5B 8
St. Georges Rd., Twickenham 1A 18
St. Georges Rd., Salfords 4F 109
St. George's Rd., Weybridge 2B 50
St. George's Rd., Wimbledon 5B 20
St. Germans Rd. 2F 23
St. Gothard Rd. 4C 22
St. Helens Cr. 4D 43
St. Helens Rd. 1A 40
St. Helier Av. 4C 38
St. Helier Cl. 3D 25
St. Helier's Av. 1C 16
St. Hilda's Av. 4C 14
St. Hilda's Cl., Horley 2B 128
St. Hilda's Cl., Three Bridges 2F 147
St. Hilda's Cl., Woking 2A 64
Saint Hill Rd. 3C 150
St. Hughes Cl. 2F 147
St. Hugh's Rd. 5E 23
St. James Av., Cheam 1E 55
St. James Av., Elmers End 2F 41
St. James Av., Epsom 4B 54
St. James' Av., Farnham 3B 96
St. James Cl. 2B 64
St. James Rd., Cheam 1E 55
St. James Rd., East Grinstead 2C 150
St. James' Rd., Kingston 1B 36
St. James' Rd., Purley 5E 57
St. James' Rd., Surbiton 3B 36
St. James Rd., The Wrythe 5D 39
St. James Rd., Tooting 5E 21
St. James' Ter. 3A 96
St. James Wk. 1B 7
St. James's Av., Hampton Hill 4D 17
St. James's Cl. 5A 54
St. James's Dr. 2D 21
St. James's Pk. 4B 40
St. James's Pl. 1B 140
St. James's Rd., Croydon 4B 40
St. James's Rd., Hampton Hill 4D 17
St. Joan Cl. 2C 147
St. Johns Av., Epsom 4B 54
St. John's Av., Leatherh'd. 4A 70
St. John's Av., Putney 1A 20
St. John's Cl., Guildford 1B 100
St. John's Cl., Horsham 5C 158
St. John's Cl., Leatherhead 4A 70
St. John's Ct. 4E 63
St. John's Dr. 4B 34
St. Johns Gro. 5B 8
St. Johns Hill, Coulsdon 2B 74
St. Johns Hill, Purley 1B 74
St. Johns Hill, Wandsworth 1C 20
St. John's Hill Rd. 3B 64
St. John's Lye 3A 64
St. John's Meadow 5F 111
St. John's Rise 3B 64
St. John's Rd., Earlswood 1D 109
St. John's Rd., East Grinstead 2C 150
St. John's Rd., E. Molesey 2E 35
St. John's Rd., Goldsworth 2B 64
St. Johns Rd., Guildford 1B 100
St. Johns Rd., Hampton Wick 1A 36
St. Johns Rd., Hanworth 4C 16
St. John's Rd., Kingston 2D 37
St. John's Rd., Leatherh'd 4A 70
St. John's Rd., N. Holmwood 3A 106
St. John's Rd., Penge 5E 23
St. John's Rd., Richmond 5B 8
St. John's Rd., Sandhurst 4D 43
St. John's Rd., Sutton Common 5B 38
St. John's Rd., The Wrythe 5D 39
St. Johns Rd., West Heath 4B 60
St. John's Rd., Westcott 2D 105
St. Johns Rd., Wimbledon 5A 20
St. John's Rd., Wrecclesham 5A 96
St. John's St. 1D 119
St. John's Ter. Rd. 1D 109
St. Jude's Cl. 4C 12
St. Jude's Rd. 4C 12
St. Julians Cl. 4B 22
St. Julians Farm Rd. 4B 22
St. Katherines Rd. 1A 92
St. Leonard's Hill 1D 11
St. Leonard's Rd., Burgh Heath 3F 71
St. Leonard's Rd., Claygate 2C 52
St. Leonard's Rd., Hinchley Wood 3F 35
St. Leonards Rd., Horsham 5C 158
St. Leonards Rd., Long Ditton 3A 36
St. Leonards Rd., North Sheen 5C 8
St. Leonards Walk 1B 7
St. Louis Rd. 4C 22
St. Luke's Rd., Old Windsor 1B 12
St. Luke's Rd., Whyteleafe 2D 75
St. Margarets 5A 82
St. Margarets Av., Ashford 4E 15
St. Margaret's Av., Cheam 5A 38
St. Margaret's Av., Dormans Park 5F 131
St. Margaret's Gro. 1F 17
St. Margaret's Rd., Chipstead 4E 73
St. Margarets Rd., Coulsdon 4E 73
St. Margarets Rd., East Grinstead 1C 150
St. Margaret's Rd., Elmers End 2F 41
St. Margarets Rd., Richmond 1F 17
St. Mark's Hill 3B 36
St. Marks Pl. 1A 96
St. Mark's Rd., Burgh Heath 2A 72
St. Mark's Rd., Mitcham 1E 39
St. Marks Rd., Popeswood 1B 26
St. Marks Rd., Teddington 5A 18
St. Martha's Av. 4D 65
St. Martin's Av. 5B 54
St. Martin's Cl., E. Horsley 3C 84
St. Martin's Cl., Epsom 5B 54
St. Martin's Dr. 5B 34
St. Marys Av., Hackbridge 5E 39
St. Mary's Av., Shortlands 2C 42
St. Mary's Av., Stanwell 2C 14
St. Mary's Av., Teddington 5F 17
St. Mary's Cl., Chess'n 2E 53
St. Mary's Cl., Fetcham 5E 69
St. Mary's Cl., Oxted 3F 93
St. Mary's Cl., Stanwell 2C 14
St. Mary's Cl., Upper Halliford 2A 3
St. Mary's Cl., West Ewell 2B 54
St. Mary's Cres. 2C 14
St. Mary's Dr., Crawley 3F 147
St. Mary's Dr., E. Bedfont 2E 15
St. Mary's Gdns. 2E 45
St. Mary's Gro., Barnes 5F 9
St. Mary's Gro., Biggin Hill 2E 77
St. Mary's Gro., Chiswick 3C 8
St. Mary's Gro., Richmond 5B 8
St. Mary's Hill 3C 28
St. Mary's Rd., Ash Vale 3C 78
St. Mary's Rd., Camberley 5A 44
St. Mary's Rd., Ealing 1A 8
St. Mary's Rd., East Molesey 3E 35
St. Mary's Rd., Horsell 2C 64
St. Mary's Rd., Leatherhead 5A 70
St. Mary's Rd., Mead Vale 1C 108
St. Mary's Rd., Merton 1B 38
St. Mary's Rd., Sanderstead 3F 57
St. Mary's Rd., South Ascot 3C 28
St. Mary's Rd., South Norwood 2C 40
St. Mary's Rd., Southborough 4A 36
St. Mary's Rd., Weybridge 1B 50
St. Mary's Rd., Wimbledon 4A 20
St. Mary's Rd., Worcester Pk. 5E 37
St. Mathews La. 4A 14
St. Matthews Av. 4B 36
St. Matthew's Rd., Brixton Hill 1A 22
St. Matthews Rd., Redhill 5A 90
St. Michaels Av., Guildford 3C 80
St. Michaels Cl. 5B 34
St. Michaels Rd., Ashford 4D 15
St. Michael's Rd., Beddington 2C 56
St. Michael's Rd., Camberley 5A 44
St. Michael's Rd., East End 5A 78
St. Michaels Rd., Caterham 4C 74
St. Michaels Rd., Farnborough Street 4D 61
St. Michaels Rd., Woking 5C 48
St. Mildreds Rd., Guildford 5A 82
St. Mildreds Rd., Hither Green 2C 24
St. Monica's Rd. 4B 72
St. Nicholas Av., Eastwick 1A 86
St. Nicholas Cl. 1C 140
St. Nicholas Dr. 4D 33
St. Nicholas Glebe 4E 21
St. Nicholas Hill 4A 70
St. Nicholas Rd. 3F 35
St. Nicholas Way 1F 55
St. Nicolas Av., Cranleigh 1C 140
St. Normans Way 3C 54
St. Olave's Cl. 5A 14
St. Omer Ridge 1E 101
St. Omer Rd. 1E 101
St. Oswald's Rd. 1B 40
St. Paul's Cl., Ashford 4E 15
St. Paul's Cl., Chessington 1E 53
St. Paul's Gate 2D 25
St. Paul's Rd., Brentford 3A 8
St. Paul's Rd., Dorking 2F 105
St. Paul's Rd., Hythe 4F 13
St. Paul's Rd., Maybury 2E 65
St. Paul's Rd., Richmond 5B 8
St. Paul's Rd., Thornton Heath 2C 40
St. Peters Cl., Byfleet 4F 49
St. Peter's Cl., Old Windsor 1B 12
St. Peter's Cl., Old Woking 3E 65
St. Peter's Cl., Staines 5A 14
St. Peters Mead 5C 78
St. Peter's Rd., Hammersmith 2E 9
St. Peter's Rd., Kingston 1C 36
St. Peter's Rd., Richmond 1A 18
St. Peter's Rd., South Croydon 1F 57
St. Peters Rd., West Green 4C 146
St. Peter's Rd., Woking 4E 65
St. Peter's Sq. 2E 9
St. Peter's St. 1F 57
St. Peters Way, Addlestone 5B 32
St. Peters Way, Frimley 3E 61

| Street | Ref. | Street | Ref. |
|---|---|---|---|
| Selworthy Rd. | 3A 24 | Shaw Way | 2D 57 |
| Selwyn Av. | 5B 8 | Shawbury Rd. | 1D 23 |
| Selwyn Rd. | 3D 37 | Shawfield La. | 5B 78 |
| Semaphore Rd. | 1D 101 | Shawfield Rd. | 5B 78 |
| Semley Rd. | 1A 40 | Shawford Rd. | 2A 54 |
| Send | 5F 65 | Shawley Cres. | 2A 72 |
| Send Barns La. | 5F 65 | Shawley Way | 2F 71 |
| Send Cl. | 5F 65 | Shaws Rd. | 3D 147 |
| Send Hill | 5F 65 | Shaxton Cres. | 3E 59 |
| Send Marsh Rd. | 5F 65 | Sheath's La. | 5A 52 |
| Send Rd. | 4E 65 | Sheen Common Dr. | 1C 18 |
| Sendmarsh | 5A 66 | Sheen Court Rd. | 5C 8 |
| Seneca | 2B 40 | Sheen Gate Gdns. | 5D 9 |
| Senga Rd. | 4E 39 | Sheen La. | 1D 19 |
| Senhouse Rd. | 5A 38 | Sheen Pk. | 5B 8 |
| Serpentine Green | 3C 90 | Sheen Rd. | 1B 18 |
| Serrin Way | 3C 158 | Sheendale Rd. | 5B 8 |
| Seven Hills Cl. | 3C 50 | Sheene Wood | 4E 23 |
| Seven Hills Rd. | 5C 50 | Sheep House | 5A 96 |
| Sevenoaks Rd. | 1F 23 | Sheep Wk., Headley | 4D 71 |
| Severn Cl. | 4D 43 | Sheep Wk., Shepperton Green | 4D 33 |
| Severn Dr., Hinchley Wood | 5F 35 | Sheepbarn La. | 4F 59 |
| Severn Dr., Walton-on-Thames | 5B 34 | Sheepfold Rd. | 4E 81 |
| Severn Rd. | 4B 60 | Sheephatch La. | 1A 116 |
| Seward Rd. | 1F 41 | Sheephouse Green | 3C 104 |
| Sewell Av. | 1D 25 | Sheephouse La. | 3C 104 |
| Sewill Cl. | E4 127 | Sheephouse Way | 4D 37 |
| Seymour Av., Ewell | 3C 54 | Sheeplands Av. | 4C 82 |
| Seymour Av., Morden | 4A 38 | Sheepwalk La. | 5C 84 |
| Seymour Cl. | 3D 35 | Sheerwater Av. | 4D 49 |
| Seymour Gdns., Hanworth | 4A 16 | Sheerwater Rd. | 4C 48 |
| Seymour Gdns., Surbiton | 3B 36 | Sheet Street Rd. | 4D 11 |
| Seymour Gdns., Twickenham | 2F 17 | Sheffield Cl. Crawley | 5E 147 |
| Seymour Rd., Carshalton | 1B 56 | Sheffield Cl., Stanwellmoor | 1A 14 |
| Seymour Rd., Chiswick | 2D 9 | Shefford Cres. | 1E 25 |
| Seymour Rd., Crawley | 5C 146 | Shelbury Rd. | 1E 23 |
| Seymour Rd., East Molesey | 3D 35 | Sheldon Cl. | 1C 108 |
| Seymour Rd., Hackbridge | 4E 39 | Sheldrick Cl. | 1C 38 |
| Seymour Rd., Hampton Hill | 4D 17 | Shelley Av. | 1E 27 |
| Seymour Rd., Hampton Wick | 1A 36 | Shelley Cl., Banstead | 1A 72 |
| Seymour Rd., Headley Down | 5A 134 | Shelley Cl., Three Bridges | 3F 147 |
| Seymour Rd., Ockford Ridge | 2C 118 | Shelley Rd., E. Grinstead | 2B 150 |
| Seymour Rd., Wandsworth | 1B 20 | Shelley Rd., Horsham | 4A 158 |
| Seymour Rd., Wimbledon | 3A 20 | Shellwood Rd. | 4D 107 |
| Seymour Villas | 1E 41 | Shelson Av. | 3F 15 |
| Seymour Way | 5F 15 | Shelton Av. & Cl. Warlingham | 2E 75 |
| Shackleford | 5D 99 | Shelton Cl., Guildford | 3E 81 |
| Shackleford Rd., Elstead | 2E 117 | Shelton Rd. | 1B 38 |
| Shackleford Rd., Shackleford | 5D 99 | Shelvers Green | 4F 71 |
| Shackleford Rd., Woking | 4E 65 | Shelvers Hill | 4F 71 |
| Shacklegate La. | 4E 17 | Shelvers Spur | 4F 71 |
| Shackleton Rd. | 5D 147 | Shelvers Way | 4A 72 |
| Shackstead La. | 2C 118 | Shelwood Dr. | 3A 106 |
| Shadbolt Cl. | 5E 37 | Shepherd Cl. | 5D 147 |
| Shadyhanger Rd. | 1D 119 | Shepherd's Cl., Bagshot | 3D 45 |
| Shaftesbury Av. | 2A 16 | Shepherds Cl., Shepperton | 3D 33 |
| Shaftesbury Cl. | 3D 27 | Shepherds Hill, Haslemere | 3A 152 |
| Shaftesbury Cres. | 5C 14 | Shepherds Hill, Merstham | 1C 90 |
| Shaftesbury Rd., Beckenham | 1A 42 | Shepherd's Hill, Stoughton | 4E 81 |
| Shaftesbury Rd., Bisley | 1E 63 | Shepherd's La. | 4E 81 |
| Shaftesbury Rd., Woking | 2E 65 | Shepherds Wk., Ashtead | 3C 70 |
| Shaftesbury Way | 3E 17 | Shepherds Walk, Fox Lane | 3B 60 |
| Shaftsbury Rd., Richmond | 5B 8 | Shepherds Way, Selsdon | 2C 58 |
| Shaftsbury Rd., The Wrythe | 4D 39 | Shepherds Way, Tilford | 2A 116 |
| Shakespeare Av. | 1A 16 | Shepley Cl. | 5E 39 |
| Shakespeare Rd., Addlestone | 1F 49 | Shepley Dr. | 3F 29 |
| Shakespeare Rd., Herne Hill | 1B 22 | Shepley End | 3F 29 |
| Shakespeare Way | 4B 16 | Shepperton | 3E 33 |
| Shalbourne Rise | 5B 44 | Shepperton Ct. Dr. | 3D 33 |
| Shaldon Dr. | 3A 38 | Shepperton Grn. | 2D 33 |
| Shaldon Way | 5B 34 | Shepperton Rd. | 2B 32 |
| Shale Green | 3C 90 | Sheraton Cl. | 1B 60 |
| Shalford | 3D 101 | Sheraton Dr. | 4A 54 |
| Shalford Rd. | 2C 100 | Sherborne Cl. | 4B 7 |
| Shalston Villas | 3B 36 | Sherborne Cres. | 4D 39 |
| Shalstone Rd. | 5C 8 | Sherborne Rd., East Bedfont | 2E 15 |
| Shambles, The, Guildford | 159 | Sherborne Rd., South Farnborough | 1A 78 |
| Shamley Grn. | 2D 121 | Sherborne Rd., Sutton Common | 5B 38 |
| Shamrock Cl., Fetcham | 4E 69 | Sherbourne Cl. | 2F 71 |
| Shamrock Cl., Frimley | 3E 61 | Sherbourne Dr. | 3A 30 |
| Shamrock Rd. | 3A 40 | Sherbourne Rd., Chessington | 1E 53 |
| Shandon Rd. | 1F 21 | Shere | 2D 103 |
| Shandys Cl. | 5A 158 | Shere Av. | 3C 54 |
| Shap Cres. | 4D 39 | Shere Cl., Chessington | 1E 53 |
| Shardcroft Av. | 1B 22 | Shere Cl., Dorking | 3A 106 |
| Sharon Cl., Bookham | 5C 68 | Shere La. | 3D 103 |
| Sharon Cl., Crawley | 5E 147 | Shere Rd., Albury | 1B 102 |
| Sharon Cl., Epsom | 5A 54 | Shere Rd., Ewhurst | 4B 122 |
| Sharon Cl., Long Ditton | 4A 36 | Shere Rd., W. Horsley | 3B 84 |
| Shaw Cl., Ewell | 4B 54 | Sherfield Gdns. | 1E 19 |
| Shaw Cl., Ottershaw | 2C 48 | Sheridan Pl. | 2B 150 |
| Shaw Cl. | 4A 58 | Sheridan Rd., Eastwick | 1A 86 |
| Shaw Ct. | 1B 12 | Sheridan Rd., Frimley | 3D 61 |
| Shaw Cres. | 4A 58 | Sheridan Rd., Ham | 3A 18 |
| Shaw Pk. | 2D 43 | Sheridan Rd., Merton | 1B 38 |
| Shaw Rd., Southend | 3C 24 | | |
| Shaw Rd., Tatsfield | 3E 77 | | |

| Street | Ref. | Street | Ref. |
|---|---|---|---|
| Sheridans Rd. | 1A 86 | Shurbland Gro. | 5F 37 |
| Sheringham Av., Feltham | 3A 16 | Shute End | 2D 25 |
| Sheringham Av., Whitton | 2C 16 | Sibthorp Rd. | 1D 39 |
| Sheringham Rd. | 2E 41 | Sibton Rd. | 4D 39 |
| Sherland Rd. | 2F 17 | Sickle Mill Rd. | 3E 151 |
| Sherrydon | 1D 141 | Sickle Rd. | 3F 151 |
| Sherwin Cres. | 3D 61 | Siddons Rd., Croydon | 5B 40 |
| Sherwood Av. | 5F 21 | Siddons Rd., Lewisham | 3F 23 |
| Sherwood Cl., Bracknell | 1F 27 | Side View | 5A 128 |
| Sherwood Cl., Fetcham | 4D 69 | Sidlaws Rd. | 3B 60 |
| Sherwood Cres. | 2C 108 | Sidney Rd., Beckenham | 1F 41 |
| Sherwood Park Rd., Mitcham | 2F 39 | Sidney Rd., Staines | 4A 14 |
| Sherwood Park Rd., Sutton | 1E 55 | Sidney Rd., Twickenham | 1F 17 |
| Sherwood Rd., Addiscombe | 4E 41 | Sidney Rd., Walton | 5A 34 |
| Sherwood Rd., Hampton Hill | 4D 17 | Sidney Rd., Woodside | 3D 41 |
| Sherwood Rd., Woking | 2A 64 | Signal Cl. | 2F 131 |
| Sherwood Rd., Woodmansterne | 1F 73 | Silkham Rd. | 2F 93 |
| Sherwood Wk. | 5E 147 | Silkmore La. | 2A 84 |
| Sherwood Way | 5B 42 | Silo Cl. | 5B 100 |
| Shetland Cl. | 3A 148 | Silo Dr. | 5B 100 |
| Shield Rd. | 4E 15 | Silo Rd. | 5A 100 |
| Shilburn Way | 2B 64 | Silver Birch Cl. | 4D 49 |
| Shildon Cl. | 1A 62 | Silver Birches Way | 2E 117 |
| Shillinglee La. | 4A 154 | Silver Cres. | 2C 8 |
| Ship Alley | 4D 61 | Silver Dr. | 1A 62 |
| Ship Hill | 4E 77 | Silver Hill | 4E 43 |
| Ship La., Farnborough Street | 4D 61 | Silver La., West Wickham | 5B 42 |
| Ship La., Mortlake | 4D 9 | Silver La., Woodcote | 4C 56 |
| Ship St. | 3C 150 | Silver Tree Cl. | 1D 51 |
| Shipfield Fl. | 4E 77 | Silverdale | 4E 23 |
| Shipka Rd. | 2E 21 | Silverdale Av., Oxshott | 5A 52 |
| Shipley Church Rd. | 5F 41 | Silverdale Av., Walton | 5F 33 |
| Shipley Rd. | 3B 146 | Silverdale Cl., Beckenham | 5A 24 |
| Shipleybridge | 5D 129 | Silverdale Cl., Cheam | 1E 55 |
| Shipleybridge La. | 1A 148 | Silverdale Cl., Strood Green | 2C 106 |
| Shipman Rd. | 3F 23 | Silverdale Ct. | 4B 14 |
| Shire Cl. | 3E 45 | Silverdale Dr. | 1A 34 |
| Shires Cl. | 2A 70 | Silverlea Gdns. | 3C 128 |
| Shires Ho. | 5F 49 | Silverleigh Rd. | 2A 40 |
| Shirley Av., Addiscombe | 4E 41 | Silvermere Rd. | 2A 24 |
| Shirley Av., Belmont | 3E 55 | Silversmiths Way | 2C 64 |
| Shirley Av., Carshalton | 1A 56 | Silverstone Cl. | 4A 90 |
| Shirley Av., Old Coulsdon | 3B 74 | Silverwood Dr. | 4C 44 |
| Shirley Av., Salfords | 3E 109 | Silvester Rd. | 1D 23 |
| Shirley Church Rd. | 1C 58 | Silwood | 4B 26 |
| Shirley Cl. | 1D 17 | Silwood Cl. | 1D 29 |
| Shirley Cres. | 2F 41 | Silwood Rd. | 2E 29 |
| Shirley Dr. | 1D 17 | Simmil Rd. | 1B 52 |
| Shirley Hills Rd. | 1B 58 | Simms Cl. | 5D 39 |
| Shirley Park Rd. | 4E 41 | Simondstone La. | 2B 124 |
| Shirley Pl. | 2F 63 | Simone Dr. | 1C 74 |
| Shirley Rd., Addiscombe | 4E 41 | Simons Cl. | 2B 48 |
| Shirley Rd., Woodcote | 3C 56 | Simons Walk | 5C 12 |
| Shirley Way | 5F 41 | Simplemarsh Rd. | 1D 49 |
| Shophouse La. | 1F 121 | Simpson Rd., Ham | 4A 18 |
| Shoppe Hill | 4D 139 | Simpson Rd., Whitton | 1C 16 |
| Shord Hill | 1C 74 | Sine Cl. | 3C 60 |
| Shore Cl. | 2A 16 | Sinhurst Rd. | 1C 60 |
| Shore Gro. | 3C 16 | Sion Rd. | 2F 17 |
| Shoreham Cl. | 3E 41 | Siskin Cl. | 3C 158 |
| Shoreham Rd. | 1C 14 | Sispara Gdns. | 1B 20 |
| Shoreham St. | 1C 20 | Sistova Rd. | 2E 21 |
| Shores Rd. | 5A 48 | Siward Rd. | 3C 20 |
| Shorndean St. | 2B 24 | Sixth Cross Av. | 3D 17 |
| Short Cl. | 3D 147 | Skeena Hill | 2A 20 |
| Short La., Hurst Green | 4A 94 | Skelbrook St. | 3C 20 |
| Short La., West Bedfont | 2D 15 | Skidhill La. | 5F 59 |
| Short Way | 2D 17 | Skiff Rd. | 5A 156 |
| Shortcroft Rd. | 2B 54 | Skimped Hill | 1C 26 |
| Shortdale Rd. | 2D 97 | Skimpedhill La. | 1C 26 |
| Shortfield Rd. | 3D 115 | Skinner's La., Lower Ashtead | 2A 70 |
| Shortheath Cres. | 1C 114 | Skinners La., Chiddingfold | 4A 138 |
| Shortheath Rd. | 5A 96 | Skipton Way | 1B 128 |
| Shortlands | 3D 115 | Slade Ct., | 2C 48 |
| Shortlands Gdns. | 1C 42 | Slade Rd., Brookwood | 3D 63 |
| Shortlands Gro. | 2B 42 | Slade Rd., Ottershaw | 2C 48 |
| Shortlands Rd., Kingston | 5C 18 | Slapleys | 3D 64 |
| Shortlands Rd., Shortlands | 2B 42 | Slines Grn. | 2A 76 |
| Short's La. | 3C 154 | Slines New Rd. | 3F 75 |
| Shorts Rd. | 1A 56 | Slines Oak Rd. | 3A 76 |
| Shortsfield Cl. | 3B 158 | Slinfold Wk. | 4B 146 |
| Shortwood Av. | 4B 14 | Slip Rd. | 4D 99 |
| Shotfield | 2B 56 | Slipshatch Rd. | 2A 108 |
| Shottermill | 3E 151 | Slipshoe St. | 5E 89 |
| Shottermill Rd. | 3E 151 | Sloane Walk | 3F 41 |
| Shrewsbury Cl. | 5B 36 | Slough La., Buckland | 4C 88 |
| Shrewsbury Rd., Elmers End | 2F 41 | Slough La., Headley | 1A 88 |
| Shrewsbury Rd., Redhill | 5A 90 | Slyfield | 3A 82 |
| Shrewsbury Rd., St. Helier | 4D 39 | Slyfield Green | 3F 81 |
| Shrivenham Cl. | 4E 43 | Smallfield | 3E 129 |
| Shroffold Rd. | 4C 24 | Smallfield Rd., Horley | 2B 128 |
| Shrubbery Rd. | 4A 22 | Smallfield Rd., Horne | 3A 130 |
| Shrubbs Hill La. | 3F 29 | Smallholdings Rd. | 5C 54 |
| Shrubbs Rd. | 2C 114 | Smallmead | 2C 128 |
| Shrubland Rd. | 1B 72 | Small's Hill Rd. | 1D 127 |
| Shrublands Av. | 5A 42 | Smalls Mead | 4C 146 |
| Shrublands Dr. | 4F 45 | Smallwood Rd. | 4C 20 |

| Street | Ref |
|---|---|
| Smarts Heath La. | 5B 64 |
| Smarts Heath Rd. | 5B 64 |
| Smeaton Rd. | 2B 20 |
| Smith Barn Cl. | 2B 128 |
| Smith Cl. | 5D 147 |
| Smith Rd. | 2B 108 |
| Smith Sq. | 1D 27 |
| Smith St. | 3B 36 |
| Smitham Downs Rd. | 5C 56 |
| Smithambottom La. | 4C 56 |
| Smithbarn | 4C 158 |
| Smithers, The | 1C 106 |
| Smithfield La. | 2F 133 |
| Smiths La. | 5B 80 |
| Smithwood Av. | 4E 121 |
| Smithwood Cl. | 2A 20 |
| Smithwood Common Rd. | 4E 121 |
| Smithy Cl. | 1E 89 |
| Smithy La. | 1E 89 |
| Smoke La. | 1C 108 |
| Smokejack Hill Rd. | 3B 142 |
| Smugglers Way | 5E 97 |
| Snailslynch | 4B 96 |
| Snatts Hill | 3F 93 |
| Snell Hatch | 4C 146 |
| Snellings Rd. | 1E 51 |
| Snow Hill | 1D 149 |
| Snow's Ride | 1F 45 |
| Snowdenham La. | 1A 120 |
| Snowdenham Links Rd. | 1F 119 |
| Snowdrop Way | 2E 63 |
| Snowerhill Rd. | 1E 107 |
| Snows Paddock | 5C 28 |
| Soames Walk | 1E 37 |
| Solartron | 5C 60 |
| Soldiers Rise | 5E 25 |
| Sole Farm Av. | 1F 85 |
| Sole Farm Rd. | 1F 85 |
| Solecote | 1F 85 |
| Solent Rd. | 1D 15 |
| Solom's Court Rd. | 2D 73 |
| Somerfield Cl. | 3A 72 |
| Somers Rd., Reigate | 5E 89 |
| Somers Rd., Tulse Hill | 1A 22 |
| Somerset Av., Chessington | 1D 53 |
| Somerset Av., Raynes Pk. | 1F 37 |
| Somerset Cl., Ewell | 3A 54 |
| Somerset Cl., Malden | 3E 37 |
| Somerset Rd., Acton | 1D 9 |
| Somerset Rd., Brentford | 3A 8 |
| Somerset Rd., Fulwell | 4E 17 |
| Somerset Rd., Kingston | 1C 36 |
| Somerset Rd., Redhill | 1D 109 |
| Somerset Rd., South Farnborough | 1A 78 |
| Somerset Rd., Wimbledon | 3A 20 |
| Somerset Way | 1B 7 |
| Somerswey | 4D 101 |
| Somerton Av. | 5C 8 |
| Somerton Cl. | 1B 74 |
| Somertons Cl. | 4B 81 |
| Somerville Dr. | 2F 147 |
| Somerville Rd., Oxshott | 5A 52 |
| Somerville Rd., Penge | 5F 23 |
| Somme Rd. | 2A 62 |
| Sommerfield La. | 5A 36 |
| Sondes Place Dr. | 1E 105 |
| Soning Rd. | 3D 41 |
| Sopwith Way | 2D 57 |
| Sorrel Bank | 3C 58 |
| Sorrel Dr. | 4E 45 |
| Sorrel Rd. | 3C 158 |
| Sorrento Rd. | 5B 38 |
| South Albert Rd. | 5E 89 |
| South Av., Carshalton | 2B 56 |
| South Av., Hale | 2B 96 |
| South Av., Thorpe Lea | 5F 13 |
| South Bank | 3B 36 |
| South Border | 4D 57 |
| South Cl., Woking | 1C 64 |
| South Cl., Wokingham | 2E 25 |
| South Close Green | 3B 90 |
| South Croft Av. | 5B 42 |
| South Croxted Rd. | 3C 22 |
| South Dr., Banstead | 5A 56 |
| South Dr., Cheam | 3D 55 |
| South Dr., Cotmandene | 1A 106 |
| South Dr., Virginia Water | 4B 30 |
| South Dr., Wokingham | 2E 25 |
| South Dr., Woodmansterne | 5A 56 |
| South Ealing Rd. | 1A 8 |
| South Eden Park Rd. | 3A 42 |
| South End, Bookham | 1A 86 |
| South End, South Croydon | 1F 57 |
| South Gdns. | 5D 21 |
| South Godstone | 3F 111 |
| South Gro., Chertsey | 3A 32 |
| South Grove, Horsham | 5B 158 |
| South Hill, Godalming | 2D 119 |
| South Hill, Guildford | 1C 100 |
| South Hill Rd., Easthampstead | 3D 27 |
| South Hill Rd., Shortlands | 2C 42 |
| South Holmwood | 5A 106 |
| South La., Ash | 5C 78 |
| South La., Kingston | 2B 36 |
| South La., Malden | 2D 37 |
| South Lane West | 2D 37 |
| South Lodge Av. | 2A 40 |
| South Lynn Cres. | 3C 26 |
| South Munstead La. | 4E 119 |
| South Norwood Hill | 1D 41 |
| South Nutfield | 1A 110 |
| South Parade, Bedford Park | 2D 9 |
| South Parade, Horley | 2B 128 |
| South Park Cres. | 2C 24 |
| South Park Gro. | 2D 37 |
| South Park Hill Rd. | 1F 57 |
| South Park Rd. | 5B 20 |
| South Pl. | 4B 36 |
| South Ridge | 3A 50 |
| South Rise | 3A 56 |
| South Rd., Bisley | 1E 63 |
| South Rd., Bracknell | 4B 26 |
| South Rd., Brentford | 2A 8 |
| South Rd., Brooklands | 3A 50 |
| South Rd., Englefield Grn. | 5C 12 |
| South Rd., Hampton | 5C 16 |
| South Rd., Hanworth | 4B 16 |
| South Rd., Horsell | 1C 64 |
| South Rd., Lewisham | 2F 23 |
| South Rd., Mead Vale | 1C 108 |
| South Rd., Stoughton | 4E 81 |
| South Rd., Twickenham | 3E 17 |
| South Rd., Weybridge | 1B 50 |
| South Rd., Wimbledon | 5C 20 |
| South Side, Stamford Brook | 1E 9 |
| South Side, Tongham | 1E 97 |
| South St., Dorking | 2F 105 |
| South St., Epsom | 5A 54 |
| South St., Farnham | 4A 96 |
| South St., Godalming | 2D 119 |
| South St., Horsham | 5B 158 |
| South St., South Farnborough | 1B 78 |
| South St., Staines | 4A 14 |
| South Terrace, Dorking | 2F 105 |
| South Ter., Surbiton | 3B 36 |
| South Vale | 5C 22 |
| South View Rd., Ashtead | 3B 70 |
| South View Rd., Beech Hill | 4A 134 |
| South View, Selsdon | 3C 58 |
| South Wk., W. Wickham | 5C 42 |
| South Walk, Reigate | 5F 89 |
| South Way, Blackwater | 1C 60 |
| South Way, Shirley | 5F 41 |
| South Western Rd. | 1F 17 |
| South Worple Way | 5D 9 |
| Southampton Cl. | 5D 43 |
| Southampton Rd. | 1D 15 |
| Southampton St. | 2A 78 |
| Southbank | 4A 36 |
| Southborough Cl. | 4B 36 |
| Southborough Rd. | 4B 36 |
| Southbridge Pl. | 1E 57 |
| Southbridge Rd. | 1E 57 |
| Southbrook Rd., Hither Green | 1C 24 |
| Southbrook Rd., Norbury | 1A 40 |
| Southcote | 1C 64 |
| Southcote Av. | 4C 36 |
| Southcote Dr. | 5C 44 |
| Southcote Rd., Merstham | 3C 90 |
| Southcote Rd., Selsdon | 3A 58 |
| Southcote Rd., Woodside | 3E 41 |
| Southcroft Rd. | 5E 21 |
| Southdean Gdns. | 3B 20 |
| Southdown Rd., Carshalton | 3B 56 |
| Southdown Rd., Hersham | 1E 51 |
| Southdown Rd., Wimbledon | 1A 38 |
| Southdown Rd., Woldingham | 4F 75 |
| Southend La. | 4A 24 |
| Southend Rd. | 5A 24 |
| Southerland Cl. | 1B 50 |
| Southern Av., Feltham | 2A 16 |
| Southern Av., Salfords | 4E 109 |
| Southern Av., Shortlands | 2D 41 |
| Southern Rd. | 5A 44 |
| Southerns La. | 5C 72 |
| Southerton Rd. | 2F 9 |
| Southey Rd. | 5B 20 |
| Southey St. | 5F 23 |
| Southfield Gdns. | 4F 17 |
| Southfield Pl. | 2A 50 |
| Southfield Rd., Acton | 1D 9 |
| Southfield Rd., Wandsworth | 1B 20 |
| Southfields | 3E 35 |
| Southfields Av. | 5E 15 |
| Southfields Rd. | 5A 76 |
| Southgate Av., Ashford | 4E 15 |
| Southgate Av., Crawley | 5D 147 |
| Southgate Dr. | 5D 147 |
| Southgate Rd. | 5D 147 |
| Southland Way | 1E 17 |
| Southlands | 3C 150 |
| Southlands Av. | 2B 128 |
| Southlands Cl., Ash | 5C 78 |
| Southlands Cl., Coulsdon | 2A 74 |
| Southlands Cl., Wokingham | 2E 25 |
| Southlands La. | 5D 93 |
| Southlands Rd., Ash | 5C 78 |
| Southlands Rd., Wokingham | 3E 25 |
| Southly Cl. | 5B 37 |
| Southmead, Ewell | 2B 54 |
| Southmead, Redhill | 4A 90 |
| Southmead Rd., Aldershot | 1D 97 |
| Southmead Rd., Southfields | 2A 20 |
| Southmont Rd. | 5E 35 |
| Southsea Rd., Croydon | 4B 40 |
| Southsea Rd., Kingston | 2B 36 |
| Southside Common | 5A 20 |
| Southview Ct. | 2D 65 |
| Southview Gdns. | 2C 56 |
| Southview Rd., Downham | 4B 24 |
| Southview Rd., Whyteleafe | 3E 75 |
| Southview Rd., Woldingh'm | 5A 76 |
| Southville | 2F 15 |
| Southville Cl., Ewell | 3A 54 |
| Southville Cl., Feltham | 2F 15 |
| Southville Cres. | 2F 15 |
| Southville Rd., E. Bedfont | 2F 15 |
| Southville Rd., Long Ditton | 4F 35 |
| Southway, Cannon Hill | 2A 38 |
| Southway, Carshalton Beeches | 3A 56 |
| Southway, Wallington | 1C 56 |
| Southway, Woodbridge Hill | 5E 81 |
| Southwell Park Rd. | 5A 44 |
| Southwell Rd. | 3B 40 |
| Southwick Cl. | 4F 147 |
| Southwick Rd. | 2B 150 |
| Southwold | 4B 26 |
| Southwood Av., Coombe | 1D 37 |
| Southwood Av., Knaphill | 2A 64 |
| Southwood Av., Ottershaw | 2C 48 |
| Southwood Av., Woodmansterne | 1F 73 |
| Southwood Cl. | 4A 37 |
| Southwood Dr. | 4D 37 |
| Southwood Gdns. | 5F 35 |
| Southwood La. | 5A 60 |
| Southwood Rd. | 5B 60 |
| Spa Dr. | 5F 53 |
| Spa Hill | 1C 40 |
| Space Way | 1A 16 |
| Spalding Rd. | 4E 21 |
| Sparrow Farm Dr. | 2B 16 |
| Sparrow Farm Rd. | 1C 54 |
| Sparrow Row | 2C 46 |
| Sparvell Rd. | 3F 63 |
| Spats La. | 3F 133 |
| Speedwell Cl. | 4B 82 |
| Speer Rd. | 4F 35 |
| Speke Rd. | 1C 40 |
| Speldhurst Rd. | 1D 9 |
| Spelthorne Gro. | 5F 15 |
| Spelthorne La. | 1E 33 |
| Spence Av. | 5F 49 |
| Spence Pk. | 1D 21 |
| Spencer Cl., Frimley Grn. | 4E 61 |
| Spencer Cl., Langley Vale | 3E 71 |
| Spencer Cl., Sheerwater | 5C 48 |
| Spencer Gdns. | 4C 12 |
| Spencer Hill | 5A 20 |
| Spencer Rd., Bromley Hill | 5C 24 |
| Spencer Rd., Caterham | 4C 74 |
| Spencer Rd., Chiswick | 3D 9 |
| Spencer Rd., Cobham | 1A 68 |
| Spencer Rd., Croydon | 1F 57 |
| Spencer Rd., East Molesey | 3E 35 |
| Spencer Rd., Hackbridge | 4E 39 |
| Spencer Rd., Mitcham | 2E 39 |
| Spencer Rd., Raynes Park | 1F 37 |
| Spencer Rd., Twickenham | 3E 17 |
| Spencer Way (Mason's Bridge Rd.) | 3E 109 |
| Spencer's Pl. | 4A 158 |
| Spencer's Rd., Horsham | 4A 158 |
| Spencer's Rd., West Green | 4C 146 |
| Spenser Av. | 2A 50 |
| Spenser Rd. | 1B 22 |
| Spiceall | 4F 99 |
| Spicer Cl. | 3B 34 |
| Spicers Field | 5B 52 |
| Spiers Cl. | 3E 37 |
| Spiers Way | 3B 128 |
| Spindle Way | 4D 147 |
| Spindlewood Cl. | 5E 71 |
| Spinis | 4B 26 |
| Spinner Green | 3C 26 |
| Spinney Cl. | 4A 52 |
| Spinney Dr. | 2E 15 |
| Spinney Hill | 1D 49 |
| Spinney, The, Camberley | 5D 45 |
| Spinney, The, Cheam | 1C 54 |
| Spinney, The, Crawley | 5C 146 |
| Spinney, The, Crawley Down | 3E 149 |
| Spinney, The, Fetcham | 5D 69 |
| Spinney, The, Grayshott | 5C 134 |
| Spinney, The, Guildford | 2E 83 |
| Spinney, The, Horley | 1B 128 |
| Spinney, The, Purley | 4E 57 |
| Spinney, The, Streatham | 3F 21 |
| Spinney, The, Sunbury | 1A 34 |
| Spinney, The, Sunningdale | 3E 29 |
| Spinney, The, Tatt. Corner | 3F 71 |
| Spinning Walk | 3D 103 |
| Spital Heath | 1A 106 |
| Spoil La. | 1E 97 |
| Spook Hill | 4A 106 |
| Spooner Wk. | 1C 56 |
| Spooners Rd. | 3C 158 |
| Sportsbank St. | 2B 24 |
| Spout Hill | 1D 59 |
| Spout La. | 5C 7 |
| Spratts Alley | 2C 48 |
| Spratts La. | 2C 48 |
| Spreighton Rd. | 3D 35 |
| Spring Av. | 5D 13 |
| Spring Cl. | 5A 100 |
| Spring Clears | 4E 45 |
| Spring Ct. | 3E 81 |
| Spring Cres. | 2C 8 |
| Spring Farm Rd. | 3E 151 |
| Spring Gdns., Biggin Hill | 2D 77 |
| Spring Gdns., Camberley | 5C 44 |
| Spring Gdns., Dorking | 1F 105 |
| Spring Gdns., E. Molesey | 3D 35 |
| Spring Gdns., South Ascot | 3C 28 |
| Spring Gro., Fetcham | 5D 69 |
| Spring Gro., Northbourne | 5A 100 |
| Spring Grove Rd. | 1B 18 |
| Spring Haven Cl. | 5B 82 |
| Spring La., Cheam | 2D 55 |
| Spring La., Folly Hill | 2F 95 |
| Spring La., Oxted | 4E 93 |
| Spring La., Woodside | 3E 41 |
| Spring Park Av. | 5F 41 |
| Spring Park Rd., Beckenham | 2B 42 |
| Spring Park Rd., Shirley | 5F 41 |
| Spring Plat | 4F 147 |
| Spring Rise | 5D 13 |
| Spring Rd. | 3A 16 |
| Spring St. | 3B 54 |
| Spring Well Cl. | 4A 22 |
| Spring Woods, Sandhurst | 3D 43 |
| Spring Woods, Virginia Water | 2B 30 |
| Springbank Rd. | 1C 24 |
| Springbottom La. | 2E 91 |
| Springcopse Rd. | 1C 108 |
| Springcross Av. | 1B 60 |
| Springfield, Ashford | 4C 14 |
| Springfield, Camberley | 4A 44 |
| Springfield, Elstead | 2D 117 |
| Springfield, Oxted | 3E 93 |
| Springfield Av., Hampton Hill | 5D 17 |
| Springfield Av., Morden | 2B 38 |
| Springfield Cres. | 5A 158 |
| Springfield La. | 1A 50 |
| Springfield Meadow | 1A 50 |
| Springfield Park Rd. | 5B 158 |
| Springfield Rise | 3E 23 |
| Springfield Rd., Ash Vale | 3C 78 |
| Springfield Rd., Camberley | 5C 44 |
| Springfield Rd., East Ewell | 3C 54 |
| Springfield Rd., Guildford | 5A 82 |
| Springfield Rd., Horsham | 5B 158 |
| Springfield Rd., Kingston | 2B 36 |
| Springfield Rd., Norbury | 1B 40 |
| Springfield Rd., Sydenham | 4E 23 |
| Springfield Rd., Teddington | 4F 17 |
| Springfield Rd., Wallington | 1B 56 |
| Springfield Rd., West Grn. | 4C 146 |
| Springfield Rd., Westcott | 2D 105 |
| Springfield Rd., Whitton | 2D 17 |
| Springfield Rd., Wimbledon | 4B 20 |
| Springfield Way | 2D 117 |
| Springhill | 2E 119 |
| Springholm Cl. | 2E 77 |
| Springrice Rd. | 1B 24 |
| Springvale Av. | 2B 8 |
| Springwell Rd., Beare Green | 2D 125 |

| | | | |
|---|---|---|---|
| Springwell Rd., Streatham | 4A 22 | Stanley Gdns., Beddington | 2C 56 |
| Springwood | 3B 118 | Stanley Gdns., Sanderstead | 4A 58 |
| Spruce Dr. | 4E 45 | Stanley Green | 3B 40 |
| Sprucedale Gdns., Upper | 1C 58 | Stanley Park Rd. | 2A 56 |
| Shirley | | Stanley Rd., Ascot | 1C 8 |
| Sprucedale Gdns., Wallington | 3C 56 | Stanley Rd., Ashford | 4C 14 |
| Spur Rd. | 1A 16 | Stanley Rd., Acton | 1C 8 |
| Spur, The | 2F 63 | Stanley Rd., Carshalton | 2B 56 |
| Spurfield | 2D 35 | Stanley Rd., Caterham | 4C 74 |
| Spurgeon Rd. | 1C 40 | Stanley Rd., Cheam | 2E 55 |
| Spy La. | 3A 156 | Stanley Rd., Croydon | 4B 40 |
| Square, The | 1B 56 | Stanley Rd., Fulwell | 4E 17 |
| Square, The, Bagshot | 2E 45 | Stanley Rd., Morden | 2B 38 |
| Square, The, Camberley | 5A 44 | Stanley Rd., North Sheen | 5C 8 |
| Square, The, Caterham | 5D 75 | Stanley Rd., Tooting | 5E 21 |
| Square, The, Lightwater | 3F 45 | Stanley Rd., Wimbledon | 5B 20 |
| Square, The, Tatsfield | 3E 77 | Stanley Rd., Woking | 2D 65 |
| Square, The, Weybridge | 1B 50 | Stanley Rd., Wokingham | 2E 25 |
| Square, The, Wisley | 1C 66 | Stanley Sq. | 3B 56 |
| Squire's Bridge Rd. | 2D 33 | Stanley St. | 4C 74 |
| Squire's Hill La. | 2A 115 | Stanley Walk | 5B 158 |
| Squire's Rd. | 2D 33 | Stanmore Gdns., Richmond | 5B 8 |
| Squirrel Cl. | 2C 146 | Stanmore Gdns., Sutton | 5C 38 |
| Squirrel's Cl. | 4A 100 | Stanmore Rd. | 5B 8 |
| Squirrels Grn., Fetcham | 5C 68 | Stanstead Cl. | 3C 42 |
| Squirrels Grn., Wrc. Pk. | 5E 37 | Stanstead Rd., Caterham | 5D 75 |
| Squirrels Lo. | 1F 45 | Stanstead Rd., Lewisham | 2F 23 |
| Squirrels Way | 1D 71 | Stanstead Rd., W. Bedfont | 1D 15 |
| Stace Way | 3A 148 | Stanthorpe Rd. | 4A 22 |
| Stackfield Rd. | 4A 146 | Stanton Av. | 5E 17 |
| Staff College Rd. | 5F 43 | Stanton Cl., Cheam | 5A 38 |
| Stafford Cl., Caterham | 5D 75 | Stanton Cl., Cranleigh | 1B 140 |
| Stafford Cl., Cheam | 2D 55 | Stanton Cl., Ruxley | 1F 53 |
| Stafford Gdns. | 1D 57 | Stanton Rd., Barnes | 4E 9 |
| Stafford Rd., Caterham | 4D 75 | Stanton Rd., Croydon | 4B 40 |
| Stafford Rd., Ifield Vill. | 2B 146 | Stanton Rd., Sydenham | 4F 23 |
| Stafford Rd., Kingston | 2D 37 | Stanton Rd., Wimbledon | 1A 38 |
| Stafford Rd., Twickenham | 2F 17 | Stanwell | 1C 14 |
| Stafford Rd., Waddon | 2D 57 | Stanwell Cl. | 1C 14 |
| Stag Hill | 1B 100 | Stanwell Gdns. | 1C 14 |
| Stag La. | 3E 19 | Stanwell Moor Rd., Longford | 4C 7 |
| Stag Leys | 3B 70 | Stanwell Moor Rd., Staines | 3A 14 |
| Stag Ride | 3F 19 | Stanwell New Rd. | 3B 14 |
| Stagbury Av. | 2D 73 | Stanwell Rd., Ashford | 3C 14 |
| Stagbury Ho. | 3D 75 | Stanwell Rd., East Bedfont | 2E 15 |
| Stagelands | 3C 146 | Stanwellmoor | 1A 14 |
| Stainash Cr. | 4B 14 | Staple Hill Rd. | 2D 47 |
| Stainbank Rd. | 2E 39 | Staple La. | 1D 103 |
| Staines | 4A 14 | Staple Rd. | 4F 83 |
| Staines Av. | 5A 38 | Stapleford Cl. | 2A 20 |
| Staines By-Pass | 3F 13 | Staplehurst | 4B 26 |
| Staines La. | 2A 32 | Staplehurst Cl. | 2C 108 |
| Staines Rd., East Bedfont | 2E 15 | Staplehurst Lane | 3F 109 |
| Staines Rd., Feltham | 1A 16 | Staplehurst Rd., Carshalton | 2A 56 |
| Staines Rd., Laleham | 1B 32 | Staplehurst Rd., Hither Green | 1C 24 |
| Staines Rd., Twickenham | 3D 17 | Staplehurst Rd., Woodhatch | 2C 108 |
| Staines Rd., Wraysbury | 2D 13 | Stapleton Gdns. | 1E 57 |
| Staines Road East | 5A 16 | Stapleton Rd. | 3E 21 |
| Staines Road West | 5D 15 | Star and Garter Hill | 2B 18 |
| Stainford Cl. | 4E 15 | Star Hill, Churt | 2B 134 |
| Stainton Rd. | 2B 24 | Star Hill, Woking | 3C 64 |
| Staithes Way | 3F 71 | Star Hill Dr. | 2B 134 |
| Stake La. | 4C 60 | Star La., Ash | 5C 78 |
| Stakescorner Rd. | 4B 100 | Star La., Hooley | 4E 73 |
| Stambourne Way, Norwood | 1D 41 | Star Post Rd. | 4B 44 |
| Stambourne Way, W. | 5B 42 | Starborough Rd. | 1B 132 |
| Wickham | | Starfield Rd. | 1E 9 |
| Stamford Av. | 2E 61 | Starmead Dr. | 2E 25 |
| Stamford Brook | 1E 9 | Starrock La. | 3E 73 |
| Stamford Brook Av. | 1E 9 | Starrock Rd. | 3F 73 |
| Stamford Green Rd. | 5F 53 | Starwood Cl. | 4E 49 |
| Stamford Rd. | 5B 34 | Station App., Ash Vale | 2C 78 |
| Stan Hill | 3D 127 | Station App., Ashford | 4C 14 |
| Standen Rd. | 2B 20 | Station App., Chipstead | 2D 73 |
| Standford La. | 5E 133 | Station App., Coulsdon | 1F 73 |
| Standon La. | 2C 142 | Station App., Dorking | 5D 87 |
| Stane St., Mickleham | 2D 87 | Station App., Earlswood | 1E 109 |
| Stane St., Ockley | 5B 124 | Station App., Epsom | 5A 54 |
| Stane Way | 3B 54 | Station App., Godalming | 2C 118 |
| Stanford Cl. | 5C 16 | Station App., Gomshall | 3E 103 |
| Stanford Rd. | 1A 40 | Station App., Hinchley W'd | 5F 35 |
| Stanford Way | 1F 39 | Station App., Horley | 3B 128 |
| Stanfords Pl. | 2E 131 | Station App., Horsley | 1C 84 |
| Stanger Rd. | 2D 41 | Station App., New Oxted | 3F 93 |
| Stanhill Rd. | 2B 126 | Station App., Ockley | 5C 124 |
| Stanhope Gro. | 3A 42 | Station App., Shepperton | 3E 33 |
| Stanhope Heath Way | 1B 14 | Station App., Staines | 4A 14 |
| Stanhope Rd., Camberley | 1C 60 | Station App., Sunbury | 1A 34 |
| Stanhope Rd., Carshalton | 2B 56 | Station App., Upper | 2D 75 |
| Stanhope Rd., Croydon | 5C 40 | Warlingham | |
| Stanhopes | 2A 94 | Station App., Wanborough | 5F 79 |
| Stanley Av., Malden | 3E 37 | Station App., West Byfleet | 4D 49 |
| Stanley Av., Shortlands | 2B 42 | Station App., West Clandon | 3E 83 |
| Stanley Cl., Coulsdon | 2A 74 | Station App., Woking | 2D 65 |
| Stanley Cl., Crawley | 5D 147 | Station Approach North | 1A 110 |
| Stanley Gardens Rd. | 4E 17 | Station Approach Rd. | 4F 71 |
| Stanley Gdns., Acton | 1D 9 | Station Approach South | 1A 110 |
| | | Station Av., Caterham | 5D 75 |

| | | | |
|---|---|---|---|
| Station Av., Ewell | 3B 54 | Stembridge Rd. | 1E 41 |
| Station Av., Walton | 5A 34 | Stents La. | 3C 68 |
| Station Cres. | 3C 14 | Stepgates | 4B 32 |
| Station Estate Rd. | 2A 16 | Stephen Cl. | 5F 13 |
| Station Hill, Ascot | 2B 28 | Stephendale Rd. | 3B 96 |
| Station Hill, Farnham | 4A 96 | Stephens Field | 5E 137 |
| Station La. | 3B 118 | Stephenson Dr. | 3C 150 |
| Station Par., E. & W. Horsley | 1C 84 | Stephenson Pl. | 4E 147 |
| Station Parade, Virginia Water | 2C 30 | Stephenson Rd. | 2C 16 |
| Station Rd., Addlestone | 5C 32 | Stephenson Way | 4E 147 |
| Station Rd., Ash Vale | 2C 78 | Sternhold Av. | 3F 21 |
| Station Rd., Ashford | 4C 14 | Sterry Dr., Thames Ditton | 3E 35 |
| Station Rd., Bagshot | 2E 45 | Sterry Dr., Worcester Park | 1A 54 |
| Station Rd., Barnes | 4E 9 | Stevens Cl., Beckenham | 5A 24 |
| Station Rd., Belmont | 3E 55 | Stevens Cl., Epsom | 4B 54 |
| Station Rd., Betchworth | 5A 88 | Stevens Cl., Hampton | 4C 16 |
| Station Rd., Bracknell | 1D 27 | Stevens' Lane | 2C 52 |
| Station Rd., Carshalton | 1B 56 | Stewards Cl. | 5F 95 |
| Station Rd., Chertsey | 4A 32 | Stewart | 4A 72 |
| Station Rd., Chessington | 1E 53 | Stewart Av. | 2D 33 |
| Station Rd., Chobham | 4D 47 | Stewart Cl. | 4C 16 |
| Station Rd., Claygate | 1B 52 | Steyning Cl., Coulsdon | 1B 74 |
| Station Rd., Crawley | 4D 147 | Steyning Cl., Crawley | 3D 147 |
| Station Rd., Crawley Down | 3E 149 | Stile Hall Gdns. | 2C 8 |
| Station Rd., Croydon | 4B 40 | Stile Path | 2A 34 |
| Station Rd., Dorking | 1F 105 | Stilland La. | 4E 153 |
| Station Rd., Dormans Pk. | 4F 131 | Stillart Gr. | 4E 17 |
| Station Rd., Earlswood | 1D 109 | Stillingfleet Rd. | 3E 9 |
| Station Rd., E. Grinstead | 2C 150 | Stillness Rd. | 1A 24 |
| Station Rd., Egham | 4D 13 | Stirling Cl. | 2B 72 |
| Station Rd., Esher | 5E 35 | Stirling Rd., Acton | 1C 8 |
| Station Rd., Farncombe | 5A 100 | Stirling Rd., Stanwell | 1C 14 |
| Station Rd., Farnham | 4A 96 | Stirling Rd., Whitton | 2D 17 |
| Station Rd., Frimley | 2D 61 | Stirling Walk | 3C 36 |
| Station Rd., Godalming | 2D 119 | Stirling Way, Croydon | 4A 40 |
| Station Rd., Gomshall | 3E 103 | Stirling Way, Horsham | 4C 158 |
| Station Rd., Hampton | 1D 35 | Stites Hill Rd. | 3B 74 |
| Station Rd., Hampton Wick | 1A 36 | Stoatley Hollow | 2F 151 |
| Station Rd., Horley | 3B 128 | Stoatley Rise | 2F 151 |
| Station Rd., Horsham | 5B 158 | Stoats Nest Village | 1A 74 |
| Station Rd., Kenley | 5F 57 | Stock Hill | 2E 77 |
| Station Rd., Leatherhead | 4F 69 | Stockbridge Dr. | 2D 97 |
| Station Rd., Lingfield | 1F 131 | Stockbury Rd. | 3E 41 |
| Station Rd., Loxwood | 4A 156 | Stockers La. | 3D 65 |
| Station Rd., Merton | 1C 38 | Stockfield | 2C 128 |
| Station Rd., Mugswell | 1A 90 | Stockfield Rd., Esher | 1B 52 |
| Station Rd., New Oxted | 3F 93 | Stockfield Rd., Streatham | 3A 22 |
| Station Rd., North | 5C 60 | Stockport Rd. | 1F 39 |
| Farnborough | | Stockton Rd. | 2B 108 |
| Station Rd., Norwood | 2D 41 | Stockwell Rd. | 3C 150 |
| Station Rd., Penge | 5E 23 | Stockwood Rise | 5C 44 |
| Station Rd., Redhill | 5A 90 | Stocton Cl. | 5F 81 |
| Station Rd., Rudgwick | 2F 157 | Stocton Rd. | 5F 81 |
| Station Rd., Shalford | 3D 101 | Stodart Rd. | 1E 41 |
| Station Rd., Shepperton | 3E 33 | Stoke Cl. | 1C 68 |
| Station Rd., Shortlands | 1C 42 | Stoke D'Abernon | 2C 68 |
| Station Rd., Stoke D'Abernon | 2C 68 | Stoke Hills | 3B 96 |
| Station Rd., Sunbury | 5A 16 | Stoke Rd., Guildford | 1C 100 |
| Station Rd., Sunningdale | 3E 29 | Stoke Rd., Kingston | 5D 19 |
| Station Rd., Teddington | 5F 17 | Stoke Rd., Stoke D'Abernon | 1B 68 |
| Station Rd., Thames Diton | 4F 35 | Stoke Rd., Walton | 5B 34 |
| Station Rd., Twickenham | 2F 17 | Stokes Ridings | 5A 72 |
| Station Rd., Warnham | 2A 158 | Stokes Rd. | 3F 41 |
| Station Rd., West Byfleet | 4D 49 | Stokesby Rd. | 2E 53 |
| Station Rd., Whyteleafe | 2D 75 | Stokesheath Rd. | 4A 52 |
| Station Rd., Wokingham | 2D 25 | Stompond La. | 5A 34 |
| Station Rd., Woldingham | 4F 75 | Stonards Brow | 2C 120 |
| Station Rd., Wonersh | 5D 101 | Stone Bridge Field | 4C 100 |
| Station Rd., Wraysbury | 1D 13 | Stone Bridge Wharf | 4C 100 |
| Station Road East, Ash Vale | 2C 78 | Stone Court Cl. | 2C 128 |
| Station Road East, Oxted | 3F 93 | Stone Gate | 5D 45 |
| Station Road North | 2C 90 | Stone Hill Rd., Lightwater | 3E 45 |
| Station Road South | 2C 90 | Stone Park Av. | 2A 42 |
| Station Road West | 3F 93 | Stone Pl. | 5F 37 |
| Station View | 2C 78 | Stone Rd. | 3C 42 |
| Station Way, Cheam | 2D 55 | Stone St., Aldershot | 1D 97 |
| Station Way, Claygate | 2B 52 | Stone St., Waddon | 1D 57 |
| Station Way, Crawley | 4D 147 | Stone's Rd. | 4B 54 |
| Station Yard | 2F 17 | Stonecot Cl. | 4A 38 |
| Staunton Rd. | 5B 18 | Stonecot Hill | 4A 38 |
| Staveley Gdns. | 4D 9 | Stonecroft Way | 4A 40 |
| Staveley Rd., Ashford | 5F 15 | Stonecrop Rd. | 4C 82 |
| Staveley Rd., Chiswick | 3D 9 | Stonefield Cl. | 4D 147 |
| Staveley Way | 2A 64 | Stonehill Cl., Gt. Bookham | 1F 85 |
| Stavordale Rd. | 4C 38 | Stonehill Cl., Richmond | 1D 19 |
| Stayne End | 2B 30 | Stonehill Rd., Botleys | 5E 31 |
| Stayton Rd. | 5B 38 | Stonehill Rd., Headley Down | 5A 134 |
| Steele Rd. | 1D 9 | Stonehill Rd., Roehampton | 1D 19 |
| Steels La. | 5A 52 | Stonehills Ct. | 3D 23 |
| Steep Hill | 2C 46 | Stonehouse Gdns. | 1F 91 |
| Steeple Cl. | 4A 20 | Stonehouse Rise | 2E 61 |
| Steepways | 4D 135 | Stoneleigh | 1B 54 |
| Steerforth St. | 3C 20 | Stoneleigh Av. | 1C 54 |
| Steers Hill | 4D 145 | Stoneleigh Ct. | 2E 61 |
| Steers La. | 1F 147 | Stoneleigh Cres. | 1B 54 |
| Steers Mead | 1D 39 | Stoneleigh Pk. | 2B 50 |
| Stella Rd. | 5E 21 | Stoneleigh Park Av. | 3F 41 |

| | | | | | | | | |
|---|---|---|---|---|---|---|---|
| Farnborough | | Tangley Park Rd. | 4C 16 | Temple Rd., Epsom | 4A 54 | Thompson Av. | 5C 8 |
| Sycamore Way | 3B 40 | Tanglyn Av. | 3D 33 | Temple Rd., Kew | 4B 8 | Thompson Rd. | 1D 23 |
| Sydenham Av. | 4E 23 | Tangmere Rd. | 4B 146 | Temple Rd., Lammas Park | 1A 8 | Thompsons La. | 3D 47 |
| Sydenham Hill | 3D 23 | Tanhouse La. | 2D 25 | Temple Sheen Rd. | 5C 8 | Thomson Cres. | 4A 40 |
| Sydenham Pk. | 3E 23 | Tanhouse Rd. | 4E 93 | Temple Way | 5D 39 | Thorkhill Gdns. | 4F 35 |
| Sydenham Park Rd. | 3E 23 | Tanhurst La. | 4F 123 | Templecombe Way | 3A 38 | Thorkhill Rd. | 4F 35 |
| Sydenham Rise | 3E 23 | Tankerton Rd. | 5B 36 | Templedene | 5E 33 | Thorley Cl. | 5D 49 |
| Sydenham Rd., Croydon | 4C 40 | Tankervale Rd. | 5A 22 | Templedene Av. | 5B 14 | Thorley Gdns. | 5D 49 |
| Sydenham Rd., Guildford | 1C 100 | Tankerville Rd. | 5F 21 | Templefield Cl. | 2E 49 | Thorn Bank | 1B 100 |
| Sydenham Rd., Sydenham | 4E 23 | Tanners Dean | 4A 70 | Templeman Cl. | 1B 74 | Thorn Cl. | 2C 114 |
| Sydney Cl. | 5A 26 | Tanners Field | 4D 101 | Templemere | 5E 33 | Thorn Rd. | 2C 114 |
| Sydney Cres. | 5D 15 | Tanners Hill | 1C 106 | Temple's Cl. | 4D 97 | Thornash Cl. | 1C 64 |
| Sydney Rd., Cheam | 1E 55 | Tanners La., Haslemere | 3A 152 | Templeton Cl. | 1C 40 | Thornash Rd. | 1C 64 |
| Sydney Rd., Felsham | 2A 16 | Tannery La., Send | 5F 65 | Ten Acres | 1B 86 | Thornash Way | 1C 64 |
| Sydney Rd., Guildford | 1D 101 | Tannery La., Wonersh | 5D 101 | Ten Acre La. | 1E 31 | Thornbank Cl. | 1A 14 |
| Sydney Rd., Raynes Park | 1A 38 | Tannery, The | 5A 90 | Tenby Rd. | 3F 61 | Thornburn Way | 1C 38 |
| Sydney Rd., Richmond | 5B 8 | Tannsfield Rd. | 4F 23 | Tenchley's La. | 4B 94 | Thornbury Cl. | 1D 43 |
| Sydney Rd., Teddington | 4F 17 | Tansy Cl. | 4C 82 | Tenham Av. | 3F 21 | Thornbury Rd. | 1A 22 |
| Syke Ings | 1B 7 | Tantallon Rd. | 2E 21 | Tennison Rd. | 2D 41 | Thorncliffe Rd. | 1A 22 |
| Sykecluan | 1B 7 | Tanyard Way | 2B 128 | Tennyson Av., Motspur Park | 3F 37 | Thorncombe Rd. | 1D 23 |
| Sylvan Cl., Limpsfield | 3A 94 | Tapestry Cl. | 2F 55 | Tennyson Av., Twickenham | 2F 17 | Thorncombe St. | 4F 119 |
| Sylvan Cl., Selsdon | 3B 58 | Tapner's Rd | 3E 107 | Tennyson Cl., Old Coulsdon | 3B 74 | Thorncroft | 5C 12 |
| Sylvan Cl., Woking | 2E 65 | Tarbert Rd. | 1D 23 | Tennyson Cl., Pound Hill | 3F 147 | Thorncroft Rd. | 1F 55 |
| Sylvan Estate | 1D 41 | Tarham Cl. | 1A 128 | Tennyson Rise | 2B 150 | Thorndon Gdns. | 1B 54 |
| Sylvan Gdns. | 4A 36 | Tarmac Way | 3C 7 | Tennyson Rd., Ashford | 4C 14 | Thorndown La. | 2A 46 |
| Sylvan Hill | 1D 41 | Tarn Rd. | 5E 135 | Tennyson Rd., Penge | 5F 23 | Thorne Cl., Ashford | 5E 15 |
| Sylvan Rd., Penge | 1D 41 | Tarragon Dr. | 3E 81 | Tennyson Rd., Weybridge | 1F 49 | Thorne Cl., New Malden | 2D 37 |
| Sylvan Rd., Tilgate | 5E 147 | Tarrington Cl. | 3F 21 | Tennyson Rd., Wimbledon | 4C 20 | Thorne Rd. | 2D 37 |
| Sylvan Way, Redhill | 1E 109 | Tartar Hill | 5D 51 | Tennyson's La. | 4A 152 | Thorne St. | 5E 9 |
| Sylvan Way, W. Wickham | 1F 59 | Tartar Rd. | 5E 51 | Tenterden Rd. | 4D 41 | Thornes Cl. | 2B 42 |
| Sylvanus | 4B 26 | Tasman Ct. | 5F 15 | Tern Rd. | 4A 146 | Thorney Hedge Rd. | 2C 8 |
| Sylvaways Cl. | 1D 141 | Tate Cl. | 5A 70 | Terrace Rd. | 4A 34 | Thorney La. | 1B 7 |
| Sythwood | 1B 64 | Tate Rd. | 1E 55 | Terrace, The, Addlestone | 1F 49 | Thorney Mill Rd. | 1B 7 |
| Szabo Cres. | 5F 79 | Tates Way | 2E 157 | Terrace, The, Barnes | 4E 9 | Thorneyhurst Rd. | 5F 61 |
| | | Tatnell Rd. | 1F 23 | Terrace, The, Camberley | 5F 43 | Thornfield Rd., Banstead | 2B 72 |
| | | Tatsfield | 3E 77 | Terracotta Rd. | 2E 111 | Thornfield Rd., Hammersmith | 1F 9 |
| | | Tattenham Corner Rd. | 2E 71 | Terrapin Rd. | 3E 21 | Thornford Rd. | 1B 24 |
| T | | Tattenham Cres. | 2E 71 | Testard Rd. | 1C 100 | Thornhill, Bracknell | 2E 27 |
| | | Tattenham Gro. | 3F 71 | Testers Cl. | 4A 94 | Thornhill Av. | 5B 36 |
| | | Tattenham Way | 2A 72 | Tetworth Cl. | 5C 37 | Thornhill Rd., Aldershot | 4B 78 |
| Tabarin Way | 1F 71 | Tattersall Cl. | 2F 25 | Tewkesbury Av. | 2E 23 | Thornhill Rd., Croydon | 4C 40 |
| Tabor Gdns. | 2E 55 | Taunton Av., Caterham | 5D 75 | Tewkesbury Cl. | 4F 49 | Thornhill Rd., Hook | 5B 36 |
| Tabor Gro. | 5B 20 | Taunton Av., Raynes Park | 1F 37 | Tewkesbury Rd. | 4D 39 | Thornhill Way | 3D 33 |
| Tabor Rd. | 1F 9 | Taunton Cl. | 4B 38 | Thackeray Cl. | 5A 20 | Thornlaw Rd. | 4B 22 |
| Tachbrook Rd. | 2F 15 | Taunton La. | 3B 74 | Thames Bank | 4D 9 | Thornloe Gdns. | 1E 57 |
| Tadmor Cl. | 3F 33 | Taunton Rd. | 1C 24 | Thames Cl., Chertsey | 4B 32 | Thorns Flush | 5E 121 |
| Tadorne Rd. | 4F 71 | Tavistock Cl. | 5C 14 | Thames Cl., Hampton | 1D 35 | Thornsbeach Rd. | 2B 24 |
| Tadworth | 4F 71 | Tavistock Cres. | 2A 40 | Thames Cl., West Heath | 4B 60 | Thornsett Rd. | 1E 41 |
| Tadworth Av. | 3E 37 | Tavistock Green | 4C 40 | Thames Ditton | 3F 35 | Thornton Av., Croydon | 3A 40 |
| Tadworth St. | 5A 72 | Tavistock Rd., Croydon | 4C 40 | Thames Mead | 4A 34 | Thornton Av., Streatham | 2F 21 |
| Taffys How | 2D 39 | Tavistock Rd., St. Helier | 4D 39 | Thames Meadow | 1D 35 | Thornton Av., Turn. Green | 2E 9 |
| Tait Rd. | 4C 40 | Tavistock Wk. | 4D 39 | Thames Rd. | 3C 8 | Thornton Cl., Guildford | 4E 81 |
| Talbot Cl., Horsham | 5B 158 | Tawfield | 4B 26 | Thames Side, Laleham | 2B 32 | Thornton Cl., Horley | 2A 128 |
| Talbot Cl., Mychett | 5F 61 | Tayben Av. | 1E 17 | Thames Side, Teddington | 5A 18 | Thornton Cres. | 3A 74 |
| Talbot Cl., Reigate | 1C 108 | Taylor Av. | 4C 8 | Thames St., Hampton | 1D 35 | Thornton Gdns. | 2F 21 |
| Talbot Pl. | 2E 45 | Taylor Cl. | 4D 17 | Thames St., Kingston | 1B 36 | Thornton Hill | 5A 20 |
| Talbot Rd., Ashford | 4C 14 | Taylor Rd., Ashtead | 2A 70 | Thames St., Portmore Pk. | 5D 33 | Thornton Pl. | 2A 128 |
| Talbot Rd., Carshalton | 1B 56 | Taylor Rd., Tooting | 5D 21 | Thames St., Staines | 4A 14 | Thornton Rd., Croydon | 4A 40 |
| Talbot Rd., Farnham | 5A 96 | Taylor Rd., Wallington | 1B 56 | Thames St., Sunbury | 2A 34 | Thornton Rd., Hackbridge | 4D 39 |
| Talbot Rd., Lingfield | 2E 131 | Taylors Cres. | 1D 141 | Thames St., Walton | 4F 33 | Thornton Rd., Mortlake | 5D 9 |
| Talbot Rd., Selhurst | 2C 40 | Taylors La., Lindford | 4D 133 | Thamesfield Ct. | 4E 33 | Thornton Rd., Streatham | 2F 21 |
| Talbot Rd., Twickenham | 2E 17 | Taylors La., Upper Sydenham | 4E 23 | Thamesgate Cl. | 4A 18 | Thornton Rd., Wimbledon | 5A 20 |
| Taleworth Cl. | 3B 70 | Taymount Rise | 3E 23 | Thanescroft Gdns. | 5D 41 | Thornwood Rd. | 1C 24 |
| Taleworth Rd. | 3B 70 | Taynton Dri. | 3C 90 | Thameside Rd. | 5A 14 | Thornycroft Cl. | 3B 34 |
| Talisman Sq. | 4D 23 | Tealing Dri. | 1A 54 | Tharp Rd. | 1C 56 | Thorold Cl. | 3C 58 |
| Talisman Way | 1F 71 | Teasel Cl. | 5C 146 | Thatcher's Cl. | 2B 128 | Thorold Rd. | 3A 96 |
| Tall Trees | 4A 7 | Teazlewood Pk. | 2F 69 | Thatchers La. | 2D 81 | Thoroughfare, The | 5F 71 |
| Tally Rd. | 4C 94 | Tebbit Cl. | 1D 27 | Thayers Farm Rd. | 1F 41 | Thorpe | 2E 31 |
| Talma Gdns. | 1E 17 | Tedder Cl. | 1D 53 | The Mount | 2F 51 | Thorpe Bypass | 2E 31 |
| Tamarind Cl. | 3E 81 | Tedder Rd. | 2B 58 | Theobald Rd. | 5B 40 | Thorpe Cl. | 4E 59 |
| Tamesis Gdns. | 5E 37 | Teddington Cl. | 3A 54 | Theodore Rd. | 1B 24 | Thorpe Lea | 5F 13 |
| Tamworth | 3E 27 | Teddington Pk. | 4F 17 | Thepps Cl. | 2A 110 | Thorpe Lea Rd. | 1E 31 |
| Tamworth La. | 1E 39 | Teddington Park Rd. | 4F 17 | Therapia La. | 3A 40 | Thorpe Rd., Chertsey | 3F 31 |
| Tamworth Pk. | 2E 39 | Teesdale | 5C 146 | Therapia Rd. | 1E 23 | Thorpe Rd., Kingston | 5B 18 |
| Tamworth Rd. | 5B 40 | Teevan Rd. | 4D 41 | Theresa Rd. | 2E 9 | Thorpe Rd., Staines | 4F 13 |
| Tanbridge Cl. | 5A 158 | Tegg's La. | 1A 66 | Thesiger Rd. | 5F 23 | Thorpes Cl. | 4E 81 |
| Tandridge | 5D 93 | Tekels Av. | 5A 44 | Thetford Rd., Ashford | 4C 14 | Thorpewood Av. | 3E 23 |
| Tandridge Gdns. | 5A 58 | Tekels Pk. | 1E 61 | Thetford Pk., Malden | 3D 37 | Thorsden Cl. | 3D 65 |
| Tandridge Hill La. | 3D 93 | Tekels Way | 1E 61 | Theydon Cl. | 5E 147 | Thorsden Ct. | 3D 65 |
| Tandridge La. | 1A 112 | Telegraph La. | 2C 52 | Thibet Rd. | 4D 43 | Thrale Rd. | 4F 21 |
| Tandridge Rd. | 3E 75 | Telegraph Rd. | 2A 20 | Thicket Cres. | 1F 55 | Three Arch Rd. | 2E 109 |
| Tanfield Ct. | 5A 158 | Telferscot Rd. | 2F 21 | Thicket Rd., Penge | 5D 23 | Three Bridges Rd. | 4E 147 |
| Tanfield Rd. | 1E 57 | Telford Av. | 2A 22 | Thicket Rd., Sutton | 1F 55 | Three Gates La. | 2A 152 |
| Tangier Rd., Guildford | 1E 101 | Telford Pl. | 4D 147 | Thickhorne La. | 5B 14 | Three Pears Rd. | 5C 82 |
| Tangier Rd., North Sheen | 5C 8 | Telford Rd. | 2C 16 | Third Cl. | 2D 35 | Three Stiles Rd. | 3F 95 |
| Tangier Way | 2A 72 | Tellisford | 1A 52 | Third Cross Rd. | 3E 17 | Threeacres | 5A 158 |
| Tangier Wood | 2A 72 | Temperley Rd. | 2E 21 | Thirlmere Cl. | 5B 60 | Threegates | 5C 82 |
| Tangledak | 1F 149 | Tempest Rd. | 5E 13 | Thirlmere Rd. | 4F 21 | Threshfield | 3C 26 |
| Tanglewood | 3A 16 | Templar Pl. | 5C 16 | Thirsk Rd., Selhurst | 2C 40 | Thrift Vale | 4C 82 |
| Tanglewood Cl., Longcross | 5B 30 | Temple Av. | 5F 41 | Thirsk Rd., Tooting | 5E 21 | Thrigby Rd. | 2F 53 |
| Tanglewood Cl., Shirley | 5E 41 | Temple Bar Rd. | 3A 64 | Thistlecroft Rd. | 1E 51 | Throwley Rd. | 1F 55 |
| Tanglewood Cl., Woking | 1F 65 | Temple Cl. | 4A 54 | Thistledene, Thames Ditton | 3E 35 | Thrupps Av. | 1E 51 |
| Tangley Dri. | 3D 25 | Temple Croft | 5F 15 | Thistledene, W. Byfleet | 5D 49 | Thrupps La. | 1E 51 |
| Tangley Gro. | 2E 19 | Temple Gdns. | 1A 32 | Thistley La. | 1C 140 | Thundery Hill | 3E 97 |
| Tangley Hill | 4F 101 | Temple La. | 5E 125 | Thomas Av. | 4C 74 | Thurbarn Rd. | 4A 24 |
| Tangley La., Wonersh | 4E 101 | Temple Rd., Acton | 1D 9 | Thomas La. | 2A 24 | Thurbarns Hill | 3E 125 |
| Tangley La., Worplesdon | 3D 81 | Temple Rd., Croydon | 1F 57 | Thomas Rd. | 3D 9 | Thurban's Way | 5F 95 |

| | | | |
|---|---|---|---|
| Twelve Acre Cres. | 4B 60 | Upper Beulah Hill | 1C 40 |
| Twickenham | 3E 17 | Upper Borne La. | 1D 115 |
| Twickenham Cl. | 5A 40 | Upper Bourne Vale | 1D 115 |
| Twickenham Rd., Richmond | 1A 18 | Upper Bridge Rd. | 5A 90 |
| Twickenham Rd., Teddington | 4F 17 | Upper Brighton Rd. | 3B 36 |
| Twickenham Rd., Twickenham | 1F 17 | Upper Butts | 3A 8 |
| Twilley St. | 2C 20 | Upper Charles St. | 5A 44 |
| Twining Av. | 3D 17 | Upper Chobham Rd. | 5D 45 |
| Twinoaks | 5A 52 | Upper Church La. | 4A 96 |
| Twinned | 1F 149 | Upper College Ride | 4B 44 |
| Twitten La. | 1F 149 | Upper Court Rd., Epsom | 4A 54 |
| Twycross Rd. | 5A 100 | Upper Court Rd., Woldingham | 5A 76 |
| Twyford La. | 1D 115 | Upper Dunnymans Mews | 5E 55 |
| Twyford Rd., St. Helier | 4D 39 | Upper Dri. | 2E 77 |
| Twyford Rd., Wokingham | 1D 25 | Upper Eashing La. | 2E 115 |
| Twyne Cl. | 5B 146 | Upper Edgeborough Rd. | 1D 101 |
| Twynersh | 3F 31 | Upper Elmers End Rd. | 3A 42 |
| Twynham Rd. | 5A 44 | Upper Fairfield Rd. | 4F 69 |
| Tybenham Rd. | 2B 38 | Upper Farm Rd. | 2C 34 |
| Tychbourne Dr. | 4C 82 | Upper Gordon Rd. | 5A 44 |
| Tydcombe Rd. | 3E 75 | Upper Grotto Rd. | 3F 17 |
| Tye La. | 2A 88 | Upper Green, E. & W. | 1D 39 |
| Tylecroft Rd. | 1A 40 | Upper Grove | 2D 41 |
| Tylehost | 3E 81 | Upper Guildown Rd. | 2C 100 |
| Tyler Rd. | 5D 147 | Upper Hale Rd. | 1A 96 |
| Tyler's Cl. | 3B 92 | Upper Haliford Bypass | 3F 33 |
| Tyler's Ct. | 1C 140 | Upper Haliford Grn. | 2F 33 |
| Tyler's Grn. | 3B 92 | Upper Halliford | 2F 33 |
| Tylner Cl. | 4D 23 | Upper Halliford Rd. | 3F 33 |
| Tyndals | 5F 135 | Upper Ham Rd. | 4B 18 |
| Tynedale Rd. | 2C 106 | Upper High St. | 5A 54 |
| Tynemouth Rd. | 5E 21 | Upper House La. | 3D 121 |
| Tynley Gro. | 2F 81 | Upper Jordan Goose Rye | 1D 81 |
| Tyson Rd. | 2E 23 | Upper Mall | 2F 9 |
| | | Upper Manor Rd., Farncombe | 5A 100 |
| | | Upper Manor Rd., Milford | 3B 118 |
| **U** | | Upper Mount | 1B 152 |
| | | Upper Mulgrave Rd. | 2D 55 |
| Uckfield Gro. | 1E 39 | Upper Palace Rd. | 2E 35 |
| Udney Park Rd. | 5F 17 | Upper Park Rd., Camberley | 5A 44 |
| Uffington Dri. | 2E 27 | Upper Park Rd., Kingston | 5C 18 |
| Uffington Rd. | 4B 22 | Upper Pillory Downs | 5B 56 |
| Ullathorne Rd. | 4F 21 | Upper Pines | 2D 73 |
| Ullswater | 4B 26 | Upper Pinewood Rd. | 4D 79 |
| Ullswater Av. | 5B 60 | Upper Richmond Rd. | 5F 9 |
| Ullswater Cl., Kingston Vale | 4D 19 | Upper Richmond Road W. | 5C 8 |
| Ullswater Cl., Lightwater | 3F 45 | Upper Rd., Wallington | 1C 56 |
| Ullswater Cr., Coulsdon | 1A 74 | Upper Rose Hill | 2F 105 |
| Ullswater Cres., King. V. | 4D 19 | Upper St. Michael's Rd. | 1C 96 |
| Ullswater Rd., Barnes | 3E 9 | Upper Sawley Wood | 5E 55 |
| Ullswater Rd., Lightwater | 3F 45 | Upper Selsdon Rd. | 3A 58 |
| Ullswater Rd., W. Norwood | 3B 22 | Upper Shirley Rd. | 5E 41 |
| Ulstan Cl. | 5A 76 | Upper South View | 3A 96 |
| Ulverscroft Rd. | 1D 23 | Upper Springfield | 2D 117 |
| Ulwyn Av. | 5F 49 | Upper St., Shere | 3D 103 |
| Underhill Cl. | 2D 119 | Upper Stanford | 1B 80 |
| Underhill La. | 5A 96 | Upper Star Post Ride | 5C 26 |
| Underhill Park Rd. | 4E 89 | Upper Sunbury Rd. | 1C 34 |
| Underhill Rd., Camberley | 1D 23 | Upper Tooting Pk. | 3E 21 |
| Underhill Rd., Newdigate | 3F 125 | Upper Tooting Rd. | 4D 21 |
| Undershaw Rd. | 3C 24 | Upper Tulse Hill | 2A 22 |
| Underwood | 2E 59 | Upper Verran Rd. | 1E 61 |
| Underwood | 3B 26 | Upper Village Rd. | 3D 29 |
| Underwood Av. | 5B 78 | Upper Way | 5A 96 |
| Underwood Rd., Caterham | 1A 92 | Upper West St. | 5E 89 |
| Underwood Rd., Shottermill | 2F 151 | Upper Weybourne La. | 1B 96 |
| Undine St. | 4D 21 | Upper Woodcote Village | 4C 56 |
| Unham Rd. | 5C 22 | Upperton Rd. | 1C 100 |
| Union Pl. | 4D 147 | Upshire Gdns. | 2E 27 |
| Union Rd., Croydon | 4C 40 | Upshot La. | 2A 66 |
| Union Rd., Farnham | 4A 96 | Upton Rd. | 1C 40 |
| Union St., Farnborough Park | 5C 60 | Upwood Rd. | 1A 40 |
| Union St., Kingston | 1B 36 | Utterton Way | 2D 109 |
| University Rd. | 5D 21 | Uvedale Cl. | 4E 59 |
| Unstead La. | 5C 100 | Uvedale Cres. | 4E 59 |
| Unstead Wood | 4C 100 | Uvedale Rd. | 3F 93 |
| Unwin Av. | 1F 15 | Uxbridge Rd., Hampton Hill | 4D 17 |
| Updown Hill | 2A 46 | Uxbridge Rd., Hanworth | 3B 16 |
| Upfield, Addiscombe | 5E 41 | Uxbridge Rd., Kingston | 2B 36 |
| Upfield, Horley | 3B 128 | | |
| Upfield Cl., Horley | 3B 128 | | |
| Upfold Cl., And La. | 1B 140 | | |
| Upfolds | 3B 82 | | |
| Upfolds Cl. | 5E 121 | | |
| Upham Park Rd. | 2E 9 | **V** | |
| Upland Rd., Camberley | 4A 44 | | |
| Upland Rd., Camberwell | 1D 23 | Vachery La. | 3C 140 |
| Upland Rd., Carshalton | 2A 56 | Vaillant Rd. | 1B 50 |
| Upland Rd., South Croydon | 1F 57 | Vale Cl., Lower Bourne | 2E 115 |
| Upland Way | 2F 71 | Vale Close, Purley | 5D 57 |
| Uplands, Beckenham | 2A 42 | Vale Cres. | 4E 19 |
| Uplands, Leatherhead | 3B 70 | Vale Dri. | 4A 158 |
| Uplands Cl. | 2A 152 | Vale Farm Rd. | 2D 65 |
| Uplands Cl. | 2C 74 | Vale Rd., Camberley | 1C 60 |
| Uplands Rd., Compton | 4B 96 | Vale Rd., Cheam | 1E 55 |
| Uplands Rd., Woldingham | 3A 76 | Vale Rd., Claygate | 3B 52 |
| | | Vale Rd., Mitcham | 2F 39 |
| | | Vale Rd., Stoneleigh | 1B 54 |

| | | | |
|---|---|---|---|
| Vale Rd., Weybridge | 5E 33 | Vicarage La., Ewell | 3B 54 |
| Vale Rd., Worcester Park | 5E 37 | Vicarage La., Farnham | 4A 96 |
| Vale Road North Cl. | 5B 36 | Vicarage La., Heath End | 1A 96 |
| Vale Road South | 5B 36 | Vicarage La., Laleham | 2B 32 |
| Vale St. | 3C 22 | Vicarage La., Leatherhead | 4F 69 |
| Vale, The, Feltham | 1A 16 | Vicarage La., Lower Bourne | 5B 96 |
| Vale, The, Shirley | 5F 41 | Vicarage La., Sendgrove | 1C 82 |
| Vale, The, Woodcote | 5C 56 | Vicarage La., Shottermill | 3E 151 |
| Valeswood Rd. | 4C 24 | Vicarage La., Wraysbury | 2D 13 |
| Valetta Rd. | 1E 9 | Vicarage Rd., Blackwater | 1B 60 |
| Valewood Dri. | 2E 115 | Vicarage Rd., Chobham | 4D 47 |
| Valewood La. | 5D 135 | Vicarage Rd., Crawley Down | 3D 149 |
| Valian Leas | 2C 42 | Vicarage Rd., East Sheen | 1D 19 |
| Valley Cres. | 1D 25 | Vicarage Rd., Egham | 4E 13 |
| Valley End Rd. | 2B 46 | Vicarage Rd., Hampton Wick | 1A 36 |
| Valley La. | 5A 96 | Vicarage Rd., Horley | 2A 128 |
| Valley Mews | 3F 17 | Vicarage Rd., Kingston | 1B 36 |
| Valley Rd., Frimley | 3F 61 | Vicarage Rd., Lingfield | 2E 131 |
| Valley Rd., Kenley | 1C 74 | Vicarage Rd., Staines | 3F 13 |
| Valley Rd., Shortlands | 1C 42 | Vicarage Rd., Sunbury | 5A 16 |
| Valley Rd., Streatham | 4A 22 | Vicarage Rd., Sutton | 5B 38 |
| Valley, The, | 2C 100 | Vicarage Rd., Teddington | 4F 17 |
| Valley View, Biggin Hill | 2E 77 | Vicarage Rd., Twickenham | 3E 17 |
| Valley View, Godalming | 2C 118 | Vicarage Rd., Waddon | 5B 40 |
| Valley View Gdns. | 1C 74 | Vicarage Rd., Westfield | 4D 65 |
| Valley Wk. | 5E 41 | Vicarage Way | 3A 7 |
| Valleyfield Rd. | 4A 22 | Vicars Oak Rd. | 5C 22 |
| Vallis Way | 1D 53 | Victor Rd., Fulwell | 4E 17 |
| Valnay St. | 4D 21 | Victor Rd., Penge | 5F 23 |
| Valroy Cl. | 5A 44 | Victoria Av., Hackbridge | 5E 39 |
| Vamburgh Dr. | 3B 34 | Victoria Av., Hurst Park | 2D 35 |
| Van Dyck Av. | 4D 37 | Victoria Av., Long Ditton | 3A 36 |
| Vanbrugh Rd. | 1D 9 | Victoria Av., Sanderstead | 3F 57 |
| Vancouver Ct. | 4A 54 | Victoria Av., Whitton | 1C 16 |
| Vancouver Rd. | 3F 23 | Victoria Av., York Town | 5F 43 |
| Vanderbilt Rd. | 2C 20 | Victoria Cl., Horley | 2B 128 |
| Vandyke | 3B 26 | Victoria Cl., Walton | 5F 33 |
| Vandyke Cl., Putney | 1A 20 | Victoria Cl., W. Molesey | 2D 35 |
| Vandyke Cl., Redhill | 4A 90 | Victoria Cres. | 5C 22 |
| Vanguard Cl. | 4B 40 | Victoria Dri., Blackwater | 1B 60 |
| Vanguard Way | 2D 57 | Victoria Dri., Southfields | 2A 20 |
| Vann La. | 4B 138 | Victoria Gdns. | 1E 77 |
| Vanners | 3D 147 | Victoria Pl. | 4B 54 |
| Vant Rd. | 4E 21 | Victoria Rd., Addlestone | 1F 49 |
| Vapery La. | 4D 63 | Victoria Rd., Aldershot | 5A 78 |
| Varna Rd., Deadwater | 5D 133 | Victoria Rd., Cranleigh | 1C 140 |
| Varna Rd., Hampton | 1D 35 | Victoria Rd., Crawley | 4C 146 |
| Vaughan Rd. | 4A 36 | Victoria Rd., Earlswood | 1E 109 |
| Vaux Cres. | 2D 51 | Victoria Rd., Farnham | 4A 96 |
| Vectis Rd. | 5E 21 | Victoria Rd., Feltham | 2A 16 |
| Vegal Cres. | 4C 12 | Victoria Rd., Godalming | 2D 119 |
| Vellum Dr. | 1B 56 | Victoria Rd., Horley | 2B 128 |
| Venetia Rd. | 1A 8 | Victoria Rd., Kew | 4B 8 |
| Venner Rd. | 5E 23 | Victoria Rd., Kingston | 1B 36 |
| Ventnor Rd. | 2F 55 | Victoria Rd., Knaphill | 2A 64 |
| Venton Cl. | 2B 64 | Victoria Rd., North | 5C 60 |
| Verdant La. | 2C 24 | Farnborough | |
| Verdayne Av. | 5D 41 | Victoria Rd., Oatlands Park | 5F 33 |
| Verdayne Gdns. | 1E 75 | Victoria Rd., Owlsmoor | 3E 43 |
| Verdun Rd. | 3E 9 | Victoria Rd., South Ascot | 3C 28 |
| Vereker Dri. | 2A 34 | Victoria Rd., Staines | 3F 13 |
| Vermont Rd., Sutton Common | 5C 38 | Victoria Rd., Surbiton | 3B 36 |
| Vermont Rd., Upper Norwood | 5C 22 | Victoria Rd., Sutton | 1F 55 |
| Vermont St. | 1C 20 | Victoria Rd., Tooting | 5D 21 |
| Vernon Av. | 1A 38 | Victoria Rd., Twickenham | 2D 17 |
| Vernon Cl., Ewell | 2A 54 | Victoria Rd., Woking | 2D 65 |
| Vernon Cl., Horsham | 3C 158 | Victoria Rd., Woodmansterne | 1F 73 |
| Vernon Cl., Ottershaw | 2C 48 | Victoria St. | 5C 12 |
| Vernon Dr. | 1A 28 | Victoria Terr., Dorking | 160 |
| Vernon Rd., Feltham | 3F 15 | Victoria Villas | 5B 8 |
| Vernon Rd., Mortlake | 5D 9 | Victoria Way | 3C 150 |
| Vernon Rd., Sutton | 1F 55 | Victoria Way, Woking | 2D 65 |
| Vernon Wk. | 3A 72 | Victors Dr. | 5C 16 |
| Vernon Way | 5E 81 | Victory Av. | 3C 36 |
| Verona Dri. | 5B 36 | Victory Park Rd. | 1E 49 |
| Veronica Gdns. | 1F 39 | Victory Rd., Chertsey | 4A 32 |
| Veronica Rd. | 3E 21 | Victory Rd., Horsham | 4B 158 |
| Verran Rd., Balham | 2E 21 | Victory Rd., Merton | 5C 20 |
| Verran Rd., Camberley | 1D 61 | Victory Rd., Twickenham | 2F 17 |
| Verulam Av. | 4C 56 | View Cl. | 1E 77 |
| Vespan Rd. | 1E 9 | View Terr. | 3A 132 |
| Vestris Rd. | 3F 23 | Viewfield Rd. | 1B 20 |
| Vevey St. | 3F 23 | Vigilant | 4D 23 |
| Veyers Rd. | 2C 108 | Viking | 3B 26 |
| Vibart Gdns. | 2A 22 | Village Gdns. | 3B 54 |
| Vicarage Av. | 4E 13 | Village Green Av. | 2F 77 |
| Vicarage Cl., Gt. Bookham | 1F 85 | Village Green Way | 2F 77 |
| Vicarage Cl., Kingswood | 5A 72 | Village Rd. | 2E 31 |
| Vicarage Ct., East Bedfont | 2E 15 | Village Row | 2E 55 |
| Vicarage Ct., Egham | 5E 13 | Village St. | 3F 125 |
| Vicarage Cres. | 4E 13 | Village Way, Ashford | 4D 15 |
| Vicarage Fields | 3A 34 | Village Way, Beckenham | 1A 42 |
| Vicarage Gdns. | 2D 39 | Village Way, Camberwell | 1C 22 |
| Vicarage Gate | 1B 100 | Village Way, Cranleigh | 2C 140 |
| Vicarage Hill | 5B 96 | Village Way, Sanderstead | 5A 58 |
| Vicarage La., Bagshot | 1C 44 | Villers Av., Whitton | 2C 16 |
| Vicarage La., Capel | 5D 125 | Villers Rd., Elmers End | 1F 41 |

| | | | | | | | |
|---|---|---|---|---|---|---|---|
| York Hill | 3B 22 | York Rd., Selsdon | 3C 58 | York Way, Sandhurst | 4D 43 | **Z** | |
| York Rd., Ash Wharf | 4C 78 | York Rd., South Ealing | 1A 8 | Yorke Gdns. | 5E 89 | | |
| York Rd., Biggin Hill West | 3D 77 | York Rd., South Farnborough | 1A 78 | Yorke Rd. | 5E 89 | | |
| York Rd., Brentford | 2A 8 | York Rd., Twickenham | 4E 17 | Yorkshire Rd. | 2A 40 | Zennor Rd. | 2F 21 |
| York Rd., Byfleet | 4F 49 | York Rd., Weybridge | 1B 50 | Yorktown Rd. | 4D 43 | Zermatt Rd. | 2B 40 |
| York Rd., Camberley | 5A 44 | York Rd., Woking | 3C 64 | Youldon Dr. | 5C 44 | Zigzag Rd. | 1C 74 |
| York Rd., Cheam | 2E 55 | York St., Beddington Corner | 4E 39 | Young St. | 1B 86 | Zigzag, The | 3D 87 |
| York Rd., Croydon | 4B 40 | York St., Twickenham | 2F 17 | Youngs Dr. | 5C 78 | Zinnia Dr. | 1E 63 |
| York Rd., Guildford | 1C 100 | York Way, Chessington | 2E 53 | Youngstroat La. | 4A 48 | Zion Place | 2C 40 |
| York Rd., Kingston | 5C 18 | York Way, Hanworth | 3C 16 | Yukon Rd. | 2E 21 | Zion Rd. | 2C 40 |

For the index of towns and villages, see pages 4-5.